Fuseli to Menzel

*Drawings and
Watercolors
in the Age of Goethe
from a
German Private Collection*

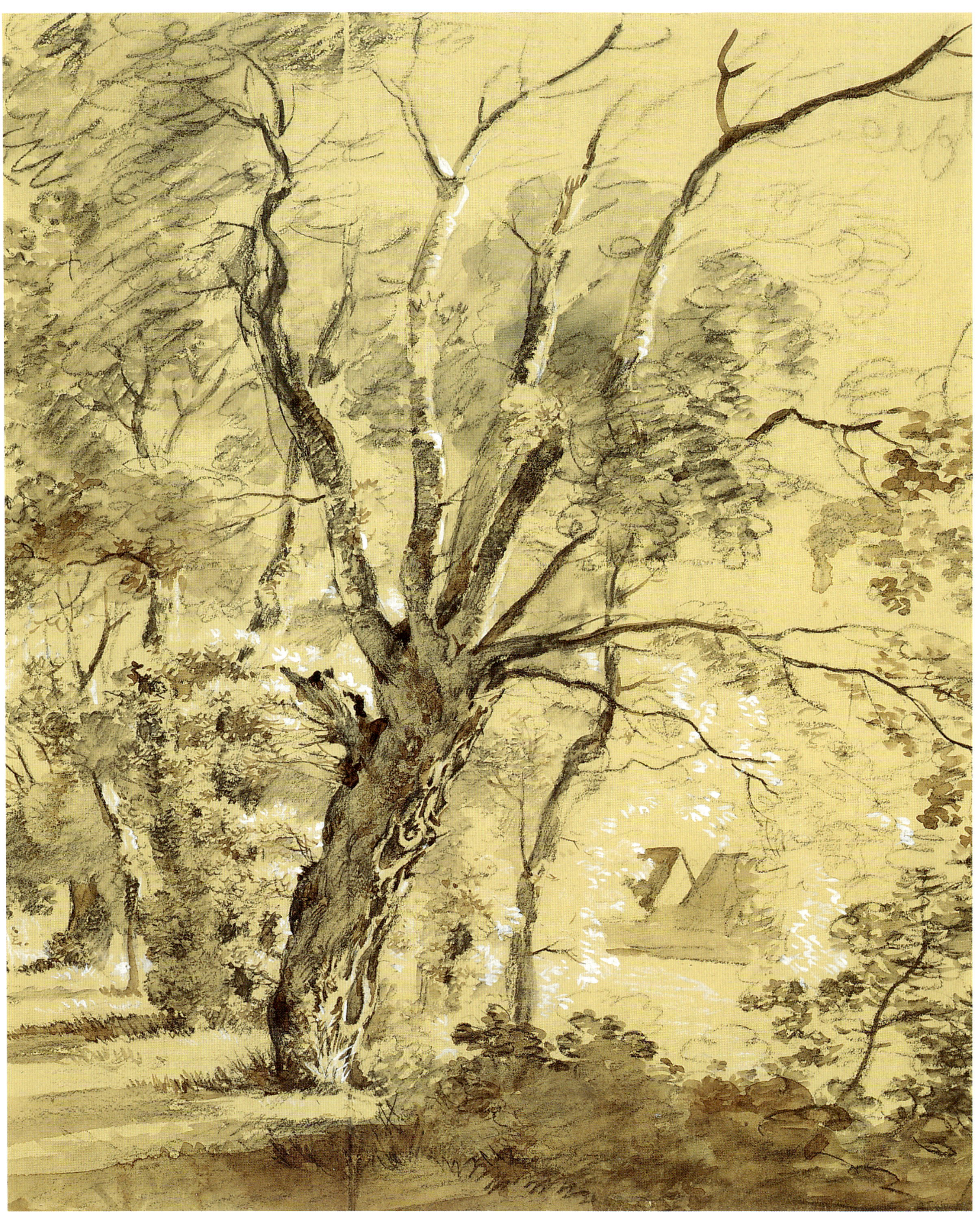

Books From California
51 W. Easy St
Simi Valley, CA 93065
UNITED STATES
customerservice@booksfromca.com

Books From California
51 W. Easy St
Simi Valley, CA 93065
UNITED STATES

To: Alibris APEX DC 76524090-23 - APEX
800 Avondale Ave.

Grandview Heights, OH 43212-3473
UNITED STATES

If this order is shipping from the US to an international buyer, remember to attach proper documentation. Complete and attach USPS Form CN-22 for all Priority Mail International Envelopes or First-Class Mail International shipments (available at your post office).

Order Number:	33164288
Ship Method:	Standard
Customer Name:	Alibris APEX DC 76524090-23 - APEX
Order Date:	7/6/2026
Alibris Order #:	76524090-23
Email:	

Items:

Qty	Item	Locator	Item ID	Condition
1	Fuseli to Menzel: Drawings and Watercolors in the Age of Goe...a German Private Collection Sieveking, Hinrich SKU: mon0004054346 ISBN: 0916724972 - Books	D -1-01-224-001-284	76524090-23	Good

Notes:

Good Very Clean Copy-Over 500, 000 Internet Orders Filled. Paperback

If you have any questions or concerns regarding this order, please contact us at customerservice@booksfromca.com
Thanks for your order!

Hinrich Sieveking

Fuseli to Menzel

*Drawings and Watercolors
in the Age of Goethe
from a German Private Collection*

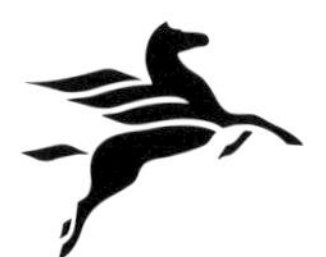

Prestel

Munich · New York

In cooperation with the
Busch-Reisinger Museum
Harvard University Art Museums,
Cambridge, Massachusetts

This book appeared on the occasion of the exhibition of the same name,
organized by the Busch-Reisinger Museum, Harvard University Art Museums, and held at:

Busch-Reisinger Museum, Cambridge, from April 4 to June 7, 1998
The Frick Collection, New York, June 23 to August 30, 1998
The J. Paul Getty Museum, Los Angeles, from September 15 to November 29, 1998.

This exhibition and publication have been made possible
by the generous support of Merck, Finck & Co., Privatbankiers,
a member of the Barclays Group, with additional support
from the Friends of the Busch-Reisinger Museum.

MERCK FINCK & CO
PRIVATBANKIERS

Unless otherwise stated, all drawings and graphic works form part of the Winterstein Collection.

On the cover: Caspar David Friedrich, *The Source of the Elbe in the Riesengebirge*, c. 1830, (detail, see cat. 21)
Frontispiece: Johann Georg von Dillis, *Common White Willows on Prater Island*, c. 1820-30 (detail, see cat. 64)

© Prestel-Verlag, Munich · New York,
and The President and Fellows of Harvard College, 1998

Photographic credits: see page 231

Library of Congress Cataloging-in-Publication Data is available.

Edited by William W. Robinson and Peter Nisbet.
Copy-edited by Jenny Barber, Tawney Becker, Dawn Carelli, Nicole Chaison, Marsha Pomerantz, and Evelyn Rosenthal.

Translated from the German by Thomas Dunlap (essays and catalogue entries), and John Gabriel (biographies).
English translation of "The Loreley" on p. 200 is published by arrangement with the Carol Publishing Group.

Prestel-Verlag, Mandlstrasse 26, D-80802 Munich
Tel.: (+ 49-89) 38 17 09-0, Fax: (+49-89) 38 17 09-35
and 16 West 22nd Street, New York, NY 10010 USA
Tel.: (212) 671 8199, Fax: (212) 627 9866

Prestel books are available worldwide. Please contact your nearest
bookseller or write to either of the above addresses for information
concerning your local distributor.

Color lithography: Karl Dörfel, Munich
Black-and-white lithography: Wilhelm Vornehm, Munich
Typesetting: Max Vornehm, Munich
Font: Walbaum (Monotype)
Printing: Buchdruckerei Holzer, Weiler im Allgäu
Binding: Oldenbourg, Kirchheim bei München

Printed in Germany on acid-free paper

ISBN 0-916724-97-2 (paperback, not available to the trade)
ISBN 3-7913-1929-9 (cloth)

Foreword

It is with great pleasure that the Busch-Reisinger Museum presents this exhibition of German drawings from the period 1760 to 1850 from the Munich collection of Alfred Winterstein. Long known but little seen, the collection is among the most important of its kind in the world. Celebrated for both its quality and depth in representing the distinguished achievements of German drawings from the time of Goethe, it was begun in 1925 by Alfred Winterstein and has been continued by his son, Wilhelm.

Out of great respect for the eye, knowledge, and accomplishment of Alfred Winterstein, and as such collections do not exist in the United States, where French and Italian drawings have been widely collected, we proposed organizing this exhibition and touring it to major cities in America and to Germany as well, where the Winterstein drawings are especially prized.

For his generous and enthusiastic participation in our endeavor, as well as for his trust in us, we are deeply grateful to Wilhelm Winterstein, and to his wife, Haidi.

We are also grateful to Hinrich Sieveking, the exhibition curator, whose knowledge of German drawings from this period is unsurpassed and who has written a definitive catalogue, rich in original scholarly contributions to the field. This has been a project of many years for Dr. Sieveking, and we are sincerely grateful for his dedication, humor, and good friendship.

At Harvard, the exhibition has been organized by Peter Nisbet, Daimler-Benz Curator of the Busch-Reisinger Museum, and William W. Robinson, the Fogg Art Museum's Ian Woodner Curator of Drawings; while Jane Montgomery, the Harvard University Art Museums' registrar, and Rebecca Wright, our manager of grants and traveling exhibitions, coordinated its tour with care, precision, and diplomacy. The German text has been ably translated into English by Thomas Dunlap, edited by Bill Robinson and Peter Nisbet, and copyedited by Jenny Barber, Tawney Becker, Dawn Carelli, Nicole Chaison, Marsha Pomerantz, and Evelyn Rosenthal. The biographies were translated by John Gabriel, Worpswede, Germany.

Of course, the exhibition would not be possible without the financial support of the Friends of the Busch-Reisinger Museum, led by Timotheus R. Pohl, and Merck, Finck & Co., Munich; or without the enthusiastic participation of our colleagues, Rolfe Bothe and Hermann Mildenberger of the Staatliche Kunstsammlungen Weimar; Christoph Vitali of the Haus der Kunst, Munich; Herbert Beck and Margret Stuffmann of the Städelsches Kunstinstitut und Städtische Galerie, Frankfurt am Main; Charles A. Ryskamp of the Frick Collection, and his successor, Samuel Sachs, New York; and John Walsh of the J. Paul Getty Museum, Los Angeles.

To all who have contributed so much to the success of this exhibition, especially to Wilhelm and Haidi Winterstein, we are sincerely grateful.

James Cuno
Elizabeth and John Moors Cabot Director
Harvard University Art Museums

The Collector Alfred Winterstein

Collecting is one of the essential prerequisites for a superior education: it awakens and develops powers of the soul and the mind that would otherwise be dormant, it allows an emotional contact with the mysterious nature of knowledge and art, and a glimpse into their workshop, it opens a path to things and into things, and it fills one with a calm, pervasive, and radiant feeling of joy, a feeling that is usually experienced only by the scholar or artist.... The collector, whose actions transcend his own person, has shown himself to be the indispensable foundation of all artistic creation. And as the center of inspiration for the circle in which he lives, he helps to transmit the artist's power, translated into a thousand cultural and economic values, to the entire nation.

Alfred Lichtwark (1852–1914)
Director of the Kunsthalle, Hamburg

In the nineteenth century and at the beginning of the twentieth, Germany, unlike France and especially England, had no mature tradition of collecting drawings. With few exceptions, such as members of the royal house of Saxony, German princes neglected this branch of art, which is rather quiet, and not suitable for political representation. Outside the public institutions, collecting graphic art in the broader sense was confined to a small circle of connoisseurs and amateurs, drawn primarily from the educated middle class. Moreover, in contrast to the other European schools, German art, with the exception of the Dürer period, was not collected internationally. Since the turn of the twentieth century, Germany's political entanglements have also contributed to this situation, which helps to explain why even today many museums outside of Germany have a lot of catching up to do. German drawings of the eighteenth and nineteenth centuries have remained, until recently, the domain of a few German collectors.

Beginning at the turn of this century, profound economic and social upheavals, driven by World War I and the worldwide economic crisis of the Great Depression, caused a redistribution of old wealth and art collections in Germany. One person who benefited was the legendary collector and banker Franz Koenigs, who had both the good fortune and financial resources. He was able to add even splendid pieces by Grünewald and Dürer to his incomparable collection of drawings by European old masters. It was during this time, as well, that the few significant private collections of early nineteenth-century drawings went on the market: in 1908, the part of Eduard Cichorius's outstanding collection of drawings that had not passed into the Kupferstichkabinett in Dresden; in 1911, the collection of Baron Adalbert von Lanna of Prague; in 1913, that of Alexander Flinsch of Berlin; in 1914, the collection of Arnold Otto Meyer of Hamburg, famous for its size and quality; and in 1921, that of the Princess Caroline zu Sayn-Wittgenstein. Cichorius and Meyer had been on friendly terms with Julius Schnorr von Carolsfeld, Moritz von Schwind, Ludwig Richter, Philipp Veit, and Edward von Steinle, and had been able to purchase even early works directly from the

artists. To gather a comparable collection from the early nineteenth century in the hands of a single person no longer seemed possible.

Beginning in the early 1920s, an unstable inflationary period following World War I, the lawyer Alfred Winterstein spent five decades assembling, with love and dedication, a collection of drawings, watercolors, and prints of the Goethe period (c. 1750 – c. 1850). Although smaller in scale, it followed the tradition of the great collections from the late nineteenth century.

During Alfred Winterstein's lifetime, opportunities for the collector were strongly influenced by political and economic conditions. In the period between the two world wars, the sources for a collector of German drawings remained largely limited to Germany, where much remained in private hands, and many artists' estates were still held by the descendants. The relevant market was concentrated in Germany and Austria. Until 1945, the most important place where art changed hands was the venerable auction house of C. G. Boerner in Leipzig, which specialized in drawings and prints; its beginnings reached back to the time of Goethe. It was here that most of the collections of note came under the hammer. The beautifully printed and carefully researched catalogues still provide valuable source material.

During the Nazi period, the value of German art was driven up excessively because the National Socialists considered it "national art." Since there was little international art on offer, the market was flush with German works of every period and style. Jewish collectors who read the signs of the times early enough sold their holdings or emigrated with them, which is how German art on a larger scale first made its way abroad, especially to the United States. During those years, in the back room of the Graphisches Kabinett Günther Franke in Munich, Alfred Winterstein occasionally acquired works by artists whose work was proscribed as "degenerate" during the Nazi period.

After 1945, to the extent that public collections were able to resume collecting at all, they were primarily concerned—at least in western Germany—with making up for losses they had suffered in early twentieth-century art under the Hitler regime. Consequently, the small circle of private collectors of early nineteenth-century German drawings still remained "undisturbed," so to speak. That would only change toward the end of the sixties, in the wake of a far-reaching social movement of reflection and reassessment. This situation also affected the art market, which was becoming increasingly international. German auction houses entered a difficult period as less and less material became available, while at the same time a new, dynamic art market specializing in old master drawings developed. For the most part, this change was precipitated and fostered by scholarship and the growing field of exhibitions, which now focused increasingly on the art of the nineteenth century. Let us cite, for example, the ambitious research project of the Fritz Thyssen Foundation, which produced numerous monographs on the history of nineteenth-century art, and the series of exhibitions on art from the period around 1800 that Werner Hofmann organized so successfully at the Hamburg Kunsthalle in the 1970s. This new focus can be traced in the bibliography of the present catalogue. The wealth of new publications diffused knowledge of the period more widely, and, given the growing competition among collectors and art dealers, it has become more difficult to make new finds.

Alfred Winterstein was born on 7 July 1895 in Dillingen on the Danube, and died on 21 April 1976 in Munich, at the age of eighty. The two world wars, which he experienced as soldier and officer, marked significant breaks in his life. Immediately after graduating from the humanistic Wilhelmsgymnasium in Munich in 1914, he volunteered for military service. After the war he studied law, obtaining his doctorate *juris utriusque* in 1923, and his assessor qualification in 1924. In 1925 he married Elisabet von Finck in Regensburg, who shared his interest in art. Elisabet, the daughter of the banker Wilhelm von Finck, a direct descendant of Stephan Freiherr von Stengel (1750–1822), the art-collecting cabinet secretary of the electorate of the Palatinate and Bavaria, an amateur draftsman and friend of Johan Georg von Dillis, not only understood her husband's passion for collecting, but contributed enthusiasm of her own. After spending some years gaining experience in the business world, Alfred Winterstein settled as a lawyer in Munich in 1927. He pursued his profession with pleasure well into old age, serving during his last years on the board of directors of the Isar-Amper-Werke and the Vereinigte Werkstätten für Kunst im Handwerk.

In World War II., Winterstein served on various fronts, first as a captain, later as a major. While his collection escaped destruction, tied into a bundle and placed for safekeeping with farmers in the countryside, he himself was taken prisoner and interned in Yugoslavia; he did not return until 1951. During those hard years of forced labor, he gave lectures on art (inspired by memories of his collection) and law in the prisoner-of-war camp, as part of a so-called barbed-wire university.

Winterstein hailed from a Franconian family from the Würzburg region. His father was an upper-level Bavarian civil servant who for many years held a leading position in the ministry of culture. A home in which art was appreciated, together with a humanistic education, provided the fertile soil in which Winterstein's early penchant for art collecting first sprouted. From the outset he was interested in drawings, initially of the early German period. Drawings by Dürer and his contemporaries, however, were exceedingly rare and unaffordable, even during the inflationary twenties. It was easier to pur-

sue his interest in prints of the incunebula and Dürer periods, an interest to which relevant literature and the first edition of Sebastian Brant's *Ship of Fools*, illustrated with woodcuts by the young Dürer, in his library continue to attest. This interest may have been awakened by contemporary expressionist art, which invoked its roots in early German woodcuts in such publications as Kandinsky's almanac *Der Blaue Reiter* [The Blue Rider] or Carl Georg Heise's *Genius*.

The ground for Alfred Winterstein's decision to embrace German drawing of the eighteenth and nineteenth century had also been prepared by the 1906 centennial exhibition in Berlin, organized by Alfred Lichtwark and Hugo von Tschudi: it was a gigantic inventory of the art of the German-speaking lands between 1775 and 1875, with a focus on the early nineteenth century. It had led to a rediscovery of many outstanding but long-forgotten talents from the Goethe period. But specialized follow-up exhibitions were not mounted until about ten years after the first world war—in 1925 in Heidelberg, a monographic exhibition on the work of Carl Philipp Fohr, and in the following year in Lübeck, Carl Georg Heise's exhibition *Friedrich*

Alfred Winterstein in summer 1975

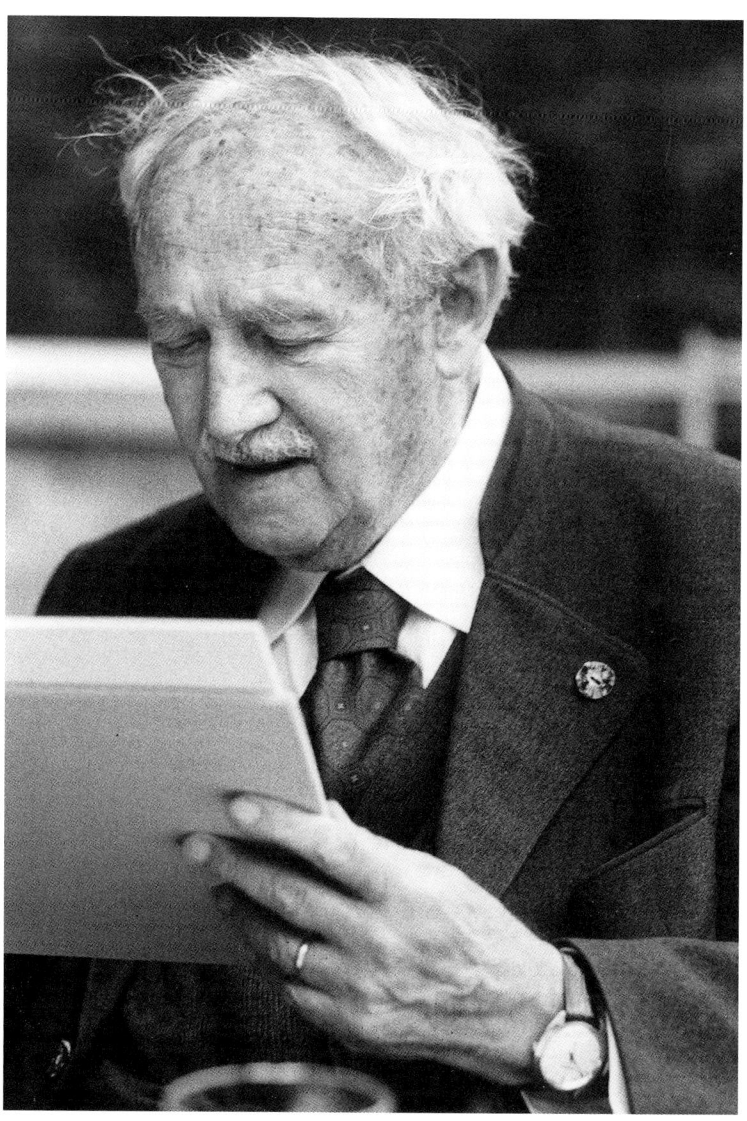

Overbeck and His Circle. Both shows were pioneering achievements in diffusing knowledge about early nineteenth-century drawing. Also important was the 1931 Munich exhibition of masterpieces of German Romantic painting, *From Caspar David Friedrich to Moritz von Schwind*, which was totally destroyed in the Glass Palace fire.

The Fohr exhibition in Heidelberg was a key experience for Alfred Winterstein, recently married and working in Mannheim at the time. Fohr's brilliant draftsmanship awoke in Winterstein the desire to collect works of the Romantic period. It is possible that he detected parallels to the drawings of the Dürer period. Winterstein was fascinated by the cultural flowering of the Romantic era in music, literature, and the visual arts; in its drawings he felt the pulse of that exciting time. The diversity of artistic directions and stylistic developments, from Fuseli to the young Menzel, captivated him. Winterstein also felt a close bond to the work of Goethe, whose life had spanned the period, and many connections could be made between his growing collection and the life of the great poet. Winterstein created a "Goethe room" in period style, with original furniture, pictures, porcelain, and—most importantly—a small library of first editions of classic German literature, in his country home in the foothills of the Bavarian Alps, not far from where Goethe had stayed in early September of 1786, on his way to Italy. Collecting drawings of the age of Goethe followed naturally. Within this scope Winterstein did, however, focus on the Romantic period, with the chronological end point set, with some exceptions, at around 1830. It was still possible to find important drawings and watercolors of the Goethe period, even at affordable prices. By sticking to fixed and relatively low limits at auctions, Winterstein, who collected throughout his life with limited funds, pursued an astonishing price policy that is hard to imagine today. What made this possible in the first place was relatively weak competition at auctions: apart from the public museums, there was only a small circle of private connoisseurs and collectors, most of whom knew each other and were even friends.

Collecting is a learning process in taste and awareness of quality. In the beginning, Winterstein was not concerned with amassing only masterpieces, but was fascinated first of all by an artist's characteristic touch, which could also be found in more modest sheets. His demand for quality grew rapidly, along with his knowledge, and his affinity for the artistically extraordinary led to an early interest in Carl Philipp Fohr and Johann Georg von Dillis. Winterstein compiled small, specialized holdings of works by both artists, who are represented in his collection by superb pieces from various stages of their development. Artists in whom he took a particular interest included Julius Schnorr von Carolsfeld, Ludwig Emil Grimm, and Moritz von Schwind, whose development and versatility from their early to their mature works can be studied in this collection. Winterstein made every effort to obtain the exceedingly rare works of other artists for whom he had a special fondness as well: Franz Horny, Fohr, Franz Pforr, August Heinrich, and Johann Evangelist Scheffer von Leonhardshoff. Because these artists had died young, they had left behind relatively small oeuvres, usually of works on paper, and for that reason had often fallen into obscurity. Not all these drawings that Winterstein acquired are masterpieces in themselves, but each is important for understanding the artist's overall career. Obtaining works by the major figures of German Romanticism, Philipp Otto Runge and Caspar David Friedrich, had always been difficult, but characteristic works by both artists ended up in the collection, and Friedrich is better represented here than in some public collections.

Winterstein was also fond of artist portraits, self-portraits, and above all, landscapes. He appreciated the drawing of the early Nazarenes because of its outstanding quality, and felt a particular attraction to the art of the Munich school. In the circle of collectors of the Munich group "Mappe," energetically led by Lotte Roth-Wölfle, Alfred Winterstein showed originals from his collection and spoke about some of his favorite themes that run through it, which also render the bounds of his collection more transparent: "Artists discover the Salzburg countryside," "The English Garden in Munich," "German artists see Italy," "The portrait in the Goethe period and in the Romantic era," "Goethe and his contemporaries in book and image: Autographs and portraits," "Select prints from around 1800: Graphic art of Neoclassicism and Romanticism," "On the 150th anniversary of the death of Carl Philipp Fohr: A report on his life and work," and "Austrian drawings of the nineteenth century." Winterstein also devoted himself actively to the art of Austrian watercolor, which had reached its acme in the work of Rudolf von Alt during the nineteenth century, and had taken on the unique characteristics of a national school.

Winterstein was greatly influenced by his friendly contacts with other collectors, such as Paul Arndt in Munich, Carl Heumann in Chemnitz, and not least Eugen Roth in Munich, who expressed the psychology of art collecting with such keen perceptiveness and humor in his book *Sammelsurium*. Winterstein's active exchanges with many art historians, museum professionals, and art dealers were of importance, and bonds of friendship tied him to curators who were particularly knowledgeable in the field of drawing: men like Edmund Schilling, the former director of the Kupferstichkabinett at the Städelsches Kunstinstitut, Frankfurt, who emigrated to England; Ludwig Grote, the supporter of the move of the Bauhaus to Dessau and later director of the Germanisches Nationalmuseum in Nuremberg; and especially Peter Halm, the first postwar director of the Staatliche Graphische Sammlung in Munich, who mounted the first exhibition of the Winterstein collection in 1958. Later came friendly ties to Keith Andrews, director of the prints and drawings collection at the National Gallery of Scotland in Edinburgh, and to his student, the English art historian Colin Bailey. For years Winterstein maintained close contact with Jens Christian Jensen in Heidelberg. Ever since his schooldays, he had been good friends with the art dealer Fritz Nathan, the former owner of the Ludwigsgalerie in Munich, who was forced into Swiss exile by the political situation. It was through Nathan that some lovely and important pieces, like the double portrait of Overbeck and Cornelius (cat. 29), entered the collection after the war.

Winterstein regarded the collecting of drawings, which allow such a direct insight into the process of artistic work, as a creative and culturally important activity. The older he became, the more intensively he devoted himself to it, and it gave him great and obvious joy. He liked to interest young people in the art of drawing, and he tried, with demonstrated success, to awaken in them a passion for collecting. Winterstein loved to look at the original works with others who shared his interest, and to them his collection was always open and accessible. He understood collecting also as a research mission. Along with his collection, he systematically built up a specialized library of artist monographs, essays, and exhibition and auction catalogues; around the collection and library a small cultural center developed in his Munich home, where lively research took place in exchanges with art historians and with collectors. In the early nineteenth century, many artists, including those who have not become so well known, had used the same drawing media and had often worked collectively, drawing in almost indistinguishably similar fashion; problems of attribution have therefore been inevitable. Borderline cases—is it Dillis or Dorner, Overbeck or Pforr, Fohr or Horny, Wassermann or Janssen—were discussed and resolved within the Winterstein collection. The collector took special pleasure in helping students of art history, who sought his aid in questions relating to their dissertations. In many cases he provided the impulse behind dissertations and followed their progress with encouragement through years of personal contact. In this way, much of what he knew was able to find its way into scholarship. Winterstein himself did not put his knowledge and experiences into writing; self-critical and modest, he left scholarly interpretation of his insights to others. In grateful recognition of this fact, a number of publications, including such substantial ones as Siegfried Wichmann's important monograph on Wilhelm von Kobell, were dedicated to him as a collector. Winterstein's careful notes on the old mats, where the latest state of scholarship was recorded, have also survived, and these notes formed the scholarly basis on which Peter Halm and Peter Vignau-Wilberg compiled the catalogues for the 1958 and the 1969 exhibitions, respectively; these two shows made the Winterstein collection known to the public. The notes are also reflected in the current catalogue.

The first exhibition in 1958, *Deutsche Zeichenkunst der Goethezeit: Handzeichnungen und Aquarelle aus der Sammlung Winterstein, München* [German Drawing from the Goethe Period: Drawings and Watercolors from the Winterstein Collection, Munich], comprised a selection of 175 pieces, supplemented by seven works by Austrian artists, chiefly watercolors. The beautiful catalogue was issued by the publishing house of Winterstein's friend Max Hirmer, a professor of botany and a photographer. In 1958–59, the exhibition traveled from Munich to Nuremberg, Hamburg, Heidelberg, Hagen, Stuttgart, and Cologne, and to Berne in Switzerland. The second exhibition, *Deutsche Zeichnungen 1800–1850* [German Drawings 1800–1850], with a selection of 198 works, was mounted in 1969 only in Lübeck, on the occasion of the hundredth anniversary of the death of Friedrich Overbeck. Since that time there have been more requests for loans made on a frequent basis. Winterstein generously made photographs available for scholarly use, and supported exhibitions with key loans. Given that many museums today are increasingly reluctant to lend, his activities highlighted one important function of an actively managed private collection.

With the genuine curiosity of a scholar and a well-trained eye, Winterstein acquired such a high degree of connoisseurship and such an unerring feel for quality that art historians, museum people, collectors, and dealers were always soliciting his advice. He also placed his rich stock of experience in service to the public. As a specialist in the nineteenth century, his judgment carried weight in the State Art Acquisitions Committee of Bavaria, on which he served, initially under Eberhard Hanfstaengl, for twenty-five years. In 1952, he was among the founding members of the Verein zur Förderung der Alten Pinakothek [Association for the Promotion of the Alte Pinakothek]; he was active on its board, and for a time was also its chairman. He worked on behalf of contemporary art on the board of trustees of the Munich Kunstverein, and to the end of his life was on the board of the Munich Galerie-Verein.

Open-mindedness and a capacity for enthusiasm characterized Alfred Winterstein; the charisma, kindness, and humanity he radiated will always be remembered. Exquisite quality and a broad intellectual range characterize his collection, which was carried on after his death with great commitment first by his widow, Elisabet Winterstein, and after her death in 1989 by his son, Wilhelm Winterstein. This next generation of the family is not guarding the collection as something immutable and complete, but is continuing to add to it, guided by the principles set by its founder, and with high standards of quality; at the same time, it is keeping the collection accessible. About a quarter of the works shown in the present exhibition were acquired after Alfred Winterstein's death, some by Elisabet Winterstein. In the spirit of its founder, this collection is being shown again, in a concentrated selection. The fact that the initiative came from Harvard University's Busch-Reisinger Museum would have pleased him. When his collection was first presented in Germany and Switzerland, Winterstein also considered a venue in the United States, but that did not happen. Instead, in 1972 he supported an exhibition of German master drawings of the nineteenth century at the Busch-Reisinger Museum with significant loans, some of which are now returning (cat. 29, 57, 63). The present selection of eighty drawings offers a representative overview of the collection and is a kind of anthology.

As Hugo von Hofffmannsthal said, "Among all the works of the fine arts, the drawing is the most spiritual in nature and allows the most spiritual relationship to art." To Alfred Winterstein, Weimar had been something like the spiritual center of his collection. The Cold War and the partition of Germany made it impossible in 1958 to exhibit his collection there. That the present exhibition is now not only possible in Weimar, but can begin its tour there, is of special significance, and nothing could better honor the memory of Alfred and Elisabet Winterstein. From there it will travel to various venues in Germany and the United States.

Fuseli to Menzel

Aspects of German Drawing in the Age of Goethe[1]

Moritz von Schwind, looking back over his life, wrote to the Hamburg merchant Arnold Otto Meyer, an important collector of drawings: "I do not think I err in believing that in our time more of what is important and rich in ideas is captured in drawings than in paintings." Making a general point that was not restricted to conditions in Munich under King Ludwig I of Bavaria, he went on to say: "Under Ludwig I a terrible practice was introduced and has since become firmly established, namely, that the execution of a picture is entrusted without hesitation to someone other than the person who conceived it. This is sufficient to explain why these works have inevitably been worse than the drawings."[2]

Let me begin my remarks with the thesis that Schwind's assessment of drawing as an essential expression of the age, along with the notion that it held an extremely high rank among the various genres of art, is valid for the entire age of Goethe, even from our perspective today. Drawing was the leading medium of pictorial art during that period. To no small degree this was the result of the literary character of the era, eloquent testimony of which is the fact that the entire period is named after its preeminent poet and writer. Its outstanding cultural achievements came in the areas of music, philosophy, and literature, and art and literature are intimately interrelated. Evidence of this interrelation is, not least, the existence of identical terms in art history and the history of literature (e.g., "idyll"), as well as the phenomenon of many individuals who were talented as both artists and writers, the best known example being Goethe himself. When it came to illustrating the written word, the art of drawing had a key role to play.

The Age of Goethe

The Goethe period in the narrower sense coincides with the life dates of the great German poet, 1749 to 1832. Here I use the phrase in a wider sense to refer to the century between 1750 and 1850, when Goethe's artist-contemporaries—who belonged to different generations, from Daniel Chodowiecki to Adolph Menzel—lived and worked. The title of the exhibition, *Fuseli to Menzel*, identifies two outstanding personalities who were polar opposites as artists. They stand, respectively, at the beginning and the end of this epoch in the German-speaking lands, and are included in this exhibition with representative works (cat. 10, 11, and 78–80).

Goethe's life spanned an era of intellectual, social, economic, and political transformation. The turn of the century marked the transition from the court-dominated eighteenth century to the burgher-dominated nineteenth century. In 1803–06, the Holy Roman Empire of the German nation dissolved under pressure from Napoleon. Goethe lived through the Enlightenment and secularization, absolutism and constitutional monarchy, the French Revolution, the Napoleonic occupation and the Wars of Liberation, Restora-

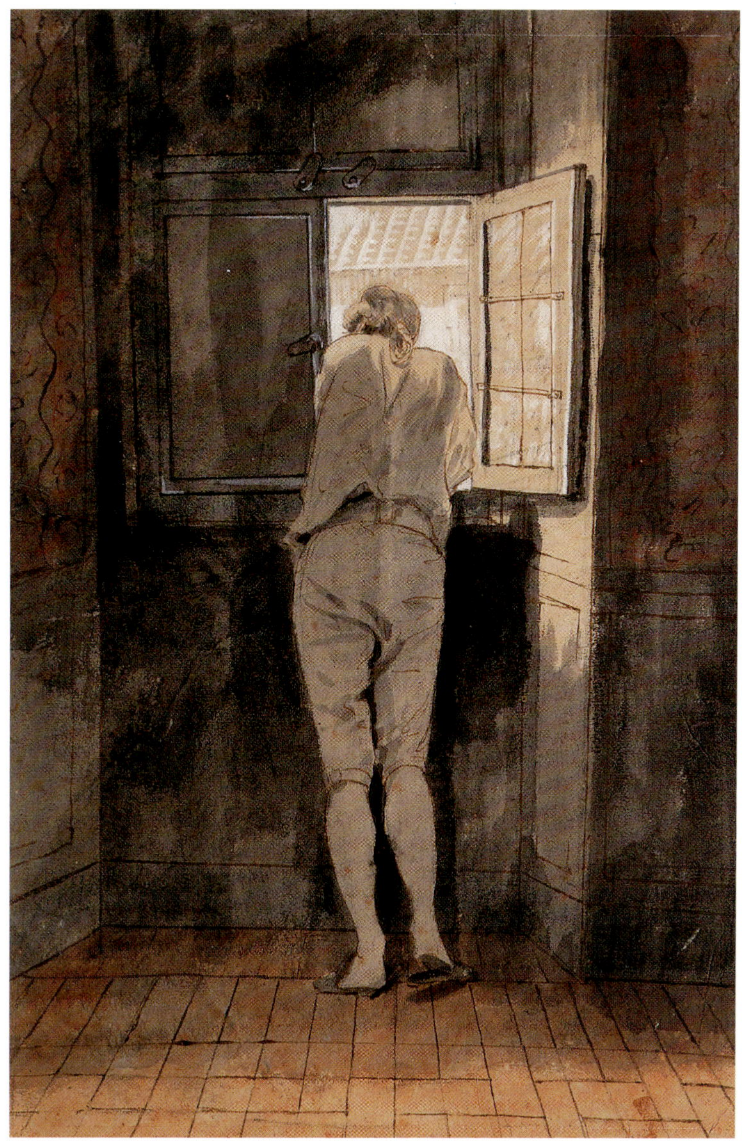

1 Johann Heinrich Wilhelm Tischbein,
Goethe at the Window of the Roman Apartment on the Corso, 1787.
Watercolor, chalk, and pen over pencil, on laid paper; 415 x 266 mm.
Frankfurt am Main, Freies Deutsches Hochstift/Frankfurter Goethe-Museum

tion, Sturm und Drang, Romanticism, and Biedermeier. The changes in the lives and consciousness of the people of his time found expression in a multitude of artistic trends that narrow stylistic terms such as rococo, neoclassicism, and realism cannot begin to define.

Moreover, artistic creation in the German-speaking lands showed differences in approach and style. Germany was not a centralized state like France, but was politically splintered into a colorful palette of large, medium-sized, and numerous small states.[3] More significant than any territorial boundaries were the effects of the religious division into the Protestant north and the Catholic south. The conditions for artistic work in the independent, republican trading cities were different from those in the absolute monarchies of Bavaria, Prussia, and Saxony. No one national center of art like Paris, Copenhagen, London, or Rome existed at that time in the German lands, and the way in which artistic taste in Germany oriented itself toward these foreign centers varied according to geography. This was especially true in the second half of the eighteenth century, though it carried over even into the early nineteenth century. The academies of these foreign centers were magnets for aspiring artists from neighboring German territories: for example, the Academy in Copenhagen attracted Caspar David Friedrich from Greifswald and Philipp Otto Runge from Hamburg; the Academy in London drew Johann Heinrich Ramberg from Hannover; and the Academy in Paris attracted Johann Anton Ramboux from Trier.

The leading academies in the German-speaking lands were those in Berlin, Vienna, Dresden, and Munich;[4] Düsseldorf did not join their ranks until the middle of the nineteenth century. These academies were supported by the courts, and their mission was to train the next generation of artists. Strict academic rules allowed aspiring artists little room for individual development. In response, many outstanding talents, such as Henry Fuseli or Joseph Anton Koch, sought their own path outside the academy and abroad, especially in liberal Rome, where differences of social class mattered little and Germans of every regional background considered themselves simply Germans. The first—albeit unspectacular—secession from an academy was instigated by the Nazarenes in Vienna.

With the end of the traditional form of patronage and the development of an art market in the modern sense, the social position of the artist was changing. The middle class played a more prominent role alongside the traditional patrons, the Church and the nobility. But artists without any connection to a court often lived at the edge of poverty. Because they were working increasingly without patronage, especially in the field of graphic arts, they needed new ways to sell their works of art. That was precisely the purpose of the exhibitions mounted by the newly established artist and art unions.[5]

The Age of Dürer/The Age of Goethe

In German art history there were two periods in which drawing assumed a leading role: the period around 1500, the age of Dürer; and the period around 1800, the age of Goethe or the Romantic era, especially the early nineteenth century. The visual arts of both periods show strong graphic tendencies, and their most eminent artists produced important work as draftsmen. Many artists—and this applies particularly to the Goethe period, largely because a number of artists died young—are documented primarily as draftsmen, and it was as draftsmen that they created the very essence of their work. These periods have parallel historical developments that led to the autonomous position of drawing. The age of Dürer and the age of Goethe were times of radical intellectual, social, economic, and political change. The Dürer period witnessed the transition from the late Gothic to the early Renaissance with the spread of humanism

and the Reformation. In the Goethe period rococo, neoclassicism, various permutations of romanticism, and realism succeeded one another rapidly under the banner of the Enlightenment. Both periods saw equivalent changes in the situation of the artist, which resulted from the loosening of traditional bonds and conventions: the constraints of the guilds and the anonymity of the collective workshop in the Dürer period, and the strict regimen of the academies in the Goethe period. This process of liberation had consequences for artistic creation that are still important today. The model sheet or model book of the anonymous medieval craftsman was only gradually replaced, during the Dürer period, by the nature study drawn by the artist's individual hand and by the personal sketchbook. Similarly, during the age of Goethe, the direct study of nature gradually replaced the practice of copying from models at the academy. In both periods, the individualization of artists and their artistic self-awareness developed in tandem with the rise of an educated and affluent middle class. A related development led to the autonomous drawing, i.e., drawings created for their own sake as independent works of art, which did not serve an auxiliary function in the creative process. Drawings were appreciated in their own right and became collectible. The emancipatory changes in the lives and consciousness of people corresponded to the development of a personal style on the part of the artist.

Drawings are also signs of their times. The art of drawing is, figuratively speaking, the handwriting of its respective era, and historical discontinuities and changes are reflected more subtly in drawing than in other forms of art. Later, in a retrospective context, I will discuss parallels in the development of autonomous draftsmanship and the interesting phenomenon that aspects of the Dürer period were frequent themes in drawings of the age of Goethe.

The huge number of talented draftsmen in the Goethe period, so large that it is hard for us to fathom, is unique in the history of German art and comparable only to the appearance of the many outstanding painters in the Netherlands during the seventeenth century. For example, several hundred German artists lived in Rome during the first three decades of the nineteenth century. Most of these were draftsmen who worked at a high level, but whose individual style is often impossible to discern. Many German artists of the Goethe period were primarily draftsmen, even if they called themselves painters. The body of work they left behind consists chiefly of drawings, and it is above all as draftsmen, not as painters, that they assert their rank as artists. One should also mention the phenomenon of countless dilettante draftsmen: among the nobility, drawing lessons were as much a part of traditional education as music lessons. The ability to draw was an expression of a higher education, in keeping with one's social status. By the Goethe period, private drawing instruction had also established itself among the upper middle class as an important component of education and a means of self-improvement (fig. 9).[6]

Drawing in the Goethe period is a vast and complex field. This introductory essay can be no more than a simplified survey of some important innovations and aspects of this art; examples are drawn chiefly from the genres of portraiture and landscape. My discussion of the varied developments and stylistic trends of the period is based mainly on the present selection of characteristic drawings and watercolors from the Winterstein collection. I will also address changing

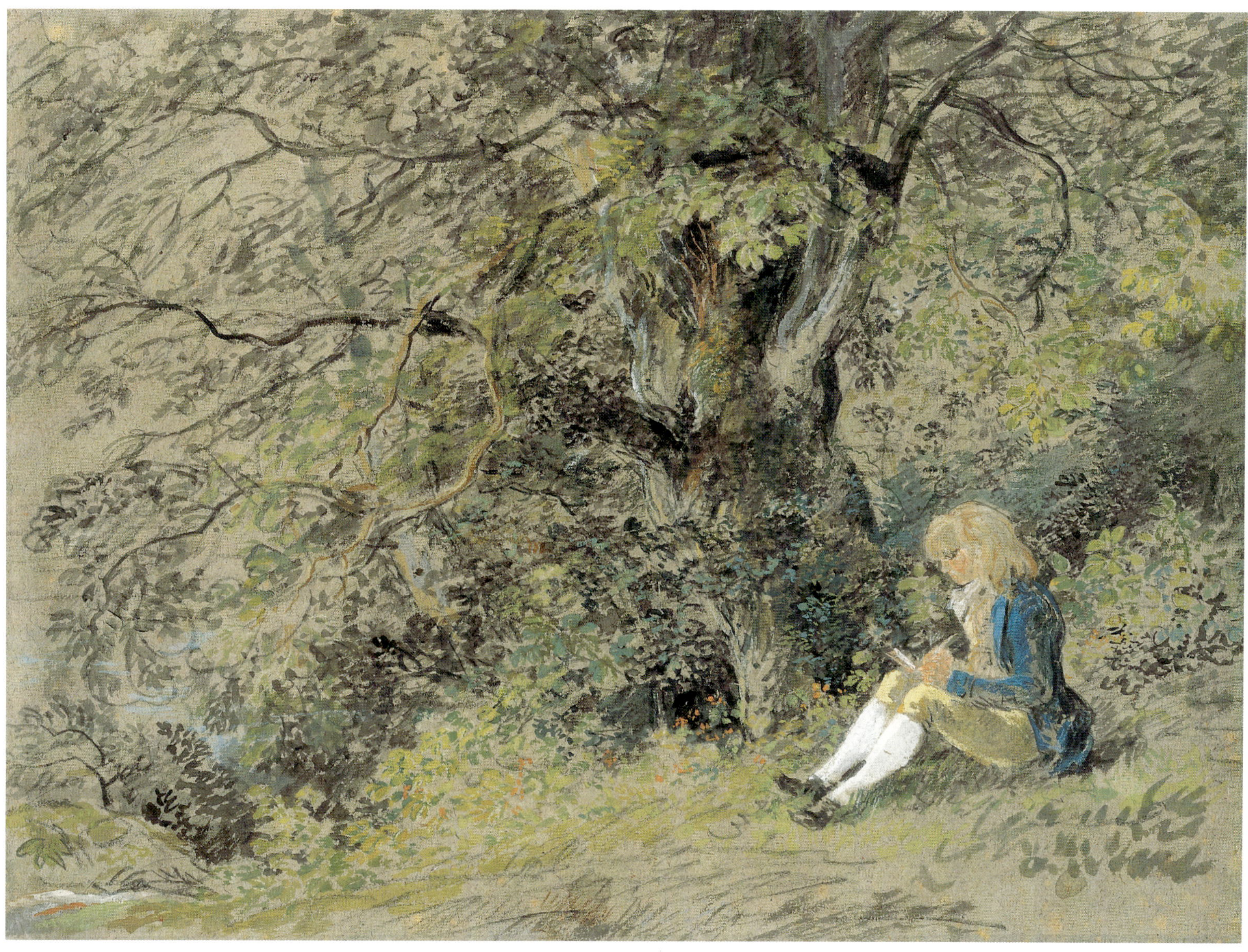

5 Johann Georg von Dillis, *A Draftsman Outdoors, Presumably Cantius Dillis,
Drawing in the English Garden*, c. 1790.
Black chalk, pencil, watercolor, and gouache, on gray-tinted laid paper; 240 x 313 mm

Philipp Otto Runge; much later even Max Ernst would continue to draw inspiration from it. Arcadian elements, central motifs in the work of Reinhart (cat. 4), are also hinted at in the figural staffage of the otherwise rather conventionally composed, classical-idealized landscape by the Mannheim-Munich artist Franz Kobell (cat. 3).

The Swiss Henry Fuseli, a man of many talents who exploded all conventions, is one of the most fascinating artists of the age of Goethe (cat. 10, 11). As a writer and visual artist he was a chief exponent of Sturm und Drang and its cult of the genius. He settled in England and is today considered a member of the English school, an example of an artist from the German-speaking lands who assimi-

lated in a foreign country. His self-portrait from around 1790, executed in black chalk, represents a compelling and impressive dialogue with himself (fig. 6). Fuseli, about forty years of age in the drawing, portrayed himself in the pose of melancholy, of self-questioning and self-analysis, mirroring the awakening of a new self-awareness. A parallel in terms of development and motif can be found in Albrecht Dürer's Erlangen self-portrait of circa 1492, which for the first time, with expressive power, addressed the theme "Know thyself" (fig. 7).[20] In the age of Dürer, the individual portrait as an artistic category developed only slowly from various roots, through, for example, the individualization of saints' figures, traditionally stylized in a formulaic way, or from the donor portrait. In the age of Goethe, by contrast, the portrait fulfilled a classic artistic purpose, as it had done since the Renaissance.

Moreover, a new image of the individual, freed from the boundaries of class and social position, the kind of image that had already characterized the realistic middle-class art of the northern Netherlands in the seventeenth century, established itself during the Sturm und Drang period. The rise of the middle class went hand in hand with German artists taking the art of Rembrandt and his contemporaries as a point of reference. Working in Rembrandt's manner became fashionable and manifested itself also in portrait painting. Georg Friedrich Schmidt (1712–1775), a draftsman and engraver from Berlin, had done much to spread Dutch influence through his copies of Rembrandt's etchings. The impact of Dutch genre painting is particularly strong in Friedrich Müller (1749–1825) from the Palatinate, who called himself "Maler Müller" [Painter Müller] and, as a poet and a *peintre-graveur*, is one of the most interesting dual talents of the Sturm und Drang. The artistic ambitions of this "hothead" ranged from a realistic, popular, coarse "low style" to an aristocratic "high style."[21] Using fairly rough brush strokes with watercolors and gouache over red chalk, Müller portrayed members of the lower class, whose features are marked by hard work and a life of poverty.[22] His generalizing, blunt realism, which reflects his human sympathy, heralds a new and fundamental interest in the human being. Johann Georg Dillis demonstrated a similar sympathy for the socially marginalized in his depictions of the sick, the old, and the poor.[23] A social awareness of human misery, sharpened by the Enlightenment, also led to the growth of philanthropic activity and the goal of improving living conditions. The new philanthropic attitude was exemplified by Count Rumford, who, in Munich alone, did a great service by founding a poorhouse and a workhouse, by rehabilitating beggars, and by inventing heating devices such as cost-saving stoves and fireplaces (fig. 8).

Portrait and Physiognomy

Anton Graff of Zurich, who taught for decades at the Dresden Academy, made a name for himself as the leading portraitist of the

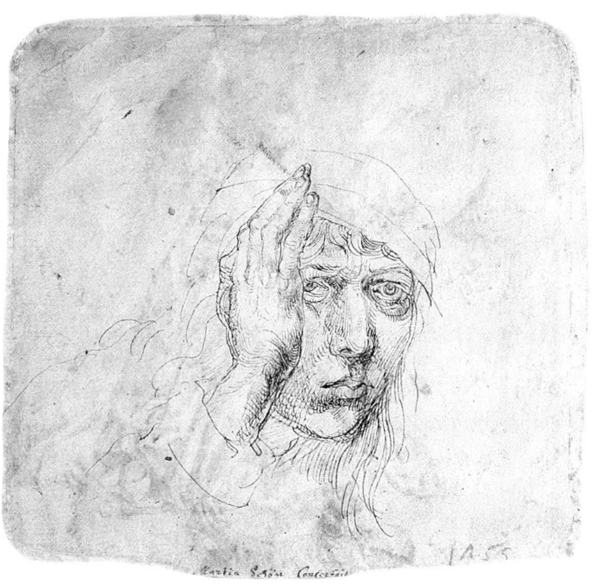

7 Albrecht Dürer, *Self-Portrait*, c. 1492.
Pen and gray-brown ink; 204 x 208 mm.
Erlangen, Graphische Sammlung der Universitätsbibliothek
Erlangen-Nürnberg

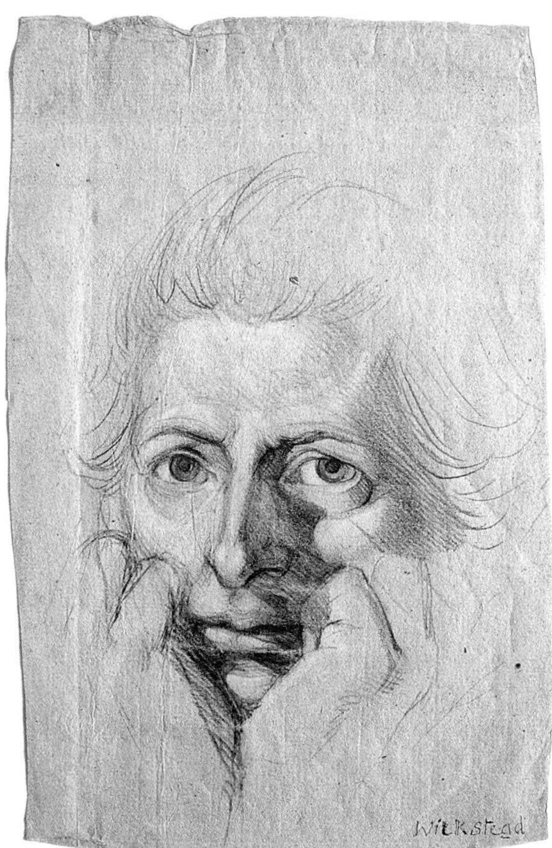

6 Henry Fuseli, *Self-portrait*, c. 1780–90.
Black chalk, heightened with white, on laid paper; 270 x 200 mm.
London, Victoria & Albert Museum

upper class in German-speaking countries. His self-portrait, circa 1784, executed in watercolor on vellum, is proof of his talent in capturing an individual soberly and objectively, a gift that was appreciated by the nobility and the middle class alike (cat. 13). His work testifies to two social trends that were characteristic of his time: the nobility was acquiring middle-class characteristics, and the economically successful and educated bourgeoisie was being raised to a more dignified level. Only a few years later, in 1792, Johann Georg von Dillis created, in a similar spirit, the portrait of the previously mentioned American Benjamin Thompson, on the occasion of his elevation to the title of Count Rumford (fig. 8).[24] A faint hint of the chromatic richness of the waning Bavarian Rococo is detectable in the colored chalks. Dillis has vividly captured the personality and alert gaze of this eminent man—scientist and inventor, philanthropist and champion of the English Garden. At the time, Rumford was serving as the minister of war at the court of the elector of Bavaria, after having fought in the American War of Independence on the side of the English (cf. cat. 8).[25]

French and Dutch influence combined in Daniel Chodowiecki's middle-class art; in the second half of the eighteenth century, Chodowiecki was a leading figure in Berlin's artistic and cultural life. An immensely prolific draftsman, he was the leading master of the middle-class genre scene, of the bourgeois Rococo in the Berlin of Frederick the Great, and a portraitist of the *Zopfstil*. Influenced by seventeenth-century Dutch interior genre paintings, he created in 1759 an intimate domestic scene of ladies at a social, playing cards, the earliest work in the present exhibition (cat. 12). In 1781, using colored chalks, he drew the family of the Hamburg wine merchant and senator Johann Valentin Meyer (fig. 9).The portrait represents the family as the source of human happiness, the parents as educators, and training in the art of drawing as part of the children's upbringing. Education in general was an important topic of discussion in middle-class circles during the Enlightenment. The sheet also sheds light on the relationship between artist and patron, who face each other as independent entrepreneurs, individuals of equal rank. Standing confidently though modestly at the right edge of the picture, Chodowiecki presents the family portrait to the collector. Thus, the circumstance of the commission has been made a subject in the drawing itself. The work also addresses an aspect of the history of collecting. With its growing importance as an autonomous medium of artistic expression, the drawing became an object of collecting in its own right, although this happened later in the German lands than in, say, England or France. Johann Valentin Meyer assembled a significant collection of drawings by old masters and by contemporary artists with whom he had friendly relations, including Goethe (cat. 6). In the late eighteenth century, when Hamburg did not yet have a public museum, his collection was considered an attraction, and he made it accessible to anyone who was interested. Still extant is Meyer's *album amicorum* (friendship album, or in German, *Stammbuch)*, the microcosm of a collection with entries by his artist-friends. Friendship albums, precursors of poetry albums, are treasure troves for the cultural history of the art of drawing, especially for the Goethe period. Drawings in an *album amicorum* of that time are also monuments to friendship.[26] Chodowiecki inscribed his drawing in Meyer's album with the words: "the inner side of my brain" (fig. 10). Evidently his head was abuzz with physiognomies. As on a model sheet, he drew the most diverse faces, from primitive and animal likenesses on the lower right to the bright faces of his collector friend and his wife and children in the center, an echo of William Hogarth's etching *3 Characters and 4 Caricatures* (1743).[27]

Interest in physiognomy was in the air at the time. Johann Heinrich Wilhelm Tischbein, for example, who had scientific ambitions, participated in the lively discussion on physiognomy. He saw anthropomorphic features in animals and animal features in humans, and established associations between animal physiognomies and human personality traits. The Zurich preacher Johann Caspar Lavater (1741–1801) endeavored to infer the qualities of a person's soul and character from the external shape of the face, a fateful idea which the contemporary philosopher Georg Christoph Lichtenberg (1742–1799) had already denounced as unscientific. In his *Physiognomische Fragmente zur Beförderung der Menschenkenntnis und der Menschenliebe* [Physiognomic Fragments to Further the Knowledge and Love of Humanity, published 1775–78], Lavater read and interpreted the silhouettes of prominent living personalities.

The portrait silhouette, in its reduction to a single color and to the pure profile outline, offered the highest degree of abstraction and simplification of the individual likeness. Easy to produce mechanically and therefore inexpensive, it was very widely disseminated. This special form of the 'reduced' portrait responded well to the

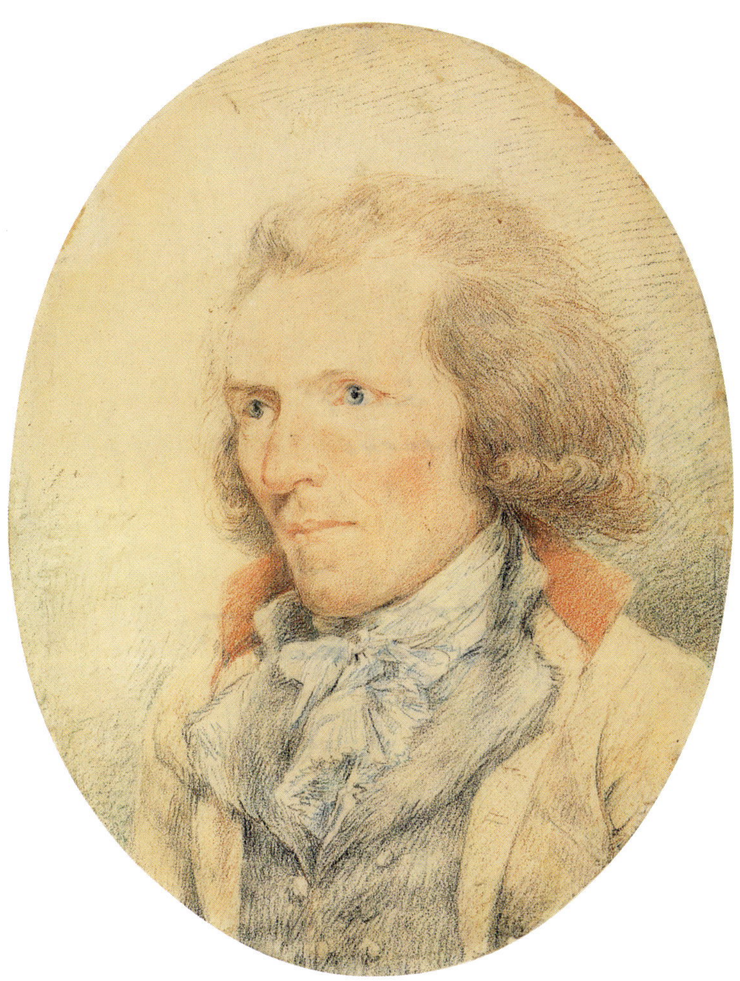

8 Johann Georg von Dillis,
Sir Benjamin Thompson, Count Rumford, 1792.
Colored chalks; 169 x 128 mm.
Munich, Staatliche Graphische Sammlung

growing demand for the individual likeness in the age of Goethe, and it enjoyed such popularity that it became the insignia of the age.

Outline and Reduction of Colors

Along with the silhouette (also called *Schattenriss*, or "shadow cut," in German), Pliny the Younger's legend of the invention of drawing, recorded in his *Historia naturalis*, became a popular subject in the visual arts. A girl in Corinth, so the legend goes, saw the shadow of

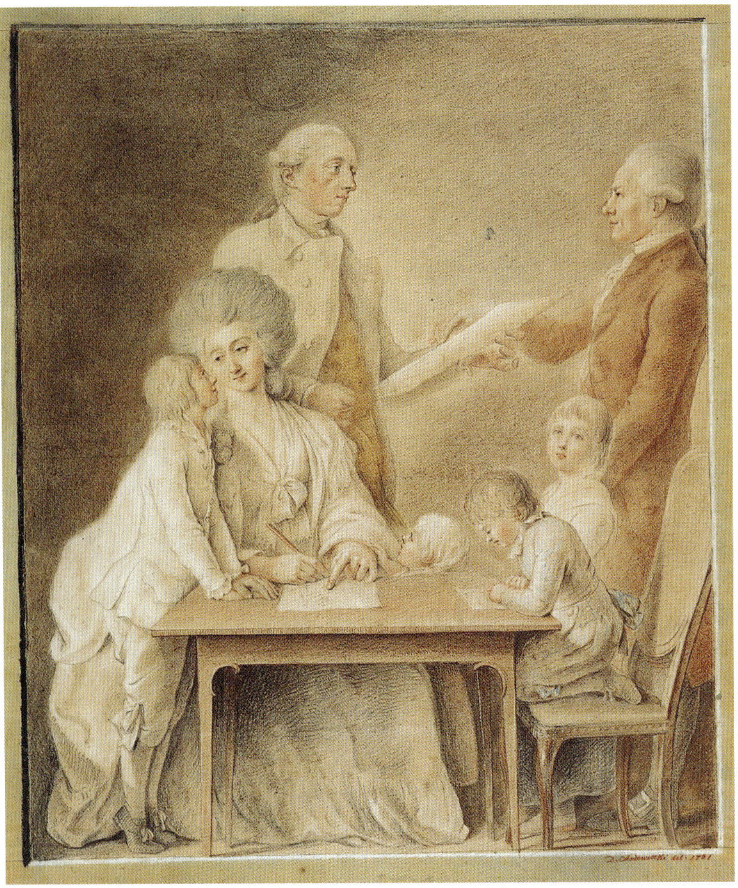

9 Daniel Chodowiecki,
Self-Portrait with the Family of Johann Valentin Meyer, 1781.
Colored chalks; 588 x 492 mm.
Hamburg, Museum für Hamburgische Geschichte

her beloved in the light of the candle as he was bidding her farewell
to go to war. To preserve at least his shadow image, she quickly
scratched the contours into the wall: drawing had been invented. The
girl's father, a potter, shaped a clay relief of the figure of the depart-
ing young man: the birth of sculpture. In the age of Goethe, this legend was still invoked in the debate about the preeminence of drawing over other artistic genres.[28]

In its essential characteristics—reduction to a single color and to
the pure outline—the silhouette coincided with basic artistic trends
of the period around 1800, the era of Neoclassicism and Romanticism (cat. 1, 2, 4–6, 14; 16–19, 28). Let me illustrate this with two
examples from the work of Philipp Otto Runge. In 1800, while at the
Copenhagen Academy, Runge drew the *Triumph of Amor* (fig. 11).
With its painterly distribution of light and shadow, this triumphal
procession of the god of love still belongs to the tradition of Baroque
ceiling painting. The handling of chiaroscuro, the reduction of color
to grisaille, and the modeling of the nude children after the example
of antique sculpture reveal characteristic traits of Neoclassical academic practice. The poem by Johann Gottfried Herder (1744–1803)
on which this work is based, the visual image into which it was translated, and the implied musical sound of the lyre produce a synesthesia of the arts of poetry, painting, and music. This fusion of art forms
already expresses an essential concern of the Romantic era.

Around 1800, the abstracting contour had established itself as the
characteristic international handwriting technique of Neoclassicism,
one that transcended that of individual artists. It derived from
antique Greek vase painting, knowledge of which had been popularized through excavations in Herculaneum and Pompeii, cities buried
by the eruption of Mount Vesuvius, and by publications such as the
one that reproduced Wilhelm Tischbein's drawings after Greek vases
in the Hamilton collection, which appeared in Naples from 1790 on.

10 Daniel Chodowiecki,
"the inner side of my brain,"
entry in the *album amicorum* of Johann
Valentin Meyer, 1781.
Pen and brown and gray-black ink,
watercolor; 115 x 182 mm.
Hamburg, Museum für
Hamburgische Geschichte

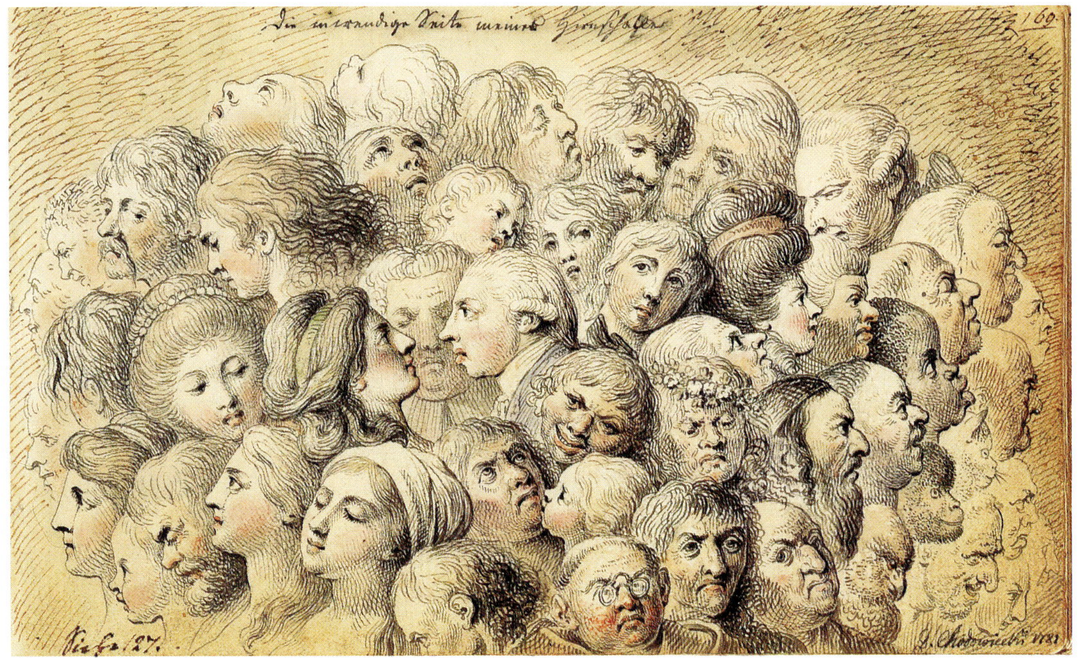

It was above all the Englishman John Flaxman (1755–1826) who helped this style to triumph with his outline illustrations of Homer and Dante, published in 1793 and widely circulated. In Germany, the Flaxman manner was adopted early on by the Riepenhausen brothers, Friedrich Overbeck, Runge, and Franz Pforr, a nephew of Wilhelm Tischbein. Tischbein was probably influential through personal contacts after his return from Naples in 1799. Runge, who had participated unsuccessfully in Goethe's neoclassically oriented Weimar competition in 1801, only a few years later used the pure, classicistic outline in his studies and finished drawings for the cycle *Times of Day*. This series of four drawings captures the essence of Runge's artistic vision. It was reproduced in engravings and was supposed to be translated into a monumental fresco. A monumentally conceived study of a lily stem with flowers and buds, executed in

Horny (cat. 49–51) and Friedrich Nerly (cat. 53), is portrayed as a spirited, important personality, an effect achieved by the turn of the head and the sweep of the hair across the forehead, which was modeled after representations of Napoleon (cf. cat. 53, 55). Gottfried Schadow, the director of the Berlin Academy, drew the likeness of the wife of Johann Andreas Schlegel, director of the mint in Berlin (cat. 14). Both portraits refer to the Neoclassicistic marble portrait bust: this is evident in the sculptural character of the forms and in the reduction of color. Both show echoes of antique portraits in their treatment of clothes. While the Munich-based von Langer idealized his subject, the Berliner Schadow stayed closer to nature.

The Austrian miniature painter Moritz Michael Daffinger drew a portrait of the duke of Reichstadt and king of Rome, Napoleon's son from his marriage to Marie-Louise of Austria (cat. 55). He is seated,

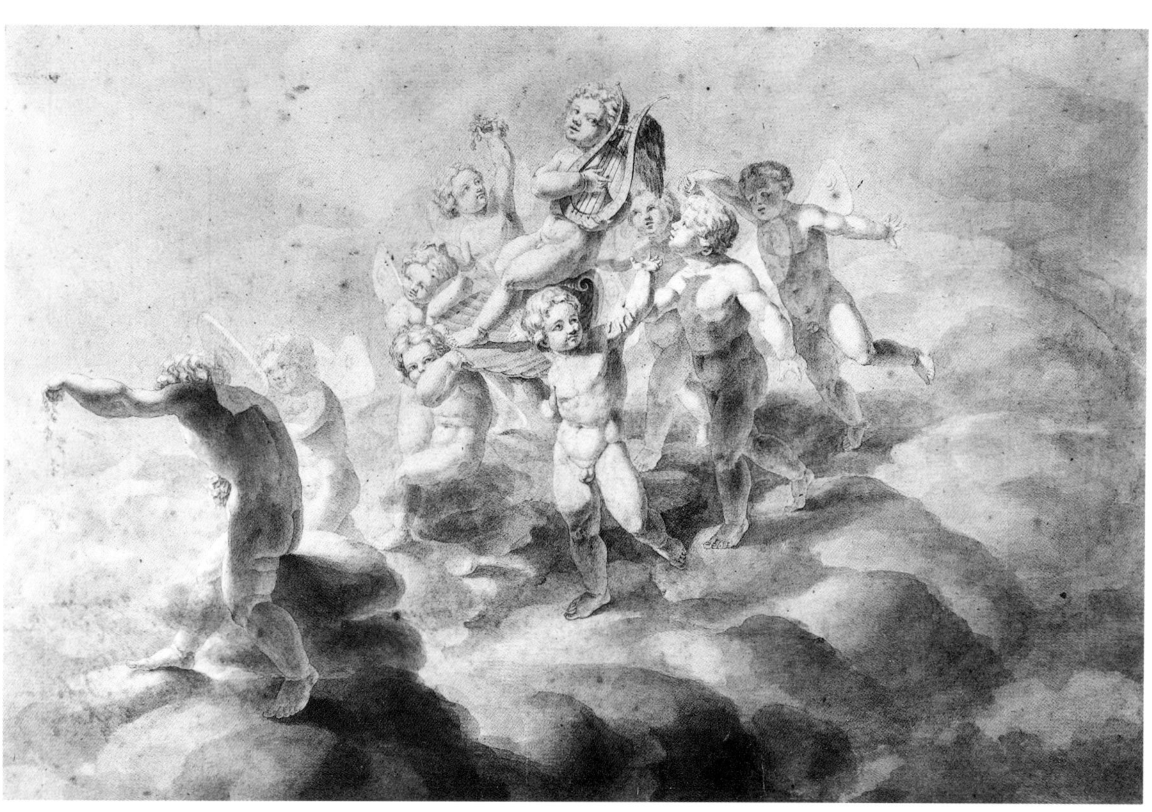

11 Philipp Otto Runge,
Triumph of Amor, 1800.
Brush and gray wash;
263/65 x 393/96 mm.
Private collection

1808 with pen and black ink, was evidently intended as a model for transfer into a painted version of *Morning*, and possibly also for the fresco planned for later (cat. 19).[29] In contrast to the even, neutral classicistic line of Flaxman, for example, Runge's dynamic, swelling and tapering line lets us feel something of the organic life of the plant and of the forces of nature.

It was above all the academies that were the standard bearers of Neoclassicistic taste around 1800. The director of the Munich Academy, Johann Peter von Langer (1756–1824), drew a portrait of Carl Friedrich von Rumohr (1785–1843), one of the fathers of the historical-critical study of art (fig. 12). Rumohr, himself a gifted draftsman and patron of outstanding artistic talents such as Franz

in a contemplative pose, in front of a Neoclassical marble bust of his father modeled in the style of a Roman emperor. In the realistic depiction of the scene notwithstanding, the artist retained conventional signs of lordship, such as the antique column in the background, lest there be any doubt about the social rank of the sitter. In the sheet strikes one as a meditation on the Empire and Neoclassical styles, an epoch which came to an end with Napoleon's fall.

The Pencil Drawing

The emergence of the color-neutral pencil as the favorite medium promoted the wide diffusion of realistic drawing styles at the beginning of the nineteenth century. In the wake of the French Revolution, the Frenchman Jacques Louis Conté, a man involved with many technological innovations, had discovered in 1795 that graphite powder and clay could be combined, resulting in various degrees of hardness. He thus invented the modern pencil, which quickly established itself internationally as a drawing tool. Prior to 1800, artists had used mainly lead point, graphite, or the so-called "English" pencil (a graphite from Borrowdale in England), the stroke of which is barely distinguishable from that of the modern pencil. (For simplicity's sake, I therefore use only the term *pencil* in the technical information for each work). As soft drawing styles and chalks gave way to pencil, smooth wove paper came to be preferred over laid papers. High-quality paper made from rags was generally used in the Goethe period; machine-made paper of wood pulp, which deteriorates easily, did not come into use until about 1840. That most sheets in the present exhibition remain fresh despite being nearly two hundred years old is due in no small measure to the quality of the paper. Most types of paper came from Dutch paper mills (*I & C Honig, D & C Blauw*). The smooth wove paper that was superbly suited for sharp pencil and watercolor came primarily from England (*J. Whatman*).

German artists, too, soon took a liking to the sharp pencil. Ludwig Richter reports from the early 1820s in Italy that French artists set out with brush and palette to paint *en plein air*, while German artists drew with the pencil: "We preferred drawing over painting. The pencil could never be too hard or too sharp to outline the contours firmly and definitely down to the finest detail. Each one sat hunched over his painting box, which was no bigger than a small sheet of paper, and tried to execute with an almost painstaking diligence what he saw before him. We fell in love with every blade of grass, with every delicate twig, and did not want to miss a single appealing feature. The effects of air and light were avoided rather than sought out; in short, everyone strove to reproduce the subject with the greatest possible objectivity, as faithfully as in a mirror."[30] For the most part, sketches from nature were done in pencil.[31] During his time in Italy, Ernst Fries of Heidelberg went on frequent outings into the countryside around Rome, accompanied by Ludwig Richter and Camille Corot, among others. During one of those outings he created a masterpiece in the subtle handling of pencils of various hardness: a true-to-nature view of Olevano, a work of splendid, light-suffused clarity in the perspectival rendering of spatial depth (cat. 52). Another precious example of a precise but soft handling of the pencil is found in the compelling portrait of the Holstein painter Theodor Rehbenitz by the engraver Carl Barth (cat. 54). Its charm comes from its immediacy and naturalness. The small-format portrait study presumably served as a preparatory drawing for an engraving. Wilhelm Hensel (1794–1861) drew portraits in pencil almost exclusively, assembling them into a collection.[32] His art of small-format portraiture, which he developed in the Berlin Empire style, shows a parallel, though on a more modest level, with the work of the Frenchman Jean-Auguste-Dominique Ingres, whose elegant portraiture, brilliant and highly refined in its artistry, was drawn exclusively in pencil. Probably due to his marriage to Fanny Mendelssohn, the sister of the composer Felix Mendelssohn-Bartholdy, Hensel became not only Prussian court draftsman but also the portraitist of the 'spiritual countenance' of his time (cf. cat. 13).

Carl Christian Vogel von Vogelstein (1788–1868) created an extensive collection of pencil portraits of contemporary artists (Dresden, Kupferstichkabinett). In this context we should also mention two portrait collections that are outstanding for their artistic quality but smaller in size. The first is Carl Philipp Fohr's series of portraits of German artists in the Café Greco in Rome (Heidelberg, Kurpfälzisches Museum); drawn in silvery pencil, these likenesses were intended for reproduction in an etched group portrait that was never executed. The second is the *Roman Portrait Book* of Julius Schnorr von Carolsfeld, who made the drawings around 1820 with pen and brown ink (cat. 35).

The Nazarenes

In contrast to the individual personalities in the northern German/Protestant strand of Romanticism, with its central figures of Philipp Otto Runge and Caspar David Friedrich, the Catholic-influenced Nazarene strand, which initially led to Italy, developed as a collective movement. The way was prepared for its appearance and development by literature. Wilhelm Heinrich Wackenroder's tract *Herzensergiessungen eines kunstliebenden Klosterbruders* [Outpourings from the Heart of an Art-Loving Monk], which he published in 1797 at the age of twenty-three (fig. 13), was profoundly influential. In it he placed art close to religion and compared the contemplation of art to worship. Wackenroder saw art as a form of devotion anticipated in

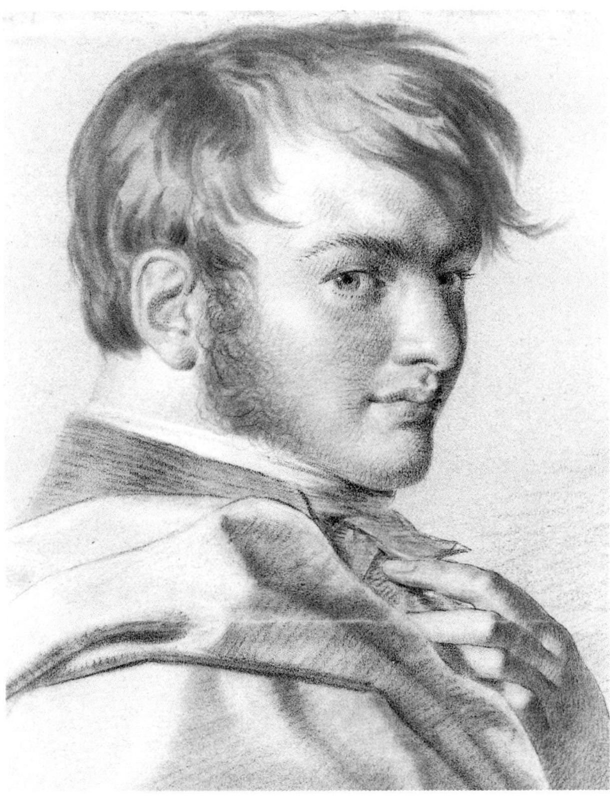

12 Johann Peter von Langer, *Portrait of Carl Friedrich von Rumohr*, c. 1810. Colored chalks, heightened with white, on blue tinted paper; 391 x 304 mm. Munich, Staatliche Graphische Sammlung

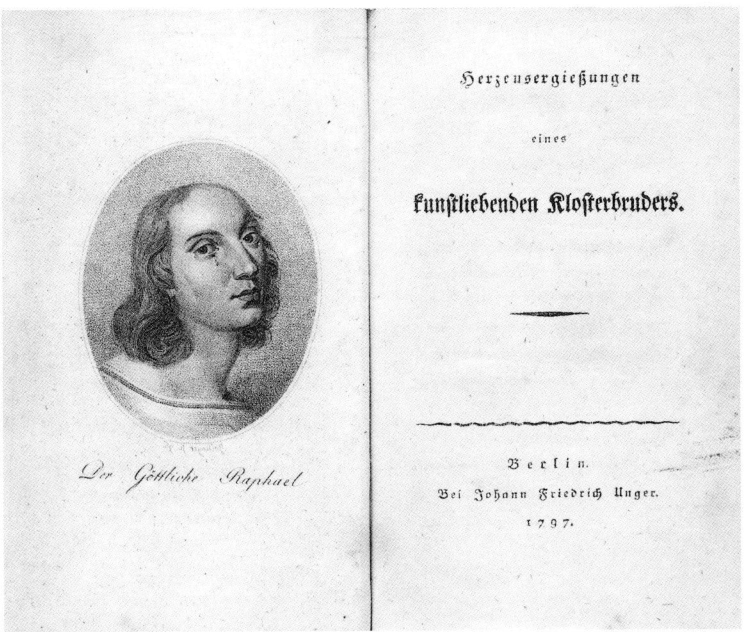

13 Wilhelm Heinrich Wackenroder, *Herzensergiessungen eines kunstliebenden Klosterbruders*, ed. Ludwig Tieck, Berlin 1797 (1796).
Frontispiece and title page

the Pantheon. That exhumation was the climax of the cult of Raphael, and it came at a time when the Nazarene artistic vision had already been pushed to the margins by newer trends.

The Nazarene movement had begun in 1809 with a peaceful secession from the Vienna Academy. The following year the Nazarenes established themselves as a collective community in the abandoned monastery of San Isidoro in Rome. There they lived from September 1810 to September 1812, trying to put into practice their ideal of a monastic, ascetic life devoted to art and faith. The Zurich artist Ludwig Vogel (1788–1879) painted a view of the monastery from the

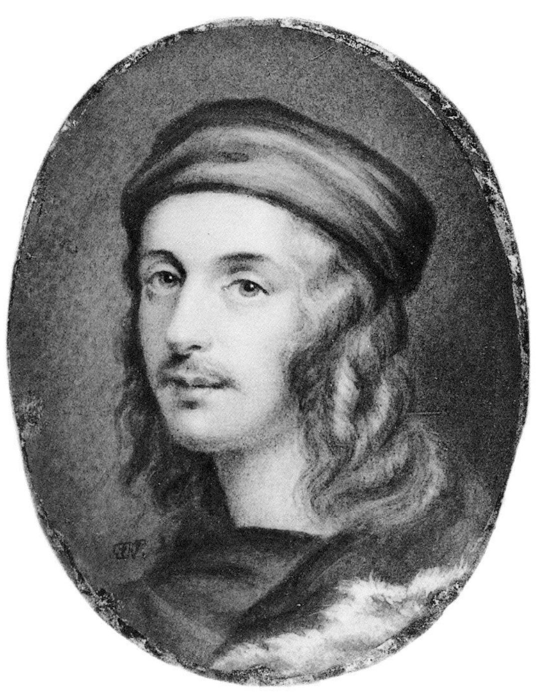

14 Friedrich Nerly, *Self-Portrait*, c. 1833.
Watercolor; 120 x 94 mm. Private collection

exemplary fashion in the art of the Dürer period and of the Italian Renaissance. His *Outpourings* awakened a desire to renew German religious art after the model of Dürer and Raphael (cf. cat. 43, 44); the romantic cult of Dürer and Raphael began with this book. An 1833 self-portrait by Friedrich Nerly of Holstein, who portrayed himself with the features of Raphael as they appear in the frontispiece of Wackenroder's booklet, confirms that this cult still influenced the second generation of Nazarene-inspired artists (fig. 14). Nerly's likeness, a programmatic image that makes a personal statement, attests to the artist's desire to resemble Raphael in external appearance through strict imitation in his own life and work. The "imitatio Raphaeli" is here analogous to the "imitatio Christi," an idea of the late medieval mystic Thomas à Kempis, to which Dürer, among others, had given visual expression in his Christlike self-portrait from 1500 (Munich, Alte Pinakothek). Nerly evidently was alluding to this idea in his self-portrait. Much in the way that late medieval religiosity expanded on the story of Jesus' family life through apocryphal legends, the cult of personality surrounding Raphael and Dürer during the Romantic era fostered an imaginative elaboration of their undocumented private lives. Vasari's mention of the Fornarina, Raphael's lover, provided the impulse for the growth of various legends. Jean-Auguste-Dominique Ingres's first version of his painting *Raphael and the Fornarina* takes as its point of departure Raphael's lovely portrait of the Fornarina in the Palazzo Barberini. Johannes Riepenhausen's later watercolor on the same theme was based on Ingres's first version. Riepenhausen's composition was published in 1833 as part of a series of twelve outline etchings on Raphael's life (cat. 43), coinciding chronologically with Nerly's self-portrait, and nearly with the exhumation of Raphael's remains in

Villa Malta during these early years (fig. 15). The Nazarenes called themselves the Brotherhood of St. Luke, the 'Lukasbund,' an allusion to the late medieval guilds of painters whose patron saint was St. Luke. It is significant that in Rome, the capital of the Christian world, the Nazarenes looked for inspiration and guidance less to antiquity than to the Christian art of the Middle Ages and the Renaissance (cf. cat. 44). The leading and most influential members of this circle were Friedrich Overbeck of Lübeck, the son of a senator and a convert to Catholicism, and Peter Cornelius of Düsseldorf. In Rome, presumably at San Isidoro, the two men drew each other in a mutual double portrait, which seems like an echo of Raphael's self-portrait with Sodoma in the *School of Athens* (cat. 29). This sheet is important testimony to the friendships among artists that were widely conducted with cultic fervor, and a key early example of an independent category of works that arose from these bonds, the so-called friendship pictures of the Romantic era. On the left of the double portrait, with features reminiscent of Dürer, is Overbeck, the intellectual and spiritual head of the movement, who lived out his long life in Rome. On the right, dressed in the style of the Italian Renaissance, is Cornelius, the great inventor of historical themes and compositions, mostly in drawings that others translated into murals. It was Cornelius who later conveyed the ideas of the Nazarenes to Germany, initially in the service of King Ludwig I of Bavaria, preparing the way for their monumental murals.

The artist collective of the Nazarenes in Rome strikes one as a precursor to groups of German artists that were formed a hundred years later, like the Brücke in Dresden and Berlin, the Blaue Reiter in

the Tasso room entirely by himself. With this work he caught the eye of Crown Prince Ludwig of Bavaria. Immediately upon assuming the throne, Ludwig called him to Munich as a professor at the Academy and commissioned him to paint monumental murals in the new additions to the Residenz.

The pen drawing, with its precise line and resemblance to the brilliant engraving technique of the Dürer period, is also characteristic of Nazarene art. One example is Overbeck's masterful scene of Roman family life, drawn in 1819 directly with pen and light reddish brown ink (cat. 31). It strikes us as a secularized portrayal of the Holy

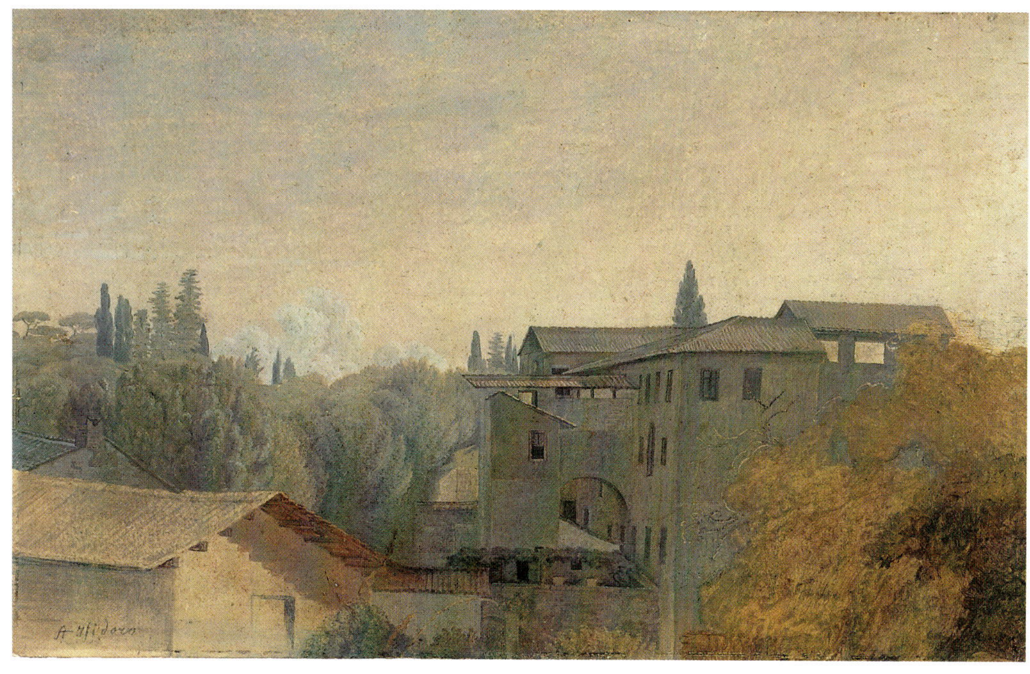

15 Ludwig Vogel,
The Monastery of San Isidoro in Rome, c.
1810. Oil on paper; 227 x 355 mm

Munich, or the Bauhaus in Weimar, Dessau, and Berlin. It began as a community that shared working and living space in the monastery of San Isidoro. Later, the Nazarenes held evening classes with artistic assignments for the group as a whole. Finally, the Brotherhood achieved self-realization through the collective design and execution of monumental murals. First came the frescoes in the Casa Bartholdy (Palazzo Zuccari) in 1816–17, involving Cornelius, Overbeck, Philipp Veit, and Wilhelm Schadow. This was followed by their major surviving work, the decoration of three rooms in the Casino Massimo with themes from classic Italian literature. The latter project dragged on for more than a decade, from 1818 to 1829. Work in the Dante room involved Cornelius for a short period until his departure for Munich in 1818; Philipp Veit (cat. 41), who continued and built on Cornelius's compositional design for the ceiling; and finally Joseph Anton Koch, who was close to the Nazarenes and painted scenes from the *Inferno*. Overbeck began the Ariosto room, but left its completion to Joseph von Führich. Only Julius Schnorr von Carolsfeld worked alone, designing and executing the decoration of

Family on the terrace of an Italian country home in a Renaissance composition. It is also an expression of the Nazarene concern to use religious sensibilities to impart significance even to a genre scene. In an early composition from 1825, Julius Schnorr von Carolsfeld depicted a scene from the Old Testament, *The Creation of Eve* (cat. 37). The figural types are derived not least from those used by Raphael, as in the Vatican *Loggie*. Schnorr's drawing stands at the beginning of a nearly forty-year-long involvement with the project of illustrating the Bible, which the Nazarenes saw as a central task of their artistic work. The brothers of St. Luke originally began it as a collective effort, but it was Schnorr, one of their most talented draftsman, who eventually finished it on his own. His drawings, carefully executed as fully detailed pictorial compositions, served as direct models for transfer into woodcuts, which allowed the production of a large edition. Schnorr's illustrated Bible, published in parts between 1852 and 1860 and bound in popular and luxury editions, sold in huge numbers. His own religiosity was accompanied by a deep yearning to overcome the religious division in Germany. It must

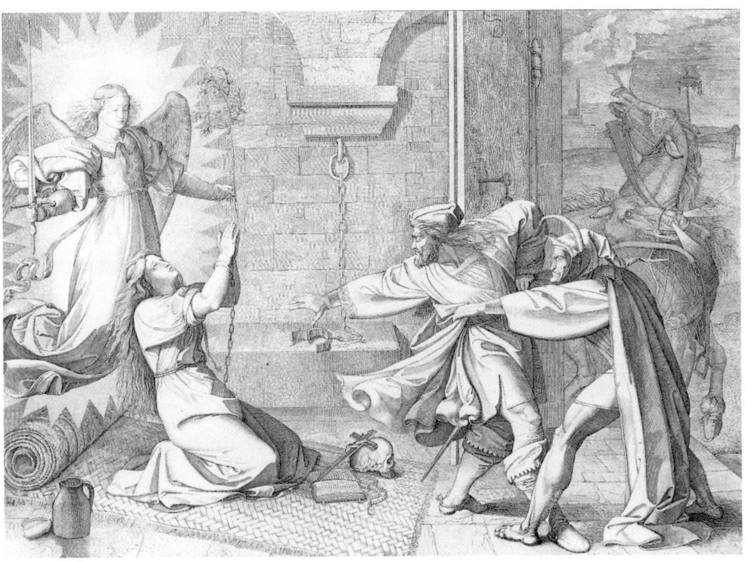

16 Peter Cornelius, *Gretchen in the Dungeon*, final scene of Goethe's *Faust* (Rome, 1815). Engraving by Ferdinand Ruscheweyh, 1817; approx. 390 x 501 mm (platemark)

line endows the face with a generalizing, coolly distant, and timeless expression that transcends individual features and is reminiscent of carved marble. Julius Schnorr von Carolsfeld's outstanding achievement in portraiture remained limited to his early years in Italy, around 1820. At that time he created a type of portrait drawing executed in brown ink and wash. This portrait type was modeled after Florentine Renaissance busts in its formal composition, and after Albrecht Dürer's printed likenesses in its engraving-like precision and separate field for the inscription at the bottom. In addition to recording the physiognomies of the people he portrayed, Schnorr strove to convey their spiritual countenances. He created a graphic monument to his friends in his *Roman Portrait Book* (cat. 35).

The Nazarenes did not produce their own school of landscape art; their real field was that of figural history painting (cf. cat. 44). Still, some of them did create landscape masterpieces. The Protestant Ferdinand Olivier belonged to the Brotherhood of St. Luke, even though he never traveled to Italy. His study of the Hohensalzburg Citadel, drawn with a sharp, hard pencil, shows a view of the landscape that is *veduta*-like in its rendering but at the same time infused with a higher meaning through the rigor of its line (cat. 34). The sheet dates from the years around 1818, the period when German artists began to discover the beauty of the Salzburg countryside. Olivier's refined study was drawn in the context of his suite of seven crayon lithographs, printed with tone, of Salzburg landscapes, one for each

therefore have given him great satisfaction, late in life, to see his Bible used in both Protestant and Catholic religious instruction in the schools. With this work, Schnorr fulfilled the missionary goal of the Nazarenes to renew art from the spirit of religion and to awaken a new sense of religiosity. It has shaped pictorial representations of biblical events to this day.

In addition to the Bible, patriotic themes from history and literature provided the richest source for illustration in the wake of a growing national self-awareness during the Romantic era. The Germanic Niebelung legend replaced the Homeric epics preferred by Neoclassical illustrators. Peter Cornelius's twelve drawings for Goethe's *Faust* (1808), published as etchings beginning in 1816, constitute the incunabula of Romantic illustration.[33] These etchings show accentuated outlines, little interior modeling, and an evenly pale tonal effect. One characteristic example is the final scene in the dungeon (fig. 16). Gretchen appears in the pose of the repentant Mary Magdalen with uplifted arms, as she was often depicted at the foot of the cross in early German altarpieces of the Crucifixion; Faust and Mephistopheles comport themselves like late Gothic Morris dancers. Goethe initially liked this approach because it reflected the time of the historical Faust, but later he rejected it as an excess of medieval Germanomania. He thought that Eugène Delacroix, the chief representative of the French Romantic school, understood him better. Delacroix's lithograph of 1828 staged the same scene with much more dramatic effects of light and shadow, and is theatrically expressive and sensuous (fig. 17).[34]

The Nazarenes also produced important work in the field of portraiture. Among the most beautiful is the frontal half-figure likeness of a young boy, formerly attributed to Peter Cornelius (cat. 33). It is drawn with the sharp and hard pencil the Nazarenes preferred. Though realistic in its details, the sharp calligraphy of the portrait's

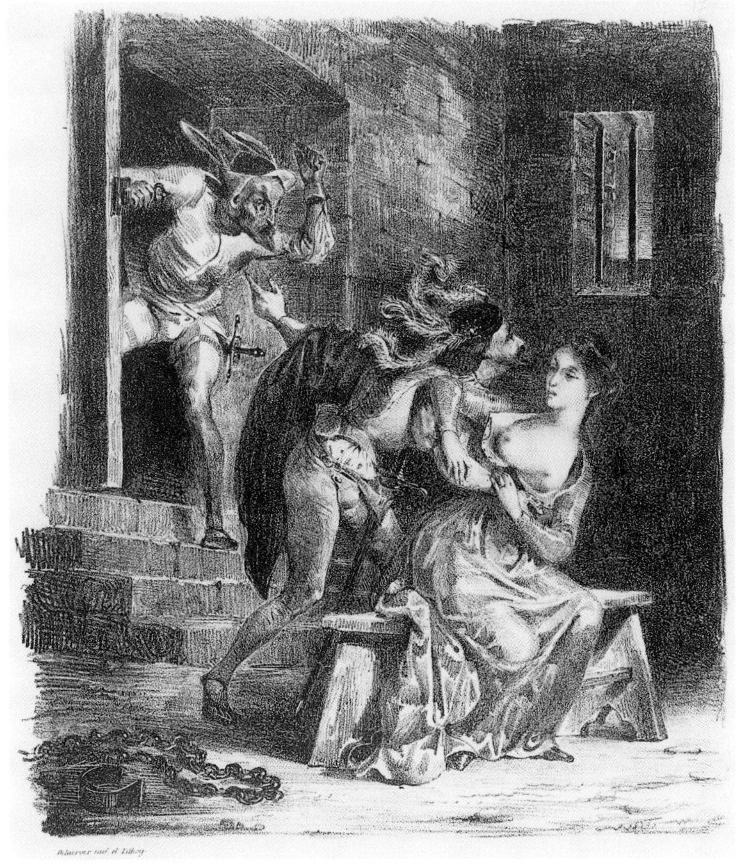

17 Eugène Delacroix, *Gretchen in the Dungeon*, scene from Goethe's *Faust*, 1828. Lithograph; approx. 253 x 198 mm (image). Munich, Staatliche Graphische Sammlung

day of the week. Together with two allegorical sheets that frame the suite, these landscapes are early German examples of the use of lithography as a medium of artistic expression.

An important friend and supporter of Nazarene art was Joseph Anton Koch from Tyrol. In 1793, as a brilliant young member of the Sturm und Drang generation who had escaped the Hohe Carlsschule in Stuttgart in 1791 and who sympathized with the French Revolution, he made a vivid drawing directly from nature that captured his experience of the Bernese High Alps: a view through the Lütschin Valley to the Jungfrau massif (cat. 2). Sepia-brown pen strokes fill the entire, highly finished drawing with a vibrant energy that evokes the primeval forces of nature. To Koch, the high and extensive Swiss mountains were a symbol of human freedom. Echoes of the landscape drawing of the Danube school emerge, the steady rhythm of freely oscillating lines suggesting parallels with the technique of Albrecht Altdorfer. By contrast, in Rome an older Koch drew an invented landscape as the setting for his *Rest on the Flight into Egypt* (cat. 28) with much greater detachment. He executed it in pale gray-black, Neoclassicist contours, his characteristic style from about 1800 on. This work served as a preparatory study or cartoon for an oil painting of identical format:[35] a devotional picture in the Nazarene spirit, and simultaneously an example of an ideal landscape, a type of painting whose diffusion Koch did much to promote through the model of his own art (cat. 28, fig.).

Carl Philipp Fohr and Franz Horny, two of the most important German draftsmen of the period, were close to the Nazarenes and influenced by Koch, who was also their teacher. Inspired by the experience of the light and landscape of Italy, they developed a vivid conception of nature expressed in draftsmanship infused with a calligraphic energy and liveliness. One example from Fohr's oeuvre is his famous self-portrait of 1816, now in Heidelberg; examples from Horny's work are his free tree studies (cat. 50) and his boldly washed drawing with its fresh morning atmosphere, executed in the Aequi Mountains east of Rome (cat. 51). Though both artists died young, their calligraphic, clear, rhythmic line found imitators down to the twentieth century within the Dresden school, thanks to the decisive mediating role played by Ludwig Richter. In his youth in Italy, Richter absorbed the style of Horny and Fohr by directly studying and copying it. Later, in Dresden, he passed their artistic legacy on to a small circle of highly gifted students and their successors, including Heinrich Dreber (1822–1875), Albert Venus (1842–1871), and Victor Paul Mohn (1842–1911). Nowhere else in German draftsmanship of the age of Goethe can we observe with such clarity the creation of a school on the basis of a specific technical feature, a process that is characteristic of Italian artistic circles of earlier centuries.

Printmaking

In contrast to their French counterparts, German artists were rather late in discovering the lithograph as an original artistic medium. In Germany it was initially used chiefly for reproduction. The year 1806 saw the publication of Johann Nepomuk Strixner's lithographic reproductions of Albrecht Dürer's marginal drawings in the prayer book of Emperor Maximilian I. They were extremely important in disseminating a knowledge of Dürer's draftsmanship and for the assimilation of his technique by artists such as Carl Philipp

Fohr (cat. 45), Ferdinand Olivier (cat. 34), Julius Schnorr von Carolsfeld (cat. 35), and Moritz von Schwind (cat. 59). Through the circulation of these lithographic reproductions, the calligraphy of Dürer's vine ornaments and of the imaginative genre figures that surround the text exerted a crucial influence on nineteenth-century book illustration. Witness, for example, Eugen Napoleon Neureuther's (1806–1882) marginal drawings to Goethe's ballads and romances, which were published during the poet's lifetime. It is noteworthy that in the wake of the intense preoccupation with the art of engraving of Dürer and his contemporaries, engraving in the Dürer style experienced a revival through printmakers like Samuel Amsler, Carl Barth, Ferdinand Ruscheweyh, and Julius Thaeter, all of whom, significantly, primarily reproduced Nazarene compositions.

Moritz von Schwind

Within the art of the Romantic period, with its literary-illustrative character, Moritz von Schwind assumes a special place, not least by virtue of his affinity for music and fairy tales. A few examples from his important early drawings of circa 1820 to 1840 illustrate the point; these works also reveal various connections to the Dürer period. The forest, with all its connotations, is a central theme in Schwind's work. *The Apparition in the Forest*, the subject of a major drawing that still awaits conclusive interpretation, leads into the imaginative world of the German fairy tale (fig. 18).[36] A knight in early German dress, riding through a forest in the dark of night, encounters the graceful figure of a fairy floating beneath the crescent moon. The drawing, with rounded upper corners, was done as an autonomous work. Thirty-five years later, the aging Schwind reused this composition in an oil painting (fig. 19), with some of the details altered.[37] This is an example of anachronistic artistic creation, similar to that found in Overbeck and Schnorr: in old age, they also used works created in their youth as an archive of ideas without being able to bring a particular theme up to date. At the same time, this comparison between works from Schwind's youth and old age reveals that one aspect of *The Apparition in the Forest* could be adequately conveyed only in the drawing and was lost in the execution in oil: the transparency and transcendence of the weightlessly floating fairy in the drawing has been demystified in the painting into a bodily, material, and heavy female figure who seems in danger of falling down with a crash.

In *The Boy's Magic Horn* or *Forest Solitude* (c. 1840–43), Schwind, in the scene of the youth lying on the forest floor blowing his horn, created an image of blissful solitude in the forest as a positive counterpart to the city dweller at a time of growing industrialization (cat. 60). The forest was also an image of the infinite; it aroused yearnings and spurred the imagination. It has been a theme of German artists from Albrecht Altdorfer to Moritz von Schwind, from Max Ernst to Anselm Kiefer. Elias Canetti wrote in 1960: "In no other modern country of the world has the feeling for the forest remained as alive as it has in Germany . . . . One must not underestimate the impact of this early forest romanticism on the Germans. They expressed it in countless songs and poems, and the forest that appears in them was often a German one."[38]

The legend of the Lorelei, whose seductive song robbed boatmen on the Rhine of their reason, thereby leading them to destruction on

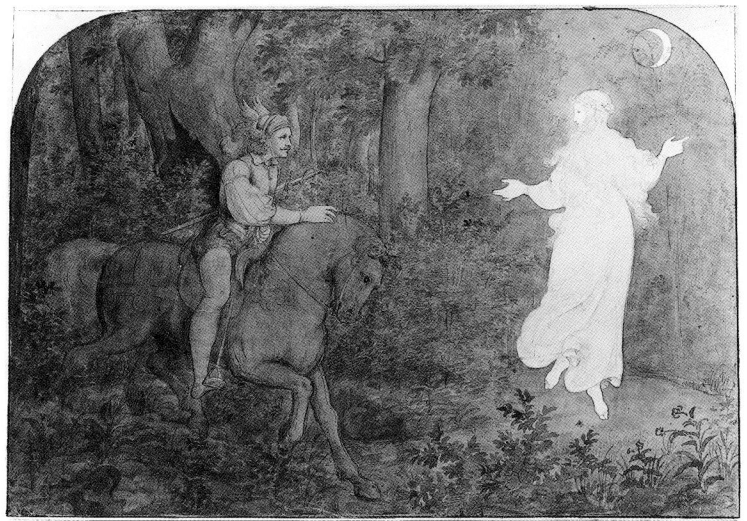

Maiden to music in a song in 1817, and between 1823 and 1826 in his late D-minor string quartet. He was inspired by the verses of Matthias Claudius, which describe death consolingly as a gentle friend. Schwind, who was part of Schubert's inner circle, illustrated these verses in a drawing (fig. 20). The scene is set at night time in a middle-class bedroom of the period. Death in the form of a skeleton has entered through the window by the light of the moon and approaches the startled girl, who sits up in her bed—an image adapted from Annunciation scenes in early Netherlandish and German painting. The theme was also popular during the age of Dürer in the context of illustrations of the Dance of Death. In his drawing of this theme, executed on dark brown, prepared paper and heightened with white, Hans Baldung depicted death as a sensually aggressive man who lustfully embraces the vital young woman vainly regarding herself in a mirror (fig. 21). While Baldung imparted a

18 Moritz von Schwind,
The Apparition in the Forest,
23 April 1823.
Pen and brown ink, brown wash;
335 x 470 mm.
Vaduz, Ratjen Foundation

19 Moritz von Schwind,
The Apparition in the Forest, 1858.
Oil on canvas; 40.2 x 63.9 cm.
Munich, Bayerische
Staatsgemäldesammlungen,
Schack-Galerie, inv. no. 11584

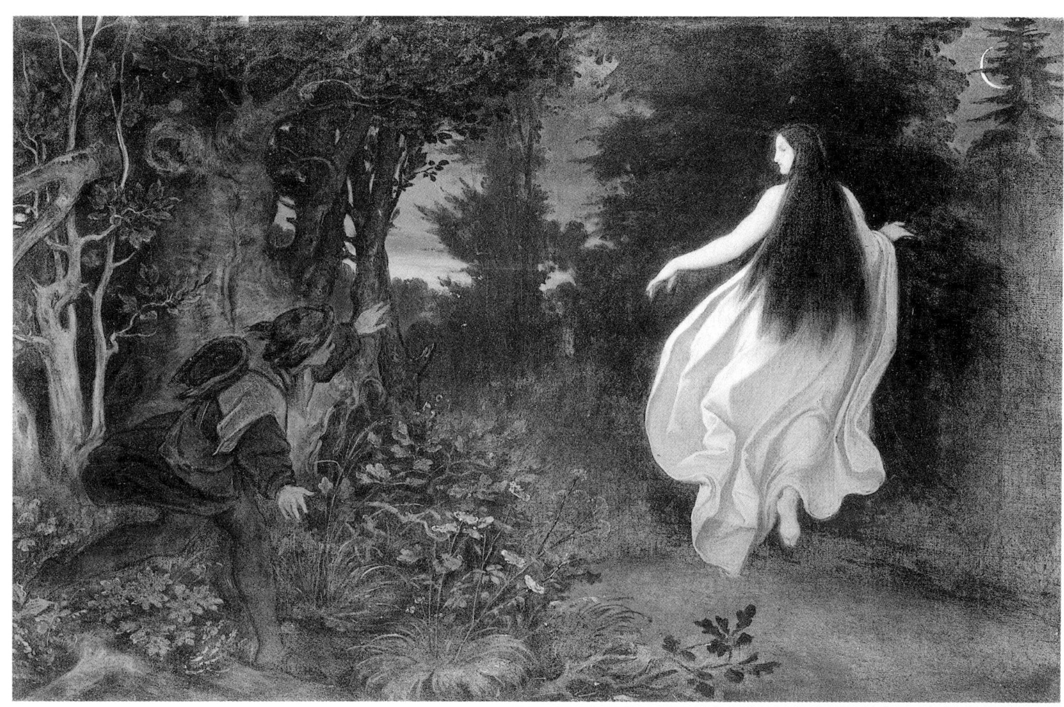

the rocks, was transformed into poetic verses by, among others, Clemens Brentano in his *Märchen vom Rhein* [Rhine Legends] and Heinrich Heine, in verses that were set to music ("Ich weiss nicht was soll es bedeuten" [I know not what it must mean]; see Appendix A). Schwind chose this legend for a drawing of vertical format that is dominated by a steeply rising rock face (cat. 59). At the bottom, close to the rock, the boatman risks a fateful look up toward the Lorelei, who can be heard but not seen. The hard, jagged rock face, layered like crystal, appears chiseled. It has been drawn in a manner appropriate to the material depicted, with metal-sharp, precise pen strokes reminiscent of the engraving technique of the Dürer period.

A central theme in the music, literature, and art of the Romantic period was death. Franz Schubert set the theme *Death and the*

strong erotic component to the *vanitas* motif, Schwind's conception of the theme remains chaste, as though he wanted to fulfill Overbeck's demand that art should be chaste. Obedience to Overbeck's commandment not only affected the creative work of the Nazarenes; it may also explain why German art of this period so often makes a somewhat lifeless impression.

Interiors

The history of motifs in the nineteenth century is a highly productive field for art historians. Among the leitmotifs of the Goethe period—which appear again and again, in different contexts and with different meanings—is the interior with an opening to the out-

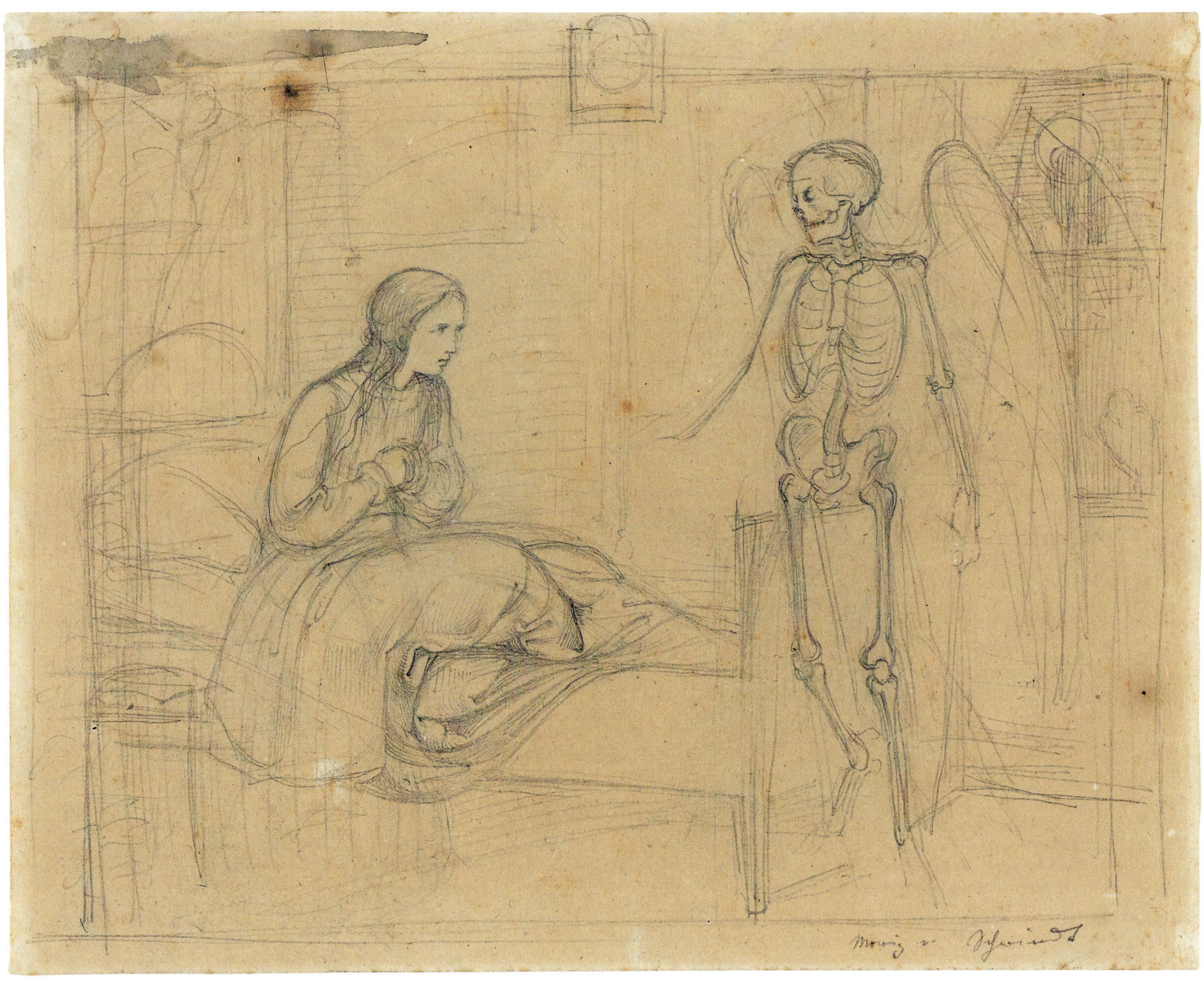

20 Moritz von Schwind, *Death and the Maiden*, c. 1823/24.
Pencil; 186 x 228 mm. Private collection

side, a door or a window that is simultaneously a source of light (cf. fig. 1).[39] Caspar David Friedrich's entryway into a chamber in the choir of the ruined monastery church of the Holy Cross near Meissen, a drawing in sepia wash, shows the artist's interest in the finely nuanced shadows cast by the light falling from the back toward the front into the dark, empty room (cat. 22). The steps to the door and the door as an opening to the light become metaphors for the transition from earthly life to a higher existence after death. The atmospheric scene of emptiness and solitude has become a devotional image.

In 1821, Ludwig Emil Grimm, a younger brother of Jacob and Wilhelm Grimm and a diligent draftsman, produced a watercolor of an interior with his sister Lotte busy at her needlework in her room in the Grimm family's house in Cassel: a typical picture of the modest but tasteful middle-class lifestyle of the Biedermeier period (cat. 57). Plaster casts of antique sculptures, such as the bust of the *Apollo Belvedere* on top of the cupboard on the right, assert the family's intellectual interests and status.

Friedrich and Grimm shared an interest in the subtle diffusion of light inside a room with Franz Pforr (cat. 32) and Georg Friedrich

30

Kersting (cat. 24). In variations on the theme of the "woman's room," Pforr and Kersting chose closed, dark interior rooms illuminated by an internal light source, namely the glow of a table lamp (cf. cat. 12). Presented almost as still lifes, these women are wives of idealized imagination, engrossed in their needlework, virtuous, observed in their social roles as homemakers, without any distraction or outside threat. They are dream images of secluded, tranquil, middle-class life.

Caricature

Caricature offered a rich field for drawing. Prior to the Revolution of 1848, German artists rarely used caricature as a weapon in the struggle for better social conditions or lithography as the medium for the unlimited reproduction of caricatures with the goal of influencing the masses. In the metropolis of Paris, where social conflicts developed earlier than in the German cities and led to political turmoil, lithography was put to use early on as a suitable artistic medium for caricature. Although caricature in the German lands did address social questions, these were chiefly questions concerning the artists themselves and the deplorable state of affairs at the academies. Three strong and stubborn personalities—Johann Gottfried Schadow, Joseph Anton Koch, and Johann Christian Reinhart, whose temperaments (rooted in Sturm und Drang) and irrepressible will to freedom had landed them in early opposition to the academies and had led them to Rome—vented their scorn for the academies, for writing on art, and for the constraints of an artist's life in countless caricatures. For example, the exceedingly sharp-tongued painter Reinhart, to whom the members of the Brotherhood of St. Luke probably owe the derisive name "Nazarenes," mocked the relationship between artist and patron in a pen drawing that contrasts the submissiveness of a gaunt, bowing artist with the artistic ignorance of the patron, here a pompous lady of enormous girth wearing a tall, elaborate headpiece.[40] Reinhart inscribed the sheet: "a young, hopeful artist is introduced to a lady who is a *strong* patron of the arts." In a pen drawing worked up with watercolor, he derided the artificiality of history painting—the leading subject taught at the academies—by showing a painter with a pigtail wig drawing a lively cavalry scene from a stiff mannequin seated on a wooden block (cat. 26). Only the Berliner Schadow, who would return to the academy as a teacher, also addressed the political conditions of the day as a caricaturist. In oppressed Prussia he took aim at Napoleon with his pictorial satires in the style of James Gillray. Years of war and occupation made Napoleon a broad target of caricature in the German lands.[41]

German Schools of Painting

I shall conclude my comments with a brief survey of the most important schools of German painting in the first third of the nineteenth century, looking at representative artists and, for the most part, the field of landscape watercolor painting. I have not included the Düsseldorf school, whose motifs and style were oriented toward seventeenth-century Dutch art because of its geographic proximity to the Netherlands, since it did not play a leading role in German art until the middle of the nineteenth century. With the exception of a few drawings, the Düsseldorf school is not represented in the Winterstein collection. Neither is the Austrian school of watercolor included in this survey, even though it produced so many notable works (some of which are in the Winterstein collection), since it falls outside the chronological boundaries of this selection.

Dresden

Among the Romantic schools, the northern German, Protestant-oriented school in Dresden holds an eminent place, chiefly through its outstanding representative, Caspar David Friedrich. In one of his loveliest landscape watercolors, based on a pencil drawing done from nature during a hike in 1810, Friedrich depicted the morning atmosphere in a pristine and expansive landscape in the Riesengebirge (cat. 21). The source of the Elbe springs from the lush meadow in the right foreground; Friedrich's companion Kersting sits on the stone

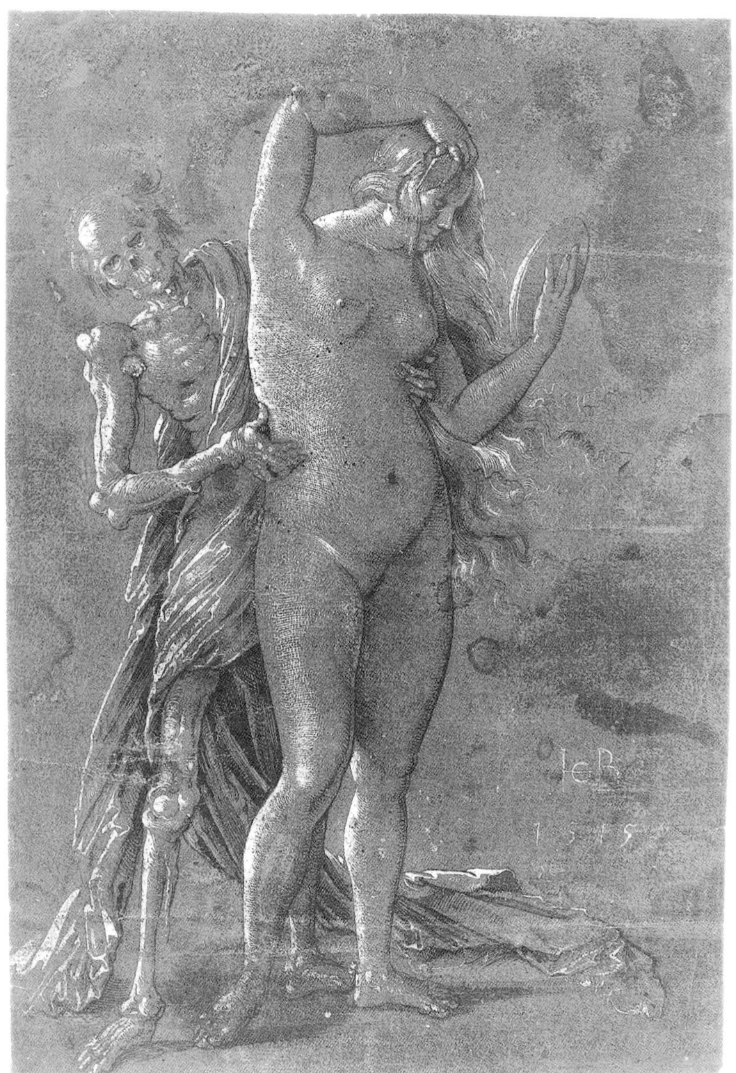

21 Hans Baldung, *Death and the Maiden*, 1515.
Pen and black ink, brown wash, heightened with white, on brown prepared paper; 307 x 207 mm.
Berlin, Staatliche Museen Preussischer Kulturbesitz, Kupferstichkabinett

structure on top of the source, leaning on his walking stick in a pose of deep reflection. The source is symbolic of life; the landscape is both a *veduta* and a devotional image. Characteristic of Friedrich's work are the strong emotional content in the landscape and the depiction of processes in nature. Friedrich's portrait of his brother Christian (c. 1801/02), who translated some of the artist's drawings into woodcuts, bespeaks an exceptional spirituality, an inner concentration, and a seriousness of expression (cat. 20). The parallel, broad black chalk strokes and the cross-hatching still reflect academic training.

A similar expressiveness informs a portrait study of Caspar David Friedrich by his friend Georg Friedrich Kersting (cat. 23), a work executed with great precision, like a miniature. It was drawn in pencil, partly incised, as if with a silverpoint, on card primed with white chalk—a difficult technique that demands a sure hand and does not permit corrections. During the age of Goethe, Anton Graff in Dresden especially promoted the use of this medium, and it was frequently used for portraits in miniature. In the early part of the Dürer period, as in the work of Hans Holbein the Elder, silverpoint had been a preferred drawing tool, particularly for portraits. Kersting used his study from nature as a preliminary drawing for a painting (Berlin, Nationalgalerie) that shows Friedrich alone in front of his easel in his sparsely furnished studio (cat. 23, fig.).

A small, important group of Friedrich's students also emphasized close imitation of nature and a strong mood in their art—hallmarks of the Dresden school. Unlike their teacher, however, they were drawn to Italy. This group included Carl Gustav Carus, a naturalist and physician; August Heinrich, a highly gifted exponent of a meticulously naturalistic style, who died of tuberculosis on his way to Italy at the age of twenty-eight (cat. 74); and Ernst Ferdinand Oehme (cat. 73), Heinrich's friend and traveling companion. Oehme's *Forest Chapel in the Snow* awakens symbolic associations, though these are muted, compared to similar themes in the work of Friedrich. Characteristically, Carus chose for his view of the Castel dell'Ovo in Naples an underlying mood that is rather melancholy, in accord with the approach of his school (cat. 72). What fascinated him was not, perhaps, the luminous color contrasts in the bright light of the sun, but rather the broken, diffuse light of a foggy and hazy midday atmosphere in which the sky and the surface of the water seem to merge: a subtle experience of color perceived through the eyes of a northerner.

Munich

Artists of the Munich landscape school show great individual variations in their tendency to choose bright tonalities. This school produced some great talents and masterpieces, especially in watercolor; examples include Max Joseph Wagenbauer, with his atmospheric pictures of the Bavarian Forest (cat. 62), and Wilhelm von Kobell, with his splendidly painted, cool, clear landscapes of the Alpine foothills at the Tegernsee, with compositions layered like stage scenery and still, porcelain-like figures in the foreground (cat. 67).

At a time when decorative gouache painting and monochrome techniques such as sepia and gray-black wash were the dominant fashions in the German-speaking lands, Johann Georg von Dillis was the first to promote the art of transparent watercolor, which had already played an important role as an autonomous genre in England during the eighteenth century. From the late 1780s, and also after 1808, as the first teacher of landscape painting at the newly founded Academy, Dillis prepared the way for watercolor within the Munich school. He himself created masterful "impressions" in his highly individual, loose combination of watercolor and drawing; his works recall those of the English draftsmen Richard Wilson and Thomas Gainsborough (fig. 5 and cat. 63) and, at the same time, seem to anticipate Adolph Menzel and Max Liebermann (cat. 64). The encounter with nature in the English Garden played an important role in the development of landscape painting in Munich. It was here that Dillis early on forged his characteristic, energetic style (fig. 5 and cat. 8, 9). By contrast, Simon Klotz, with his atmospheric *Excursion in the English Garden*, was still under the spell of the coloristically decorative-picturesque *veduta* painting of the so-called Swiss *Kleinmeister*, in the style of Johann Ludwig Aberli (cat. 61).

Three decades later, the Heidelberg native Carl Rottmann shifted the emphases in his views of the most beautiful landscapes in Italy and Greece, places that were rich in history and myth, and which he visited for that very reason. Italy and Greece were the spiritual home of his patron, the great philhellene King Ludwig I of Bavaria. For example, Rottman interpreted the deserted landscape of Marathon —where the Athenians defeated the Persians—as a site of great historical significance by making dramatic use of natural forces such as a thunderstorm (cat. 71). This vibrantly atmospheric watercolor belongs to a series of finished designs, based on studies from nature that were originally intended as preparation for murals in the Munich Hofgarten, though eventually they were executed for display in the old Neue Pinakothek. We are indebted to the court painter Joseph Karl Stieler for a lively portrait of the crown prince and later king, Ludwig I of Bavaria (cat. 68). This was a study for the official coronation picture (painted in 1826) of the monarch who would lead the arts in Bavaria to new heights. I have already had occasion to mention Stieler's portrait of Goethe (fig. 2).

The Bavarian court architect Leo von Klenze and Karl Friedrich Schinkel, who served the Prussian court, were rivals, but an artistic kinship and parallels can be found in their work. Both men were excellent painters and draftsmen. The art of both shows the characteristic traits of the schools to which they belonged. While Klenze played a role within the Munich school with his architectural pieces and landscape *vedute* (cat. 69), Schinkel, with the nearly inexhaustible imagination that he also manifested as a painter, was a central figure in Berlin in the field of landscape painting.

Berlin

Both Klenze and Schinkel revered Friedrich Gilly in Berlin as their teacher. Gilly, who died young, was a brilliant architect whose designs reflect the grand spirit of French revolutionary architecture. He caused a big stir at the Berlin Academy in 1795 with his watercolor views of Marienburg. In his painterly and luminous view of the castle church of Marienburg, a recently discovered sheet and the most beautiful in the series, Gilly conveyed the simple grandeur and sublimity of Gothic architecture, giving it an equal place alongside ancient or neoclassical architecture (cat. 75). Gilly's sympathetic embrace of the architecture of the German Middle Ages follows in the footsteps of Goethe's eulogy *Of German Architecture* of 1772/73, a hymn celebrating the legendary builder of Strasbourg Cathedral, Erwin von Steinbach. It also shows spiritual kinship and parallels with Wilhelm Heinrich Wackenroder. Gilly had met him in 1793 and the two had established a friendly relationship. Around the same time that Gilly produced his watercolors, Wackenroder recorded in letters his impressions of the medieval city of Nuremberg, which still looked the way it had in Dürer's day.

Political repression under Napoleon and the Wars of Liberation may account for the persistence of patriotic themes and attitudes as important components within the Berlin school. During the age of Goethe, Gothic architecture, which originated in France, was erroneously believed to be of German origin. Goethe reinforced this historical misperception with his hymn to Erwin von Steinbach. The frequent depiction of Gothic architecture as an allusion to the "German" Middle Ages thus reflected patriotic sentiment. The Gothic style may also have expressed—as it did in Schinkel's many visions of Gothic cathedrals—the longing for a reunification of the Catholic and Protestant confessions. Schinkel drew up plans for the erection of a "German" cathedral on the battlefields of Leipzig, as a memorial to the Wars of Liberation and a symbol of the German unity yet to be attained. Later the cathedral in Cologne took on that role during the drive to complete it. The architect Karl Friedrich Schinkel, the most important representative of the Berlin school, had in his artistic repertoire both a neoclassical element (cat. 76) and a romantic, patriotic, Gothicizing one. In a lithograph from around 1810, he depicted a cemetery as a grove with a German oak and a Gothic church: a memorial to patriotic sentiment during the time of the Wars of Liberation (fig. 22).[42] Schinkel inscribed the work: "An attempt to express the sweet and wistful melancholy that fills the heart at the sounds of worship coming from the church." By incorporating a reference to music to deepen the experience, Schinkel showed himself an exponent of Romanticism akin to Philipp Otto Runge.

The faculty of the Berlin Academy included the sculptor Gottfried Schadow (cat. 14) and Friedrich Georg Weitsch. In 1813, Weitsch drew from life the closely observed portrait of a young volunteer in the Wars of Liberation against Napoleon (cat. 15). The youth's candid face, eyes wide with fear and anticipation, expressively mirrors his own difficult situation and the distress of his homeland. The aged Weitsch still used pastels for the portrait, a medium that had been popular in his youth.

Goethe had once criticized the art of Berlin for its prosaic rendering of reality and close adherence to nature. His criticism did in fact identify the fundamental characteristics of the Berlin school. I will end this survey with a look at its most important representatives (apart from Schadow and Schinkel), innovators whose work rises above a certain monotony inherent in the realism and naturalism that were persistent and highly valued features of this school.

The experience of light characterizes the landscapes that Carl Blechen drew with loose brush strokes in watercolor or wash. Sketched from nature or composed in a stagelike manner, sparing in their use of color and with an impression of spontaneity, these works capture the direct experience of landscape. In addition, they create symbolic references in motifs such as the ruins of Gothic churches or medieval castles in the forest (cat. 77). With his fresh, painterly real-

ism, Blechen was a precursor of this same movement in art, which developed toward the end of the nineteenth century.

Adolph Menzel, a stupendous draftsman who sketched an astonishing range of subjects, closes the circle around the age of Goethe, the period that had begun with the Berliner Chodowiecki, whom Menzel acknowledged as his sole "teacher." Menzel took a profound interest in the eighteenth century, which he illustrated as a chronicler of Prussian history. He felt a particular affinity for the Baroque, especially of the late eighteenth century (cat. 79, fig.). Menzel was enchanted by the playful effects of light and shadow, with their ability to suggest the material quality of the concrete world. It is significant that on a visit to the Glyptothek in Munich, Menzel chose, from among the many important originals of Greek art, to make various studies of the Hellenistic *Barberini Faun*. This statue is baroque in character—it had once been restored by Gianlorenzo Bernini—and its pose presented Menzel with the most challenging model.

Using the versatile carpenter's pencil, capable of evoking color with its broad range of black tones, around 1840 Menzel vividly por-

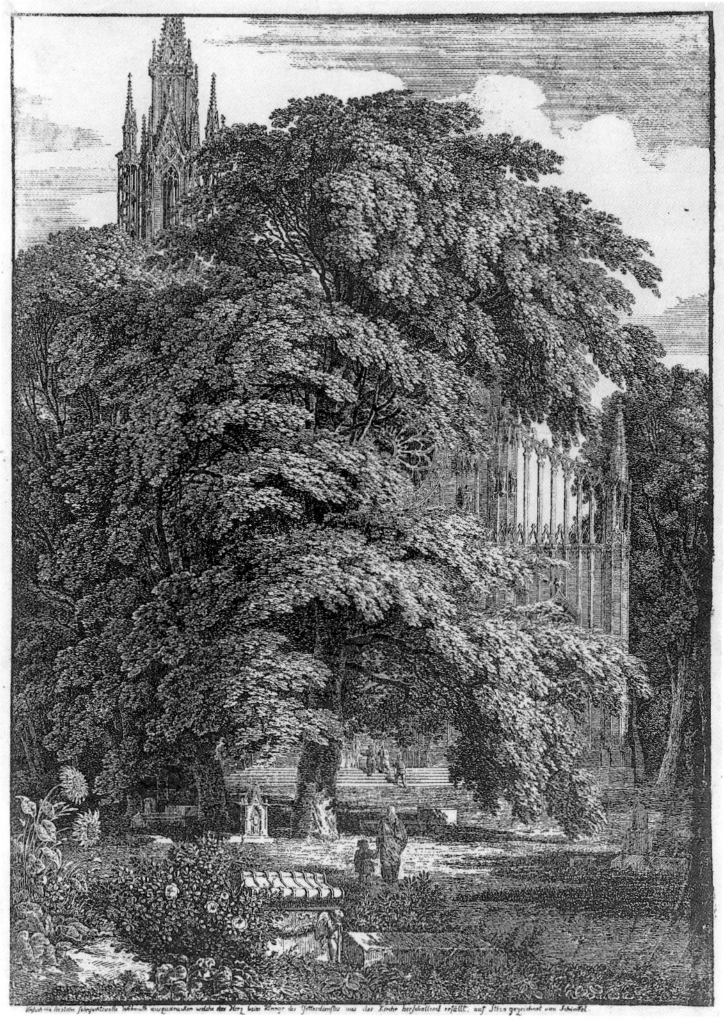

22 Karl Friedrich Schinkel, *Gothic Church in an Oak Grove with Graves*, 1810. Pen lithograph on brown-tinted paper

trayed the iridescent, precious silk of the baroque vest of King August II ("the Strong," 1670–1733),[43] and forty years later he used the same medium to depict baroque sandstone sculpture, the *Atlantes* at the Dresden Zwinger.[44] With his skill and dedication he was a role model for artists as late as Lovis Corinth or the young Max Beckmann. After the carpenter's pencil, Menzel's favorite medium was pastel, which reached the height of its popularity at the beginning of the Goethe period. Menzel used it especially around 1850 and during the rococo revival—the climax of the eclectic historicism of the *Gründerzeit* (the decades after 1871)—for portraits, or to capture moments of experience or memory.

Some of the pastels we most admire today were created for Menzel's private use and were not exposed to public scrutiny. His pastel *The Opera Glass* of around 1850, which he drew from memory and which concludes the present exhibition (cat. 80), has a highly modern effect. From a seat above her in the opera house, he observed a woman who was looking intently at the stage through her opera glass. It was not the action on the stage that fascinated the artist, but the spectator's reaction, and he captured the scene spontaneously. In the choice of subject matter as well as in its artistic execution—the boldness of the perspective from above, of the framing of the view, and of the composition with blank surfaces—Menzel here shows himself, more than a decade before the influence of Japanese woodcuts on avant-garde European art, as the precursor of Degas and Toulouse-Lautrec. His work, which had begun to develop with such promise during Goethe's lifetime,[45] establishes a direct link between the art of the Goethe period and that of the twentieth century.

1 This essay is based on my lecture in Alsfeld to the Arbeitskreis Stadtzeichner, which was subsequently published by Bernd Growe; Sieveking 1990.

2 Letter of 10 July 1869, in Stoessl 1924, p. 492.

3 Cf. Bruford 1979, pp. 314–17: statistical overview of Germany before the Napoleonic Wars.

4 See Paul Ortwin Rave and Ernst Herbert Lehmann, "Akademie," in *RDK*, vol. 1 (1937), cols. 243–62; Nikolaus Pevsner, *Die Geschichte der Kunstakademien* (Munich, 1986), chap. 4, pp. 141–86, chap. 5, pp. 187–236 Grotkamp-Schepers 1980; Steffi Röttgen, "Hofkunst-Akademie-Kunstschule-Werkstatt. Texte und Kommentare zur Kunstpflege von August III. von Polen und Sachsen bis zu Ludwig I. von Bayern," in *Münchner Jahrbuch der bildenden Kunst*, vol. 36 (1985), pp. 131–81.

5 An important role in collecting and in the exposure given to works of art was played especially by the *Kunstvereine* [art unions] with their sales exhibitions, lotteries, and yearly gifts of prints; cf. Langenstein 1983.

6 Cf. Kemp 1979.

7 *Zopfstil*, literally, "pigtail style," after the men's hairstyle of the second half of the eighteenth century.

8 Cf. Frankfurt 1994, p. 163, no. 113 (repr. in color).

9 Inscribed, lower right: "der Frau Geheimen Räthin Göethe zur Erinnerung von Joseph Stieler" [To Frau Privy Councillor Göethe in remembrance from Joseph Stieler]; Von Hase 1971, p. 133, no. 134; Angelika Lenz, "Erwerbungsbericht (Museum), Freies Deutsches Hochstift, Jahresbericht 1972/73," in *Jahrbuch des Freien Deutschen Hochstifts* (1974), pp. 393–433, here 398–401, repr. frontispiece (in color); Christian Lenz, "Stielers Bildniszeichnung von Goethe," *Pantheon* 42 (1984): pp. 90 f. (repr.).

10 Johann Wolfgang von Goethe, "Die Luisenburg bei Alexandersbad," in *Zur Naturwissenschaft*, vol. 1.3 (1820) (*Ausgabe letzter Hand*, vol. 51, p. 157).

11 Scheidig 1958; Ernst Osterkamp, "'Aus dem Gesichtspunkt reiner Menschlichkeit': Goethes Preisaufgaben für bildende Künstler 1799–1805," in Frankfurt 1994, pp. 310–22, 323–42, cat. nos. 199–217.

12 Scheidig 1958, pp. 437–88, 454 f., 477 f., 484 ff., nos. 8, 9, figs. 46, 47.

13 A characteristic example, a red chalk study for the figure of Ceres in a fresco in the royal palace of Madrid, is in Vaduz, Ratjen Foundation; cf. *Hundert Zeichnungen aus fünf Jahrhunderten*, published by the Galerie Kurt Meissner (Zurich, 1984), p. 31, no. 9 (repr. in color).

14 An example is the "Fall of the Rebel Angels" or the "Fall of the Damned through Archangel Michael," a crucial theme of the Counter Reformation. It symbolizes the triumph of faith over unbelief or of the Church over paganism, and was continued into the late eighteenth century on countless altarpieces and ceiling paintings in churches.

15 Denis Diderot and Jean L. d'Alembert, *Encyclopédie: Reçueil de planches sur les sciences et les arts, Dessein* (Paris, 1763), pl. 1.

16 Nuremberg 1980, pp. 60 f., no. 45; p. 73, no. 55; pp. 84 f., nos. 62, 63; p. 94, no. 73; p. 95, no. 77.

17 Diderot and d'Alembert (n. 15), pl. 24.

18 Charles le Brun, *Méthode pour apprendre à dessiner les passions* (Paris, 1667).

19 *Tree study*, inscribed, lower left: „den 1. April 1801." Pencil; 203 x 210 mm. Private collection. Cf., for example, *Neuerwerbungen*, exh. cat., Staatliche Graphische Sammlung München (Munich, 1982), p. 13, no. 13, fig. 3.

20 Friedrich Winkler, *Die Zeichnungen Albrecht Dürers*, vol. 1 (Berlin, 1936), no. 26 (repr.).

21 Friedrich Gross, "Zwischen niederem Stil und klassischem Ausdruck: Die Revolte des Malers Müller," *Idea: Jahrbuch der Hamburger Kunsthalle* 4 (1985): pp. 9, 83–106, here 97 f., 99.

22 *Bust-Length Portrait of a Peasant Woman in Profile*, signed and dated 1775. Red chalk, gouache, watercolor; 222 x 179 mm. Munich, Staatliche Graphische Sammlung, inv. no. 31806. Ingrid Sattel-Bernardini and Wolfgang Schlegel, *Friedrich Müller 1749–1825: Der Maler* (Landau/Pfalz, 1986), p. 170, Z 47, p. 95, color pl. 11.

23 Cf. Hardtwig 1984, pp. 157–88.

24 *Sir Benjamin Thompson, Count Rumford (1753–1814)*, 1792. Colored chalks; 169 x 128 mm (upright oval). Munich, Staatliche Graphische Sammlung, inv. no. 24514. Munich 1991, p. 126, no. 37 (Hinrich Sieveking). Cf. also the rather official, distinguished portrait of Rumford by Thomas Gainsborough from 1783. It was probably painted in connection with Rumford's elevation to British knighthood in 1784; Cambridge, Massachusetts, Fogg Art Museum, inv. no. 1922.1; cf. Louise Todd Ambler, *Early Science at Harvard: Innovators and Their Instruments 1765–1865*, exh. cat., Fogg Art Museum, Harvard University (Cambridge, Mass., 1969), pp. 50 f., no. 55 (repr.).

25 In addition to those already mentioned, Rumford's most important accomplishments in the service of the Bavarian elector Carl Theodor included military reform and, in conjunction with that, the design of the English Garden (1789–92); the introduction of a healthful diet (so-called Rumford soup and the propagation of the potato as a staple); saving the city of Munich in 1796 from occupation and plundering by French and Austrian troops; and, finally, the defortification of Munich as a prerequisite for the future development of the city.

26 Cf. Lankheit 1952, pp. 65 ff.

27 Ronald Paulson, *Hogarth's Graphic Works*, 2nd, corrected ed. (New Haven and London, 1970), no. 162; Gerhard Langemeyer *et al.*, eds., *Bildnis als Waffe und Motive der Karikatur in fünf Jahrhunderten*, exh. cat., Münchner Stadtmuseum (Munich, 1984), p. 39, no. 15 (repr.). Cf. Chodowiecki's etching "la cervelle d'un peintre"; Bauer 1982, p. 235, no. 1629 (repr.), E 696.

28 While this so-called Debutades legend gradually disappeared from the literature on art theory, its pictorial illustration reached its climax between 1770 and 1830; cf. Hans Wille, "Erfindung der Zeichenkunst," in *RDK*, vol. 5 (Stuttgart, 1967), cols. 1235–41, 1237, 1239.

29 Traeger 1975, p. 429, no. 399, p. 427 (repr.).

30 Ludwig Richter, *Erinnerungen eines deutschen Malers* (Frankfurt am Main, 1885), p. 159.

31 Ludwig Emil Grimm, whose oeuvre consists essentially of pencil drawings, is a characteristic example of a draftsman who stayed close to nature.

32 Hensel's portrait collection consists of 47 albums with a total of 1,082 portrait drawings. Except for one, all of the albums were acquired by the Nationalgalerie in Berlin in 1956, through the mediation of Paul Ortwin Rave; today they are in the Berlin Kupferstichkabinett. Cf. Berlin 1981, pp. 9 ff. (Lucius Grisebach); Paul Ortwin Rave, "Wilhelm Hensel: Ein Porträtist im Mendelssohnschen Hause," in Rave 1965, pp. 148–55.

33 *Bilder zu Goethe's Faust von P. Cornelius, gestochen von F. Ruscheweyh* (Frankfurt am Main, 1816–26) (Berlin, 1845); Stephan Seeliger, "Zur Editionsgeschichte der Faust-Bilder von Peter Cornelius," *Aus dem Antiquariat* 7 (1988): pp. 277 ff.; Mainz 1993, pp. 136–39, nos. 55, 56; original drawings in the Städelsches Kunstinstitut in Frankfurt am Main; Frankfurt, 1977, pp. 208 f., nos. E.84–E.90, pp. 250–52 (repr.); Frankfurt 1991 (Martin Sonnabend); additional original drawings in the Kunstmuseum Düsseldorf, the Goethemuseum Düsseldorf, and private hands.

34 *Faust: Tragédie de M. de Goethe*, trans. into French by M. Albert Stapfer (Paris, 1828). Loys Delteil, *Le peintre-graveur illustré*, vol. 5 (Paris, 1908), nos. 57–74.

35 Stuttgart, Staatsgalerie, inv. no. L 1227. Christian von Holst, *Staatsgalerie Stuttgart: Malerei und Plastik des 19. Jahrhunderts* (Stuttgart, 1982), p. 96 f. (repr.); Stuttgart 1989, p. 132, no. 16, fig. 77 (in color).

36 C. G. Boerner/Arnold Otto Meyer, vol. 1, p. 3, no. 20, pl. 5.

37 Schack-Galerie 1969, pp. 366 ff., fig. 44.

38 In *Masse und Macht*, quoted by Inken Nowald in "Wie Maler den Wald gesehen," in Berlin 1987, p. 99.

39 Cf. Schmoll 1970.

40 Feuchtmayr 1975, p. 377, Z 401, fig. 36.

41 Friedrich Schulze, *Die deutsche Napoleon-karikatur* (Weimar, 1916). Lammel 1992, pp. 19–29, 104–186, figs. 35–122. Sabine and Ernst Scheffler, in collaboration with Gerd Unverfehrt, *So zerstieben getraeumte Weltreiche: Napoleon I. in der deutschen Karikatur* (Stuttgart, 1995).

42 Berlin 1980/81, pp. 44 f., no. 93, p. 47 (repr.).

43 Vaduz, Ratjen Foundation. Hamburg 1982, pp. 48 f., no. 6 (repr.).

44 *Ibid.*, p. 206, no. 126 (repr.).

45 In 1833, the year after Goethe's death, Menzel, who had already made a name for himself as a lithographer, drew and published the series of lithographs to *Künstlers Erdenwallen* after Goethe's poetry. Through this work, he attracted the attention of the historian and art historian Franz Kugler, with whom he later collaborated as illustrator on Kugler's *Geschichte Friedrichs des Grossen* [History of Frederick the Great].

Acknowledgments

Many thanks to my American colleagues at Harvard University in Cambridge, Massachusetts, who initiated this exhibition: James Cuno, Elizabeth and John Moors Cabot Director of the Harvard University Museums; Peter Nisbet, Daimler-Benz Curator of the Busch-Reisinger Museum; and William W. Robinson, Ian Woodner Curator of Drawings at the Fogg Art Museum. I am also grateful to Charles A. Ryskamp, director of the Frick Collection in New York, whose passion for European drawings opened his house to this exhibition, and to John Walsh, director of the J. Paul Getty Museum, Nicholas Turner, curator of drawings, and his assistant Lee Hendrix, who enthusiastically offered the exhibition space in the Getty Museum's new home in Los Angeles.

I would like to thank those in charge of the German sites of the exhibition for their spirited participation in this project from the very beginning: Director Rolf Bothe, Hermann Mildenberger, and Thomas Föhl of the Staatliche Kunstsammlungen Weimar; Director Christoph Vitali, Hubertus Gassner, and Bernhart Schwenk of the Haus der Kunst, Munich; and Director Herbert Beck and Margret Stuffmann of the Städelsches Kunstinstitut, Frankfurt am Main. My gratitude goes to colleagues and friends who helped me in the preparation of this catalogue. The photographer, Engelbert Seehuber, deserves special recognition. His great commitment and photographic work laid the foundation for high-quality reproductions. I am grateful to Michael Horster for his help with computer questions, and to Andreas Heese of Berlin and Michaela Schmitt and Andrea Lukas of Munich for their support. For clarifying and wide-ranging discussions I would like to thank Jens Christian Jensen of Hamburg, Peter Märker of Darmstadt, Petra Maisak and Margret Stuffmann of Frankfurt, Siegmar Holsten of Karlsruhe, and Helmut Börsch-Supan of Berlin, as well as Frank Büttner, Konrad Feilchenfeldt, Ulrike von Hase, and Stephan Seeliger of Munich. A special thank-you to the Staatliche Graphische Sammlung, Munich, and its director, Tilman Falk, as well as Wiebke Tomaschek, Hermann Mayr, and Hermann Mischke for help in a variety of ways, in view of their long-standing, friendly contacts with the Winterstein collection. Konrad Laudenbacher of the Doerner-Institut of the Bayerische Staatsgemäldesammlungen, Munich, answered a number of difficult questions concerning painting and drawing technique. Ursula Küpper and Peter Reimpell in Munich, as well as my brother Klaus in Bremen, contributed active interest and constant support, and I am deeply grateful to them. With gratitude I remember the collector Alfred Winterstein and his wife Elisabet, who live on so vividly in their collection and who were in my thoughts as I worked on this catalogue. Alfred Winterstein was one of those who opened my eyes to the art of drawing. Finally, I extend special thanks to the Winterstein family for the trust they have placed in me over so many years.

CATALOGUE

1

Caspar Wolf

Baptized Muri/Aargau 3 May 1735 – 6 October 1783
Heidelberg

Waterfall in the Mountains, c. 1770 – 80

*Pen and black ink, gray wash, black border, on laid paper;
watermark: lily on crowned escutcheon, below it, V/J
HONIG; partially trimmed, laid down on its old mount;
314 x 211 mm*

Right up into the eighteenth century, the Alps had the reputation of being inaccessible, dangerous, and terrifying. But naturalists and geologists who studied their formation gradually laid the groundwork for a new way of looking at these mountains. A complete reappraisal came in the hymnic poem "Die Alpen" by the Bernese poet and polymath Albrecht von Haller.[1] It appeared in 1732 and triggered a genuine wave of Alpine enthusiasm. Haller saw Arcadia in the world of the mountains, a place where people, uncorrupted by civilization, lived a simple and free life in harmony with nature. His critique of civilization was popularized throughout Europe in Jean Jacques Rousseau's epistolary novel *Julie ou la Nouvelle Héloïse* (published in 1761), with its magnificent descriptions of the Alps, whose panorama was familiar to Rousseau from his childhood in Geneva. The Sturm und Drang period—also influenced by Rousseau—promulgated a new, elemental experience of nature that was strongly shaped by emotions. This experience also led to the discovery of the beauty of the landscapes of the Swiss high Alps and to the development of an early form of tourism.[2] The effect of the "sublimity" of nature on the human mind became a topic of philosophical debate. Edmund Burke examined it for the first time in his essay "A Philosophical Enquiry into the Origin of Our Ideas of the Sublime and Beautiful," published in 1757. In 1771, the Swiss aesthete Johann Georg Sulzer, in his *Allgemeine Theorie der Schönen Künste* [General Theory of the Fine Arts], wrote this under the key word "Sublime": "The beauty of inanimate nature teaches the person whose thinking is still untrained that he is no mere mortal composed only of matter. More definitive feelings of an ethical and passionate kind are also developed through the contemplation of lifeless nature. She shows us scenes in which we learn to admire what is great, new, and extraordinary. She has landscapes that arouse fear and trembling…. Who would not [feel] his own weakness and subordination to higher powers as he beholds the mighty mass of overhanging rocks?"[3]

Caspar Wolf was the first artist to make depicting the Alps his chief artistic concern.[4] Wolf—and after him, Joseph Anton Koch (cat. 2)—experienced the wild, primeval force and sublimity of the Alps also as a refuge of freedom, though each man did so in a very different way. Wolf chose the motif of the raging waterfall, which became in the age of the French Revolution a metaphor for liberty and for an irrepressible will to freedom, as a counterimage to the immovable rocks, which represented petrified social systems.[5] It is possible that Wolf based his composition on an actual topographical motif in the Swiss high Alps.[6] Be that as it may, in this work, the symbolically expressive elements of nature seem to have been mounted, with great artistry, as a mighty spectacle on a stage. The black border confirms that the drawing's steep, high format is the original one, and Wolf employed it to intensify the expressiveness of the height of the mountains on the one hand, and the precipitous plunge of the waterfall on the other. Wolf "used the sweep of the rocaille to impart rhythm" to the staggered rock formations jutting out in every direction, and this technique "reveals his background in the decorative art of the southern German Rococo."[7] The gloomy rock formations frame the entire left edge of the drawing in the manner of a *repoussoir*. On the top, they jut out menacingly toward the right. The view of the waterfall seems to open up like a semicircle toward the right, as from an enormous shaded grotto.[8] As a result, the human figure in the lower edge of the drawing, which provides an indication of scale, seems puny, as though crushed by the force of the steep rocks and the raging waterfall. The man, on his knees on an anthropomorphic rocky ledge, is groping his way toward the center of the picture in the foreground, careful lest he slip and fall. His stooped posture suggests that he is looking into an abyss that plunges down into even greater depths. He is directly exposed to the tremendous happenings in nature; he is a precursor of Caspar David Friedrich's figures, who stand with their backs to the viewer, pulling us into the picture.

The close-up view and the narrowly circumscribed perspective focus the picture on the battle of the elements, and this further accentuates the isolation of and danger to the sole human witness. Earth-shaping forces become perceptible in the fanned-out, bizarre rock formations washed by water. Here Wolf reveals his geological interests. By the power of its descent, the water has carved out a path through the mountains. Where it encounters resistance, the water spurts upward and vaporizes, and the light is caught in countless reflections in the rising cloud of spray. Wolf heightens the experience of nature by the imagined roar and the sound of its echo as the primeval elements of water and stone collide. By incorporating the acoustic into the visual experience, he expands the encounter with nature by means of synesthesia. This already suggests a romantic sensibility of nature.

1 Cologne 1984, p. 162, no. 103.
2 Cf. Monika Wagner, "Die Alpen: Faszination unwirtlicher Gegenden," in Tübingen 1981, pp. 67–86.
3 Sulzer 1771, vol. 1, p. 653.
4 Wegmann 1993, pp. 20–29. Between 1773 and 1779, at the request of the Bernese publisher Abraham Wagner, Wolf created his famous cycle of more than 150 oil paintings that were to serve as a model for an extensive compendium of engravings of the Alps, which remained unfinished. The first series of ten etchings based on his paintings was published in Bern in 1777; a second series of twenty-four color aquatints by J. F. Janinet appeared in Paris in 1779. We know that Wolf began his paintings of scenic Alpine views in his studio, but finished them on-site. He ruined his health by painting outdoors even in the winter, which is why he died so young. Cf. Beat Wismer, "Malerei und Geologie, Anmerkungen zu Caspar Wolf und Per Kirkeby," in *Skreiner-Festschrift*, 1992, pp. 241–251.
5 Warnke 1992, p. 118.
6 For related compositions and the associated question of dating, cf. Willi Raeber, *Caspar Wolf 1735–1783. Sein Leben und sein Werk. Ein Beitrag zur Geschichte der Schweizer Malerei des 18. Jahrhunderts* (Aarau, Frankfurt am Main, Salzburg, and Munich, 1979), pp. 187–304, nos. 121, 134, 144, 171, 180, 182, 183, 221, 227, 237, 243, 250, 251, 253, 254, 273, 276ff., 332, 333, 335, 339, 340, 352, 383.
7 Wegmann 1993, p. 28.
8 Because Wolf was fond of depicting grottoes and caves, he was also jokingly called "cave wolf."

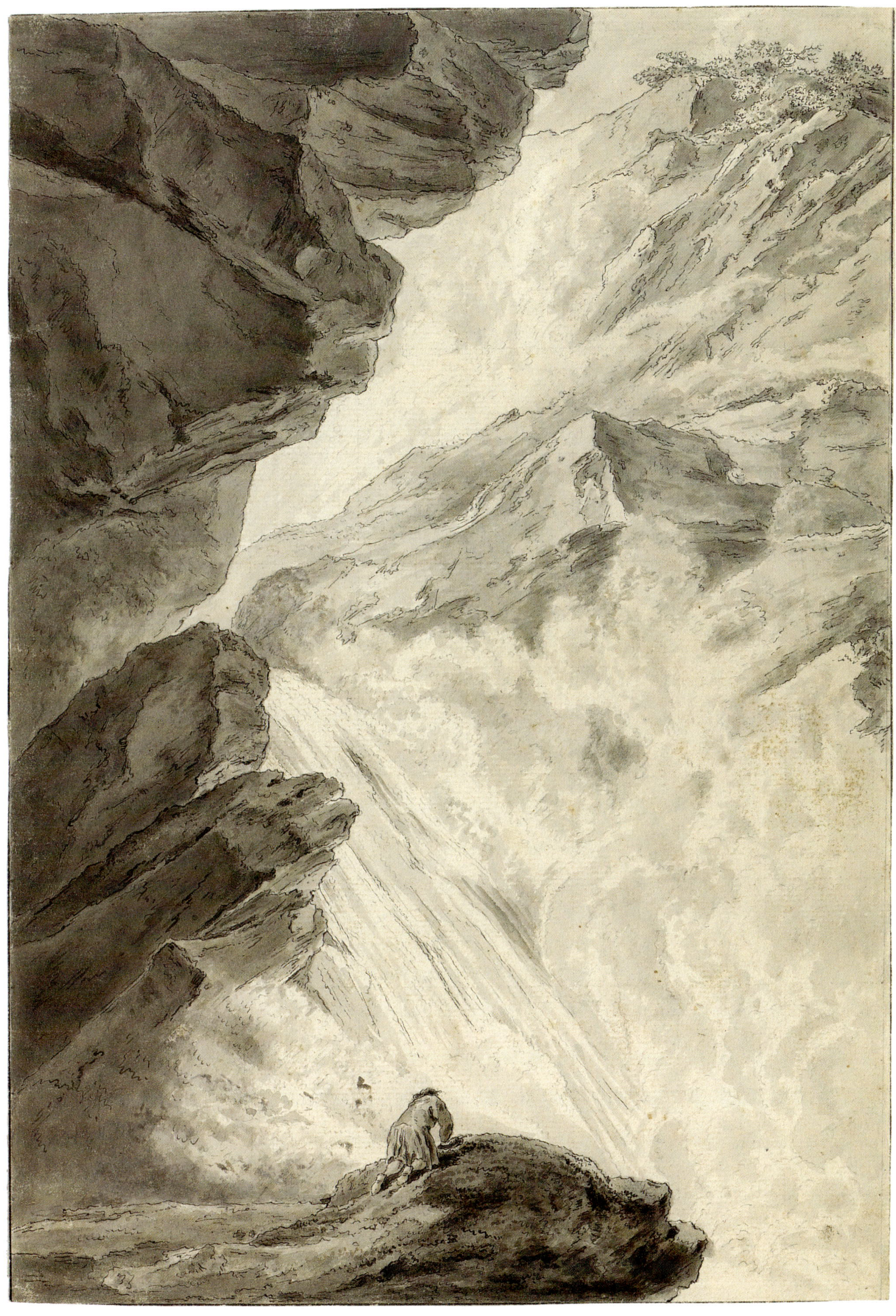

2

Joseph Anton Koch

Obergibeln/Tyrol 27 July 1768–12 January 1839
Rome

View of the Jungfrau from the Lütschin Valley,
c. 1793

Pen and brown ink, on laid paper; 190 x 237 mm

*Selected bibliography: Berlin 1939, p. 45, no. 87; Lutterotti
1940, pp. 15, 271, no. 564, pl. 63, fig. 103; Lutterotti 1944,
pp. 23 f., fig. 6; Winterthur 1955, p. 60, no. 254; Munich 1958,
p. 39, no. 93, fig. 8; Heise 1959, p. 53, fig. 34; Lübeck 1969,
pp. 52 ff., no. 88 (repr.); Lutterotti 1985, pp. 32 f., 353, Z 564,
p. 196, fig. 81; Stuttgart 1989, pp. 132 f., no. 16, fig. 77 (in color)*

In the age of the French Revolution, the notion
of the Alps as a refuge of freedom was a relevant
and explosive idea in terms of social politics.
Nature in its primeval, untouched state became
the symbol of a better society. William Tell was
known everywhere as a hero of liberty, and
Schiller created a monument for him in his
drama *Wilhelm Tell*. It was Schiller, too, who
said, "In the mountains there is liberty!"[1] Koch
lived in Switzerland from 1792 to 1794, under the
political system of the republican Swiss Confed-
eration, which he considered a liberal one, and in
the midst of the primeval landscape of the Alps,
which symbolized freedom: first in Basel, then in
Bern—where, suspected of revolutionary activities, he was not tolerated for long—and, finally,
in Biel. As a young adherent of the Sturm und
Drang movement, Koch had become enthusiastic
about the ideas of the French Revolution. In
1791, he had escaped the military discipline of
the Hohe Carlsschule in Stuttgart, as Friedrich
Schiller had done eleven years earlier, and had
gone to Strasbourg. Along the way, on the Rhine
Bridge (according to another version, it was dur-

ing a speech at the Strasbourg Jacobin Club), he
cut off the pigtail that was required at the Carlsschule and sent it to his former superiors in Stuttgart. His revolutionary enthusiasm expressed itself also in the way he signed his works, for
example, "Koch 1792 im 4. Jahr der Freyheit"
[Koch 1792 in the fourth year of liberty].[2]
On hikes in the high Alps of Switzerland, Koch
drew landscape studies from nature. In part, they
were also expressions of the freedom he thought
the Alps symbolically embodied. We know for
certain that Koch spent the summer of 1794 in
the Jungfrau region and "clambered around in
the mountains like a mountain-goat hunter."
Something of his passion for liberty can be felt in
the spirited strokes of this landscape of the
Bernese Oberland, which he sketched from
nature and possibly finished in the studio. The
topographical situation of the forested valley
through which the Lütschin flows—with a view
of the Jungfrau massif towering in the distance
—has been faithfully rendered, as in a *veduta*,
except for a few simplifying deviations (for
instance, the depiction of the mountain ridge).
The compositional structure reveals the traditional gradation of foreground, middle ground,
and background, which grow lighter with distance. Figures, such as the wanderers on the path
that winds along the river, set the scale in order
to illustrate the vast depths and heights of
the mountains. Sketchy sepia pen strokes fill the
entire, pictorially executed drawing with a
vibrant energy. These strokes embody the unifying primeval force of nature. The landscape is
alive and pulsating with a steady rhythm of
freely resonating lines and hatchings. Parallels to
the art of drawing in the period of Dürer are
evident, as seen in the landscape art of the
Danube school, an expression of an artistic desire
whose roots lie in the primal Danubian and
Alpine landscape, in late medieval piety, and in
the humanism that radiated from Vienna. For
example, there are landscape drawings by
Albrecht Altdorfer that depict actual topographical situations and show a similar rhythm, with
short strokes and hatching. In format and technique, in its vigorous penmanship, and in the use
of motifs from the Bernese Oberland, this view of
the Lütschin Valley relates to five other drawings by Koch.[3] In all these drawings, Koch's concern extended beyond the faithfulness of the
veduta to the dramatized effect of the picture,
which also encompasses light-dark contrasts and
cloud formations in the sky. The pictorial execution and engraving-like graphic treatment of the
drawings suggest that Koch may have been planning a series of engravings or etchings.[4] In fact,
he did correspond with the publisher and art
dealer Johann Friedrich Frauenholz in Nuremberg concerning the production and sale of landscape etchings, which he hoped would open up a

new source of income for him. On 25 July 1797,
he offered Frauenholz, among other works, this
series of early Alpine landscapes, but Frauenholz
did not place an order for them.[5] In 1810, however, Koch would publish his series of twenty
etchings of "Roman Views" himself, his most
important effort in the field of printmaking.
Koch's drawing was the model for a copy in pen
and ink by Otto Count Baudissin (fig.), who
defused Koch's energetic draftsmanship and
moved the work closer to being a *veduta*.[6] This
copy attests that the special quality of Koch's
work was recognized early on, and that Koch may
readily have lent his drawings and sketchbooks
to art lovers and students for drawing exercises
and copying. The future general Count Baudissin
(1792–1865), who was an amateur painter and
etcher, had been in contact with Koch and had
been one of his patrons in Rome around 1819.
Since Baudissin made his copy in Florence in
1820, we can assume that he acquired Koch's
drawing in Rome, directly from the artist. A
number of Baudissin's own drawings from Italy
were exhibited in Copenhagen between 1829 and
1837 (see cat. 28).

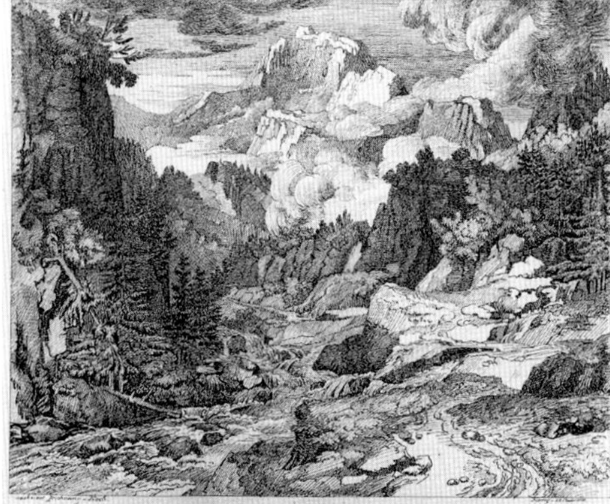

Otto Graf Baudissin, *View of the Jungfrau from the
Lütschin Valley*, 1820. Pen and black ink; 194 x 236 mm.
Kiel, Kunsthalle, inv. no. 1953-V77

1 Friedrich von Schiller, *Braut von Messina*, IV, 17.
2 Stuttgart 1989, pp. 123 ff., nos. 8, 9.
3 *Ibid.*, pp. 131–34, nos. 14–18, figs. 75–80.
4 *Ibid.*, p. 131, no. 14.
5 On 25 July 1797, Koch wrote from Rome, "I have many
   studies of the Swiss Alps, chiefly from the Lauterbrunn,
   Grindelwald, Unterseen, and Oberhasli valleys, drawn
   from nature and in part with watercolor. I have several
   of the most interesting waterfalls of these regions: for
   example, the Staubbach, Schmadrigletscherbach . . .; many
   wild mountain and glacier views: for example, the
   Jungfrau, the glaciers in the Grindelwald . . . . Since there
   is little passable work of the Swiss Alpine regions, either
   etched or engraved, I think one could put together a collection that would attract interest, especially since I have
   tried to draw each view from its most diverse and picturesque vantage point. I would draw these studies either
   in pure coloration or in a single color with sepia, and etch
   them myself. Or I could send you the drawings and you
   could have them etched or engraved." Lutterotti 1940, p.
   138; cf. Edith Luther, *Johann Friedrich Frauenholz
   (1758–1822), Kunst-händler und Verleger in Nürnberg*
   (Nuremberg, 1988), p. 65.
6 Sheet size: 314 x 416 mm. Inscribed underneath the drawing on the left: "nach einer Zeichnung v. Koch" [after a
   drawing by Koch]; on the right: "Florenz, d. 29 Novbr
   1820"; Martius 1956, p. 125, fig. 64.

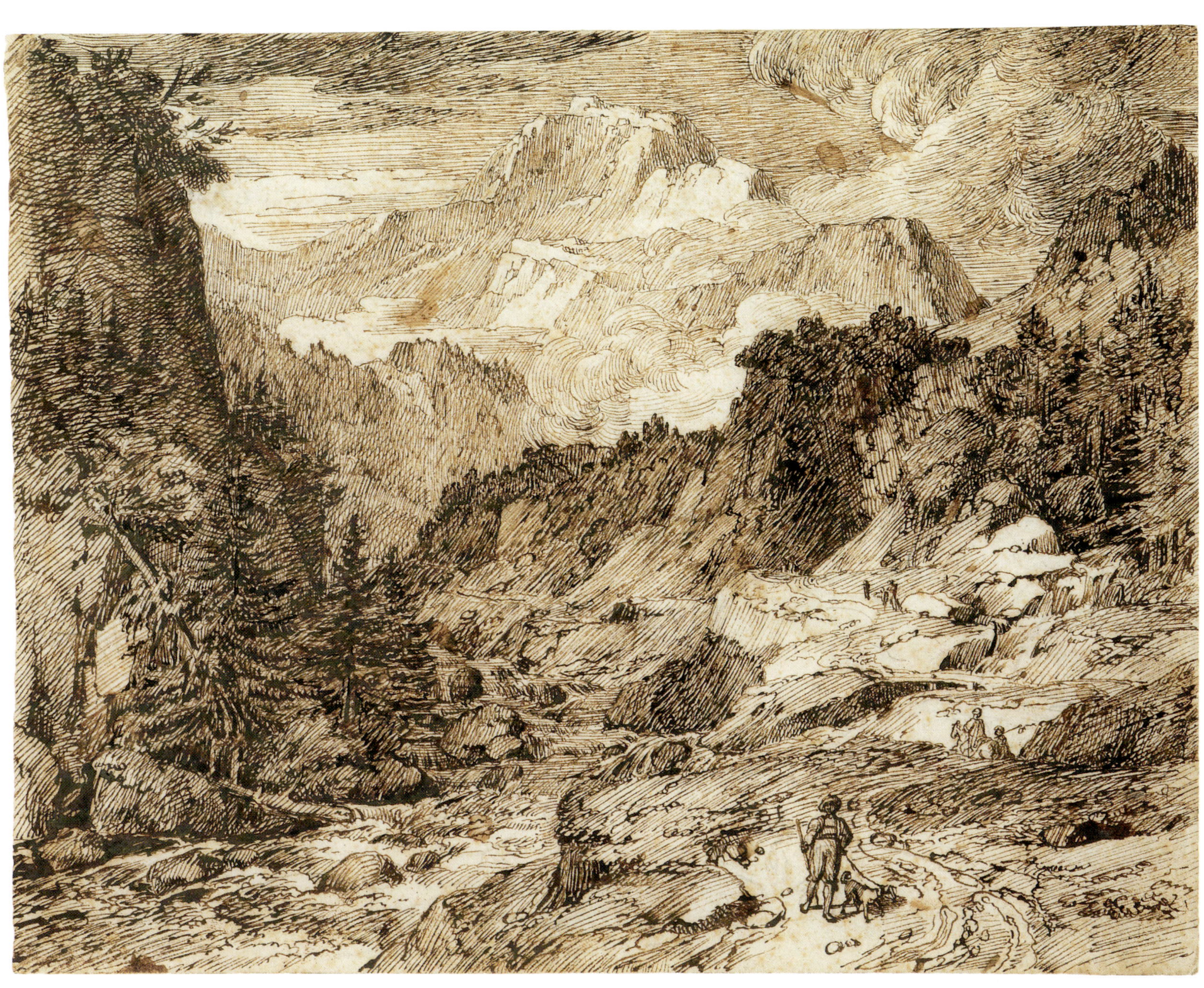

3

Franz Innocenz Kobell

Mannheim 23 November 1749–14 January 1822
Munich

Idealized Southern Landscape, c. 1780

*Pen and black and gray ink, watercolor, border in black
pen (partially trimmed on the bottom), on laid paper;
watermark: J Honig/&/Zoonen; laid down on its old
mount; 249 x 308 mm*

Bibliography: Munich 1958, p. 37, no. 82

Franz Kobell represents a type of artist characteristic of the Goethe period: someone who made his living almost entirely through his drawings. He was probably the most prolific draftsman of his time.[1] Although he did little painting and etching, and that only occasionally, he drew incessantly and with an almost manic obsessiveness. Johann Nepomuk Ringseis, the personal physician of the crown prince and, later, king Ludwig I of Bavaria, recounted in his memoirs, "Having spent the entire day drawing, he would have a book of paper laid out every evening and go on to fill it with compositional ideas."[2] Pen and brush drawings, mostly of small and miniature format, flowed quickly and easily from Kobell's hand. He preferred to use a pen, with all the gradations of brown ink, bister, and sepia, and only occasionally added watercolor to his drawings. In technique and form, the present watercolor, painted primarily in green and blue tones, is part of a small group of pictorially executed, pure aquarelles in the manner of oil painting. It is possible that Kobell intended to obtain commissions for executing them in oil. He may also have produced them on commission, for sale, or as presents, for they were highly prized by collectors. Goethe, who wanted to acquire drawings by Franz Kobell, approached his brother Ferdinand in a letter of 3 December 1780: "Please order a dozen drawings from your brother in Rome, I have 24 ducats for that purpose. But he should draw them at least partially from nature, and then finish them as he wishes.... "[3]

Since Kobell adhered to classical landscape motifs for decades and rarely dated his works, it is very difficult to place them chronologically.[4] Kobell's prompt delivery of the drawings for Goethe,[5] therefore, provides a valuable aid for dating the sheet exhibited here. Although it is a more mature work, the present drawing relates to the others in both its strong mood and a certain hardness in the treatment of the trees. These suggest that the watercolor was executed not long after the drawings commissioned by Goethe.

In this piece, Kobell presents us with an impressive and quite magnificent southern landscape.

With its massive, steep, and towering rock formations overgrown with brush and trees on the one hand, and its infinitely broad vista on the other, it conveys the sublimity, magnificence, and beauty of nature. Nevertheless, this is not a landscape that was drawn from nature and that can therefore be topographically located. Instead, Kobell—undoubtedly inspired by his experience in Italy and its southern light—conceived of an idealized Mediterranean landscape in the studio and assembled it from elements suitable for conveying a heroic impression. Kobell had a fairly small repertory of such motifs, and he continuously rearranged them into new compositions. The picture is dominated in the middle ground by the massive rock formation on the left, with its cave openings and grottoes, and the natural spectacle of a waterfall in the center (see cat.1). Kobell frequently used variations of such rock formations as dramatic landscape elements, often in conjunction with clouds and thunderstorms. Apparently he was inspired by the starkly architectonic, layered rocks in quattrocento panel painting, such as those seen in the works of Mantegna or Giovanni Bellini.

In his composition's stagelike structure—achieved by overlapping the foreground, middle ground, and background like stage scenery and, in accordance with aerial perspective, lightening the tonality toward the pale blue mountain ranges in the distance—he followed the classical landscape artists Claude Lorrain and Gaspard Dughet. Revealingly, Goethe recommended such Kobellian compositions as models for theatrical stage scenery.[6] In the present work, staffage figures in classical dress are fully integrated and can be seen only on close inspection. In the left foreground, a couple resembling effigies on Etruscan sarcophagi face a solitary man with a Bacchic belly who reclines on the ground next to a jug of wine. In front of the waterfall in the middle ground, noticeably smaller and seen at a greater distance, a woman bends to draw water while three other female figures stand nearby; this awakens associations with the Graces or the Judgment of Paris. Here, the staffage serves to clarify perspective and scale, and simultaneously transports the landscape into a timeless Arcadian idyll. Invented out of heroic and idyllic elements, Kobell's landscape and its mood show the artist's strong feelings for nature, which had their roots in Sturm und Drang and were highly cherished among his contemporaries. In this regard, we see a kinship with the compositions of Jacob Philipp Hackert, for whose works, in fact, Kobell's are occasionally mistaken. Goethe criticized and praised Franz Kobell's artistry with keen insight: "I know Franz Kobell through his drawings, which he executes in a style all his own, with great speed and in extraordinary numbers. One often finds in them hints that he has understood

and felt nature with a highly trained eye, but soon he goes on to undo and completely destroy what was good in the distance with thoughtless and quite impossible masses, which are meant to serve as his foregrounds. The main thrust of his compositions tends toward a conglomeration of many incompatible objects, which cannot possibly find their ground in the narrow space in which he brings them together.... Otherwise, his style is intelligent and agreeable."[7]

1 After Franz Kobell's death, Friederike Hartmann wrote in a letter of January 1822, "One can hardly calculate how many of his drawings exist, though one can gauge their number from the report that the Probst Stengel, alone, owns 6,000 of them.... It would surely be no exaggeration to estimate the number of his drawings at 100,000." She also reported that even on his deathbed, Kobell continued to draw right up to his last breath; see *Erinnerungen des Dr. Johann Nepomuk v. Ringseis*, collected, supplemented, and edited by Emilie Ringseis, vol. 1 (Regensburg and Amberg, 1886), pp. 564 f. Kobell's friend Johann Georg von Dillis alone owned some 15,000 of his drawings, cf. Robert Brulliot, *Verzeichnis der von dem verstorbenen Königl. bayer. Central-Gemälde-Gallerie-Direktor Georg von Dillis hinterlassenen Sammlung von Holzschnitten, Kupferstichen, Radirungen und Handzeichnungen* (Munich, 1843), nos. 1067–1127, 1143.

2 His female cook always sold these drawings in a tavern in Munich, cf. Ringseis (n. 15), p. 298.

3 Cf. *Goethes Briefe*, published on commission from the Grand Duchess Sophie von Sachsen, sect. 4, vol. 5 (Weimar, 1889), p. 12.

4 I would like to thank Thomas Herbig of Munich, who prepared the monographic exhibition on Franz Kobell for Traunstein and Reutlingen in 1997/98, for graciously allowing me to look at his material and for helping me to place the work chronologically. Cf. Thomas Herbig, *Franz Kobell, Ein Landschaftszeichner um 1800: Watercolors, drawings, etchings*; exh.cat Städtische Galerie Traunstein und Kunstverein Reutlingen, (Stein, 1997). A first attempt at a chronology of the artist's vast body of graphic work can be found in Siegfried Wichmann, *Franz Kobell, 1749–1822: Erste Ansätze einer chronologischen Ordnung des graphischen Werks* (Munich and Starnberg, 1974).

5 Now in *Weimar, Staatliche Kunstsammlungen*, cf. Schuchardt, 1848, vol. 1, p. 271, no. 590. 1–10; Goethe confirmed receipt of the pieces as early as 5 February 1781, cf. *Goethe-Corpus 1978*, vol. 6B, p. 22, under no. 45. See *Goethes Briefe* (n. 17), pp. 46 f.; Thomas Herbig of Munich kindly called my attention to this.

6 Goethe, *Kunsttheoretische Schriften und Übersetzungen* (Berlin edition), ed. Siegfried Seidel, vol. 17 (Berlin and Weimar, 1984), p. 142.

7 Quoted in Adolf Feulner, *Münchner Malerei um 1800*, exh. cat., Galerie Heinemann (Munich, 1920), p. 12.

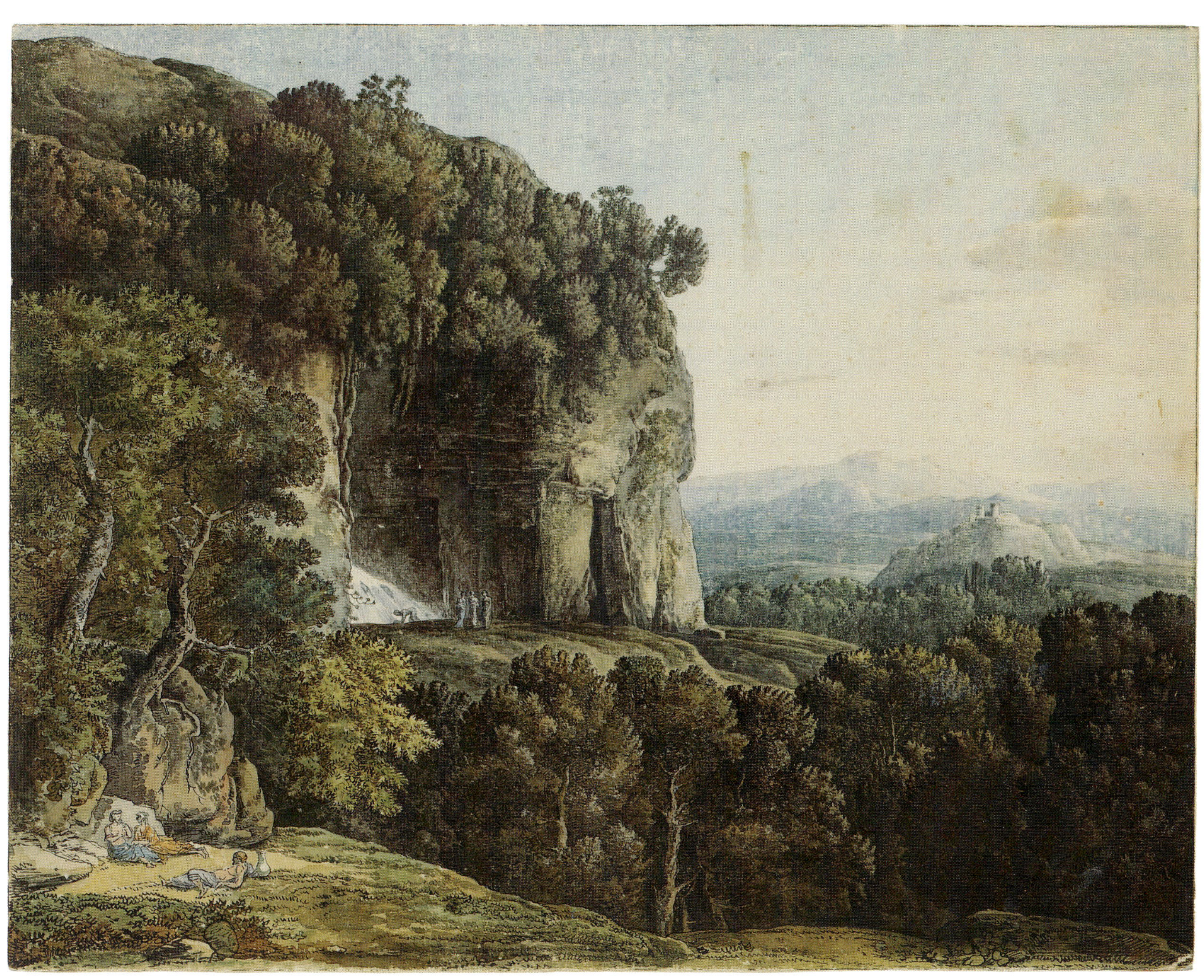

4

Johann Christian Reinhart

Near Hof 24 January 1761–9 June 1847 Rome

I, Too, Was in Arcadia (ΚΑΓΩ ΗΝ ΕΝ ΑΡΚΑΔΙΑ), 1785

Pen and brown ink, brush and gray, black, and ochre wash, on laid paper; watermark: C R & C o (illegible), two decorative rectangular fields, in one a trumpeter, in the other a man with a dancing bear
Dated by the artist in pen and brown ink, lower left: "d. 22 Juli 1785"; 284/86 x 398/400 mm

Provenance: Prof. Dr. Edwin Redslob, Berlin; Prof. Dr. Friedrich Winkler, Berlin; Eva Dencker-Winkler, Zurich

Bibliography: London 1972, p. 410, under no. 767; Feuchtmayr 1975, pp. 61–63, 376f., Z-399, fig. 206; Gisela Bergsträsser, "Johann Christian Reinhart's Zeichnung: Et ego in Arcadia," in Kunst in Hessen und am Mittelrhein 1, no. 2 (1962): 126ff., fig. 8

In his pastoral poems, the ancient author Virgil transfigured Arcadia, the remote and wild mountain region in the Peloponnesus, into a land of human longing, where people, far from urban civilization, lived together peacefully and in harmony with nature. Over the centuries that followed, Arcadia was increasingly equated with Magna Graecia in southern Italy, and in the age of Goethe, finally, with Italy as a whole. Beginning in the seventeenth century, we find the "Et in Arcadia ego" theme always formulated in Latin in the visual arts, first by Guercino and then by Poussin. The words were traditionally depicted as inscriptions on tombstones. Originally they represented a *memento mori*: even in Arcadia, death spares no one. They were also understood as a reminder of the transitory nature of happiness, which the deceased had enjoyed during his or her lifetime ("I, too, once lived in Arcadia and enjoyed Arcadian happiness").[1] When Goethe published *Italienische Reise*, he used "I, too, in Arcadia!" as a motto at the beginning.

In his spirited drawing, Reinhart has depicted the tomb in the form of a sarcophagus. Instead of the usual shepherds and shepherdesses, he has placed only "shepherdesses around the tomb of their playmate" (Christian Ludwig Hagedorn), in keeping with the elegiac conventions of his time. While a tomb and figures are usually incorporated into an Arcadian landscape as mood-setting staffage, Reinhart has closely focused on the mourning women surrounding the sarcophagus. In the classical manner, he has composed them on a foreground stage very much in the spirit of Greek antiquity; parallel to the picture plane, the figures stand in a row and overlap, which is reminiscent of Greek votive and funeral reliefs. Reinhart has reduced the colors in imitation of what was believed to be the ancient treatment of marble. Six young women—like sisters of the same age, whether nymphs, Graces, or Muses—are wearing classical Greek dress, as is the seventh young woman, the deceased, whose reclining figure crowns the sarcophagus, and whose gesture immortalizes melancholy.

In a second drawing, larger in format, Reinhart repeated the group of three women in the foreground: at the base of the tomb, a seated figure who solemnly plays a kind of lyre, and two standing figures, one scattering flowers, the other turning away in grief.[2] The sarcophagus, on which the stone sculpture of the deceased rests as on an Etruscan tomb, is in the shape of a boat, which is a reference to Charon's bark and the crossing of the river Styx. The inscription carved into the tall base is in Greek: "ΚΑΓΩ ΗΝ ΕΝ ΑΡ-ΚΑΔΙΑ" [I, too, was in Arcadia] (ΚΑΓΩ is a contraction for ΚΑΙ ΕΓΩ).

Reinhart's drawing is dated 22 July 1785. He therefore created it during the period when he was close friends with the poet Friedrich Schiller in Gohlis, near Leipzig.[3] On 8 December 1787, Schiller wrote from Meiningen to his friend Körner in Dresden, "I've spent a lot of time with Reinhart, he is still the good old fellow he's always been…. We got to know each other even better here [in Meiningen], I quite like him…. He is now painting a large landscape in oil on the theme *Et ego in Arcadia*. He is going to give me the smaller model, also in oil, as a present."[4] Schiller's poem "Resignation—A Fantasy" is dated to 1785/86. Tellingly, it opens with the words "I, too, was in Arcadia born." In all likelihood, the two friends exchanged ideas on the Arcadia theme. Although Reinhart did not illustrate Schiller's poem, he did give visual expression to the sorrow over irretrievably lost time that Schiller reflects upon in the last lines of "Resignation": "You could have of the Wise inquiry made/The minutes from the hour struck/Are given back by no Eternity." However, Reinhart's drawing does not show resignation, but rather a summoning to life in the image of these women, who are still in their prime in sun-drenched Arcadia.

Reinhart undoubtedly was inspired to execute this theme in the Greek style by his teacher, Adam Friedrich Oeser, and, indirectly, by Oeser's friend, Johann Joachim Winckelmann. Oeser was imbued with the thought of the early Neoclassical period, which was reinforced by his intense exchange of ideas with Winckelmann. A painting by Oeser of circa 1770 on the theme of *Et ego in Arcadia* was the first in which an artist depicted this inscription on the sarcophagus of the deceased in Greek.[5] Otherwise, he adhered faithfully to the Baroque tradition in terms of iconography and composition: shepherdesses stand in front of the sarcophagus and decipher the inscription, a *memento mori* in the midst of the blissful life in an idyllic Arcadian landscape. The permanent exhibition in the Goethe-Museum Düsseldorf includes, under Reinhart's name, a watercolor—faded by daylight—on the Arcadia theme. It is closely related to Oeser's oil painting.[6] A close examination of the work, however, rules out Reinhart as the artist. The theme is treated entirely in Oeser's style as a landscape idyll, and the soft brushwork is typical of Oeser's touch, which contrasts with the younger Reinhart's firmer and less calligraphic handling.[7] The work is one of Oeser's own variations on the same theme. The nearly identical format of the two pieces is also a good argument for this attribution. Details of the motif in the drawing that differ from those in the painting are likewise inventions in the spirit of Oeser.

1 Cf. Erwin Panofsky, "Et in Arcadia Ego: Poussin and the Elegiac Tradition," in *Meaning in the Visual Arts: Papers in and on Art History* (Garden City, New York, 1955), pp. 295–320; Max Denzler, "Et in Arcadia Ego," *RDK*, vol. 6 (Munich 1973), cols. 117–31; Marbach 1966; Petra Maisak, "Et in Arcadia Ego: Zum Motto der Italienischen Reise" (Düsseldorf, 1986), pp. 133–45; *Arkadien, Landschaft vergänglichen Glücks*, ed. Petra Maisak and Corinna Fiedler (Frankfurt am Main and Leipzig, 1992), epilogue by Petra Maisak and additional bibliography.

2 Pen and brown ink, watercolor, 365 x 470 mm; Feuchtmayr 1975, p. 381, right col. Cf. Karl & Faber, sale 80, 14–16 May 1962, no. 328; Denzler (n. 1), col. 130 (repr.). In 1786, Reinhart etched the pair of standing figures in a tondo, A.13, Feuchtmayr 1975, p. 391, fig. 205.

3 A humorous drawing by Reinhart that shows Schiller smoking a pipe and seated on a donkey dates from the years of their close personal contact, 1785–87; Feuchtmayr 1975, pp. 347f., Z-82.

4 *Briefwechsel zwischen Schiller und Körner*, ed. Ludwig Geiger (Stuttgart, 1892), vol. 1, p. 168.

5 Circa 1770, oil on canvas, 38.5 x 46.0 cm; Hannover, Niedersächsisches Landesmuseum. Cf. Börsch-Supan 1988, pp. 108, 117, fig. 10 (in color); Frankfurt 1994, p. 237, no. 165 (repr. in color; Petra Maisak).

6 See Feuchtmayr 1975, p. 373, Z-352, fig. 202; *Goethe in seiner Zeit*, ed. Volkmar Hansen, cat. of permanent exhibition, Goethe-Museum Düsseldorf, Anton-und-Katharina-Kippenberg-Stiftung (Düsseldorf, 1993), p. 192, no. 5, 103.

7 The "limpness of the bodies" (Börsch-Supan 1988, p. 108) and the formulaic cast of the face and eyes have no parallels in Reinhart's early independent work as a draftsman. Bergsträsser's attribution of this piece to Reinhart is therefore not convincing. Bergsträsser 1962, pp. 126ff., fig. 7.

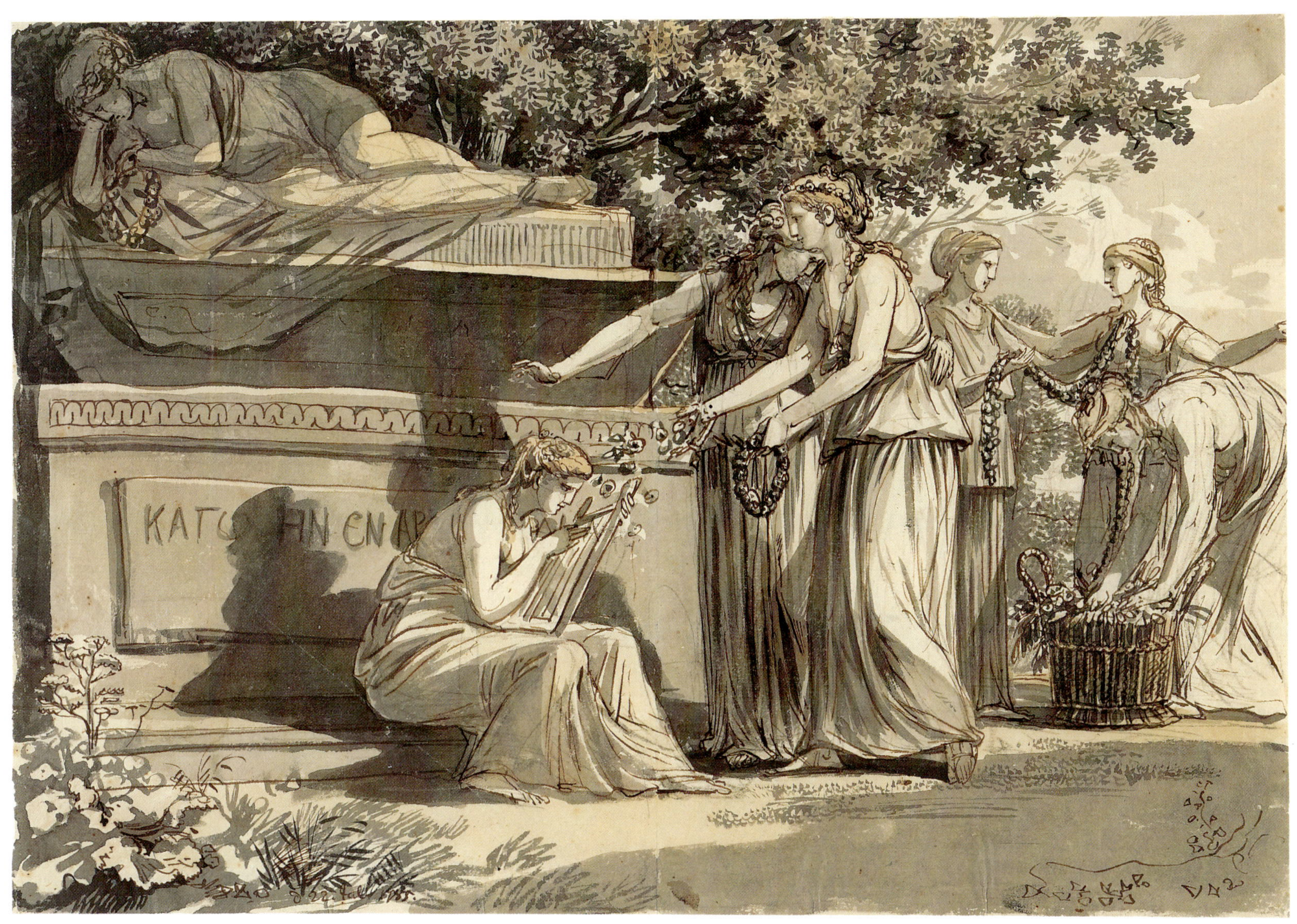

KATΩ ΗΝ ΕΝΑΡ

5

Carl Wilhelm Kolbe the Elder

Baptized Berlin 9 November 1759–13 January 1835
Berlin

Arcadian Landscape with an Offering to Pan,
c. 1808

*Black chalk, border line in pen and black ink, on wove
paper, laid down on its old mount; 405 x 517 mm
Signed in black chalk, upper right: "C W Kolbe f."*

*Provenance: Graphisches Kabinett Günther Franke,
Munich*

*Bibliography: Ulrich Christoffel, "Zu einer Romantik-
Ausstellung," Die Kunst 77, no. 39, pt. 1 (Munich, 1938): 55
(repr.); Munich 1958, pp. 39f., no. 97, fig. 7; Lübeck 1969, p.
57, no. 95; Ulf Martens, Der Zeichner und Radierer Carl
Wilhelm Kolbe d. Ä. (1759–1835) (Berlin, 1976), pp. 33f.,
87f., under no. 97/J. 215, pl. 25, fig. 48 (Offering to Pan)*

Beginning in about 1800, Kolbe drew a series
of monumental compositions of wildly exuberant swamp vegetation, so-called *Kräuterstücke*
[herbage pieces]. Although they form only a
small part of his oeuvre, it is here that the creative power and originality of his art reach their
heights. In these pieces, one senses Kolbe's roots
in the Sturm und Drang, which found a late echo

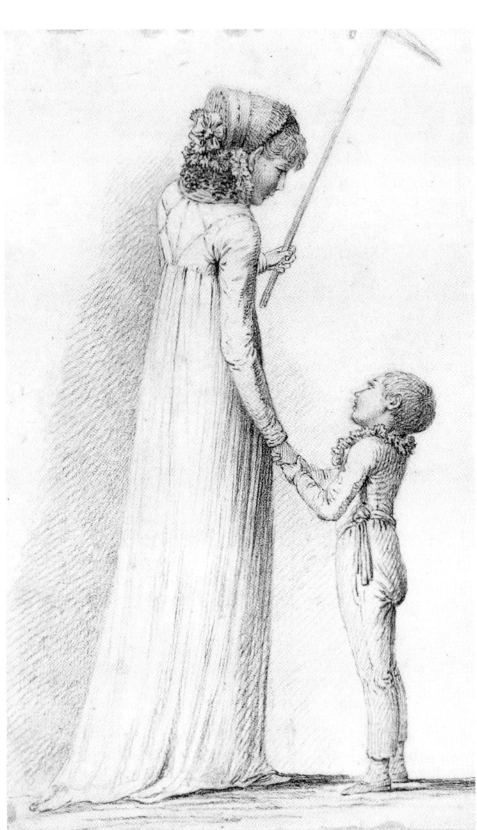

Carl Wilhelm Kolbe the Elder, *Young Woman with Boy*,
c. 1800–1810. Black chalk; 335 x 198 mm

in this series. There is no vista into a broad landscape. Rather, the landscape has been condensed
into a closed composition of plants, not in the
sense of a *nature morte*, but of a still life in the
true meaning of the phrase. He made his plants
into primal models of their botanical genera.
From a limited repertory of such primeval
plants, we can recognize in Kolbe's drawing the
leaf-cups of the burdock in the left foreground;
above it, the reeds with their long, lancelike
leaves; and at the right edge, hedge bindweed
and wild grapevine, which entwine an antique
herm of Pan.

At the foot of the dead trunk of a mighty willow[1]
hollowed out by the elements, a pair of young
people in front of a cavelike bower present their
offering to the god Pan, whose home was Arcadia. Both figures, variations of which also appear
in other herbage pieces—especially in *Et in
Arcadia Ego*[2]—seem, in their posture, to be modeled after classical statues. The naked young man
is playing the flute in homage to the inventor of
this instrument, and, in view of the presence of
his female companion and of the mighty reeds,
he calls to mind the myth of Pan's wooing of the
nymph Syrinx. Associations with Arnold Böck-
lin's painting *Pan among the Reeds* arise. Like
Adam and Eve in Paradise, this young couple is
integrated into the exuberant flora in a state of
eternal summer, removed from civilization and
time—but only seemingly so, for the dead willow and the large holes eaten into the leaves by
insects indicate impermanence.

Kolbe's idyll has parallels in the figurative drawings he did for commercial purposes—for example, in the image of an elegantly dressed woman
influenced by the "Grecism of the republican
women" in Paris, a charming design possibly for
the *Journal des Luxus und der Moden*, which
Justin Bertuch published in Weimar and modeled after French fashion magazines (fig.).

In our drawing—a primeval forest of the imagination, in which Kolbe, influenced by Gessner,
combined the basic Arcadian mood with the
idyll—we can almost hear the riotous growth of
the foliage and the rustling of the reeds. Kolbe
observed nature with its different sounds and
voices; he saw and heard processes such as
growth and decay: the cycles of birth and death
(synesthesia). Kolbe's roots in Sturm und Drang
expressed themselves in his inventiveness and
imagination. From precise botanical observation,
his imagination conjured up gigantic, fossil-like
plants. Kolbe exploded the natural relationships
of scale; the plants are unreal, surreal, and look
genetically manipulated. Kolbe's experience of
the mystery of nature found its expression here.
His exaggeration of nature into a surreal realm,
which stimulates the viewer's imagination,
would find a much later continuation in early
twentieth-century art—for example, in Henri

Rousseau's jungle images or the fantastic vegetation in Max Ernst's surrealistic work.[3] Kolbe's
profound feelings for nature's forces deeply influenced Philipp Otto Runge. His lasting impact,
especially on the younger generation of artists—
among them, Carl Philipp Fohr in his early plant
studies (cat. 49, fig.)—was due to the wide circulation of his masterful etchings, for which he prepared in careful drawings, mostly in black chalk.
The present pictorially executed drawing was
also a direct model for an etching, though only a
few impressions of it are known to exist.[4] While
his drawings—with their subdued coloration,
porous chalk strokes, and soft contours—retain
the character of grisailles, his etchings draw their
power from the starkly contrasting coloration of
light-dark and black-white, combined with a
brilliant precision and sharpness of motif. In the
etchings, Kolbe raised his expressive power to an
uncanny level.[5]

1 The gnarled tree, specifically the oak, whose very crooked-
ness fired the imagination, remained a leitmotif in his
work, earning him the nickname "oak Kolbe." Kolbe, a
former forestry official (*Forstsekretär*), found his motifs in
the oak forest around Dessau.
2 Martens 1976, pl. 21, figs. 39, 40, pl. 23, fig. 42, pl. 25,
figs. 47, 48.
3 I see parallels in Max Ernst's fantastic Arizona landscapes
from the early 1940s and a possible influence, for example,
in the painting with the very allusive title *Joy of Living*,
1936; cf. Rosenblum 1975, p. 170, fig. 252.
4 Martens 1976, pp. 87f., no. 97 (J.215).
5 His great talent as a *peintre-graveur* was soon recognized.
In 1795, he was made a full member of the Berlin Academy, and in 1798, he was summoned to Dessau as a court
engraver and drawing teacher at the Hauptschule. In
Dessau, he was also active in the Chalcographische
Gesellschaft [Society of Engraving]; the Olivier brothers
were among his students. In 1805, he accepted an invita-
tion from the Gessner Bookshop and went to Zurich,
where he stayed until 1807, to produce etchings after the
late Salomon Gessner's gouaches. This work made him
known in even wider circles. Martens 1976, pp. 29f.

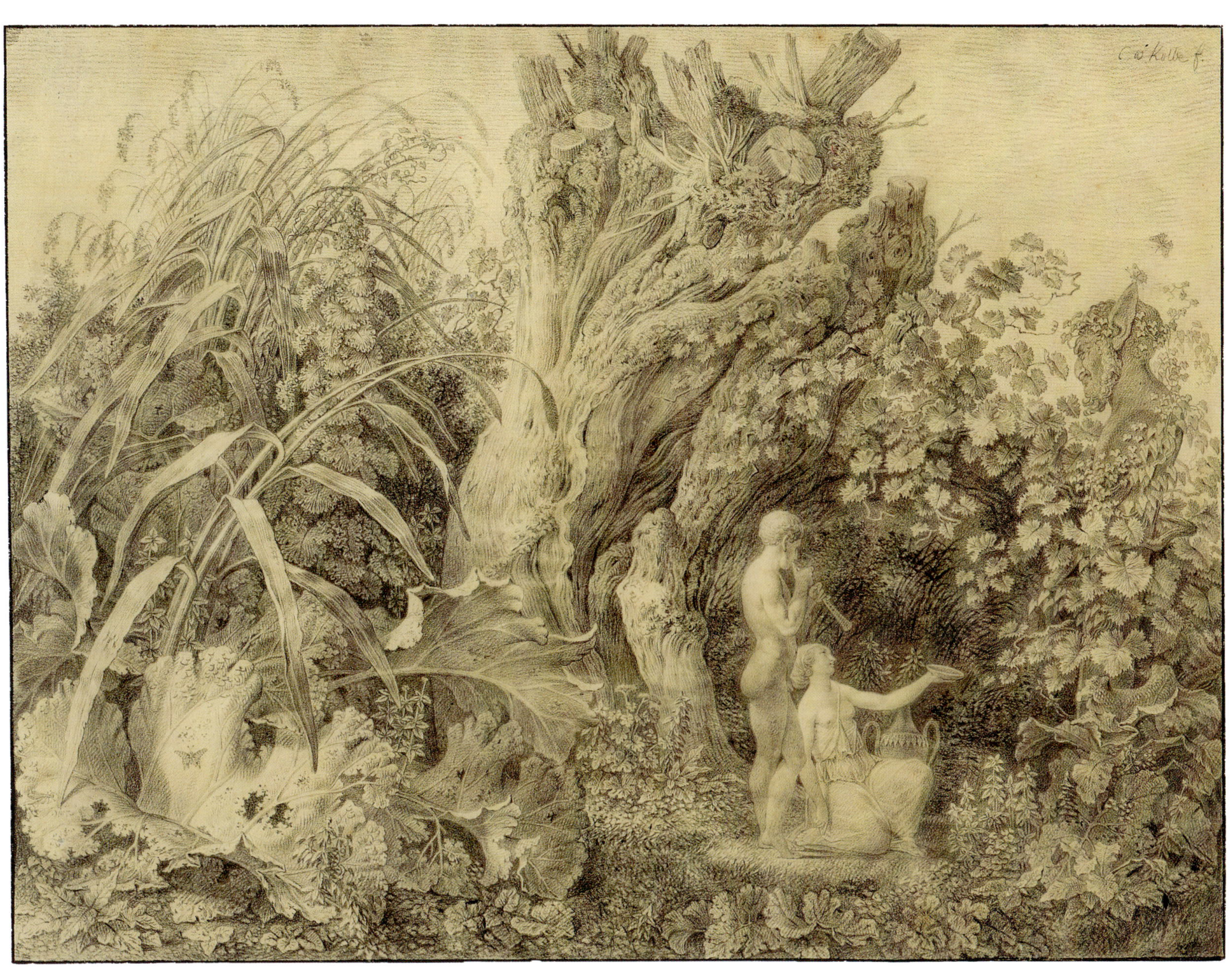

Cw Kolbe f.

Johann Wolfgang von Goethe

Frankfurt am Main 28 August 1749 – 22 March 1832
Weimar

*Landscape with Neoclassical Chapel and Cross
on a Rock*, 1785/86

*Pen and brush in gray, on laid paper, laid down on an
old mount with a decorative molding in wash, foxing;
183 x 222 mm*
*Verso inscribed by Friedrich Johann Lorenz Meyer in pen
and brown ink. Below left: "Wahrheit erkennen—Schön-
heit lieben—/das Beste wollen—das Gute thun./Denken
Sie, Werthester, mit Freundschaft meiner/wie ich Ihrer
denken werde. Hamburg, 21. Juni 1829 Meyer";[1] below
right: "Umstehende Handzeichnung Göthe's ist mir/durch
meinen Bruder Johann Valentin, der/sie von ihm selbst
empfangen hatte, überbracht. M."[2] Inscribed on the backing by Goethe himself (?) in pen and gray ink: "Goethe"*

*Provenance. Senator Johann Valentin Meyer, Hamburg
(Lugt 1551a); Domherr Friedrich Johann Lorenz Meyer,
Hamburg*

*Bibliography: Munich 1958, p. 30, no. 51; Lankheit 1959, pp.
65, 73 (repr.); Goethe-Corpus 6B (1971), p. 24, no. 49 (repr.);
Hamburg 1974, pp. 58f., fig. 191; Düsseldorf 1986, p. 321, no.
284 (repr.)*

During his numerous trips to take the waters,
Goethe stayed repeatedly in Karlsbad, the first
time in 1785. It was from here, the following
summer, that he secretly set out on his trip to
Italy. While traveling, he drew prolifically, as his
many landscapes of Karlsbad, among other subjects, attest.[3] The drawing exhibited here has
often been identified as a Karlsbad scene.[4] The
Swiss landscapist and engraver Adrian Zingg
(1734–1816) produced a faithful rendering of the
topographical situation in a Karlsbad view of the
wooden bridge across the Tepl River, at the foot
of the Johannes Rock. He frequently published
his landscape *vedute*, usually executed with gray
and brown wash, as outline etchings worked up
with watercolor or wash. This was the case with
the latter work, which has its counterpart in a
landscape Goethe drew, in a simplified manner,
from a nearby vantage point (fig. 1),[5] and it is
possible that Goethe used Zingg's etching to ori-
ent his own drawing. The gatelike structure
between the bridge and the rock has been interpreted as a chapel, though it looks more like an
architecturally elaborate roadside cross or well.
A small neoclassical temple—the kind that, as a
friendship temple, gives English gardens a sentimental accent—does not appear in these landscapes. Yet evidently, such a structure—whether
it was a roadside chapel, a Station of the Cross, a
gatehouse, or a wellhouse—did exist in Karlsbad, for Goethe drew it on several occasions. For
example, the structure appears in a later drawing
from around 1812, at the foot of the Johannes
Rock behind the sweeping curve of the Prager
Strasse across the new stone bridge over the Tepl
(fig. 2).[6] But the small temple there, as in the
exhibited drawing, was probably an addition. In
both cases, Goethe was evidently drawing not
from nature but from memory. His decision to
incorporate the small temple into these landscapes was intentional: the drawing not only
reminds the viewer of Karlsbad; it also awakens
feelings and thoughts about nature and the humble motifs created by human hands. Perhaps the
jagged and weathered rocks indicate the age of
the earth and the history of its creation, while the
wild growth of trees and bushes indicate living
nature. The small temple suggests antiquity. A
cross rises to the sky on top of the rock. This was
a common motif, and twenty years later, in the
spirit of romanticism, Caspar David Friedrich
elevated it to a devotional image in the so-called
Tetschener Altar. In the present drawing, unlike
Adrian Zingg's work, the cross on the rock is not
a crucifix. Rather, it is an abstract sign of the
Church—built on rock—and of Christianity.
Goethe frequently occupied himself with
thoughts about nature, antiquity, and Christianity as sources of art, and about questions concerning natural, human, and redemptive history and
the interconnections between them. Perhaps this
simple drawing was a playful musing on these
themes.

The unresolved overall impression of the drawing suggests that it was done before Goethe's trip
to Italy. The spatial and lighting relationships
are indicated rather than clarified. We cannot
really determine whether a river is flowing from
the lower left corner, as it does in the topographical Karlsbad landscapes (figs. 1, 2). Also, our
drawing does not yet show the resolute handling
of line that Goethe acquired in Italy. With a
loose pen, he scribbled short, suggestive strokes,
which—with the exception of the small temple
—do not structure the world through clear lines,
but let it dissolve into an atmospheric realm. Yet
in spite of its sketchlike character, the sheet is
highly finished. Later, Goethe himself characterized sketchlike drawing as the mark of dilettan-
tism.[7] Goethe also reduces color, and his manner
of handling the gray wash—in this case, not very
rich in contrast—was in keeping with the fashion of the time, modeled after seventeenth-century Dutch draftsmanship. This style is typical of
Goethe's early drawings. These observations on
draftsmanship and style apply equally to the
Karlsbad landscape in the Henckel-Donners-
marck collection (fig. 1), which is nearly identical
in format and is the one most closely related to
our drawing. It is dated 1785/86. In all likelihood, our drawing, too, was therefore made
shortly before Goethe's hasty departure for Italy.
Goethe later had it mounted with a decorative
border in colored washes and presented it as a gift
to the Hamburg wine merchant Johann Valentin
Meyer.

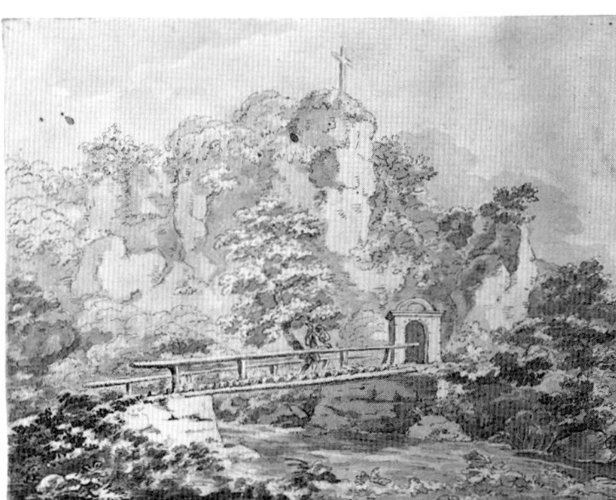

1 Johann Wolfgang von Goethe, *Wooden Bridge over the
Tepl and the Johannes Rock in Karlsbad*, c. 1785/86. Pen
and gray ink, gray wash, over pencil; 185 x 227 mm.
Weimar, Stiftung Weimarer Klassik, loan from Henckel-
Donnersmarck, inv. no. 2280

2 Johann Wolfgang von Goethe, *Karlsbad—Johannes
Rock and Chapel at the Bridge over the Tepl*, c. 1812. Pen
and brown ink, wash, over pencil on blue paper;
82 x 102 mm. Weimar, Stiftung Weimarer Klassik, inv.
no. 1267

1 [To recognize truth—to love beauty—/—to want the
best—to do good./My dearest friend, think of me in
friendship/as I will think of you. Hamburg 21 June 1829
Meyer.]
2 [The drawing by Goethe on the reverse was handed to
me/by my brother Johann Valentin, who/received it from
him in person. M.]
3 *Goethe-Corpus*, vol. 1 (1958), pp. 99f., nos. 279 (repr.), 285
(repr.); vol. 4A (1966), pp. 49f., nos. 150 (repr.), 152 (repr.),
pp. 57ff., nos. 176 (repr.), 180–82 (repr.); vol. 6A (1969),
p. 70, no. 259 (repr.); vol. 6B (1971), pp. 55ff., nos. 150–53
(reprs.), 158 (repr.), 160 (repr.), 163–64 (reprs.), 169 (repr.).
4 *Goethe-Corpus*, vol. 6B (1971), p. 24, no. 49 (repr.); Düsseldorf 1986, p. 321, no. 284 (repr.).
5 *Goethe-Corpus*, vol. 1 (1958), p. 100, no. 285 (repr.); Femmel 1955, p. 27, no. 8 (repr.).
6 *Goethe-Corpus*, vol. 4A (1966), p. 50, no. 152.
7 Frankfurt 1994, p. 106 (Petra Maisak).

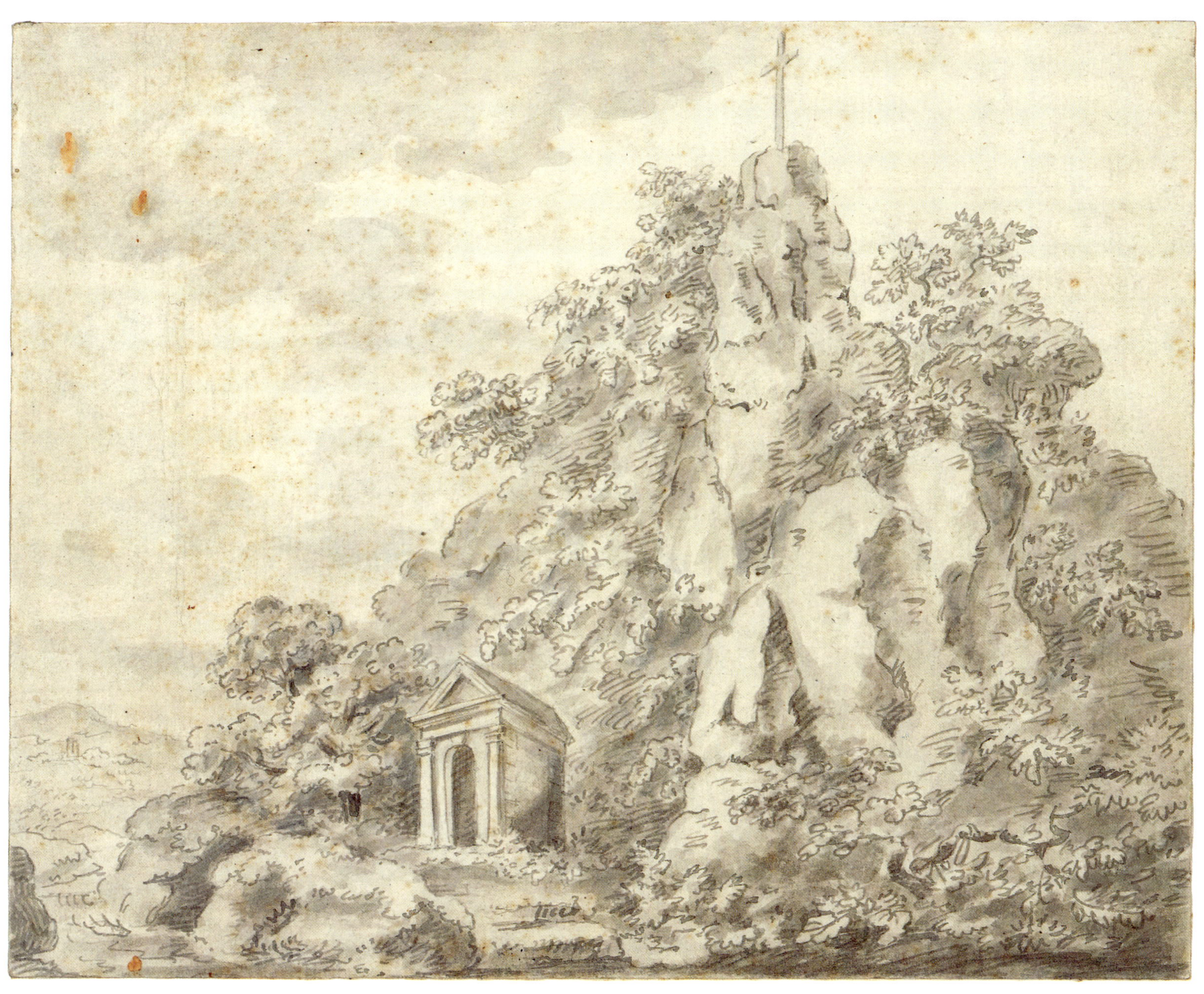

Johann Wolfgang von Goethe

Weathered Blocks of Granite on the Luisenburg, 1820

Pen and brown ink, blue-gray and brown wash, on ochre-gray laid paper, trimmed on all sides; 103/11 x 172 mm
Inscribed (not by the artist) in pen in brown ink, upper left: "Goethe's Handzeich-/nung. GSchueler." On the verso, inscribed by Goethe himself in pen and brown ink (line cut): "… wertheste Verein [most esteemed association]!" and several (illegible, partially cut) lines in graphite

Provenance: Prof. Gustav Schueler, Jena

Bibliography: Johannes Walther et al., Goethe als Seher und Erforscher der Natur *(Halle an der Saale, 1930),* p. 271; Munich 1958, pp. 29f., no. 50, p. 7 (repr.); *Goethe-Corpus, vol. 5B (1967), p. 91, no. 214 (repr.) and cover; Lübeck 1969, p. 39, no. 57;* Johann Wolfgang von Goethe, Sämtliche Werke *(Frankfurt edition), vol. 25:* Schriften zur allgemeinen Naturlehre, Geologie und Mineralogie, *ed. Wolf von Engelhardt and Manfred Wenzel (Frankfurt am Main, 1989), p. 1108, fig. 18; Otto Krätz,* Goethe und die Naturwissenschaften *(Munich, 1992), p. 53 (repr., Schueler's handwriting retouched); Frankfurt 1994, p. 147, no. 107 (repr. in color); Maisak 1996, p. 265, no. 193 (repr.)*

In search of insight into the creation of the earth, Goethe devoted himself intensively to geological studies throughout his life, especially during his travels, and in the process, he frequently made drawings of natural phenomena. From the late eighteenth to the beginning of the nineteenth century, theorists vigorously debated about the creation of the earth. The so-called Neptunists (named after the Roman god of the sea) explained the creation and formation of the layers of the earth and of the atmosphere as a gradual developmental process resulting from a receding primal sea. Through chemical processes, granite and other primeval rocks supposedly first crystalized in the original ocean.[1] The Plutonists or Vulcanists (named after the god of the netherworld) recognized the decisive role that fire had played in shaping the earth—the flow of fire from the earth's core and the great upheavals caused by the cooling and solidification of the earth's crust. Despite growing evidence that the water theory was untenable, Goethe professed himself a Neptunist to the end. According to Busch, "In 1819, he published, with some feeling of resignation, *Eines verjährten Neptunisten Schlussbekenntnis* [The Final Confession from an Aged Neptunist]. For him, Vulcanism was and remained an unpleasant, revolutionary model. Evolutionary Neptunism was not only more to his liking; it also corresponded much more readily to his entire world view in political, scientific, and artistic terms."[2]

The question concerning the origins of granite, recognized as a primary rock, had already preoccupied Goethe during his early trips to the Harz Mountains in 1777 and 1783. In 1784, he wrote his essay "Über den Granit, 'die Grundfeste unserer Erde'" [On Granite, the Foundation of Our Earth]. On his third trip to the Harz in the fall of the same year, he kept a "geognostic" diary, and he had his companion Georg Melchior Kraus draw granite rocks in order to prove their crystallization in water by observing the regular jointing. During his first trip to Karlsbad in 1785, Goethe had already noticed the "strange fragments of a granite mountain" on a hill of the Fichtelgebirge, called Luisenburg,[3] near Alexandersbad and Wunsiedel in Upper Franconia. Twenty-five years later, during another trip to Karlsbad on 25 April 1820, he passed the site again and examined the granite blocks at length. On 1 May 1820, he noted in his diary, "Sketches of cloud drifts, as well as of granite rocks, to explain the debris of the Luisenburg,"[4] and on 4 May 1820, more "drawings and an essay on Luisenburg."[5] The energetic sketch exhibited here could therefore have been made either from nature, on-site, or afterwards—as mentioned above—to clarify his thinking.

The relationship of this sketch to a second drawing in Weimar, which is very similar in motif, is an open question.[6] Scholars generally believe that the Weimar version began with a drawing by Goethe, essentially no longer recognizable, which was then carefully reworked by Carl Lieber, a teacher at the drawing school in Weimar, who added a lovely landscape to it.[7] I suspect that Lieber made the drawing entirely by himself, using the sketch exhibited here as a model.[8] The drawing then served as the model for an etching by Lieber with which Goethe illustrated his essay "Die Luisenburg bei Alexanders-Bad" [The Luisenburg near Alexandersbad] in his writings on natural science.[9] The letters shown on the rocks in this sketch, however, are missing in the Weimar drawing, since they would have spoiled the "pleasant landscape." Lieber took them directly from this sketch. In the etching, the drawing appears like a head vignette in the upper field. The fields below it were also etched from one of Goethe's drawings reworked by Lieber.[10] They depict phases in the weathering process; the unweathered condition appears on the left and the weathered condition on the right. In the present drawing, Goethe was not concerned with clarifying how granite was created, but with furnishing the "correct" proof that the position and form of the rocks were caused by "calm and slow" deterioration (an evolutionary process) and not by "violent means" such as volcanoes and earthquakes (a revolutionary process). His essay includes a precise explanation based on the granite blocks already identified with the letters in our drawing: "Above all, the reader should familiarize himself with the letters written on the rocks in the landscape drawing above. First of all, he should imagine the various rocks *a. b. c. d. e.* together forming an upright section, somewhat inclined toward the horizon. Now, when one of the middle masses *a* weathers, the upper *b* will slide down and come to rest approximately as *bb*. Next, the lower rear *c* weathers, and the obelisk *d*, because of its top-heavy weight, will topple and come to rest as *dd*. Only the mass *e* will have remained in its place unmoved and unchanged."[11]

Our sheet comes from the estate of the Bergrat Gustav Schueler, who collected a number of geological studies drawn by Goethe. Schueler studied at the Bergakademie in Freiburg and later taught at the University of Jena as a professor of geology. Goethe maintained a scientific correspondence with him.[12]

1 The chief proponent of this theory was the geologist Abraham Gottlob Werner (1750–1817), who taught at the Freiburger Bergakademie.

2 Busch 1994, p. 489.

3 Originally, this hill-site of geological interest, discovered early on, was named after the ruined Castle Luchsburg nearby. Following the visit of Queen Luise of Prussia, the hill-site was renamed Luisenburg in her honor in 1805. For an early drawing from 1785, cf. H. von Maltzahn, "Eine Handzeichnung Goethes aus dem Fichtelgebirge," in *Neuntes Rundschreiben des Freien Deutschen Hochstifts* (Frankfurt am Main, 1953), pp. 24 ff.

4 The restless naturalist Goethe was interested in the formation and metamorphosis of fleeting clouds as much as he was interested in solid rock formation.

5 *Goethe-Corpus*, vol. 5B (1967), p. 91, no. 214; Maisak 1996, p. 265, no. 193.

6 *Goethe-Corpus*, vol. 5B (1967), pp. 90f., no. 213 (repr.).

7 Precisely for the purpose of reproduction, Goethe frequently had his nature sketches carefully reworked pictorially by Carl Lieber, whose work he appreciated for "its extreme neatness and finish."

8 This view is shared by Ludwig Münz, *Goethes Zeichnungen und Radierungen* (Vienna, 1949), pp. 49f., 120, n. 48.

9 *Die Luisenburg bei Alexanders-Bad*, etching by Carl Lieber after his own reworkings of Goethe's drawings, in Goethe, *Werke: Vollständige Ausgabe letzter Hand* (Stuttgart and Tübingen, 1833), vol. 51, illustration to p. 157; cf. *Goethe-Corpus*, vol. 5B (1967), pp. 90ff., no. 213, 214a; Goethe, *Werke* (Frankfurt edition), pp. 332f., 1106–8, figs. 18–20.

10 *Goethe-Corpus*, vol. 5B (1967), pp. 91f., no. 214a (repr.).

11 Goethe, *Werke* (as n. 9), p. 157, illustration to p. 157.

12 For a letter of Goethe's from Dornburg to Gustav Schueler, dated 28 August 1829, see Goethe, *Sophienausgabe*, vol. 44, letter no. 224, and p. 471.

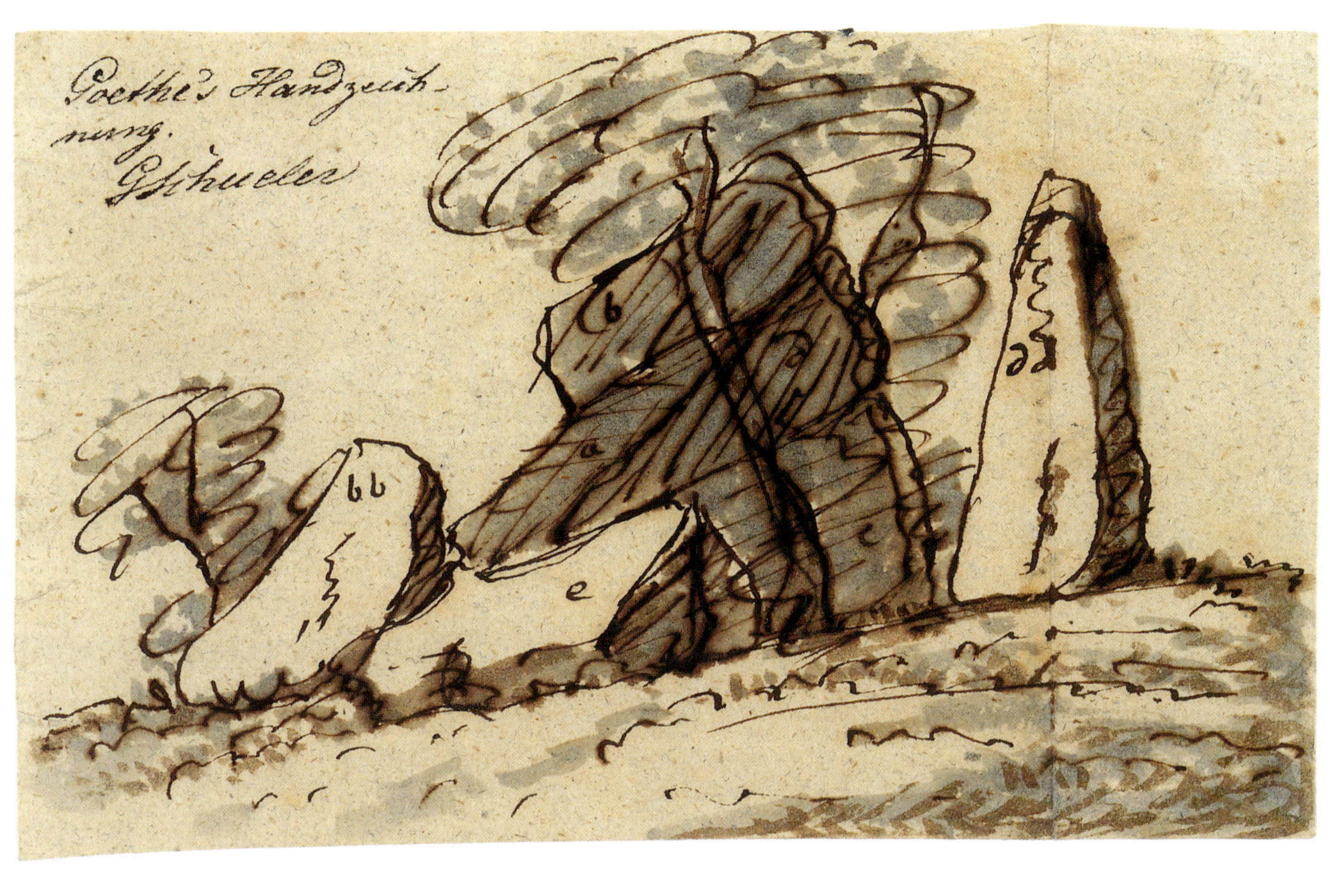

Goethe's Handzeich-
nung.
Gschueler

8

Johann Georg von Dillis

Grüngiebing above Schwindkirchen near Haag,
Upper Bavaria 26 December 1759 – 28 September
1841 Munich

*An Excursion to the Country — Count Rum-
ford and Countess Baumgarten, 1791*

*Watercolor over pencil, black chalk, border in black left
and below, on laid paper; 283/86 x 201/3 mm
Signed and dated in pen and brown ink, below left: "Georg
Dillis 1791"*

Provenance: Dr. Richard Messerer, Munich

*Bibliography: Munich 1959, p. 23, no. 69; Munich 1979,
p. 229, no. 78 (repr.); Karl & Faber, Auction 180, Munich,
28 – 29 November 1990, cat. no. 337, pl. 8 (repr. in color);
Barbara Hardtwig, "Der Mensch in der Natur: Dillis'
Landschaftskunst," in Munich 1991, pp. 57f., fig. 12
(in color), n. 46*

Dillis occasionally portrayed excursionists in the
countryside.[1] In this very vivid watercolor from
1791, he painted two small groups of wandering
townspeople on a sunlit forest path in the mountains. An old inscription on the original mount of
the sheet allows us to identify two of the people
in the foreground: Count Rumford and Countess
Baumgarten.[2] Maria Josepha Countess of Baumgarten, née von Lerchenfeld, is apparently the
woman seen from the back in the shaded foreground on the right. Recently widowed, she is
dressed in black; her husband had drowned in the
river Inn on 26 October 1790. The art-loving and
highly musical Countess Baumgarten was a passionate and talented soprano.[3] In 1780, at the
young age of eighteen and newly married, she
had already played a key role as intermediary in
Elector Carl Theodor's commission to Mozart to
compose *Idomeneo*.[4] At that time, she was a celebrated beauty and was considered the elector's
mistress; in 1784, she had helped Sir Benjamin
Thompson to win the elector's favor.[5] Her love
affair with Thompson, an American, led to the
birth of a daughter, Sophy, in 1788.[6] A portrait
by Moritz Kellerhoven from the year 1787,
presumably painted for Thompson, shows the
countess in the English style, in front of a nature
scene.[7]
Early on, Dillis was a frequent visitor at the
Baumgarten house and gave the children drawing lessons.[8] Perhaps it was here that he made
the—for him, fateful—acquaintance of the
future Count Rumford, though he might have
met him in the circle of free-thinking men in the
Order of the Illuminati, to which Joseph Karl
Count of Baumgarten (Maria Josepha's husband)
as well as Benjamin Thompson and Dillis himself, belonged.

In the watercolor, the "Yankee" Benjamin
Thompson (1735–1814) is easy to recognize from
his energetic posture. In 1792, Carl Theodor
would elevate Thompson to the rank of Count of
Rumford in recognition of his services. The
American had begun with a mercantile apprenticeship, graduated from Harvard, and then risen
in the English military service. After his flight to
England in 1776, he advanced swiftly in society
and had an adventurous career as a scholar,
inventor, officer, politician, and philanthropist.
From 1784 to 1798, in the service of the Bavarian
elector Carl Theodor, he pursued activities that
were of great significance, especially for the city
of Munich. The Bavarian metropolis remembers
him with gratitude and, above all, as the founder
of the English Garden. Rumford also deserves
credit for having recognized the young Dillis's
talent and fostered his career. Rumford's efforts
were momentous; in 1790, Dillis was hired as
inspector of the picture gallery at the Hofgarten.
In 1792, Dillis created a tribute to his mentor
with a masterfully drawn portrait, which was reproduced as a print shortly after he completed it.
The portrait vividly conveys Rumford's appearance and outstanding personality (see essay,
"From Fuseli to Menzel," fig. 8).
Our watercolor is also valuable testimony to
Count Rumford's and Countess Baumgarten's
friendship with Dillis, who accompanied them
on their outing as a confidant and draftsman-
chronicler. Revealingly, Dillis was not concerned
with portraying his prominent companions, nor
with placing them next to a significant natural
site,[9] nor with depicting a landscape that expressed the grandeur of nature. Rather, he spontaneously and unpretentiously sketched his companions from the back, walking ahead of him, as
they paused in a sunny spot, leaning on their
walking sticks. As a result, the sheet clearly
reveals the quick method of watercolor painting
that Dillis used to capture a fleeting moment.
The transparency of the working process is a typical and particularly attractive feature of his
draftsmanship. All steps of Dillis's work process
remain visible and contribute to the piece's free,
loose overall effect: an outlining preliminary
drawing beneath the watercolor; reworking
alternately with pencil and brush, frequently
done anew, without fixing the contours, instead
leaving them open; frayed transitions; and a handling of the light in delicate watercolor accents,
with the white of the original paper left untouched in parts. In this way, he created a light-
suffused, atmospheric picture, an "impression"
of wandering townspeople in the country.
Of particular importance in this case is the artist's
own dating of the sheet, since it attests that by
around 1790, Dillis had long since developed his
characteristic fluid touch and brushwork.
This is important for answering questions about

the origin of Dillis's style, its development, and
its sources of influence. The answers lie primarily in the artist's free-thinking, enlightened
mind as well as in his temperament, dynamic
creative urge and sensitivity to nature, the roots
of which can be found in Sturm und Drang. His
sense of color, though, was shaped by the cheer-
ful chromatic harmonies of the late Rococo in his
native land.
The pictorial finish of the sheet, the artist's complete signature, and the partially preserved pen-
and-ink border suggest that this watercolor was
intended as a gift.

1 Cf. Munich 1991, p. 148, no. 52 (*A Group of Wanderers in
 the Mountains*, c. 1790/95); pp. 152 ff., no. 56 (*Company on
 the Hesselberg*, 1801); pp. 202 f., no. 87 (*Company at the
 Riverbank*, c. 1790).

2 The sheet comes from an old album and was inscribed
 "Dillis, Graf Rumford u. Gräfin Paumgarten"[Dillis,
 Count Rumford, and Countess Baumgarten]; Munich 1979,
 p. 229, no. 78 (Barbara Hardtwig).

3 Robert Münster, "Mozarts Münchener Aufenthalt 1780/81
 und die Uraufführung des *Idomeneo*," in *Wolfgang
 Amadeus Mozart — Idomeneo — 1781–1981: Essays, For-
 schungsberichte*, exh. cat., Bayerische Staatsbibliothek
 (Munich, 1981), pp. 74, 265 f., nos. 41–44.

4 *Ibid.*, pp. 71, 74, 82, 85, 88, 103. In gratitude, Mozart
 dedicated a concert aria to her; *ibid.*, p. 265, no. 41.

5 *Ibid.*, p. 74.

6 Larsen 1961, pp. 159, 162 f. Cf. Munich 1991, p. 132, no. 41
 (Hinrich Sieveking).

7 Münster (n. 3), p. 265, no. 40, p. 116 (repr. in color). The
 original is in the Shaefe Walker Collection, Concord, New
 Hampshire. It was created at the same time that Rumford
 was trying to escape the intrigues of the Munich city
 administration and at court through a transfer to England.

8 He painted a watercolor of Sophy as Flora in front of
 Schloss Ammerland, and he drew the son, Karl, repeatedly;
 cf. Munich 1991, p. 132, no. 41, n. 5. Dillis's estate contained two drawings that were copies of prints after
 Claude Lorrain, inscribed "Baumgarten"; *ibid.*, n. 4.

9 As, for example, the distinguished Prussian party on the
 Hesselberg near Ansbach (1801), with Queen Luise, King
 Frederick William III of Prussia, Friederike, the princess
 of Solms-Braunfels, with her husband, State Minister Karl
 August Count of Hardenberg, and others, who are enjoying the view of the Alps in the early evening—notable
 testimony to early tourism; *ibid.*, pp. 152 ff., no. 56 (repr.
 frontispiece in color) (Hinrich Sieveking).

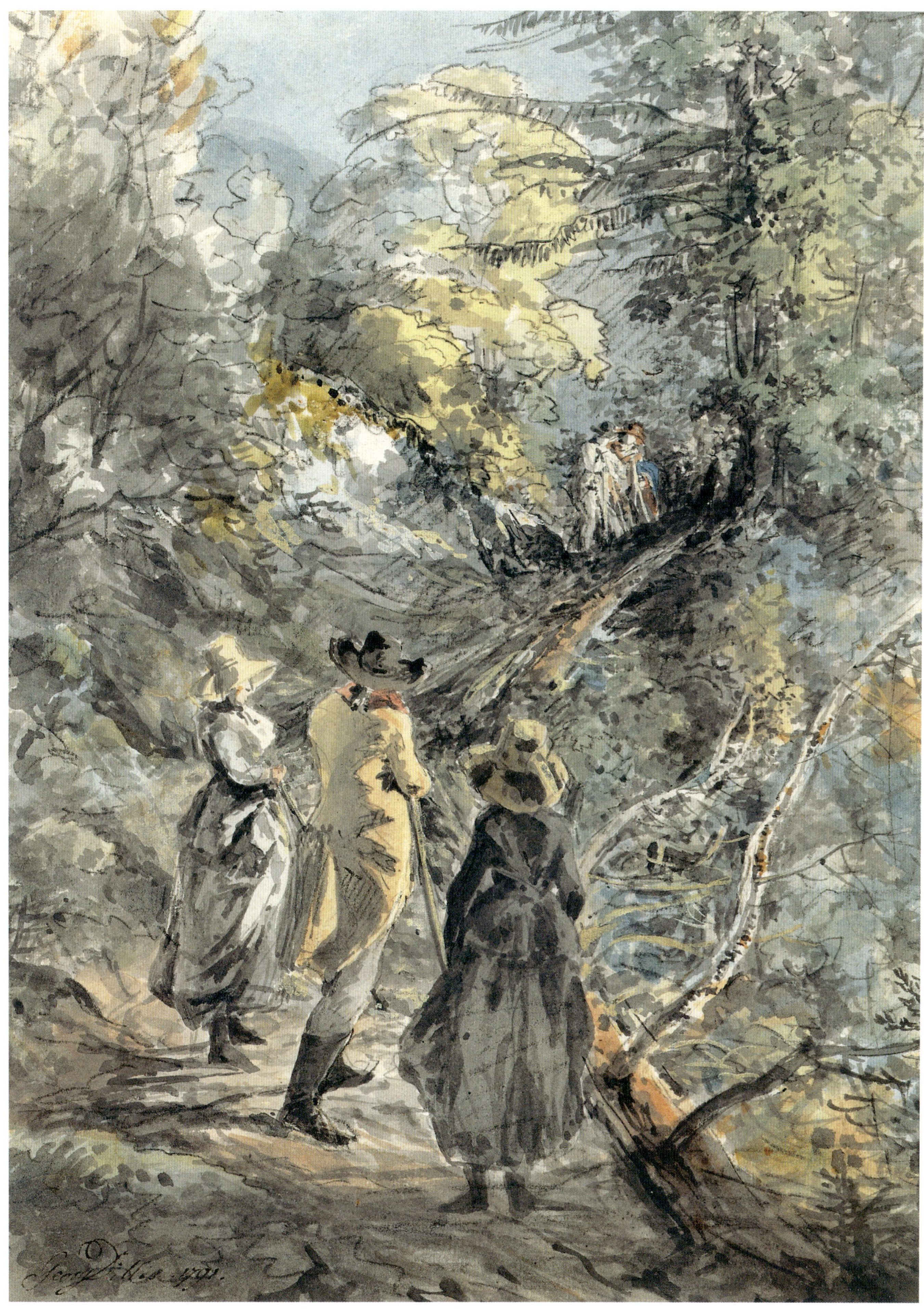

9

Johann Georg von Dillis

The Temple of Apollo in the English Garden in Munich, c. 1795

Watercolor over pencil, pen and gray-black ink, incised with a stylus, on laid paper; watermark: I T A Y L O R, verso blackened; 271/73 x 415/18 mm

Bibliography: Winterthur 1955, p. 58, no. 239; Munich 1958, p. 22, no. 16, cover and p. 15 (repr. in color); Munich 1959, p. 25, no. 95; Larsen 1961, pp. 128f. (repr. in color); Lübeck 1969, p. 24, no. 20, p. 25 (repr. in color); Denys Sutton, "Munich: City of the Arts," Apollo n.s. 94, no. 117 (1971): 332 (fig. 2), 337; Richard Messerer, "Georg von Dillis, Ein Entdecker der Münchner Landschaft," in Der Englische Garten zu München, ed. Theodor Dombart (Munich, 1972), p. 291 (repr., detail); Bayern, Kunst und Kultur, exh. cat., Stadtmuseum Munich (Munich, 1972), p. 467, no. 1535; Ingrid Weibezahn, Geschichte und Funktion des Monopteros: Untersuchungen zu einem Gebäudetyp des Spätbarock und des Klassizismus, pt. 2 (Hildesheim and New York, 1975), pp. 54–58, 55, 58, C/b.2; Munich 1979, pp. 212f., no. 17 (repr.); Sieveking 1988, pp. 160f. (repr. in color); Munich 1991, pp. 88f., no. 12 (repr. in color)

As part of the design of the English Garden in Munich (cf. cat. 61), the Temple of Apollo—commonly called the Doric Temple—was erected in 1789/90, not far from the Chinese Tower. One of the first "sentimental" architectural ornaments, it was built in the form of a Tuscan monopteral temple with ten columns, and topped with a high, semidomed cupola of wood.[1] In 1791, a statue of Apollo was placed in the temple, an allegorical reference to the love of art and patronage of the elector Carl Theodor, founder of the park.[2] The designers chose a picturesque site for the temple, under high elm and ash trees in the old Hirschanger Forest, on the bank of the Eisbach, where it makes a loop.[3] The temple seems to stand on an island or a spit of land and is reflected in the water on several sides. Decades later, it became dilapidated and was torn down. King Louis I commissioned Leo von Klenze to erect a semicircular bench of white marble on the temple's foundation.[4] Between 1832 and 1837, again at the king's behest, Klenze erected a monopteral temple on an artificial hill nearby. Modeled on the Temple of Apollo, it has remained to this day the landmark of the English Garden and offers one of the most beautiful views of the Old Munich skyline. The strong mood that the ancient grove with the original Doric Temple evoked in the learned visitor at the time is revealed in the earliest description of the English Garden prior to its official opening. It comes in a report on the elector's first tour of the garden, in the company of Count Rumford, on 25 May 1790: "The dome of the temple reaches into the branches of the majestic stand of trees that surrounds it; a sense of terrifying awe characterizes these surroundings, and at the Greek temple in the Celtic grove of bards one can almost hear the strings of Homer and Ossian sing in sweet harmony."[5]

Depictions of the temple were especially frequent during the first years after its erection, when its many symbolic allusions were still understood. It was shown in simple *vedute* or in the moody atmosphere of moonlight, the earliest example of which is the 1790 aquatint-etching, printed in brown, by Simon Gassner. In the print, Gassner took his view of the temple, drawn by day on-site, and transformed it into a moonlight scene in sepia, in close imitation of Hendrick Goudt's widely spread engraving reproducing on Adam Elsheimer's painting *Flight to Egypt*.[6] This sheet, in which the imagined experience of nature and academic model overlap, had its intended effect. One critic, in the mistaken belief that the artist had observed the temple at night in moonlight, extolled Gassner's artistic accomplishment and praised the grounds of the English Garden as useful for training the next generation of artists: "This first example will certainly attract the attention of our young artists, and they will do much better studying life, which is so very vigorous in this park, than copying even the best of paintings."[7]

Dillis, too, considered the "significant" motif of the Temple of Apollo important. But what attracted him even more than the myth-laden, classicistic, Arcadian grove was the direct encounter with nature. He went there on a summer day seeking to capture the mood of the early morning hour just before sunrise. The blush of day on the horizon at the left grows lighter toward the upper edge of the picture. A clear light suffuses the freshness of dawn. Even the temple, reflected in the water, is transparent, and—freed from its didactic ballast—has become part of nature. The rather cool watercolors, which blend across the contours, are masterful: accentuated by the pen and by the reserved areas of white paper, they were applied with a free and sure hand in only a few tones. The momentary impression of nature has been captured so vividly that it is recreated in the viewer's mind. This authentic view of the Temple of Apollo from the northwestern side is an astonishingly early example of the reception of nature *en plein air* and, at the same time, is one of Dillis's most mature and loveliest creations. The sheet is incised with a stylus and blackened on the reverse. Apparently, Dillis was thinking of transferring the image into an oil painting or, more likely, of reproducing it as an outline etching that he could color by hand.[8]

In its early years, especially during the first decade of its existence, the English Garden frequently attracted artists and inspired a wide range of representations. A small circle, mostly of local artists, went to the garden in search of a direct experience of nature (cf. cat. 61).[9] This circle formed the nucleus of the Munich school of landscape painting that flourished in the nineteenth century. Dillis, the most eminent artist in the group, played a key role in this development. It was, above all, through his work that the English Garden became artistically relevant. Dillis was also the only artist whose free, unconventional composition and touch, which he developed early on, gave creative expression to the sense of freedom and sovereignty which the English Garden, according to the original sociopolitical intent behind its creation, was supposed to convey.

1. Its architect was Johann Baptist Lechner; cf. Elmar D. Schmid, *Englischer Garten München: Amtlicher Führer* (Munich, 1989), p. 42, no. 45.
2. The wooden statue was the work of Joseph Nepomuk Muxel, sculptor at the electoral court, from 1791; cf. Dombart 1972, pp. 57, 172f.
3. Weibezahn 1975, pp. 54ff., no. 17.
4. The king had the following words engraved on the bench: "HIER WO IHR WALLET DA WAR SONST WALD NUR UND SUMPF" [Here where you roam there once was only forest and swamp].
5. *Der baierische Landbot*, no. 43 (Munich, 26–30 May 1790). Reprinted in *Skizze des neu angelegten englischen Gartens oder Theodors Parks zu München* (Munich, 1793), p. 14, with an etched illustration by Simon Gassner, c. 1791, 148 x 170 mm, reprinted in Freyberg 1988, p. 89.
6. Simon Gassner, *The Surroundings of the Doric Temple in the Newly Designed English Garden or Theodor Park in Munich ...*, 1790; aquatint etching; reprinted in Sieveking 1988, p. 146; cf. von Buttlar 1979, p. 169. The painting by Elsheimer was in the Electoral Picture Gallery at the Hofgarten in Munich (today Bayerische Staatsgemäldesammlungen, Alte Pinakothek, Munich, inv. no. 216).
7. *Der baierische Landbot*, no. 29, 20 February 1791.
8. Perhaps as part of a series he was planning of the "most interesting views of the English Garden in Munich, drawn from nature." It is possible that this series—like the 1786 series commissioned by Count Rumford, with "Views of the Most Interesting Landscapes of the Bavarian Mountains"—was to be reproduced and sold by Simon Warnberger as hand-colored outline etchings; cf. Sieveking 1988, pp. 160f.
9. Among them were Simon Warnberger (1769–1847), Max Joseph Wagenbauer (1775–1829), Johann Jacob Dorner the Younger (1775–1852), and Simon Klotz (cf. cat. 61).

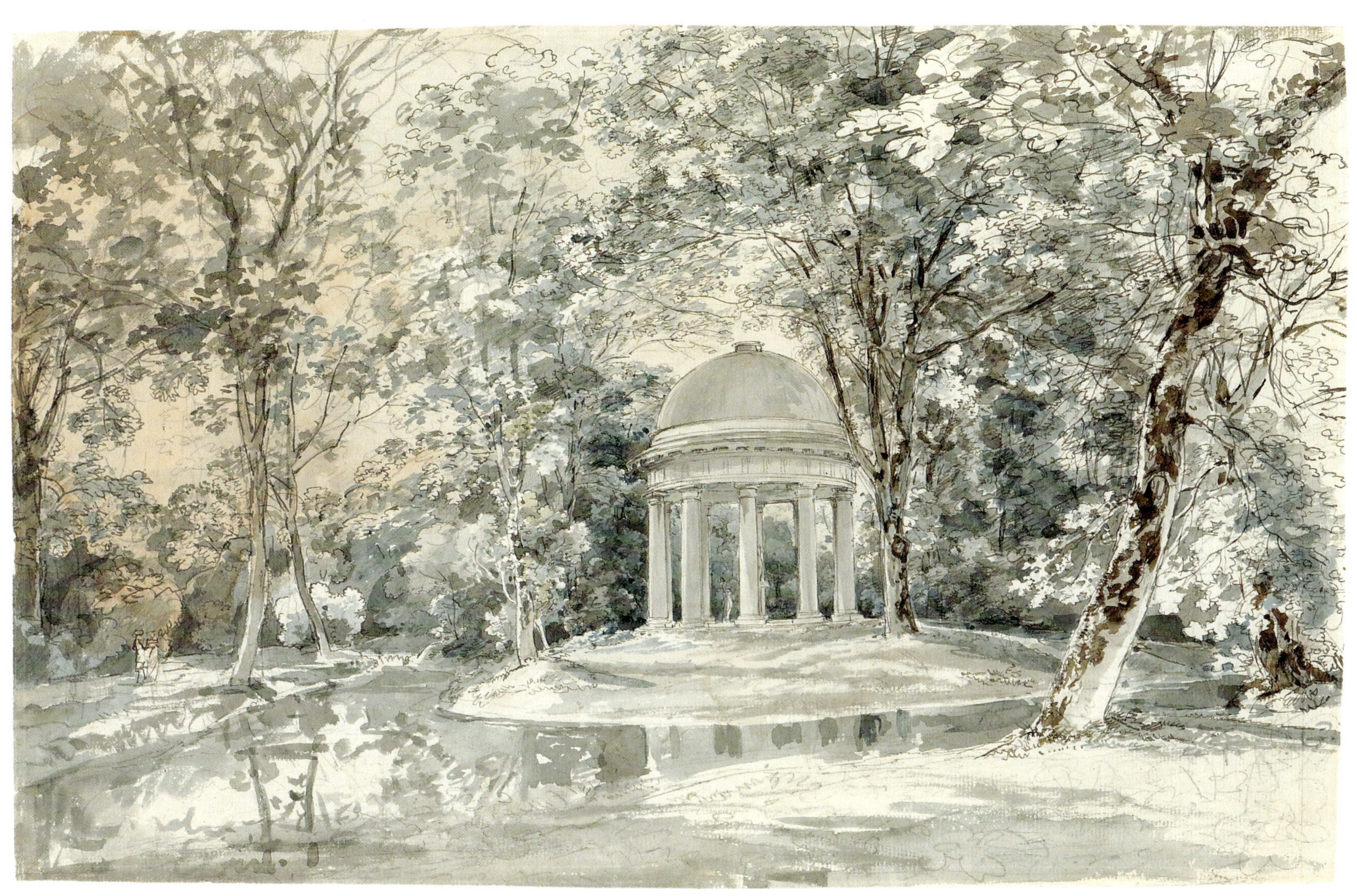

10

Henry Fuseli

Zurich 6 February 1741–16 April 1825 Putney Hill
outside London

Perseus with the Graeae, 1771/72

*Mixed technique, gouache, coarse graphite, minimal
heightening with oil on heavy laid paper, right lower corner extended; 336/44 x 401/10 mm*

Provenance: Henry B. Hoyt, Boston, Massachusetts

*Bibliography: Munich 1958, p. 29, no. 49 (as "Allegorical
Scene"); Schiff 1973, vol. 1, pp. 443f., no. 405 (oil print),
vol. 2, no. 405 (repr.);* Kunst um 1800: Johann Heinrich
Füssli, 1741–1825, ed. Werner Hofmann, with essays by
Werner Hofmann, Gert Schiff, and Georg Syamken, exh.
cat., Hamburger Kunsthalle *(Munich, 1974), p. 113, no. 17a
(repr.);* Johann Heinrich Füssli, *ed. Gert Schiff, exh. cat.,
Musée du Petit Palais (Paris, 1975), no. 52; David H.
Weinglass,* Prints and Engraved Illustrations by and after
Henry Fuseli: A Catalogue Raisonné *(Aldershot, England,
1994), pp. 22f., no. 23 (repr.; erroneously identified as a
monotype)*

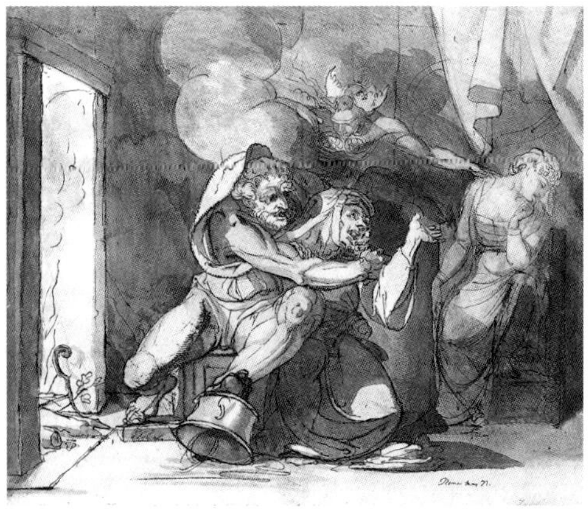

Henry Fuseli, *Perseus with the Graeae*, 1771.
Pen and brown ink over pencil, gray wash; 440 x 520mm.
Hamburg, Kunsthalle, Kupferstichkabinett

According to the Greek myth, Polydectes, the
king of the island of Seriphos, fell in love with
Danaë, the mother of Perseus, but she did not
return his love. As Polydectes was pondering how
to gain power over Danaë, he decided to get rid
of Perseus, whose physical prowess was a threat.
He therefore asked Perseus to give him, instead
of the usual tribute from a subject to his ruler, the
head of Medusa. Perseus, the offspring of Danaë
and Zeus, who had appeared to Danaë in a
shower of gold, enjoyed the favor of the gods.
Athena advised him first to search out the
Graeae, the ugly sisters of the Gorgons. The two
Graeae, gray-haired from birth, had only one eye
and one tooth between them.[1] By stealing their
eye, Perseus forced them to reveal the way to the
dreadful Gorgons and to give him the imple-
ments he would need to defeat Medusa: the cap

of invisibility, winged shoes, and a bag. At the
frightful place where the Gorgons dwelled, Perseus saw humans and beasts turned to stone by
Medusa's countenance, and he found the Gorgons sleeping. He approached Medusa backward,
following her reflection in his shield, and cut off
her head. Having stuffed the head into his bag he
escaped her sisters with the help of the cap of
invisibility.

On the way back, he freed Andromeda from the
clutches of the sea monster, which he turned to
stone with the head of Medusa. Eventually, he
also rescued his mother from Polydectes, who
was still trying, unsuccessfully, to bend her to his
will by threatening to starve her out of a sanctu-
ary. Again Perseus used the head of Medusa and
turned him into stone.[2]

Fuseli chose the key scene from the myth for his
illustration. The work depicts Perseus trying to
steal the shared eye of the two Graeae. From
above, Athena, who hurried to the scene, points
to the sleeping sister on the right, who has the
eye. Perseus having seated himself next to the
old sister in the foreground and is holding her
tightly around the head and chin with his left
arm. Since she is blind at the moment, she turns
around toward her sleeping younger sister and
holds out her open hand to receive the eye, which
she needs in order to see who is grabbing her.
Perseus waits tensely—as though ready to
leap—with right arm outstretched to intercept
the eye the moment it is handed over. His left
foot rests on a vessel from which water flows,
symbolic of a river or lake and probably the Tri-
tonian Sea where the Graeae lived.[3]

In the gloomy and eerie place, the magnificent
naked body of young Perseus stands out against
the women, who turn away from him. There is a
pale and ghostly light, reminiscent of the reflection of a fire. With his sense for the cataclysmic,
Fuseli composed this scene in a masterfully theatrical way and staged it dramatically with his
handling of the light.

Fuseli made a second version of this theme.
According to the artist's own inscription, it was
drawn in Rome in May of 1771 on a larger sheet
of paper with pen and brown ink and gray wash.
Here, Fuseli executed some details with greater
narrative content: the owl crowning Athena's
helmet with wings outspread, for example, and
the missing tooth in the open mouth of the sister
held by Perseus (fig.). Moreover, the source of
light on the left becomes recognizable as the fire
in an open fireplace. Perseus appears here as an
older, partially dressed man. The scene, which in
the exhibited sheet has given way to a tense
pause following the initial assault, depicts the
moment of attack and the frightened reaction of
the sister in the foreground. These observations
suggest that our version is more focused on the
figures, drawn in a more severely rhythmical

way, and is a further development of the Hamburg composition.[4] Fuseli probably created it not
long after the first version, while in Rome; it was
there that he pursued a wide range of activities,
including archeology, and repeatedly occupied
himself with themes from Greek mythology.
The virtuosic, unconventional mixed technique
of the work further supports this argument:
Fuseli did not use the unusual combination of
media to reinvent the composition, but to execute his design pictorially with verve, based on a
secure conception of his theme.

This drawing allows insight into Fuseli's creative
process. Evidently, he used every graphic technique at his disposal to work on the thick paper.
First he moistened the paper or covered entire
sections with wet color. Then he reworked it with
a relatively thick pencil, probably a graphite stylus, pressing down on the paper so strongly that
the colored medium collected in the grooves he
created. Through layered heightenings he drew
those aspects of the narrative that he wanted to
highlight against the mysterious darkness. The
plastic effects of the shadows and heightenings
give the sheet a special tactile appeal. Fuseli also
proved himself a truly original artist in the way
he handled the tools of his art.

I am grateful to David H. Weinglass, Kansas City, Mis-
souri, for answering my numerous questions concerning
the closer identification of the two images reproduced
here.

1 According to Hesiod, *Theogony*, pp. 273ff., and Ovid,
   Metamorphoses, vol. 4, pp. 770ff.

2 Cf. Herbert Jennings Rose, *Griechische Mythologie: Ein
   Handbuch* (Munich, 1961), 2nd ed., pp. 26f., 277ff.

3 Schiff 1973, vol. 1, p. 444, no. 405 (information from
   Andreas Rumpf).

4 David Weinglass also lists our drawing as the second
   version after the Hamburg sheet in his revised English
   edition of Gert Schiff's catalogue raisonné of Fuseli's work,
   in preparation.

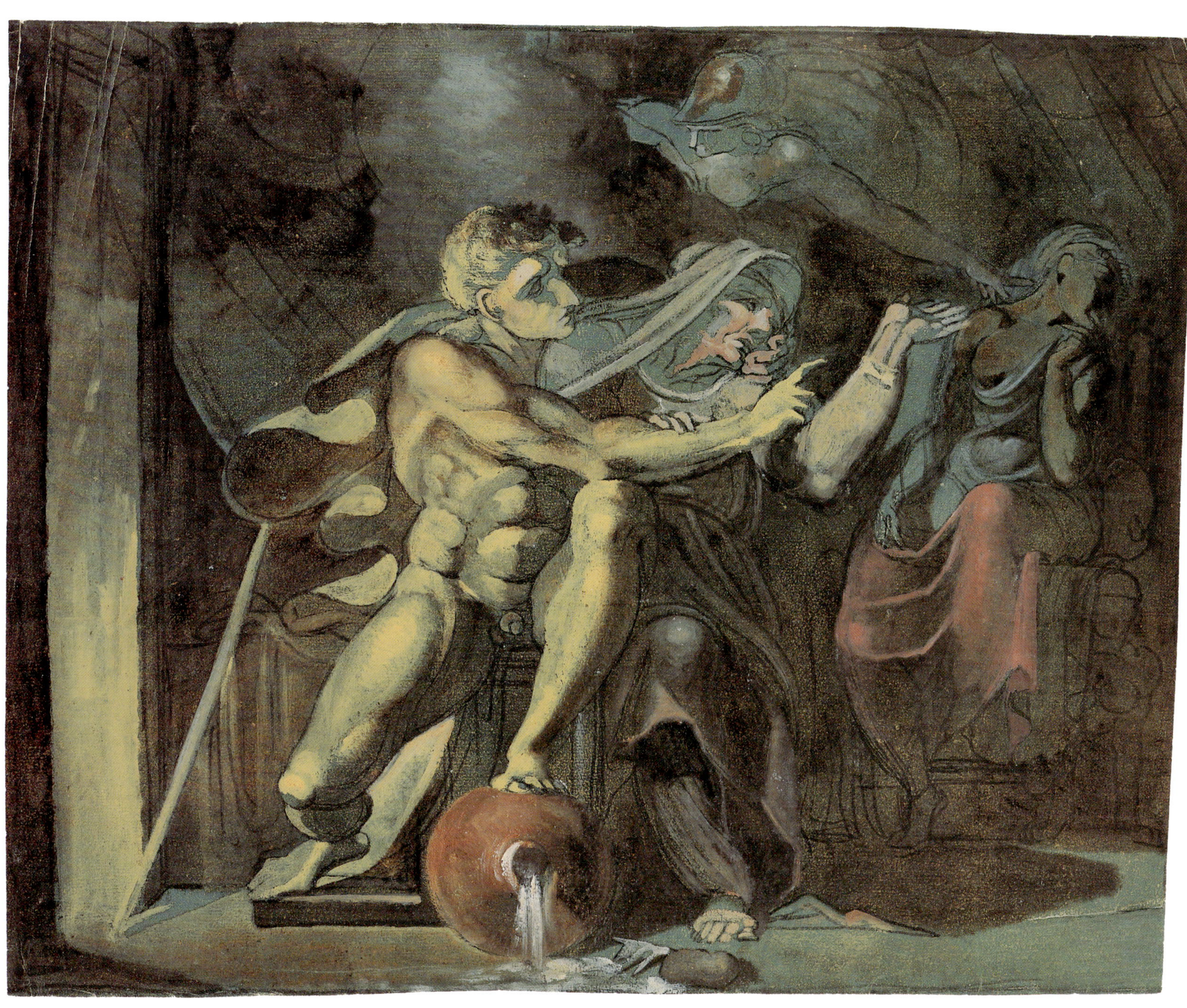

11

Henry Fuseli

Portrait Study of the Artist's Wife, Sophia Rawlins, c. 1793

Black chalk, heightened with white, on laid paper; watermark: Strasbourg lily; vertical crease; 313/39 x 307/285 mm Verso in pencil: two leg studies with knee and lower leg

Provenance: Robert Henri Randall Davies, London (Lugt 2903a)

Bibliography: Paul Ganz, Die Zeichnungen Hans Heinrich Füsslis (Henry Fuseli) (Bern-Olten, 1947), pp. 55, 67, no. 55 (repr.) (erroneously identified as a gift of Ganz to the Kunsthaus, Zurich)

With delicate chalk strokes that follow the flow of the hair, and a subtle heightening in white, Fuseli vividly captured the likeness of his young wife. We view her from below; Sophia's head is gently tilted and turned backward to her right. Her face, framed by a transparent scarf, the hat-

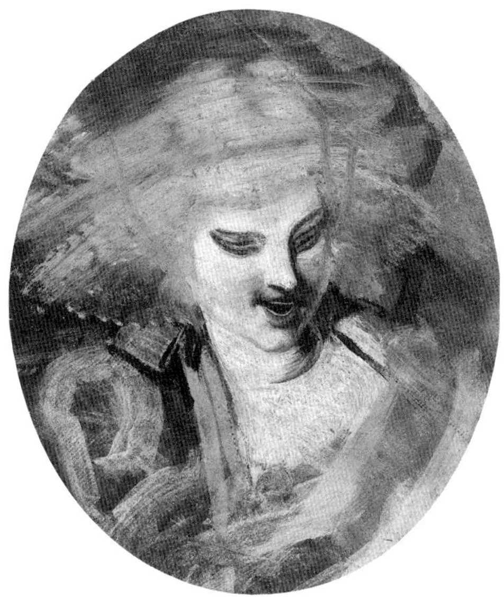

Henry Fuseli, *Portrait Study of the Artist's Wife, Sophia Rawlins,* 1790–92. Oil on laid paper; 220 x 185 mm (upright oval); laid down on its old mount

band under her chin, and her imaginative coiffure, are lightly shaded to eye level by the widely fanned-out brim of the hat, while her nose, cheeks, mouth, and chin are illuminated. Her pose and face express gentle devotion and grace; her affectionate gaze emanates sensuousness and a hint of coquettishness. This is Sophia Fuseli as seen through her husband's loving eyes.

In 1788, at the height of his artistic career, Fuseli, then forty-seven years old, married the attractive twenty-five-year-old Sophia Rawlins, an

Englishwoman from Bath who had been his model. Our unusually tender portrait drawing can be assigned to a whole series of portrait studies that the artist made of his young wife from 1790 to 1800. Between 1790 and 1810, Fuseli executed over 140 likenesses of women, for the most part with exotic coiffures and headpieces; many of these works were previously classified as fantasized portraits of courtesans. Gert Schiff has identified about 120 of these drawings as variations on a single theme: the representation of Fuseli's wife.[1] Schiff realized this on the basis of a single portrait of Sophia from the year 1798, documented as her likeness by the artist's own inscription.[2] Fuseli made these drawings—intimate evidence of the fascination and attraction he had for his wife and, simultaneously, essays on "woman" as such—as the occasion arose, and used every conceivable graphic medium (fig.). In these likenesses, Fuseli portrayed Sophia not so much as a lovingly devoted housewife, but as an erotic, seductive creature, as a goddess from classical antiquity, a grande dame or prostitute, and, above all, a woman seduced by fashion: the image of vanity. Associations with similar themes in the work of his sixteenth-century Swiss countryman Urs Graf are apparent.

Fuseli shared his wife's pleasure in extravagant fashion. Thanks to the illustrated Paris fashion journals, we are well informed about the excesses and the sartorial silliness of the ancien régime, and about the sobering changes brought about by the French Revolution. These changes affected hairstyles especially, but also accessories like hats and headpieces. Fuseli clearly took his cues from the excessive fashion of his day, but went far beyond it in his inventiveness.

In a painting he executed around 1793/94, entitled *Titania Caresses Bottom's Donkey Head,* Fuseli illustrated a forest scene from Shakespeare's *Midsummer Night's Dream* (4.1).[3] The fairy Peaseblossom, whom Bottom has called, appears above his donkey head and, as requested, scratches between his ears to relieve the itch caused by the donkey hair. This benevolent and charming fairy not only bears the features of Fuseli's wife, but she is also wearing a hat that is pointed at the top and has a broadly fanned-out brim, which is exactly the way the hat in our drawing would look if we completed it in our minds. It is as though Fuseli used this portrait drawing of Sophia as the inspiration for the fairy's depiction, where Peaseblossom raises her head slightly and turns it in the opposite direction. For his painted compositions, Fuseli did in fact draw upon the rich supply of figurative sketches and portraits he had created for their own sake.

A comparison between the present chalk study and an oil sketch in the Winterstein collection (fig.) may be indicative of Fuseli's rather am-

bivalent attitude toward his wife and toward women in general. In the virtuosic oil sketch, his wife's animated likeness appears with masklike theatricality. Fuseli also dramatized color and gesture and masterfully rendered the piece, focusing on the expression of the head.[4] In addition to the slanted eyes, the nose, chin, and mouth (open for speaking) also show caricatured, pointy features. Perhaps Fuseli saw Sophia as a Fury, as a witch or sorceress, or more likely, as a femme fatale. David H. Weinglass has pointed out that the hair has been sculpted to resemble the wings on Medusa's head, a repellent symbol.[5] Such an allusion to Medusa is suggested by the ashen white color of the flesh, reminiscent of marble, with the accentuation of the rosy cheeks. In a washed, lightly watercolored brush drawing from 1799, Fuseli portrayed his wife in full figure seated in front of a fireplace, above which her portrait appears once again in a fictive relief of upright oval format. She is depicted here in full frontal view with facial features that have been stylized into the head of Medusa.[6] The surrounding inscription in Greek reads unmistakably, "The head of fair-cheeked Medusa."

Fuseli began his professional career as a theologian, like J. G. von Dillis and J. C. Reinhart, and led the restless life of a freelance artist. Like no other visual artist of the Sturm und Drang, he made statements about human drives and passions in his work. He loved life, art, and human freedom. Much like Goya, he dealt with basic human experiences: loneliness and fear, horror and terror, as well as every permutation of the passion between the sexes. Throughout his work runs a strongly erotic component in search of a primal humanity, freed from all constraints and conventions.

1   David H. Weinglass, *Women Observed: Twenty Master Drawings. Thomas Le Claire,* cat. 10 (Hamburg, 1996), no. 11. As Fuseli confessed, "Restlessly, through fleeting fashions, I sought the picture of my dream." Cf. Schiff 1973, p. 231.

2   1 July 1789; pencil, 138 x 89 mm; Schiff 1973, no. 1110.

3   Zurich, Kunsthaus; Schiff 1973, no. 885.

4   In format, technique (oil sketch on paper), and its use of the cut-out upright oval, it is nearly identical to *Sophia Fuseli in Profil Perdu,* 1790–92; oil on paper, 222 x 165 mm; Schiff 1973, no. 1087 (repr.). In context with the upright-oval portrait of Mrs. Fuseli, 1792; cf. Schiff 1973, no. 930 (repr.).

5   Weinglass (n. 1).

6   Nuremberg, Germanisches Nationalmuseum, inv. no. Hz 3599; cf. *Die Handzeichnungen des 18. Jahrhunderts: Kataloge des Germanischen Nationalmuseums Nürnberg,* ed. Monika Heffels, vol. 4 in *Die deutschen Handzeichnungen* series (Nuremberg, 1969), pp. 102 f., no. 126, p. 105 (repr. in color).

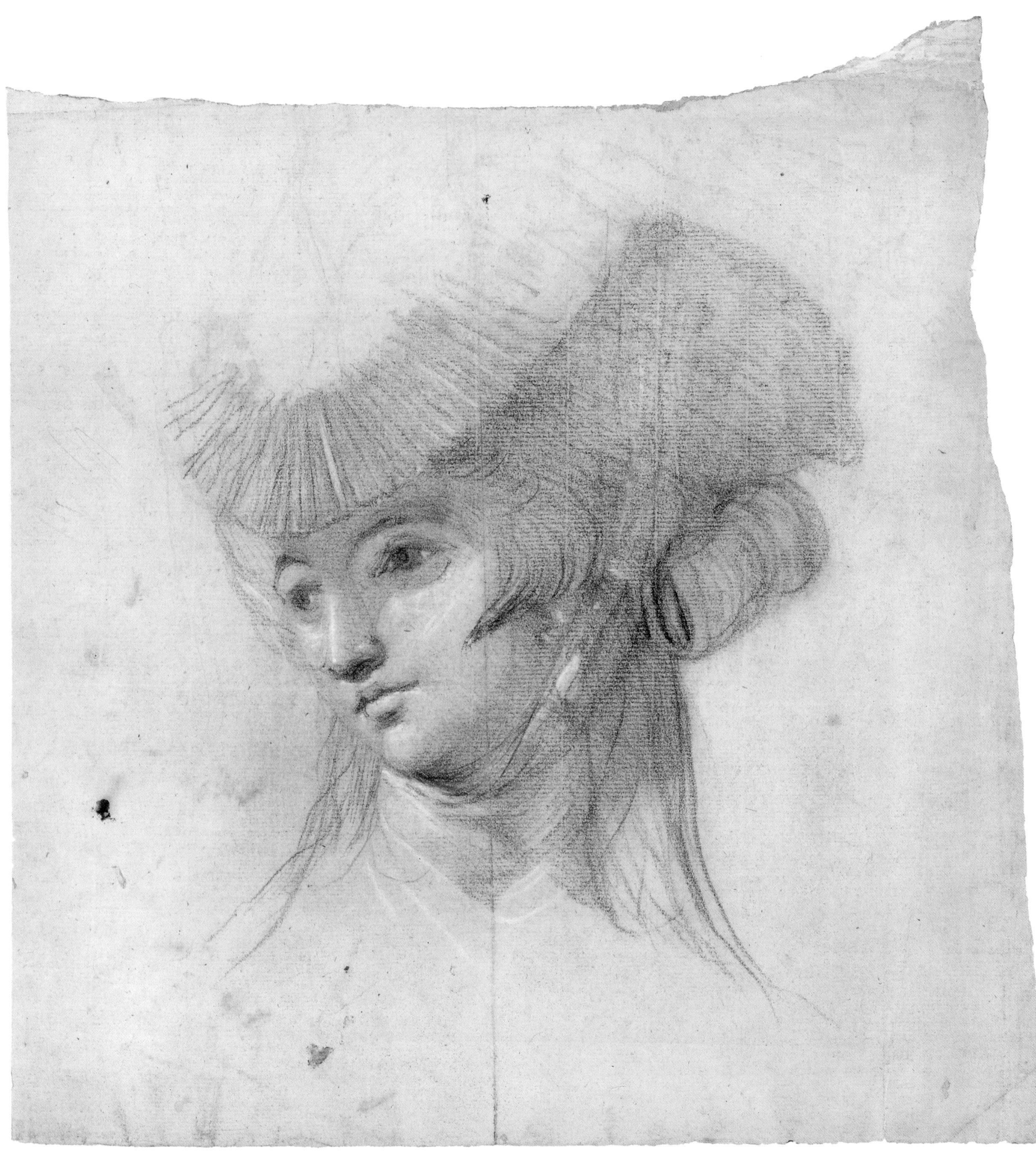

12

Daniel Nikolaus Chodowiecki

Danzig 16 October 1726 – 7 February 1801 Berlin

Ladies' Social at the L'Hombre Table, 1759

Pencil, on laid paper, incised with a stylus, verso reddened with chalk
Inscribed by the artist in pencil, lower right: "den 6 8bre 59"; 104 x 167 mm
Provenance: Wilhelm Engelmann; Mme. M. Stechow, Berlin (Lugt 2371)

Bibliography: C. G. Boerner, Das radierte Werk des Daniel Chodowiecki vollständig und durchweg in frühesten Zuständen, Ätzdrucken oder Probedrucken; Miniaturen und Emaillemalereien; Sammlung von Originalzeichnungen; Briefe, Tagebücher, Sammlung M. Stechow; auction sale, Berlin, 10–13 December 1919 (Leipzig), cat. no. 55; Munich 1958, p. 20, no. 7

Chodowiecki's real artistic career did not begin until the Seven Years' War (1756–63). Prior to that, he worked primarily in commercial art as a miniaturist and enamel painter. Now he trained himself also as a painter and draftsman. During this early phase, he devoted himself passionately to the study of nature through graphite drawings, and his first experiments in etching belong to the same period. Only after 1763, under financial pressure, did Chodowiecki develop into a professional graphic artist in the vast field of book illustration for the public market. It is for this work that he is known today.

In his autobiography, Chodowiecki described his manner of drawing during this early period: "I drew incidentally. If I was in a social gathering, I would sit where I could see the whole gathering, or a group within it, or merely a single figure. I

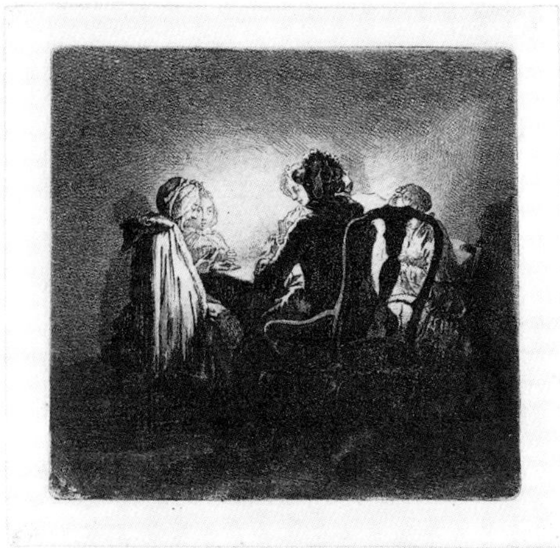

Daniel Chodowiecki, *The Large L'Hombre Table*, 1765. Etching and aquatint; the plate: 118 x 118 mm (E.22 II, Ba.24). Berlin, Staatliche Museen Preussischer Kulturbesitz, Kupferstichkabinett

then drew as quickly and with as much diligence as time or the steadiness of the people would permit. I never asked for permission, but rather tried to do everything as clandestinely as possible. For if a woman (and sometimes also a man) knows that one is trying to draw her, she wants to present herself favorably and ruins everything; her posture becomes forced. I didn't let it bother me if people ran off when I was only half done, for I had gained so much! What wonderful groups with light and shadow I sometimes entered in to my pocketbook, with every advantage that Nature has over all the vaunted ideals if left to herself. I also did this frequently in the evening by light; there is no better practice for bringing out large sections, light and shadow. I drew standing, walking, riding on horseback; through the keyhole I sketched girls in bed in the most lovely positions left entirely to themselves .... I drew very little from paintings, slightly more from plaster, and much from Nature. In Nature I found the most satisfaction, the greatest usefulness; she is my only guide, my benefactress."[1]

On the evening of 6 October 1759, Chodowiecki drew this intimate domestic scene of a ladies' card game, the earliest work in the present exhibition. Five young women sit grouped around a table, absorbed in a card game and illuminated by a hidden source of light (the glow of a candle). They are playing L'Hombre, a Spanish card game which, today, has almost completely been replaced in Germany by Skat.[2] Chodowiecki's chief interest was not so much the individual likenesses of the women as the distribution of the light, which binds the card players together into an intimate, isolated gathering.[3] The silvery pencil, which Chodowiecki used to place accents here and there, allows no deep black, only gray tones. Depending on the firmness or lightness of the stroke, these gray tones become more closely packed in parallel lines and crosshatchings, gentle echoes of the light-dark effects of seventeenth-century Dutch paintings of interiors.

The drawing, in the format of a family album leaf, soon served as the model for an aquatint-etching, in which the scene was faithfully reproduced (fig.).[4] Here, the composition, in a square format, is tightly focused on the group of figures. Once again, Chodowiecki was interested in the distribution of the light in the dark room. In the process, he was trying to create the effect of a wash drawing. In this piece, he was still experimenting with aquatint technique, which had been developed in France only a short time before.[5] The plate appears to be lightly bitten, and we can detect the crosshatching that Chodowiecki used to achieve darker shadows. Chodowiecki was one of the first German artists to adopt the new aquatint technique. This extremely rare print, with its mysterious light-dark effect, is a characteristic example of work

done in the manner of Rembrandt, a popular style at the time.

Chodowiecki's art of bourgeois genre stood in clear contrast to the official, French-oriented court art of the Frederician Rococo. His world was that of the simple bourgeoisie, whose values he conveyed through his art, and his interest lay in the accurate rendering of reality. His early drawings, which mirror bourgeois social life with its changing fashions in dress and hairstyles, already reveal a sense of reality that established a Berlin tradition that would continue through Schadow to Menzel. Chodowiecki had close ties to the French colony in Berlin by birth and marriage. This immensely industrious draftsman and small-format illustrator, full of simple grace and charm, seems a very German counterpart to the contemporary French vignette artists of the utmost refinement and aristocratic elegance, such as Nicolas Cochin the Younger, Hubert François Gravelot, and Charles Eisen.

1 From his autobiography, quoted in Märker 1978, pp. 59f.
2 Elisabeth Wormsbächer, *Danzig 1726–1801 Berlin. Daniel Nikolaus Chodowiecki. Erklärungen zu seinen Radierungen. Ein Ergänzungsband zum Werkverzeichnis der Druckgraphik*, ed. Jens-Heiner Bauer (Hannover, 1988), p. 3, no. Ba.15/E.15, p. 4, no. Ba.24/E.22.
3 Cf. also cat. 24 (Kersting), 32 (Pforr), and 22 (Friedrich).
4 For transfer, the drawing was reddened with red chalk on the verso and incised with a stylus on the recto. "A playful idea led me to make an attempt at an etching in the year 1756 .... As badly as this attempt turned out, I did like the advantage of being able to reproduce a work through the print, and this gave me the desire to do more. During leisurely hours I made various small sheets, most of which represent objects from daily life, which I had previously drawn from nature." Quoted by Märker 1978, p. 65. Chodowiecki's early family etchings are exceedingly rare, since they were entirely private and experimental works. Prints from this plate, two states of which exist, are in Berlin and Stuttgart. It was only later family scenes, such as the *Cabinet d'un peintre* (1771), that the artist released for public circulation after he had mastered his technical skills.
5 In a handwritten note on a proof of the aquatint-etching of *Small L'Hombre Table* (1758), Chodowiecki stated, "An attempt to imitate the aquatint technique, which at the time was little known outside the works of Leprince, Saint-non, and Charpentier"; cf. Bauer 1982, p. 9, no. 15 (E.15 2).

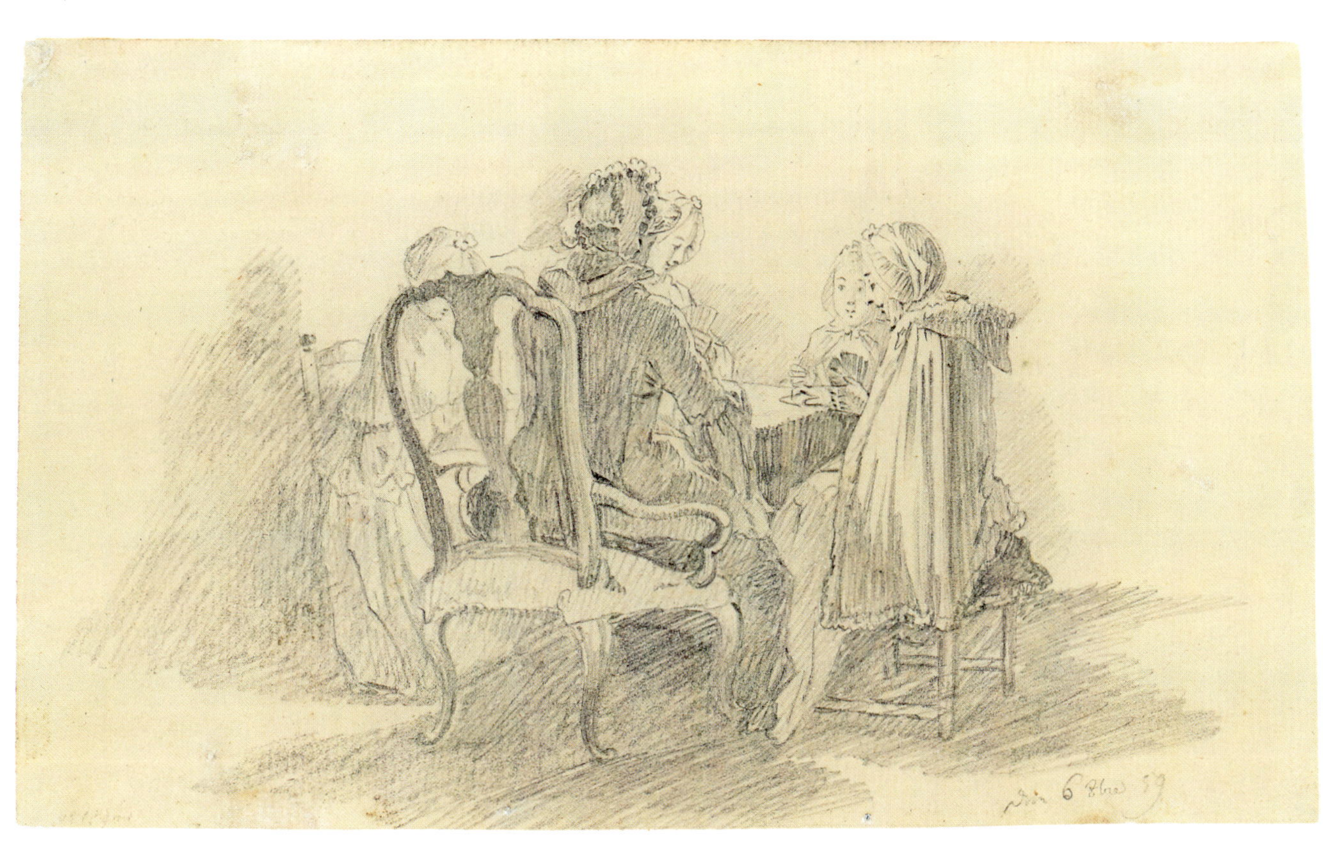

13

Anton Graff

Winterthur 18 November 1736 – 22 June 1813
Dresden

Self-Portrait, c. 1784

*Watercolor and gouache on parchment, border in black,
laid down on its old mount; 159 x 115 mm*

Like no other portraitist, the Swiss painter Anton Graff captured the "intellectual face" of his time in numerous likenesses of leading social figures in the German-speaking lands. In his work, infused with the spirit of the Enlightenment and mirroring the changing times, he transcended the conventions of the artificial portraiture of the Baroque and Rococo, with its emphasis on representation. Graff was interested in the way a person naturally appeared, and his talent for depicting the individual soberly and objectively was appreciated by the nobility and the bourgeoisie alike. His work is testimony to two important social trends of the Enlightenment: the nobility was becoming bourgeois, and the economically successful and educated bourgeoisie was being ennobled. Graff primarily created life-size portrait paintings in addition to—as shown here—miniature portraits on parchment and drawings, some in silverpoint.

Graff painted more self-portraits than any other artist of his generation. Over eighty are known, from the earliest, showing him at age seventeen, to the last, completed in the year of his death.[1] Unlike his countryman Henry Fuseli, Graff did not regard the self-portrait as a medium of self-analysis or as an expression of existential searching and doubt. Rather, he saw self-portraiture as an objective way to take stock of his mental and physical condition and to situate his artistic development within the passage of time.

In the present work, Graff depicted himself half-length, turned to the right, bareheaded, in a narrow pictorial space in front of a neutral background. He dispensed with the usual painter's props, such as an easel and palette; the sole reference to his profession is that he points a brush or chalkholder at himself.[2] Nothing distracts from the personality of the sitter. In conventional fashion, he turns his head to look at the viewer over his right shoulder as his body faces sideways. The artist's face—set off against the dark, dull colors of the gray-black background and his simple, reddish brown coat—is clear and bright. He placed himself as if lit from the front and finely modeled his features in the manner of a miniaturist. Compositionally, Graff concentrated on the study of his own physiognomy. His eyes are wide open, and his lucid, observant, and inquisitive look is directed both at the viewer, whom he scrutinizes like a model, and at the mirror, in which he examines himself.

Johann Georg Sulzer, Graff's father-in-law, described the artist's intense gaze: "I have remarked more than once that a number of people who had themselves painted by our Graff, who has the splendid gift of portraying the entire physiognomy true to nature, could hardly bear the keen and emotion-laden looks he directed at them, for each one seemed to penetrate to the innermost part of their soul…."[3]

Graff's countryman Johann Caspar Lavater, in his widely discussed *Physiognomic Fragments* (published in 1775–78), had spoken of the human face as the mirror of the soul and as the primary place where individual personality expressed itself. In the present self-portrait, Graff gives us a key for understanding not only him but also his conception of the art of portraiture, which is in harmony with the demands that Lavater and Sulzer made of this art. Graff's self-portrait testifies to a spiritualization in the rendering of the human face, and in this he shows himself to be the precursor of Caspar David Friedrich (cat. 20), Georg Friedrich Kersting (cat. 23), and Friedrich Georg Weitsch (cat. 15). Comparisons with other dated self-portraits suggest that the artist was about forty-eight when he painted this piece. The high degree of similarity with a half-length portrait from 1784 (fig. 1,)[4] makes it likely that the present piece was executed in the same year and that it actually served as the model for this portrait and for a replica now in Munich (fig. 2).[5] The freshness and vividness of the brush drawing suggest that Graff made it directly from life. His drawings with watercolor and wash were usually intended for friendship albums.[6] The same was probably true for the sheet exhibited here: its format, pictorial execution, and black border seem to indicate as much.[7]

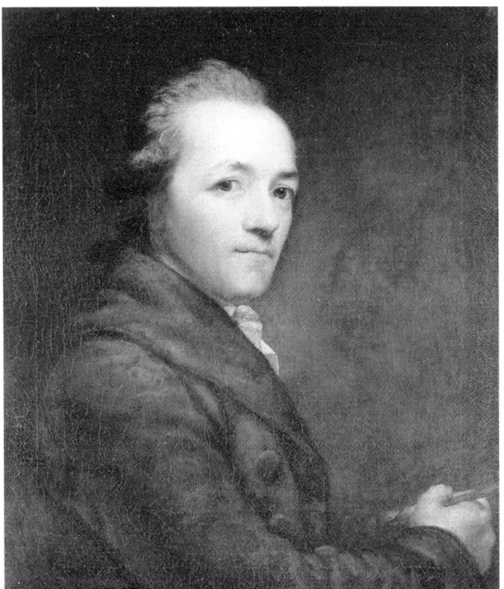

1 Anton Graff, *Self-Portrait*, 1784. Oil on canvas. Winterthur, Kunstmuseum, inv. no. 120

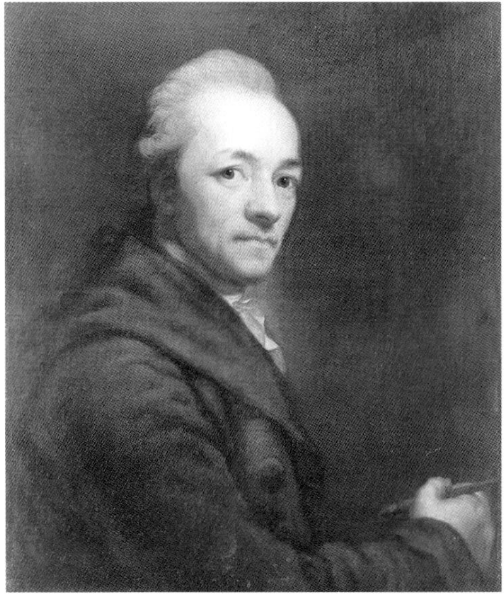

2 Anton Graff, *Self-Portrait*, c. 1784, replica. Oil on canvas. Munich, Bayerische Staatsgemäldesammlungen, inv. no. 1055

1 Berckenhagen 1967, nos. 473–553; *Anton Graff, Meisterwerke aus dem Museum der bildenden Künste Leipzig: Dokumentation & Interpretation* (Leipzig, 1986); Zurich 1990, pp. 11–23, 14.

2 During that period, when painters wanted to highlight their own intellectual achievement and the creative process, they often portrayed themselves in front of an easel holding a piece of chalk, a drawing tool, instead of a brush; cf. Brunhilde Rothbauer, "Selbstbildnisse der Graff-Zeit," in *Anton Graff, Meisterwerke* (n. 86), pp. 20, 22 f.

3 Sulzer 1774, vol. 2, pp. 918 ff., 920.

4 Berckenhagen 1967, no. 490.

5 *Ibid.*, no. 491, see also nos. 492–94. *Nachbarock und Klassizismus: Bayerische Staatsgemäldesammlungen, Gemäldekataloge*, vol. 3, ed. Barbara Hardtwig, (Munich, 1978), pp. 115 ff. (repr.), inv. no. 1055 (Wolfgang Hauke).

6 Berckenhagen 1967, p. 32.

7 Assuming it was completed in 1784 or even earlier, the portrait exhibited here could be the one that Daniel Chodowiecki mentioned in a letter of 27 October 1784 to his friend Graff as the latter's gift to Countess Christine von Solms-Laubach; cf. *ibid.*, no. 493.

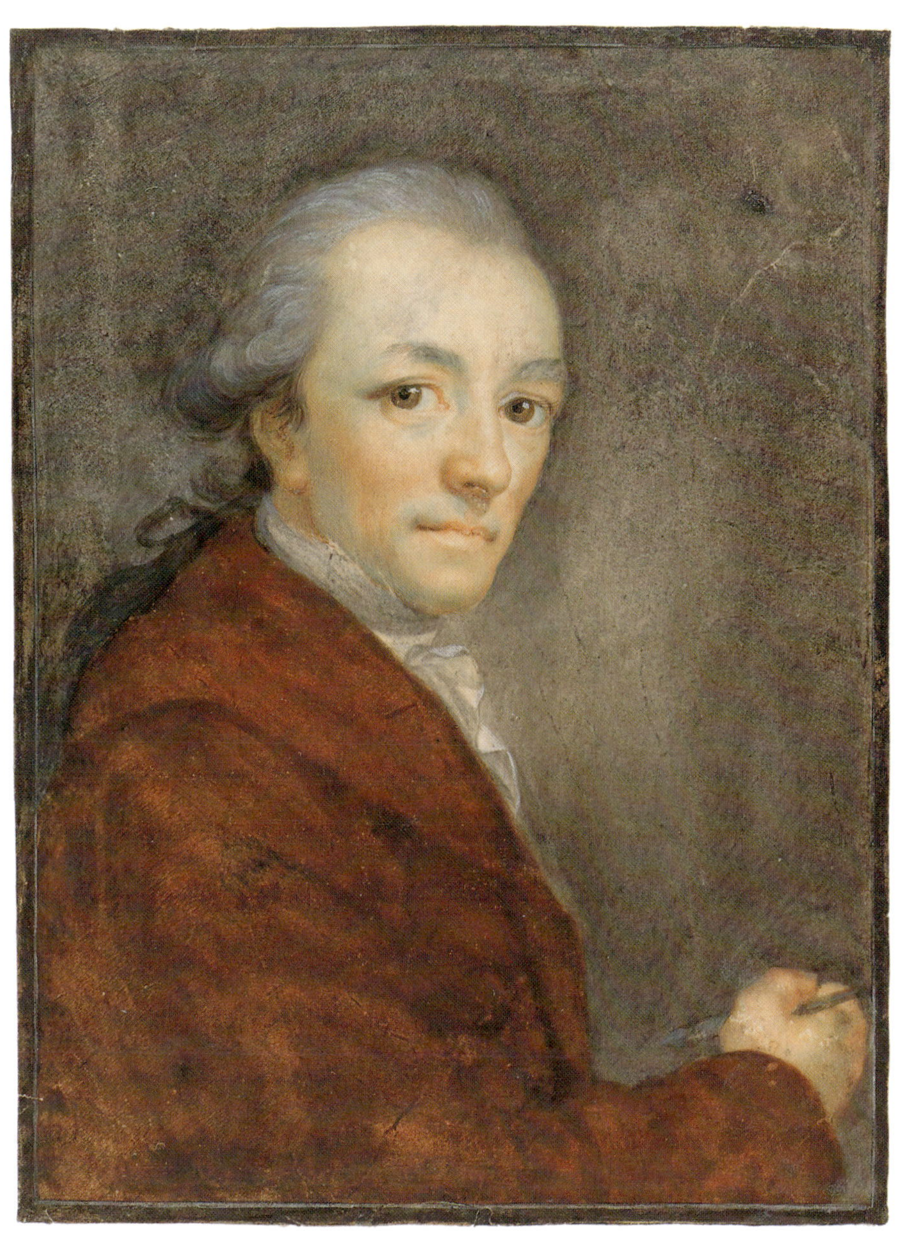

14

Johann Gottfried Schadow

Berlin 20 May 1764 – 27 January 1850 Berlin

Portrait of Marie Christine Schlegel, 1803

Black and colored chalks on laid paper, laid down on its old mount; 221/22 x 173/75 mm
Signed and dated by the artist, lower left: "G. Schadow 1803"

Bibliography: Winterthur 1955, p. 62, no. 270; Lübeck 1957, p. 57, no. 158; Munich 1958, p. 52, no. 148, fig. 42; Lübeck 1969, pp. 84ff., no. 166 (repr.); London 1972, p. 421, no. 804; Bailey 1987, pp. 142f., under no. 121; Lübeck 1990, p. 66, under no. 19 (Sieveking); Sieveking 1990, p. 54, p. 117, fig. 9

Between 1788 and 1805, the families of the sculptor Johann Gottfried Schadow and of the director of the mint Johann Andreas Schlegel lived in the same house, the new mint in the Berlin suburb of Spandau.[1] Schadow's studio and Schlegel's administrative offices of the royal mint were located in this building, which Gentz had designed. In 1800, Schadow had executed an extensive figural frieze based on a design by Friedrich Gilly on its façade.

Many of Schadow's genre and portrait drawings attest to friendly relations between the two families, especially portraits of Frau Schlegel, née

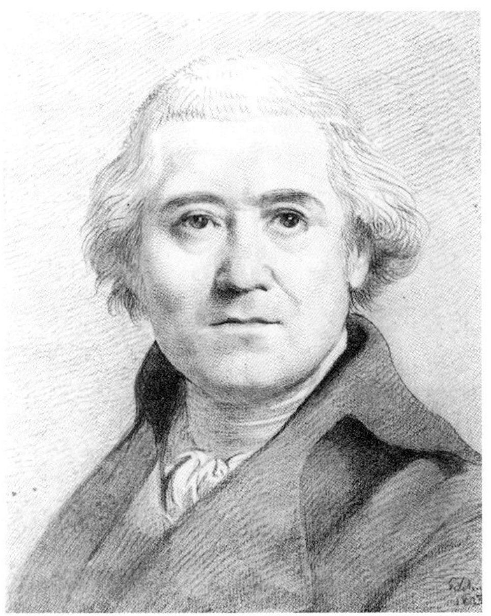

Johann Gottfried Schadow, *Portrait of the Mint Director Johann Andreas Schlegel*, 1803. Black and colored chalks; 224 x 177 mm. Germany, private collection

Luckow, and her daughter Marianne, Schadow's godchild.[2] A number of these pieces are in the so-called Schadow family album, which is housed today in the Berlin Kupferstichkabinett.

As a special memorial to this friendship, Schadow drew the portraits of Johann Schlegel and his wife in 1803 as pendants. That the drawing of Frau Schlegel belongs in this context was recognized for the first time a few years ago, when the portrait of her husband reappeared (fig.).[3] No doubt these two portraits belong together: format, technique, date, signature, and the old mounting on gray-brown card are completely identical. Although both likenesses have been carefully finished as independent half-length portraits *en face*, they are clearly related. In each one, the head is placed frontally and is aligned symmetrically on the central vertical axis of the composition, while the bust is set at an angle to the picture plane. Both likenesses reveal the hand of the sculptor with his distinctive sense of plastic form; moreover, both are inspired by Neo-classicistic marble portrait busts, this being apparent in the treatment of light and the use of light in modeling the form, as well as in the reductive palette. The representation of social status plays a minimal role in these works. Schadow imparted an official character to the portrait of Johann Schlegel, then general mint assistant, by showing him in his gray-black coat. In contrast, he imbued the portrait of his wife, a "full-figured bourgeois woman," with a certain dignity by treating her dress in the classical style. With "a gift of observation bordering on the cunning," Schadow, who had a sense of humor, combined the simplicity of this bourgeois face with a dignified sculptural form. And yet the likeness of Frau Schlegel emanates the naturalness and vitality characteristic of Schadow's art. During the period when this drawing was made, Schadow's precise observations of nature and his prosaic matter-of-fact depictions offended Goethe, who maintained that artistic representation should pursue idealization in the classical sense. This gave rise to a debate about art theory that was carried on publicly from 1800 to 1803.[4]

When Schadow created the Schlegel portraits, his talent was at its height, as was his early fame as a sculptor. This was also a phase during which the focal point of his work began to shift to the graphic arts. The Schlegel portraits also clearly reflect Schadow's scientific interest in the study of human physiognomy. On each face he drew a system of coordinates with axes that intersected at the base of the nose; traces of this system are still visible, as in the portrait of Frau Schlegel, where we can still see the remains of the vertical line above the upper lip and on the tip of the nose.

Schadow published his *National Physiognomies* in 1835.[5] In it, he reproduced, in zinc etchings, portrait drawings he had done over the course of decades: on top of each, *en face* or in profile, he drew the same system of coordinates in order to make the human proportions easier to read, mea-

sure, and thus teach. It is possible that, when drawing the Schlegel portraits, he was thinking of one day including them in his book.

1 As far as we know, the family of the mint director Schlegel and the learned brothers August Wilhelm and Friedrich Schlegel, frequent guests in the Schadow household, were not related.

2 For example, the full-length portrait of Frau Schlegel, in Bailey 1987, pp. 141 ff., no. 121 (repr.). Schadow painted Marianne for the first time in 1802, as *Mignon*, a character from Goethe's *Wilhelm Meister's Apprenticeship* (Berlin, 1795); cf. New York 1988, p. 74, no. 19 (repr. in color). In 1805, he created a sculptural portrait bust of the girl; cf. Bernhard Maaz, ed., *Johann Gottfried Schadow und die Kunst seiner Zeit*, exh. cat. (Cologne, 1994), pp. 243 f., no. 93 (repr.), p. 258, no. 122 (repr.), p. 261, no. 129 (repr.). Additional drawings and portraits of various members of the Schlegel family can be found, for example, in Berlin 1906, p. 109, nos. 5010–12, p. 112, nos. 5037, 5040.

3 Lübeck 1990, p. 66, no. 19 (repr. in color).

4 Cf. Maaz, *Johann Gottfried Schadow* (n. 94), pp. 141–48.

5 Johann Gottfried Schadow, *National Physiognomien oder Beobachtungen über den Unterschied der Gesichtszüge und der äusseren Gestalt des Kopfes, in Umrissen bildlich dargestellt auf 29 Tafeln, als Fortsetzung des Polyclet oder Lehre von den Verhältnissen des menschlichen Körpers* (Berlin, 1835).

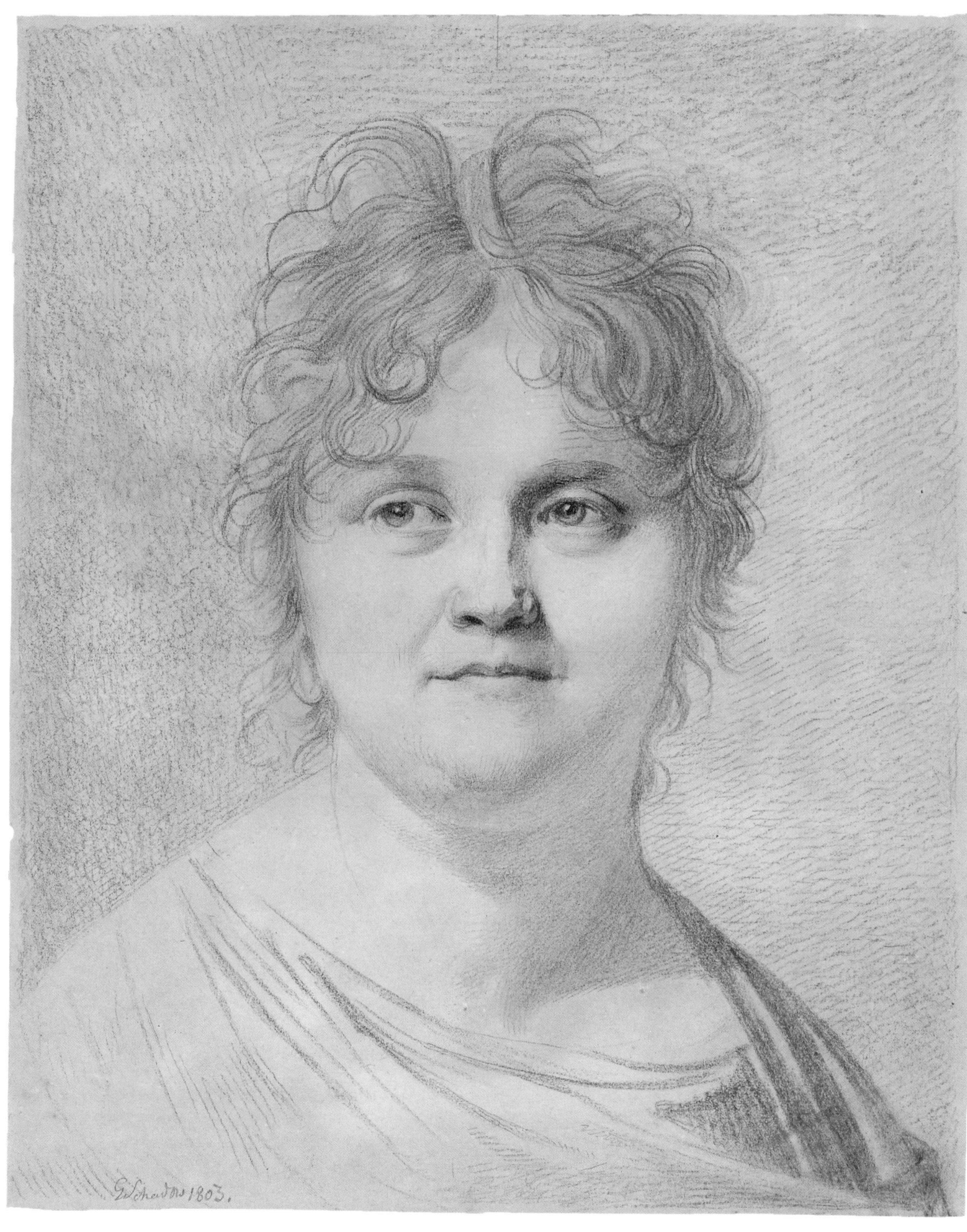
GSchadow 1803.

15

Friedrich Georg Weitsch

Brunswick 8 August 1758 – 30 May 1828 Berlin

Portrait of the Volunteer Friedrich Adolf Klaatsch, 1813

Pastel, border in black chalk, on gray-tinted laid paper; watermark: F. JOHANNOT; 274 x 218/20 mm Monogrammed and dated, lower left: "F.W.f./1813"

Provenance: Elisabeth Klaatsch, Trier

Bibliography: Jahrhundertfeier der Freiheitskriege, exh. cat., enlarged and revised 4th edition (Breslau, 1913), p. 97, no. 37; Gerd Rosen, Graphik, Handzeichnungen, Gemälde, Antiquitäten, 39th auction sale, Berlin, 5–10 November 1962, cat. no. 1006 (repr.); Lübeck 1969, p. 103, no. 197

Prussia had been humiliated by the Peace of Tilsit in 1807 and by the French occupation that followed. The cries for restoration of the state's sovereignty and for national unity grew louder, especially among representatives of the German intelligentsia. Let us recall Johann Gottlieb Fichte's daring lectures *Reden an die deutsche*

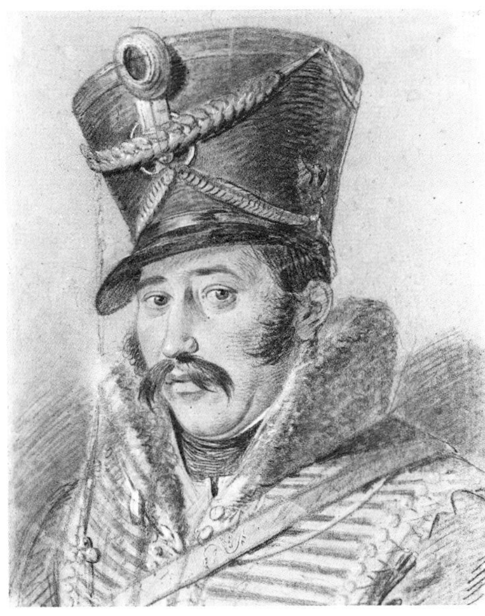

Karl Ludwig Buchhorn, *Portrait of Ferdinand von Schill*, 1809. Black and red chalks, charcoal, heightened with white; 552 x 414 mm. Berlin, Staatliche Museen Preußischer Kulturbesitz, Kupferstichkabinett

Nation [Talks to the German Nation], delivered in the winter of 1807/08 in French-occupied Berlin, and Ernst Moritz Arndt's many writings and songs about Germany's liberation. Scattered uprisings, like that of Andreas Hofer in Tyrol or of Major Schill (fig.) in Stralsund in 1809, rekin-

dled the hope that Germany would be freed from the French yoke. Under pressure of public opinion, King Frederick William III of Prussia eventually published the *Call to My People* on 17 March 1813 in Breslau. In it, he urged the Germans to join the common struggle against the French and appealed to their willingness to make sacrifices ("I have given gold for iron"). Many volunteers answered the appeal and served in units such as the Lützow Free Corps; even youngsters like Friedrich Adolf Klaatsch signed up, as did numerous artists.[1] In the fall of that year, the allies defeated Napoleon in the fateful Battle of the Nations near Leipzig (16–19 October 1813), a defeat that marked the beginning of the end of Napoleon's hegemony.

Weitsch drew this compelling portrait of the volunteer Friedrich Adolf Klaatsch prior to the beginning of the campaign of 1813. The young soldier is depicted in the black fur jacket of the Second Regiment of the King's Own Hussars, with upturned collar. Normally this fur jacket was worn over the left shoulder, which indicates that this drawing was done in the winter. Judging from the height of the fur collar, Klaatsch held the rank of a cornet or ensign, so he was an officer cadet.[2] Ludwig Buchhorn (1770–1856), later an instructor at the Berlin Academy, drew the freedom fighter Ferdinand von Schill in a similar winter fur; the work dates from 1809, when Schill had become commander of the Second Hussar Regiment, a few months before his death (fig.).

We know little about F. A. Klaatsch aside from the dates of his life (25 August 1798-July 1836 Berlin). In 1813, at age fifteen, he entered the Second Regiment of the King's Own Hussars and later rose to the rank of captain. Although no further information about the Klaatsch family has so far been unearthed, the catalogue of the 1962 auction where this drawing was sold brought to light, from the same source, a number of additional family portraits. They include a second pastel by Weitsch, also drawn at the beginning of the campaign: it represents Carl Heinrich Klaatsch (1794–1845), who joined the Battalion of Guard Jaegers as a volunteer in 1813 and may have been a brother of Friedrich Adolf.[3] Of particular interest, in addition to Conrad L'Allemand's portrait, dated 1844, of Franziska Elisabeth Klaatsch (1801–1879) seated on a sofa,[4] is the frontal half-length likeness of Eduard Friedrich Klaatsch (1801–1879), who held the post of Geheimer Archivrat. The Prussian court painter Franz Krüger (1797–1857) drew him in his characteristic style in black chalk, heightened with white on brown paper.[5] Perhaps the Klaatsch family was known at court. Eduard Friedrich is depicted wearing the Iron Cross of 1813 in his buttonhole. In all likelihood, then, there were three Klaatsch brothers, all of whom fought in

the War of Liberation. That our portrait of the youngest of the three brothers was shown at the Historical Exhibition in Breslau in 1913 in room 8, which was dedicated to the families of the heroes, corroborates this argument.

Weitsch's drawings attest to his eclectic approach, and they vary greatly in their originality and quality. His landscapes were influenced by seventeenth-century Dutch and French art, especially the work of Claude Lorrain and Gaspard Dughet. Red-chalk drawings from his Italian period reveal that he followed the forms and style of the French Academy in Rome and, in particular, the art of Hubert Robert. As a portraitist, to be sure, Weitsch produced notable and even highly significant works, such as the portrait of Alexander von Humboldt.[6] His likenesses, often drawn spontaneously, are characterized by a lively, natural approach. The present portrait of the young Friedrich Adolf Klaatsch stands out as one of the loveliest by virtue of the vibrant sense of life it exudes. Weitsch drew it in airy pastel, a technique that had been popular during his youth. The fashionable hairstyle hints at French Neo-classicistic taste. It is masterful in its expression of naiveté and childlike innocence in the soft, rounded facial features on the one hand, and the youthful sincerity of patriotism on the other: a mix of a love of adventure and stubbornness, of curiosity and an unsuspecting nature. The wideopen eyes mirror not only the fatherland's predicament and Friedrich Adolf's fear, but also courage and determination.

1 Among those who took up arms as volunteers were the artists Johann Gottfried Schadow, Wilhelm Hensel, Carl Friedrich Zimmermann, Ferdinand Flor, Georg Friedrich Kersting, Philipp Veit, Friedrich Olivier, and Johann Evangelist Scheffer von Leonhardshoff. In Berlin, the *Landsturmverordnung* [Home Reserve Decree] was published on 21 April 1813; the entire citizenry was ready (and had been before this) to join, especially men in the sciences and the arts, university professors, members of the Academy, actors, and musicians.

2 I would like to thank the military historian Hugo F. W. Schulz, Düsseldorf, for his kind research into the Klaatsch family and for answering questions relating to the uniform depicted here.

3 Rosen 1962, p. 156, no. 1007.

4 *Ibid.*, p. 88, no. 658.

5 *Ibid.*, p. 107, no. 817, p. 106 (repr.).

6 *Portrait of Alexander von Humboldt*, 1806, Wirth 1990, pp. 51, 53 (repr.).

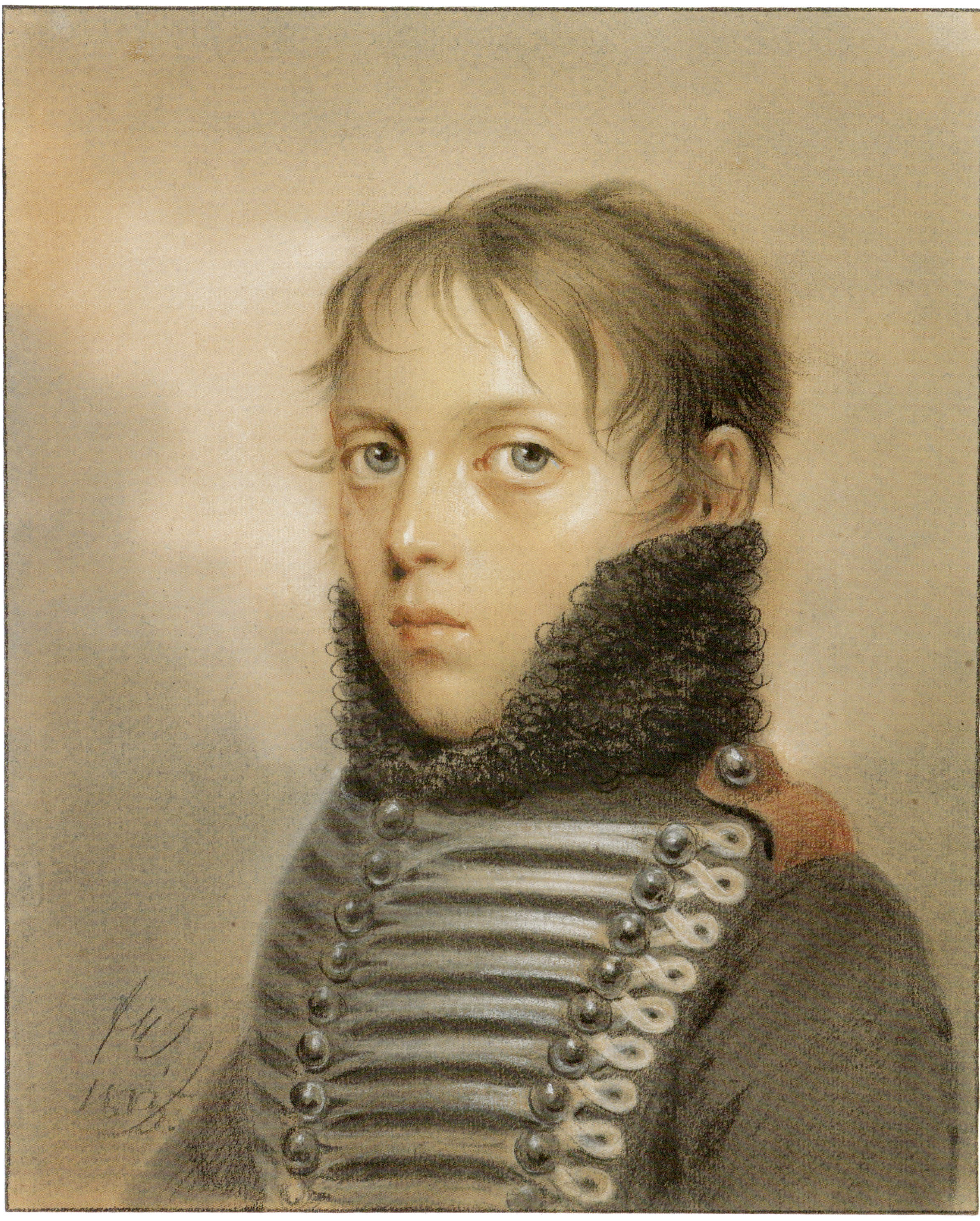

16

Johann Heinrich Wilhelm Tischbein

Haina 15 February 1751 – 26 June 1829 Eutin

The Miracle of Blossoms, after 1813

*Pen and black and brown ink over pencil, watercolor,
on laid paper; watermark: C & 1H, on the lower side of
the sheet: C & 1 Honig with beehive, framed by sprays;
219 x 345/50 mm
Inscribed in pen and brown-black ink, lower left:
"Ernestine Tischbein"
Inscription on the verso of the sheet, which has been folded
backward, in the artist's hand in pen and brown ink:*
*1 "Als die Franzosen die umliegenden Gärten von Ham-
burg zerstörten, die schönen Obstbäume derselben im Winter umhauten und so liegen liessen, schlugen einige im
Frühjahr doch Laub und trieben Früchte. Es soll sogar ein
Besitzer von einem Kirschbaume, der noch ein wenig mit
der Borke am Stumpfe sass, Kirschen gegessen haben.
Flor² sagte mir, dass in seinem Garten ein, im Winter
abgehauener Siringenbaum im Frühjahr reichliche
Blüthen getrieben habe; und unter dem Schutte der zerstörten Gebäude, blüheten die, in den Gartenhäusern gezo-
genen ausländischen Gewächse hervor; sogar in dem Kothe
des Fuhrweges, wo das Vieh darauf trat sah man die sel-
tensten ausländischen Blumen. So kräftig strebt die Natur
das Schöne wieder hervorzubringen. —Sollten die
deutschen Geistes-Treibhäuser, und die schönen Geister
die unter die Füsse getreten wurden auch wohl wie diese
mit den Zeiten wieder aufblühen? Es geht ihnen wie jenen,
die innere Kraft treibt öfters noch Blüthen, hin und wieder
auch wohl noch eine Frucht."
2 "Was in ruhigen Zeiten erlernt ist, treibt noch schwache
Blüthen und möchte gerne noch Früchte tragen."
3 "Der schöne Tod.
Du nährender Freund warst gütig im Leben und bist
schön, selbst im Tode. Dein Mörder war scheuslich im
Leben und bleibt es auch im Tode."*

Provenance: Legationsrat von Zehender, Oldenburg

*Bibliography: Geller 1955, pp. 8–10, fig. 2; Munich 1958,
p. 58, no. 167*

Wilhelm Tischbein the draftsman repeatedly
returned to depicting scenes from the French
Revolution, Napoleon's occupation of Germany,
and the Wars of Liberation in his work.[3] He
made no secret of his patriotic feelings. After all,
he had been threatened by the French more than
once: in 1799 when they took Naples, in 1806
when they occupied Hamburg, and in 1811 when
they drove his new patron, Duke Peter of Oldenburg, into exile in St. Petersburg.
Tischbein was inclined to interpret such historical events as well as everyday occurrences as
imbued with profound meaning. He liked to
illustrate his thoughts on folded sheets of hand-
made letter paper; on the verso he would write
explanations. The present watercolor is based on
a historical event from the period of the Wars of
Liberation.
The French occupied Hamburg in November of
1806, and two months later, Napoleon imposed
the Continental Blockade against England, with
disastrous consequences for Hamburg's economy,
which relied on trade. In 1811, the French marshal Louis Nicholas Davout began his reign of
terror in Hamburg, which had been incorporated
into the French Empire. In May of 1813, two
months after the city had been briefly liberated
by Russian soldiers under the command of
Colonel Tettenborn, Davout reoccupied it and
proclaimed a state of siege. To create a clear line
of fire, he ordered that all houses in a wide swath
around the fortified city be razed and all trees cut
down.
Tischbein's watercolor alludes to these events.
Under a dark and gloomy sky, we can make out
the ruins of destroyed houses in the background
and a wasteland as far as the eye can see. In the
foreground, the blossoming branches of a felled
fruit tree and a woman's head, bathed in sunlight, stand out brightly against the dull-colored
background. The effect of a brilliant white in her
head and in the blossoms was not achieved
through the application of color, but by reserving
areas of the paper. The woman, shown in profile,
stands before the magnificent blossoms on the
central vertical axis of the picture; with her head
lowered and her arms folded below her chest, she
appears deeply absorbed in thought. Tischbein
projected his own naive amazement at this miracle of nature and his own melancholic reflections
on its more profound meaning onto the figure of
the standing woman, much as Caspar David
Friedrich projected the experience of the landscape onto the figures that stand with their backs
to the viewer in his pictures. The tree that was
cut down in the winter of 1813[4] and yet sprouted
blossoms in the spring of 1814 symbolized the fall
of the fatherland at the hands of Napoleon, and
faith in its resurrection. Tischbein used the same
motif in the lower right corner of his large historical painting *General von Bennigsen and His
Staff,* which he executed in 1816 on commission
from the Hamburg Senate in remembrance of the
liberator of Hamburg and victor at the Battle of
Leipzig.[5] The watercolor was presumably created
in the spring of 1814, in response to events of
immediate relevance. Its thematic context and,
therefore, likely chronological proximity to the
Bennigsen picture support this view. It is conceivable that Tischbein, in direct response to
events, sketched out the sheet in pencil and later,
in the 1820s, worked it up into a finished watercolor. Since he frequently finished in old age
works he had begun in his earlier years—*The
Idylls,* for example—it is difficult to establish a
chronology of his drawings, especially since he
had developed his characteristic touch early on.
On the basis of the watercolor's inscription,
Tischbein's daughter Ernestine, born in 1806,
has previously been identified as the standing
female figure; in 1814 she would have been eight
years old; in 1829, the year of Tischbein's death,
she would have been twenty-two. The close
stylistic similarity to Tischbein's 1822 portrait of
her younger sister Angelika may indicate that he
depicted Ernestine here at the age of sixteen
years.[6] But in light of the fact that Tischbein
depicted a mature woman "wearing a bonnet"
(i.e. married), it is more likely that we are looking at his wife, Anna Martha Ketting,[7] whom he
married in 1806 when she was pregnant with
Ernestine. The inscription "Ernestine Tischbein"
below the branch of blossoms and the sentence at
the end of the first paragraph on the verso are
obviously allusions to this circumstance.

1 1. [When the French destroyed the gardens surrounding
Hamburg, cutting down their beautiful fruit trees in the
winter and leaving them where they fell, some of them
still sprouted leaves and fruit in the spring. It is even said
that one owner of a cherry tree, which was still barely
attached to the stump with a little bark, ate some cherries.
Flor (see n. 105) told me that a lilac tree in his garden,
which had been chopped down in the winter, sprouted
plenty of blossoms in the spring, and under the rubble of
the destroyed buildings there bloomed the foreign plants
that had been raised in the greenhouses; even in the drop-
pings on the carriage roads, where the animals stepped,
one saw the strangest foreign flowers. With such energy
does nature strive to bring forth beauty once again. Could
it be that the German greenhouses of the spirit and the
beautiful spirits that are being trampled underfoot should
also bloom again in time? They are like the plants, the
inner power frequently brings forth blossoms, and now
and then no doubt also a fruit.]
2. [What was learned in peaceful times is still bringing
forth weak blossoms and still wants to bear fruit.]
3. [A beautiful death.
You nourishing friend, you were kind in life and are beautiful even in death. Your murderer was horrid in life and
remains such even in death.]
2 "Flor" was the Hamburg portraitist Ferdinand Flor
(1793–1881), who had gone through his first training
with Tischbein in Eutin; cf. Geller 1955, p. 10.
3 Cf. Hermann Mildenberger, "Johann Heinrich Wilhelm
Tischbein (1751–1829). Historienmalerei und niedere
Bildgattungen vereint im Dienste monarchischer Restau-
ration," *Idea* 8 (1989): pp. 75–94, 79, 89; Hinrich
Sieveking, "Undeutliche Striche—erste Gedanken. Zu
bisher unveröffentlichten Zeichnungen Johann Heinrich
Wilhelm Tischbeins," *Kunst und Antiquitäten* 5 (1994):
pp 28 ff., fig. 1.
4 Cf. Warnke 1992, pp. 148 ff., figs. 146, 147.
5 General von Bennigsen's entry into Hamburg on 31 May
1814, painted 1816; oil on canvas, 350 x 538 mm; Hamburg,
Kunsthalle (depot); Landsberger 1908, no. 150.
6 Oil on canvas, 191 x 122 mm; Hamburg, Kunsthalle; Landsberger 1908, no. 172, repr. following p. 152.
7 No doubt in consideration of his imminent employment as
court painter to the duke of Oldenburg, Tischbein decided
to marry the daughter of a childhood friend.

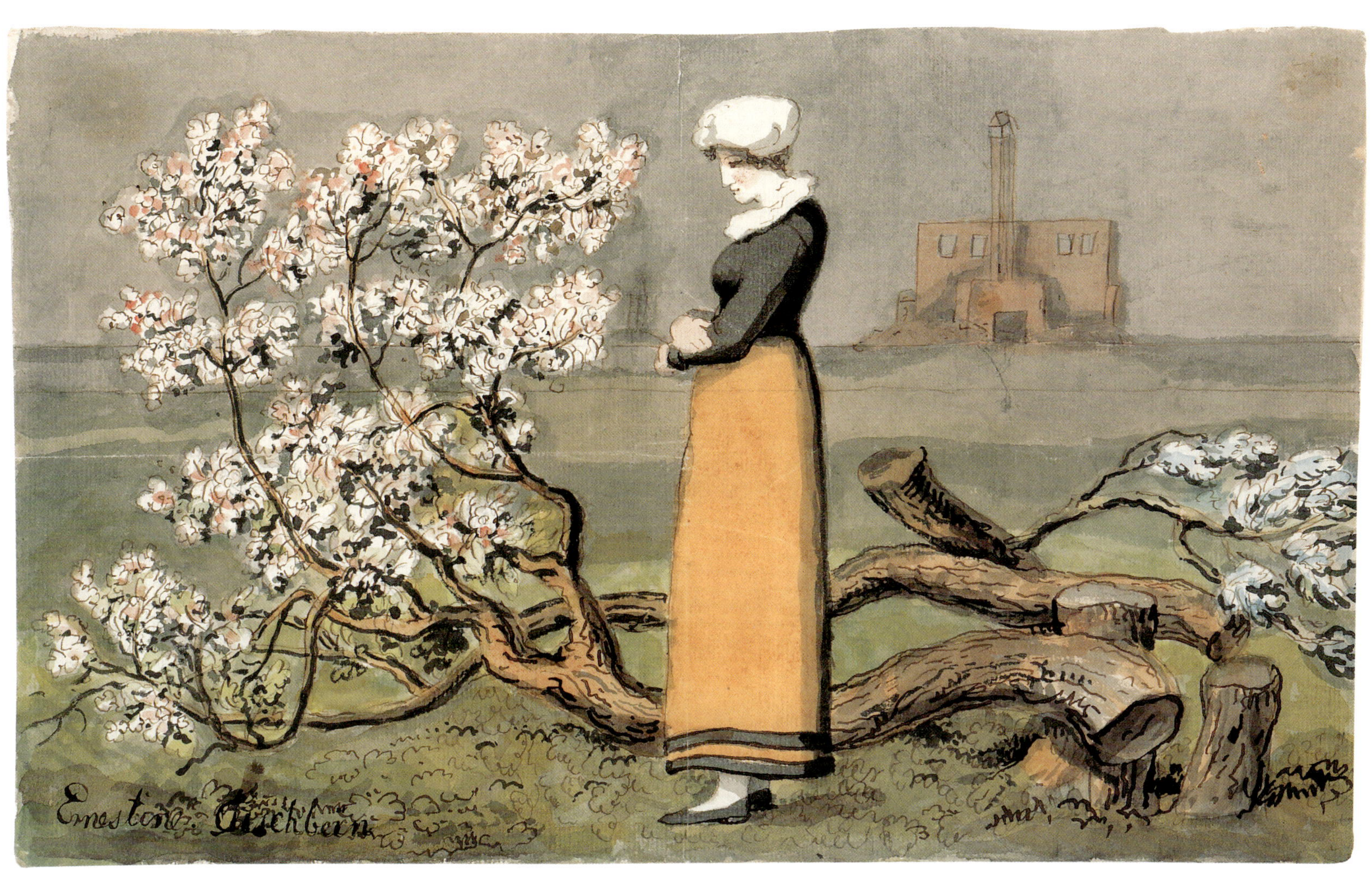

Ernestine Schickhardt

17

Philipp Otto Runge

Wolgast 23 July 1777 – 2 December 1810 Hamburg

Rose, Thistle, Pear

Découpages, white laid paper, laid down on their old mount of blue laid paper; 325 x 397 mm

Provenance: Estate of Otto Speckter, Hamburg; Marie-Luise Sieveking, née Duncker (granddaughter of Otto Speckter), Hamburg; Ludwigsgalerie, Munich

Bibliography: Munich 1958, p. 51, no. 147.a; Lübeck 1969, p. 81, no. 161.a; Cornelia Richter, Philipp Otto Runge: Ich weiss eine schöne Blume: Werkverzeichnis der Scheren-schnitte *(Munich, 1981), p. 133, no. 168*

In its essential characteristics—reduction to a single color and pure outline—découpage overlaps with basic artistic trends of the period around 1800, the era of Neoclassicism and Romanticism.

The découpage, or silhouette, signified a fundamental creative principle in Runge's work. He developed his pictorial ideas and concept of space out of the flat surface and the contrast of light

Philipp Otto Runge, *Cornflowers and Lilies of the Valley*, c. 1804–06. Folded paper découpage, white laid paper, laid down on the old mount of laid paper, toned with black wash; 411/13 x 320 mm

and dark. The contour line has an essential place in his oeuvre. Insofar as they exhibit these characteristics, the three works presented here (cat. 17–19) are intimately and profoundly related.

Runge devoted himself to découpage from his early childhood, and he continued to practice this art form throughout his artistic life. He created a wealth of highly decorative plant and flower cut-outs, also using the folded-cut technique, in which the paper is folded over one or more times (fig.). These silhouettes also served practical purposes (for example, as decorations for lamp shades or as wall ornaments in the manner of classicistic lotus-palmette friezes [see cat. 57]). Runge, who used to cut playfully and, as the occasion arose, with great ease and confidence, was also thinking of using découpages as a source of income and a means of shaping public taste through broader circulation. In 1803, he met Johann Heinrich Wilhelm Tischbein in Hamburg. They shared an interest in the applied arts and made plans to set up a school to promote craftsmanship, with workshops in which elements for interior decoration would be mass-produced after the designs of both men and sold commercially. Runge considered using his cut-outs with plant motifs in this enterprise, but his early death in 1810 put an end to the project.

In his individual plant cut-outs, Runge was able to capture the natural and living image of a flower. He also combined its structure and disposition with a nearly heraldic abstraction, which seems to impart to the individual plant the primeval character of its genus. Drawing on a knowledge of the internal geometry of the plants, his découpages show objectified primal specimens. Even in his most humble cut-outs a higher meaning occasionally resonates. For instance, the viewer can watch the processes of growth and decay in nature through several stages of plant development on a single stem or branch, from the blossom to the fruit (here, for example, the bud and flower of a rose). In the cut-outs exhibited here, Runge depicted the rose, thistle, and pear in blossom. It was surely in nature's blooming that Runge saw its great mystery most clearly revealed.

Runge's art of découpage was widely popular. Goethe, who had asked for some cut-outs for room decorations and was given a few as a present, felt transported into a pleasant state when looking at them.

Karl August Varnhagen von Ense called the "quiet art" of découpage a "splendid substitute for sculpture"; of Runge's cut-outs, which he had never seen but knew from descriptions, he said, "We must count them among the best, and perhaps they are the only works in which a higher meaning has indeed been expressed in these delicate carvings. There can only be unanimity about this fairy-tale painter's taste, about the profundity, richness, and loveliness of his thoughts. But his cut-outs are in larger formats, and therefore less artistic and difficult."[1]

1 Karl August Varnhagen von Ense, "Vom Ausschneiden," first printed in *Morgenblatt für die gebildeten Stände* 9 (9 March 1814): 229–31; reprinted in *Werke*, vol. 4: *Biographien, Aufsätze, Skizzen, Fragmente*, ed. Konrad Feilchenfeldt and Ursula Wiedenmann (Frankfurt am Main, 1990), pp. 384, 387. I am grateful to Konrad Feilchenfeldt, Munich, for calling my attention to this essay.

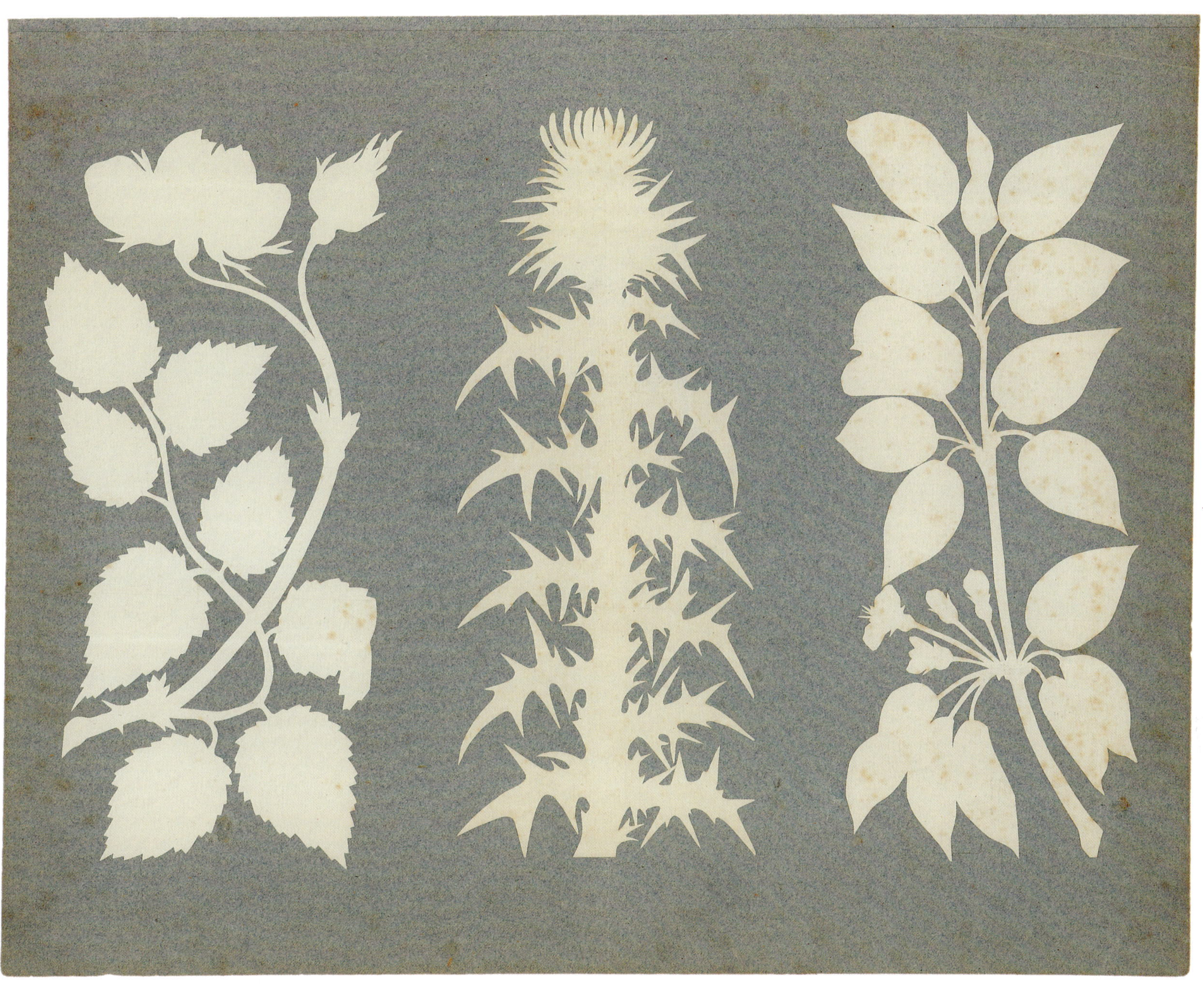

18

Philipp Otto Runge

View from a Window over the Alster River,
1805

Black wash over pencil, on laid paper; watermark:
J . H O N I G / & / Z O O N E N and a decoratively
framed beehive coat of arms/J. H. & Z; 434 x 311 mm
Inscribed on the verso by Daniel Runge, in pen and black
ink: "Original von Philipp Otto Runge 1805"

Provenance: Felicie Runge, Berlin

Bibliography: C. G. Boerner, 199th Auction, 25 May 1938
(Leipzig), p. 12, no. 101; Christian Adolf Isermeyer, Philipp
Otto Runge (Berlin, 1940), p. 128, no. 33/2; Munich 1958,
p. 51, no. 145, fig. 2; Lankheit 1959, p. 65; Marcel Brion,
Kunst der Romantik (Munich and Zurich, 1960), p. 55,
fig. 16; Gunnar Berefelt, Philipp Otto Runge zwischen
Aufbruch und Opposition 1777–1802 (Stockholm, Göte-
borg, and Uppsala, 1961), p. 138, n. 3; Lübeck 1969, p. 81,
no. 160; Traeger 1975, pp. 91, 149, 376, no. 309 (repr.); Ham-
burg 1977, pp. 231f., 234f. (repr.), no. 227 (Hanna Hohl);
Jensen 1978, p. 183, no. 82, fig. 26

The circle of Daniel and Philipp Otto Runge's
closest friends, whose minds were open to literature and the arts, included the distinguished publisher Friedrich Perthes in Hamburg. He was
married to Caroline Claudius, the daughter of
the poet Matthias Claudius (also known as the
"Wandsbecker Bote," or "herald of Wandsbeck").
On 10 January 1802, Caroline gave birth to their
second daughter, Luise Perthes, who later lived

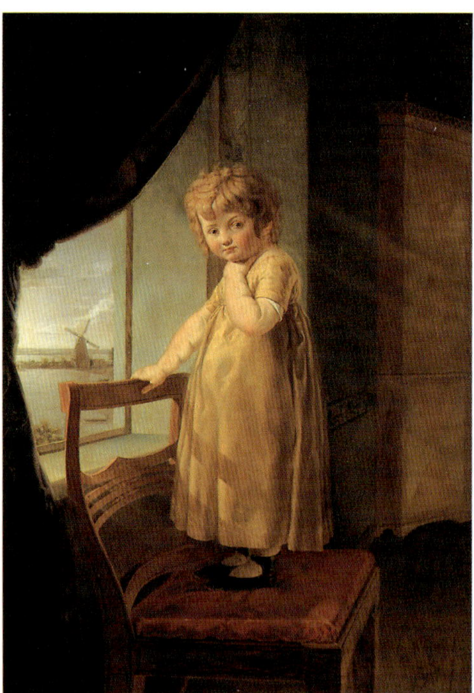

Philipp Otto Runge, *The Little Perthes Girl*, 1805. Oil on
canvas; 1435 x 950mm. Weimar, Kunstsammlungen zu
Weimar, inv. no. G.948

in Gotha under her married name, Agricola. In
1805, Runge painted a portrait of Luise, not yet
four years old, for his friend Friedrich Perthes;
Daniel Runge, Philipp Otto's brother, called it a
"composed portrait" (that is, a likeness which, by
incorporating the environment, surpasses the pure
portrait and conveys a general allegorical meaning).[1] That same year, Runge painted a number
of his most important portraits of this type: in the
spring and summer his masterpiece, *We Three,*
which was burned in the Munich Glaspalast fire,
and in the fall and winter his preeminent children's portrait, *The Hülsenbeck Children.* Between these two works he painted *The Little*
Perthes Girl (fig.), for which three preliminary
drawings are known: a head study, which is lost,
a full-length graphite study of the girl in Berlin,
and the present wash drawing of the view from
the window.[2]

Runge painted little Luise Perthes in her parents' home at the Jungfernstieg in Hamburg.
The view from the window sweeps across the
Inner and Outer Alster River to the Lombard
Bridge and the windmill at the city walls, and on
into the rural outskirts. Luise has climbed a chair
to look out onto the landscape, but she turns her
head somewhat self-consciously toward the painter and viewer. Standing on the soft cushion without firm footing, she reaches with her chubby
right arm to steady herself on the back of the
chair. She holds her left arm inquiringly under
her large, strangely mature head and gazes pen-
sively, a playful variant of the gesture signifying
melancholy. Her yellow empire dress is aglow in
the golden light of what we recognize through
our knowledge of the topographical setting as the
morning sun. The girl herself seems to reflect a
golden radiance, receiving sunlight and passing
it on like another source of light. The depiction
of a child in the morning sun recalls the subject
of *Morning* in the cycle entitled *Four Times of*
Day, the central theme in Runge's oeuvre. According to Daniel Runge, in August 1805—that is,
while he was working on *The Little Perthes*
Girl—Philipp Otto began work on the painting
Rest on the Flight into Egypt, "because it was to
have a close affinity to his *Morning,* which would
have to be the first among his *Times of Day.*"[3]
The color gold also played a role for Runge in
connection with the cycle of the *Times.* After finishing the drawings, he thought about painting
the entire series in large format against a gold
ground color. Only a single experiment with the
central group, the *Caritas of Midday* from the
painting *Day,* has survived.[4] In addition to its
inherent meaning as a symbol of light, the gold
ground was also supposed to make the colors
superimposed on it radiate from within.[5] In the
portrait of Luise Perthes, the image of a child in
a golden dress also carries a symbolic meaning:
namely, proximity to the original state of Par-

adise. The child, like the flower, is a leitmotif
and guiding symbol in Runge's oeuvre. Börsch-
Supan has interpreted the portrait's interior setting as representative of the safety and security of
the parents' home, the view into the landscape
outside as a view into the world and the future,
and the river with boats as an emblem of life.[6]
The drawing in black wash exhibited here prepares only one area of the finished painting: the
curtain, the back of the chair, and the window
jamb frame the view into the landscape, which is
rendered as a pencil sketch of the topographical
setting, like a picture within the picture. However, the compositional principle of the entire
painting is adumbrated in the light-dark contrast
of the study: from the interior's dark frame to the
luminous inner motif with the child at the center,
and the view of the landscape. Runge developed
his spatial ideas from the surface, the silhouette.
He subsequently used this "découpé" or "silhouette" principle in the preparatory work for his
painting *Rest on the Flight into Egypt,* specifically in his study in gray wash of the landscape of
the Nile valley.[7] The polarity of light and dark
also recalls Runge's preoccupation with the poles
of black and white in his color sphere. Beginning
in 1804, leading up to the transformation of the
drawings for the *Times* cycle into paintings,
Runge gave a lot of thought to color theory.

The painting of Luise reflects the milieu of the
educated bourgeoisie. It is reminiscent of the
middle-class world of seventeenth-century Holland, which was captured in interior portraits,
such as Rembrandt's 1647 dry-point of Jan Six,
who is standing in a window below a pulled-back
curtain (B.285). While the painting alludes to
these seventeenth-century models, a tradition
that had been revived at the end of the eighteenth century (cf. essay "From Fuseli to Menzel," fig. 1), in its abstraction, the wash drawing
points ahead to Edvard Munch's expressionist-
symbolic etchings *Girl in a Shirt at the Window*
(1894) and *Night at St. Cloud* (1895).[8]

1 Cf. Hamburg 1977, p. 231 (Hanna Hohl).

2 Traeger 1975, pp. 375f., nos. 307–9.

3 Quoted in Traeger 1975, p. 382, nos. 316–22. Runge called
his *Rest on the Flight* the "morning of the East," and associated it with the painting *Source and Poet,* which he
called "evening of the West"; Traeger 1977, p. 108, no. 17.

4 Traeger 1975, p. 362, no. 285, color pl. 6.

5 *Ibid.,* p. 82, no. 4.

6 Börsch-Supan 1972, p. 27.

7 The tree silhouette in the left foreground of the study,
for example, was transformed in the painting into the figures of Joseph and the donkey; cf. Traeger 1975, pp. 384f.,
no. 320 (repr., and p. 386, no. 322, color pl. 10). Koerner
believes that the transformation occurred the other way
around: Koerner 1990, pp. 156f., figs. 68, 69.

8 Cf. Schmoll 1970, p. 55 (fig. 80), p. 76 (fig. 112).

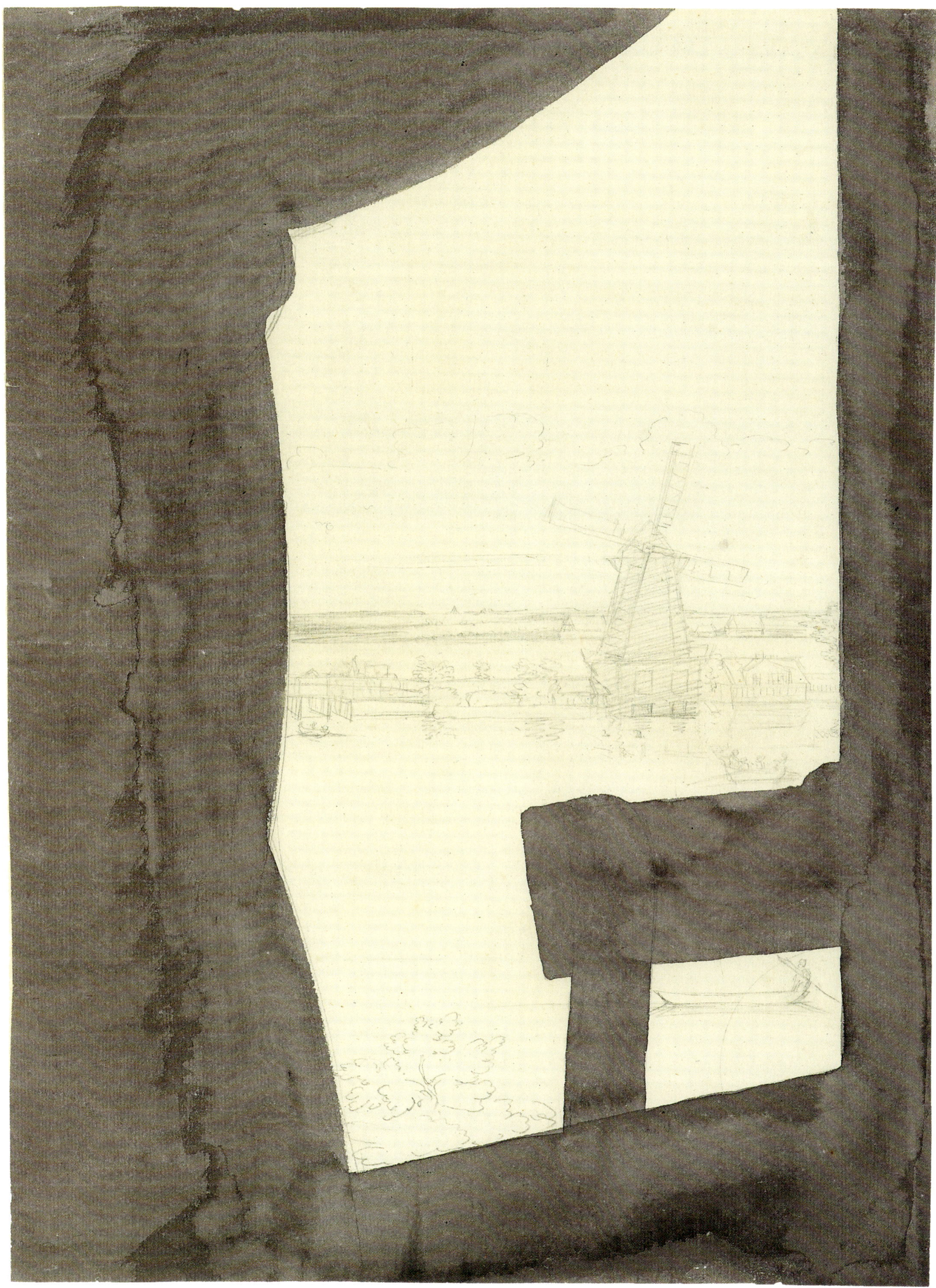

19

Philipp Otto Runge

Lily Blossoms, c. 1808

*Pen and black ink over pencil, on laid paper; watermark:
D & C. BLAUW (trimmed); trimmed on all sides;
327/30 x 253/58 mm
Verso: pencil study of broad leaves (fig. 1); inscribed in pen
and gray ink by Daniel Runge: "PORunge"*

*Provenance: Otto Sigismund Runge, estate of the artist;
Künstlerverein, Hamburg*

Bibliography: Philipp Otto Runge, Hinterlassene Schriften,
ed. Daniel Runge, 2 vols. (Hamburg, 1840–41), vol. 1,
p. 237; Stephan Waetzoldt, "Philipp Otto Runges 'Vier
Zeiten'" (Ph.D. diss., Hamburg, 1951), pp. 127, 144, n. 348,
fig. 47; Hamburg 1969, p. 285 (under no. 3.k.); Spring
Exhibition 1935 of the Hamburg Künstlerverein in the
Kunstverein Hamburg, 6 April to 5 May 1935, exh. cat.,
p. 8, no. 112; C. G. Boerner, 195th Auction, Neuere deutsche
Handzeichnungen: Neun Originalzeichnungen von
Philipp Otto Runge, 19 June 1937, auction cat. (Leipzig),
p. 17, no. 185, pl. 4 (repr.); Traeger 1975, p. 429, no. 399,
p. 427 (repr.)

Around 1800, the abstracting contour line had
established itself internationally as the characteristic drawing technique of Neoclassicism. It
derived from Classical Greek vase painting,
which had been popularized by the excavations
at Pompeii and Herculaneum, and by publications such as Johann Heinrich Wilhelm Tischbein's copies after Greek vases in the Hamilton
collection, published in Naples starting in 1790.
With his widely circulated outline illustrations
of the works of Homer and Dante, which began
to appear in 1793, the Englishman John Flaxman
did more than any other artist to promote the
technique of contour drawing.

Through personal contacts, Tischbein influenced
the younger generation of artists, including
Runge in Hamburg after 1803. Following awk-
ward beginnings, Runge had practiced drawing
with great effort prior to meeting Tischbein,
eventually developing such confidence and perfection that he attained the highest mastery in
outline drawing, as he did in découpage. In 1801,
he had participated unsuccessfully in Goethe's
classically oriented Weimar competition, but during the following years, he began to use the pure,
classicizing contour line in his studies and finished drawings for the *Four Times of Day* cycle.
The essence of Runge's artistic intent can be read
from this cycle of four abstract outline drawings.
They were reproduced in engravings, and Runge
planned to convert them into paintings and
eventually into monumental murals in an architectural setting specifically constructed for this
purpose. It is within the context of the great
artistic complex of the *Times* cycle—the idea of a
total work of art—that we should also locate the
drawing exhibited here: a large-scale study of a
lily stem with flowers and buds, executed in outline with great precision in pen over pencil, with
leaf studies on the verso (fig. 1). It is intended to
reproduce the momentary natural state of the
plant as well as capture its general and regular
features: the budding, blossoming, and falling of
the petals, with the free-standing pistils left
behind. In this drawing, Runge was also concerned "to highlight especially the plant's sexual
characteristics."[1] In contrast to the even, neu-

tral classicizing line of Flaxman, for example,
Runge's dynamic, swelling and receding line lets
us feel something of the organic life of the plant
and of the forces of nature.

The lily was undoubtedly the plant most heavily
imbued with symbolic meaning in Runge's treasury of forms; he made numerous studies of it
(fig. 2). The white lily is an ancient Christian
symbol of purity and innocence. As a symbol of
divine light, it assumes the role of the spiritual
center in the *Four Times of Day* cycle.[2] Once
again, there are hints of the polarity of light and
darkness in Runge's intellectual and spiritual
edifice (cf. cat. 18).

Judging from its format, our study belongs to the
later group of drawings that may have been
intended as models for translation into a painted
version of *Morning*, or into other paintings
planned in this context, or possibly even for the
murals planned for the future. It has also been
seen as a direct study for a lily stem in the painting *Morning (Small Version)*.[3]

1 *Philipp Otto Runge, Hinterlassene Schriften* (Hamburg,
1840–41), p. 240.
2 Traeger 1977, p. 152, no. 37.
3 Hamburg 1969, p. 285, under no. 3.k.

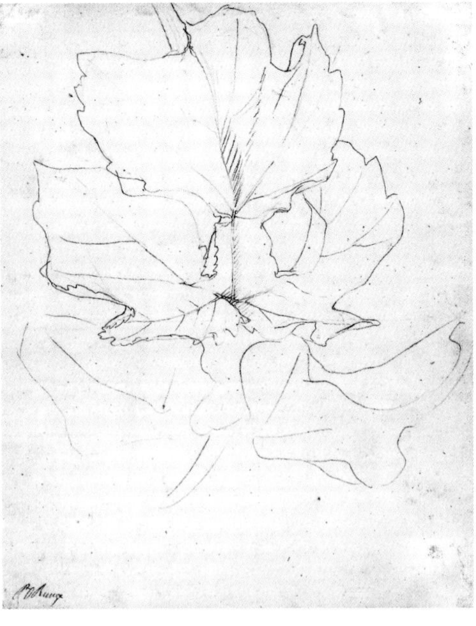

1 Verso: *Leaf Studies*, c. 1808. Pencil

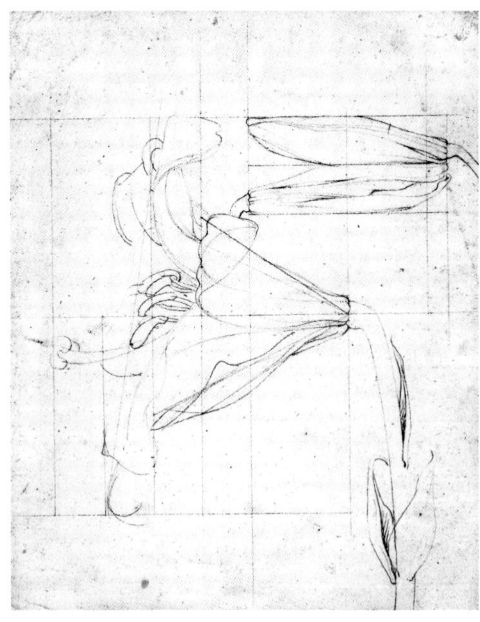

2 Philipp Otto Runge, *Lily Blossom and Bud*, c. 1807.
Pencil, 298 x 235 mm

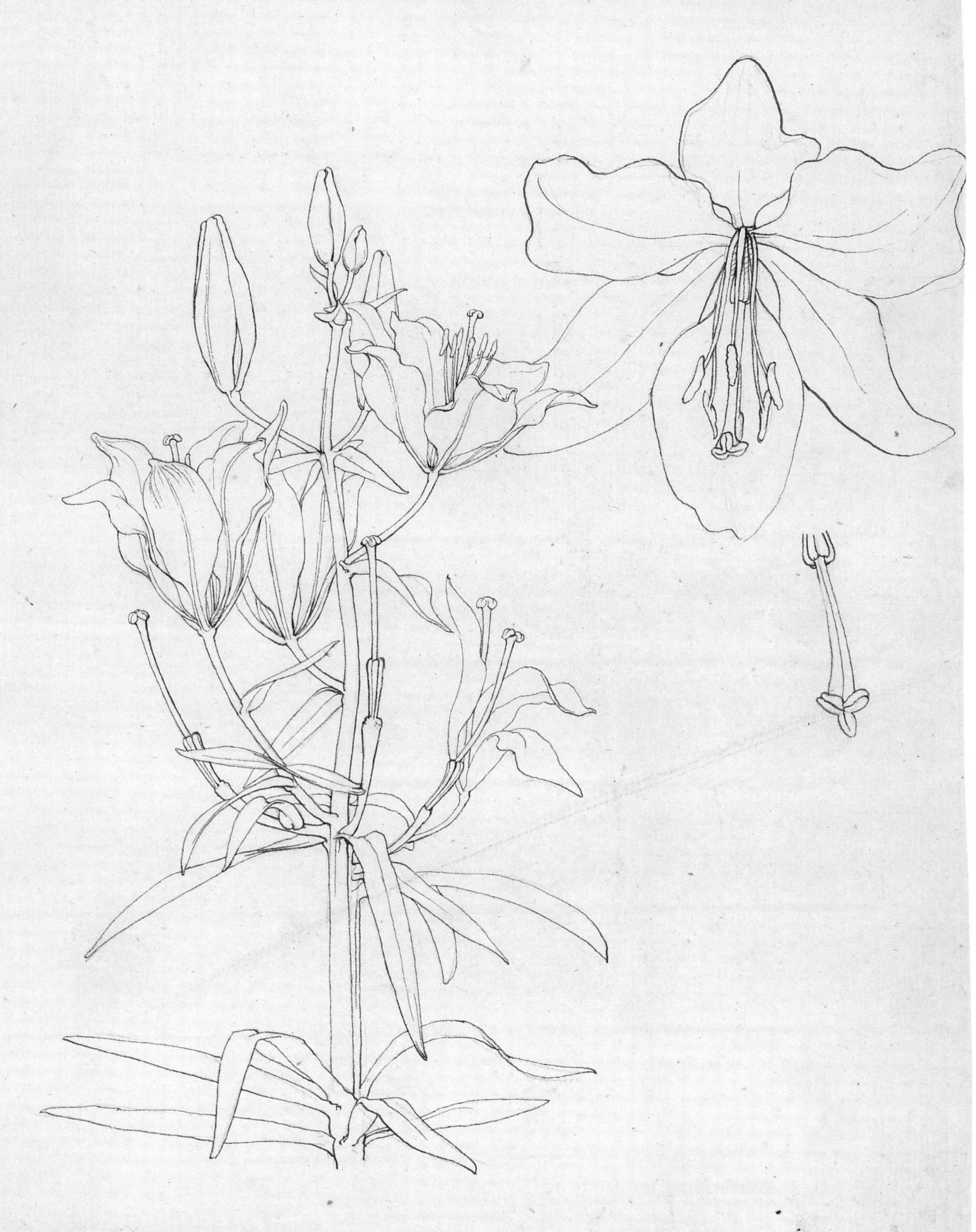

20

Caspar David Friedrich

Greifswald 5 September 1774 – 7 May 1840 Dresden

Portrait of the Artist's Brother Christian Friedrich, 1801/02

Black chalk on thin wove paper, upper left corner restored; 235 x 185 mm

Provenance: The artist's descendants; Ludwigsgalerie, Munich

Selected bibliography: Kurt Wilhelm-Kästner, Ludwig Rohling, and Karl Friedrich Degner, Caspar David Friedrich und seine Heimat (Berlin, 1940), pp. 35, 65, no. 9, p. 35, no. 8 (repr.); Kurt Karl Eberlein, Caspar David Friedrich, der Landschaftsmaler: Ein Volksbuch deutscher Kunst (Bielefeld and Leipzig, 1940), pp. 21, 67, no. 13 (repr.); Winterthur 1955, p. 58, no. 243; Lübeck 1957, p. 13, no. 35; Munich 1958, p. 27, no. 39, fig. 3; Gert von der Osten, "Kleine Gemäldestudien II: Caspar David Friedrichs Bildnis eines älteren Mannes," Niederdeutsche Beiträge zur Kunstgeschichte 1 (1961): 276–83, 282f., fig. 220; Heidelberg 1964, p. 52, no. 152; Hinz 1966, no. 71; Lübeck 1969, pp. 34f., no. 46 (repr.); Sumowski 1970, pp. 46, 51, 176; Börsch-Supan and Jähnig 1973, p. 260, no. 67 (repr.); London-Tate 1972, p. 56, no. 14; Bernhard 1974, p. 338 (repr.); Bernhard (Hinz) 1974, p. 60 (repr.); Hamburg 1974, p. 117, no. 9 (repr.); Jensen 1974, p. 17, fig. 4; Paris 1984, p. 174, no. 123 (repr.)

There are few portraits from the hand of Caspar David Friedrich, and they all belong to his early work: a few paintings, nine self-portraits, and about fifteen portraits exclusively of family members or persons close to him that he drew circa 1801/02 or circa 1806.[1] Friedrich spent the period from the beginning of March 1801 to the end of July 1802 at his family home in his native city of Greifswald, having returned from Dresden via Neubrandenburg. During this time, he displayed his extraordinary talent in very different ways in works that employ a variety of graphic techniques. It was here that he evidently created the family portraits in rapid succession, executing them in black chalk in the crayon manner, the technique used in the present likeness of his youngest brother, Christian Friedrich. He modeled the faces with delicate gradations of light and, in striking contrast, drew the clothing in broad, parallel hatchings that follow the shape of the body—as though patterned with alternating black and white stripes—against a neutral background summarily evoked with crosshatching. This chalk technique, which models the figures in the round, reflects the drawing tradition of the Copenhagen Academy, which aimed at achieving painterly effects. Consequently, in the literature prior to the publications of Börsch-Supan and Jähnig, this portrait was dated to the period around 1798, when Friedrich left the Copenhagen Academy, especially since its style is

very closely related to that of the entire group of family portraits. The purest example of this group is the portrait of Ernst Theodor Johann Brückner.[2] It has also been dated to 1798, because Friedrich inscribed his name in the family album of Brückner's daughter Margarete during a visit to the Brückner household in Neubrandenburg on August 7th of that year. However, Friedrich's older brother Adolf married Margarete Brückner on 13 November 1801, thus establishing ties of kinship, so it is more likely that Brückner's portrait was completed later than 1798, perhaps on the occasion of the wedding.

Moreover, in their style and touch, this series of family portraits shows a development beyond the academic character of Friedrich's drawing in 1798, and a higher degree of artistic maturity. Börsch-Supan, arguing from "a more consistent system in the handling of the line," convincingly assigns these portraits—including the present example—to 1801/02.[3]

Christian Joachim Friedrich (1779–1843), the painter's youngest brother and closest to him among the siblings artistically and personally, was *Amtsmeister* and alderman of the joiners' guild in Greifswald. He worked primarily as a wood carver.[4] Making woodcuts was something he probably did only occasionally, at first primarily for his brother Caspar David, who did not employ this technique himself but may have wanted to provide his brother with a chance to broaden his professional opportunities. At that time, the art of xylography had fallen into obscurity in Germany; during these same years, Johann Christoph Gubitz in Berlin was making the first efforts to revive it, following the leading English wood engraver, Thomas Bewick. From letters to his brother, we know that Caspar David gave Christian careful technical instructions: how to work either along or against the grain by using the burin, and details about paper, printing, and impressions. Christian Friedrich showed he had the sensitivity as a woodcutter to feel his way into his brother's artistic intention.[5] Four woodcuts, impressions of which are in the Winterstein collection, substantiate this assertion. One is a self-portrait; the other three, well known because of their symbolic content, are after drawings from the so-called Mannheim sketchbook: a boy sleeping on a grave mound, the *Woman with the Spider Web (Melancholy)*, and the *Woman with the Raven at the Abyss*. It has been repeatedly conjectured—and there is much to support this—that these images were intended as illustrations for a planned volume of Caspar David Friedrich's poems, with the self-portrait in profile possibly serving as an author portrait at the beginning of the book.[6] It was presumably Caspar David himself who developed his sketches into finished pen drawings on the woodblocks and prepared them for the wood engraver during

his Greifswald period, working from models he had created there. The characteristic changes between the sketches and the printed compositions provide clear evidence of this. His brother's careful cutting was then carried out during the following months, and in March 1804, the three allegorical woodcuts were shown at the Dresden Academy Exhibition.[7]

In the present portrait of his brother, Friedrich has turned the right half of the face further toward the viewer, a dialogic element that enlivens the image.[8] Drawn with an unadorned, lifelike truthfulness, the head is serious in its expression and imbued with a strong spiritual content; it is a landscape of the soul. In this and other portraits, Friedrich achieved a spiritualization of the human face, as did Philipp Otto Runge, whom he had met in Greifswald in 1801, around the same time. Although Caspar David Friedrich had a pronounced talent for portraiture, which might have brought him some income from his art, unlike Runge, he did not take advantage of it.

1 Börsch-Supan and Jähnig 1973, dated c. 1801/02: pp. 259–62, nos. 63–71; dated 1806: pp. 287–89, nos. 135–39, 141.

2 Ibid., pp. 259–62, nos. 63–71, Brückner portrait, p. 261, no. 68. Brückner was a pastor, poet, and member of the Göttingen Hainbund, a coterie of undergraduates interested in poetry, which existed from 1770 to 1774.

3 Ibid., pp. 259–62, nos. 63–71, 63.

4 For example, in the Nikolai Church in Greifswald, where he removed the Baroque additions from the organ, the pulpit, and the altar and restored them in the Gothic style.

5 Cf. Hans Zeeck, "Der Holzschneider Christian Friedrich," Gebrauchsgraphik 16 (Berlin, 1939): pp 17–21, and an expertise by Werner Sumowski (1996) of a newly discovered woodcut by Christian Friedrich, after a lost self-portrait drawing by Caspar David, now owned by Gallery H. W. Fichter, Frankfurt am Main.

6 Cf. Börsch-Supan and Jähnig 1973, pp. 257ff., nos. 60–62, p. 263, nos. 73, 74.

7 Ibid., p. 257, no. 60. Cf. Sumowski 1970, p. 138. Impressions are very rare; some of the woodblocks have been preserved.

8 Franz Pforr executed his painted self-portrait, now in the Städelsches Kunstinstitut und Städtische Galerie in Frankfurt am Main, in a similar way.

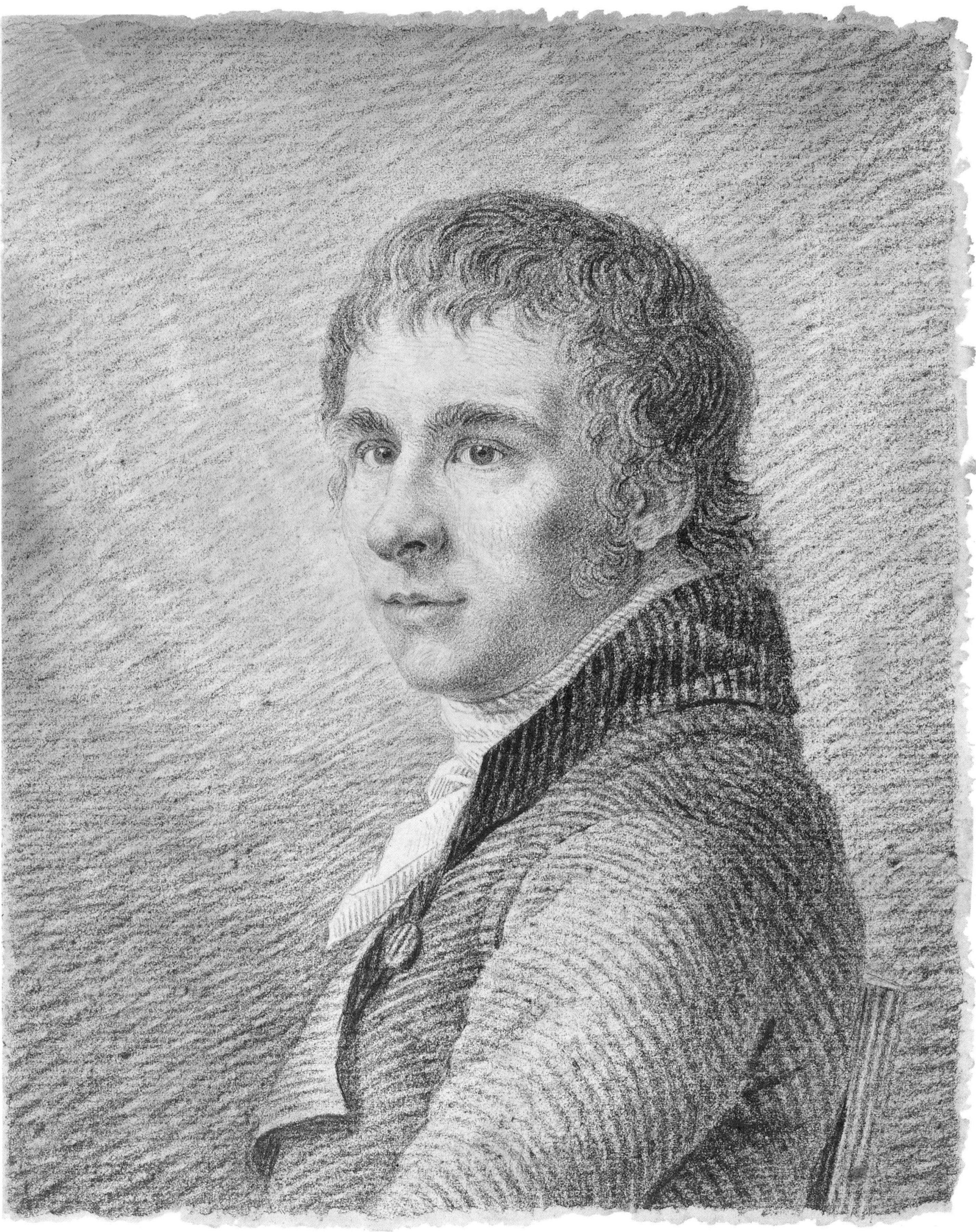

21

Caspar David Friedrich

The Source of the Elbe in the Riesengebirge,
c. 1830

Watercolor on wove paper; 250 x 344 mm

Provenance: Prince Johann Georg von Sachsen, Berlin; Galerie Paul Rusch, Dresden, 1924; Wurster, Berlin-Zehlendorf; Ludwigsgalerie, Munich

Selected bibliography: Günther Grundmann, Das Riesengebirge in der Malerei der Romantik (Breslau, 1931), pp. 85f., fig. 56; Munich 1958, p. 27, fig. 41, p. 9 (repr. in color); Hinz 1966, no. 544; Lübeck 1969, pp. 36f., no. 49 (repr. in color); Sumowski 1970, pp. 164, 241 (under no. 462); London-Tate 1972, p. 86, no. 96; Börsch-Supan and Jähnig 1973, pp. 422f., no. 386 (repr., with older literature); Bernhard (Hinz) 1974, p. 525 (repr.); Hamburg 1974, p. 286, no. 202 (repr.); Paris 1976, pp. 68f., no. 77 (repr.); Paris 1984, p. 287, fig. 261 (in color); Börsch-Supan 1987, pp. 196f., no. 63 (repr. in color); Koerner 1990, pp. 171, 253, no. 90 (repr. in color)

The scenic beauty and primal character of the Riesengebirge mountain range strongly attracted Dresden artists at the beginning of the nineteenth century.[1] Christoph Nathe's *Picturesque Wanderings through the Riesengebirge,* published in 1806, may have stimulated their interest. In the summer of 1810, Friedrich and his friend Georg Friedrich Kersting undertook a walking tour through the Riesengebirge, which is documented in detail in Friedrich's extant travel

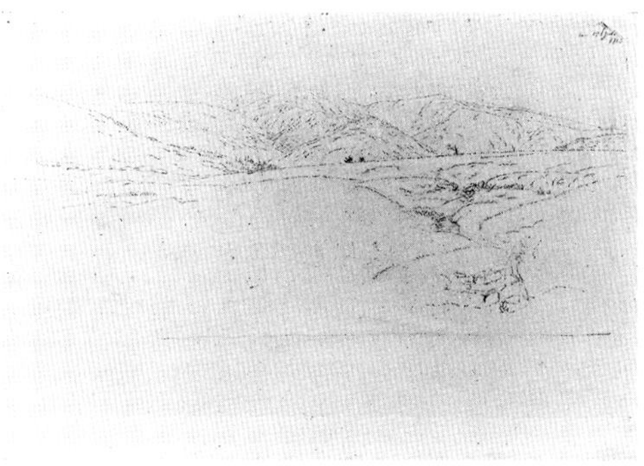

Caspar David Friedrich, *The Source of the Elbe in the Riesengebirge,* 10 July 1810. Pencil; 262 x 363 mm. Essen, Museum Folkwang

sketchbook.[2] In a high marshland in the western part of the mountains, at a height of 1,346 meters, lies a small brook that is the source of the Elbe. As it winds its way down to the North Sea, the Elbe passes the cities of Dresden and Hamburg and swells into a mighty river. On 10 July 1810, Friedrich made a pencil sketch of the view across the source of the Elbe and the meadow to the mountain chain in the background; from right to left we see the Planur, the Ziegenrücken, the Silberkamm and, towering above it, the Schnee-

koppe (fig.). The next day, the two hikers signed their names in the visitors' book at the summit of the Schneekoppe.

Considering how often Friedrich depicted the Riesengebirge, it may seem surprising that he made only one trip to these mountains. But that encounter left a deep impression; later, in the quiet of his studio, he drew upon the rich stock of motifs in the drawings he had made to create sepias, watercolors, and oil paintings. As he got older, Friedrich often returned to earlier nature studies. Starting from these studies, he created from his inner vision what he called "a free, spiritual reproduction of nature," thereby realizing his own maxim that a painter "should not paint only what he sees before him, but also what he sees within himself." In the present watercolor, he carefully and faithfully reproduced the topographical setting at the source of the Elbe from the pencil study; he only increased the relative height of the mountains.

An 1830 etched *veduta* by Friedrich August Tittel, a student of Adrian Zingg, shows the same view toward the east, with the source of the Elbe in the foreground along with the crumbling stone monuments that had been erected in remembrance of the visits by the Hapsburg archdukes Joseph and Rainer in 1804 and 1806, respectively. Tittel's work attests that the artistic discovery of the Riesengebirge had gone hand in hand with the development of tourism there.[3] Friedrich, by contrast, shows the sublimity of the landscape. Nothing suggests civilization or human intervention in the bare heights above the sparsely vegetated tree line. Solitude and desolation prevail in the wide expanse of nature. Faint morning light shimmers in a light haze on the mountain slopes, the silhouettes of which Friedrich rendered in a transparent manner. Friedrich reduced his staffage to a single hiker, his friend Kersting; with his left hand resting on his hiking stick, he pauses above the Elbe's source and reflects, in a posture that indicates profound meditation.[4] By placing the figure with his back toward us, Friedrich draws the viewer into the picture and encourages contemplation. The source is symbolic of life; brightly reflecting the sky, it disappears into the shady meadow. It is a picture of a solitary dialogue between the wanderer and the infinite. In the left background rises the highest peak, the Schneekoppe, and in the right lower foreground springs the Elbe. Both poles of this view are diagonal and refer to each other conceptually. With the most subtle treatment of light and color—from the dark lower edge of the picture to the bright upper edge—Friedrich, working in the medium of transparent watercolor, has achieved a transcendent quality that surpasses the *veduta.* Börsch-Supan surmises that Friedrich imbued the picture with allegorical meaning: the shaded foreground as a metaphor of the earthly

world with the river as the symbol of life, contrasting with the mountains illuminated by morning light as a metaphor of the hereafter.[5] On stylistic grounds, Sumowski and Börsch-Supan date the present watercolor to the period 1828–30.[6] This dating is also supported by its technical similarity to the watercolor that Friedrich contributed in 1828 to the album commemorating Dürer's three-hundredth birthday (cf. cat. 24), based on an earlier pencil study.[7]

A group of related watercolors of the same size with motifs from the Riesengebirge suggests that Friedrich was thinking of a cycle similar to that of Rügen landscapes, which would have preceded the painted Riesengebirge series from around 1830.[8] These sheets share a strong mood. Friedrich may have conceived them in the context of a cycle of the seasons and the times of day. What unites all the works is that they are simultaneously *vedute,* devotional images, and contemplative pictures.

The present watercolor and the pencil study are of special significance for two paintings with very similar landscapes. In *Morning Mist in the Riesengebirge* (1820; Munich, Neue Pinakothek), the same mountain range appears, but without the valley of the Elbe's source; it is also seen from a vantage point that is higher and shifted to the left, and dramatized by a fanciful higher mountain ridge in the distance that transforms the landscape into an Alpine vista. In a later painting, *Recollection of the Riesengebirge* (c. 1835; St. Petersburg, Hermitage), a variation of the Munich picture, Friedrich once again incorporated the Elbe's source as a way of imbuing the work with an allegorical meaning.[9]

1 Carl Gustav Carus (cf. cat. 72) traveled to the Riesengebirge in August of 1820; cf. Carl Gustav Carus, *Lebenserinnerungen und Denkwürdigkeiten,* new edition by Elmar Jansen (Weimar, 1966), vol. 1, p. 251.

2 Grundmann 1931, pp. 52, 68–72, 85.

3 Cf. *Das Riesengebirge in der Graphik des 18. und 19. Jahrhunderts,* exh. cat., Riesengebirgs-Museum (Marktoberdorf/Allgäu, 1993), pp. 36ff., nos. 83–87.

4 In the watercolor sketch *Boulders at the Kochel Fall* (Dresden, Kupferstichkabinett), he had depicted Kersting on 17 July in the same attire; cf. Grundmann 1931, p. 74, fig. 46. A work from this trip that has become well known is Kersting's rendering on 18 July 1810 of the wandering Caspar David Friedrich seen from the back; cf. Berlin 1994, p. 37, no. 21.

5 Börsch-Supan and Jähnig 1973, p. 422, no. 386.

6 Börsch-Supan sees a connection to the Riesengebirge watercolor *Recollection of Nollendorf Heights,* exhibited in Dresden in 1829, and points out that Friedrich did not exhibit any watercolors in Dresden before 1829; letter to the author, 14 March 1997. Börsch-Supan and Jähnig 1973, pp. 114 and 442, no. 368; Sumowski 1970, pp. 164f.

7 Mende and Hebecker 1973, pp. 74ff., no. 23.

8 Börsch-Supan and Jähnig 1973, nos. 385–88, 491–93.

9 *Ibid.,* pp. 442f., no. 418 (repr.).

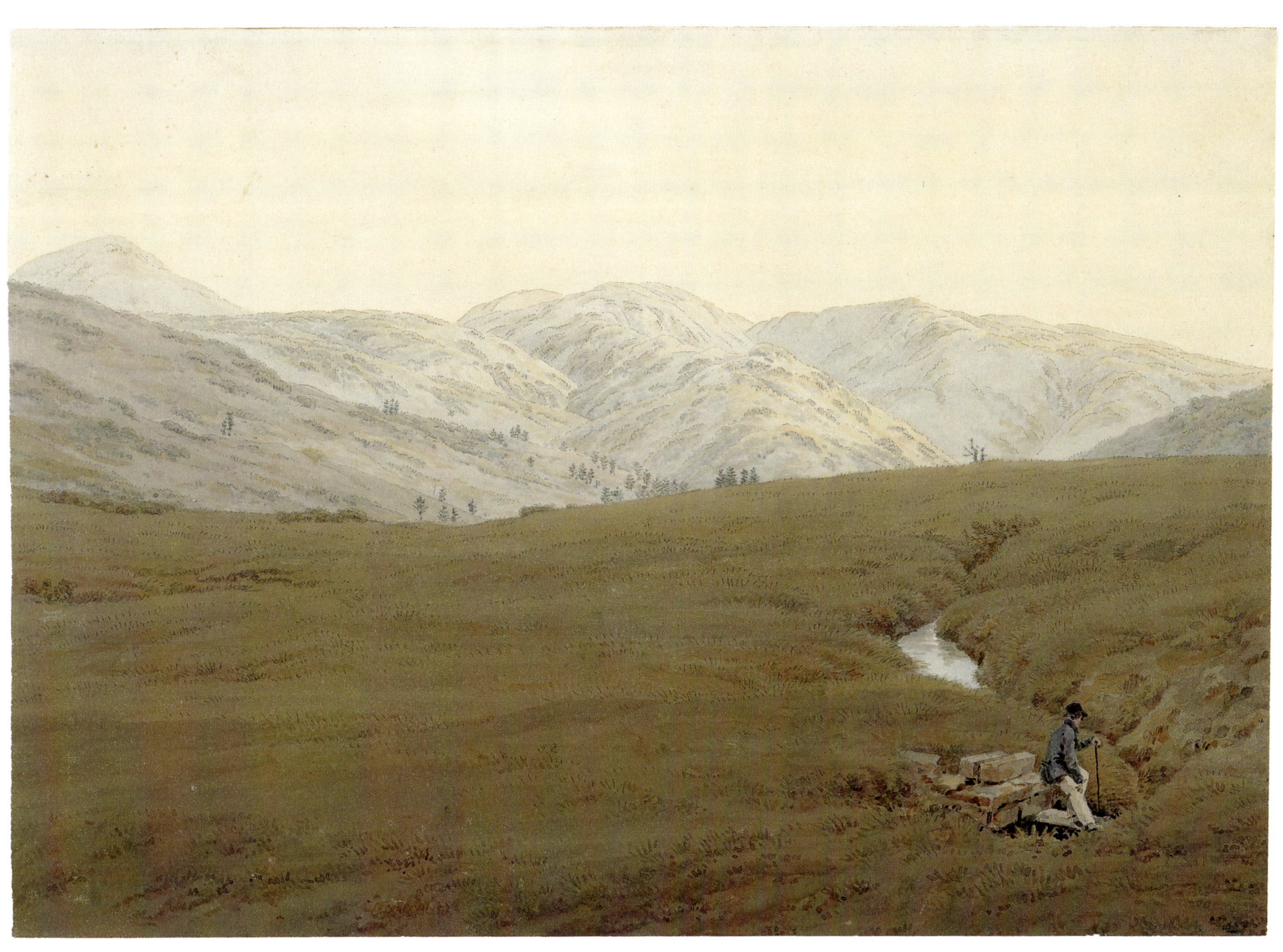

22

Caspar David Friedrich

*Entrance to a Chamber in the Convent Church
of the Holy Cross near Meissen, c. 1835–37*

Brush in sepia over pencil on wove paper, 228 x 194 mm
Provenance: Auktionshaus Hugo Helbing, Munich
*Selected bibliography: Munich 1958, p. 27, no. 40, fig. 4;
Lübeck 1969, p. 36, no. 50; Sumowski 1970, p. 153; Börsch-
Supan and Jähnig 1973, p. 461, no. 458 (repr.); Bernhard
(Hinz) 1974, pp. 723 (repr.), 813 (Hans H. Hofstätter);
Jensen 1974, p. 107, fig. 39; Paris 1984, p. 307, no. 281 (repr.
in color); Munich 1985, pp. 87f., no. 32 (repr.); Petra
Kuhlmann-Hodick, "Zwei Aquarelle Caspar David
Friedrichs in Dresden und Angers," Dresdner Kunstblät-
ter 4, no. 4 (1996): 123ff., fig. 9*

Passages or openings in solid walls, whether doors or windows, run through Friedrich's oeuvre like a leitmotif. He depicted this same entrance in nearly identical fashion in three technically different versions: in a pencil drawing worked up with watercolor, done directly on the spot (Hamburg, Kunsthalle)[1] in the present sepia, and in an oil painting in the Gemäldegalerie in Dresden. On the basis of the inscription on the Hamburg sheet, the title *Entrance to the Fürstenschule in Meissen* was established long ago for all three versions, though the exact location was never identified.

The site depicted in these three works does, in fact, still exist, but it was only recently discovered and published by Petra Kuhlmann-Hodick of Dresden.[2] It is in the ruins of the former Convent of the Holy Cross on the left bank of the Elbe, north of Meissen. The site is a chamberlike, completely enclosed, vaulted room at the edge of the still extant enclosure tract, which is located on the Elbe side and adjoins the choir of the church.[3] The Benedictine Convent of the Holy Cross, a thirteenth-century Cistercian foundation, was dissolved in the middle of the sixteenth century and left to decay. The early nineteenth century saw the first measures to secure the convent ruins, whose picturesque site enticed Caspar David Friedrich to capture a number of views as early as 1800.[4] The inscription on the Hamburg pencil drawing came about because the Fürstenschule in Meissen, which had been given the convent's most important buildings after it had been dissolved, was still using parts of the monastic compound in the nineteenth century.[5]

Comparison of the actual site with the study Friedrich made of it shows how conscientious he was, and it sheds light on his method of working. He deliberately chose the view from inside the dark room to the open door, through which the gaze leads to daylight and the facing wall of the nave of the church with the recognizable window

corner on the left. The entrance is in the center of the composition; it forms a small passageway in the thick wall, and is framed on the sides by cut stone blocks and above by bricks. On the Hamburg sheet, Friedrich faithfully recorded all these details in pencil. He even captured the varying dimensions of the stone blocks framing the entrance and the crack in the ceiling of the narrow passageway, which, still unchanged, can be seen today.[6] Friedrich lightly washed the pencil study with watercolor; evidently, his original intention was to execute the composition as a finished watercolor. It was only later that he chose the Hamburg drawing from his study material and carefully translated it in the studio into a pictorially executed composition in sepia and into an oil painting.

In the present sepia, only the foliage in the light-filled exterior has been identified more precisely as two young fir trees. Otherwise, it is identical to the drawing. In the oil painting, the motif's spatial situation underwent a slight change, which altered the content and made the space into a dungeon: the door-passage leads into an anteroom with a barred window, beyond which is the light source. The painting was, in fact, entitled *The Prison*.[7] Sumowski has dated the Hamburg study, with its "deliberate drawing style rich in hatchings and an emphasis on the prismatic aspect of the architecture," to around 1820 or a little later.[8] It was probably done around 1822–24 during one of Friedrich's documented visits to Kersting, after the latter had moved to Meissen with his family (cf. cat. 23, 24). Perhaps Kersting's pictures of interiors inspired Friedrich to take up the motif, from which he banned any human presence.

Friedrich had his first successes with sepias.[9] Initially, he was influenced by the Zingg school of the Dresden Academy and by the fashionable brown tonality of the aquatint. He preferred the sepia technique, which he practiced with growing mastery, until he took up oil painting in 1807. Even thereafter, Friedrich continued to produce sepias throughout his creative life. It became particularly important in his later years, when his deteriorating health no longer let him paint in oil. All this makes it difficult to date the present sepia. It most likely belongs to one of two phases during which Friedrich worked intensively in this technique: the period around 1826, to which the cycle of the stages of life in the Hamburg Kunsthalle has been assigned and which Sumowski tends to favor, or the period around 1835–37, which Börsch-Supan prefers because of the work's delicate tonal gradations. Because the present sheet's brushwork and motif are close to the sepia *Owl in a Gothic Window*, which is dated 1836,[10] and because it is also similar in conception to an 1837 Bohemian landscape in sepia,[11] I agree with the later dating.

Friedrich appears to have made the waning reflections of light the theme of the present work. He used delicately nuanced gradations of sepia with great mastery in capturing the way the light entering through the doorway is diffused in the dark room. The brightest areas of light are those suggested by the reserved areas of the white paper. The steps to the door and the door as an opening into the light have become metaphors. The monochromatic, highly painterly picture of solitude and emptiness has become an allegory and a devotional image. Börsch-Supan, who has studied the artist's pictorial vocabulary, finds in the present work an existential interpretation of the poetry of Friedrich's pictorial language: the dark room in the foreground symbolizes earthly life, the door opening into a light-filled space represents death, the young trees are a promise of resurrection, and the sun-flooded space outside signifies life after death.[12]

1 Pencil, watercolor, color trial strokes on the edge of the sheet; 275 x 215 mm. Inscribed by another hand: "Eingang zur Fürstenschule in Meissen" [Entrance to the Fürstenschule in Meissen], Hamburg, Kunsthalle, inv. no. 41107; Hamburg 1974, p. 261, no. 169 (repr.).

2 Kuhlmann-Hodick 1996. I would like to thank the author for clarifying various points, and Horst Hodick for his photo of the site today.

3 The room directly underneath the gallery may have served as a vestry, a treasury, or a stockroom; today it is used as a storage room.

4 Kuhlmann-Hodick 1996, pp. 118ff., fig. 4.

5 *Ibid.*, p. 125.

6 What is different now compared to Friedrich's time is that the door and steps have been replaced by new ones. A wooden door with the same kind of handle as in Friedrich's depiction has been preserved in a neighboring room; cf. *ibid.*, pp. 124f.

7 Cf. Börsch-Supan and Jähnig 1973, pp. 408f., no. 354 (repr.).

8 Sumowski 1970, p. 153.

9 P. O. Runge acquired two of his sepias around 1802. In 1805, Friedrich won a half prize at the Weimar competition with two sepias; cf. Scheidig 1958, pp. 437–88, 454f., 477f., 484ff., nos. 8, 9, figs. 46, 47.

10 Börsch-Supan and Jähnig 1973, p. 461, no. 459 (repr.).

11 Lübeck 1990, p. 112, no. 42 (Gerhard Gerkens).

12 Börsch-Supan and Jähnig 1973, p. 461, no. 458 (repr.), in connection with pp. 408f., no. 354 (repr.). Cf. research by the American doctor Raymond Moody, to whom clinically dead patients who had been brought back to life described the experience of death as a dark passageway with an opening into the light; Raymond A. Moody, *Life after Life: The Investigation of the Phenomenon of Survival of Bodily Death* (Covington, Ga., 1975); *Leben nach dem Tode* (Reinbek near Hamburg, 1977), 1995, pp. 57f., 65.

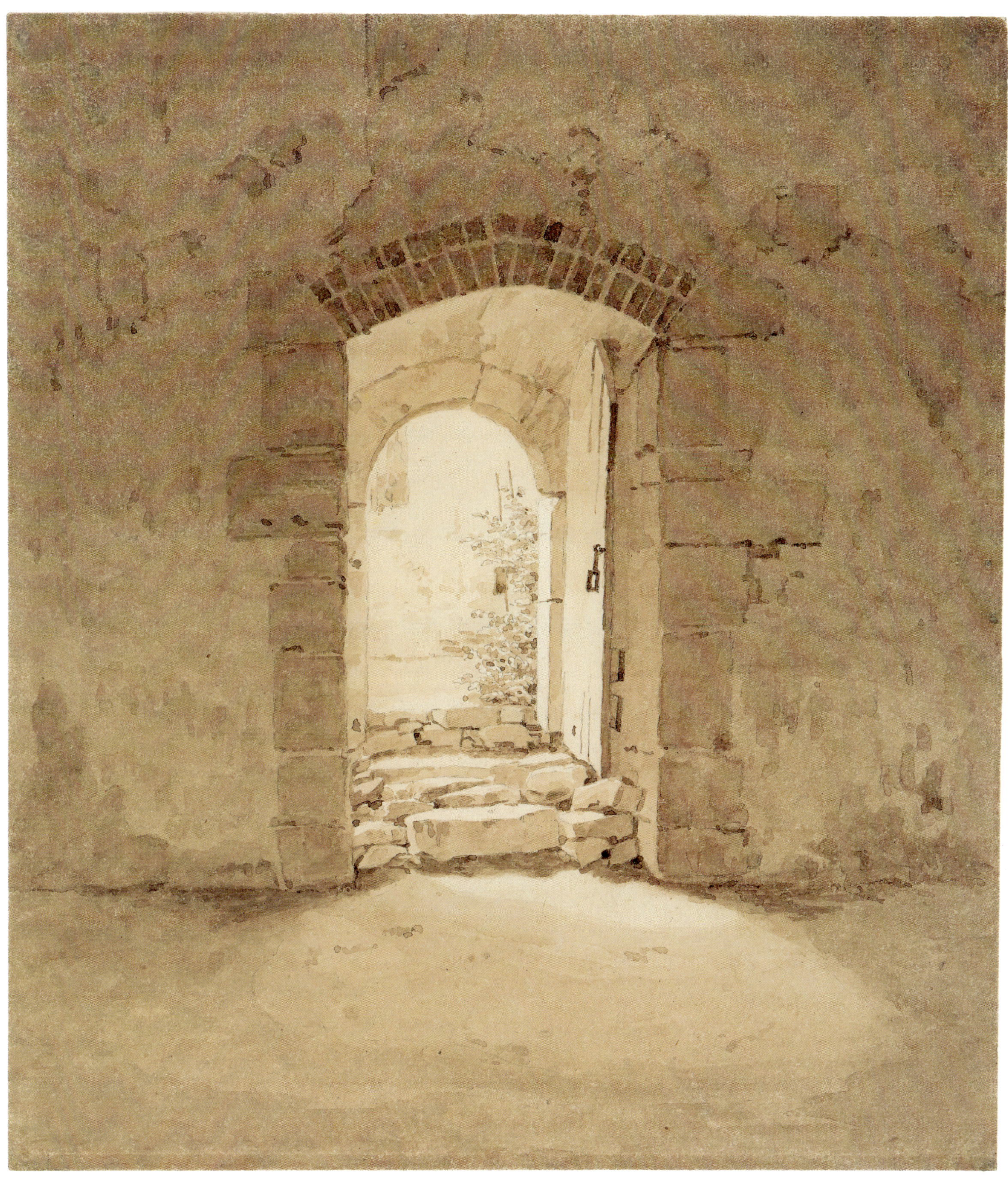

23

Georg Friedrich Kersting

Güstrow 23 October 1785–1 July 1847 Meissen

Portrait of Caspar David Friedrich, c. 1812

Pencil, lightly stumped, on card prepared with a white chalk ground (recto and verso); 148 x 96 mm

Provenance: Louise Seidler, Rome (?); album of the painter Johann Caspar Schintz; Graphisches Kabinett Günther Franke, Munich

Bibliography: Lübeck 1957, p. 27, no. 73; Munich 1958, pp. 34f., no. 71, fig. 1; Lankheit 1959, p. 65; Heidelberg 1964, p. 78, no. 284 (repr.); Lübeck 1969, p. 49, no. 78; Helmut Börsch-Supan, L'opera completa di Friedrich (Milan, 1976), p. 85, fig. 17; Schnell 1994, pp. 26f., 40, 306, no. A47

Kersting drew this bust-length portrait of his friend from life. It served as the model for his 1812 oil painting *Caspar David Friedrich in His Studio*, today in Berlin (fig.).[1] Kersting had already portrayed his artist friend in his studio the year before (Hamburg, Kunsthalle).[2] Between 1814 and 1819, possibly on commission, he executed the subject again, relying closely on this first Hamburg version.[3] It is conceivable that the present study from life, and other studies now lost, were made as early as 1811 in connection with the first version of the painting, although that work shows Friedrich in profile, sitting on a chair in front of his easel, at work on a landscape. The drawing exhibited here depicts Friedrich's face in three-quarter view, looking attentively ahead, with a pensive, serious expression. Despite the small format, the drawing mov-

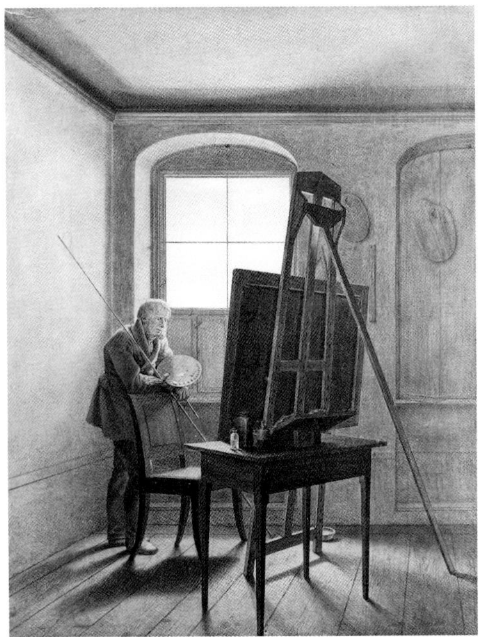

Georg Friedrich Kersting, *Caspar David Friedrich in His Studio*, 1812. Berlin, Nationalgalerie

ingly conveys the sitter's presence. The rounded truncation of the bust is reminiscent of a portrait miniature in an (imagined) upright oval. In placing the portrait in an unusually small format for a study from life, Kersting was presumably initially thinking of a miniature. This would also seem to be indicated by his support—card prepared with chalk on both sides—and by the drawing media, a soft, partly stumped pencil, and a sharp pencil (or lead point?) that slightly incises the chalk ground—a rather difficult technique, since it is not easy to erase or correct. Kersting probably owed this technique—reminiscent of the silverpoint used by the old masters—to Dresden's aged Anton Graff, whom he regarded highly, and who had successfully revived it for miniature portraits (cf. cat. 13). It was not customary to use these media to sketch spontaneous studies from life.

Kersting depicted his friend in the Berlin painting exactly as he had drawn him here, with the upper body leaning slightly forward. I am almost inclined to say that this portrait drawing was the point of departure for the entire painting, which was composed around it (fig.). The dimensions of the head are identical in the drawing and the oil painting.[4] Unlike the Hamburg version, Friedrich stands in front of his easel behind a chair and leans on the back of the chair as he contemplates a fairly large, oblong painting that the viewer cannot see; only the painting's back and the stretcher are visible. Friedrich, who is holding a brush in his right hand and a palette and additional brushes in his left hand, has evidently risen from his chair and stepped behind it in order to examine his painting critically and intensively from a distance. The obliquely positioned easel and the table in front of it—with open paint box, oil bottles, and color bottles—seem to set Friedrich apart and crowd him into the corner; this suggests the withdrawn artist, who like an ascetic, works in isolation from society. Here, the painting is the compositional center, whereas in the Hamburg version, the artist at work is the focus. In the drawing, we can clearly discern a source of light falling from above right, its reflections indicated as reserves of the blank paper on the highest points of the shoulders and head. This seems to indicate that Kersting composed the study in precisely the same studio setting, with the *contre-jour* effect of the light coming from the upper window.

Kersting painted his Hamburg studio portrait as a pendant to his studio portrait of Gerhard von Kügelgen.[5] Contemporaries already felt that both work spaces, depicted with all their contents in exacting detail, revealed much about their occupants' personalities and methods of working. Friedrich's austere and bare atelier was a space ruled by reason: a place for contemplation and concentration to which he withdrew alone.

Kügelgen kept his studio, which was overflowing with sensual stimuli, locked. His son, Wilhelm von Kügelgen, described his father's studio as a rather chaotic place crammed with all manner of objects and curios, where he felt comfortable "since any imagination would wither amidst bare walls and in tidied-up rooms." "Friedrich's studio, in contrast, was so completely bare that [the writer] Jean Paul could have compared it to the disemboweled corpse of a prince. There was nothing in it except an easel, a chair, and a table. Above the table hung a solitary ruler as the only wall decoration, and no one could figure out how it had attained that honor .... Friedrich felt that all external objects disturbed the inner pictorial world."[6]

Gotthilf Heinrich von Schubert's description of Friedrich's appearance attests to Kersting's true-to-life portrayal of his friend in the present drawing (Schubert had met the artist repeatedly in Dresden between 1806 and 1809): "He was by no means what you would call handsome, rather pale and gaunt. But each muscle, even when he was not moving, embodied a powerful character trait .... The melancholy seriousness that spoke from the lines of his forehead was softened by the guileless, childlike gaze of his blue eyes; over the mouth there hovered a faint hint of suffering."[7]

1 Schnell 1994, pp. 306f., no. A48 (repr.). See also New York 1981, p. 118, no. 37f. (repr. in color).

2 First version 1811 in Hamburg, Kunsthalle; cf. Schnell 1994, pp. 301f., no. A29 (repr.).

3 Third version between 1814 and 1819 in Mannheim, Kunsthalle; cf. Schnell 1994, p. 312, no. A72 (repr.).

4 Height c. 3 cm. I am grateful to Birgit Verwiebe of the Nationalgalerie, Berlin for taking measurements of the original.

5 Both paintings, the first that Kersting exhibited publicly, were shown at the 1811 exhibition of the Dresden Academy under the same title: *A Painter's Studio, Painted in Oil*; cf. Schnell 1994, p. 19.

6 Wilhelm von Kügelgen, *Jugenderinnerungen eines alten Mannes* (Ebenhausen near Munich, 1920), pp. 106f.; cf. Seidler 1922, p. 43.

7 Quoted in Schnell 1994, p. 27.

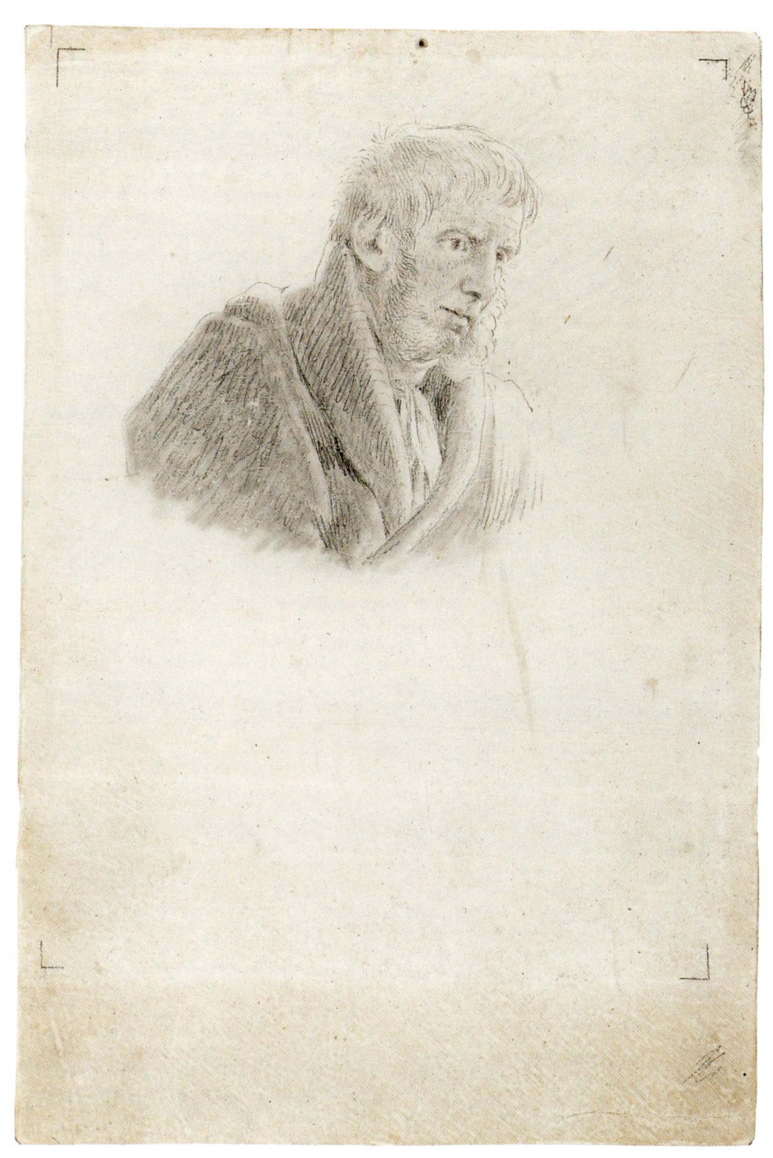

24

Georg Friedrich Kersting

Young Woman Sewing by Lamplight, c. 1828

Transparency; recto: brush in gray-black wash over pencil; verso: watercolor over pencil; on wove paper; 235 x 183 mm
Bibliography: Munich 1958, p. 35, no. 72; Mende and Hebecker 1973, p. 89, under no. 35; Hannelore Gärtner, Georg Friedrich Kersting (Leipzig, 1988), pp. 116ff., fig. 74; Schnell 1994, pp. 93, 124, 140, 323, no. A124; Birgit Verwiebe, Lichtspiele. Vom Mondscheintransparent zum Diorama. Zur Archäologie des Kinos (Stuttgart, 1997), pp. 51ff., figs. 30, 31 (in color)

Unlike his friend Caspar David Friedrich, early in his career Kersting began to concentrate on his characteristic, still-life-like interiors. In these works, he depicted people engaged in quiet activities such as reading, writing, painting, embroidering, or braiding hair. We observe them in their own precisely rendered environments, mirroring their personalities and emotional states. These are pictures of a general spiritualization; they depict the meditative spaces of a circumscribed, limited life.

In 1828, Kersting composed three variations on the theme of a young woman sewing by lamplight in an enclosed room: a chalk drawing (Nuremberg), the present work, worked up on both sides with wash and watercolor (figs. 1, 2), and an oil painting (Munich). Kersting made the drawing from life; it served as the model for both the oil painting and the present sheet, which, if somewhat simpler in design, follows the drawing in most details. According to Hermann Büne-mann, the woman depicted is the artist's wife, Agnes Sergel, daughter of the chief postmaster of Dresden.[1] Kersting had married Agnes in Dresden in 1818 when she was seventeen years old. In the drawing, Kersting showed her in an unspecified, enclosed space. Only in the oil painting was the room more fully characterized; there, the woman sits in front of a window with drawn shade. In the present transparency, Kersting leaves the room undefined, suggesting protection and safety as well as a disquieting confinement and isolation from the outside world. Monotonous walls without any windows or doors, and with sparse furnishings, suggest an ascetic cell. The young woman sits alone and works on a white (bridal?) dress by lamplight. In what is probably an image of his wife, Kersting also offers a "woman's portrait" typical of his era, a picture of a woman's social role similar to Ludwig Emil Grimm's painting of his sister Lotte (cat. 57). Wearing a high-necked dress, the woman sits, with lowered eyes, absorbed in her needlework as though in a pose of pious devotion. The only book in the room is a Bible on the small, plain, Biedermeier table. The woman is therefore chaste, virtuous, pious, gentle, submissive, and obedient. As a housewife, she is busy caring for clothes, a conventional role assigned early on and learned through activities such as spinning, knitting, darning, and sewing.[2]

Kersting had a special interest in depicting light in interior spaces. Around 1828, it was a widespread custom to hang transparencies—translucent pictures made of various materials—in windows or to place them on a stand, in a lampshade frame, or in front of a candle or some other light source. Lithopanes (translucent porcelain plates) were also produced for these purposes. Invented in 1827 in Paris, by the following year they were being produced in large quantities by the porcelain factory in Meissen, and with even more economic success in Berlin, by the Royal Porcelain Manufactory (KPM).[3] Thus, the transparent image was a topical theme in 1828, and it is no coincidence that Kersting chose the motif of his drawing, with the artificially lit interior, for a transparency.[4] The peculiar character of the present work, wash on one side worked up with watercolor on the other, leaves no doubt that he created it as a transparency. Its state of preservation, with traces of glue and torn on the edges, attests that it was originally mounted as a light screen. The front is composed monochromatically with pencil and brush in gray wash; it shows in fine tonal nuances the gradations of light in the room. Viewed in normal, reflected light, it appears rather dry and cool (fig. 1). On the verso, Kersting used watercolor to describe the corresponding motifs (fig. 2). When illuminated from behind by a direct source of light, the colors shine through and we see a charming picture in warm colors, with the reddish-purple dress and yellow apron shimmering delicately. The large reproduction on the right-hand page shows the intended effect of the transparency. The colors are concentrated in the figure and the furnishings. They differ from those in the oil painting, especially in the woman's dress.

In the same year (1828), Kersting took the drawing that had served as a model for the two other versions to Nuremberg, where he donated it to the so-called *Dürer-Stammbuch*, the album produced to commemorate the three-hundredth anniversary of Dürer's death.[5]

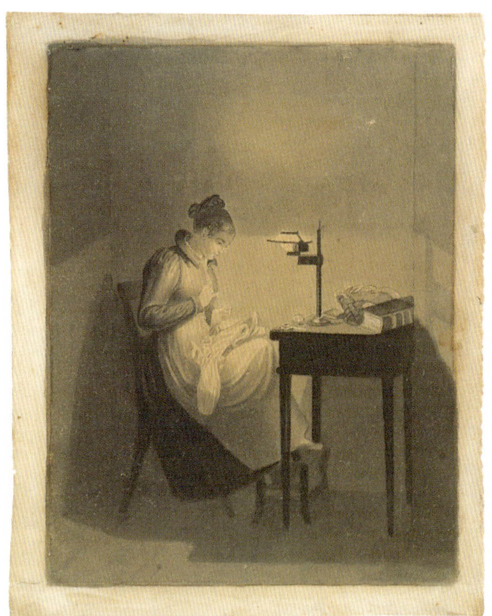

1 Georg Friedrich Kersting, *Young Woman Sewing by Lamplight*, recto

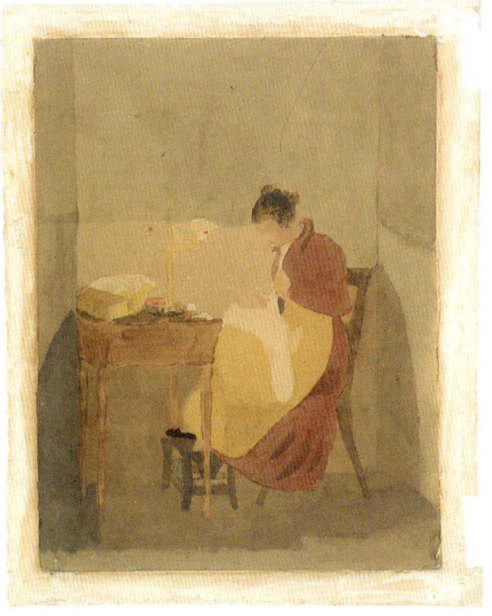

2 Georg Friedrich Kersting, *Young Woman Sewing by Lamplight*, verso

1 Hermann Bünemann, "Kersting, der Maler des Nahen," *Die Kunst und das schöne Heim* 56 (1958): 41–45.
2 Cf. Münster 1995, pp. 114, 141f., 148, 165ff., 167; Ulrike Krenzlin, "Zu Georg Friedrich Kerstings Frauenbild im Innenraum(1812–1821), *Georg Friedrich Kersting—Zwischen Romantik und Biedermeier*, 5. Greifswalder Romantik-Konferenz, *Wissenschaftliche Zeitschrift der Ernst-Moritz-Arndt-Universität Greifswald* 35, 1986, vols. 3–4, pp. 46–49; cf. also Cordula Grewe, "Shaping Reality through the Fictive: Images of Women Spinning in the Northern Renaissance," *RACAR* 19, nos. 1–2 (1992): 6–19.
3 Verwiebe 1997, p. 93; Erich Köllmann, *Berliner Porzellan*, 2 vols. (Brunswick, 1966), pp. 80, 141, 208, 249; Hans Leichter, "Berliner Lithophanien, eine fast vergessene graphische Technik des Biedermeier," *Der Bär von Berlin: Jahrbuch des Vereins für die Geschichte Berlins* (Berlin, 1974), pp. 50–69.
4 Verwiebe 1997, pp. 51ff.
5 Cf. Mende and Hebecker 1973, pp. 89f., no. 35 (repr.).

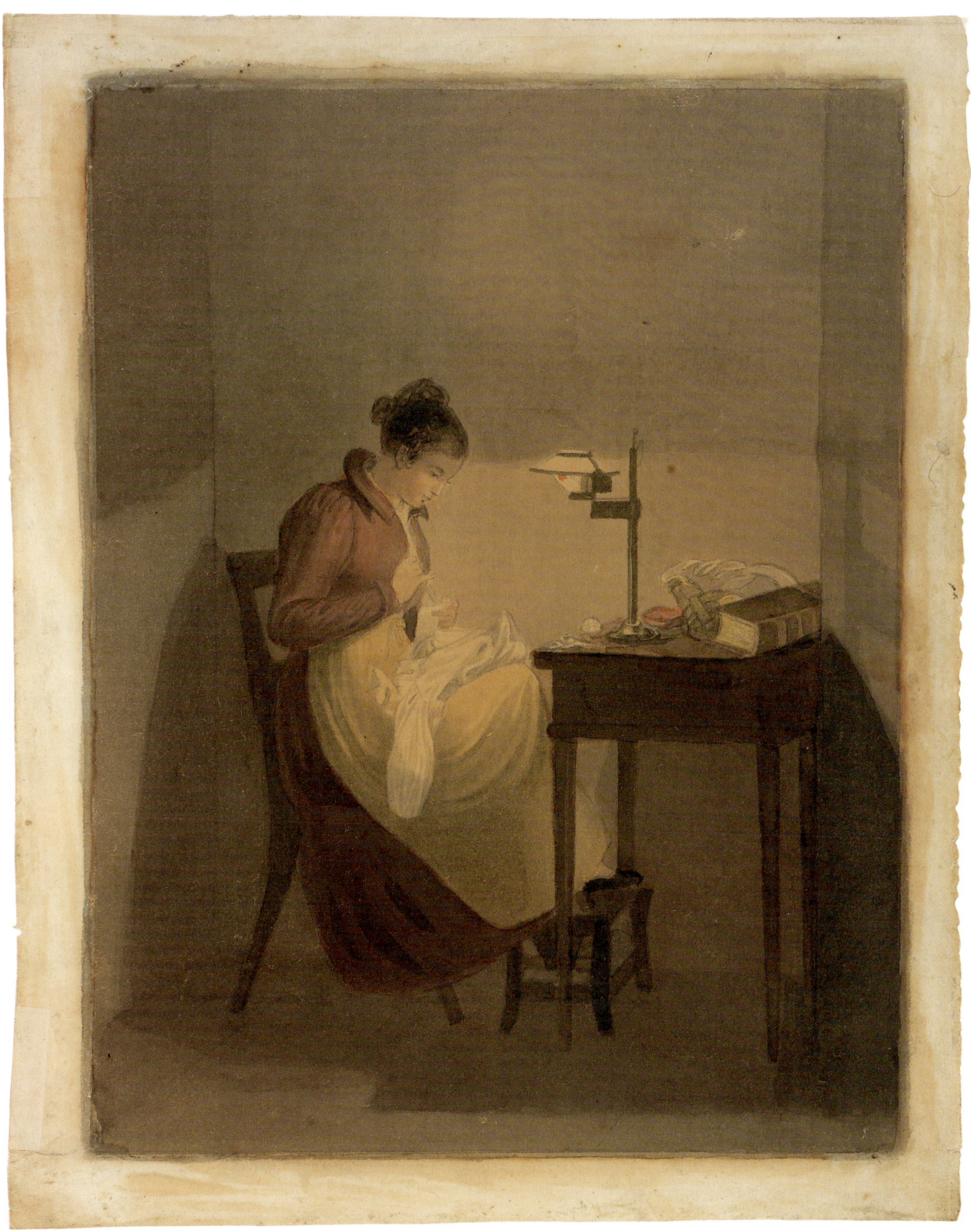

25

Johann Christian Reinhart

Near Hof 24 January 1761 – 9 June 1847 Rome

Ruins of Hadrian's Villa, 1796

*Pen and gray-black ink, watercolor over pencil, on wove paper; watermark: J WHATMAN; 338/41 x 484/86 mm
Inscribed in pencil, lower right (partially trimmed): "Reinhart R[oma]"*

Provenance: August Grahl, Dresden (without his stamp, Lugt 1199)

Bibliography: Wiesbaden 1936, p. 40, no. 535; Dörries 1943, pp. 18, 107 (repr.), 159; Munich 1958, p. 47, no. 126, fig. 6; Heidelberg 1965, p. 63, no. 259; Lübeck 1969, p. 73, no. 138; London 1972, p. 411, no. 769; Bernhard 1974, vol. 2, p. 1286 (repr.); Robels 1974, pp. 47, 90, pl. 10; Feuchtmayr 1975, p. 378, Z-422, fig. 321; Munich 1979, p. 306, no. 258; Munich 1981, p. 76, no. 84, p. 132, fig. 29; Washington 1996, p. 68, fig. 8 (Sarah Faunce)

Beginning in the eighteenth century, the varied landscape around Tivoli, near Rome, became an attraction for those on educational trips or on the "Grand Tour." At the same time, it was a favorite destination for artists, who—like Jacob Philipp Hackert, highly esteemed by Goethe—created views of this area to satisfy the demand for souvenirs that came with early tourism.

Among the most splendid villas of the Roman rulers was that of the art-loving emperor Hadrian (AD 117–136). In the late eighteenth century, only scattered ruins marked the site of its former glory. The picturesque abundance of nature and historical sites in and around Tivoli had, earlier in the eighteenth century, attracted artists like Piranesi and the Frenchmen Jean Honoré Fragonard and Hubert Robert, inviting them to depict the area in works of art.[1] What fascinated them was how nature had taken possession of the derelict monuments of antiquity. In 1792, Friedrich Johann Lorenz Meyer, a canon of Hamburg, gave this description of the situation: "The present view of the ruined buildings is vast and picturesque; it too offers a stirring image of the frailty and changeability of all things human, a picture so oft repeated in these parts."[2] During the first ten years he spent in Rome, Reinhart was often drawn to the area around Tivoli, where he liked to hunt as well as to make studies for his etchings and paintings.[4] At that time, he began a commercial relationship as *peintre-graveur* with the Nuremberg publisher J. F. Frauenholz.[3] In 1794, Frauenholz published Reinhart's series of six etchings of Italian landscapes with ruins of ancient tombs overgrown with ivy, grass, and bushes. Reinhart also etched twenty-four landscapes for the extensive series of *72 Picturesquely Etched Views of Italy*, which he proposed and which Frauenholz brought out in

twelve installments between 1792 and 1798.[5] Reinhart was chiefly concerned with rendering picturesque views of nature from the area around Rome, including Tivoli, which had not previously been depicted. His etchings are characterized by their fresh and vigorous representation of nature, as compared to the flat-looking, conventional *vedute* in contemporary engravings. We can observe a change between 1790 and 1800 in Reinhart's drawings and etchings in his conception of the landscape from the natural to the invented, heroic, and idealized. This development, which would henceforth characterize his style, was given a theoretical foundation by Carl Ludwig Fernow.[6] Revealingly, Reinhart would not take part in further ambitious collaborative projects with Frauenholz.

In the summers of 1795 and 1796, a time of political unrest in Rome as a result of the French Revolution, the gardens of Hadrian's Villa were Reinhart's chief place of study, and there he created a rich store of nature studies and landscape scenes as material for future paintings.[7] The well-preserved watercolor exhibited here was probably also produced on the site. It shows the large *thermae* structure in the center of Hadrian's villa, with a view into the *frigidarium*, the central section of the bath.[8] On 16 June 1796, Fernow wrote from Rome to the writer Johann Pohrt that Reinhart was going to Tivoli and would be spending the better part of the summer there making studies, since he had been commissioned by Countess Lichtenau, the mistress of King Frederick William II of Prussia, to execute two paintings with views of Hadrian's Villa. On 7 October 1796, he wrote again to Pohrt, "Reinhart has now returned from Tivoli with a nice harvest of superb studies, so lovely they surpass anything he has done before."[9]

Beginning in the summer of 1795, Rome was also home to the young, rising landscapist Johann Martin von Rohden (1778–1868). Reinhart soon took him under his wing and they became close friends, especially since they were both passionate hunters. In the summer of 1796, Rohden, too, was in Tivoli at Hadrian's Villa, where he produced an oil painting, now lost, with a ruin very similar to that in Reinhart's watercolor.[10] The Kunsthalle in Bremen has a drawing that shows the same view onto the same wall remnants of Hadrian's Villa as Reinhart's watercolor.[11] It should be attributed to Martin von Rohden; the horizontal and diagonal hatching in the shaded areas, in particular, indicate his touch.[12] Evidently, the artists drew the same motif from nature at the same time, which is another argument for dating Reinhart's watercolor to 1796. Stylistically, too, the watercolor fits in his early Roman period, when Reinhart, still fresh from his experience of nature, produced naturalistic studies.[13] In the present sheet, he was palpably

excited by the reddish ruins of Roman brick buildings. Picturesquely overgrown with green plants, bushes, and trees, they had become part of nature: a magnificent landscape in the clear light of the sun. Reinhart saw the ruins close up, in a narrow, panorama-like composition, and he left the foreground and sky blank, to be worked up in the studio or added if and when he executed an oil painting of the motif.

1 As part of his *Vedute di Roma*, Piranesi (1720–1778) created landscapes of Tivoli and its countryside: the so-called Temple of Sybil (1761) and the waterfalls of the Aniene (1765 and 1769). Artists on stipends from the French Academy often spent time in the region of Tivoli (for example, in 1761, Honoré Fragonard [1756–1761 in Rome] at the Villa d'Este and Hubert Robert [1754–1765 in Rome] also at the Villa d'Este); cf. also Tübingen 1981, pp. 39–46.

2 Friedrich Johann Lorenz Meyer, *Darstellungen aus Italien* (Berlin, 1792), p. 270.

3 Etchings of Tivoli (reprs. in Feuchtmayr 1975): *Villa Maecenate*, 1792 (A.54, fig. 373); *Ruins of the Villa Basso*, 1793 (A.61, fig. 376); *Tempio della Torse*, 1793 (A.62, fig. 377); *In Tivoli*, 1794 (A.70, fig. 588); *Remains of the Library in Hadrian's Villa*, 1798 (A.74, fig. 392); *Ponte Aquoreo*, 1798 (A.75, fig. 593).

4 Luther 1988, pp. 124–33.

5 The other landscapes were done by Albert Christoph Dies and Jakob Wilhelm Mechau.

6 Carl Ludwig Fernow, *Sitten- und Kulturgemälde von Rom* (Gotha, 1802), pp. 260 ff.; *idem*, "Über die Landschaftsmalerei," in *Römische Studien*, vol. 2 (Zurich, 1806).

7 Otto Baisch, *Johann Christian Reinhart und seine Kreise: Ein Lebens- und Culturbild. Nach Originalquellen dargestellt* (Leipzig, 1882), p. 107.

8 Cf. *Von Mannheim nach Italien: Peter Ferdinand Deurer, 1777–1844. Ludwig Deurer, 1806–1847. Landschaftszeichnungen der Romantik*, exh. cat., Städtische Kunsthalle Mannheim (Mannheim, 1997), p. 158, no. 53, p. 159 (repr. in color) (Sabina Wagner).

9 Feuchtmayr 1975, p. 329, G55, 56.

10 Unfinished. Oil on paper, 395 x 530 mm, Ludwigsgalerie. Otto H. Nathan, *Die Sammlung Bernd Grönvold*, exh. cat., Munich, 5–31 October 1931, no. 66, repr.; Pinnau 1965, pp. 111 f., G-5; cf. p. 140, G-43.

11 Brush and gray wash over pencil, heightened with white, on bluish paper; 308 x 402 mm. Bremen, Kunsthalle, Kupferstichkabinett, inv. no. 5418.

12 Cf. Pinnau 1965, Z-87, Z-102, Z-166. Additional early drawings from in and around Tivoli, *ibid*.: Z-7, Z-8, Z-11, Z-17. Identical in technique, type of paper used, and format is Z-8: *Tivoli*, pencil, wash, heightened with white, on blue-green paper; 308 x 400 mm. Unsigned. Dresden, Kupferstichkabinett, inv. no. 1920:213. Cf. Bernhard 1974, vol. 2, pp. 1414 ff., 1418 ff.

13 Later, he generally invented his often dramatic classical landscapes. Reinhart reduced their color, drawing mostly with pen and brown ink and with brush in brown and gray wash, and occasionally also in blue-gray wash, heightened with white. Cf. the related watercolor by Ernst Fries from the year 1826; Jensen 1978, pp. 122, 165 f., cat. no. 34, fig. 72 in color.

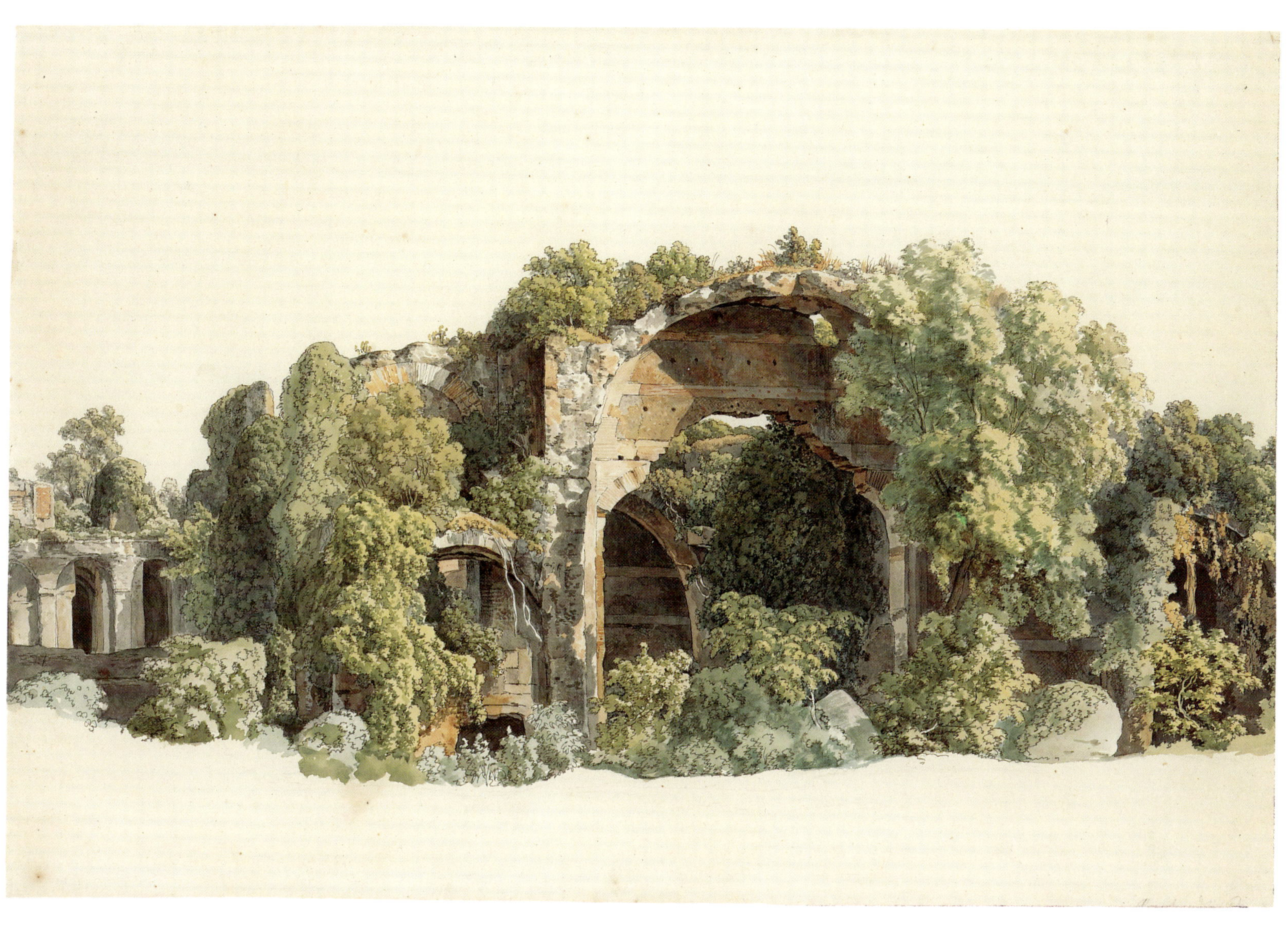

26

Johann Christian Reinhart

The History Painter, Caricature, c. 1800

Pen and brown ink over pencil, watercolor, on laid paper; watermark: PRO PATRIA and coat of arms: a crowned lion—with a sword and seven arrows, which represent the provinces of Holland—defends the Maid of Holland in the stockade; 198/201 x 243/45 mm

Bibliography: Geller 1955, pp. 24f., fig. 7; Feuchtmayr 1975, p. 378, Z-425, fig. 34 (following p. 124); Nuremberg 1991, pp. 177f., fig. 16 (Ursula Peters)

Reinhart—a man of earthy and forceful artistic temperament and a thoroughly Baroque figure—had a sense of humor, was quarrelsome, and was always in the mood for jokes. He shared his penchant for caricature with other artistic personalities, particularly Joseph Anton Koch and Bonaventura Genelli, who were original, of independent mind, and highly self-conscious.

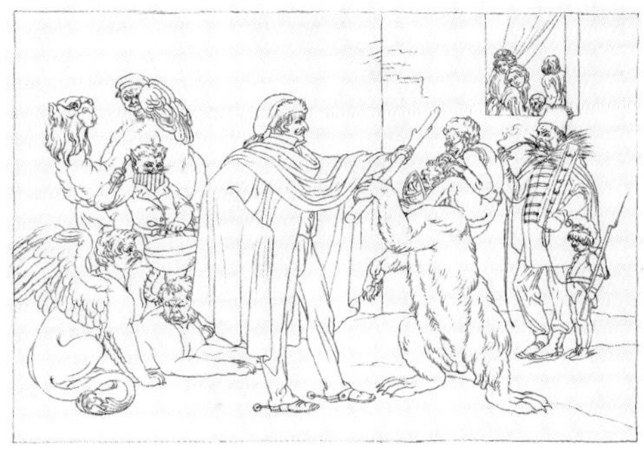

Bonaventura Genelli, *King Ludwig I of Bavaria as Animal Tamer*, c. 1822–32. Pen and brown ink over pencil; 363 x 499 mm

Reinhart had a sharp mind and an equally sharp tongue; he never minced words. Even very late in his life (on 26 June 1830), in a circular letter from Rome, he responded acidly to the art critic Dr. Ludwig Schorn in Munich, who, in reviewing one of Reinhart's paintings for his journal *Kunstblatt*, had described it as "licked" (i.e., painted with fastidious finish).[1] "A Frank by birth," wrote Reinhart, "I will also speak the truth frankly and freely."[2]

During his early years of friendship with Schiller, Reinhart had tried his hand at poetry. Reinhart's command of language was powerful and original, and possessed real literary quality, which stayed with him into old age, while his later pictorial art reveals a certain exhaustion. His penchant for verbal excess and exaggeration had a visual counterpart in his talent for caricature. Above all, he aimed his ridicule at the artist

in society: his dependency and precarious living, his vanity, and the various styles of artistic expression. Reinhart especially liked to castigate the academies, which were training the next generation of artists. As a member of the Sturm und Drang generation, Reinhart, much like Koch, had an irrepressible yearning for freedom and an insatiable desire to grapple with nature, which is why he could not endure the academic environment for very long. Like Koch, he felt a deep distrust, even loathing, for the dominant academic establishment, which is reflected in the present caricature.[3] The watercolor is distantly reminiscent of the satirical drawings of the Englishman Thomas Rowlandson, but unlike Rowlandson, with his elegantly smooth pen, Reinhart, in keeping with his temperament and style, drew more stiffly, simplifying the motif and the forms of the history painter's studio with rather crude, scratchy pen strokes.

In this watercolor, the landscapist Reinhart, who loved nature and the natural, mocks history painting, which played a leading role in the academies during the Goethe period. He ridiculed it as being ludicrous, false, artificial, posed, and fabricated. The pigtails worn by the model and artist underscore the utterly outdated and obsolete state of this genre. The artist sits as stiffly as his model, wedged into his tight, throne-like chair that leaves no room for artistic freedom of movement. Before him, on the huge, angled canvas (positioned to make it easier to reach all parts of the surface), he is painting a lively figure on horseback—presumably for a battle scene—from the lifeless model: a mannequin dressed in elegant clothes or a uniform, sitting stiffly on a cloth-covered wooden stand.[4] It is revealing that Reinhart kept his distance from the history painters in Rome. He also didn't care for the artistic intentions of the members of the Brotherhood of Saint Luke, who worshipped Dürer and Raphael and who injected new life into religious history painting. Supposedly, it was Reinhart who first gave them the derisive nickname "Nazarenes."

Reinhart himself was repeatedly the target of caricatures. One example is a satirical drawing by his friend Bonaventura Genelli (1798–1868), even though Reinhart appears only marginally (fig.).[5] The drawing pokes fun at King Ludwig I of Bavaria's patronage of the arts. Although Reinhart enjoyed the favor of the Bavarian crown prince and king, he was not dependent on the Bavarian court; hence, Genelli gave him a spectator role in the drawing. Reinhart appears at the right below the window with his son Erminio, born in 1811.[6] On the left, behind the king, sits Peter Cornelius—well tamed and submissive—in the form of a griffin. Because of its use as a heraldic emblem, the griffin alludes to Cornelius's role in the king's service as a designer

of monumental decorations. On the dromedary's back, the wise Joseph Anton Koch (in the form of an owl) watches the animal tamer, Ludwig I, and smiles from behind his wing. The king tames a wild bear rearing up on its hind legs: the sculptor Johann Martin von Wagner, Ludwig's constant confidant in Rome. The bear in turn is being groomed by a monkey sitting on its back: the previously mentioned art critic Schorn. From his position of independence, Genelli mocks King Ludwig's patronage and the artists he has tamed and rendered submissive. As an added touch, the caricature—probably executed during the artist's years in Rome, from 1822 to 1832—was drawn in the same characteristic, classicistic outline style he used to illustrate Homer and Dante.[7]

1 Printed in *Drei Schreiben aus Rom gegen Kunstschreiberei in Deutschland: Erlassen und unterzeichnet von Franz Catel, Jos. Koch, Friedr. Riepenhausen, Joh. Riepenhausen, von Rohden, Alb. Thorwaldsen, Ph. Veit, Joh. Chr. Reinhart, Friedr. Rud. Meyer. Mit einem lithographirten Blatte, nach einer Zeichnung von J. C. Reinhart* (Dessau, 1833), pp. 27–52.

2 Ibid., p. 52.

3 Cf. *Moderne Kunstchronik: Briefe zweier Freunde in Rom und der Tartarei über das moderne Kunstleben und Treiben; oder die Rumfordische Suppe, gekocht und geschrieben von Joseph Anton Koch in Rom*, edited and with introduction by Hilmar Frank (reprint Leipzig and Weimar, 1984; orig. Karlsruhe, 1834), pp. 43–47. Reinhart worked on parts of this pamphlet.

4 Koch expressed his disgust about working from dressed wooden mannequins in his thoughts about older and newer painting, printed in David Friedrich Strauss, "J. Kochs Gedanken über die neuere Malerei," in *Kleine Schriften* (Leipzig, 1862), pp. 303ff. This practice lasted long into the nineteenth century in the field of history painting, as Anton von Werner's 1870 painting *General von Moltke and His Staff before Paris* attests. In that picture, the monument-like rigidity of the chief of staff resulted from the artist's use of a photograph showing Moltke astride a wooden stand. Cf. *Anton von Werner, Geschichte in Bildern*, ed. Dominik Bartmann, exh. cat., Berlin, Deutsches Historisches Museum (Munich, 1993), p. 294, no. 398 (repr.), p. 405 (repr.). This reference was kindly furnished by Frank Büttner of Munich.

5 Cf. Lübeck 1969, p. 39, no. 56.

6 The identification of the figure as Reinhart is suggested by the board with wild boar's teeth (hunting trophies) he is holding in his left arm. His son, whom Reinhart spent little time raising, became a volunteer in a military corps.

7 Cf. Geller 1955, pp. 40ff., fig. 18. Munich 1981, p. 38, no. 34, fig. 56.

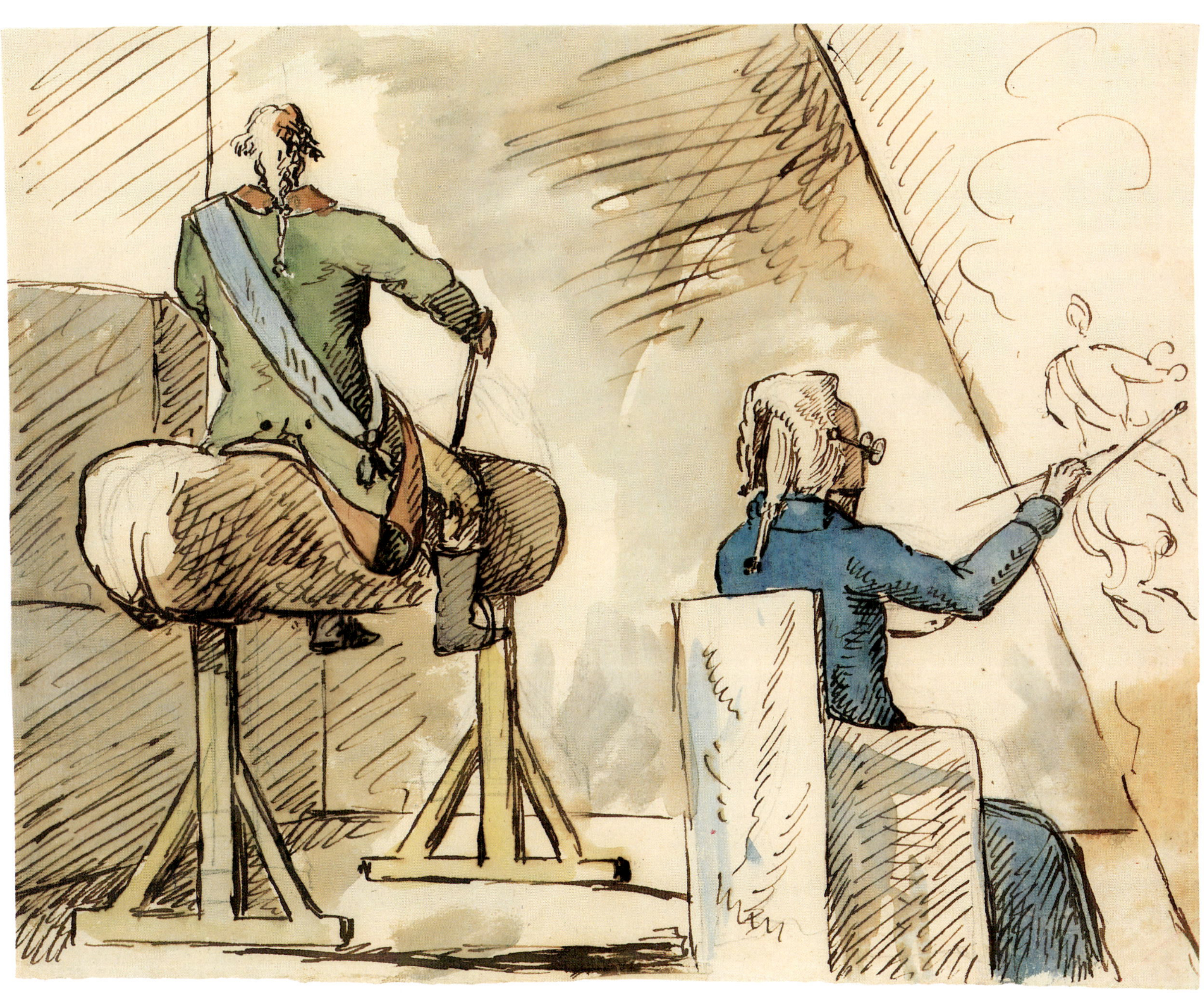

27

Philipp Veit

Berlin 13 February 1793–18 December 1877 Mainz

Portrait of Joseph Anton Koch, c. 1830

Black chalk, heightened with white, over pencil, on brown, tinted laid paper; watermark: crowned escutcheon with the letter M; 345 x 277 mm; trimmed on all sides

Bibliography: Lutterotti 1940, frontispiece preceding p. VII; Lutterotti 1944, repr. on cover; Geller 1952, p. 72, no. 683, fig. 232; Lübeck 1957, p. 76, no. 220; Munich 1958, pp. 58f., no. 169, fig. 9; Lübeck 1969, pp. 100ff., no. 191; Robels 1974, p. 97, pl. 29 (in color); Munich 1981, pp. 94f., no. 107, fig. 9; Cologne 1984, p. 18 (repr.); Lutterotti 1985, p. 7 (repr.); Stuttgart 1989, p. 21, fig. 11 (in color); Suhr 1991, pp. 77, 296, no. Z 162, p. 511, fig. 166

The present portrait, which shows Joseph Anton Koch around the age of sixty, dates from about 1830. Veit was in Rome through the summer of 1830, and then he went to Frankfurt am Main to take up an appointment as professor at the Städelsches Kunstinstitut. Perhaps he drew the portrait as a visual souvenir of the highly esteemed Koch, who played an important role for the Nazarenes as a teacher and mentor and through the example of his own art (cats. 2, 28). That Veit created a second, nearly identical version in the same technique and also on brown paper, which he kept for himself and which later found a home in the Dresden Kupferstichkabinett,[1] also suggests that he indeed made the drawing for this purpose.

A comparison with the Dresden version suggests that the present sheet was subsequently trimmed to its narrow format. A certain hardness in the heightening and in the drawing of the eyes characterizes the overall impression of the Dresden version, which is therefore more likely a copy after the present portrait than a second version from life. Gisela Scheffler has rightly noted that the "expression of lurking intrigue," which Gerstenberg believes can be detected in the Dresden version, is rather the consequence of a certain "hardening that comes with copying."[2] Compared to the Dresden sheet, the present study is notable for its naturalness and vividness, which suggest that it was done directly from life, a remarkable approach for a Nazarene. Not least because of these qualities, the portraits that Veit drew of his painter friends and colleagues in Rome are among his most compelling achievements as a draftsman.[3] He drew most of those portraits, however, with a sharp, hard pencil; they are all sketchlike in character and small in format. The two nearly identical portraits of Joseph Anton Koch are exceptional in format and technique. Since opinions on their dates range from 1820 to 1830, a comparison with other Koch portraits might be useful for a more precise dating.

Suhr proposes that a third, very similar variant of the present Koch portrait, which more strongly accentuates the model's momentary smile and is attributed to Friedrich Olivier, could have been made during the same sitting as this work.[4] Since Olivier was in Rome between 1818 and 1823, Veit's two versions would have to be dated on the earlier side, no later than 1823. Gisela Scheffler dates the present piece to circa 1825. Around that time, Koch replaced Veit in painting the murals in the Casino Massimo, and the two men probably met.[5] In fact, Veit felt hurt that the commission had been transferred to Koch, even though he had brought it about. Veit was so displeased with Koch's frescoes that he never again set foot in the room after their completion.[6] The relationship between the two men had therefore cooled at the time, which suggests that Veit made the portrait at a later date, after the tension had subsided.

Koch's forward-leaning posture, slightly raised head, upward-looking eyes, and biretta recall those in a portrait of an older Koch, similar also in physiognomy, that Carl Küchler (1807–1843) drew in 1836; it went to the Dresden Kupferstichkabinett from the Cichorius collection.[7] Particularly close to the present likeness are portraits of Koch by Friedrich Preller from 1830 and Johann Michael Wittmer from 1831; there is also a portrait by Joseph von Führich from the period 1827–29, which, despite a Nazarene restraint and stylization, conveys a vivid picture of the Tyrolean artist.[8] In a letter from Italy, Führich, who succeeded Overbeck and completed the murals in the Tasso room of the Casino Massimo, remarked about Koch, who was working at the same time in the Dante room, that "His entire character is expressed in his reddish, pleasant face, which is surrounded by white hair and crowned by a paint-spattered cap."[9] Working in proximity, Führich became very familiar with Koch's personality. The description in Führich's memoirs almost reads as an interpretation of the present portrait: "I found in him the singular man his reputation had already indicated, one of those born and not affected characters whom one forgives everything that one would take as hurtful or insulting if it came from others. Behind the stern way in which he used to express his—usually correct—opinions, there always showed through a certain honest and guileless good nature, which at times gave his anger at certain ills, especially in regard to the state of modern art, something comical. He was witty, poetical, an artist through and through. And in Rome, where only very conventional types would miss the pale and stale ways of our German salon conversation, he was, in outward appearance and the way he conducted himself, an elemental creature, with all the roughness, awkwardness, sharpness, and beauty of such a creature."[10]

1 Suhr 1991, p. 296, no. Z163 (here dated c. 1820); C. G. Boerner, *Deutsche Handzeichnungen aus der Sammlung weiland Prinz Johann Georg Herzog zu Sachsen,* cat. of the 203rd auction, 24/25 April, 1940, p. 75, no. 862 ("drawn from life in Rome in 1827"), pl. 55 (repr.); *Zeichnungen aus der Sammlung Prinz Johann Georg Herzog zu Sachsen,* ed. Matthias Kühn, exh. cat., Kupferstichkabinett, acquisitions 62 (Dresden, 1989), no. 97 (repr.).

2 Munich 1981, p. 95, no. 107; Gerstenberg and Rave 1934, p. 67.

3 Norbert Suhr, *Philipp Veit: Porträts aus dem Mittelrheinischen Landesmuseum Mainz und aus Privatbesitz* (Mainz, 1977/78), pp. 30–59. Suhr 1991, p. 76.

4 Suhr 1991, p. 77; Friedrich Olivier, *Portrait of Joseph Anton Koch.* Pencil, 190 x 150 mm. Dresden, Kupferstichkabinett. Because of the identical angle of the face and other correspondences in details, this work should be seen as a copy based on Veit's likeness from life; cf. Geller 1952, p. 72, no. 685, fig. 233; Bernhard 1974, p. 1036 (repr.).

5 Munich 1981, p. 95, no. 107.

6 Suhr 1991, p. 62.

7 Cf. Christian Dittrich, *Vermisste Zeichnungnen des Kupferstichkabinettes Dresden* (Dresden, 1987), p. 68, no. 676 (repr.). Küchler etched it as part of a series of six "Portraits of the most famous artists of our time," published in 1839 by G. G. Lange in Darmstadt. The preliminary drawings from life were made in the years 1836/37, which is why the present portrait, by comparison, can be dated late, to the period around 1830.

8 Cf. Geller 1952, no. 701, fig. 227 (Preller), no. 696, fig. 225 (Wittmer), no. 689, fig. 230 (Führich).

9 Quoted in Gerstenberg and Rave 1934, p. 67. Koch was a real character; no other member of the German colony of artists was caricatured as often as he was; cf. Geller 1955, p. 45.

10 Quoted in Munich 1958, pp. 58f., no. 169. The writer Beda Weber has left us a very apt description of Koch's personality at age sixty: "Koch in Rom, niedergeschrieben nach Notizen 1847" [Koch in Rome, written from notes in 1847], in *Charakterbilder* (Frankfurt am Main, 1853); abbreviated reprint in *Hochland* 32 (1934/35): 436f.

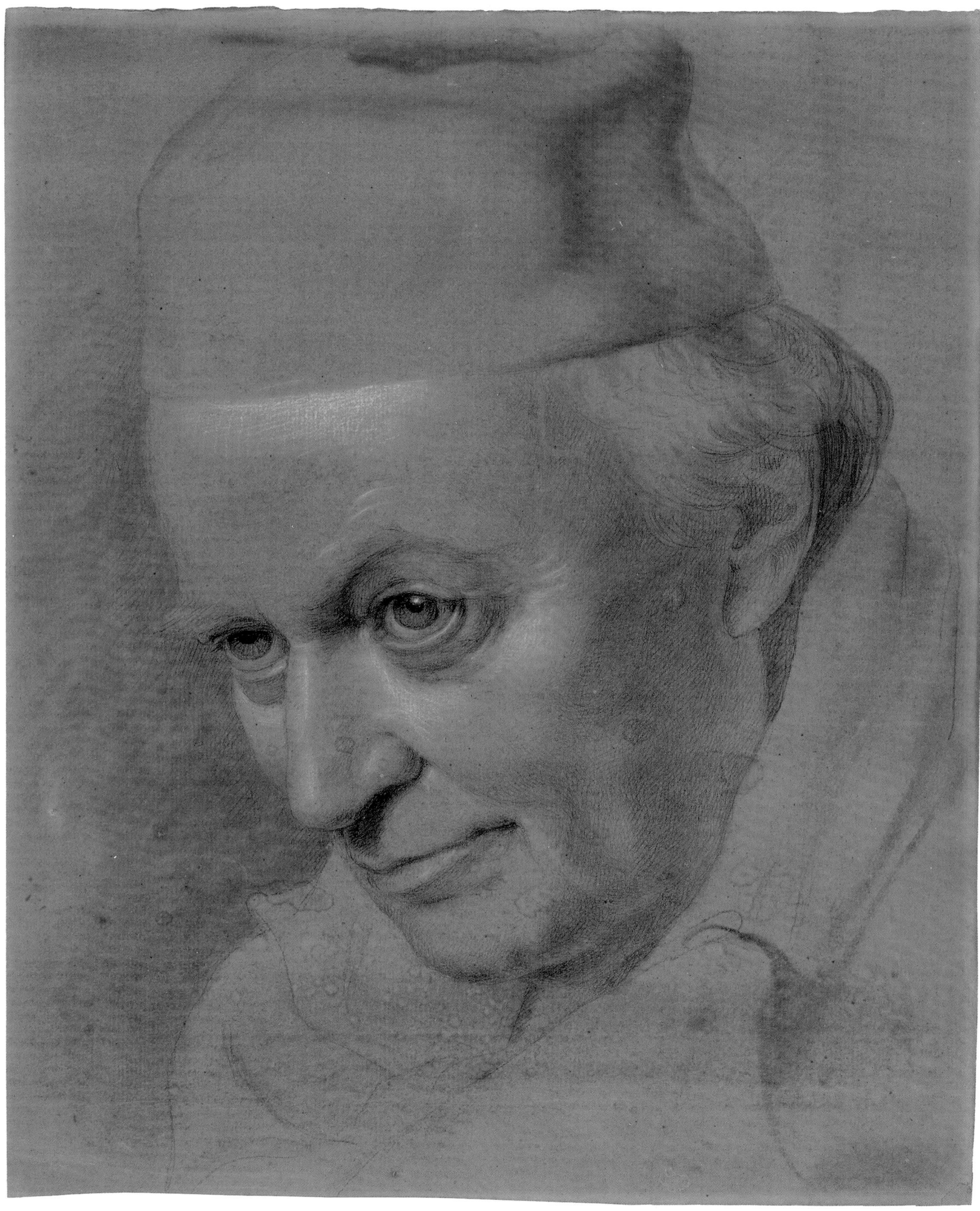

28

Joseph Anton Koch

Obergibeln/Tyrol 27 July 1768 – 12 January 1839
Rome

Rest on the Flight into Egypt, c. 1815 – 20

*Pen and black ink over pencil, on thin, transparent, laid
paper; watermark: Shell 1808; 309 x 411/13 mm (size of
sheet); 297 x 400 (size of image)*

Provenance: Ludwigsgalerie, Munich

Bibliography: Kunstwerke aus Karlsruher Privatbesitz,
*exh. cat., Badische Kunsthalle (Karlsruhe, 1922), no. 501;
Lutterotti 1940, p. 271, no. 570, fig. 245; Munich 1958, p. 39,
no. 95; Lübeck 1969, p. 55, no. 91; Bernhard 1974, vol. 1, p. 789
(repr.);* Staatsgalerie Stuttgart: Malerei und Plastik des
19. Jahrhunderts, *ed. Christian von Holst (Stuttgart, 1982),
pp. 96 f.; Lutterotti 1985, pp. 93, 353, Z570, fig. 206; Stuttgart
1989, p. 266, no. 115, fig. 191*

In contrast to his very personal and spirited early
Alpine landscape, executed in dark brown ink
(cat. 2), Koch drew this work with a summary,
pure outline in pale black ink, simplifying the
preliminary pencil sketch and defining it with
greater precision. Beginning in the late 1790s
and influenced by John Flaxman's outline illustrations as well as by his friend Asmus Jacob
Carsten's drawing style, Koch assimilated this
new, rather generalizing neoclassicistic technique,
which would remain his immutable, characteristic style.[1]

Using a simple outline, he incorporated the foreground, middle ground, and background—the

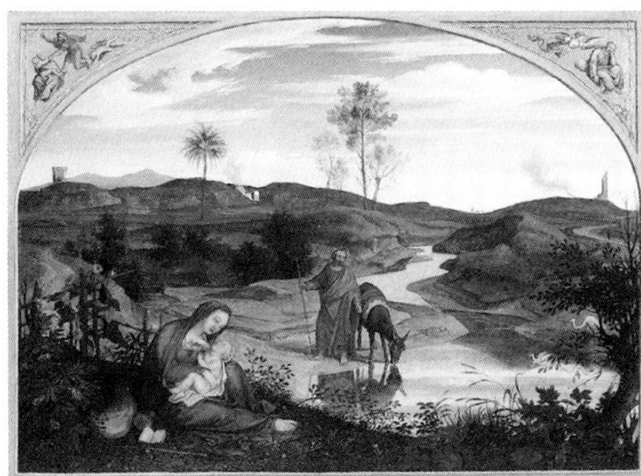

Joseph Anton Koch, *Rest on the Flight into Egypt*, c. 1820.
Oil on wood; 517 x 415 mm. Stuttgart, Staatsgalerie

earth and sky of his composition—into the surface plane, giving each equal value. Only the figures in the foreground have been given slightly
more emphasis. This sheet served as the direct
preliminary drawing, or "cartoon," for a small,
meticulously executed panel painting of identical format (fig.).[2] This radiantly colored painting

demonstrates the level of abstraction in Koch's
drawing. The small, previously unknown wood
panel, a collector's private devotional image and
cabinet piece, appeared about fifteen years ago
on the London art market and belongs today to
the Stuttgart Staatsgalerie.[3] According to an inscription, it comes from the estate of Dr. George
Nott (1767–1841), an English theologian who, as
Koch's patron and friend, acquired over a period
of decades an entire collection of paintings,
Dante illustrations, and drawings by the artist.
Nott funded Koch's trip to Italy in 1794 and paid
his expenses for three years.

From the sixteenth century on, the Flight into
Egypt and Rest on the Flight into Egypt had
been popular themes in landscape painting, especially in the work of Claude Lorrain. According
to the *Liber veritatis*, Claude depicted the first
theme in five paintings, and the second in four.[4]
The Nazarenes, too, were fond of these themes,
especially in the circle of artists around Ferdinand Olivier in Vienna, which included Julius
Schnorr von Carolsfeld for many years and
Joseph Anton Koch from 1812 to 1815.[5] These
artists occupied themselves intensively with the
art of the late Middle Ages and, in particular,
with apochryphal narrative scenes from the life
of Mary and the childhood of Jesus.[6] Possibly
influenced by the early German paintings in
Vienna's public collections, in this picture Koch
directly followed the late medieval, typological
narrative style, inserting in the spandrels scenes
that predetermine and clarify the main picture's
action. In the upper right spandrel, the angel
appears to Joseph in a dream to warn him of
Herod and advise him to seek refuge in Egypt
(Matt. 2:13, 16); the upper left spandrel portrays
the Massacre of the Innocents in Bethlehem,
which the Holy Family escaped by fleeing to
Egypt. In the left foreground of the main scene,
Mary sits in a small garden plot reminiscent of a
rose bower or enclosed garden (*hortus conclusus*),
which is an image of the Virgin from the *Song of
Songs* and a reference to the garden of Paradise.
Koch modeled the setting on the Tiber Valley in
the Roman Campagna without making it a portrait of a specific landscape. Scattered trees—
among them a palm—in the style of quattrocento Florentine painting identify this as a
Biblical scene. Koch placed the staffage more
prominently in the foreground than in his other
landscapes, so that the setting and figures carry
equal weight. The figures are based on the
Raphael canon, and the arched format of the picture also alludes to Renaissance painting. It suggests an architectural context, as in an altarpiece,
and was frequently used by the Nazarenes,
specifically for altar panels in connection with
the revival of the devotional image.[7] Ferdinand
Olivier was the first to use this architectural
frame with an arched top as a leitmotif in his

landscapes to elevate his pictures to a sacral
realm (cf. cat. 34). It was probably in Olivier's
house that Koch, during his Vienna years, was
inspired to use this kind of frame. It was rare in
Koch's other work, but he did use it immediately
after his return to Rome in 1816 in his painting
The Return of Jacob.[8] In this work, Koch created
a devotional picture in the Nazarene spirit as well
as a model for the type of idealized landscape
that his work subsequently helped to popularize.
Because it is so closely related to Nazarene conceptions of art, Koch's painting and the preliminary drawing exhibited here on which it is based
should be dated to the years immediately following his return to Rome from Vienna (1815 – 20).

1 Koch's 1803 copies after trecento and quattrocento figural
wall paintings in Florence and Pisa—for example, the
frescoes at the Camposanto of Pisa—also reveal his talent
for the clear, abstracting outline; cf. Ulrike Jenni, "Joseph
Anton Kochs Auseinandersetzung mit der Kunst des Trecento und Quattrocento: Zur romantischen Komponente
seines Schaffens," in *Römische Historische Mitteilungen*,
ed. Hermann Fillitz and Otto Kresten, vol. 37 (Vienna,
1995), pp. 163 – 91, figs. 1 – 30.
2 The laid lines of the thin paper have been misinterpreted
as traces of squaring; cf. Munich 1958, p. 39, no. 95.
3 Sotheby's, *Important Nineteenth Century European Paintings*, auction cat., 25 November 1981, lot. 13 (repr. in
color).
4 Cf. Munich 1991, p. 296, no. 146, nn. 1, 4 (Hinrich Sieveking).
5 In 1819, Overbeck drew and painted a version of *Rest on
the Flight into Egypt*; cf. Steinle 1977, pp. 152 f. We should
also recall Philipp Otto Runge's treatment of the theme
in a large altarpiece; Traeger 1975, p. 386, no. 322, color
pl. 10.
6 See Steinle 1977, pp. 152 – 61; cf. Munich 1994, p. 46, no. 6;
p. 56, no. 10; p. 58, no. 11.
7 Recall Scheffer von Leonhardshoff's major work, the
Death of Saint Cecilia, 1820/21, in the Österreichischen
Galerie, Vienna; cf. Andrews 1967, pl. 58 (in color); or Ferdinand Olivier's *The Holy Family on a Working Day*, 1817,
in the Georg Schäfer collection, Schweinfurt; cf. Schweinfurt 1966, p. 120, no. 104, color pl. 104.
8 Stuttgart 1989, pp. 253 ff., no. 109. fig. 182 (in color).

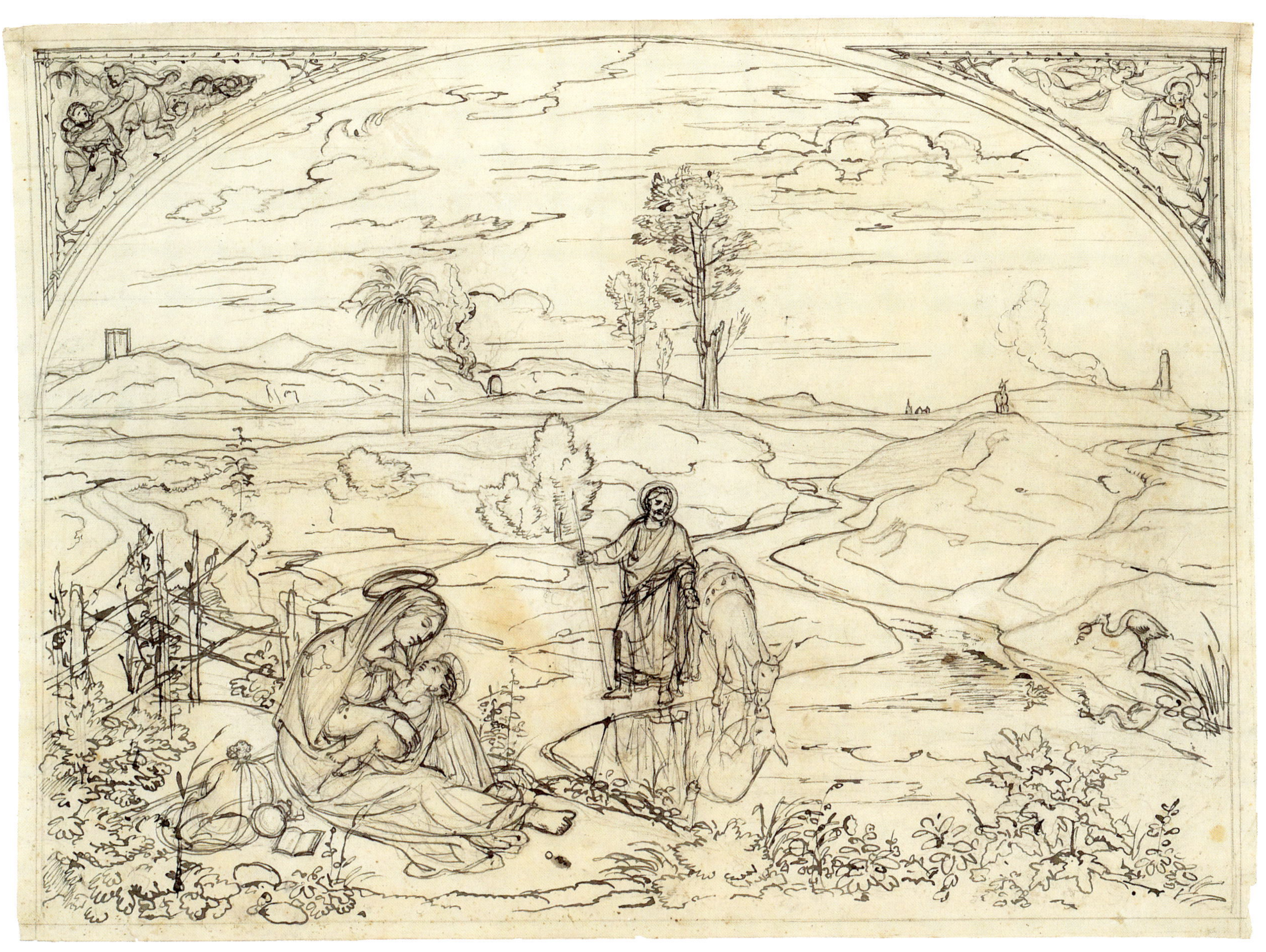

29

Friedrich Overbeck

Lübeck 3 July 1789–12 November 1869 Rome

Peter Cornelius

Düsseldorf 23 September 1783–6 March 1867 Berlin

Mutual Double Portrait, 1812

Pencil on wove paper; a strip of 19 mm added on the bottom; 424 x 370 mm
Inscribed, lower right: "Zur Erinnerung an unsern Freundt C. F. Schlosser, von F. Overbeck und J. P. Cornelius in Rom. d. 16 März 1815" [As a remembrance for our friend C. F. Schlosser, from F. Overbeck and J. P. Cornelius in Rome. 16 March 1815]
Verso inscribed in pen and light brown ink: "Bernus"

Provenance: Christian Heinrich Schlosser, Frankfurt am Main; Councillor Friedrich Schlosser, Stift Neuburg bei Heidelberg; until 1886, Baron Alexander von Bernus, Stift Neuburg bei Heidelberg; until 1906, Freiherr von Bernus, Heidelberg; Dr. Burg, Cologne; 1929–69, Emma Reifenberg-Lehnsen, New York; Dr. Fritz Nathan, Zurich

Selected bibliography (for additional literature, see Lübeck 1989, p. 202): Veit Valentin, "Meisterwerke des Stifts Neuburg," in Zeitschrift für Bildende Kunst mit dem Beiblatt Kunst-Chronik, ed. Carl von Lützow, vol. 17 (Leipzig, 1882), pp. 112 f. (repr.); Berlin 1906, p. 93, no. 2876; Lehr 1924, p. 176; Lohmayer 1935, p. 324; Andrews 1964, p. 91, repr., frontispiece and cover ill.; Lübeck 1969, pp. 18–20, no. 9 (repr.); Cambridge 1972, no. 9 (repr.); Kassel 1985, pp. 101–12 (Anton Merk), pp. 104 f., fig. 6; Lübeck 1989, pp. 200–202, no. 85, repr. (Hinrich Sieveking); Sieveking 1990, pp. 56, 119, fig. 13; Heidelberg 1995, p. 19 (repr.); Munich 1995, p. 114, fig. 35 (in color), p. 662, no. 107; Hofmann 1995, pp. 645, 651, fig. 538; Thomas Noll, Vincent van Gogh: Fischerboote am Strand von Les Saintes-Maries-de-la-Mer. Eine Kunstmonographie (Frankfurt am Main and Leipzig, 1996), pp. 110 f., fig. 23

Three months before the death of Franz Pforr, whose friendship with Overbeck formed the nucleus of the Brotherhood of St. Luke, Overbeck and Cornelius—the two future spiritual fathers and the driving force behind the Nazarene movement—drew these portraits of each other. This double portrait, especially notable given the prominence of the artists involved, is a compelling example of the Romantic friendship picture and has become widely known through frequent reproduction. The artists drew it in Rome on 16 March 1812,[1] after Cornelius had been admitted to the Brotherhood of St. Luke and had become close friends with Overbeck. Both artists dedicated and gave it as a gift to the physician and educator Dr. Christian Heinrich Schlosser, a nephew of Goethe's brother-in-law Johann Georg Schlosser, who associated with the Nazarenes. During evening sessions in the Monastery of San Isidoro, he read and translated Dante's poetry to his young artist friends. He had also attended the ailing Franz Pforr at the end of his life.

A single portrait of Cornelius furnishes additional insight into how the dual portrait was made. Drawn in soft pencil, it is identical to the dual portrait in posture, hairstyle, and the angle of the face, except that the eyes are turned toward the viewer (fig.). The chalky line and the disposition of hatchings show Overbeck's touch. Until now, the drawing was attributed to Philipp Veit and dated to c. 1815.[2] Gisela Scheffler surmised that Veit had drawn the likeness of Cornelius from the double portrait.[3] Norbert Suhr has shown that this was not the case and refuted the attribution to Veit.[4] It is clear that this drawing, which I attribute to Overbeck, is the direct study from life on which our double portrait was based. In the single portrait, Overbeck described the facial features more finely and three-dimensionally with interior modeling. In the double portrait, he abstracted the features by emphasizing the outlines, and adjusted them to the overall composition and the intended pictorial statement by changing the direction of the eyes. Cornelius probably drew a study of Overbeck in a similar manner and then worked it into the double portrait in a second step. Evidently, both single studies were fastened to an underlying sheet of paper for the transfer process; holes in the sheet of the Cornelius portrait suggest as much. In the transfer to the double portrait, the artists accentuated the contours and strengthened certain areas (for instance, the chins in both faces). Based on naturalistic single portraits, the two heads in the double portrait were spiritualized and elevated in the

spirit of Nazarene art. Both artists worked on the double portrait, as nuances in the hatching technique suggest. Because of the soft pencil they used and the normative handling of line, it is almost impossible to determine each artist's individual touch—testimony to the collective nature of the Brotherhood of St. Luke. The very similar postures, the heads and busts overlapping in a very shallow space, as in an image on a coin, speak of the equality and spiritual harmony of the Brothers. Still, the artists portrayed their own characters in very different ways. Although he appears close to the center foreground, Cornelius's face seems overshadowed compared to Overbeck's, and he looks intently straight ahead. Overbeck depicted his friend, six years his senior, as withdrawn and intellectual. We know from Overbeck's diary what he thought of Cornelius as a person,[5] and we learn what Cornelius thought about his friend from a letter to the history painter Carl Mosler written in March of 1812, around the time the drawing was made.[6] Overbeck's eyes are turned toward the viewer. His sincere and open face projects a combination of gentleness and personal charisma.

The solid structure of this double portrait, with its emphasis on outline, is reminiscent of carved and painted likenesses from the Italian Renaissance. The association with the sculpted portrait bust makes explicit another aspect of this masterpiece in drawing: the desire for immortalization. The composition, the posture, and the glances of both artists echo Raphael's self-portrait with Sodoma in the painting *The School of Athens*. Overbeck's countenance shows similarities to the young Dürer's, while Cornelius is dressed in Italian Renaissance style: a subtle hint of the "Italy and Germany" theme. Overbeck completed his work of that title in 1828; he had finished a cartoon for the painting in 1812, and his original intent was to call it *Friendship*.

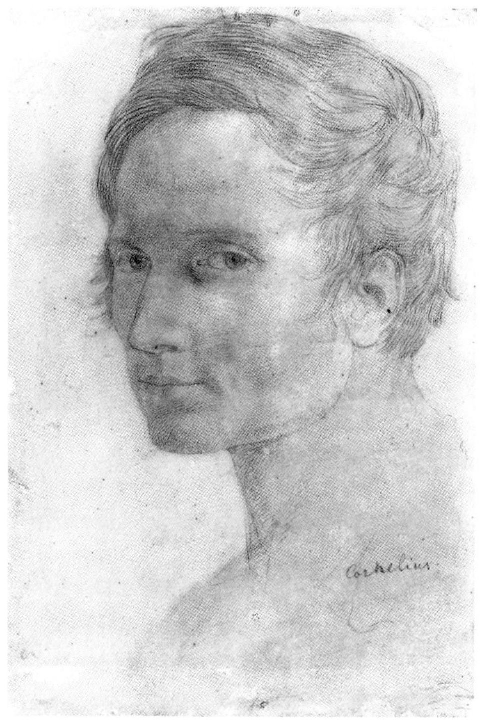

Friedrich Overbeck, *Portrait of Peter Cornelius*, 1812. Pencil; 221 x 146 mm. Munich, Staatliche Graphische Sammlung, inv. no. 1954:1 (as by Philipp Veit)

1 Contrary to the current inscription, "1815," the dating to 1812 is secure thanks to a letter from Overbeck to Joseph Sutter of 20 March 1812; cf. Howitt 1886, vol. 1, pp. 228 f. The sheet has suffered from an early restoration, during which the lower edge of the paper was added and the last digit of the date, which had become illegible, was redrawn as 5 instead of 2.
2 Lübeck 1957, p. 75, no. 217 (repr.); Bernhard 1974, vol. 2, p. 1891 (repr.); Munich 1981, p. 92, no. 105 (repr.).
3 *Ibid.*
4 Suhr 1991, pp. 77 f., 360, ZZW 29.
5 Howitt 1886, vol. 1, p. 229.
6 *Ibid.*, p. 228.

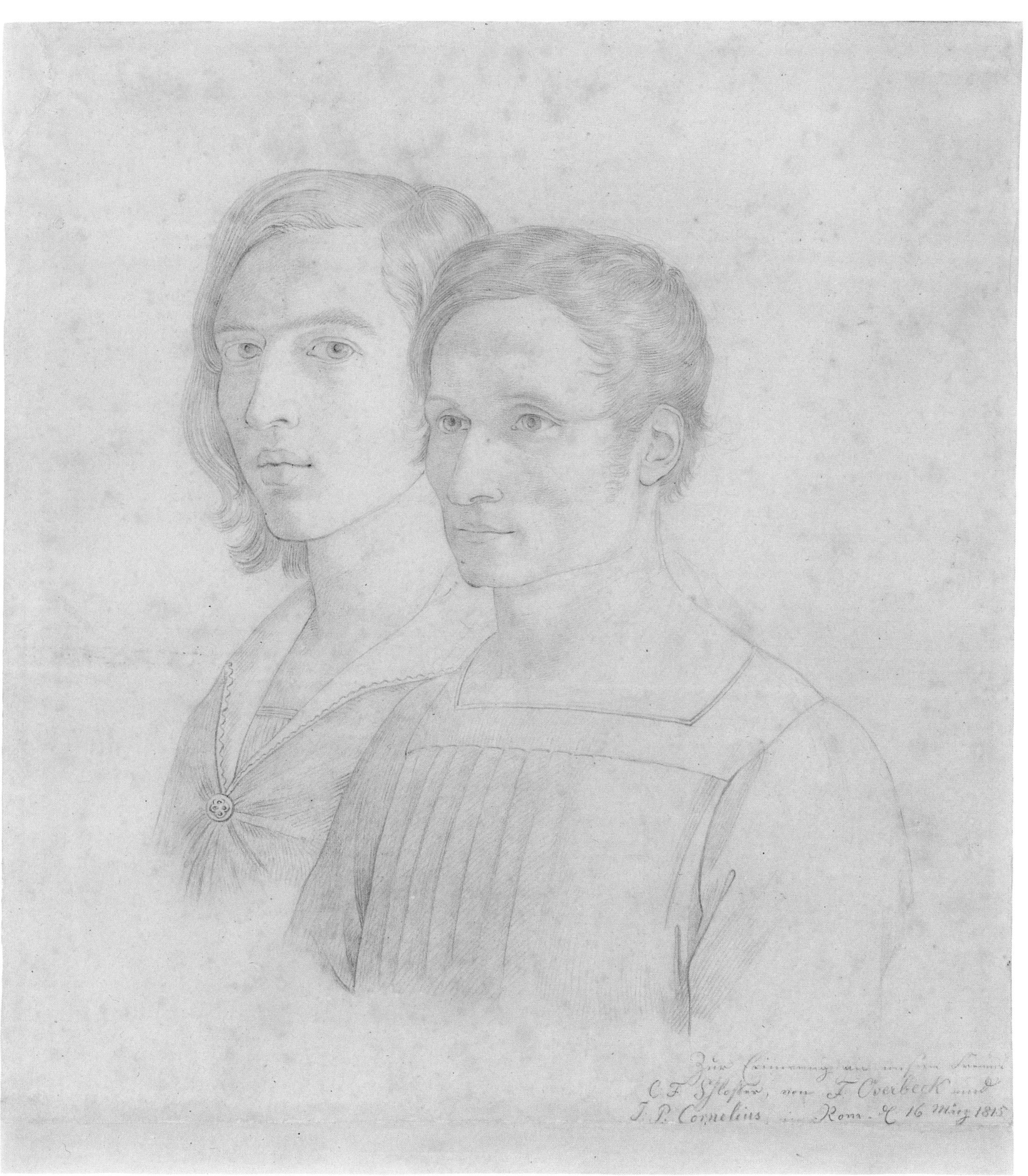
Zur Erinnerung an unsern Freunde
C. F. Schlosser, von F. Overbeck und
J. P. Cornelius, in Rom. ♃ 16 März 1815

Friedrich Overbeck

Lübeck 3 July 1789–12 November 1869 Rome

Madonna, c. 1814

Pencil on wove paper (yellowed); 297/99 x 211/12 mm;
border in pencil, trimmed on all sides
Signed and dated in pen and brown ink, lower right:
"Fr. Overbeck Romae/1866"

With his many altarpieces, Friedrich Overbeck made a significant contribution to the revival of the devotional image, a task the Nazarenes considered important. The theme of Mary and the Christ child became significant after the Nazarenes arrived in Rome, where they encountered the Madonna images of the quattrocento.[1] Confessional identity played a decisive role, since there was no worship of the virgin in Protestantism.[2] Overbeck, influenced by his conversion to Catholicism, was particularly devoted to this theme. In the present *Madonna*, composed in the narrative style of the old masters, Overbeck drew upon the early German and Netherlandish panel painting tradition he knew from Vienna; the drawing should be interpreted with this in mind. The *Madonna*, drawn in gray pencil and surrounded by stone architecture, has a grisaille effect; she is related to the early Netherlandish figures painted in a grisaille technique that suggests stone. The youthful Mother of God is seated in the light on a grassy bench in front of a stone wall with architectural features and a view through windows. The source of light in the upper right corner can be readily detected from the shadow cast by the bench on the left side. The image implicitly recalls the late medieval motif of the Madonna on a Grassy Bench. The wall behind her recalls, in this context, the *hortus conclusus*, or enclosed garden, an image from the *Song of Songs* interpreted in the Christian tradition as alluding to Mary's virginity and the garden in Paradise. The stone bench, richly ornamented in the Italian Renaissance style, resembles a throne, and the closed book to Mary's right attests to her piety, wisdom, and knowledge of scripture. Mary dominates the foreground, her figure nearly the height of the sheet itself. Overbeck has ingeniously placed her like a caryatid on the central vertical axis in front of the window opening. The image thus assumes a deeply symbolic meaning: Mary as the central pillar of the Church and, in the context of the stone bench and wall, perhaps also the pillar of the Church that was built on rock. Another innovation is Overbeck's depiction of the Christ child with the cruciform nimbus—a subtle allusion to the Passion—clasping the apple tightly with both hands, while Mary places her hand protectively yet assertively on top. Here, the apple of the Fall

is a symbol of redemption through the new Adam, Jesus Christ.

Mary and the child have rather broad, round faces, which resemble the figural types in Overbeck's painting *Christ in the House of Mary and Martha* (1813–16).[3] Mary's head, a facial type from pre-Raphaelite art, such as Perugino's, is not an idealized image of Overbeck's wife, Nina. This indicates that the work dates from before 1818, the year of their marriage. Mary's long, blond hair is chastely covered by a kerchief and a cloak. The garments with ornamented borders that are worn by mother and child hark back to Raphael's madonnas. Precedents for the statuesque posture and architecturally symmetrical composition can be found in Giovanni Bellini's Venetian paintings.[4] Overbeck's *Madonna in Front of a Wall* of 1811 was also strongly influenced by Bellini,[5] which attests to the early date of the present drawing.

The double-arched window gives a view onto two landscapes. As in many late medieval German panel paintings, these landscapes are not part of a uniform spatial continuum but are two separate scenes. On the left, we see a medieval German town with a Gothic church reminiscent of those in and around Vienna, while on the right, we find an Italian river landscape with a medieval bridge and architecture. Mary thus appears as the element uniting the two worlds symbolized by the landscapes, and as the pillar of the Church and the faith.

These separate landscapes clearly allude to the theme of Italy and Germany, a central idea for Overbeck and Franz Pforr, the founders of the Brotherhood of St. Luke, as seen in Overbeck's major work, *Italy and Germany*, and in Pforr's diptych *Sulamith and Mary* (cf. cat. 32). Pforr conceived of his composition from the very outset as a diptych, a format that goes back to early Netherlandish models and that provided the inspiration for a pencil drawing by Overbeck in 1814, showing the Annunciation and Visitation.[6] The technique of that drawing is also extremely close to that of the present work. Both drawings include a vine ornament on the arch of the window frame, which is important because of its Eucharistic symbolism, a motif that can be traced back to the decorated arch frame in Dürer's *Life of the Virgin*.[7] Compositionally, however, the present drawing is closest to Pforr's design for the concluding page of illustrations to Goethe's *Götz von Berlichingen*.[8] In that work, Christ's body on the cross appears as an Atlantean figure in place of the central pillar in an identical double-arched window frame, corresponding to Mary as a caryatid here.

The detail of the damaged and missing pieces of the brick wall on the windowsill to Mary's left reappears in Overbeck's *Italy and Germany*—the completion of which dragged on from 1811 to

1828—on the right edge in the upper part of the brick wall on Germany's side. The missing piece of wall is a sign of loss; it could refer to the recent death of Overbeck's friend Franz Pforr. Since it appears in both pictures only on the "German" side, however, Overbeck could also have intended it as a contrast to the "whole" Italian side. Perhaps he was suggesting that Italy was in good order because of Catholicism, while his German homeland was not because of its religious schism. Perhaps he used the motif to indicate reformation and secularization.

Overbeck's early draftsmanship is characterized by pronounced contours and sensitive interior modeling in the form of hatching. The dense network of strokes evokes extremely refined light-dark values that bring to mind early German drawings and prints, in particular the engravings of Lucas von Leyden. The rigorous uniform handling of line is characteristic of Overbeck's early period, and the similarity to Pforr's *Götz* composition and to the details and the initial conception of the Italy-and-Germany theme all indicate a date for this drawing of around 1814, not too long after Pforr's death. The drawing was originally unsigned, as was often the case in this early period. Overbeck's late signature, written in pen and rare in the form seen on this sheet, suggests that the artist added it only when he parted with the work.

1 Steinle 1977, p. 131.
2 *Ibid.*, p. 130.
3 Lübeck 1989, p. 124, no. 16 (repr. in color).
4 For instance, the so-called *Morelli Madonna*, who is seated in front of a curtain with a view of the landscape off to her side; cf. Rona Goffen, *Giovanni Bellini* (New Haven and London, 1989), p. 53, fig. 35.
5 For the Pietà character of the sleeping child, Overbeck was also clearly following Bellini's madonna seated on a stone throne with the sleeping child in her lap; cf. *ibid.*, p. 42, fig. 24. Friedrich Overbeck, *Madonna in Front of a Wall*, 1811; cf. Lübeck 1989, pp. 118 f., no. 15 (repr. in color).
6 The drawing is in the Kupferstichkabinett, Basel; cf. Basel 1982, p. 183, no. 95, fig. 36.
7 See, for example, the 1514 woodcut showing the meeting of Joachim and Anna at the Golden Gate (M.191).
8 Lehr 1924, p. 350, no. 129, pl. 27, fig. 42.

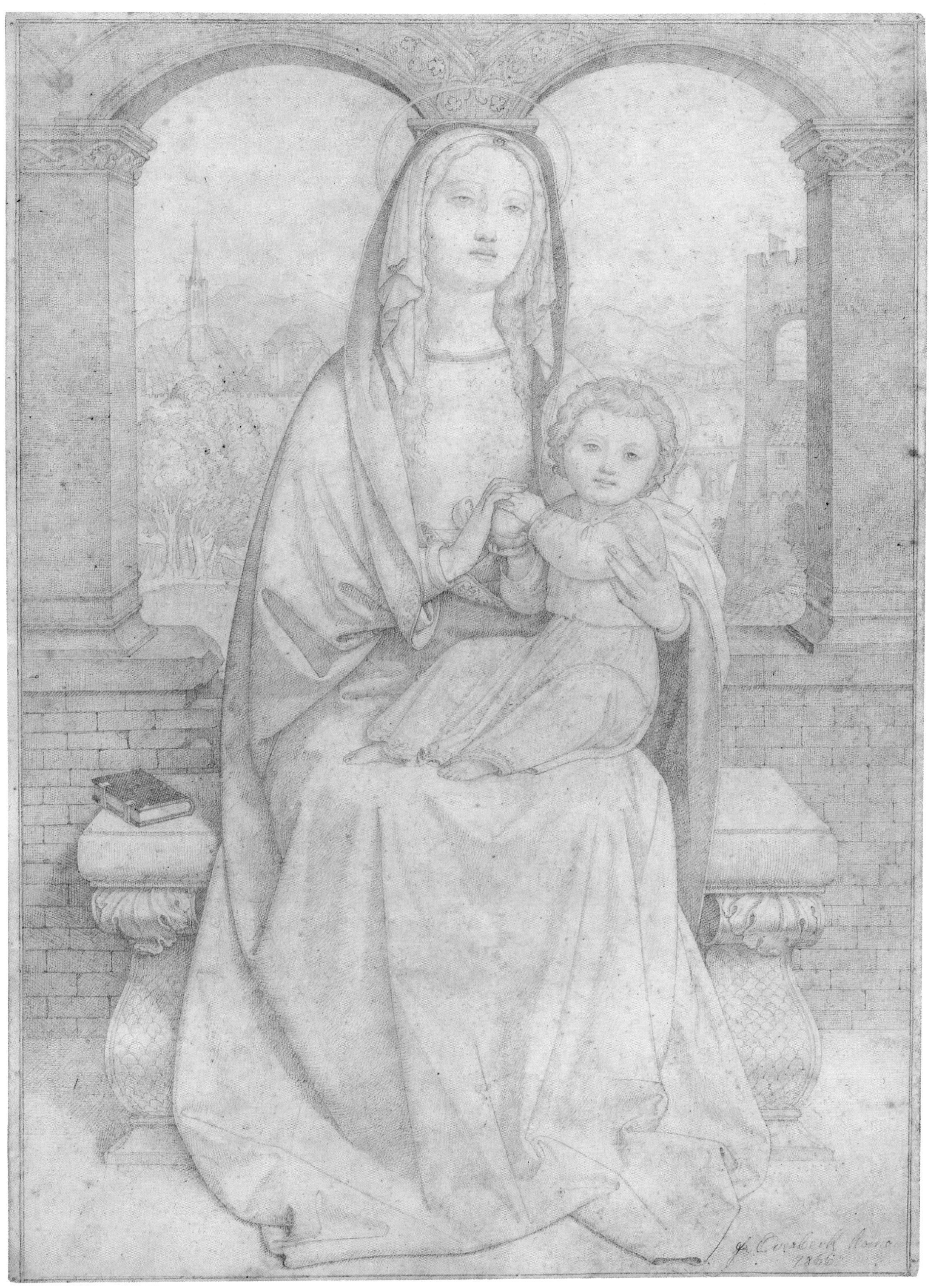

Friedrich Overbeck

A Scene from Roman Life, c. 1819

Pen and light reddish-brown ink, traces of pencil, on wove paper; 163 x 188 mm; trimmed on all sides, upper left corner restored

Provenance: Carl Friedrich von Rumohr; von Passavant-Gontard, Frankfurt am Main; Ludwigsgalerie, Munich

Selected bibliography (for additional bibliography, see Lübeck 1989, p. 217): Auction Hugo Helbing, estate of von Passavant-Gontard and others, auction cat., 3 December 1931, p. 53, no. 1093, pl. 19 (repr.); Munich 1958, p. 44, no. 117, fig. 11; Marbach 1966, p. 183, no. 260; Lübeck 1969, p. 66, no. 120; Lübeck 1989, pp. 216 f., no. 98, p. 42 (repr. in color); Sieveking 1990, pp. 56, 121, fig. 15

This genre scene of a family on the vine-covered terrace of an Italian country villa suggests a secularized depiction of the Holy Family. The drawing—with a composition and figural canon modeled after Italian Renaissance examples and with precise, calligraphic lines recalling the engraving style of the period of Dürer—is a masterpiece of Nazarene draftsmanship. The prevailing opinion is that a newly married Overbeck depicted himself with his family at the Villa Palombara on the Esquiline, where he spent a year from 1818 to 1819.[1] The villa, belonging to the marchese Massimi and surrounded by vineyards and vegetable gardens, was not far from the Casino Massimo, where Overbeck was painting the Tasso room.

In August of 1819, Overbeck's son Alfons was born; his daughter Maria followed in 1822, and in 1826, a second daughter, Agnes, was born. Both girls died soon after birth. At best, this piece would therefore be an idealized, imagined picture of Overbeck's family life. If so, the drawing could not have been executed before 1826.

Jensen was correct in assuming that the drawing is identical to one that Overbeck did for Carl Friedrich von Rumohr and mentioned in a letter to his parents on 15 January 1820: "I recently presented to Rumohr, as a token of my gratitude, a small sheet drawn with the pen. He has promised to send it soon for you to look at; it is a picture of Roman life, occasioned by impressions of our former villa."[2] This makes it clear that the persons depicted are not the Overbeck family, even though Nina, Alfons, and Friedrich Overbeck are "freely hinted at"[3] in the group on the right, a mother with her infant and a man. I follow Jensen in dating the drawing to the period after Alfons's birth, to the fall of 1819.

The drawing was not listed in the auction catalogue of Rumohr's estate.[4] Rumohr must therefore have parted with it during his lifetime. Perhaps the Overbeck family in Lübeck, to whom he sent the drawing at the artist's request, did not return it, having received it as a present.

Although Jensen (1969)[5] and Gerkens[6] have written on Overbeck as a draftsman, there is as yet no comprehensive critical study of his entire oeuvre of drawings. As a result, hardly any parallels have been suggested between the present sheet and Overbeck's other known drawings. For a variety of reasons, I questioned the attribution to Overbeck, an opinion seconded by Keith Andrews of Edinburgh, one of the leading experts on Nazarene drawings.[7] However, on the basis of recent findings, Overbeck's authorship must now be accepted without any doubt. The close similarity of the draftsmanship to that of Julius Schnorr von Carolsfeld can be plausibly explained by the intimate friendship and collaboration between the two artists in the years 1818 to 1820. Schnorr's acknowledged mastery of drawing with pen and brown ink, in which he assimilated the style of the old masters, challenged Overbeck to create some of his loveliest compositions in the same technique. In addition to the present work, two small signed and dated drawings from the period 1819/20 have recently come to light; in both cases, scholars have noted their similarity to the present work.[8] One of these in particular, *Allegory of Summer*, exemplifies the same technical characteristics as the drawing exhibited here.[9] There is also another mystery we can attempt to solve: it concerns the study of a woman's drapery, previously attributed to Franz Pforr, who died in 1812. It shows an enlarged version of the lower part of the standing female figure in the present drawing (fig.), viewed from the rear. It was probably copied by Overbeck himself, who used a sheet of paper from the monastery of San Isidoro period that was in Pforr's estate.[10] Presumably, the study was done in preparation for a painting of a larger size. In 1991, a previously unknown etching after the exhibited drawing appeared, identical in format and without inscription or date, probably a unique impression. Sketchlike in character, it completes our unfinished drawing (for instance, the artist added floor tiles and the upper left portion of the pergola). Overbeck presumably etched the drawing for himself, trying out an appropriate reproduction process, before giving it to Rumohr as a gift.

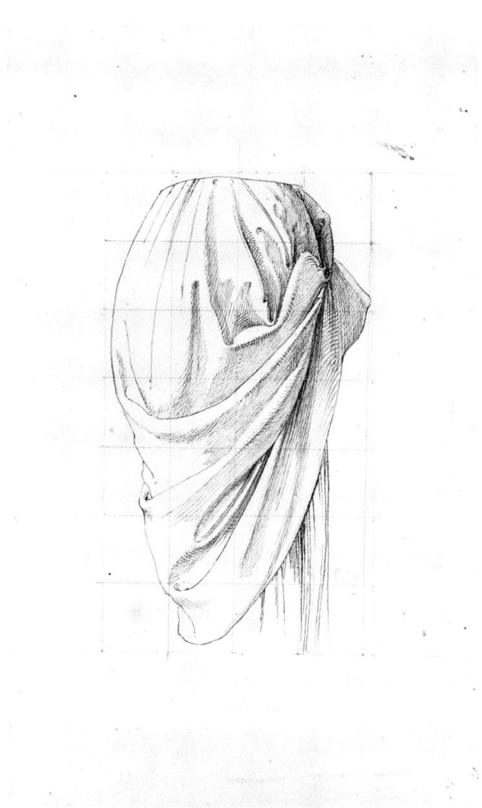

Friedrich Overbeck, *Study of a Woman's Drapery*, c. 1819. Pen and black ink over pencil; squared; 250 x 149 mm

1 The villa with pergola can be seen in Overbeck's family picture, begun in 1829, now in Lübeck; cf. Andrews 1967, p. 31, pl. 5.

2 Jensen 1962, pp. 372 f. A copy of the letter is in the Stadtarchiv Lübeck, Familienarchiv Overbeck 2, fols. 856–40. I am grateful to Jens Christian Jensen for providing me with the exact quotation from the letter. Rumohr had just recently helped Overbeck by advancing the payment for his painting *Christ's Entry into Jerusalem*; cf. Lübeck 1989, p. 216, no. 98. On C. F. von Rumohr, cf. cat. 53.

3 Jensen 1962, pp. 372 f.

4 Frenzel 1846.

5 Jens Christian Jensen, *Zeichnungen von Friedrich Overbeck in der Lübecker Graphiksammlung* (Lübeck, n. d. [1969]).

6 Gerhard Gerkens, "Overbeck als Zeichner," in Lübeck 1989, pp. 34–41 and catalogue section.

7 Lübeck 1989, pp. 216 f., no. 98 (Hinrich Sieveking). Letter from Keith Andrews to Alfred Winterstein, dated 21 November 1960: "... but it seems irrefutable to me that the drawing is by Schnorr."

8 *In Front of the Wall*, 1820. Pen and light brown ink; 124 x 140 mm. Monogrammed and dated: *FO* (in ligature)/1820. Dresden, Kupferstichkabinett, inv. no. 1896–15; Lübeck 1989, p. 218, no. 100, (repr.) (Gerhard Gerkens). *Allegory of Summer*, 1819. Pen and brown ink; 86 x 90 mm. Monogrammed and dated: *FO* (in ligature)/1819.

9 Under the title *The Four Ages of Man*, in Potsdam 1995, pp. 335 f., no. 6.21; p. 341 (repr. in color) (Gerd Bartoschek).

10 Verso: traces of a figural drawing and writing in pencil: "S. Isidoro"; additional inscription with pen in black ink: "Carissimo amico sod(?)f(?)"; Lehr 1924, p. 549, no. 119. These *pentimenti* point to Pforr's technique, thus the recto came to be attributed to him.

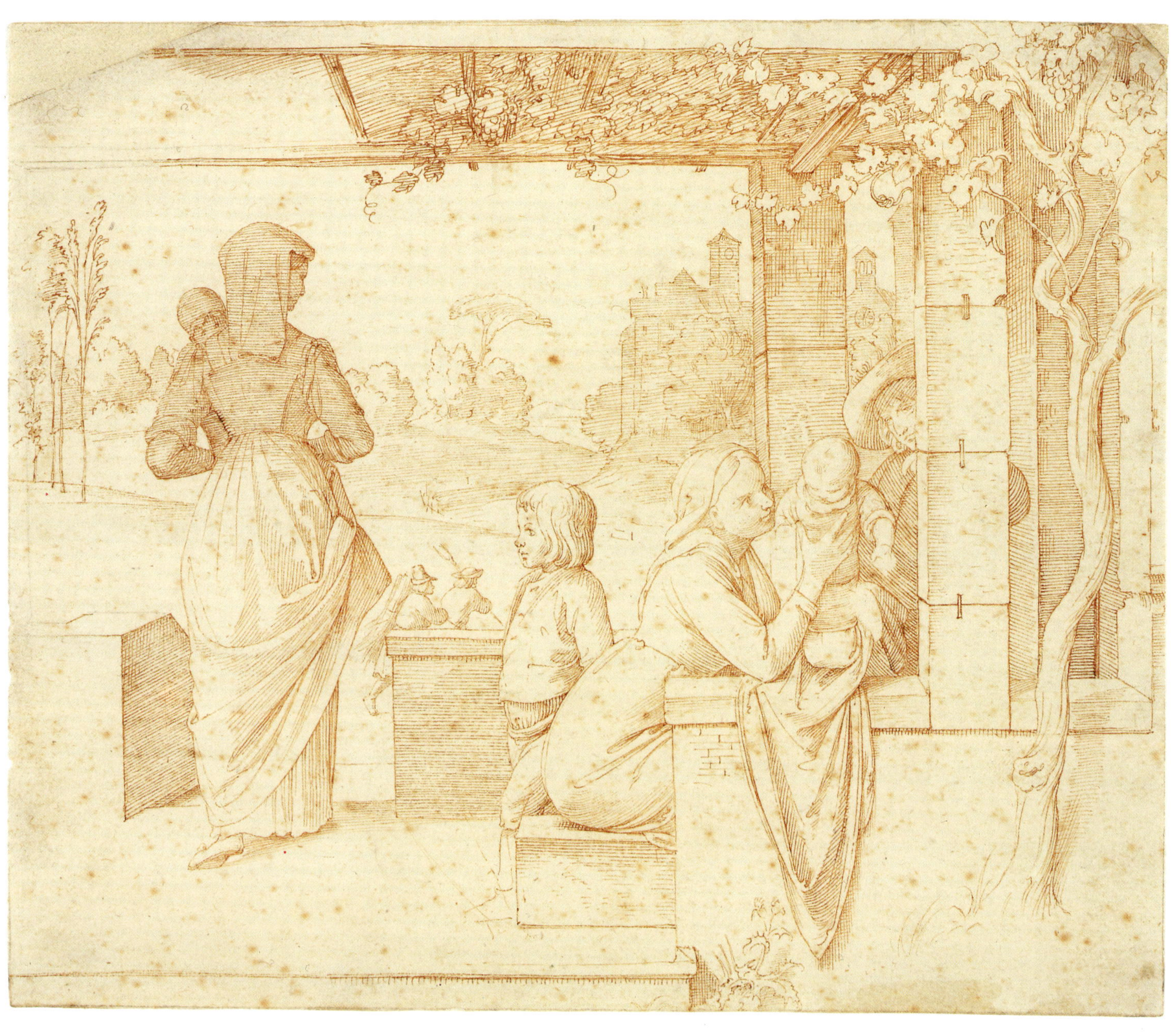

32

Franz Pforr

Frankfurt am Main 5 April 1788 – 16 June 1812
Albano, near Rome

Homecoming at Night, 1808

*Pen and black ink, brush and gray wash over pencil, on
laid paper; 156/58 x 127 mm
Verso: watercolor trial strokes*

*Bibliography: Munich 1958, p. 45, no. 118, fig. 10; Jens
Christian Jensen, "Gedenkblatt für den Maler Franz
Pforr, den Freund Friedrich Overbecks," in* Der Wagen
1963: Ein Lübeckisches Jahrbuch *(Lübeck, 1963), pp. 87,
85, fig. 2; Andrews 1964, p. 97, no. 14b (repr.); Andrews 1967,
p. 95 (repr.); Hasse 1969, pp. 303 f., fig. 4; Lübeck 1969, p. 68,
no. 124, p. 69 (repr.); Bernhard 1974, vol. 2, p. 1121 (repr.);
Steinle 1977, p. 231, fig. 187; Munich 1985, pp. 68–72, no. 21
(repr.); Manfred Jauslin, "Die gescheiterte Kulturrevolu-
tion: Perspektiven religiös-romantischer Kunstbewegung
vor der Folie der Avantgarde" (Ph. D. diss., Basel, 1988;
Munich, 1989), p. 121, n. 2*

In the summer of 1808, a group of like-minded
students at the Academy in Vienna, among them
the painter Ludwig Vogel from Zurich, formed a
friendship circle around Franz Pforr and Friedrich Overbeck. Every other week they assigned
themselves the task of inventing compositional
ideas on a given theme, and then they compared
and critically evaluated the results. One such
subject was a nocturnal "homecoming." Like the
pain of parting, the return home—as an experience of hope and longing, of expectation and the
joy of meeting again—was a popular theme in
romantic music and literature.[1] In a report on his
studies, Pforr wrote from Vienna to his guardian
Sarasin in Frankfurt am Main, "We had resolved
that each one of us would produce a painted
night piece by a certain date. I painted a small
picture: a man who returns home and finds his
wife at work. I chose this quiet, domestic scene
because battle painting no longer satisfied me.
For the representation of a scene that, despite its
impression of grandeur, shows the corruption of
humankind, no longer seemed to me a subject
quite worthy of art …."[2]
In the drawing exhibited here, Pforr presents an
escapist vision of the earthly happiness he
dreamed of. We learn this from a "dream of the
future" that he wrote for his fellow members,
presumably in the early years of the Brotherhood
of St. Luke, in which he described the life he
hoped for. He evoked a small sitting room that
was clean and pleasant and built in "the old
style": "In one bay of the windows are my easel
and painting supplies …. But the door opens and
a woman enters …. she sits down to her work at
the table, which is not far from the alcove in

which stands the pure bed consecrated to the
most loyal and chaste love …. The door opens
again and you, Overbeck, enter as well …. No,
such happiness would be too much."[3] In a letter
to J. D. Passavant, dated 6 January 1809, Pforr
wrote, "I long for a place of which I can say, this
is where you will stay …. I feel that I am not
meant for the restless, grand life. A small chamber with my easel in it, a few friends, and a livelihood, that satisfies my desires …. A quiet, bourgeois life, that is the real thing."[4]
This drawing thus depicts the happy life of
Pforr's imagination: the ideal bride in a sparsely
furnished, early German sitting room, doing her
needlework at the table by candlelight. She turns
with anticipation toward the man who enters
the room, wearing a broad-brimmed hat and a
wide cloak; this is Pforr himself, shutting the
door behind him. The paint box, palette, and
stretched canvas on the floor in the right foreground are clearly associated with the artist.
Behind his imagined bride rises a high stove,
which keeps his supper warm, and farther back,
at the end of the orthogonals of the floorboards,
is an alcove with a sleeping nook. The room and
the disposition of the figures faintly recall early-
German and Netherlandish Annunciation compositions,[5] which take place in middle-class living and sleeping chambers, a symbolic setting
derived from the mysticism of the bride in the
Christian tradition.
Pforr's programmatic reference to early German
art in his dream image of a middle-class life of
peaceful solitude continued in the major work he
painted in Italy, the friendship painting for
Overbeck entitled *Shulamit and Mary.*[6] He
shows both female figures in the diptych in their
respective environments: on the left, Overbeck's
Raphaelesque Shulamit on a bench in an enclosed Edenic garden surrounded by the southern
Italian landscape and vegetation, and on the
right, Pforr's early German Mary in a late-medieval chamber with bull's-eye glass panes, an echo
of Dürer's engraving *St. Jerome in His Study.*
Both women represent the ideal brides of the
two artist friends and embody their respective
conceptions of art. In the right wing, Pforr
introduced a variation on *Homecoming at Night,*
except Mary is alone and Pforr does not enter the
chamber. In the left panel, Overbeck approaches
Shulamit through the garden gate with shy anticipation. Evidently, Pforr deliberately left himself out of the picture. Sensing that his death was
near, he no longer believed that his dream of an
artist's life would be fulfilled (cf. cat. 30).
In his finished compositional design *Homecoming at Night,* Pforr handled the distribution of
light and shade with complete mastery, using
reserves of the white paper and subtle gradations
of gray wash that attest to his pronounced sense
of colorism.[7]

A small pencil sketch from the estate of Ludwig
Vogel served as a preparatory study for the
present wash drawing.[8] It shows the young
woman's expectant posture in even greater detail. Perhaps Pforr made other detailed preparatory drawings, which, together with the present
work, served as models for his lost oil painting.[9]
Ludwig Vogel also created a night piece: *The
Homecoming of the Swiss Soldier.* In December
1808, he began to execute it in oil.[10] Because
Vogel's work was part of the same design project
the Vienna students assigned themselves, we can
assume that Pforr also made his drawing at the
end of 1808.

1 Cf. Claude Keisch, *Abschied, Reise, Heimkehr: Eine Motiv-
   gruppe zwischen Empfindsamkeit und Biedermeier. Das
   Studio 16,* exh. cat., Staatliche Museen zu Berlin, Nationalgalerie (Berlin, 1978).
2 Printed, along with an accompanying letter, in Lehr 1924,
   pp. 32–43, quote p. 40.
3 *Ibid.,* pp. 293 f.
4 *Ibid.,* pp. 271 f.
5 For example, on the left wing of the Columba Altar by
   Rogier van der Weyden, Munich, Bayerische Staatsgemäldesammlungen (Alte Pinakothek).
6 Repr. in color in Andrews 1967, p. 33, pl. 7.
7 Using the same technique with gray wash, Pforr created
   other pictorially composed night pieces, probably as part
   of the same task: for example, a domestic scene related to
   the present piece, an illustration to Heinrich Pestalozzi's
   Lienhard and Gertrud, chap. 1; cf. Lehr 1924, p. 343,
   no. 58, pl. 13, fig. 21.
8 *Young Woman Doing Needlework,* study for *Homecoming
   at Night,* 1808. Pencil; 80 x 70 mm; estate inv. no. 693.
9 Among the lost oil paintings in Lehr 1924, p. 333, no. 8,
   V.A.5. Listed in Boetticher, vol. 2.1, p. 264, no. 1: "Genre
   scene. A garret in which a girl is seated by the light of a
   burning lamp, as a man wrapped in a cloak enters hastily.
   Pictures rest on the floor, and through the window one
   can see the rooftops of the neighboring houses. It is win-
   tertime, and here and there are scattered flashes of illuminated windows."
10 Salomon Vögelin, "Das Leben Ludwig Vogels, Kunst-
   maler von Zürich," in *Neujahrsblatt der Künstler-
   gesellschaft in Zürich 1881 und 1882,* pp. 16 f.; Steinle 1977,
   p. 231.

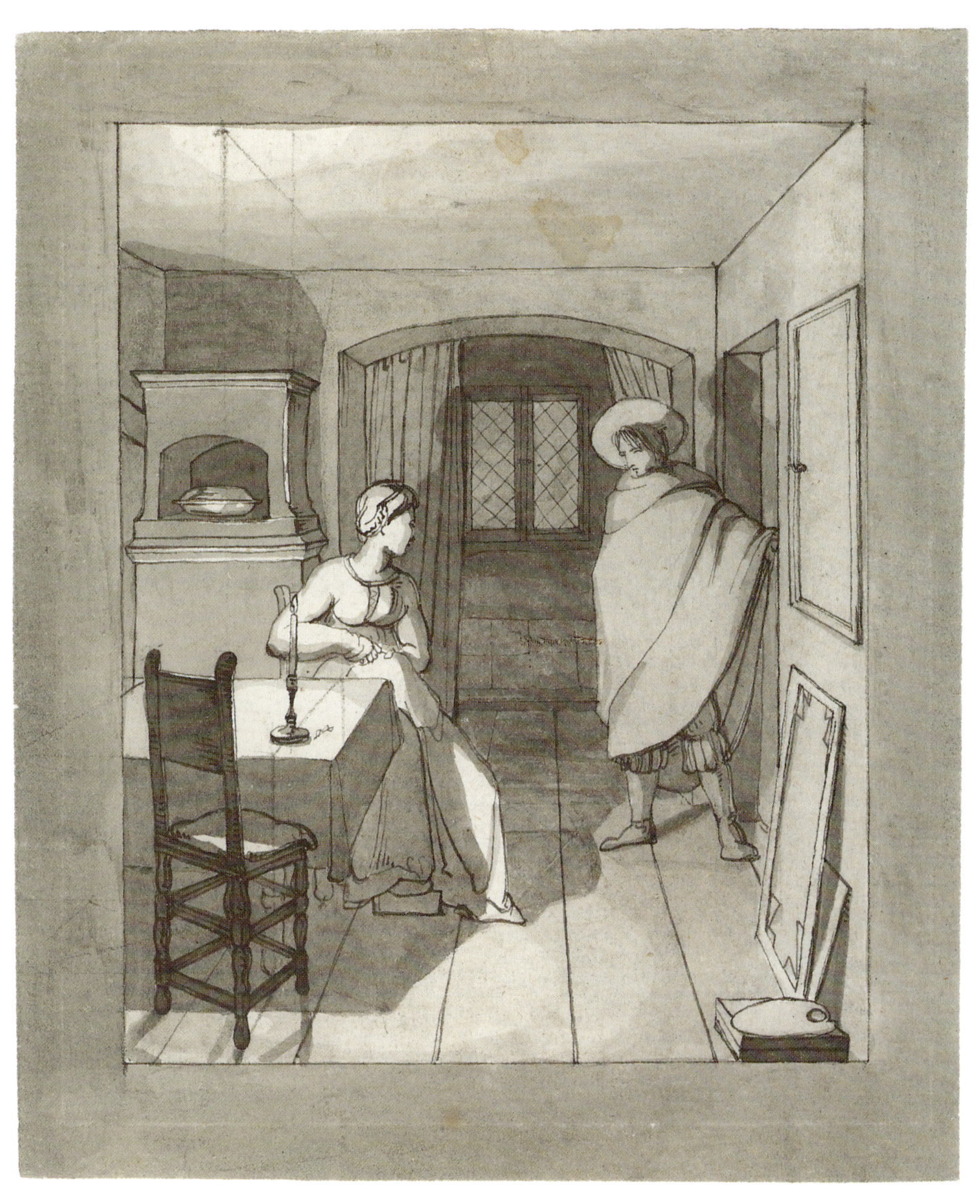

33

Peter Cornelius, formerly attributed to

Düsseldorf 23 September 1783 – 6 March 1867 Berlin

Head of a Boy, c. 1817

Pencil on wove paper; 195 x 174 mm
Inscribed verso, in pencil, by another hand: "Jul. Schnorr"

Provenance: Else Sohn-Rethel, Düsseldorf

Selected bibliography: Heise 1928, p. 36, no. 41 (repr.);
Munich 1958, p. 21, no. 10, fig. 15; Lübeck 1969, pp. 20 ff.,
no. 12 (repr.); Frankfurt 1977, p. 193, no. E.21, p. 223 (repr.);
Rome 1981, p. 78, no. 6; Frankfurt 1991, pp. 17 f. (repr.), p. 49,
no. 28; Darmstadt 1995, pp. 92 ff., fig. 7 (Jens Christian
Jensen)

This frontal, bust-length drawing of a boy is an outstanding example of the Nazarenes' achievements in portraiture. Executed in realistic detail with a pencil as sharp and hard as a metal stylus, its steely, swift, and calligraphic stroke renders a generalized, coolly distant expression that transcends individual features and has an enduring quality reminiscent of carved marble. Here, a precision recalling engravings of the Dürer period is combined with an allusion to antique sculpture. The Nazarene ideal required this evocation of the eternal in portraiture.

Carl Georg Heise first brought this portrait to public attention as a work by Peter Cornelius in his 1926 exhibition in Lübeck, a groundbreaking show of Nazarene art. Since then, the portrait has been exhibited and reproduced frequently. One of the best-known works in the Winterstein collection, it contributed to Cornelius's reputation as a first-rate portraitist. Right up through the 1991 Cornelius exhibition in Frankfurt, no one ever voiced doubt about its attribution to him. In 1995, Jens Christian Jensen, one of the preeminent experts on Nazarene drawings, was the first to raise questions about Cornelius's authorship. In the catalogue of the Fohr Exhibition in Darmstadt, Jensen not only questioned the Cornelius attribution but ascribed the drawing to Carl Philipp Fohr and explained his arguments at length.[1] Frank Büttner, who is in the process of publishing the second volume of his monograph on Peter Cornelius, will not include the present work in the catalogue of drawings. The difficulty of making a definite attribution arises in part from the Nazarenes' aspiration, during the early years of the Brotherhood of St. Luke, to sacrifice their individual styles in favor of a more general statement. That is why the Nazarenes rarely signed their studies. Individual achievements became anonymous ones in the collective atelier, an attempt to approximate the medieval workshop.

Any proposal to clarify the authorship of this sheet should seriously consider its provenance and the information about the attribution that the study of its provenance provides. It is interesting that a number of other drawings undoubtedly by the same artist also come from the Sohn-Rethel collection. These drawings, too, have thus far been attributed to Cornelius.[2] Although none of the securely documented drawings from his early Roman period show the use of a sharp, hard pencil and a similarly calligraphic line, it is conceivable that Cornelius, influenced by Overbeck, Schnorr, and Fohr, briefly adopted this idiosyncratic stroke.[3]

How else can we explain the traditional attribution? Perhaps Cornelius owned some of the drawings in question and retained them because he appreciated their quality, and because they reminded him of the artist who created them. The only candidates for the author of this group are first-rate draftsmen: Friedrich Overbeck, Julius Schnorr von Carolsfeld, Johann Anton Ramboux, Carl Philipp Fohr, and Franz Horny, all of whom had close ties to Cornelius in Rome. They all would have been capable of the kind of severe line found in the present portrait. Overbeck's early drawings have not been completely documented, so surprises are possible.[4] The inscription on the verso of the portrait indicates that Schnorr could have been the draftsman. He cannot be ruled out, since he experimented with pencil during his early years in Rome, when his work was influenced by Ferdinand Olivier's precise draftsmanship. Ramboux occasionally created astonishing drawings with a precise and abstracting line, but they lack the extreme refinement characteristic of this sheet, and the quality of Ramboux's work varied greatly. Carl Philipp Fohr demonstrated his mastery of portraiture with the series he did of German artists in the Café Greco. For these drawings, he made exclusive use of a comparatively soft, silvery pencil, which was amenable to the stumping technique he employed. His portraits, simultaneously true to nature and abstracted, show complete mastery of the architecture and volume of the heads, which would support the view that he produced the work exhibited here. However, no drawings from his Roman period display a comparably "sharp" technique, which would also have taxed his patience. Additionally, Fohr's portraits lack the marmoreal, sculptural character of the present example. I am most inclined to regard Franz Horny, whose drawings show a dynamic, calligraphic touch, as the draftsman of this portrait. The only comparable work that is securely attributed to Horny is a portrait of a young man, now in Dresden (fig.). The treatment of the hair is less precise, but the exceptionally refined handling of the lips and eyes, especially the iris, is amazingly similar.[5] The evocation of the shadow on the neck and collar with parallel lines is also identical. Perhaps Horny gave these sheets to Cornelius during their collaboration in 1817, before Cornelius left for Munich. The debate about the authorship of this masterful portrait has only just begun.

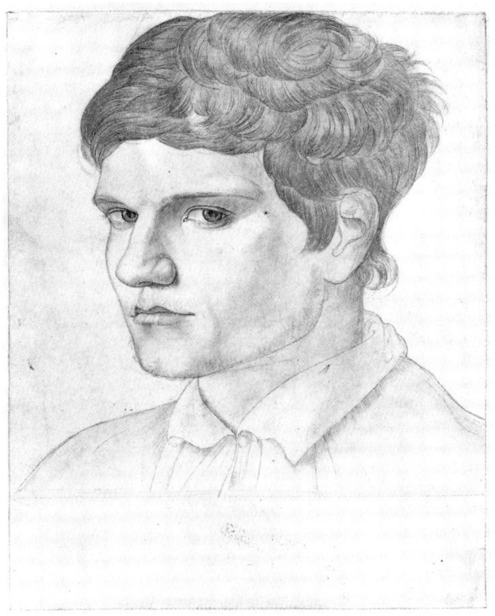

Franz Horny, *Portrait of a Young Man.* Pencil; 248 x 196 mm. Dresden, Staatliche Kunstsammlungen, Kupferstichkabinett, inv. no. C 1908 – 237

1 Darmstadt 1995, pp. 90 – 96.
2 Cf. Grimschitz 1941, p. 43, no. 29 (repr.).
3 Jensen provides examples. See Darmstadt 1995, pp. 90 – 96. See also C. G. Boerner, 185th Auction, 16 May 1934, p. 4, no. 43, pl. 1.
4 In the Städelsches Kunstinstitut, Frankfurt am Main, there is a portrait of a girl with curly hair and a necklace which functions as a boy's portrait and was undoubtedly executed by the author of the present work; it is inscribed "Overbeck" and attributed to him. Cf. Frankfurt 1977, p. 192, no. E.18, p. 222 (repr.).
5 Cf. the portrait of a girl by Horny that is now in Oxford (pencil; 242 x 207 mm); Bailey 1987, pp. 65 f., no. 58 (repr.).

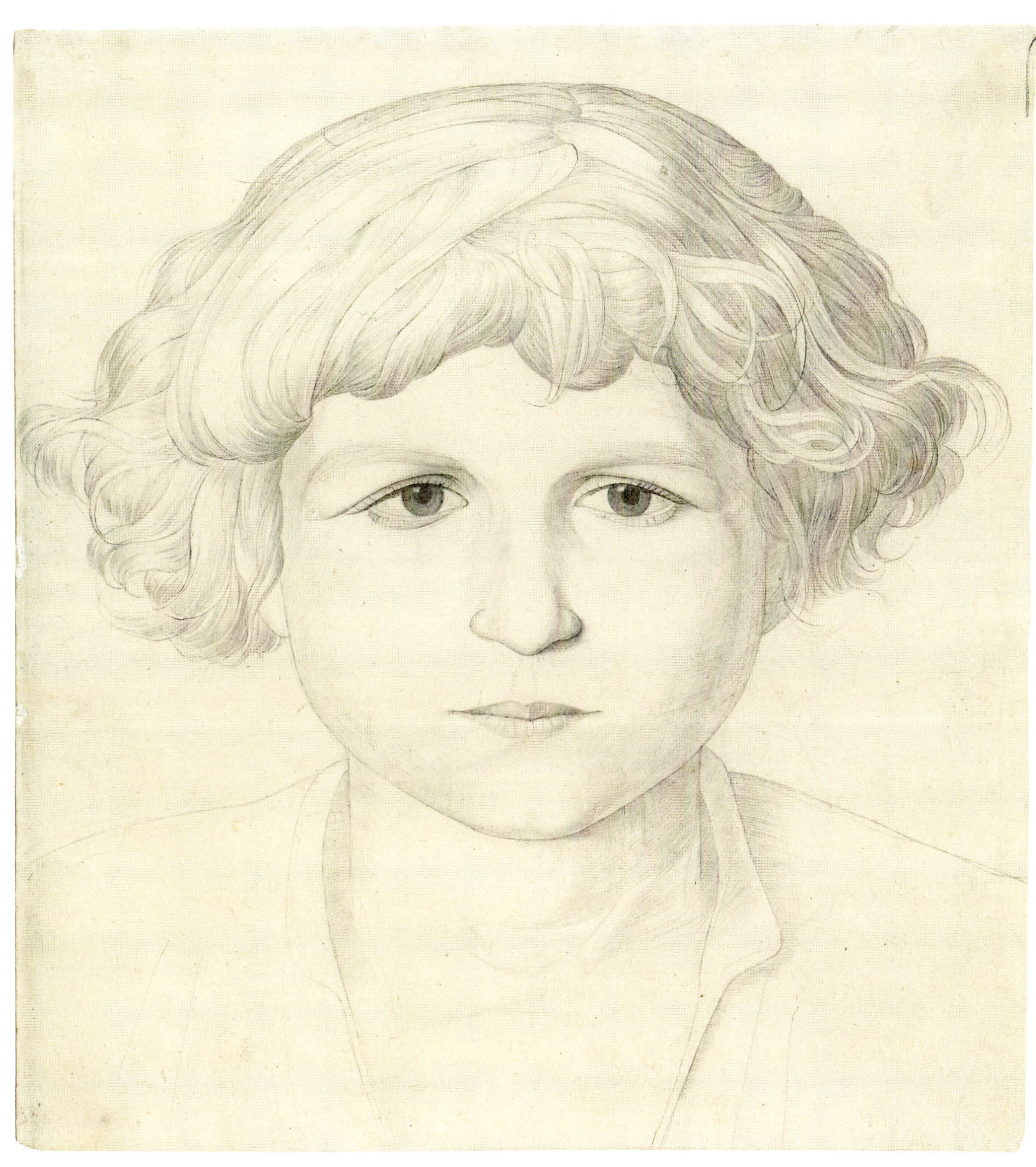

34
Ferdinand Olivier

Dessau 4 January 1785 – 2 November 1841 Munich

Hohensalzburg Citadel, c. 1817/18

Pencil heightened with white, on light gray tinted wove paper; border in pencil; 175 x 267 mm; upper corners cut to arched shape
Signed in pencil with monogram on the stone block, lower left: "FO" (in ligature)

Provenance: Franz Graf von Pocci, Munich/Starnberg; Antiquariat Emil Hirsch, Munich

Selected bibliography: Grote 1938, pp. 200, 236, fig. 144; Schwarz 1957, fig. 45; Munich 1958, pp. 53 f., no. 113, fig. 21; Lübeck 1969, p. 63, no. 112; New York 1981, p. 250, no. d25 (repr.)

Ferdinand Olivier is rightly regarded as the artist who discovered the Salzburg countryside.[1] In the summer of 1815, he made his first large group of drawings from nature in and around Salzburg, and these studies gave him the idea to publish a series of his own etchings with views of the most beautiful sites. To gather additional material, he

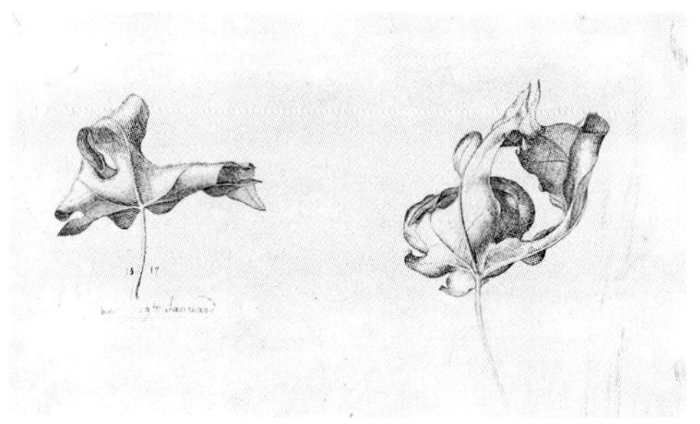

1 Friedrich Olivier, *Shriveled Maple Leaves, 19 January 1817. Pen and brown ink over pencil; 130/2 x 213/4 mm*

went to Salzburg again, from July to August 1817, accompanied by Julius Schnorr von Carolsfeld and others. The yield of drawings from this trip was so large that it kept Olivier occupied with Salzburg themes for years. In 1823, he published his lithographic masterwork, the suite *Seven Views of Salzburg and Berchtesgaden, Arranged According to the Seven Days of the Week, Linked by Two Allegorical Sheets.*[2] In this series, Olivier sought to give veiled expression to the cycle of birth and decay in nature, possibly echoing Philipp Otto Runge's *Four Times of Day* cycle. The underlying Christian idea becomes clear in the allegorical compositions that frame the series: treated as relieflike stone walls, they establish a conceptual link to Gothic church architecture that is reflected in the title of the final sheet, *Keystone.* The form of the artist's signature on

each print and in our drawing (on the stone block in the lower left corner) derives its meaning from this context: in the manner of a medieval stonemason's mark, it shows Olivier's ligated monogram in the late Gothic decorative form of a *Zweischneuss* (a circular tracery form with two *mouchettes*).

After a few attempts at etching, Olivier decided to use lithography for his series. One reason was commercial: it allowed him to produce an unlimited number of impressions. Another reason was artistic: through the use of a second tone stone, lithography allowed him to reproduce adequately the delicate tonal values of his drawings. Thus the Salzburg landscapes, originally drawn with a hard, sharp pencil, were published as exquisitely refined crayon lithographs.

Most of the Salzburg drawings associable with the production of the lithographs—including the present view of the citadel from the "midday side"—date from the winter of 1817/18. They share a hard, sharp line as well as a uniform brightness that sets them apart from the work of their time. "In love with every blade of grass," Olivier drew each detail with equal precision on light gray paper, the values graded according to atmospheric perspective from the darker, more strongly impressed pencil in the foreground to the lighter pencil in the distance, with delicate heightening in the sky to intensify the silver-gray tones. Clarity and transparency also characterize this drawing, so that foreground and background appear in equally sharp focus. The precision and sharpness of line are reminiscent of Dürer's engravings. The artists in Olivier's circle sought to incorporate a handling of line like Dürer's in their own drawings. Julius Schnorr von Carolsfeld and Friedrich Olivier, for instance, vied with each other to master early German draftsmanship in their studies of dried leaves, virtuoso pen drawings of the utmost refinement (fig. 1).

Within the series of lithographs, the present drawing is close to the landscape in *Tuesday* (fig. 2). There, however, Olivier shifted the point

2 *Ferdinand Olivier,* Tuesday, Hohensalzburg Citadel from the Midday Side, *1823. Lithograph*

of view to the right, so that the fortress appears at the left edge. In the lithograph, human figures enliven the landscape with allegorical allusions. Patriotic artists frequently used the medieval castle or palace as a monument to an idealized German past (cf. cat. 62, 75, 77). In the present drawing, the mighty medieval fortress is an undisguised reflection of the knightly age. As in an apotheosis, Olivier—possibly influenced by patriotic ideas—depicted it compositionally as a high point, thus intensifying its impact. The fortress is situated on the central vertical axis and is symmetrically framed by the upper border, which is shaped like a basket arch. Significantly, the Nazarenes used the arched format—an invention of the Italian Renaissance which suggests an architectural context, such as that of an altarpiece—especially for altar panels associated with the revival of the devotional picture. Ferdinand Olivier was the first to use this framing device as a leitmotif in his landscapes, where it serves to elevate the image to the sacral realm.[3] Although he based this view of the Hohensalzburg citadel on a study from nature, while executing the drawing in uniformly austere and precise lines, Olivier sublimated the landscape he experienced, elevating the *veduta* into a lofty, idealized vision. In the process, he spiritualized nature by translating it into a rigorously abstracting graphic language of uniform rhythm. I see a parallel here to the landscape drawings of the Danube school in the sixteenth century.

1 Grote 1938, pp. 229 f.; Schwarz 1957, p. 12; Margret Gröner, "Salzburger Land: Garten Gottes," in Tübingen 1981, pp. 87–94.
2 A suite of nine lithographs with tone stone; size of image approx. 195 x 270 mm; printed by Adolph Kunicke in Vienna. On the creation of the suite and its meaning, see Grote 1938, pp. 212–28; Peter Märker, "Selig sind, die nicht sehen und doch glauben: Zur nazarenischen Landschaftsauffassung Ferdinand Oliviers," *Städel-Jahrbuch,* n.s. 7 (1979): 178–206; *Luther und die Folge für die Kunst,* ed. Werner Hofmann, exh. cat., Hamburger Kunsthalle (Munich, 1983), pp. 482–84, no. 361 (Friedrich Gross).
3 Cf. cat. 28; Andrews 1967, pl. 38 (repr. in color); Schweinfurt 1968, p. 120, no. 104 (color pl. 104).

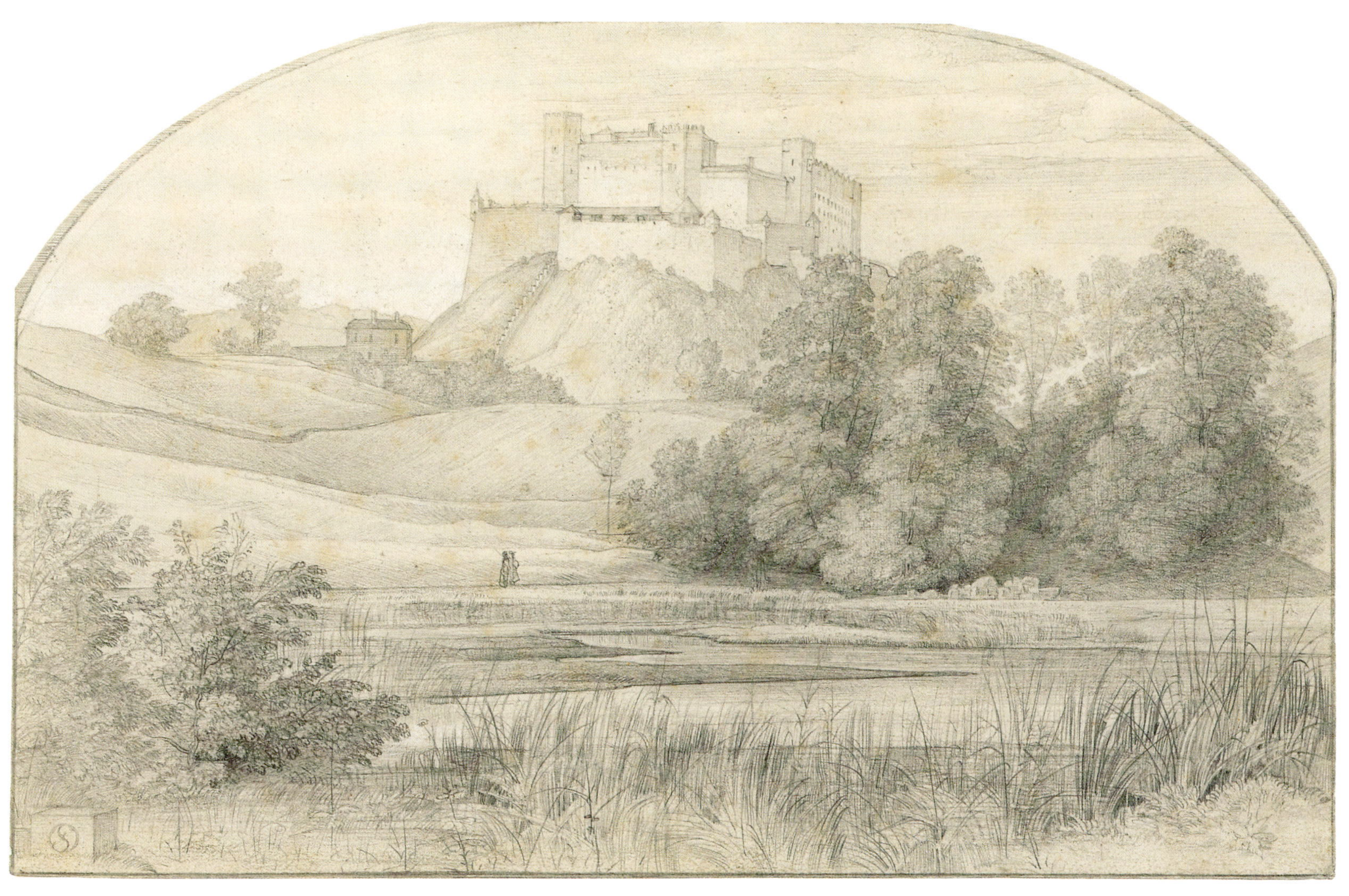

35

Julius Schnorr von Carolsfeld

Leipzig 26 March 1794 – 25 May 1872 Dresden

Portrait of Johannes Metzger, 1819

Pen and brown ink over pencil, on wove paper;
254 x 192 mm
Inscribed below the border line (height: 14 mm) in pen and
brown ink: "18 JS19 J O H A N N E S   M E T Z G E R. Florenz
d. 12. Sept."

Provenance: Prince Philipp of Hesse; Ludwigsgalerie,
Munich

Bibliography: Benz and Schneider 1939, p. 211, pl. 73; Alois
Trost, "Nachträgliches zum 'Römischen Portraitbuch'
Julius Schnorrs von Carolsfeld," Die Graphischen Künste,
n.s. 7 (1942/43): 72 f., fig. 2; Lübeck 1957, p. 64, no. 181;
Munich 1958, pp. 53 f., no. 153, fig. 17; Bremen 1961, no. 5;
Messerer 1966, no. 22, pp. 37 f. VI 21, p. 40i, fig. 6 following
p. 40; Lübeck 1969, p. 90, no. 172; Hutter and Lhotsky 1973,
p. 5, n. 5; Berhnard 1974, vol. 2, p. 1699 (repr.); Munich
1981, pp. 83 f., fig. 19; Ludwig I: Eine Darstellung seiner
Sammeltätigkeit, ed. Gisela Goldberg, exh. cat., Neue
Pinakothek (Munich, 1986), n.p. (repr.); Cornelia Syre in
Ludwig I. und die Alte Pinakothek: Festschrift zum
Jubiläumsjahr 1986 (Munich, 1986), pp. 44 ff., 47, fig. 7;
Munich 1994, pp. 78 f., no. 21 (repr. in color, with additional
literature); Cornelia Syre, Fra Angelico: Die Münchner
Tafeln und der Hochaltar von San Marco in Florenz
(Munich, 1996), pp. 16 f., fig. 5

Schnorr's masterful portraits, a few of which date from his Vienna period,[1] were mostly produced during the early years of his sojourn in Italy. There, he developed a type of portrait drawing that was uniform in format (approx. 260 x 200 mm), executed in pen and ink and brown wash over pencil, and characterized by a formal composition that emulated the portrait busts of Renaissance Florence. Both the engraving-like precision of the line and the separate inscription at the bottom were influenced by Dürer's engraved portraits. Besides capturing the likeness and individuality of the sitters, Schnorr was interested in their spiritual countenance; through this approach to portraiture he created drawn monuments to their memory.[2] Schnorr pasted a number of portraits of persons who were particularly close to him into a friendship album, known to art historians as the *Roman Portrait Book,* which today is in the Academy of Fine Arts in Vienna.[3] Although Schnorr had a pronounced talent for portraiture, as he did for landscape, he unfortunately did not pursue it. In 1867, at a very advanced age, he confessed in a letter to the Leipzig collector Eduard Cichorius that his stronger love for history painting had supplanted his "fondness" for genres such as landscape and portraiture.[4]

Johannes Metzger (1772–1844), whose portrait Schnorr drew in Florence, was a skilled repro-

ductive engraver. He came to the Italian city on a stipend from the Munich Academy to continue his training in the studio of the well-known engraver Raphael Morghen. In Florence, Metzger made a name for himself primarily as an excellent painting restorer, connoisseur, and art dealer. As a middleman, he helped various German princes—among them, the king of Prussia—build up their collections. He attained particular historical significance as the principal agent for the crown prince, later King Ludwig I of Bavaria, whose confidence he won early on. Between 1808 and 1844, he was able to satisfy Ludwig's passion for collecting by procuring forty-two paintings, mostly Italian Renaissance works, including such major pieces as Ghirlandaio's high altar from Santa Maria Novella in Florence and Raphael's *Madonna Tempi* and *Portrait of Bindo Altoviti,* which was regarded at the time as Raphael's self-portrait.[5] The extent of Metzger's activities on Ludwig's behalf is also reflected in the index of the correspondence between the king and his artistic advisor, Johann Georg von Dillis, from 1807 and 1841; Metzger's name is by far the one most frequently mentioned.[6]

Schnorr and Metzger were good friends.[7] They had met during Schnorr's first stay in Florence in November 1817. To view the city's works of art, he had placed himself "in the hands of Rumohr and Metzger, to whom he had been recommended from Rome."[8] In 1819, Schnorr, wanting to avoid a bout of Roman fever, spent the hot summer months in the more salutary climate of Florence. "Through Metzger's kind services," he was given "a spacious studio in the workshop of a sculptor of German extraction."[9] During these artistically productive months, Schnorr drew this likeness of Metzger as well as other portraits, two of which are in the *Roman Portrait Book.*[10] In composition, technique, and approximate format, Schnorr executed this portrait entirely in the *Roman Portrait Book* style. Usually, he began this type of "programmatic" likeness with a preliminary pencil drawing from life. Next, in a second sitting before the model, he worked the drawing up with the pen. Finally, at some later time, he often finished the work more firmly and pictorially by using hatching and a wash. The pencil *pentimenti* of the preliminary drawing are still clearly visible in Metzger's face, especially around the eyes, but also in the nose, mouth, and collar. This sheet may have been a commissioned work or a present that Schnorr gave away before he had a chance to rework it and make himself a copy, as he usually did. This would explain its absence from the *Roman Portrait Book,* assuming Schnorr intended to include it.[11]

Schnorr portrayed Metzger *en face* and, in contrast to other portraits in the album, dressed in monastic garb. Whether this was his artist's tunic

or an allusion to the well-liked Metzger's modesty and unpretentiousness remains an open question.[12] In any case, the dress recalls Florentine Renaissance portraits, such as that of the preacher Savonarola by Fra Bartolommeo, which Schnorr had surely seen in the Dominican monastery of San Marco.[13] In the drawing, Metzger looks directly at us with lively, telling eyes. All the human qualities he was praised for—honesty, trustworthiness, good-naturedness, and kindness—are reflected in the impressively frank and open face of this man, whose personality radiated from his eyes.

1 Cf. Munich 1990, pp. 132 f., no. 61; Munich 1994, pp. 42 f., no. 4, pp. 76 f., no. 20.
2 Munich 1994, pp. 80 f., no. 22, pp. 86 f., no. 25.
3 Hutter and Lhotsky 1973.
4 Julius Schnorr von Carolsfeld, "Zwölf Briefe zum Italienischen Landschaftsbuch an Eduard Cichorius, Dresden 1867," MS in the Kupferstichkabinett Dresden, inv. no. Ca 54 fy, letter 12.
5 Today in the National Gallery, Washington, DC; a list of the paintings that Metzger procured for Ludwig I can be found in an appendix in Messerer 1966, pp. 753–55.
6 *Ibid.,* p. 780.
7 Metzger's estate contains a letter from Schnorr, dated 11 May 1828, to "my dearest" Metzger, and signed "in old and loyal friendship"; cf. Nuremberg, Germanisches Nationalmuseum, Archiv für bildende Kunst, Nachlass Giovanni Metzger, no. 67.
8 Schnorr, "Landschaftsbuch" (as n. 4), letter 2.
9 *Ibid.,* letter 4.
10 Portrait of the geologist Rudolf Przystanewski on 21 June 1819 and portrait of the painter Carl Mosler on 3 October 1819; cf. Hutter and Lhotsky 1973, pp. 34–37, 38–41.
11 Other portraits drawn in the same style are also not included in the *Roman Portrait Book,* such as those of Johann Christoph Erhard and Barthold Georg Niebuhr, which are well known thanks to engraved reproductions; Mainz 1993, pp. 28 f., no. 7 (repr.), pp. 40 f., no. 14 (repr.).
12 Louise Seidler described Metzger in her memoirs as a "simple, unassuming, modest artist" with an "uncommon warm-heartedness"; cf. Seidler 1922, pp. 217 f.
13 Cf. Jacob Burckhardt, *Die Kultur der Renaissance in Italien* (Cologne, 1956), figs. 109, 110; cf. also Castagno's portrait of Francesco Petrarca, repr. in Marita Horster, *Andrea del Castagno* (Oxford, 1980), pl. 83.

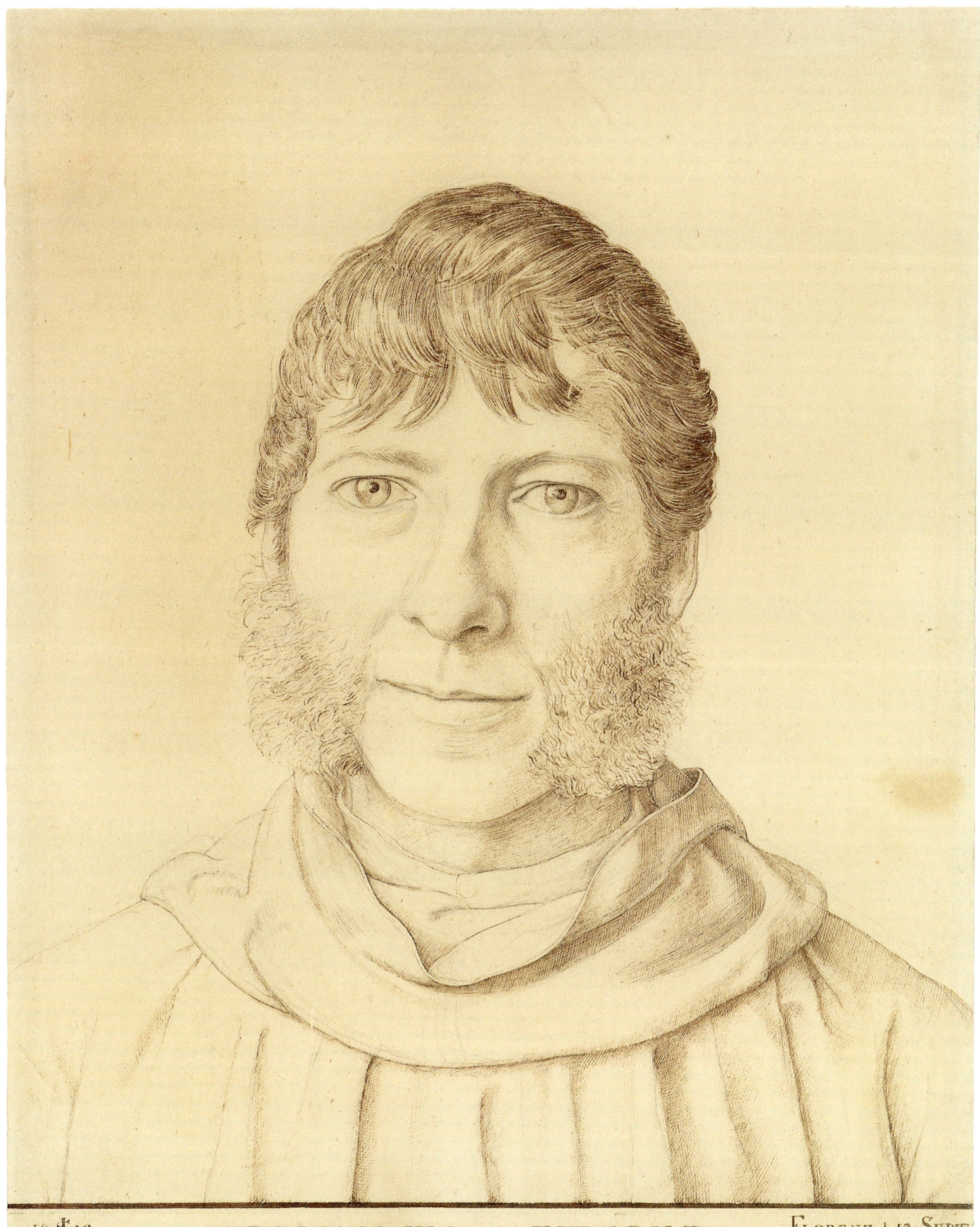

.18 19.
IOHANNES METZGER.
FLORENZ d. 12 SEPT.

36

Julius Schnorr von Carolsfeld

Seated Nude Youth, 1821

*Pencil on wove paper; 442 x 276/83 mm
Inscribed on verso (later?) in pencil by the artist:
"Gioachino—febr. 1821"*

*Provenance: Arnold Otto Meyer, Hamburg (Lugt 1994);
Graphisches Kabinett Günther Franke, Munich*

*Selected bibliography: Munich 1958, p. 54, no. 155; Lübeck
1969, p. 90, no. 173, p. 89 (repr.); Hugh Honour, Romanticism (Harmondsworth, 1981), p. 136, fig. 79a; Petra Trenk-
mann, "Julius Schnorr von Carolsfeld—Zeichnungen bis
1827" (Ph.D. diss., Weimar, 1985), pt. 1 (text), pp. 99 f.,
under no. 120; Mannheim 1993, p. 16, fig. 9, p. 84; Munich
1994, pp. 68 f., no. 16 (repr. in color; cover image; with additional literature)*

For the Nazarenes, who aspired to implement their artistic project primarily in the field of figurative history painting, drawing from the nude was an important prerequisite. In the mostly Catholic collective of the Brotherhood of St. Luke in the Monastery of San Isidoro there were, however, no studies of female models; the situation in the academies was similar. This would change only later, with the second generation of Nazarenes in the Protestant circle around Julius Schnorr von Carolsfeld. Beginning in 1819, during regular evening sessions, the Nazarenes made drawings from male and female models in rooms rented for this purpose. In contrast to academy students, who worked from professional adult models, the Nazarenes drew from nonprofessional young models who fulfilled their notion of beauty and whose natural, simple bearing matched the Nazarene ideal of pure humanity uncorrupted by education.[1]

In German academies, students still drew in the classicizing manner, using chalk on a rough, usually gray or blue, laid paper, which produced a painterly effect. The Nazarenes, by contrast, preferred to draw on smooth, white wove paper, using a pencil that was never too hard or too sharp. For a while, Schnorr, too, preferred the pencil. This was the technique he could "do the quickest," and it was "the most suitable for work done in one's free time and for pleasure."[2] This would change in 1821. That spring, Schnorr drew the nude exhibited here in pencil; in the fall, when he participated in the resumed evening drawing sessions, he confessed to his friend Quandt in a letter: "This time I will draw my nude studies with pen (after the contour has been done in pencil). As an instrument I like the pen much more than graphite."[3] Schnorr's superb mastery can best be seen in the nude studies drawn directly in pen without any preliminary pencil sketch.

The nude study has a special place in Schnorr's oeuvre. He made the most important contribution to this genre in early nineteenth-century German art. Inspired by the naturalness, grace, and beauty of the young models, he created his loveliest autonomous work during his early years in Rome. Most of his nudes, however, date from a later period and were done in preparation for monumental murals. In a report on his life, written in 1855, Schnorr addressed the role of the nude studies for the murals in the Munich Residenz: "And I did not execute a single figure without first having drawn a nude study from life for it, the evidence of which is still in my portfolio."[4] How many there must have been for the enormous murals in the *Kaisersäle* alone, which are teeming with figures![5] In these preparatory studies for murals, Schnorr had his models strike the same pose he wanted the figures in his historical compositions to assume. In so doing, he followed the academic method his venerated model Raphael had already employed: using nude studies to clarify and prepare the posture and movement of clothed figures in the paintings.

Schnorr drew the present nude as an autonomous study in February 1821, during one of the evening sessions. We can infer this from another study of the same model by Theodor Rehbenitz, Schnorr's friend and neighbor in the Palazzo Caffarelli (cf. cat. 54). Rehbenitz obviously drew his study in the same session from the opposite angle.[6] As he often did, Schnorr noted the model's name and the date of the study on the back of the sheet.[7]

The effect here is that of a single, uniform outline uniting the various parts of the body. The contours are fluid and blend with the boundaries of the body, accentuating its statuelike character. Schnorr treated the shadows of the body as in an engraving, with sweeping parallel lines and crosshatching over areas of tone created by stumping. In the viewer's eye, these shadows blend into a silvery sheen. Subtle hatching models the body in response to the light. Besides the model's posture and proportions, Schnorr was interested, above all, in the distribution of light.

We cannot exclude the possibility that he considered using this study in a painting, since the pose suggests that of an Arcadian shepherd boy or the figure of Paris from the Judgment of Paris.[8] The surface treatment of the seated nude reflects Schnorr's acquaintance with antique sculpture. In fact, when he did this study in the spring of 1821, he was drawing intensively from the ancient statues that had been set up again in the Vatican.[9] In its statuelike calm and resolution, this nude is also reminiscent of the classical nude studies by Jean-Auguste-Dominique Ingres, whose ideas about the exemplary role of antique sculpture were much like Schnorr's. Ingres used classical works of art "to learn to see and trans-late nature."[10] The two artists probably met in Rome between 1818 and 1820.[11]

This seated youth seen partially from the back is one of the loveliest of Schnorr's nudes from his early years in Rome. As if with a silver point, he sensitively modeled the slender figure in a meditative posture in the light. Naturalistic observation, refined stylization, and idealization overlap. Here, Schnorr has elevated the natural model into a vision of grace, restrained eroticism, and beauty. In this regard, he remains an exception among the brothers of St. Luke.

1 Schnorr wrote in a letter to Johann Gottlob von Quandt on 21 September 1820, "...but I have drawn a few nudes that you would like, especially since they are of the kind one does not readily have an opportunity to draw in Germany"; Schnorr-Briefe, p. 364.
2 Letter dated 23 September 1818; *ibid.*, p. 102.
3 Letter dated 16 November 1821; *ibid.*, p. 376.
4 *Julius Schnorr von Carolsfeld: Künstlerische Wege und Ziele: Schriftstücke aus der Feder des Malers Julius Schnorr von Carolsfeld*, ed. Franz Schnorr von Carolsfeld (Leipzig, 1909), p. 19.
5 In Schnorr's estate, his widow Marie Schnorr von Carolsfeld, née Heller (1807–1882), still counted 337 nudes—among them 155 male and 89 female nudes, 34 male and 17 female nudes of which had been done in Rome—and noted them in her private inventory; Dresden, Sächsische Landesbibliothek, Schnorr von Carolsfeldsches Familienarchiv, Mscr. Dresd. n. 44 I, fol. 9r.
6 Wolf-Timm 1991, pp. 361 f., no. 819 (repr.), p. 362 (repr.).
7 There is another study by Schnorr of the same model: a nude showing the back view; pencil; 419 x 262 mm; inscribed by the artist in the lower right corner: "Gioachino d. 1 n Februar 1821"; today in the Schlossmuseum, Weimar, inv. no. KK 7418.
8 Cf. the seated figure of a shepherd boy by Thorvaldsen from the years 1817–26; Honour 1981, p. 136, fig. 79b.
9 Schnorr-Briefe, pp. 243, 381. Individual studies in the Kupferstichkabinett, Dresden and in the Städtische Galerie im Lenbachhaus, Munich.
10 Cf. *Ingres: Handzeichnungen*, exh. cat., Landesmuseum (Mainz, 1983), p. 17; cf. the nude showing the back view in Ingres's painting *The Bather of Valpinçon*, 1808, Paris, Louvre; *ibid.*, p. 33 (repr.).
10 In 1826, Schnorr is said to have sent "his friend Ingres" in Paris a cycle of six drawn compositions illustrating Ariosto's *Orlando Furioso*; Boetticher, vol. 2/2, p. 615, nos. 145–50.

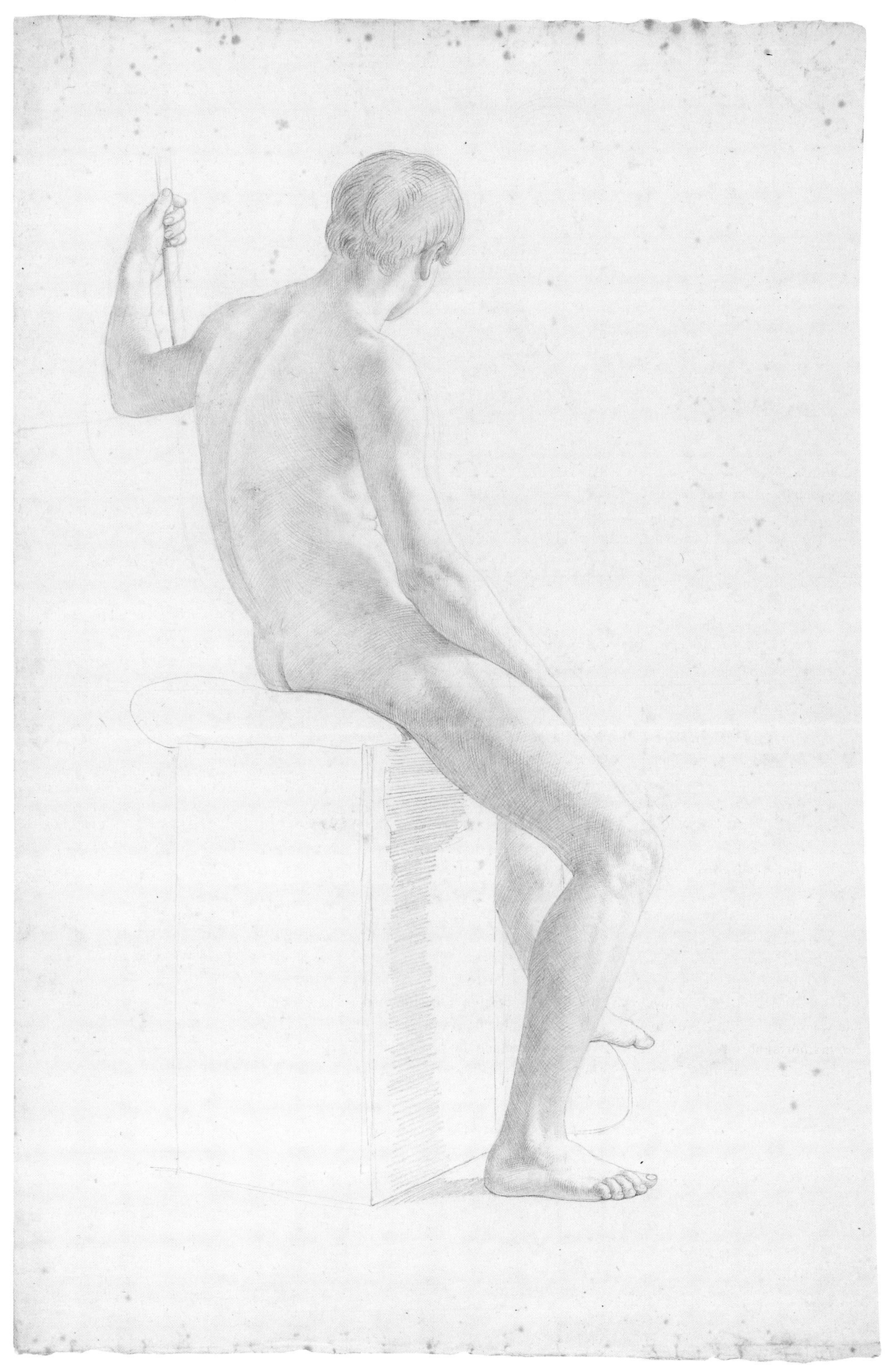

37

Julius Schnorr von Carolsfeld

The Creation of Eve, 1825

Pen and brown ink over pencil, on laid paper; 219 x 258 mm
Monogram in pen and brown ink, lower left: "IS" (in
ligature)
Verso in pencil: sketch of a standing nude female with
raised arms, seen from the back at an oblique angle

Provenance: Kurt Meissner, Zurich

Bibliography: C. G. Boerner, Lagerliste 29: Originale
Zeichnungen alter und neuerer Meister *(Leipzig, 1907),*
no. 198; Adolf Schahl, "Geschichte der Bilderbibel von
Julius Schnorr von Carolsfeld" (Ph.D. diss., Leipzig, 1936),
p. 152; Munich 1994, pp. 140 f., no. 55 (repr. in color);
Christine Riegelmann, "Die Schöpfungsdarstellungen in
der 'Bibel in Bildern' von Julius Schnorr von Carolsfeld:
Entstehung und Gestaltungsprobleme" (master's thesis,
Kiel, 1995), pp. 15 ff., 24 ff., 27 ff., fig. 4

One of the Nazarenes' principal projects was illustrating the Bible, which they began in the original collective of the Brotherhood of St. Luke as a joint enterprise. After repeated, unsuccessful attempts between 1821 and 1824 in the compositional associations (*Komponiervereinen*) they had formed for academic drawing exercises, Schnorr eventually pursued the project on his own. He worked on it with his usual perseverance for nearly forty years and brought it to a successful conclusion. In Rome, he had already laid a crucial foundation and created some of his loveliest drawings. He made a list of selected themes from the Old Testament (the so-called Roman list) and settled on a uniform format, which he followed to the end, as well as the medium of pen and brown ink, which suited his initial preference for reproducing his drawings as etchings printed in brown.

Schnorr assigned the first seven pictures to the six days of creation in Genesis, with two for the sixth day: number six, *The Creation of Adam*, and number seven, *The Creation of Eve*.[1]

In technique and format, the present finished drawing is undoubtedly the compositional design for the seventh picture in the cycle, and it should be dated to 1825.[2] A letter from Schnorr to his father, dated 2 June 1825, indicates the time frame when he was working on these related themes. In the letter, he writes of the problems he faced in inventing the images : "The most difficult will be those belonging to the creation story. I would like to copy the inimitable compositions of Michelangelo and Raphael in all humility and use them as the beginning of my cycle .... It is easiest dealing with subjects these giants passed over entirely."[3] Beginning in the early Renaissance, the great, exemplary artists had created an iconographic tradition for this central religious and art historical theme explaining the origin of the sexes that was, for Schnorr, even more canonical than the actual words in the Bible. And so the drawing's composition on a foreground stage as well as the figures' postures and types show the unmistakable influence of Jacopo della Quercia's relief on the façade of San Petronio in Bologna,[4] of Michelangelo's depiction on the ceiling of the Sistine Chapel,[5] and of Raphael's frescoes in the Vatican *Loggie*. The figures also recall, though in reverse, the relief on Ghiberti's bronze Paradise door on the Baptistery in Florence.[6] These models had already provided the basis for Schnorr's pencil drawing of the same theme, dated 3 May 1821, one of the earliest documents of a project to illustrate the Bible.[7] Schnorr probably presented it for discussion in May 1821 at the first meeting of the newly established composition club. We can barely recognize his hand in this drawing; the contours are accentuated, and the representation still seems —in the manner of Olivier—simplified and stylized. This may have grown out of Schnorr's concern, given the weighty content of the Bible, to use an abstracting and "elevating" approach, holding back his personal style in favor of a general one in this collective project.

Compared to the earlier pencil composition, in the present work Schnorr has developed the theme further in his own sensuously powerful technique. The figures, modeled with greater refinement in crosshatching and parallel strokes, have a livelier and more natural effect. In the freshness of its conception and in the strong expressive power of the pen stroke, which also support a date of 1825, the present drawing is among the finest of the early Bible illustrations. However, out of concern that the figures' nakedness would offend moral sensibilities, it was not included in the later publication of the illustrated Bible.[8]

Schnorr collected his sketches and compositional projects, created over many years and in random order, and pasted them into a large album, following the numeration of the Roman list. Only later did he decide to illustrate the New Testament as well and to use the woodcut medium for reproduction; this technique allowed the unlimited edition that was essential for a popular book. Moreover, the woodcut's expressive linear pattern favored the pedagogical goal of creating memorable images that would appeal to a mass audience. The labor-intensive process probably involved the creation of around a thousand preliminary drawings for the 240 woodcuts. Early compositional designs can be identified by their brown ink and later ones by their black ink, which was already suggestive of the black and white effect of the woodcut. *The Bible in Pictures (Bilderbibel)* was eventually published between 1852 and 1860 in individual installments by Georg Wigand in Leipzig. It can rightfully be called the artist's life work.

Schnorr's religiosity was informed by a deep longing to overcome the confessional divisions between Catholicism and Protestantism. He must have felt great satisfaction, late in life, to see his illustrated Bible used in both Protestant and Catholic religious instruction in the schools. With his illustrated Bible, Schnorr probably came closest to fulfilling the Nazarenes' missionary goal of awakening a new religiosity through their art. Widely circulated in huge numbers and reprinted to this day, his work continues to influence the way Biblical events are visualized.

1 Schahl 1936, pp. 29 ff.
2 Munich 1994, p. 140, no. 55.
3 Schnorr-Briefe, pp. 294 f.
4 Schnorr spent two days in Bologna in December 1817; Schnorr-Briefe, p. 34.
5 Schnorr had already become familiar with Michelangelo's fresco through his father's book of 1810, *Unterricht in der Zeichenkunst* [Lessons in Draftsmanship], on which Schnorr worked as a reproductive etcher (pl. 54); see Stephan Seeliger, "Die Bedeutung der Druckgraphik für das Werk Julius Schnorr von Carolsfelds," in *Julius Schnorr von Carolsfeld und die Kunst der Romantik*, ed. Gerd-Helge Vogel (Greifswald, 1996), pp. 239 f., 243, fig. 2.
6 Schnorr-Briefe, p. 33.
7 Monogrammed and dated at the lower left and right: "18JS21 Rom d. 3 t May"; cf. *Deutsche und österreichische Handzeichnungen und Aquarelle 1785–1860: Bestandskatalog in Auswahl 1.*, gen. ed. Gisela Götte, selected with commentary by Jutta Assel, Clemens-Sels-Museum (Neuss, 1985), p. 37, no. 63, fig. 58 (inv. no. Gr234); see also Schahl 1936, pp. 15 ff.
8 The ministry of Saxony did not want to recommend the work for use in schools because of "offensive" pictures (i. e., nudes); cf. Hans Wolfgang Singer, *Julius Schnorr von Carolsfeld* (Bielefeld and Leipzig, 1911), p. 111. The result would have been a considerable loss of sales. The picture *Tobias and Sarah Are Found Unharmed on the Morning after the Wedding Night*, included in the first installment of 1852, was publicly criticized as immoral and initially impeded sales of the book, which led to financial losses for the publisher; cf. Leipzig 1994, p. 240, no. 143 (Christine Riegelmann).

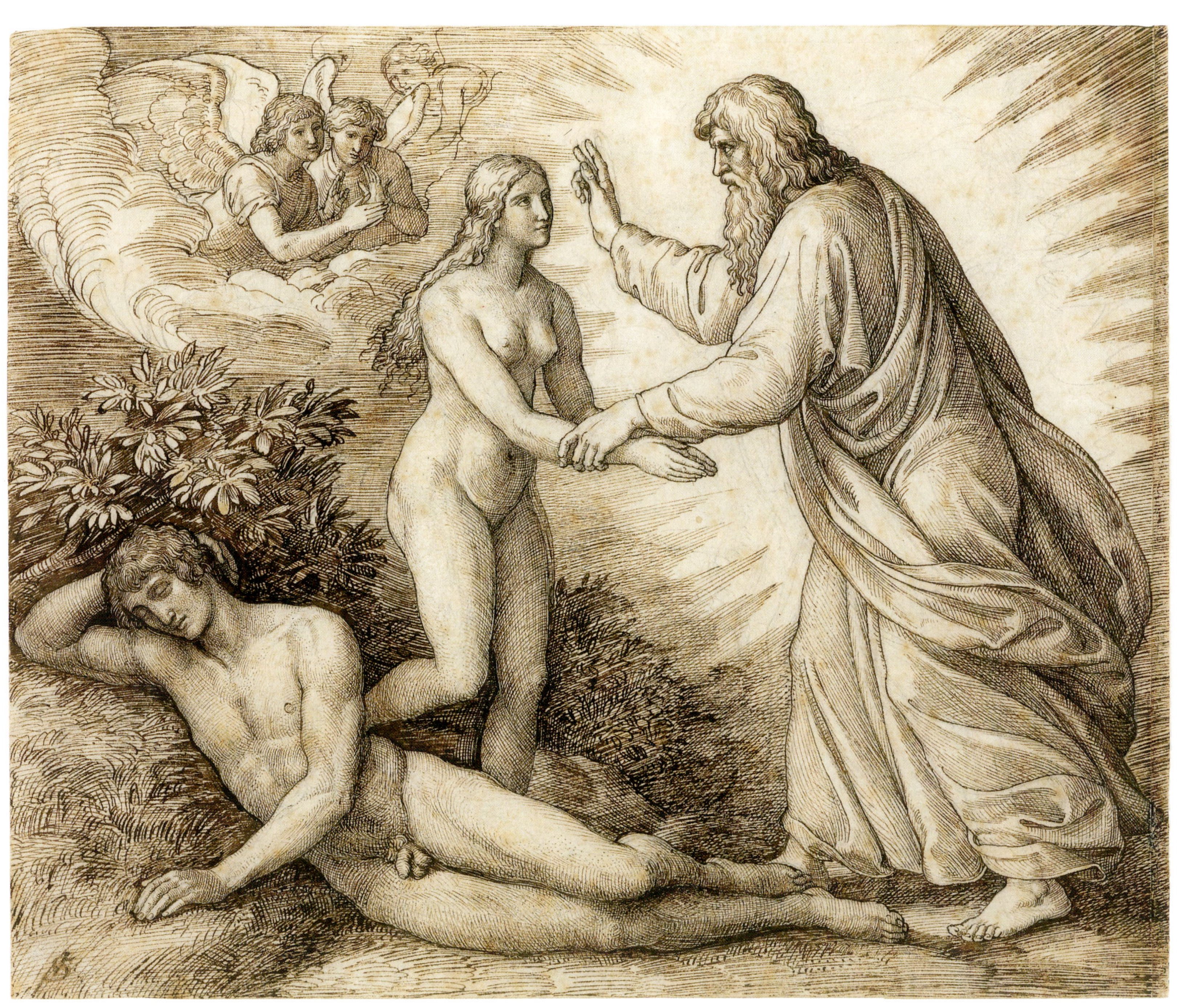

38

Julius Schnorr von Carolsfeld

Portrait of Alexander Max Seitz, 1831

Pencil on light gray, tinted, laid paper; 356 x 266 mm
Monogrammed and dated center left: "JSvC 17t
Januar 1831"
Inscribed by the artist, center: "Max Seitz"
Below that: "Studienkopf zu dem Bilde: Siegfrieds Einzug
in Worms" [Head Study for the Picture Siegfried's Entry
into Worms]

Provenance: Hele Hauptmann, Leipzig (granddaughter of
Johann Martin von Rohden); Ludwigsgalerie, Munich

Bibliography: Lübeck 1957, p. 65, no. 187; Munich 1958, p. 55,
no. 158; Bremen 1961, no. 28; Lübeck 1969, p. 93, no. 176;
Bernhard 1974, vol. 2, p. 1749 (repr.); Inken Nowald, "Die
Nibelungenfresken von Julius Schnorr von Carolsfeld im
Königsbau der Münchner Residenz: 1827–1867" (Ph.D.
diss., Kiel, 1978), pp. 102 f., 195 f., no. 43, p. 334 (repr.);
Leipzig 1994, p. 250, no. 178; Munich 1994, pp. 108 f., no. 39
(repr. in color)

Schnorr's Munich years, 1827 to 1846, which he felt were the happiest of his life in both private and professional ways,[1] were dominated by King Ludwig I of Bavaria's commission to paint monumental frescoes in the additions to the Munich Residenz built by Leo von Klenze. All the youthful dreams of Schnorr, who felt a special calling for history painting, seemed to have been fulfilled. The national awakening in the Romantic period opened up a large field of patriotic themes from history and literature. The *Nibelungenlied,* regarded as a German national epic, soon replaced the Homeric themes that had been favored by classicists. As a result of this change in taste, endorsed by the patriotic King Ludwig I himself, the subject of Schnorr's first commission for murals in the Königsbau, which he received while still in Rome, was changed from the *Odyssey* to the *Nibelungenlied.* Schnorr began preparations immediately upon his arrival in Munich and commenced painting in 1831. The work would drag on until 1867. Today, the Nibelung cycle is the only testimony to Schnorr's monumental fresco painting in Munich to survive the devastation of World War II.

The young history painter Alexander Maximilian Seitz (1811–1888) was the model for the present portrait study, which Schnorr drew in preparation for the Nibelung cycle. Seitz was a student of Peter Cornelius and Heinrich Maria Hess at the Munich Academy, where Schnorr also taught as professor of history painting. Since Seitz's talent emerged early on, Hess employed him in decorating the court church of All Saints in Munich. In 1833, Seitz went to Rome, where he associated closely with the Nazarenes. Overbeck, who thought highly of Seitz as an artist, enlisted him in 1844 to paint the private chapel of the Villa Torlonia in Castel Gandolfo. Beginning in 1869, Seitz and his son Ludwig executed various Overbeck cartoons and some of his own designs in the cathedral of Djakova in Croatia.[2]

With Schnorr's move to Munich, the focus of his activity as a draftsman shifted from free, autonomous drawings to those done in preparation for works in other media. He drew the profile of the young Max Seitz, who is looking up to the right, as a study for a page's head at the left edge of the large fresco *Siegfried's Victorious Return from the Saxon War* in the Königsbau's second hall (fig.). The model for the second page (with his right arm raised to point) was the Hamburg painter Victor Emil Janssen (1807–1845), who also studied with Cornelius in Munich (cf. cat. 52, fig. 1).[3]

Schnorr worked tirelessly on the compositional designs and cartoons for years before he began to paint in fresco in July of 1831, a few months after these head studies were done. He worked both studies into the cartoon about 1833[4] and, under time pressure and without assistants, painted the fresco in 1834. Since he considered it a failure, he demolished the fresco ten years later and executed it anew in 1844 on the basis of a painted copy he had made in 1838.[5]

It is characteristic of Schnorr's working method that he had his models assume the exact position he had in mind for the fresco (cf. cat. 36). Both studies reveal his concern about making the figures in his historical scenes look as natural and authentic as possible, even if—as in this case—the faces in the final version are almost unrecognizable. The two head studies of the pages, the only such studies for the Nibelung cycle that have come to light,[6] attest that Schnorr retained a fresh vision and a facility and virtuosity in the handling of the drawing media.

Although the head study of Max Seitz originated as a preparatory drawing, Schnorr nonetheless created a masterful portrait, and he drew it at a time when, according to Schnorr himself, he had lost all interest in portrait drawing, since he was "preparing himself to deal with the heroes of the old world."[7] Although in no way inferior to the drawings in the *Roman Portrait Book* (cat. 35), the present work does reveal a change in style that resulted from its function as a working study. It is not stylized and "spiritualized" in the Nazarene manner, but radiates vitality, naturalness, and youthful grace.

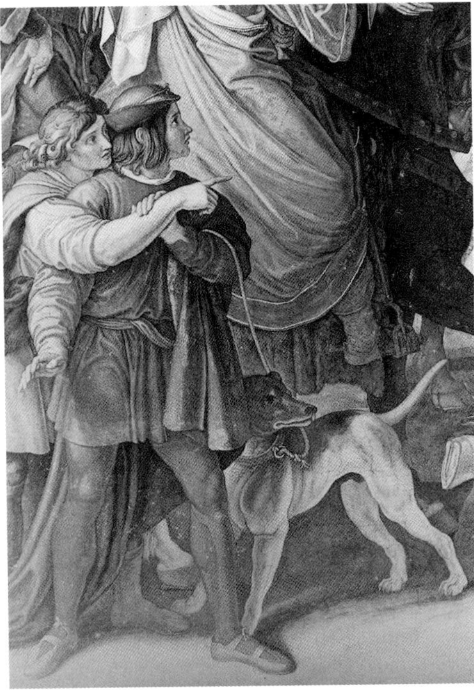

Julius Schnorr von Carolsfeld, detail from the fresco
Siegfried's Victorious Return from the Saxon War, 1844
(1834), Munich, Königsbau of the Residenz

1 On 30 October 1827, a few days before his arrival in Munich, Schnorr had married Maria Heller, the stepdaughter of his friend Ferdinand Olivier, in Vienna.

2 Cf. Howitt, vol. 2, pp. 370 ff.; Hyazinth Holland, "Alexander (Max) Seitz," in *Allgemeine Deutsche Biographie,* vol. 33 (Leipzig, 1891), pp. 655 f.; Peter Vignau-Wilberg, "Overbecks letztes Werk: Die Ausführung der Fresken durch Alexander Maximilian Seitz und Ludwig Seitz," in *Johann Friedrich Overbeck und die Kathedrale von Djakova/Kroatien,* ed. Axel Feuss, exh. cat., Ostdeutsche Galerie (Regensburg, 1994), pp. 18 ff.

3 Pen and brown ink over pencil, on light gray, laid paper; 303 x 248 mm. Hamburg, Kunsthalle, Kupferstichkabinett, inv. no. 47400; cf. Cambridge 1972, no. 84 (repr.); Leipzig 1994, p. 250, no. 178, p. 156 (repr.).

4 Cf. Nowald 1975, pp. 102 ff., 195 ff., nos. 42–47, p. 289 (repr. of fresco), pp. 333–37 (repr.).

5 *Ibid.,* pp. 107 ff., 197, no. 46; cf. *Julius Schnorr von Carolsfeld, Künstlerische Wege und Ziele: Schriftstücke aus der Feder des Malers Julius Schnorr von Carolsfeld,* ed. Franz Schnorr von Carolsfeld (Leipzig, 1909), p. 127; on the oil painting, cf. Leipzig 1994, p. 250, no. 177, p. 154 (repr. in color).

6 Nowald 1975, p. 102.

7 Julius Schnorr von Carolsfeld, *Zwölf Briefe zum Italienischen Landschaftsbuch an Eduard Cichorius, Dresden 1867,* MS in the Kupferstichkabinett Dresden, inv. no. CA 54 fy, letter 12.

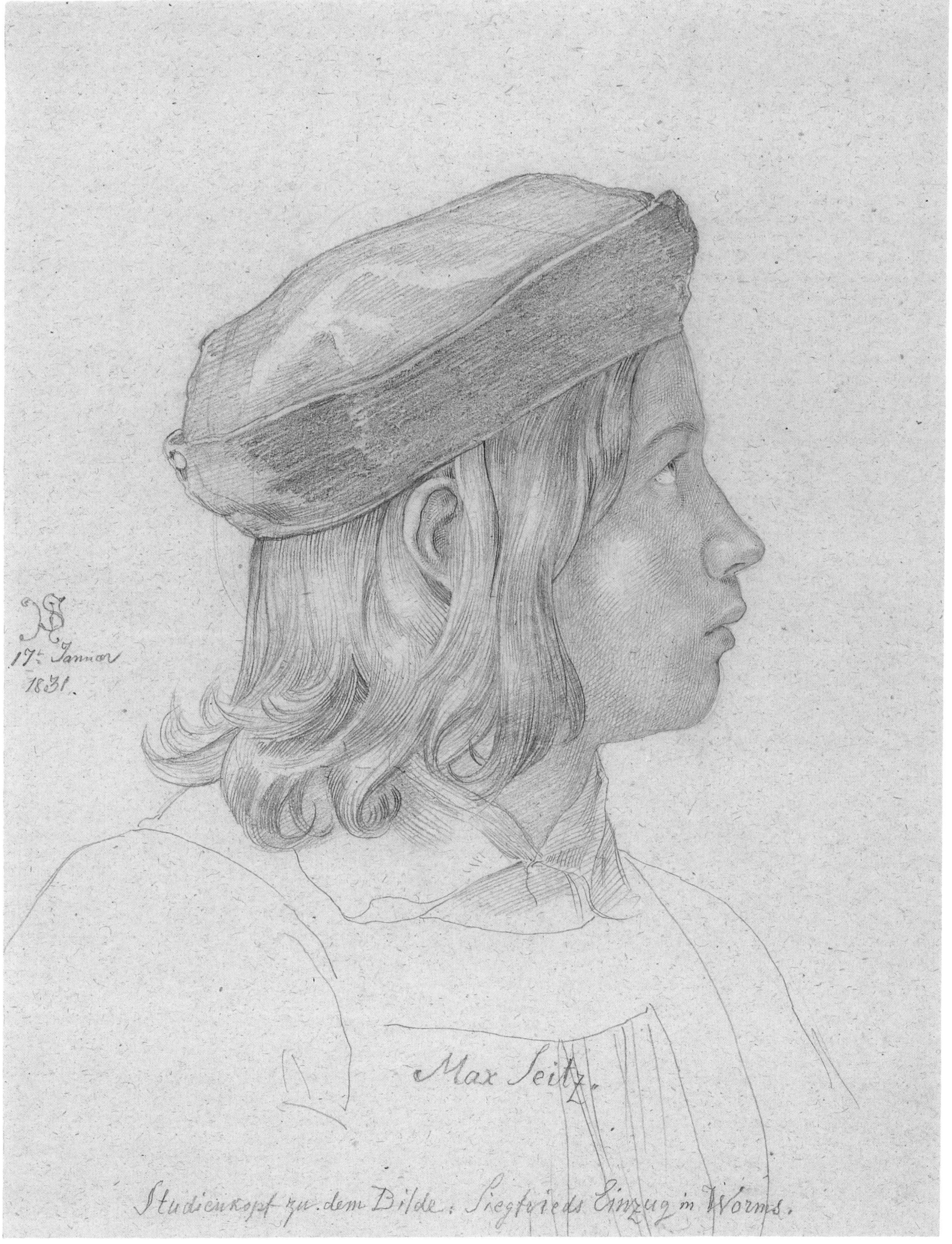
17ᵗ Januar
1831.
Max Seitz.
Studienkopf zu dem Bilde: Siegfrieds Einzug in Worms.

Johann Evangelist Scheffer
von Leonhardshoff

Vienna 30 October 1795 –12 January 1822 Vienna

Self-Portrait, "Pretty Miserable," 1815

*Black chalk, heightened with white; border in pencil, on
thick, gray-tinted, laid paper; watermark; 180 x 128 mm;
corners trimmed*
*Inscribed by the artist, lower right: "Miserabl genug / als
Riconvaliszenttt. Schaut traurig g'nug" [Pretty miserable,
as a convalescent. Looks pretty sad]*

*Provenance: Dr. August Heymann, Vienna; Ludwigs-
galerie, Munich*

*Selected bibliography: Hans Tietze, "Ausstellung von
Nazarenerzeichnungen in Wien," Kunst und Künstler 26,
no. 1 (1928): 224 (repr.)., 222; Geller 1952, p. 99, no. 1214,
fig. 471; Geller 1955, p. 59; Munich 1958, p. 52, no. 150; Keith
Andrews, "Scheffer von Leonhardshoff," in Schweinfurt
1968, p. 57; Lübeck 1969, pp. 86 f., no. 168 (repr.); Krapf 1977,
p. 112, D-123; Krapf, Johann Evangelist Scheffer von Leon-
hardshoffs "Selbstbildnis mit aufgeblasenen Backen": Von
der Karikatur zur Selbstbefragung, Festschrift Skreiner
1992, pp. 173–181, 175 (regr.), 178; Rudolf Preimesberger,
"'Sol ich so mich Mahlen wie ich wirklich bin ….' Der
Nazarener Johann Evangelist Scheffer von Leonhardshoff," Neue Zürcher Zeitung, Fernausgabe no. 51, Friday,
3 March 1995, p. 41 (repr.)*

Scheffer, who presents his countenance so directly and naturally in this drawing, frequently
depicted himself. Geller alone lists eleven self-
portraits.[1] They all attest to a unique self-absorp-

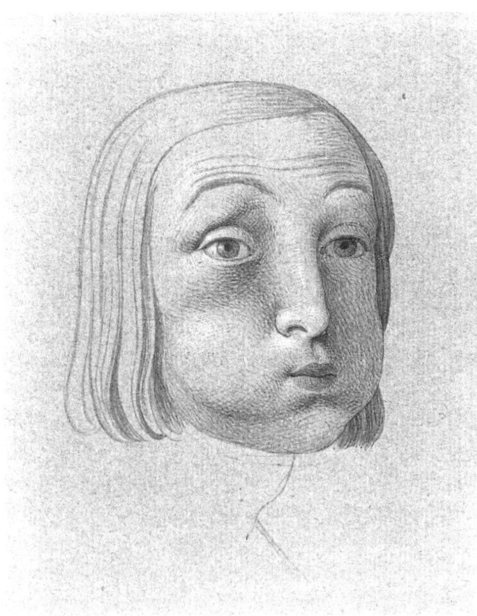

Johann Evangelist Scheffer von Leonhardshoff,
Self-Portrait with Puffed-Up Cheeks, 1815. Pen and brown
ink over pencil, heightened with white, on blue-gray
paper; 151 x 124 mm. Berlin, Staatliche Museen Preussischer Kulturbesitz, Kupferstichkabinett, inv. no. SZ.2.

tion in the sense of a self-questioning that was
not merely a momentary "stocktaking," but entailed deep reflection on that inner state of the
artist's being.

The present sheet was shown next to Schnorr's
pencil portrait of Scheffer in a 1928 exhibition of
Nazarene art in Vienna. Judging from its composition and inscription, the likeness of Scheffer
was the first drawing in Schnorr's *Roman Portrait Book.* The rest of the portraits in the album
were executed in pen and ink (cat. 35).[2] Hans
Tietze discussed the two works at length in a
review of the exhibition: "Scheffer's self-portrait, placed alongside Schnorr's drawing, characterizes the difference between the two artists;
one feels … the tribal contrast between northern
German and southern German. The self-portrait
is the more intimate, momentary, and casual creation, as the dreadfully misspelled inscription
already reveals …. The piece is delightful in its
freshness and matter-of-factness, and is surprising in its ability to grasp profoundly the melancholy of a youth and convalescent. This down-to-
earth quality is no fluke; every drawing by the
Viennese Nazarene … breathes this elemental
warmth which the thoroughly spiritualized
sphere of his companions usually lacks. One can
surely see it as the gift of his native soil."

Scheffer's self-portrait has been repeatedly
linked with another one in Berlin in which he is
puffing out his cheeks (fig) Both drawings can
be interpreted in the light of the artist's serious
illness. Geller surmises that Scheffer had jokingly portrayed himself in a "puffed-up condition": "The tubercular, pale young man probably
wanted to reassure his constantly worrying
mother about the state of his health; for once she
was to see a chubby-cheeked son." As for the present, inscribed self-portrait, Geller believes that
"Scheffer sent such sheets containing visual
reports to his mother on other occasions as well."[3]
Keith Andrews has said that Scheffer had "that
gift of self-irony which Ricarda Huch has so
aptly called the typical mark of the true romantic personality. That gift stands out in the comical self-portraits: the one with the puffed-up
cheeks and the one with the playfully sad face of
the convalescent."

Rudolf Preimesberger has recently subjected the
present drawing to a probing analysis. It was
drawn and inscribed by the artist with the same
chalk. Image and text complement each other
and, in this case, must be read together. The text
is a commentary on the image taken from the
mirror. The facial expression is rather ambigu-
ous, but the words "miserable" and "sad" sug-
gestively guide the viewer into reading it in this
particular way. The hint of a smile contradicts
the text, with a degree of irony, and creates distance. Scheffer speaks of himself in the third person, thereby objectifying his condition. The

inscription is written in dialect, which leads
Preimesberger to believe it was addressed to
someone very close to the artist. Although he was
temporarily experiencing a remission, the cause
of his "miserable" and "sad" appearance was an
illness that had broken out in Italy in 1815: tuberculosis, which would cause his death at an early
age. He probably drew the self-portrait while
still in Italy.[4] "Pretty miserable" refers to the
state of his health; "sad" reflects how he feels
about it. Poor health is the reason why he is a
"convalescent." In the word "Riconvaliszenttt,"
Preimesberger notes not only the highly original
spelling, but also "iconic traits" in the tripling of
the cruciform final consonant, *t*: Scheffer made
three crosses, as if trying to ward off a recurrence
of the illness.

Scheffer referred to the latent illness in a
manuscript document in the Winterstein collection, which he later titled "parce redemptis"
[spare the redeemed]. In it, he spoke in general
terms about the purpose of the self-portrait, and
his words have repeatedly been invoked to interpret the present drawing: "If I want to paint
myself as I really am, I must drag myself into the
light in front of everybody. I must powerfully
examine the expression of my face, to see
whether the feelings of the heart are in it truthfully. Or whether deceitful parts …." The goal of
the self-portrait is truth, not a deceptive vision.
Striving for truthfulness was one of the Nazarenes'
commandments in their work as artists. "To drag
oneself into the light in front of everybody"
means to reveal one's innermost self, to lay it
bare in the original meaning of "portrait,"
derived from the Latin *protrahere,* to draw forth.
It is in this sense that Scheffer has revealed himself in this moving, intimate self-portrait, which
very likely, as Geller believes, he sent to his
mother from Italy.

1 Geller 1952, p. 99, nos. 1207–17.
2 *Portrait of Johannes Scheffer,* 1816, pencil, 267 x 204 mm;
   Hutter and Lhotsky 1973, pp. 10 ff. (repr.).
3 Geller 1955, pp. 57 ff., 59 (repr.).
4 The dating of the present work is confirmed by a comparison with other self-portraits and with the 1816 portrait by
   Schnorr; cf. the self-portrait sketch that should also be
   dated to 1815, that is, to the Roman period Munich,
   Staatliche Graphische Sammlung, inv. no. 1940:51, there
   dated 1819; cf. Munich 1979, p. 89, no. 99, fig. 29 (Gisela
   Scheffler).

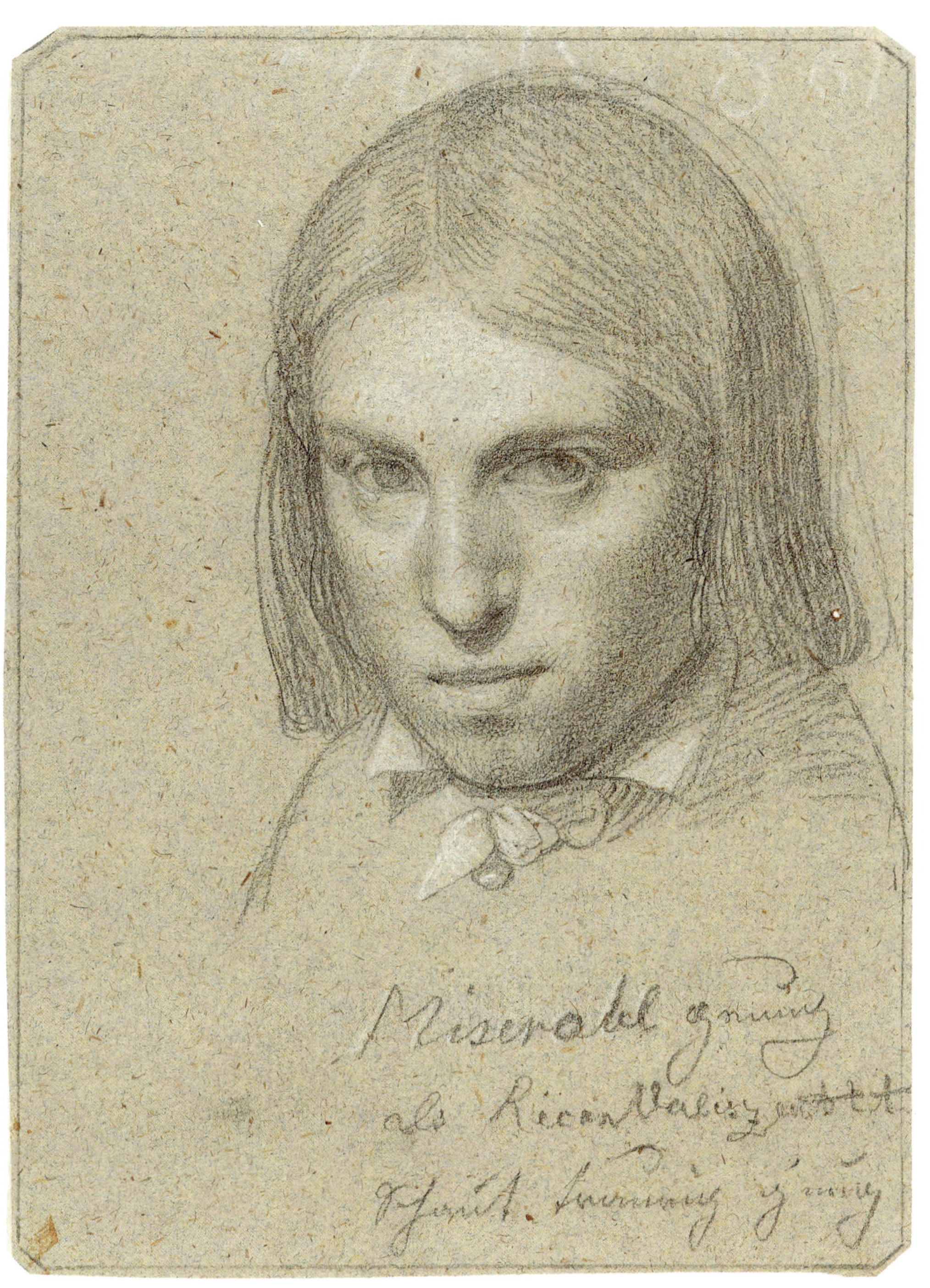

40

Johann Evangelist Scheffer
von Leonhardshoff

Dante and Virgil Meet Paolo and Francesca,
1815

Pen and brown ink, heightened with white, partial border
in pen and brown ink and pencil, on gray-tinted laid paper;
watermark; 150 x 168 mm
Verso inscribed in pen and brown ink: "Endris an Frau
Marie v. Schnorr/Zeichnung von unserem gemeinschaft-
lichen Freunde/Scheffer" [Endris to Frau Marie v.
Schnorr. A drawing by our mutual friend, Scheffer]

Provenance: Johann Christoph Endris, Vienna (Lugt 812);
Julius und Marie Schnorr von Carolsfeld, Munich and
Dresden

Bibliography: Krapf 1977, pp. 173 f., no. 71, fig. 23

In *The Divine Comedy*, Dante offers a vision of
the life of the soul after death in the three realms
of the hereafter: *inferno, purgatorio,* and *para-*
diso. As in a dream, Dante sees himself, having
lost his way, in an impenetrable forest and
threatened by wild animals. Virgil, the great
Roman poet and Dante's revered model, appears;
he will guide and protect Dante on the dangerous
journey to salvation, which leads through the
hereafter. The two begin their long journey in
hell. They progress through each of the nine
circles of hell, in which the souls of the dead suf-
fer punishment according to the severity of their
sins. In the fifth canto of the *Inferno*, they reach
the second circle of hell, where excesses of

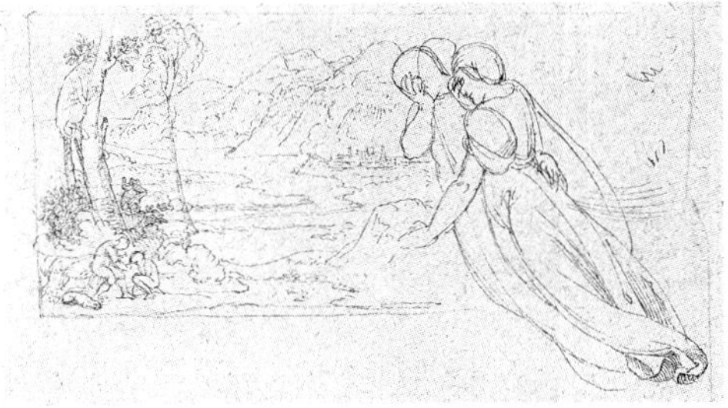

Johann Evangelist Scheffer von Leonhardshoff,
Study for "Paolo and Francesca," 1815. Pen and brown
ink; 70 x 123 mm. Vienna, Historisches Museum der Stadt
Wien, inv. no. 101.877

human conduct are punished, such as avarice
(*avaritia*), gluttony (*gula*), and lust (*luxuria*).[1]
Storm winds rage and howl, lashing the poor
souls and tossing them about like flocks of
startled birds, keeping them from finding any
rest. Dante and Virgil meet many historical
and mythical figures whose love lives led them
astray, including Helen, Dido, Cleopatra, Achilles,

Paris, and Tristan. Dante feels profound compassion. When two lovers, entwined in an embrace,
are blown along like a plaything, he speaks to
them. They are Francesca da Rimini and Paolo
Malatesta. This moment, which has inspired so
many illustrations, is the subject of Scheffer's
drawing. He based the scene on verses 73–140 of
canto 5 of the *Inferno*. Francesca was the daughter of Guido da Polenta, the ruler of Ravenna.
To end the hostilities between the houses of
Polenta and Malatesta, her father married her
off, against her will, to the misshapen and cruel
Gianciotto Malatesta, the ruler of Rimini. Francesca felt attracted to Paolo Malatesta, her husband's musical younger stepbrother, and together
they read the love story of Lancelot, the knight of
the Round Table, and Queen Guinevere, the wife
of King Arthur. When they discovered their love
for each other in the process, they were caught by
surprise and murdered by Francesca's jealous
husband. According to Dante, their souls were
banished to the second circle of hell.

For his illustration, Scheffer has chosen the
moment when Francesca—the howling wind
having died down enough to allow her to com-
municate—relates the cause of her eternal love
and her death, while Paolo sheds tears of pain
(verses 139–40), immediately before Dante,
overcome with compassion, lapses into a brief
spell of unconsciousness. Dante and Virgil,
crowned with laurel wreaths and dressed in
monastic garb, appear like brothers next to the
two hovering figures of the unhappy lovers in
their wind-whipped garments. Scheffer indulged
his acute sense of color not only in the papers he
chose, but also in the various heightenings with
white and gold in his drawings. For this scene
from the shadowy realm of hell, he chose gray-
tinted paper, on which he drew a dense net of
parallel hatching. Scheffer composed the scene
from the tragic love story in a gracefully moving
way; his unfulfilled love for the married Cäcilia
Bontzak would make the tragic love theme a very
real one during the last years of his life.

The breadth and tragic nature of Dante's *Divine*
Comedy made it an internationally popular subject for artists around the time of Goethe.[2] The
Nazarenes avidly read, translated, and illustrated
Dante during their early years in Rome in the
monastery of San Isidoro. They considered a collective project to illustrate *The Divine Comedy,*
similar to their plan for an extensive series of
Bible illustrations (cat. 37). It was realized only
in the fresco decoration of the Dante room in
the Casino Massimo by Peter Cornelius—who
provided some of the designs—Philipp Veit
(cat. 41), and Joseph Anton Koch. Scheffer's small
drawing with partial border line, reproduced
here at its original size, suggests an illustration
for the purpose of reproduction. Perhaps he also
contemplated making a series of illustrations. A

preliminary sketch for the present drawing may
provide evidence of this: it shows a summary
study of the two lovers and, within a separate
border, a landscape with a pair of figures—
Dante and Virgil—and wild animals. This could
be interpreted as the first scene of *The Divine*
Comedy (fig.).[3] Scheffer executed this drawing
during his first Roman period, from the end of
1814 to December 1815. This dating is supported
primarily by stylistic criteria. A drapery study
dated 2 January 1815, also executed with a fine,
sharp pen and showing similarly clear, wiry contours, furnishes a direct comparison.[4] Scheffer
completed the study during one of the regular
sessions at which members of the brotherhood
posed for each other wearing the late Franz
Pforr's wide Venetian cloak, as Wilhelm Schadow did in this case. In addition, for the present
drawing, Scheffer chose the same gray-tinted
paper he used for a self-portrait, datable to his
first Roman period (cat. 39).

The drawing came into the possession of Schef-
fer's close Viennese friend Johann Christoph
Endris, who presented it to Julius and Marie
Schnorr von Carolsfeld after Scheffer's death.[5]

1 I am grateful to Peter Dreyer of New York for introducing
   me to Dante's complex *Divine Comedy*, and for providing
   translations of the relevant verses.
2 Illustrations were made by, among others, Felice Giani,
   William Blake, J. H. Fuseli, Asmus Jacob Carstens,
   I. A. Koch, Peter Cornelius, Jean-Dominique-Auguste
   Ingres, Ary Scheffer, and Gustave Doré. Outline etchings
   by Tommaso Piroli were made in 1793 after John Flaxman. Cf. Stuttgart 1980, pp. 28ff; *Paolo e Francesca*, exh.
   cat., Municipal Museum (Rimini, 1994), and *Romance*
   and Chivalry—History and Literature Reflected in Early
   Nineteenth Century French Painting, exh. cat. (New York
   and Cincinnati, 1996). Cf. also Büttner 1980, pp. 97–117,
   104, 106.
3 Cf. Vienna 1977, pp. 172 f., no. 70.
4 *Wilhelm Schadow in a Venetian Cloak*, 1815. Pen and black
   ink on turquoise-tinted paper; 293/300 x 229 mm.
   Inscribed lower right: "Roma 2 tn Genajo 1815."
5 Immediately after Scheffer's death in 1822, Johann
   Christoph Endris, the executor of Scheffer's estate, asked
   Schnorr for a copy of his 1816 portrait drawing of the
   deceased; cf. cat. 39, n. 2. Schnorr made a second version
   of it, probably still in 1822 (Vaduz, Stiftung Ratjen);
   cf. Munich 1994, pp. 80 f., no. 22 (Hinrich Sieveking).

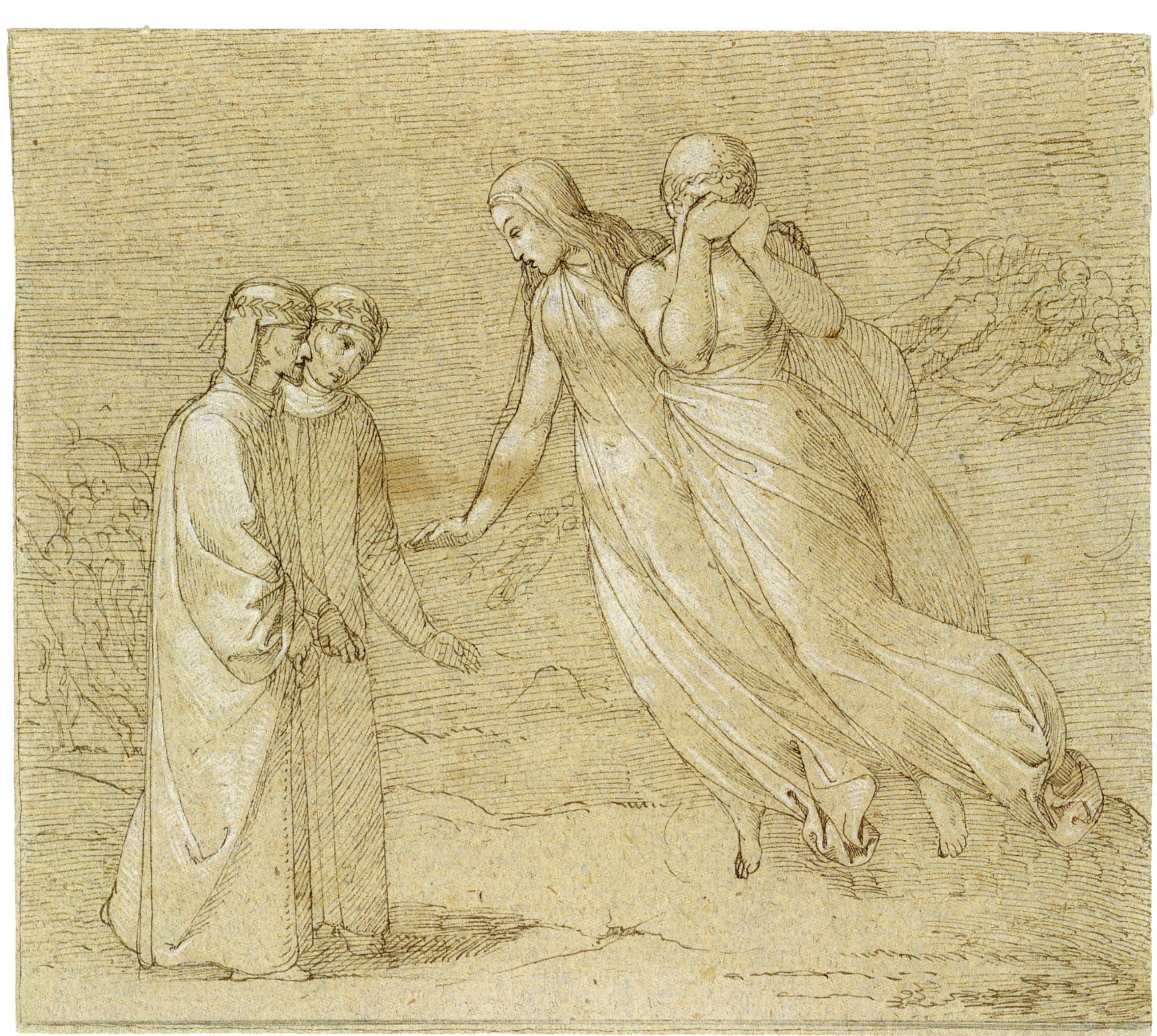

41

Philipp Veit

Berlin 13 February 1793–18 December 1877 Mainz

*Dante and Beatrice in Paradise, Design for
the Ceiling Decoration in the Casino Massimo,*
1818

*Pencil, pen and gray, brown, and colored inks, watercolor,
gold, on stiff wove paper; 205 x 355 mm; trimmed to the
shape of a vault spandrel
Signed, lower right: "ROM PVS (in ligature) 1819"*

*Provenance: Arnold Otto Meyer, Hamburg (Lugt 1994);
Prince of Liechtenstein, Vaduz*

*Bibliography: Gerstenberg and Rave 1934, pp. 58–66;
C. G. Boerner and Arnold Otto Meyer 1914, vol. 1, p. 93,
no. 834, pl. 58; Munich 1958, p. 58, no. 168, fig. 12; Lübeck
1969, p. 100, no. 189; Robels 1974, p. 97, pl. 30 (in color);
Scheffler and Hardtwig 1979, pp. 104 ff., under no. 119; Rome
1981, p. 308, II (repr.); Munich 1981, p. 93, under no. 106;
Gisela Balke, "Das Freskenwerk Philipp Veits: Ein Beitrag zur Geschichte des Freskos im 19. Jahrhundert"
(Ph.D. diss., Berlin, 1986), pp. 23, 29, 70, 246, no. 6; Suhr
1991, pp. 287 f., no. Z 68, p. 432, fig. 20; Heidelberg 1995,
p. 188*

The Casino Massimo, a seventeenth-century garden pavilion, is situated close to San Giovanni in
Laterano in Rome. Its painted decoration with
themes from the classical Italian literature of
Dante, Tasso, and Ariosto was the Nazarenes' second and most significant project of monumental
fresco painting in Rome. That a member of one
of Rome's most prominent noble families gave
such an important commission to the young Ger-

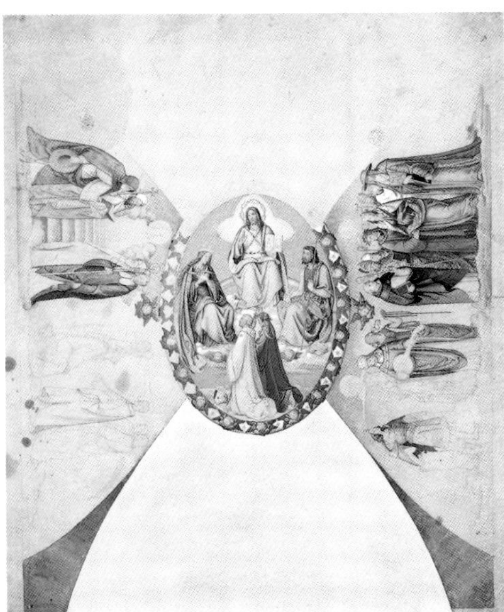

Philipp Veit, *Paradise, Design for the Ceiling Fresco in
the Casino Massimo,* 1818. Pencil, pen and brown ink,
watercolor, gouache, and gold; 552 x 458 mm. Munich,
Staatliche Graphische Sammlung

man Nazarenes attests to the reputation they had
earned through their Casa Bartholdy frescoes. In
the spring of 1817, the marchese Carlo Massimi
commissioned Peter Cornelius to paint one room
on the theme of Dante's *Divine Comedy* and
Friedrich Overbeck to decorate the Tasso room.
Later, Schnorr von Carolsfeld took over the frescoes in the Ariosto hall.

Cornelius divided the Dante room according to
the three books of *The Divine Comedy*, beginning at the bottom with the inferno, then placing
purgatory above it, and paradise on the ceiling.
His first compositional projects addressed the
representation of paradise. Instead of a pictorially illusionistic ceiling fresco in the Baroque
tradition, he designed a composition that con-
formed to the architectural surfaces and represented heaven as a mystical rose.[1] Around the
empyrean's central oval, the immutable seat of
God in the form of the Holy Trinity, the eight
circles of the heavens with the seven planets and
the firmament of fixed stars, through which
Beatrice leads Dante, rotate in concentric orbits.
In four or eight friezelike fields, Cornelius
grouped the monumental figures of the beatified, the saints, and the angels whom they meet.
Franz Horny was assigned to accentuate this
richly symbolic constellation of figures with
flower and fruit festoons, garlands, and wreaths
(cat. 49). When Crown Prince Ludwig of Bavaria
enticed Cornelius away to paint the Glyptothek
in Munich and dissolved his contract with the
marchese Massimi, the project had not pro-
gressed beyond the finished compositional
designs. After Cornelius's departure, the painting
of the Dante room was no longer carried out uniformly by a single artist. Overbeck had suggested
Joseph Anton Koch as Cornelius's successor; on
Koch's recommendation, the job was given to
Philipp Veit, who took over in the summer of
1818.

Veit found it difficult to come up with an entirely
new conception in the face of Cornelius's fully
resolved design and, in the end, he adhered to it
compositionally. With great effort, however,
Veit was able to develop Cornelius's ideas further. Decisive stimulation and support came
from his mother, Dorothea Veit-Schlegel,[2] a
daughter of the philosopher Moses Mendelssohn,
and especially from his stepfather, Friedrich
Schlegel. At the same time, though, he was intellectually overtaxed by their zealous meddling,
especially from Schlegel, a philosopher and art
theoretician, who wanted to impose his interpretation of *The Divine Comedy*.

From the outset, Veit was determined to paint
only the ceiling fresco. After he had completed it
in the summer of 1824, having definitely abandoned thoughts of continuing work on the
inferno and purgatory on the walls, Joseph Anton
Koch was eventually called upon to finish the

room, which he accomplished between 1825 and
1829.[3] Consequently, the final result lacks unity
and cohesion: with its references to Luca Signorelli's depiction of hell in the cathedral of
Orvieto, Koch's *Inferno* is heavy and dramatic,
while Veit's *Paradise* is lyrical and musical, its
coloration reminiscent of Fra Angelico.

The present watercolor is a segment cut from
Veit's complete design of 1818 (fig.).[4] In contrast
to Cornelius's project, the central transverse oval
has become an upright oval. Inside the oval, Veit
portrayed Christ making a gesture of blessing
and enthroned on a rainbow, basing his composition on representations of the *Deesis*—the iconic
image of Christ enthroned between the Virgin
and John the Baptist—and the Last Judgment.
Christ is surrounded by Mary and John the Baptist as intercessors and Dante in a prayerful pose
beside St. Bernard. In the fresco, Veit moved the
enthroned Mary, Queen of Heaven, into the center between the Holy Trinity and the two praying figures. According to the third and fourth
cantos, Dante's journey through paradise begins
in our segment of the design on the left in the
first circle with the moon, where Dante and
Beatrice encounter the beatified souls: first, the
empress Constance, the mother of Emperor Frederick II, and then the beautiful Piccarda, a nun of
the order of St. Clare from the Florentine house
of Donati. In the next sphere, of Mercury, they
meet the beatified souls who won just renown on
earth: Romeo de Villeneuve as a pilgrim and the
Roman emperor Justinian.[5] In the fresco, Veit
faithfully reproduced the arrangement and conception of the figures from this drawing,
although he left out the flower garland held by
angels, and the head of the seraph in the upper
center, which recall Cornelius's design.[6]

1 Cf. Büttner 1980, pp. 108–17, pl. 43, fig. 90.

2 Veit's monogram, *PVS* (in ligature), refers to the initials
   for Philipp Veit Schlegel.

3 Koch had occupied himself with Dante's work primarily in
   drawings; cf. Gerstenberg and Rave 1934, p. 67;
   cf. Stuttgart 1980, pp. 10 ff., 41 ff., 48 ff., nos. 30–42.

4 Suhr 1991, pp. 56f; cf. also Scheffler and Hardtwig 1979,
   pp. 104 ff., color pl. 15, fig. 55; Munich 1981, p. 93, no. 106.
   In 1870, Veit cut this trapezoid-shaped piece of his design
   out of the complete composition for the Hamburg collector
   A. O. Meyer (cf. Suhr 1991, pp. 229–33), and dated it
   incorrectly from memory (*ibid.*, p. 230, right col.).

5 I am grateful to Peter Dreyer of New York for translating
   and interpreting Dante's text.

6 Cf. Rome 1981, p. 304 (repr. in color).

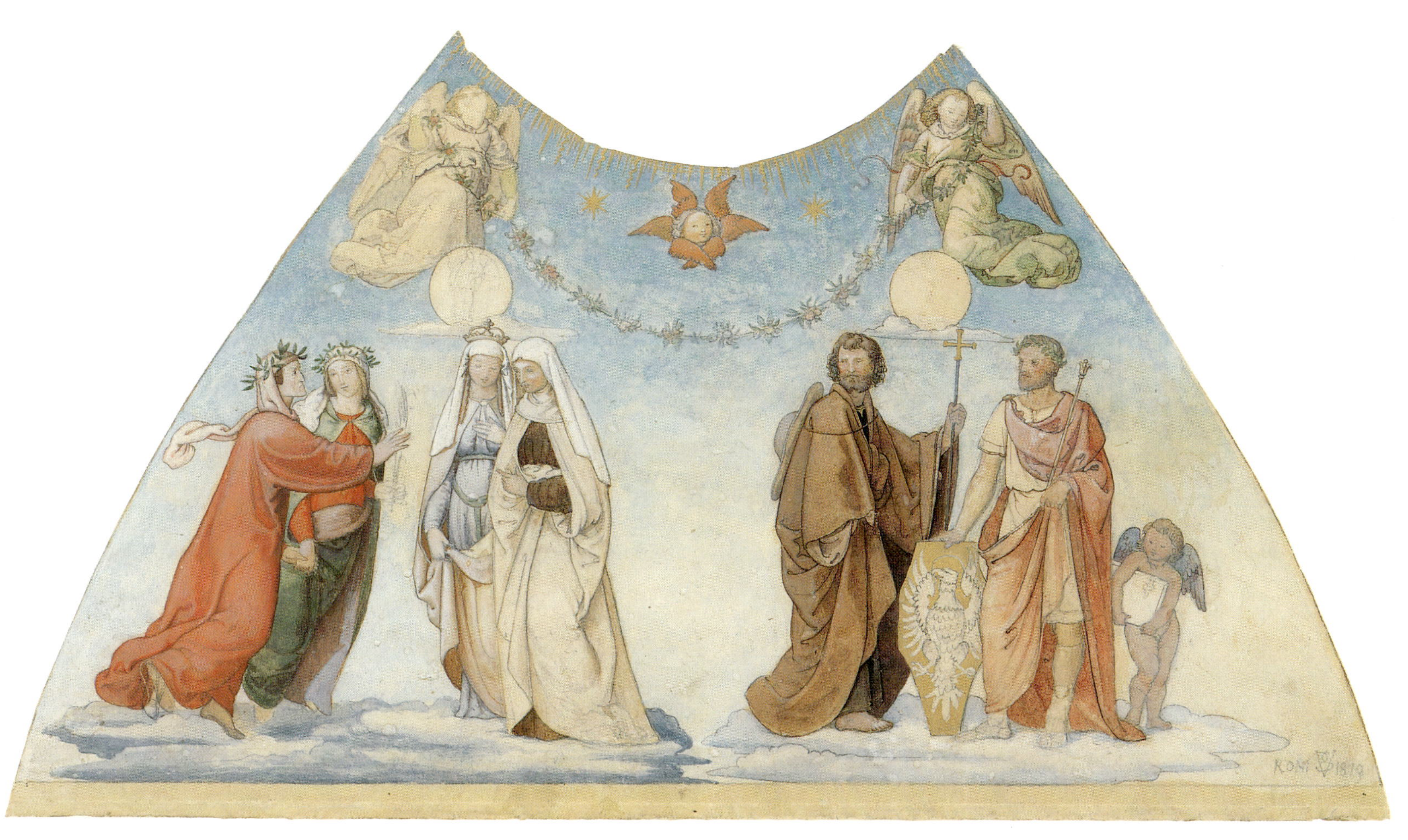

42

Johann Anton Ramboux

Trier 5 October 1790 – 2 October 1866 Cologne

Merenda in the Farnesi Gardens in Rome,
1823

Pen and brown ink, brown wash over pencil, on wove paper;
465/471 x 567 mm
Signed on the step, lower right: "AR [in ligature] f./1823"
Inscribed on the backing: "Merenda in den Farnesischen
Gärten zu Rom/Handzeichnung von Johann Anton Ram-
boux von Trier" [Merenda in the Farnese Gardens in
Rome/Drawing by Johann Anton Ramboux of Trier]

Provenance: Philipp E. von Schneider, Frankfurt am Main;
Hermann von Mumm, Frankfurt am Main; Städelsches
Kunstinstitut, Frankfurt am Main (exchanged in 1935)

Bibliography: Johann Anton Ramboux 1790–1866, exh.
cat., Rheinisches Landesmuseum (Trier, 1935), p. 13, no. 72;
Munich 1958, p. 46, no. 122, fig. 14, Andrews 1964, pl. 34b,
p. 108, no. 34b; Johann Anton Ramboux, exh. cat., Wallraf-
Richartz Museum (Cologne, 1966), pp. 13, 77 f., no. 36
(repr.); Lübeck 1969, p. 72, no. 133; Bernhard 1974, vol. 2,
p. 1211 (repr.); Robels 1974, p. 89, pl. 40 (in color); Paris 1976,
pp. 150 f., no. 174 (repr.); Eberhard Zahn, Johann Anton
Ramboux, Museumsdidaktische Führungstexte, vol. 4
(Trier, 1980), pp. 19 f., under cat. 9, p. 31 (repr.); Rome 1981,
pp. 192, 198 f., no. 96, repr. (Sigrid Metken); Heidelberg
1995, pp. 134 f. (repr. in color)

The present drawing is well documented. It was
commissioned by the Frankfurt collector Philipp
E. von Schneider, who had spent some time in
Rome in 1818, and assembled a collection of
drawings and watercolors, of large format where
possible, by artists who had been in Rome during
the same period. The artists included Friedrich
Overbeck, Johann Martin von Rohden, and
Ramboux, who lived in Rome from 1816 to 1822.
On 19 March 1822, before his departure from the
city, Ramboux wrote a letter to Schneider, in
which he proposed making a watercolor of a view
of Rome from an interesting vantage point. On
7 February 1823, Ramboux wrote again to
Schneider from Trier, where he had by now
returned: "I have the honor of sending you here-
with the drawing we agreed on, something that
Dr. Böhmer probably already informed you of. I
hope the choice of subject is to your liking, so that
it won't have to be redone. It presents a Roman
entertainment of the kind you yourself would
have had opportunity to observe in real life."[1]
Ramboux had in fact informed Dr. Johann
Friedrich Böhmer, a historian who, beginning in
1822, was also co-administrator of the Städelsches Kunstinstitut in Frankfurt. Böhmer wrote
on 1 May 1823 from Frankfurt to Johann David
Passavant in Rome: "Ramboux has done a view
of the Farnese Gardens for Herr von Schneider."[2]
Because of the clearly documented provenance, it
should be emphasized that this sheet, contrary to
a tenacious claim in the literature, was not part of
the artist's estate and therefore could not have
come under the hammer when the estate was
auctioned in 1867.[3]

In this highly finished work, Ramboux depicts
popular activities in the Farnese Gardens on the
northeastern side of the Palatine in Rome. Vineyards and gardens surrounded the Palatine Hill,
once the site of the palaces of Roman emperors.
From here, as in this drawing, one could enjoy a
wide panoramic view to the east, over the Forum
Romanum and the Arch of Titus and, on clear
days, all the way to the Sabine Hills. Surely the
beautiful view was one reason why people gathered here on warm summer evenings for a
merenda (a light repast) with music, dancing,
and wine. Ramboux first captured this scene on
the spot in a large watercolor sketch (fig.). Compared to the present sheet, it shows a narrower
view in a vertical format with the mighty shade
trees at their full height. Ramboux used this
watercolor as the starting point and model for the
present wash drawing, which he executed in his
studio in Trier as a sepia-brown grisaille. Here,
Ramboux expanded the view on both sides. He
placed the tall campanile of the medieval church
of Sta. Francesca Romana in the center of the picture, probably not only for compositional reasons. The lower edges of the crowns of the trees
close the composition at the top like a leafy
canopy, sheltering a variety of scenes of popular
life that unfold in rich narrative detail. One
could also imagine this large-format composition
as a cartoon for a painting or mural. In fact, Ramboux did create a painting on the same theme,
but it was lost in 1931 in the fire at the Glass
Palace in Munich.[4] For this painting, too, Ramboux used the watercolor sketch (fig.) as his
model. He incorporated the fountain with a vase
planted with an agave from the center foreground of the drawing exhibited here, and
shifted the perspective so far to the right that the
silhouette of the Colosseum was clearly visible at
the right edge. In the present, rigorously balanced, monumental composition, Ramboux—
very much in the Nazarene spirit—once more
brought together the experiences of his stay in
Italy in the Nazarene circle. He clearly modeled
the thoroughly pondered—though in its basic
tenor lively—composition after trecento and
quattrocento Italian fresco painting. The figural
scenes—in part invented, in part based on studies from life—show a characteristic combination
of still-life-like stylization and individuation in
their detail.—The unifying vision with which
Ramboux integrated the wealth of motifs into
his stylistic concept has a special charm.

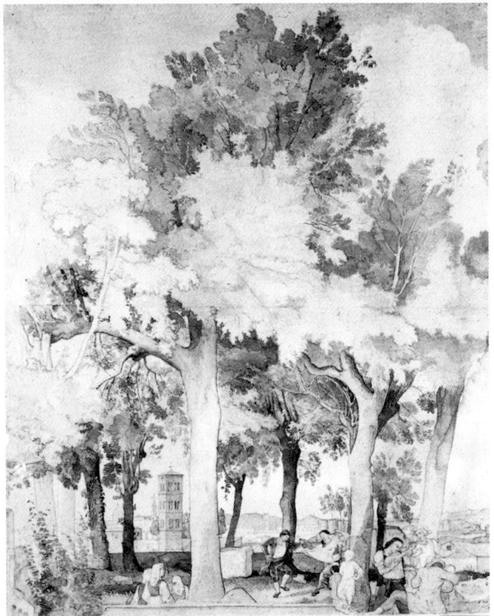

Johann Anton Ramboux, *Evening Repast in the Farnese
Gardens in Rome.* Watercolor over pencil; 540 x 450 mm.
Trier, Städtisches Museum

1 Original letters in the Kupferstichkabinett of the
   Städelsches Kunstinstitut, Frankfurt am Main.

2 *Johann Friedrich Böhmer's Briefe*, ed. Johannes Janssen,
   vol. 1 (1815–1849) (Freiburg im Breisgau, 1868), p. 123.

3 Estate auction (J. M. Heberle and J. Lempertz), Cologne
   1867, vol. 2, no. 781: "No. 781—landscapes. Villas with
   female figures playing music etc. Two watercolors done
   in Rome in 1820. 2 sheets. qu. fol. nos. 781–1/2 – 2. Also,
   Italian landscapes with staffage. 2 watercolors. fol. qu. fol."
   The catalogue makes a clear distinction between sepia and
   watercolor. This entry mentions only watercolors. For that
   reason alone, it would be incorrect to identify the present
   work with this number.

4 Cf. exh. cat., Trier 1935, p. 13, no. 72, fig. 10.

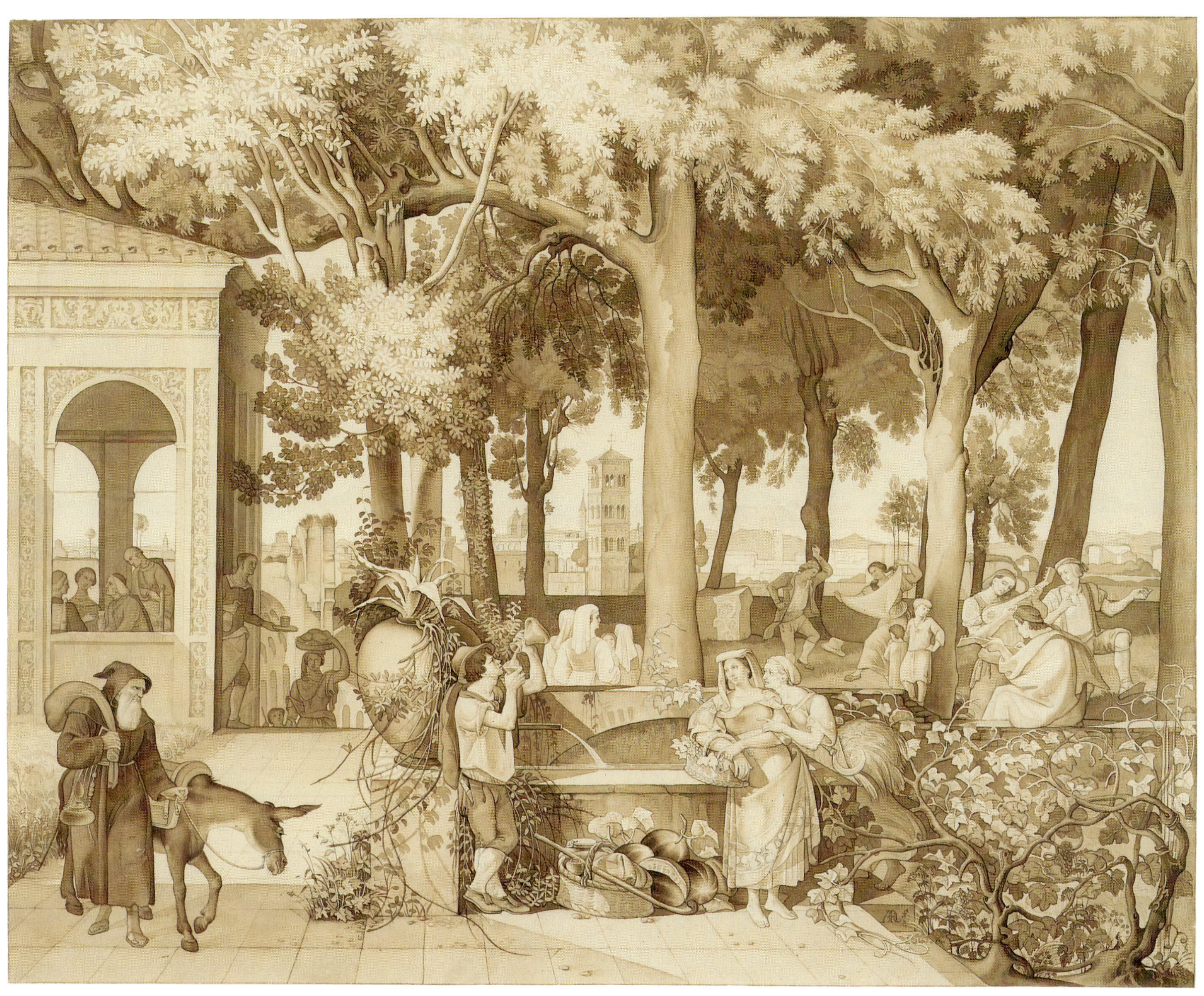

43

Johannes Riepenhausen

Göttingen 1788 – 11 September 1860 Rome

Raphael Painting the Fornarina, c. 1833

Watercolor, pen and gray and brown ink, on wove paper;
three border lines in pen and black ink;
229/231 x 281/2 mm (sheet); 222/4 x 275 mm (image)
Signed in pen and gray ink, lower left: "Riepenhausen f.
Romae"

Wilhelm Heinrich Wackenroder's *Herzenser-giessungen eines kunstliebenden Klosterbruders* [Outpourings from the Heart of an Art-Loving Monk], published in 1797 when the author was only twenty-three, awakened a desire to renew German religious art based on the models of Dürer and Raphael. The Romantic cult of Dürer and Raphael began with Wackenroder's publication, popular and widely read, especially among artists. The representation here of an apocryphal event in Raphael's life testifies to the persistence of the cult, even among the second generation of Nazarene artists.

Much as late medieval piety expanded the story of Jesus' family life through apocryphal legends, the Romantic-era personality cult centered on Raphael produced an imaginative elaboration of his undocumented private life. Vasari's mention of the Fornarina, Raphael's mistress, provided the impetus for the growth of legends. In Vasari's biography of Raphael, we read: "[He] painted the portrait of Beatrice of Ferrara, with those of other ladies; that of his own inamorata is more particularly to be specified, but he also executed many others. He was much disposed to the gentler affections and delighted in the society of

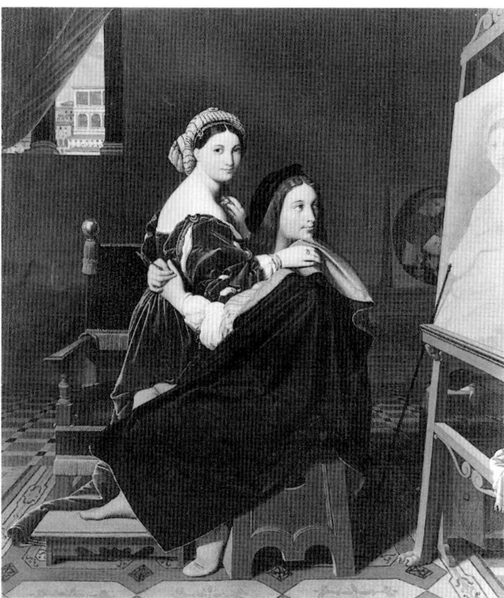

1 Jean-Auguste-Dominique Ingres, *Raphael and the Fornarina*, 1811/12. Oil on canvas; 663 x 556 mm. Cambridge, Massachusetts, Fogg Art Museum

women, for whom he was ever ready to perform acts of service. But he also permitted himself to be devoted somewhat too earnestly to the sensual pleasures of life, and in this respect was perhaps more than duly considered and indulged by his friends and admirers. We find it related that his intimate friend Agostino Chigi had commissioned him to paint the first floor of his palace, but Raphael was at that time too much occupied with the love which he bore to the lady of his choice, that he could not give sufficient attention to the work. Agostino therefore, falling at length into despair of seeing it finished, made so many

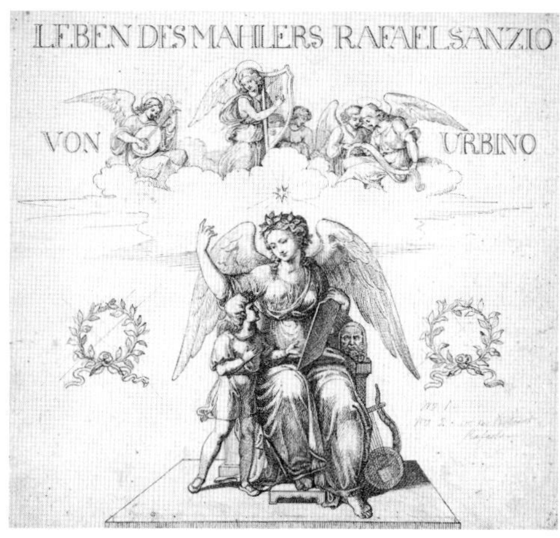

2 Franz and Johannes Riepenhausen, *Raphael and the Genius of Art*, title page to *Leben des Mahlers Rafael Sanzio von Urbino*, c. 1807. Pen and black ink over pencil; 337 x 335 mm

efforts by means of friends and by his own care, that after much difficulty he at length prevailed on the lady to take up her abode in his house, where she was accordingly installed in apartments near those which Raphael was painting; in this manner alone, the work was ultimately brought to a conclusion."[1]

Raphael's mysteriously radiant portrait of the sensuous and beautiful Fornarina—based on ancient representations of Venus—had long been accessible in the Palazzo Barberini in Rome. Nevertheless, the cleaning and restoration of the painting in 1810 was like its rediscovery. Only now was its true quality visible, so that Julius Schnorr von Carolsfeld, for example, could write to his father from Rome about the "rediscovered Fornarina."[2] Only a short time later, Ingres painted the first of his five versions—created over the course of decades—of *Raphael and the Fornarina* (fig. 1), an original contribution to the Raphael iconography. The theme soon enjoyed great popularity. From one version to the next, Ingres depicted the Fornarina wearing fewer clothes, thus approaching the model in Raphael's painting, while in compositional terms he showed her in increasingly intimate interaction

with the artist. *Raphael and the Fornarina* was conceived as part of a series of paintings of scenes from Raphael's life, which Ingres never carried out.[3] Ingres's project acknowledged the exemplary role Raphael's work played for him, and it attested to the kind of artist's life he longed for. The Riepenhausen brothers saw at least Ingres's first version of *Raphael and the Fornarina* in Rome. As early as 1807, they had offered the Nuremberg publisher Frauenholz a cycle of drawings that they had jointly created based on Raphael's life, but Frauenholz turned them down (fig. 2).[4] Friedrich Wenner in Frankfurt eventually published the cycle as a series of twelve sheets engraved by Carl Barth and others, which appeared in innumerable editions—a best seller.[5] However, the theme of Raphael and the Fornarina did not appear in this early cycle.[6] This finished watercolor, undoubtedly inspired by Ingres's painting, served as the model for an etching that was part of a new edition—based on the older work—of twelve outline etchings on the life of Raphael, after drawings and watercolors in a smaller format. The two brothers, having made changes to the pictorial program, had settled on a concept in 1831, when Franz Riepenhausen died unexpectedly. Johannes Riepenhausen must have executed the present watercolor, because the corresponding outline engraving is signed "J. Riepenhausen inv. et inc."[7] Thus, Johannes Riepenhausen produced the new edition by himself. It was published in 1833 in Rome and in 1835, in copies, by the Rocca brothers in Berlin and Goettingen.[8] Interestingly, the publication occurred close to the date of the exhumation of Raphael's remains in the Pantheon, an event that signified the climax of the Raphael cult. Riepenhausen's work seems like a final act of Nazarene artistic will, which had already been marginalized by new and modern trends.

1 Giorgio Vasari, *Lives of Seventy of the Most Eminent Painters, Sculptors, and Architects*, ed. and annotated by E. H. and E. W. Blashfield and A. A. Hopkins, vol. 3 (New York, 1926), pp. 200–201.

2 Letter from Rome dated 29 December 1820; cf. Schnorr-Briefe, p. 206.

3 Sarah B. Kianovsky, "Raphael and the Fornarina," in James Cuno et al., *Harvard's Art Museums: 100 Years of Collecting* (Cambridge, Mass., 1996), pp. 182, 183 (repr. in color).

4 Mainz 1993, pp. 129 f., no. 51.a (Stephan Seeliger).

5 Griffiths and Carey 1994, p. 173.

6 Cf. Susanne Netzer, *Raphael, Reproduktionsgraphik aus vier Jahrhunderten*, Kataloge der Kunstsammlungen der Veste Coburg, ed. Joachim Kruse, exh. cat. (Coburg, 1984), pp. 24 f., no. 21 (repr. of the complete cycle).

7 Reprinted in *Raphael Urbinas Il mito della Fornarina*, exh. cat., Palazzo Barberini, Galleria Nazionale (Rome, 1983), p. 51, no. 16.

8 Mainz 1993, pp. 129 f., no. 51.b (Stephan Seeliger).

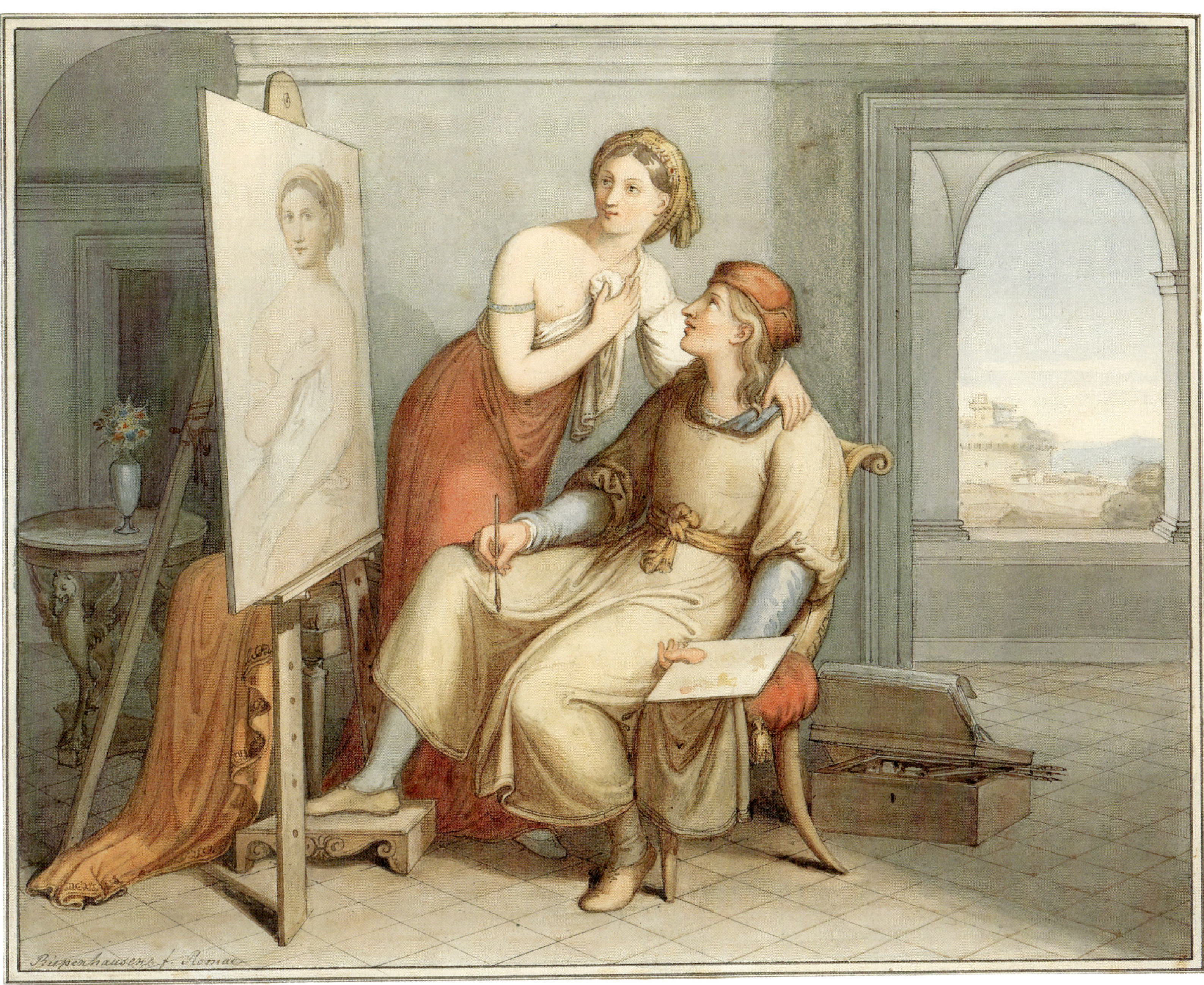

Riepenhausen f. Romae

44

Edward Jakob von Steinle

Vienna 2 July 1810 – 18 September 1886 Frankfurt am Main

Allegory of Art, c. 1828

Pen and black ink over pencil, border in ink, on wove paper; 131 x 87 mm
Monogram on a tablet, lower center: "E S" (in ligature)

Provenance: Moritz Gontard, Frankfurt am Main; von Passavant-Gontard, Frankfurt am Main

Bibliography: Edward von Steinle: Des Meisters Gesamtwerk in Abbildungen, ed. Alphons M. von Steinle (Kempten-Munich, 1910), part 2: Historische Bilder, Märchen, Genrebilder, Illustrationen zu Dichtern, Weltliche Allegorien, Titelbild; Auction Hugo Helbing, estate of von Passavant-Gontard and others, auction cat., 3 December 1931, p. 55, no. 1193; Lübeck 1969, pp. 96 ff., no. 185 (repr.); Mende and Hebecker 1973, p. 17 (repr.)

A young woman with a wreath of flowers in her long, blond hair sits on a stone bench, a subtle allusion to the late-medieval motif of the "Madonna on the Grassy Bench" (cat. 30). She personifies Art in the tradition of female allegories.[1] Steinle has equipped her and her surroundings, in a narrative manner, with a rich

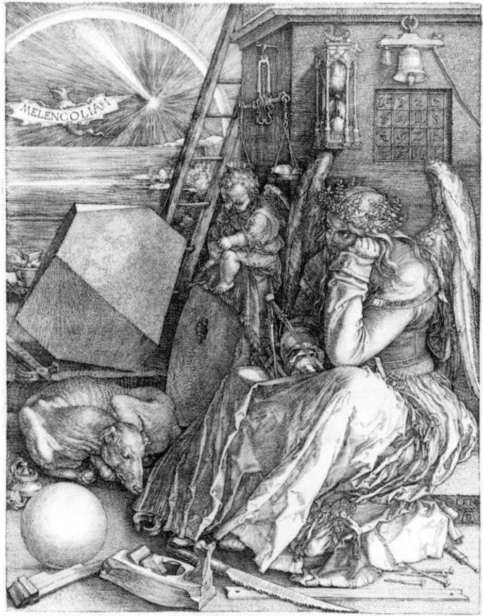

Albrecht Dürer, *Melencolia I*, 1514. Engraving. Munich, Staatliche Graphische Sammlung

stock of motifs and attributes. A cross over her chest decorates the upper part of her gown, a reference to the costume of the Crusading Orders and to the missionary significance of the cross motif. In her left hand, she holds a palette and a bunch of brushes, which together represent

Painting. She clutches a thick book, identified by the title on the spine as *Biblia Sacra* [Holy Bible]. Two other, similarly hefty volumes are propped up behind her and to her left. Their spines are inscribed with the titles *Historia* and *Legenda*. Here, Steinle has programmatically assembled the subject matter of history painting, with emphasis on the Bible.

In the right background, profiled pedestals and bases of elements of medieval church architecture with different types of columns allude to the sacred Architecture of the Middle Ages. In the left background is a pedestal with sculptor's tools, and on it we can see the bottom of a draped figure. This is a reference to Sculpture, which Steinle also represents by including fragments of an antique sculpture of a nude male on the floor on the left. It is possible that Steinle was expressing a negative opinion of both pagan Classical and Neoclassical art, as compared to the new sacral art embodied by the female figure. On the floor in the foreground lies a small tablet seen in a Gothic rhomboidal-oblique perspective, it bears the artist's ligated monogram. Dürer used this kind of tablet for his signature, and in conscious imitation of him, Friedrich Overbeck and Franz Pforr—the founders of the Brotherhood of St. Luke—used it, as did others.[2] In the lower right corner, on top of flat and rolled sheets of paper, Steinle placed compasses and an angle, symbolic references to Architecture. At the right edge, we can also see vessels, which are references to Pottery as a form of sculpture in the round.

Thus we can identify from their attributes various fields of art—"architecture, sculpture, and painting, which compete with each other and represent the most noble of the visual arts" (Karl Wilhelm Ramler). We can clearly recognize a concentrated programmatic image of Nazarene art. The way in which the figure inclines emphasizes the interconnection of painting and architecture, and it speaks to the Nazarenes' missionary desire to influence as many people as possible through monumental frescoes. Within the small format of the drawing, Steinle has created a refined allegorical female figure described with a dense arrangement of strokes, which is certainly monumental in its effect. The figure's impressive scale results in part from its placement in a constricted picture space, but it is also monumental in its reminiscence of female allegories or sibyls in an architectural context, such as those by Michelangelo on the ceiling of the Sistine Chapel.

The fine, wiry pen strokes as well as the parallel- and crosshatching recall early German engraving. It is conceivable that Steinle intended this drawing to be the model for an engraving or woodcut, most likely as an illustration in a book, which is also suggested by its small format. It

would have made a lovely frontispiece, rich in meaningful references, for a written statement of the Nazarene program. Steinle also explicitly paid homage to his revered model, Albrecht Dürer. While his draftsmanship reveals that he had assimilated Dürer's engraving style, the motif and posture of the allegorical figure embodying Art is clearly modeled after Dürer's engraving *Melencolia I* of 1514 (fig.).[3] Steinle's pensive young woman, who rests her head on her right arm and the Bible in a gesture of melancholy, undoubtedly quotes Dürer's seated allegorical figure with the flower wreath in her hair. Steinle also appropriated the motif of the pair of compasses.

The density of the strokes and the drawing's old-master style suggest that it dates from an early phase of Steinle's career, around 1828, near the beginning of his sojourn in Rome (1828–33). At that time, he associated with Friedrich Overbeck, whose early, precise graphic style Steinle seems to imitate here (cf. cat. 30, 31).[4] A stylistic comparison with Steinle's drawing *St. Eligius in His Workshop*, done in Rome in 1828, confirms this.[5] In the drawing exhibited here, Edward von Steinle created an allegory of art that could also be seen as a visual image of the Nazarene program, which he would follow into his old age.

1 Cf. the depiction of Dürer and Raphael before the throne of Art, a madonna-like figure within a radiance by Franz Pforr (etched by Hoff 1832; Lehr 1924, pl. 40, fig. 62) and Friedrich Overbeck's representation (Lübeck 1989, pp. 187 ff., no. 67, repr.), which shows Art with a cross on her chest, both works c. 1810.

2 *The Badge of the Brotherhood of St. Luke,* a vignette etched by Overbeck, shows St. Luke writing the gospel, with a small tablet in the lower left corner, left blank for the respective members' initials or monograms; cf. Jensen 1958, pp. 116 f. (repr.).

3 B.74; M., H.75; cf. Peter Klaus Schuster, "Das Bild der Bilder. Zur Wirkungsgeschichte von Dürer's Melancholiekupferstich," in *Idea, Jahrbuch der Hamburger Kunsthalle*, ed. Werner Hofmann and Martin Warnke, vol. 1 (Munich, 1982), pp. 72–134.

4 In his catalogue raisonné (where it is misidentified as a "pencil drawing"), Alfons M. Steinle (1910, p. 15) dates the present drawing without further information to the year 1835.

5 Pen and brown ink over pencil; 303 x 245 mm. Munich, Staatliche Graphische Sammlung, inv. no. 1924:74; cf. Scheffler and Hardtwig 1979, p. 103, no. 116, fig. 64.

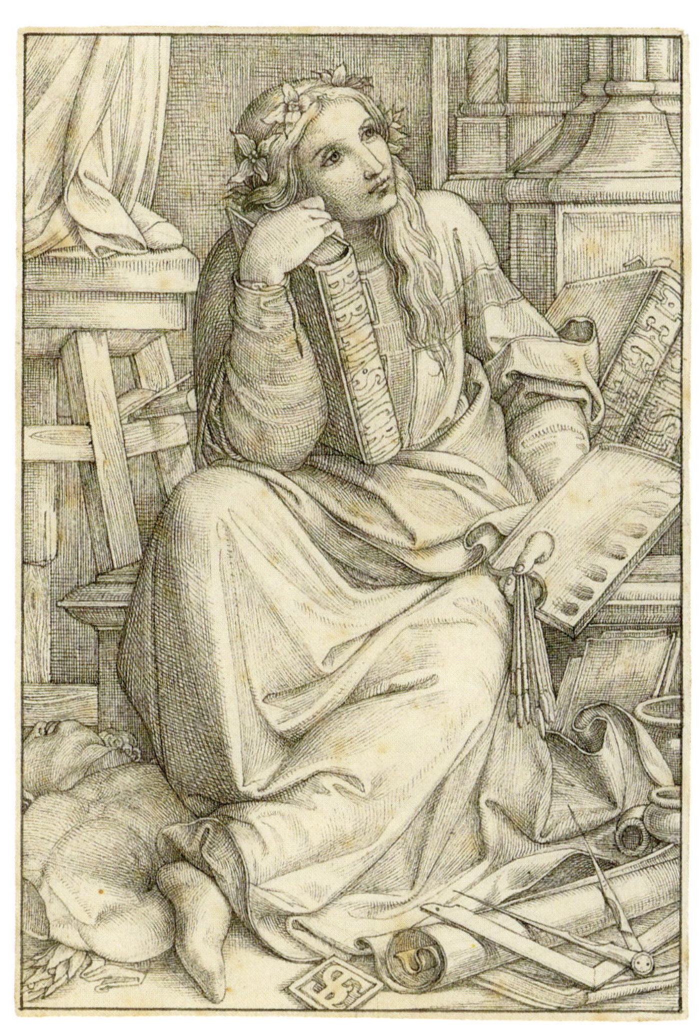

Carl Philipp Fohr

Heidelberg 26 November 1795 – 29 June 1818 Rome

Three Robber Knights on a Boar Hunt, 1813/14

Pen and green, dark green, and light turquoise blue ink over pencil, border in pencil, on wove paper; mounted on thick, laid paper; 153/4 x 225/7 mm

Provenance: Kunstversteigerungshaus Adolf Weinmüller, Munich

Bibliography: Kunstversteigerungshaus Adolf Weinmüller, 101st auction, 30 September 1966, Munich, cat. no. 1482 (anonymous, nineteenth century); Lübeck 1969, p. 30, no. 38

The present drawing depicts a forest clearing with a view at right onto a river with a Gothic church on the far bank, and at left a fanciful castle. Three horsemen in early German costume make a hasty departure; a dead wild boar is draped across the back of the last horse. From the right, a beater approaches, following his surging bloodhounds. He is just in time to see that someone else has already bagged the wild boar he

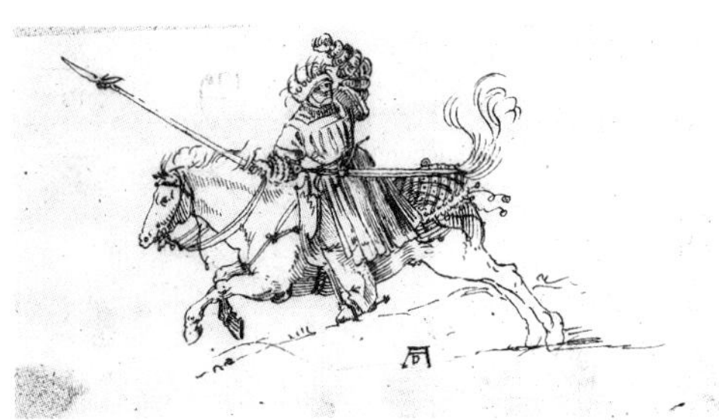

Carl Philipp Fohr, *Fleeing Horseman,* copy after J. N. Strixner after Dürer in the *Prayer Book of Emperor Maximilian,* 1813/14. Darmstadt, Hessisches Landesmuseum

has been tracking down. Here, Fohr evidently depicts one of the stories from the lives of late medieval robber knights of which he was so fond, possibly illustrating a literary text. Ludwig Tieck's *Melusine* opens with a wild boar hunt during which a fateful accident occurs, but the present drawing does not illustrate that scene. In 1813 and in the spring of 1814, as part of the preparatory work for his sketchbook of the Neckar region, Fohr had immersed himself in Goethe's *Götz von Berlichingen with the Iron Hand,* published in 1773. The Neckar sketchbook included depictions of *Götz's Castle Hornberg* and *Götz von Berlichingen in the Rathaus of Heilbronn* (pages 4 and 5), but we cannot make a direct connection between the present scene and Goethe's drama. The present drawing, like the small drawing of two knights in a forest also in

the Winterstein collection,[1] is probably a historical genre subject inspired by the spirit of the times, the kind of scene Fohr liked to invent as part of the preparatory work for his Neckar sketchbook. He may have intended it for the sketchbook, though it was never executed; it is similar to two sketchbook scenes from the life of the robber knight von Hirschhorn from the Neckar valley (pages 17 and 18).[2] The drawing's oblong format, size, and pictorial and spatial composition, as well as the border line that, in a certain sense, closes off the scene, establish a close formal connection with the Neckar sketchbook sheets, a connection that is confirmed by the technique.

The draftsmanship is remarkably similar to the drawing style of Albrecht Dürer. The inspiration for Fohr's occasional use of green ink at this time[3] evidently came from Dürer's marginal illustrations—drawn in red, green, and purpl—in the *Prayer Book of Emperor Maximilian* (cf. cat. 49, fig.); specifically, some of Dürer's scenes from the Peasants' War with fighting peasants, *lansquenets,* and knights, executed in green ink.[4] It was mistakenly believed that Fohr did not see these illustrations until 1815/16 in Munich.[5] In fact, he was familiar with them as early as 1813/14 through Johann Nepomuk Strixner's 1808 lithographic reproductions, which showed Dürer's drawings in their original colors. Fohr probably encountered them through the painter Georg Wilhelm Issel or the educator Philipp Dieffenbach, who inspired his early enthusiasm for the Middle Ages. To practice Dürer's drawing style, Fohr took seven of Dürer's motifs (after Strixner) out of their original contexts and copied them with pen and brown ink.[6] In the present drawing, Fohr freely and confidently adopted not only the use of green ink and Dürer's finely detailed style, but also the stock of copied motifs. For example, from Strixner's lithographs, Fohr copied Dürer's fleeing horseman, who is pursued by the grim reaper (fig.).[7] There is a clear variation on this horseman in the present drawing: the rider on the left who gallops off in haste, whose minutely meshed saddle blanket was also appropriated from Dürer's work. Finally, incontrovertible evidence that Fohr knew Strixner's lithographs at an early date is provided by two motifs in the Baden sketchbook, in which Fohr clearly reworked two copies he made after Strixner: the Dürer St. George on horseback,[8] which Fohr transformed into the figure of the mounted *Schirmvogt* Eberlein von Windeck;[9] and Dürer's market woman with the egg basket in her right hand and the rosary and bunch of keys hanging from her belt,[10] adapted by Fohr for the figure of the midwife of Kappel in the scene with the water spirit of Mummel Lake.[11]

Earlier, I referred to a small scene—close in subject and technique to the present drawing—of

two tired knights who have laid down their shields and swords and are warming themselves by a fire in a protected corner of the forest. Here, too, we find a detail that Fohr copied directly from Dürer's marginal drawings: the helmet with the fish-scale pattern belonging to the knight on the right.[12]

Fohr's early acquaintance with Strixner's reproductive lithographs explains how, in the present drawing, he could appropriate so congenially the lively facility of Dürer's line. It also clarifies how he was able to master complicated positions viewed diagonally, such as that of the horseman hastily galloping off or the magnificent horse in the center of the picture, impatiently rearing to go, whose mane the rider has grabbed to swing himself into the saddle. Fohr's observation of detail is fascinating, for example, in the hunting horns slung over the riders' shoulders or in the horses' physiognomy, their manes, and their hooves.

Fohr's manner of working is clearly recognizable in this drawing. He applied the ink in lighter or darker shades in keeping with chromatic perspective. At the same time, he structured his composition in a thoroughly conventional way by layering the planes of space, from the dark green at the lower edge to the light green toward the top in the background, with views of the far distance in a light turquoise blue.

1 *Two Knights Warm Themselves at a Fire in the Forest,* 1813/14. Pen and gray and black ink over pencil, on wove paper; 87 x 149 mm; mounted on laid paper. Although the two drawings are from different auctions, they show the same consignor's number; cf. Weinmüller, Munich, 109th Auction, 27 – 29 September 1967, cat. no. 2559.

2 The Gothic church visible on the right on the other side of the river could be the Ersheimer Chapel on the Neckar below Hirschhorn Castle; cf. Darmstadt 1995, pp. 148 f., nos. 14 (repr.) and 15 (repr.). This information was kindly provided by Peter Märker of Darmstadt.

3 Cf. Erwerbungen 1982 – 1989, pp. 44 f., no. 44b, fig. 21 (Gisela Scheffler).

4 *Prayer Book of Emperor Maximilian,* fols. 28r, 29v; see also 33r.

5 During his student years in Munich, Fohr surely also saw the original Maximilian prayer book in the Hofbibliothek next to the academy building; the Hofbibliothek was open to the public, and Fohr went there to copy drawings from illuminated manuscripts; cf. Darmstadt 1995, p. 289, no. 287.

6 *Ibid.,* pp. 285 – 88, nos. 279 – 85.

7 Maximilian-Gebetbuch, p. XVII, fol. 57v; Strixner 1808, pl. 26; Darmstadt 1995, p. 287, no. 281.

8 Darmstadt 1995, p. 285, no. 279 (repr.) after Strixner 1808, pl. 41.

9 Heidelberg 1968, p. 44, no. 46, fig. 41.

10 Darmstadt 1995, p. 288, no. 284 (repr.) after Strixner 1808, pl. 37.

11 Heidelberg 1968, p. 45, no. 48, fig. 43.

12 *Prayer Book of Emperor Maximilian,* fol. 28r, helmet of the knight in the lower right foreground.

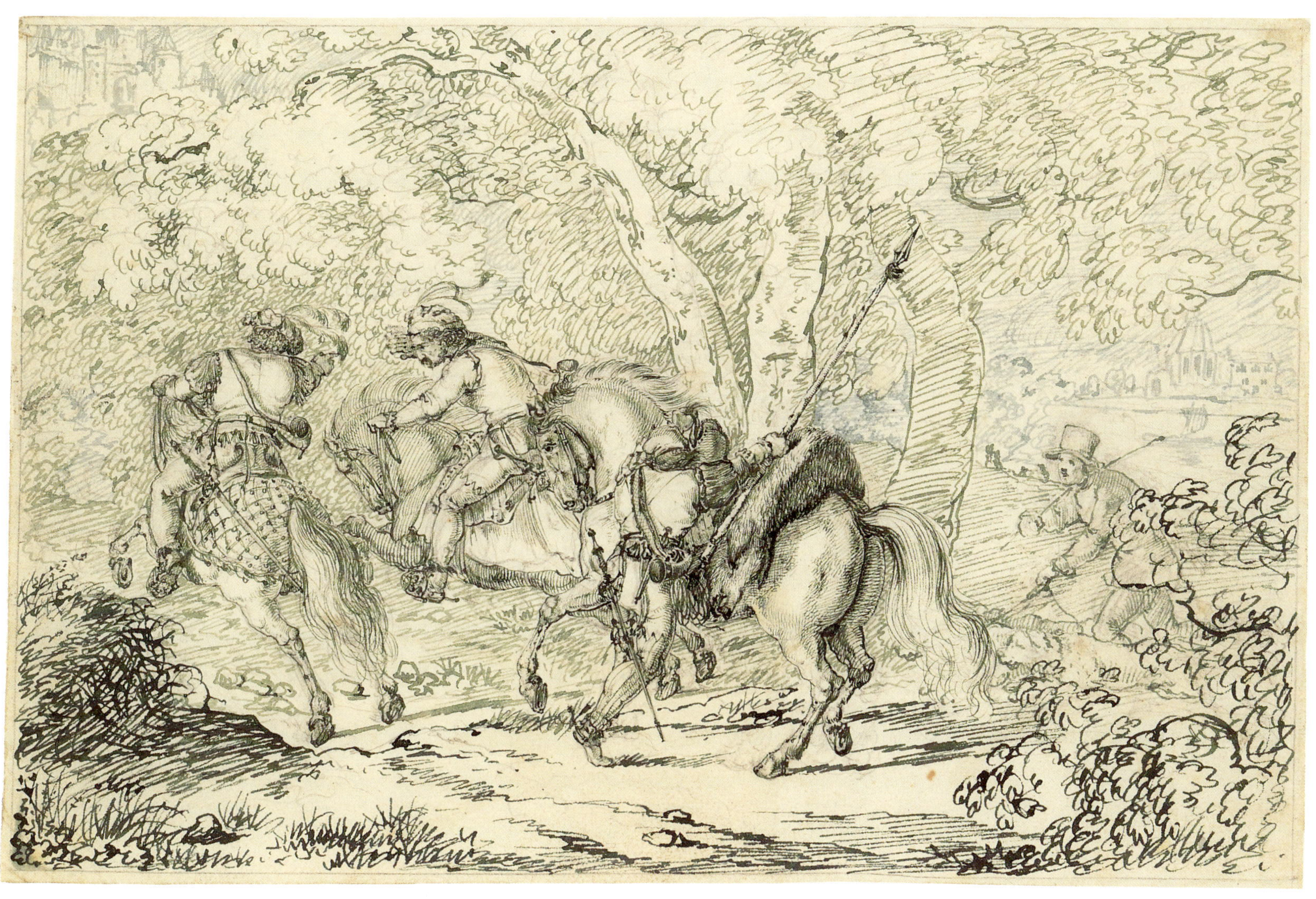

46
Carl Philipp Fohr

"Doctor Meyer's House in Baden:
A Remembrance of the Summer of 1814,"
1814/15

Watercolor, border in black-brown ink, on thin white wove
paper; 188/190 x 265/8 mm; mounted on stiff green album
paper with gilt edge
Inscribed by the artist in pen and brown ink at bottom, on
mount, in Gothic script: "Doctor Meyer's Wohnung in
Baden. Erinnerung an den Sommer 1814." [Doctor Meyer's
house in Baden. Remembrance of the summer of 1814.]
On the verso of the album sheet, a label with printed text:
"Carl Philipp Fohr (1795 –1818)/Umstehendes Blatt ist
eine Originalarbeit von Carl/Philipp Fohr und zwar
No. 4" [Carl Philipp Fohr (1795 –1818)/The sheet on the
reverse is an original piece by Carl/Philipp Fohr, namely
no. 4] (the number is written in by hand with the same
blue-gray ink as the signature); "aus dem badischen/Skiz-
zenbuch, gewidmet der Erbgrossherzogin Wil-/helmine
von Hessen. Dies wird hiermit bestätigt./München, den
1. Februar 1927/Die Direktion der Graphischen Samm-
lung" [from the Baden Sketchbook, dedicated to the Hered-
itary Grand-Duchess Wil-/helmine of Hesse. This is
hereby confirmed./Munich 1 February 1927/The office of
the director of the Graphische Sammlung]
Stamp of the Graphische Sammlung, Munich (Lugt 1093)
and signature: Dr. Weigmann

Provenance: Hereditary Grand-Duchess Wilhelmine of
Hesse; Prince Henry of Hesse; Baroness von Bassus; Lud-
wigsgalerie, Munich; Galerie Arnoldi-Livie, Munich

Bibliography: Heidelberg 1925, p. 36, Skizzenbuch aus
Badens Umgebungen Nr. 4; Ludwigsgalerie 1927, p. 4,
no. 34; Heidelberg 1968, p. 40, no. 34 (repr.); Darmstadt 1995,
p. 42, fig. 1, p. 206, under no. 105

An intimate friendship existed between Fohr
and Philipp Dieffenbach, the historian and
princes' tutor at the Hessian court, who also
became Fohr's first biographer after the artist's
early death. Dieffenbach brought Fohr into contact with the hereditary princess Wilhelmine of

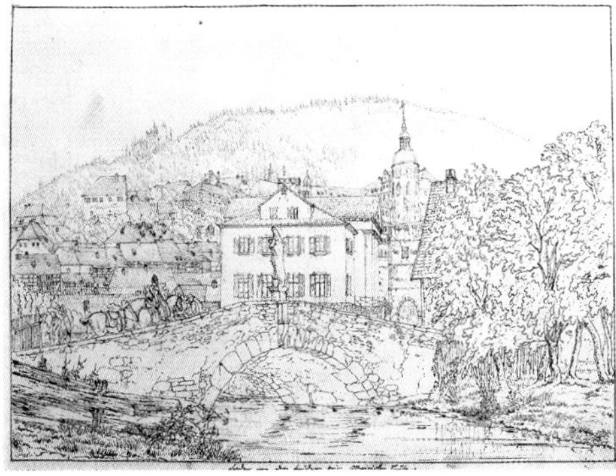

Carl Philipp Fohr, *"Baden as Seen from the Bridge at the*
Meyer House," 1814, pen and gray-black ink over pencil,
border in pen and black ink; 198 x 270 mm. Darmstadt,
Hessisches Landesmuseum, inv. no. HZ 1076

Hesse, the sister of Grand Duke Karl of Baden, a
relationship that was of great significance for
Fohr.

After Dieffenbach had repeatedly recommended
the young artist, Wilhelmine gave Fohr small
commissions for topographical landscapes. In the
summer of 1813, Fohr went on a walking tour
through the Odenwald and the Neckar Valley,
sketching landscapes along the way. During the
following winter months in Heidelberg, he carefully finished these sketches with watercolor and
compiled them into the so-called *Sketchbook of*
the Neckar Region. In the spring of 1814, he presented the sketchbook to the hereditary princess
in Darmstadt. Subsequently, the princess invited
him for six weeks to her summer residence in
Baden-Baden to record views of the surrounding
area. Fohr was at the residence from 24 June to
22 July 1814, where he and Dieffenbach explored
the city environs and the Black Forest on foot. On
these outings, he sketched selected views of
nature. During the following winter in Heidelberg, he once again reworked them into finished
watercolors and compiled them into an album,
the so-called *Baden Sketchbook*, which he sent to
the princess in the spring of 1815. These two
albums, each with thirty watercolors, are early
high points of Fohr's landscape art. They are
among the artist's few finished works. His
patron, too, was impressed: she granted Fohr an
annuity of 400 gulden, making it possible for
him to continue his training and secure his artistic livelihood.

The present watercolor is the fourth sheet from
the *Baden Sketchbook*. It is based on a study from
nature of the same view (fig.).[1] Fohr chose a picturesque vantage point for his view of Baden-
Baden. Beyond the stone bridge over the narrow
Oos River and illuminated by the morning sun, a
Neoclassical palace, with a porch with pediment
and four half-columns, rises in the middleground. The architect Friedrich Weinbrenner
built it in 1808 for the physician, Dr. Meyer, who
rented it out to distinguished visitors to the spa.[2]
On the mountain slope in the background, we
can see Schloss Hohenbaden; to the right is the
tower of the Catholic parish Church of Saints
Peter and Paul. Dieffenbach lived in the Meyer
palace during the princess's summer stays in
Baden-Baden. In all likelihood, Fohr also stayed
there.[3]

A comparison of the preparatory drawing and the
finished watercolor provides insight into Fohr's
manner of working. First, he drew the scene
from nature with pencil. Next, he carefully filled
in the details using pen and gray-black ink, especially for the architectural outlines. The drawing
seems like a pictorial grid that is laid over the
sheet uniformly. The black ink border establishes the format and thereby also delimits the
view. The size of the image in the preparatory

drawing exactly corresponds to that of the finished watercolor. Since Fohr used paper that was
bright white but extremely thin and translucent
for the watercolor, it is likely that he transferred
the drawing by simply overlaying the sheets; the
grayish-black pen and ink drawing would have
shown through. This would explain why the
overall composition and the architectural details
in the watercolor match those of the drawing
precisely. The only deviations are in the staffage
on the bridge and in some minor changes in the
riverbank vegetation. Of course, this technique
allowed for repetition, and in fact, there is a second version of this watercolor, which Fohr probably intended as a thank-you gift for Dieffenbach.[4] In the present watercolor, Fohr depicted
himself, in the red Cossack cap he started to wear
in 1814, as well as his mentor with his aristocratic
pupils.

When executing the watercolor, Fohr followed
the Classic compositional technique of a dark
foreground and an increasingly lighter tone with
the receding distance. In so doing, he seems to
have followed the tradition of decorative gouache
painting that came out of Italy in the late eighteenth century, and was fashionably popular
among artists such as Salomon Gessner and the
so-called Swiss *Kleinmeister* ["little masters"]. In
gouache, however, the light values and illumination are applied with bright-hued opaque colors
on an opaque ground, and while Fohr did occasionally use gouache, he did not do so here. In the
present work, Fohr carefully modulated the pure
watercolors from light to dark, leaving some of
the brighter areas as reserves. He created darker
areas using darker hues and repeated applica-
tions of watercolor; the white is not opaque white
but reserved areas of the paper. In this sheet,
Fohr shows himself to be a master of the difficult
watercolor technique, in which mistakes are not
easily correctable. The great charm of the
medium lies in its transparency and in the colors'
luminosity. Fohr "illuminated" his *vedute*, trans-
forming them into sumptuously dense surfaces of
color, from which the bright areas sparkle like
radiant jewels, as though they were trying to
compete with the splendor and luminosity of
medieval book illumination.

1 Cf. Darmstadt 1995, p. 205 (repr.), p. 206, no. 105.
2 The building still exists (Sophienstr. 1) and today houses
   the Städtische Sparkasse; for a picture of the city at the
   time of the early spa tourism, cf. Tübingen 1981,
   pp. 116–19 (Heide-Marie Garthe-Hochschild).
3 Darmstadt 1995, p. 206 (Peter Märker).
4 Watercolor, pen over traces of pencil on thin paper;
   166 x 224 mm. Anonymous private collection; cf. Heidelberg 1968, pp. 49 f., no. 61, fig. 50. Dieffenbach mentions
   that Fohr, as a token of his gratitude, spent days making
   additional versions for him of the most interesting and
   important views of the Baden region; Dieffenbach 1823,
   pp. 41 ff.

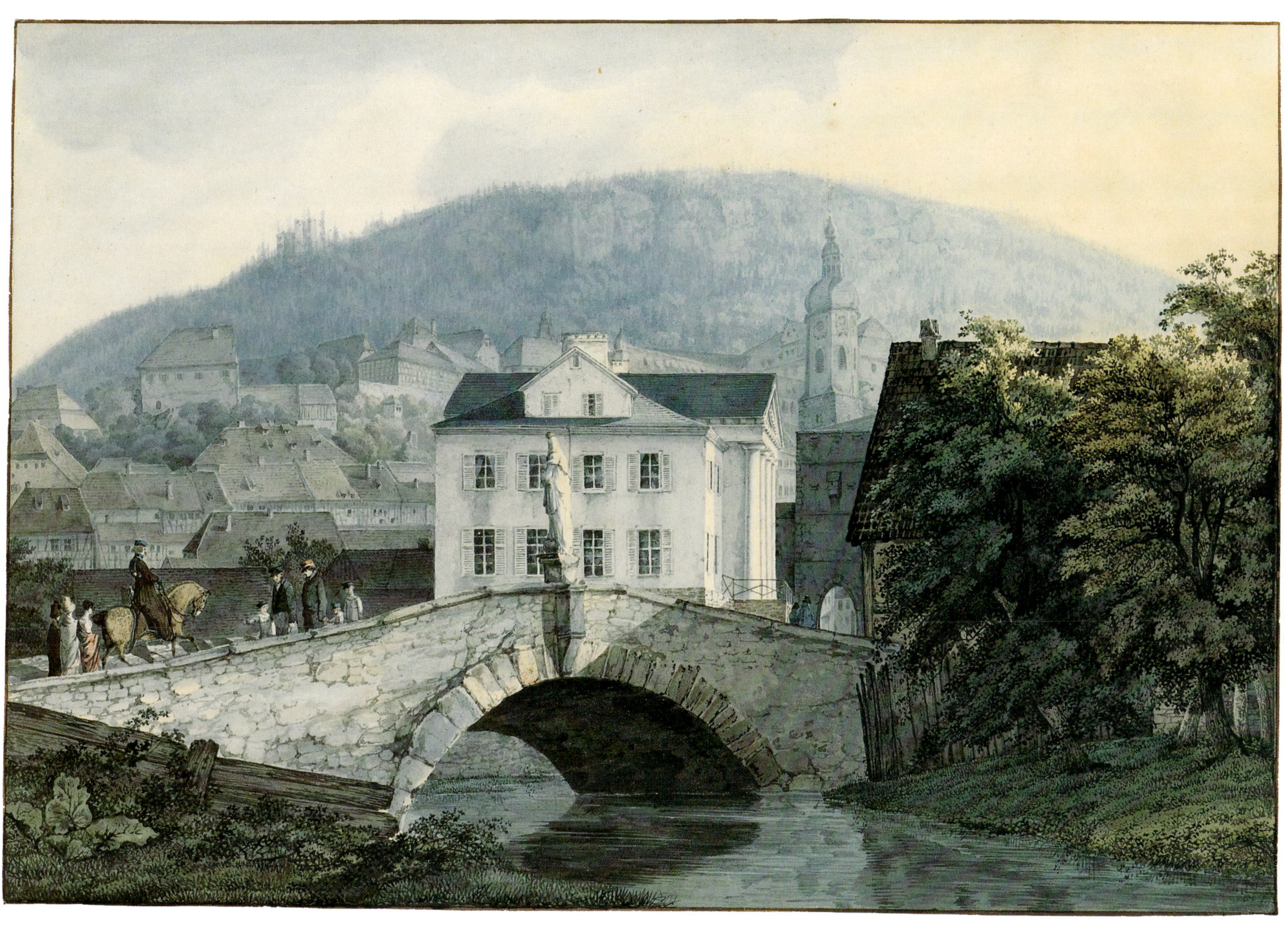

47
Carl Philipp Fohr

Self-Portrait with a Laced Coat, 1816

Brush and gray and black washes over pencil, on thin, light gray laid paper; watermark (illegible); 268/271 x 195 mm; trimmed on all sides
Verso: sketch for a scene from The Magic Circle *by Friedrich de la Motte Fouqué. Pen and black ink, gray wash, over pencil*

Provenance: Estate of Mey and Widmayer (publisher and art dealer), Munich; 1934 Antiquariat Robert Wölfle, Munich

Bibliography: Munich 1958, p. 26, no. 35, fig. 26 (Heidelberg student); Lankheit 1959, pp. 64 ff., 75, fig. 3; Jensen 1968, pp. 32 f., 52 (fig. 4), 106, no. 34 (self-portrait); Frankfurt 1968, p. 53, no. 114, pl. 38 (recto), pl. 43 (verso) (Ruhl portrait); Heidelberg 1968, p. 70 f., under no. 112; Lübeck 1969, p. 32, no. 41 (Ruhl portrait); Brigitte Rechberg-Heydegger, "Ludwig Sigismund Ruhl (1794–1887). Leben und Werk" (Ph.D. diss., Giessen, 1973), p. 209 f., B5 (Ruhl portrait); Bernhard 1974, vol. 1, p. 302 (repr.); Darmstadt 1995, p. 74, n. 35

Opinion is divided on the identity of the young man in a fashionable student costume, even though Jens Christian Jensen, as early as 1968, provided sound arguments for regarding this as a self-portrait by Fohr. Edmund Schilling had maintained that the paper and the portrait, as well as the scene on the verso, belonged to Fohr's Roman period. In 1968, Hans-Joachim Ziemke seconded that opinion; he identified the student as the Kassel painter Ludwig Sigismund Ruhl (1794–1887), an intimate friend from Fohr's years of study in Munich, with whom he had closely collaborated.[1] We have a good idea of Ruhl's appearance during the years 1815 to 1818 from a lively study of him drawing that Fohr did during their student years (fig.).[2] On the table are books whose spines bear the titles *Melusine* and

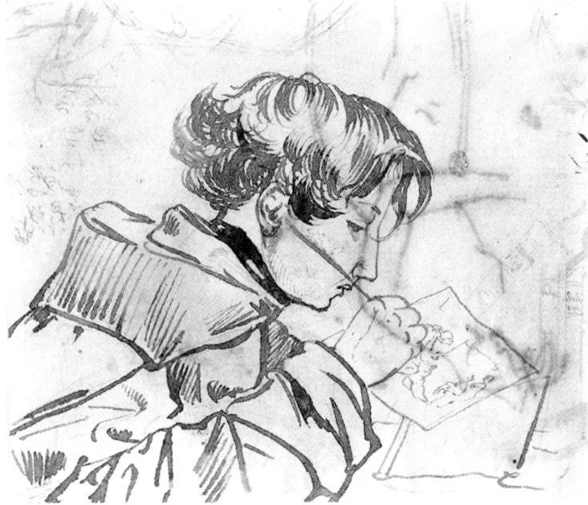

Carl Philipp Fohr, *Ludwig Sigismund Ruhl Drawing*, 1815/16. Pen and black ink over pencil; 102 x 118 mm. Heidelberg, Kurpfälzisches Museum

Zauberring [The Magic Ring]. The drawing dates from a time when the two artists worked together on a series of illustrations to Ludwig Tieck's *Melusine* and Friedrich de la Motte Fouqué's *The Magic Ring*. The sketch for *The Magic Ring* on the verso of our portrait also points clearly to this thematic context,[3] an important argument in support of the view that it was done during Fohr's Munich period.

Two additional likenesses of Ruhl, another by Fohr,[4] and one by Carl Vogel von Vogelstein dated 7 August 1818,[5] show Ruhl elegantly dressed, with a round face and medium-length hair. There is no correspondence between the present portrait and Ruhl's rounder features. On the other hand, Fohr's narrower, more chiseled features, captured in the likenesses reproduced by Geller,[6] clearly match our student portrait, where the loose touch of the brush describes the face in a more summary way. The same holds true for the length of the hair, as Ludwig Emil Grimm's portrait of Fohr, done on 11 March 1816 in Munich, confirms.[7] The face of our student expresses seriousness and self-confidence, great sensitivity and shyness—precisely the traits used to characterize Fohr in the sources. Finally, the hint of melancholy in the face also supports the argument in favor of a self-portrait. Dieffenbach emphasized this feature in his own characterization of Fohr, and remarked that it had been especially well conveyed in Amsler's well-known engraved portrait of him, based on a likeness by Barth.[8] Under the influence of the socially adept and always elegantly dressed Ruhl, Fohr had begun to place greater stock in his external appearance. In Grimm's portrait, he wears a dapper coat decorated with laces, similar to the one in the present work. It is related to the hussar coat and to the lace coat of the Lützow Fusiliers and was therefore military in origin, as was the biretta-shaped flat cap. Military dress was fashionable and popular in the circles of students returning from the War of Liberation. At some universities the administration took steps to curb it;[9] those who wore it were suspected of engaging in subversive political activities.[10] It is somewhat ironic that Fohr very nearly had to leave Munich in 1816 on the grounds that he had violated the Bavarian dress code,[11] while later, in Rome, Crown Prince Ludwig esteemed him precisely for wearing the old German coat and thus displaying his patriotism, holding him up as a model to the other German artists.[12]

In his 1814 tract *On Morals, Fashion, and Dress*, the Frankfurt journalist Ernst Moritz Arndt renounced the prevailing French taste in fashion and promulgated the black "old German" coat as an expression of support for the ideal of German unity, and long hair as an expression of individual freedom. This fashion was quickly adopted by patriotic students. When Fohr returned to Heidelberg, his politically radical student friends were now making a statement by wearing the black German coat. From then on Fohr himself wore it, even on his trip to Italy (cat. 48), where he introduced it to the German artists in Rome. The laced coat in the present drawing thus points to his earlier years in Munich or Heidelberg. Stylistically, too, the work can be dated to that period by the emphasis on the contour, which Fohr had picked up from Ruhl. Our spontaneous self-portrait is thus like a prelude to the important group of character studies of Heidelberg student friends, which reached its climax in the calligraphic self-portrait that Fohr gave to his parents as a present before his departure for Rome.[13] These portraits were drawn in the summer of 1816, mostly with pen and black ink and with emphasis on the outline.[14] They would be followed in Rome in 1817 by a second, highly important series of pencil portraits that were done for the etching—never executed—of German artists in the Café Greco.

1 Frankfurt 1968, p. 53, no. 114.
2 Jensen 1968, p. 107, no. 36a, p. 12 (repr.).
3 For a description of the subject of the sketch, see Jensen 1968, p. 106, no. 34, and Frankfurt 1968, p. 53, no. 114.
4 Pen and black ink; Berlin 1994, p. 69, no. 50 (repr.); cf. Jensen 1968, p. 107, no. 36a, p. 12 (repr.).
5 Bernhard 1974, vol. 2, p. 1477 (repr.).
6 Geller 1952, figs. 100–105, 107.
7 Koszinowski and Leuschner 1990, p. 70 f., P 120 (repr.).
8 Dieffenbach 1923, p. 103.
9 Jensen 1968, pp. 113 ff., under no. 56.
10 Cf. Bernward Deneke, "Kronprinz Ludwig und der altdeutsche Rock," in *Vorwärts, vorwärts, sollst du schauen: Geschichte, Politik und Kunst unter Ludwig I*, ed. Johannes Erichsen and Uwe Puschner (Munich, 1986), pp. 153–69, 163. See also Bernhard Bott, "Kronprinz Ludwig in altdeutscher Tracht in Rom," *ibid.*, pp. 171–84.
11 Letter from Georg Wilhelm Issel to Friedrich Schleiermacher, dated 2 June 1816; cf. Heidelberg 1925, p. 5.
12 Ludwig himself wore the old German coat in Rome and advocated it among the German artists, whom he gave money if they needed it to acquire one.
13 *Self-Portrait*, 1816. Pen and brush and a mixture of gray, blue, and brown ink and wash; 237 x 188 mm. Heidelberg, Kurpfälzisches Museum, inv. no. Z-27.
14 Among them the portraits of Ruhl; cf. Berlin 1994, p. 69, no. 50; and of Wilhelm von Harnier; cf. Frankfurt 1968, pl. 39, no. 125.

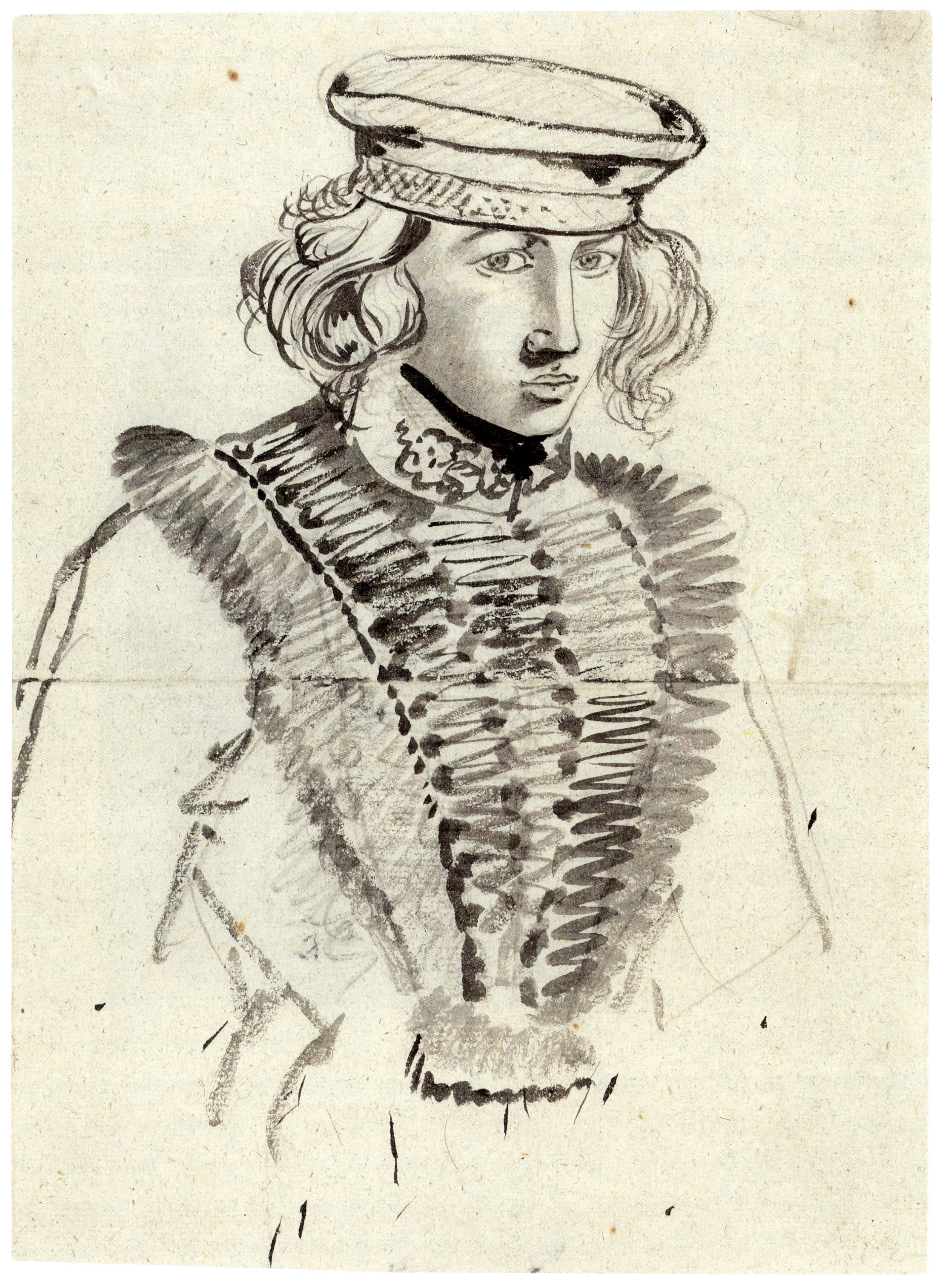

48

Carl Philipp Fohr

Fohr and His Dog Grimsel on the Way to Italy, 1816

Pen and gray ink over pencil, on wove paper; silhouetted, mounted on paper prepared with black wash; 149 x 201 mm
Inscribed in pen and gray ink, lower right: "15"

Provenance: Regierungsrat A. Fohr, Munich

Bibliography: Dieffenbach 1923, p. 67 f.; Herbert Grossberger, "Carl Philipp Fohr: Ein Umriss seiner künstlerischen Entwicklung. Mit Werkverzeichnis" (Ph. D. diss., MS, Heidelberg, 1924), p. 1, no. 4; Hardenberg and Schilling 1925, p. 25 (repr.), 69; Heidelberg 1925, p. 21 f., no. 48, cover ill.; Ludwigsgalerie 1927, p. 5, no. 72; Lohmeyer 1935, p. 263 (repr.); Grote 1944, p. 24 f., fig. 15; Geller 1952, p. 53, no. 304; Munich 1958, p. 16 (repr.), p. 26, no. 36; Andrews 1964, p. 107, under 31.b; Marbach 1966, p. 178 f., no. 252; Jensen 1968, pp. 30, 37, 44 f., 89, fig. 49, p. 107, no. 36; Frankfurt 1968, p. 52 f., no. 113; Lübeck 1969, p. 31 f., no. 40; Cologne 1973, no. 31 (repr.); Bernhard 1974, vol. 1, p. 300 (repr.); Robels 1974, p. 56, pl. 42, p. 77; Darmstadt 1995, p. 319, under no. 330

The sources describe Fohr as a nature lover, and his closeness to nature expressed itself also in his love of animals. He was especially fond of dogs, and we find them often as mood-setting staffage in his historical and contemporary genre scenes, in pictures of military-student events, and in literary illustrations. Among the animal studies now in Darmstadt is a sheet of around 1814 with representations of two of his favorite breeds in seven different positions. It is reminiscent of late medieval engraved animal playing cards that were used as model sheets, and Fohr evidently used this study in just such a way.[1] Like many students, Fohr got himself a dog, a St. Bernard,

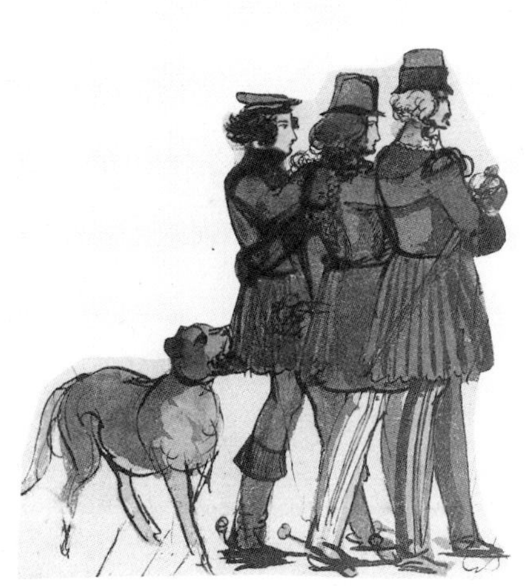

Carl Philipp Fohr, *Self-Portrait with Two Friends and the Dog Grimsel*, 1816. Darmstadt, Hessisches Landesmuseum

which he called "Grimsel" after the high mountain pass in the Bernese Alps that leads into Italy. In the present drawing, Fohr has depicted himself with this dog in October of 1816, prior to his departure for Italy. A dagger in his belt, Fohr wears the kind of old German attire favored in his circle of Heidelberg students (cf. cat. 47). The drawing has become known almost like a trademark, a leaf from the family album of the German longing for Italy: master and dog, Germania and Italia, and a Romantic friendship picture as well.

Fohr's mentor, Philipp Dieffenbach, wrote in his biography of the artist: "For a long time he had been yearning for Italy, the land of art, and for its capital, Rome, that *world within the world*. The little he had seen of Italy on his excursions from Munich had only nourished the longing in him . . . . Finally, on 16 May 1816, he received the happy news from Herr Issel that the hereditary princess approved his trip to Rome. Thoughts of the trip now preoccupied him in many ways; his imagination even painted how he would undertake the journey. And since what he thought was just as readily put on paper, one day he drew a picture of himself walking along in German dress, a small backpack on his back, and a walking stick in his hand. By his side walks a large dog, a protector on the dangerous journey and a savior in time of need. Fohr had in fact bought himself a dog (of the breed from St. Bernard Mountain) for three *carolins*, and called him 'Grimsel.'"[2] Fohr eventually made it to Rome via Freiburg, Schaffhausen, Zurich, the "ice-covered" St. Gotthard Pass, Milan, Bologna, and Florence. From the Italian capital he wrote to his parents on 15 December 1816: "I was extremely happy when I reached the tomb of Nero, the beginning of Rome, and had finished the entire journey with its endless exertions; and so, especially, was Grimsel, whose walking had also come to an end."[3]

Dieffenbach, who thought the well-known Heidelberg self-portrait drawing too cold and abstract, commented once again on the present work: "The way he appears there (in his self-portrait) is the way he may have *thought* of himself, though he did not really appear that way to anyone who knew him more closely. In this way, as I have already mentioned, he designed a small sketch of himself on the way to Italy. Who would blame the young man for this game?"[4]

A pen drawing with watercolor and black wash, also silhouetted, that shows Fohr between two friends in the same early German attire and Grimsel walking behind, seems to be a variation on our theme (fig.).[5] The huge figure on Fohr's right, girt with a sword, has been identified as Ludwig Follen.[6] Since Fohr freely invented the present drawing, it is conceivable that he also constructed a mental image of his journey to

Italy in the company of his friends: namely arm in arm with Follen on the right and—clearly identifiable—Ruhl on the left, with whom he had originally planned to travel (cf. cat. 47, fig.). In the middle of March 1817, Fohr had a severe falling out with Ruhl, the once beloved artist friend from his student years in Munich, whom he would meet again in Rome. Following the custom of Heidelberg students, Fohr let the conflict escalate to a pistol duel that ended without bloodshed. From the diary entries of the painter Wilhelm von Harnier, who was friendly with both artists, we learn that Grimsel, too, was involved in the bad feelings between the onetime friends: "Today Fohr publicly took Grimsel away from Ruhl. He told me that he had given Ruhl the dog on the condition that they would jointly have him, but since that was no longer possible, he was taking back his property. Ruhl has told me that Fohr broke his word by taking the dog he had given to him as a present."[7]

Grimsel is mentioned once more, by Francis Bunsen, née Lady Waddington, the young wife of the secretary of the Prussian delegation, in a report on Fohr's tragic death. Fohr drowned on 29 June 1818, while bathing in the swift-flowing Tiber. According to her letter, "Four days earlier, Fohr's poor dog had nearly perished at the same spot, which is why he did not dare venture into the water after his master. He ran along the bank howling and could not be moved from the spot in any way, until he was shown his master's clothes, which he then followed home."[8]

1 Darmstadt 1995, pp. 243–45, no. 186 (repr.). The varied depictions of the female animal suggest that the studies were done directly from nature; numbers 201, 278, 327 (*ibid.*) show a careful reworking of individual motifs from these studies, which is why the "model sheet" should be dated earlier.

2 Dieffenbach 1823, p. 67 f.

3 Reprinted *ibid.*, p. 133.

4 *Ibid.*, p. 104 f.

5 Darmstadt 1995, p. 319, no. 330, p. 131, pl. 31 (in color).

6 Cf. *ibid.*, pp. 319–24, nos. 331–33.

7 Entry dated 22 March 1817, quoted in Georg Poensgen, *C. Ph. Fohr und das Café Greco: Die Künstlerbildnisse des Heidelberger Romantikers im geschichtlichen Rahmen der berühmten Gaststätte an der Via Condotti zu Rom* (Heidelberg, 1957), p. 52.

8 Letter dated 1 July 1818 to her mother; quoted in *ibid.*, p. 72.

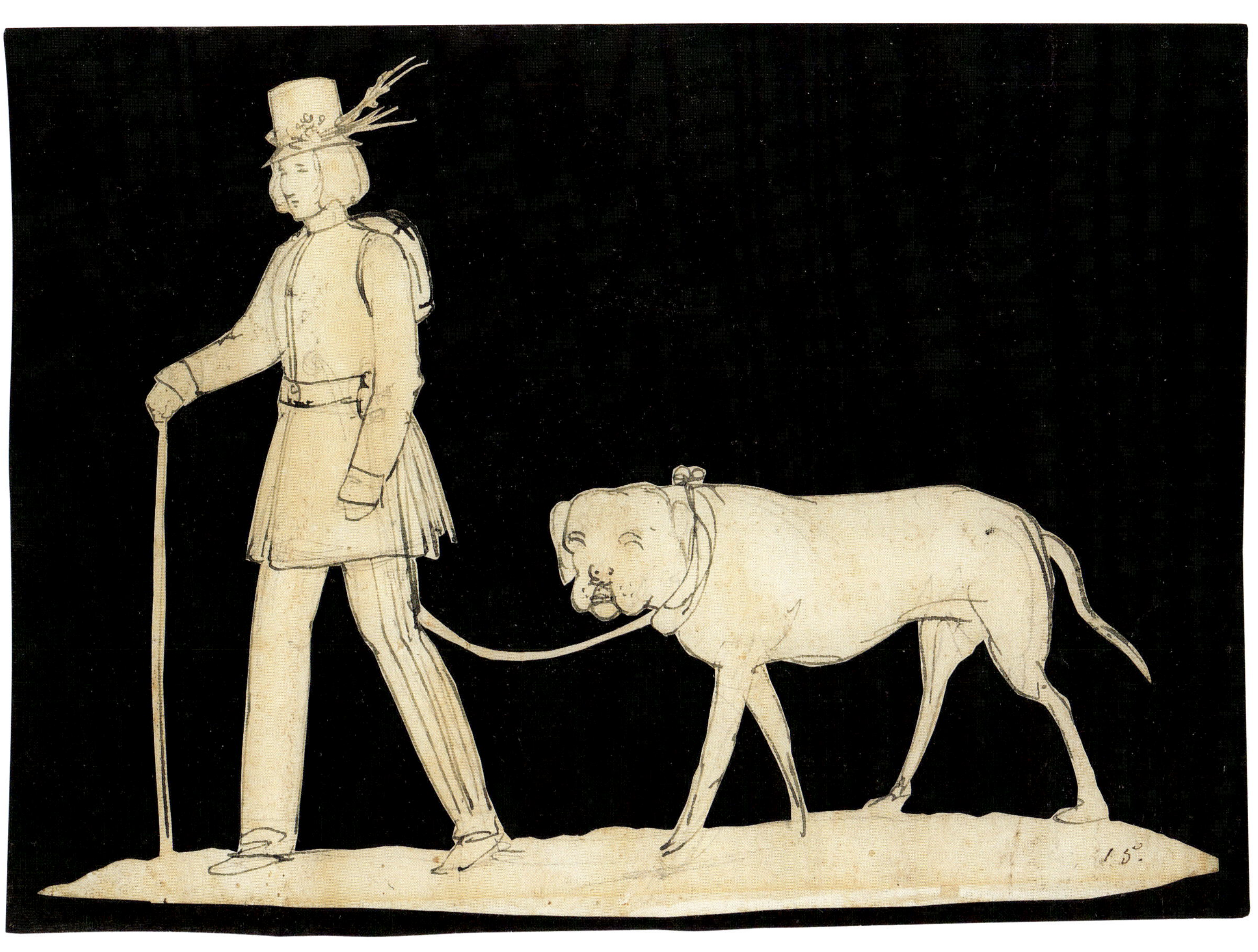

49

Franz Theobald Horny

Weimar 23 November 1798 – 23 June 1824 Olevano

Vine Branch with Green Grapes, 1817

Watercolor over pencil, on wove paper; watermark:
J RUSE; gilt border on left; 179 x 225 mm
Verso inscribed by another hand, in pencil: "Horny"

Provenance: Carl Friedrich von Rumohr, Dresden; August
Grahl, Dresden (without his stamp, Lugt 1199); Ludwigs-
galerie, Munich

Bibliography: Frenzel 1864, p. 408, no. 4026; Scheidig 1954,
p. 168, no. 168; Munich 1958, p. 33, no. 63a; Lübeck 1969, p. 45,
no. 69a; Sieveking 1975, p. 745, fig. 1 (in color); Domenico
Riccardi, "Joseph Anton Koch e Olevano: Analisi di un
rapporto preferenziale," in Römische Historische Mitteil-
lungen, ed. Otto Kresten and Adam Wandruszka, vol. 34/35
(Vienna, 1992), p. 214, fig. 30

In the fall of 1817, Horny sojourned with Peter
Cornelius in Frascati, where he executed several
hundred drawings and watercolors of plants from
nature, including this small study of green "currant grapes."¹ In this veritable frenzy of creativity, Horny displayed his prodigious and powerfully independent artistic talent for the first
time. His masterful plant studies, most of which
are lost, were the earliest pure expressions of his
keen gift of observation, his sensitive feel for the
rich diversity of nature, and his pronounced
sense of color.

Cornelius hired the young artist to collaborate on
the planned painted decoration on the theme of
Dante's *Divine Comedy* in one room in the

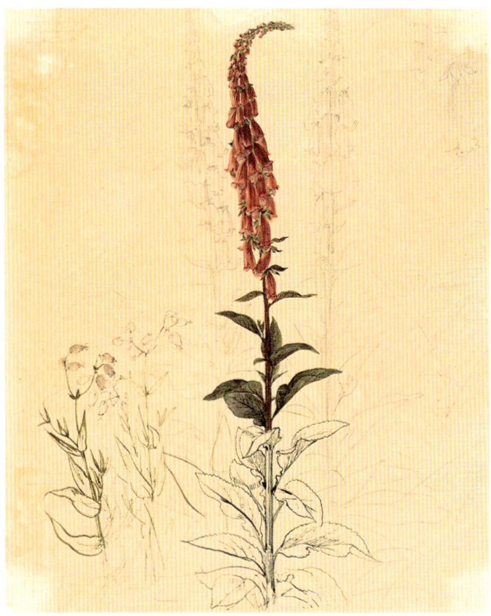

Carl Philipp Fohr, *Sheet of Studies with Blooming Fox-*
glove, 1815/16. Pen and light green, brown-green, gray-
green, and purple ink over pencil; watercolor; on thin,
light-brownish (yellowed) paper; 197/200 x 245 mm

marchese Massimi's garden pavilion in Rome.
The prospect of participating in this important
commission for a monumental painting, something many German artists at the time longed to
do, may have inspired Horny to create his luminous nature studies, which remained unequaled
in his day in their quality and individuality. In
his first design, Cornelius envisioned an oval
composition of Dante's *Paradise* as the ceiling
painting (cf. cat. 41). Festoons, garlands, and
wreaths delimited and structured his richly symbolic constellations of figures. Within these decorative elements, Horny could arrange flowers
and fruit enlivened by birds and butterflies as
suited his fancy. Horny drew his selected nature
studies and designs onto the first, extant cartoons
by Cornelius, but the cartoons were never finished or executed in fresco. Crown Prince Ludwig of Bavaria enticed Cornelius away to paint
the Glyptothek in Munich, dissolving his contract with the marchese Massimi. When Cornelius dropped out of the project, so did Horny.
Cornelius offered Horny a job as his assistant in
Munich, but he declined. He felt that he had not
yet settled into his art, and had not yet absorbed
and incorporated enough from the "cornucopia"
that was Italy.

With his deep emotional bond to nature, Horny
captured not only the particular appearance of
the plants and fruits, but also their very essence
as the perfect embodiments of their genus in a
Dantesque state of "paradise." Our small green
grapes convey a vivid impression of the exacti-
tude with which he observed nature and the skill
with which he was able to translate growth, blossoming, and ripening into delicate nuances of
color. Horny's work makes the grapes seem fresh
with dew and surprisingly real. His studies of
fruits and flowers, in particular, demonstrate his
ability to depict nature faithfully or "realisti-
cally." Although these studies were widely recognized and appreciated, especially by his mentor Carl Friedrich von Rumohr, Horny did not
continue working in this direction. Rumohr, who
had the present sheet in his collection, wrote in
his reminiscences of his travels in Italy: "The
studies that Horny did with this particular intent
in mind reveal their purpose through a certain
magnificent essence, though this doesn't mean
they were executed in a less detailed or painterly
manner. Whoever saw the ones I have was
always forced to admit that he had never encountered anything of the kind....Of course, Cornelius recognized and appreciated Horny's great
talent, which stood rather isolated at the time."²
Another watercolor study in the Winterstein collection, this one a flowering foxglove, has until
now passed as a work by Horny (fig.),³ but it is
actually by Carl Philipp Fohr. The attribution to
Horny seemed to place it conclusively within the
context of the studies for the Casino Massimo.

However, other outstanding artists devoted
themselves to the study of nature, among them
Julius Schnorr von Carolsfeld and Fohr.⁴ A close
examination of the foxglove shows that the
drawing of the contour with the pen and the use
of colored inks are characteristic of the latter's
technique (cat. 45). Fohr often used the thin,
light-brown paper with the watermark *1806/*
FHF and the gilt edge at the bottom border
during his student years in Munich and later
Heidelberg, also for plant studies.⁵ One would
hardly have encountered this northern alpine
plant in Italy. There can be no doubt that Fohr
drew the foxglove before his trip to Italy and
took the skillfully executed drawing with him: in
his report on Fohr's death and estate, the architect Franz Heger mentioned "a large book with
plants, shrubs, and studies of this sort, which he
had brought with him from Germany."⁶ In his
last drawing, completed on the morning of the
day he died, Fohr drew the huge figure of Hagen
from the *Nibelungenlied*, with the water sprites
foretelling his death. On the left, at the feet of
the warrior alongside ferns and a snake, he
depicted the poisonous foxglove.⁷

1 Cf. Gerstenberg and Rave 1934, pp. 51–54, figs. 32–37,
   p. 177; Scheidig 1954, pp. 166–68, nos. 151–72 (reprs. and
   color pls.).

2 Rumohr 1823, p. 206 f. There were about twenty sheets in
   Rumohr's estate; cf. Frenzel 1846, p. 408, nos. 4020–38,
   4108, grapes in 4024, 4026, and 4108. Under no. 4026 we
   read "blue grape and small green currant grape"; this is
   probably the present watercolor, which entered the
   collection mounted with a "blue grape" on the same passe-
   partout.

3 Cf. Scheidig 1954, p. 168, no. 171 (Franz Horny).
   Karl & Faber, 150th Auction, Munich, 28 November 1979,
   cat. no. 46 (Franz Horny), pl. 1 (repr. in color).

4 For example Schnorr, "Evergreen" (watercolor),
   30 April 1817, Berlin, Kupferstichkabinett, inv. no.
   SZ 143; and Fohr, "Anemones," 9 June 1816, cf. Bernhard
   1974, vol. 1, p. 297 (repr.); "Honeysuckle and Others," 9
   June 1816, cf. Frankfurt 1968, p. 43, no. 91 (90), pl. 29. Both
   watercolors by Fohr are on paper with gilt borders, watermark: *1806/FHF*.

5 Cf. Frankfurt 1968, p. 41, no. 82, and Darmstadt 1995,
   p. 237, no. 168, p. 319, no. 331.

6 Printed in Hardenberg and Schilling 1925, p. 64.

7 The sheet is lost (in Russia); repr. in Ludwig Grote, "Ein
   romantisches *Nibelungenlied*," *Zeitschrift des deutschen*
   Vereines für Kunstwissenschaft 8 (1941): 109, fig. 7.

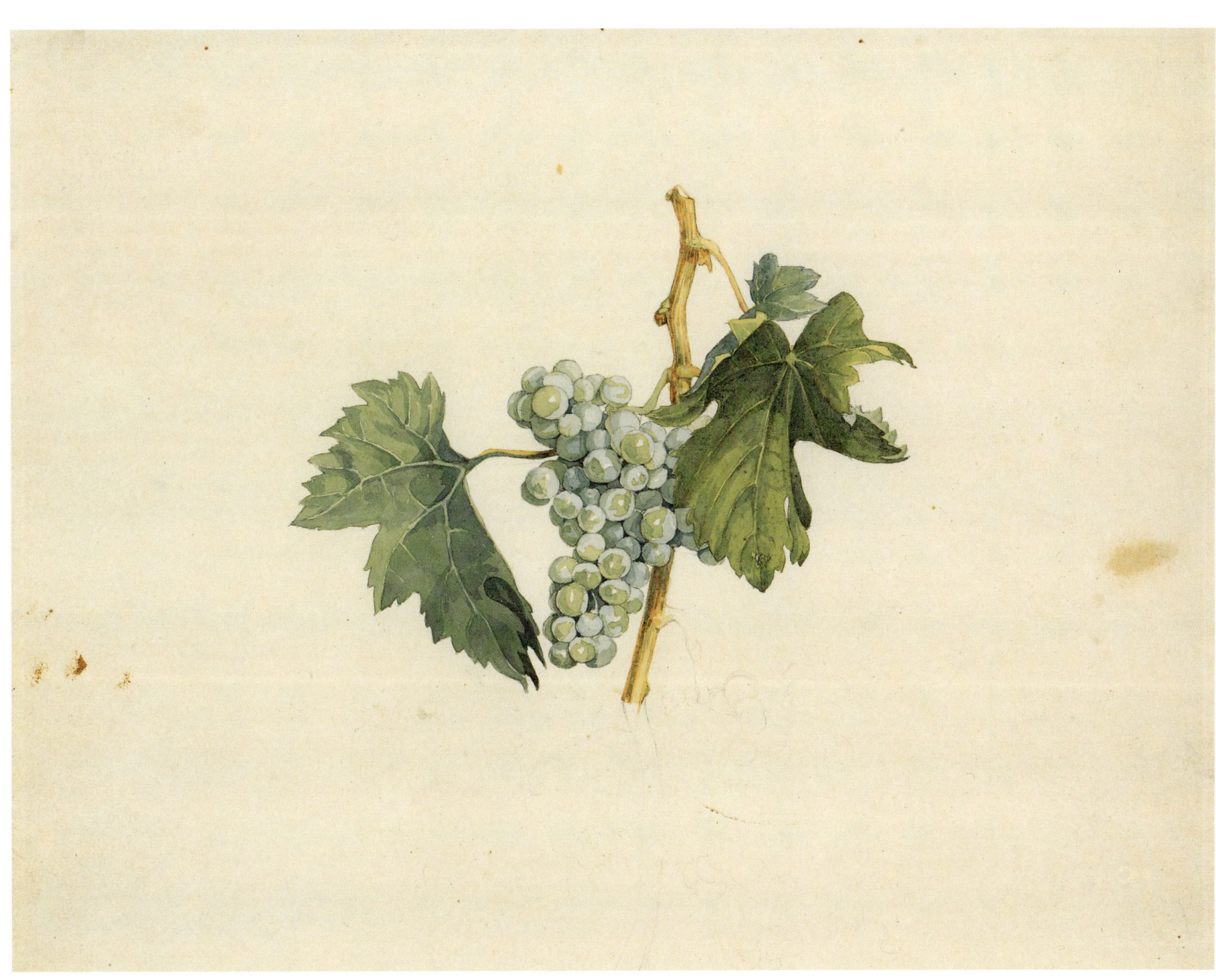

50

Franz Theobald Horny

A Stand of Trees in the Serpentara, c. 1822

Pen, brown ink, wash, over pencil, on wove paper, trimmed on all sides; 346/350 x 469 mm
Verso inscribed by another hand, in pencil: "Fohr"
Provenance: Antiquariat Emil Hirsch, Munich
Bibliography: Scheidig 1954, p. 172, no. 231; Munich 1958, p. 33, no. 65; Lübeck 1969, p. 47, no. 73; Sieveking 1975, pp. 749, 746 f., fig. 2 (in color)

Near Olevano in the mountains southeast of Rome there still stands a small patch of forest, originally an oak forest, called Serpentara. Its picturesque views attracted artists time and again, especially German artists.[1] Horny often drew at this place, and in all likelihood this study of a group of trees was also done at Serpentara. With the feathery stroke characteristic of his later years, Horny drew the trees—partly overgrown by wild creepers—showing the elastic growth of their slender trunks as they swept

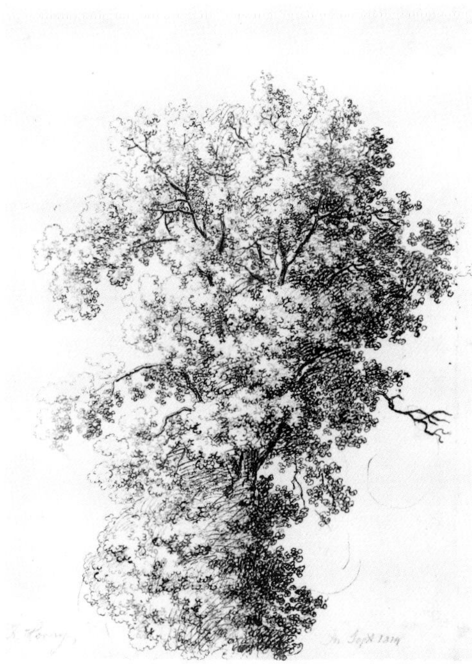

Franz Horny, *Tree Study*, 1814. Pen and black and gray ink over pencil, on laid paper; 238 x 207 mm

upward into the wide crowns. In this work, in contrast to his fruit and flower studies (cat. 49), Horny was not concerned to reproduce the trees with the painstaking attention to detail and realistic color that would allow a botanical identification; instead, he strove to capture a direct experience of nature. Horny conveys his impressions

with such freshness and immediacy that we can share in his amazement before nature. During the last years of his life he pursued larger pictorial formats in the manner of cartoons, which may have been intended as preparatory drawings for paintings. The large size of the present sheet also attests to this tend in his work.

He has confidently placed the stand of trees in the center, boldly sketched in one campaign but left unfinished, with no foreground or background, no sky or ground line, and the edges left unworked. The trees are seen as though in "sharp focus." This concentration on the essential is characteristic of many of Horny's study sheets, whose artistic statement and value lie precisely in their *non finito*. In this sketch, spontaneously drawn from nature, we recognize in the purest way the artist's technique and interest. It also provides an insight into his working process. That scholars formerly regarded the sketches and the unfinished sheets merely as preparatory material for works that were never executed has contributed to the perception that Horny's artistic estate contains only suggestions of what he wanted to do and, because of his early death, only fragmentary works. In contrast to the drawings of his Nazarene friends, who pedantically envisioned their eventual pictorial execution, the sketch takes on an artistic value all its own in the work of Horny. Unlike the Nazarenes, and removed from their collective approach, he expressed his pure sensibility in an individual manner through a sensuous calligraphy of the line. He thus attained a high degree of abstraction in stroke and color.

Nothing characterizes the development and continuity in Horny's work more clearly than a comparison with a youthful drawing, a typical early tree study that he executed in September 1814, presumably in the park in Weimar (fig.).[2] Using an almost obsessively curly stroke, Horny created an impressive image of a tree from nature, although the tree itself does not permit closer botanical identification. What typifies this tree is not its close resemblance to nature, but its character as an academic model in structure and composition, and its schematic treatment of branches and leaves, a style derived from the eighteenth century. Looking at tree studies of this kind, Carl Friedrich von Rumohr recognized Horny's special, though suppressed, talent for depicting nature. In the hope of shaping this ability in accordance with his own pedagogic ideas on how artists should be trained, Rumohr took Horny along to Italy. It was only under the impression made by the southern light, by the climate, colors, and shapes of the richly varied Italian landscape, that Horny's artistic talent could develop fully. Twice Horny had to break free from outside influences that were detrimental: in his Weimar youth from the dull academic con-

straints of Hofrat Meyer, a friend of Goethe, and during his Italian years from the well-intentioned patronizing of his Nazarene friends. The latter conflict was the most difficult on his path toward self-discovery: the Nazarenes tried to recruit his fresh and malleable talent for their own goals. In the midst of this demanding society of artists, Horny felt challenged and spurred on. The Nazarenes demanded the imagination and personal inventiveness befitting an intellectually weighty art. Horny himself confessed that he did not attain intellectual depth in his attempts to imitate and "invent" landscapes in the manner of Raphael's predecessors. In fact, these efforts, which his Nazarene friends especially praised, are among his weaker works. His mentor, Carl Friedrich von Rumohr, showed little patience with them; again and again he advised Horny to stick to nature alone. Horny had particular difficulties in depicting the human figure. Rumohr and Koch encouraged him to practice drawing the figures he needed as staffage for his landscapes. The fleetingly observed and quickly drawn study of a shepherd (cat. 51, fig. 2) reveals the mastery and ease he eventually attained in figure drawing, corresponding, for example, to this study of a stand of trees.[3] In a melodic flow, the lines capture the shepherd's posture in a playful and spontaneous way. Washes applied with a sure hand make the shepherd in his typical dress come alive in the sunlight.[4]

1 To preserve this picturesque grove for future generations of German artists, the Serpentara was purchased in 1873 —on the initiative of the painter Edmund Kanoldt— from the community of Civitella and its ownership transferred to the German Empire; cf. Noack 1927, p. 609 f. Today, the Berlin Academy of Fine Arts still lodges its stipend holders on an adjoining property.
2 Watermark: "J. Honig"; signed in pencil, lower left: "Fr. Horny"; inscribed in pencil by the artist, lower right: "In Sept 1814."
3 Scheidig 1954, p. 183, no. 527.
4 Horny used the shepherd again in a Nazarene-influenced depiction of rural folk, but here he appears harder, less natural, and less charming; Scheidig 1954, p. 183, no. 526, cf. Schellenberg 1926, p. 185 (repr.).

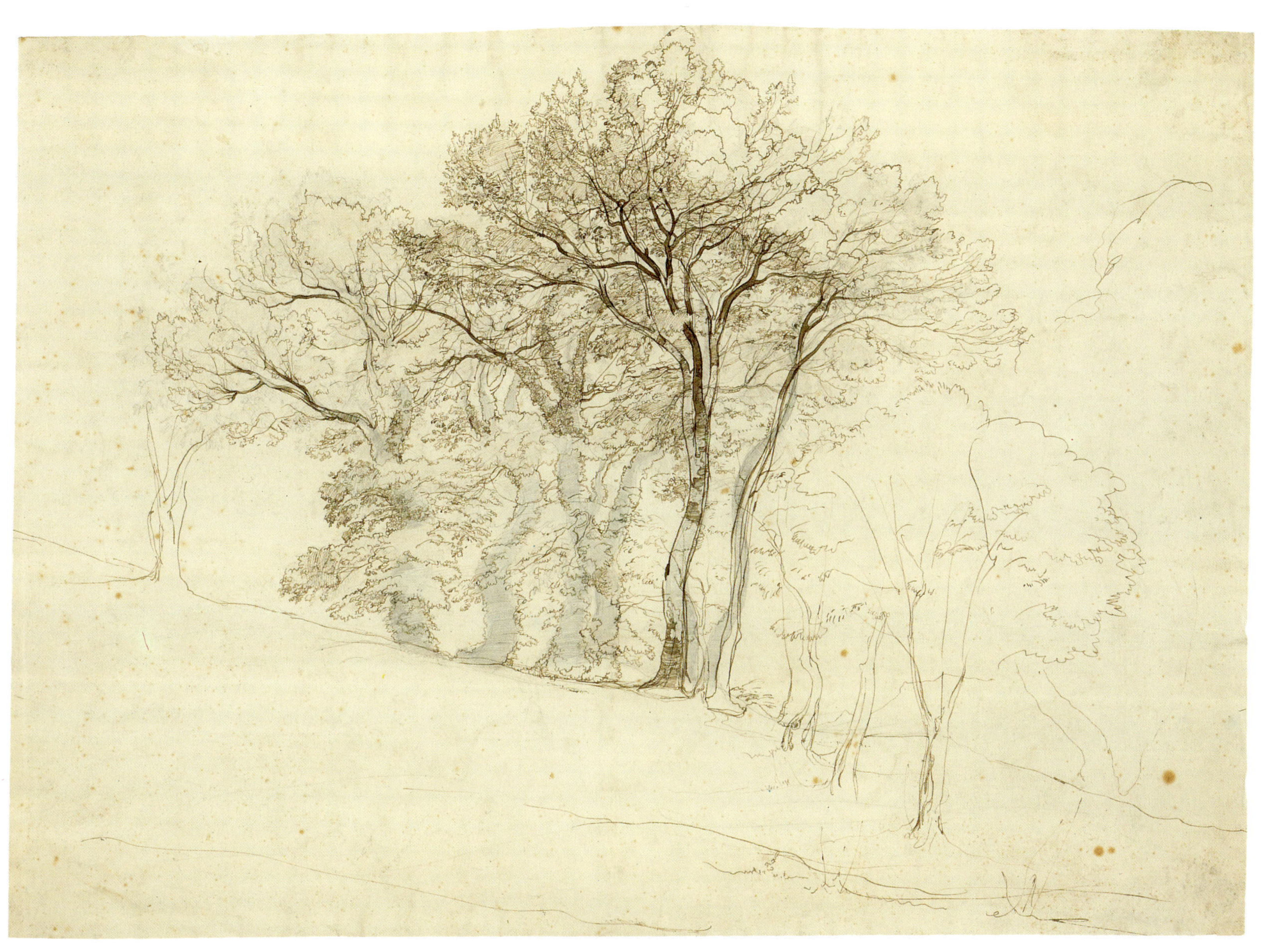

51

Franz Theobald Horny

Sunday Morning in the Aequi Mountains,
c. 1822

*Pen and brown ink over pencil and red chalk, watercolor,
on laid paper; watermark: posthorn on a crowned shield,
K&Z; 250/3 x 331/4 mm; trimmed on all sides
Verso: outline copy after Horatius Cocles in a mural by
Pietro Perugino in the audience hall of the guild of money
changers (Cambio) in Perugia
Pen and brown ink over pencil
Inscribed by the artist in pen and brown ink, lower left:
"ORAZIO COCLITE;" "143" (estate number)*

Provenance: Ludwigsgalerie, Munich

*Bibliography: Scheidig 1954, p.183, no.324; Munich 1958,
p.33, no.67, p.11 (repr. in color); Lübeck 1969, p.47, no.75;
Cologne 1973, no.36; Robels 1974, p.81, pl.47 (in color);
Sieveking 1975, pp.750f., fig.4 (in color); Paris 1976,
pp.91ff., no.104 (repr.); Munich 1981, p.44, no.41, p.147,
fig.44*

At the beginning of November 1822, Horny
wrote to his mother from Olevano, describing a
landscape painting in oil: "It is early in the day,
before sunrise, when the mountains stand out
like violet-blue velvet against the golden sky, a
color that people at home in the north have no
conception of, and that painting has no means to
reproduce."[1] This painting, which he later destroyed, can be connected to the present watercolor. Horny's Hamburg sketchbook contains a
mountain landscape jotted down in pencil; in
its outlines and in the detailed color notes, it
agrees with the finished watercolor shown here.
A handwritten entry below the sketch reads:
"The highest gradation of clarity and variety of
colors in the air and the mountains at sunrise,
16 Sept. 22."[2] The sketch suggests that our sheet
should be dated to the fall of 1822.
The locals from around Olevano have begun the
day with an early mass. Now they leave the small
mountain chapel and step out into the clear, fresh
morning. The procession of churchgoers antici-
pates the morning departures of the figures in
many of Ludwig Richter's landscapes. In the
foreground one sees a Capuchin monk convers-
ing with two women, and, in the distance, the silhouette of the Volsci Mountains.[3] A light mist
wafts through the middle ground, revealing light
or dark tree silhouettes that overlap like a col-
lage. Sky and earth, people and architecture:
these elements are artistically interwoven in various planes of space, the outlines of their forms
integrated on the picture surface. Freeform
clouds, their shape only partially defined by a
sharp outline, hurry along in a bizarre flight of
hot, dry wind from the mountains. Limitlessness
takes form in the clarity of the line, a sense of the

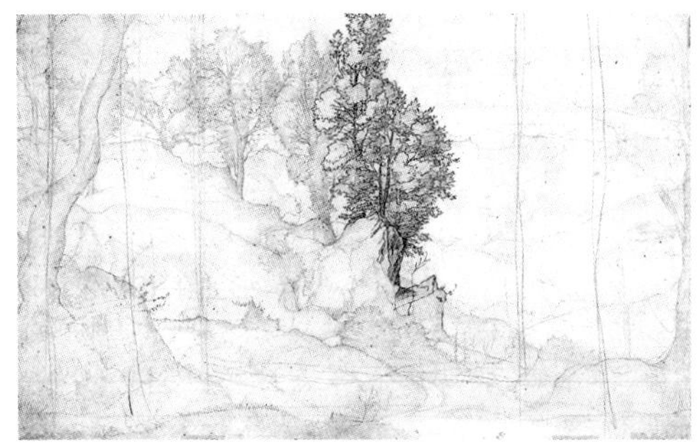

1 Franz Horny, *Landscape near Olevano,* c. 1822.
Pencil, pen and brown ink; 340 x 217 mm (recto)

infinite that Horny experienced as freedom in
the expansiveness of the landscape. He composed
the landscape in Classical-Baroque layering, a
compositional method that had become second
nature to him in his Weimar period, when he
copied Claude Lorrain's *Liber veritatis* and works
by Poussin, and which he had also learned from
his teacher Joseph Anton Koch. The bottom and
sides of the scene are framed by dark trees, earth,
and rocks in order to lead the eye to the brighter
areas in the center and in the distance. Among
several possible ways of cropping the image,
indicated by pencil lines parallel to the left and
bottom edges, the artist chose the one he preferred by trimming the sheet on all sides. The
study from nature was thus upgraded after the
fact into a finished composition. This is how one

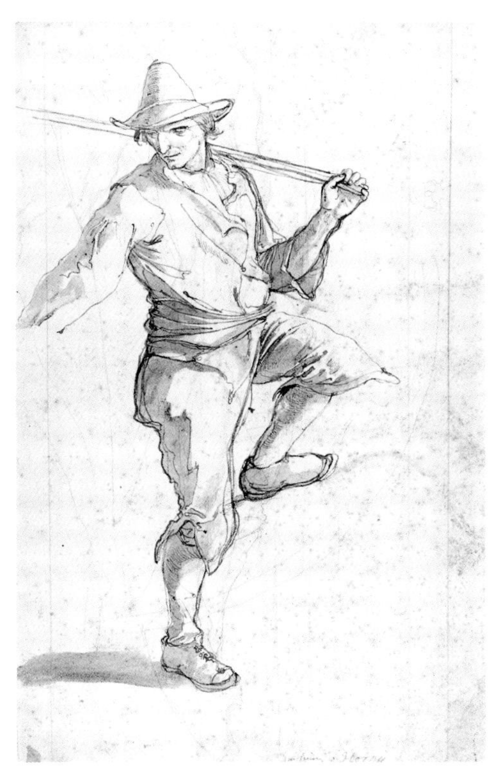

2 Franz Horny, *Study of a Shepherd,* c. 1820. Pen and
gray-brown ink; 340 x 217 mm (verso of fig. 1)

should imagine the process by which studies
would become oil paintings, a step Horny post-
poned. This concern with the choice of the right
composition is seen in another landscape study,
presumably done in Serpentara, not far from
Olevano (fig. 1). Using a sharp "Vienna pencil,"
Horny recorded a wide landscape panorama in a
uniform technique. Only a rocky outcrop overgrown with trees in the middle ground has been
sharply delineated with the pen and highlighted
three-dimensionally through hatching in a technique reminiscent of the early German engraving style. Here, as well, he indicates cropping
options that reflect the Classical conception of
landscape as a stage, with mountain ranges that
can be moved around like flats to suggest spatial
depth.
The staffage in our watercolor also serves as an
element of spatial composition, and, integrated
into nature, it helps convey mood. Horny also
achieved depth by using various drawing media.
Large areas have been broadly washed with
watercolor—in some passages disregarding the
contours that delimit the material boundaries
between objects—with light areas left as
reserves. Although the hues have been observed
from nature, they are not applied as local color.
While Horny strove to capture nature truthfully,
as the careful notes concerning color, location,
time of day, and season in his sketchbooks show,
his approach to landscape was not limited to creating a *veduta*; it also conveys the experience of
mood and atmosphere. The unfinished/finished
Sunday Morning in the Aequi Mountains, one of
his most beautiful creations, distinctly reveals his
artistic vision and technique. The uniform clarity
of his attenuated line has a surface-structuring
quality; as though electrified, the finely drawn
contours delimit the objects transmuted by light,
and, by a process of abstraction, endow them
with a sense of permanence. In Horny's work the
line springs not from reflection, as it does with
his Nazarene friends, but from reflex. In contrast
to the handling of line by the Nazarenes or by his
Neoclassical contemporaries, who were prisoners
of their strict style, Horny's line flows melo-
diously; it has a rhythmic pulse, and makes the
sketchlike concrete with its own expressive
value.

1 Schellenberg 1926, p.198.
2 Scheidig 1954, p.173, no.233.
3 Domenico Riccardi of Olevano was the first to identify
   the Volsci Mountains in this drawing.

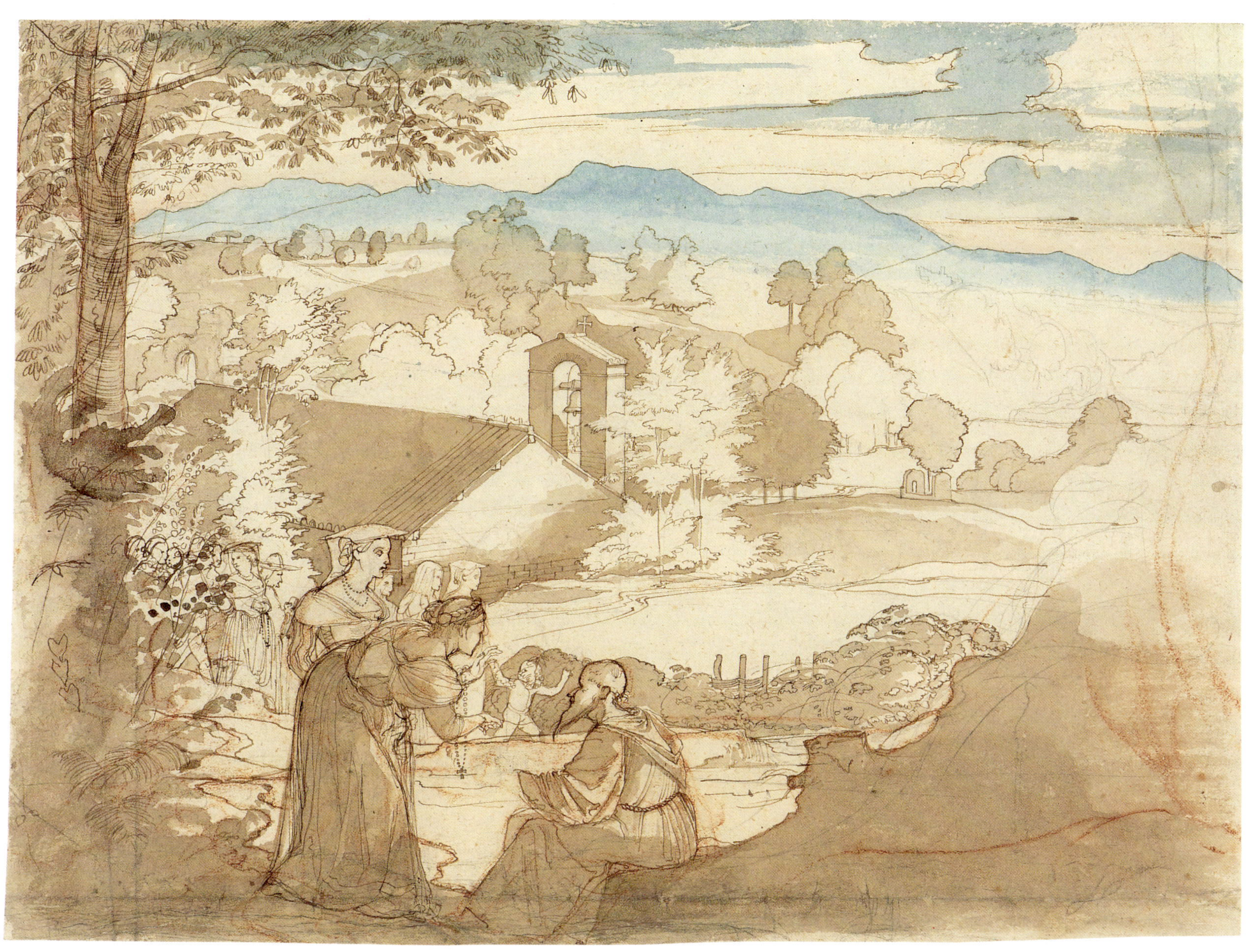

Ernst Fries

Heidelberg 22 June 1801–12 October 1833 Karlsruhe

Olevano, 1826

Pencil, border in pencil, on wove paper; watermark: 1820;
255 x 389 mm
In the lower left corner: blind stamp; EF [in ligature]
Inscribed in pencil, lower left: "Olevano 25 Sept 1826.
Abend in Campagna hie und da Rauch des kleines Hauses
auf...(?)" [Evening in the Campagna, here and there
smoke from the small house on...(?)]; upper right: "Grau-
blaue Regenwolken mit grüngelblich durchscheinenden
Stellen" [Gray-blue rain clouds with greenish yellow
patches shining through]
Verso: stamp in black ink: SJ (in a circle), below that a can-
cellation stamp in purple (in a circle)

Provenance: Städelsches Kunstinstitut, Frankfurt am Main
(Lugt 2357)

Bibliography: Munich 1958, p. 28, no. 46; Lübeck 1969,
pp. 36 f., no. 53; Bernhard 1974, p. 418 (repr.)

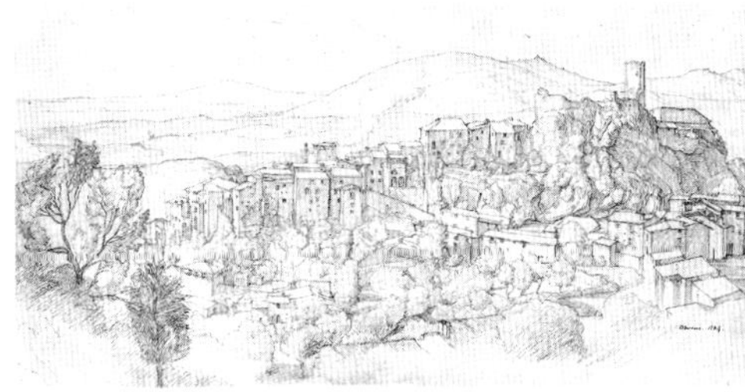

1 Victor Emil Janssen, *Olevano*, 1834. Pencil;
204/8 x 385 mm

During the course of the nineteenth century, for many German artists the small, picturesque, wine-growing town of Olevano became the embodiment of their longing for Italy. Artists from Joseph Anton Koch to Alexander Kanoldt depicted it time and again. The town sits on top of a vineyard-covered slope in the Aequi Mountains, about 45 kilometers east of Rome, and offers a panoramic view of the surrounding countryside. The densely packed, cubelike houses are piled in steps at the top of the steep slope (fig. 1). Olevano's inhabitants lived, and still live, chiefly from viniculture. Joseph Anton Koch and Johann Christian Reinhart (cat. 25) were the first, toward the end of the eighteenth century, to discover the beauty of this pristine landscape as an artistic subject; Koch met and married a local woman.

During the hot summer months artists sought to escape the unhealthy, febrile climate of Rome, retreating to the more salutary, cooler air of the mountains at Olevano, among other places. The name of Franz Horny, one of Koch's students, is especially closely tied to Olevano: because he had an advanced case of tuberculosis, he lived there in the healthier mountain climate from 1819 until his early death in 1824 (cf. cat. 49 – 51). In a letter to his mother in Weimar, dated 1 July 1821, Horny described the rapturous enthusiasm that the picturesque town, surrounded by the magnificently beautiful mountain landscape, aroused among artists. This enthusiasm found expression in innumerable views of the town, drawn from every perspective: "Olevano de Borghese is the name of the place.... It is truly a magical land, surely one of the most beautiful and significant sites in Italy ... on the whole, the entire countryside there is so fantastic that people in Germany would not believe it if they saw drawings of it. For here one is in the Sabine mountains, all towns are perched right on top of the mountains like swallows' nests....And the color! One simply cannot imagine...."[1]

Ernst Fries, who had received his first drawing lessons in Heidelberg with Carl Philipp Fohr and Carl Rottmann from Rottmann's father, turned his artistic interests early on to an accurate, naturalistic representation of landscape. During his four years in Italy (1823 – 27) he traveled throughout the country; it was there that his art matured fully. In 1826, Fries undertook several extended trips in the region around Rome. In the spring he met the eminent French landscapist Camille Corot, and apparently they spent some time and drew together;[2] in Città Castellana, Fries drew a portrait of him.[3] The drawings, watercolors, and oil studies that Fries created in 1826 are among his most beautiful and distinctive works.

The naturalistic view of Olevano exhibited here —drawn with a splendid, light-suffused clarity in its effect of depth—was executed on one of these excursions into the environs of Rome, usually undertaken with other artists, such as Lud-

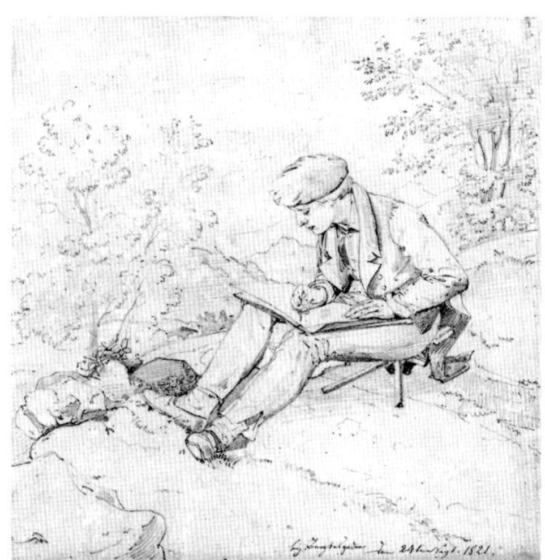

2 Ernst Fries, *Carl Sandhaas Drawing Outdoors*, 24
September 1821. Pencil; 211/7 x 208 mm

wig Richter, Ernst Welker, and the French painter Edouard Bertin.[4] Fries shows a broad vista toward the west, across the low-lying plain of the Roman Campagna, all the way to the sea. In the Classical compositional scheme, the townscape—which continues on the right up the mountain—rises at the right edge of the picture, like a *repoussoir*. On the left the view opens into the landscape, which grows lighter with increasing distance. Using pencils of varying degrees of hardness, Fries drew this landscape with great virtuosity and vigor. The modulated gray values create the light-dark perspective, from the soft pencil for the close view of the town in the wide foreground, with darker tones all the way to black depending on the pressure of the stroke, to the hard, sharp pencil, with its lighter effect, for the distance. We perceive the scene as if it were rendered in color: the artist's chromatic sense asserts itself even in the color-neutral pencil drawing. Notes on the sheet indicate Fries's awareness of color impressions; perhaps he planned to rework the drawing into an oil painting at a later time.

The contrast between the summarily sketched natural features in the foreground, on the one hand, and the detailed and exactly rendered architecture of the town and the precisely handled distance, on the other, produces a lively effect. Fries's pencil captured the picturesque view in its spatial continuum. Over the true-to-nature *veduta* lies a silvery glow that shimmers atmospherically in the light.

1 Schellenberg 1926, p. 68 f. German artists commonly— and erroneously—referred to the mountains east of Rome with the broad term "Sabine Mountains." Those mountains are in fact further north; Olevano is situated in the Aequi Mountains.
2 Jensen 1978, p. 166, no. 37.
3 Bernhard 1974, p. 409 (repr.).
4 Other views of Olevano and of Tivoli and its environs, drawn in pencil during his trip in September/October of 1826, can be found in Elisabeth Bott, "Ernst Fries (1801–1833): Studien zu seinen Landschaftszeichnungen" (Ph.D. diss., Heidelberg, 1978), pp. 227–33, nos. 113–32.

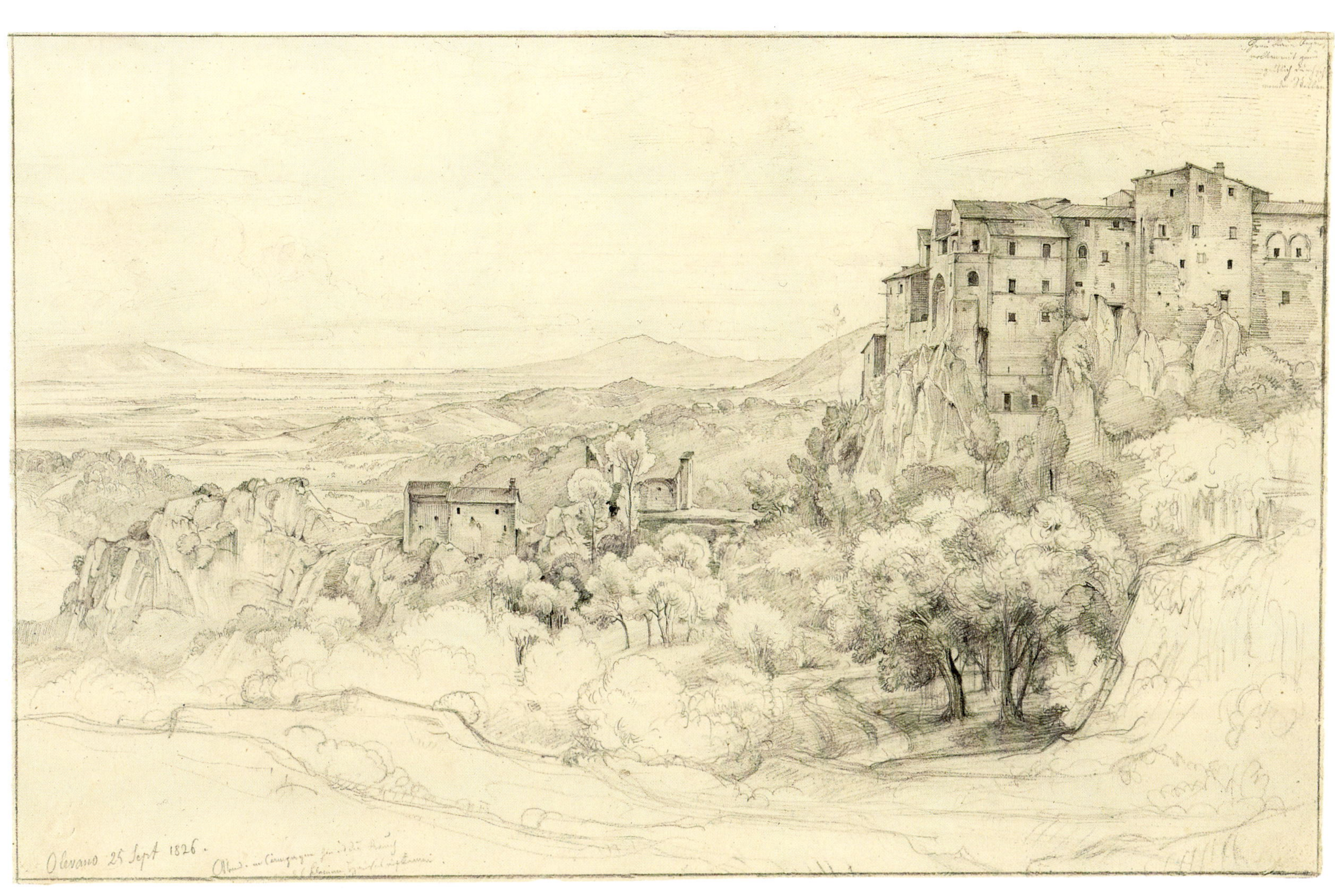
Olevano 25 Sept 1826.

Friedrich Nerly

Erfurt 24 November 1807 – 21 October 1878 Venice

Portrait of Carl Friedrich von Rumohr, 1823

*Pen and gray-black ink over pencil, heightened with white,
on brownish tinted paper; watermark (superimposed, partially cut): J/1; 278/280 x 219 mm
Inscribed by the artist, at top (partly illegible): "… auf
Ranzau … 1823 …" ("… at Ranzau … 1823 …")
Verso: academic study of the head of a young man after an
antique relief; black chalk, heightened with white*

*Bibliography: Bernhard 1974, vol. 2, p.1492 (repr.); Ger-
hard Kegel*, Carl Friedrich von Rumohr, Briefe an Johann
Georg Rist *(Buchholz, 1993), p.48 (repr.)*

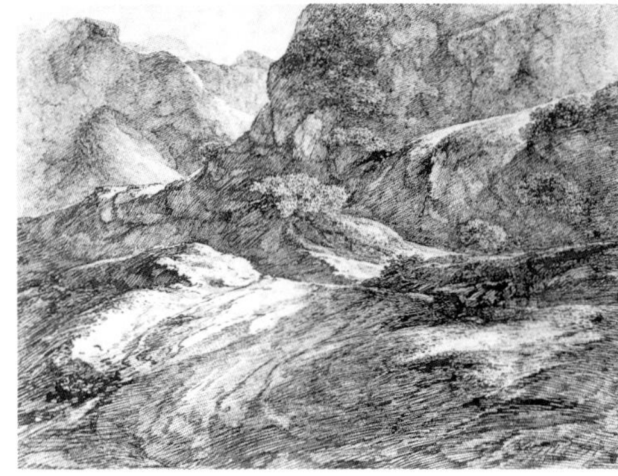

1 Carl Friedrich von Rumohr, *Landscape*, 1835.
Pen and black ink; 270 x 350 mm.
Signed and dated lower right

Carl Friedrich von Rumohr (1785–1843) is,
without a doubt, one of the most fascinating personalities of the age of Goethe.[1] Like few others,
he embodied the discontinuities and diversity of
this transitional era in the wide range of his artistic talents and interests. Descended from the old
Holstein nobility, he regularly found refuge
from his restless life on his estates in Holstein,
Lübeck, and Saxony. He was a successful scholar
and writer. His major work, the three-volume
Italian Studies (1827–31), incorporates his
method of seeing works of art in their historical
context and drawing on historical sources to
understand them. Rumohr is considered the
founder of the critical study of art. He wrote on
other matters as well: his book *Geist der Kochkunst (Spirit of the Art of Cooking)* has remained
popular to this day.[2] As an adviser on questions
relating to art and museums he served, among
others, kings Frederick William IV of Prussia
and Christian VIII of Denmark (with both of
whom he enjoyed close friendships), especially
in their efforts to build up the art collections
in Berlin and Copenhagen. Independent and
wealthy, Rumohr used his means generously as a
patron. A passionate collector, he assembled his
own important collection of drawings and
prints.[3] Rumohr himself was a talented as well as
avid draftsman and etcher. His subjects were
chiefly landscapes, created with vigorous hatchings, usually from his imagination (fig. 1), and
physiognomic studies in emulation of Hogarth
and Rowlandson. These latter he put to paper in
innumerable variations with a tendency toward
caricature, in keeping with his keen powers of
judgment and his eloquent wit.
Rumohr played a particularly important role as
the discoverer, patron, and educator of young
artistic talents such as the Riepenhausen brothers (cf. cat. 43) and especially the draftsman
Franz Horny, who died young (cf. cat. 49–51).
Friedrich Nerly was his only real pupil, but theirs

was a wonderfully successful teacher-student
relationship.
Nerly evidently drew this portrait of Rumohr at
the end of September 1823 at Castle Rantzau, the
southern Holstein estate of Rumohr's friend
Count Baudissin.[4] It is closely related to another
drawing by Nerly showing a tea or soirée in the
so-called Blue Room in Castle Rantzau, in which
Rumohr is depicted sitting at a table, drawing, in
similar posture and attire.[5] In any case, the present portrait was done during Nerly's initial
period of training under Rumohr, a few weeks
after they had met. That explains why the young
Nerly's technique closely resembles that of his
teacher: it is characterized not by a calligraphic
line, but by rather hurried though forceful

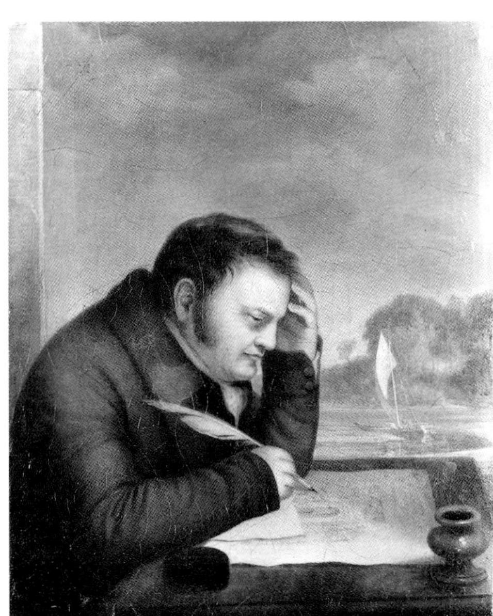

2 Friedrich Nerly, *Portrait of Carl Friedrich von
Rumohr*, dated (illegible): "182?. p." Oil on canvas;
310 x 250 mm. Berlin, Staatliche Museen Preussischer
Kulturbesitz, Nationalgalerie, inv. no. A III 725

hatching drawn with the same kind of goose
quill that Rumohr uses in the portrait on a large
landscape drawing. As for composition, Nerly
placed Rumohr's face in the center of the sheet
where the diagonals intersect, thereby emphasizing his intense concentration on the process of
drawing. The focused energy, creative restlessness, and temperament of his revered mentor are
brilliantly observed in the tense, compact posture
of the figure. Nerly used the drawing as the
model for an oil painting of slightly larger format (fig. 2). There he added a background, a
view onto a landscape reminiscent of the Elbe
River scenes around Dresden painted by Johann
Christian Claussen Dahl and Carl Gustav Carus.
The oil painting was probably executed soon
after the drawing, since Rumohr introduced his
student to this medium as well.

1 Gustav Poel, "Carl Friedrich von Rumohr," in *ADB*,
vol. 29 (Leipzig, 1889), pp. 657–61; Wilhelm Waetzoldt,
Deutsche Kunsthistoriker, 3rd ed., vol. 1 (Berlin, 1986),
pp. 292–318; Martius 1956, pp. 149–80; Gerhard Kegel,
"Carl Friedrich von Rumohr," in *Schleswig-Holsteinisches
Biographisches Lexikon*, eds. Olaf Klose and Eva Rudolph,
vol. 5 (Neumünster, 1973). On the relationship between
Rumohr and Nerly see Peter Hirschfeld, "Rumohr und
Nerly," in *Jahrbuch der Preussischen Kunstsammlungen*
52, Beiheft (1931): 261; Martius 1956, pp. 149–77; Lilli
Martius, "C. F. von Rumohr und Fr. Nerly, Lehrer und
Schüler," in *Kunst in Schleswig-Holstein* (1959), pp. 77–91;
Friedrich Nerly und die Künstler um Carl Friedrich von
Rumohr, ed. Thomas Gädeke, Mechthild Lucke, et al., exh.
cat. (Cismar, 1991).
2 Carl Friedrich von Rumohr, *Geist der Kochkunst*,
ed. Dietrich Harth (Heidelberg, 1994).
3 Frenzel 1846 catalogued this collection, which was auctioned off from Rumohr's estate.
4 Wolf-Heinrich Count of Baudissin (1789–1879) was a
writer and translator of Shakespeare. After 1827 he lived
mostly in Leipzig. Letters of Rumohr from his estate
Rothenhausen to Johannes Metzger in Florence, dated
23 September 1823 and 8 April 1824, contain references
that allow us to date Nerly's stay with Rumohr and the
visit of the two men to Rantzau. This information was
kindly furnished by Gerhard Kegel, who is working on a
monograph on C. F. von Rumohr.
5 The dating of this drawing to 1823 is confirmed by a tracing made by Auguste von Witzleben and inscribed with
the same year (Kunsthalle Kiel). In the following year,
evidently, Nerly finished the drawing and colored it, possibly as a gift for Count Baudissin. That work is today in
Rantzau in the hands of Baudissin's descendants;
cf. Martius 1956, p. 157, fig. 79.

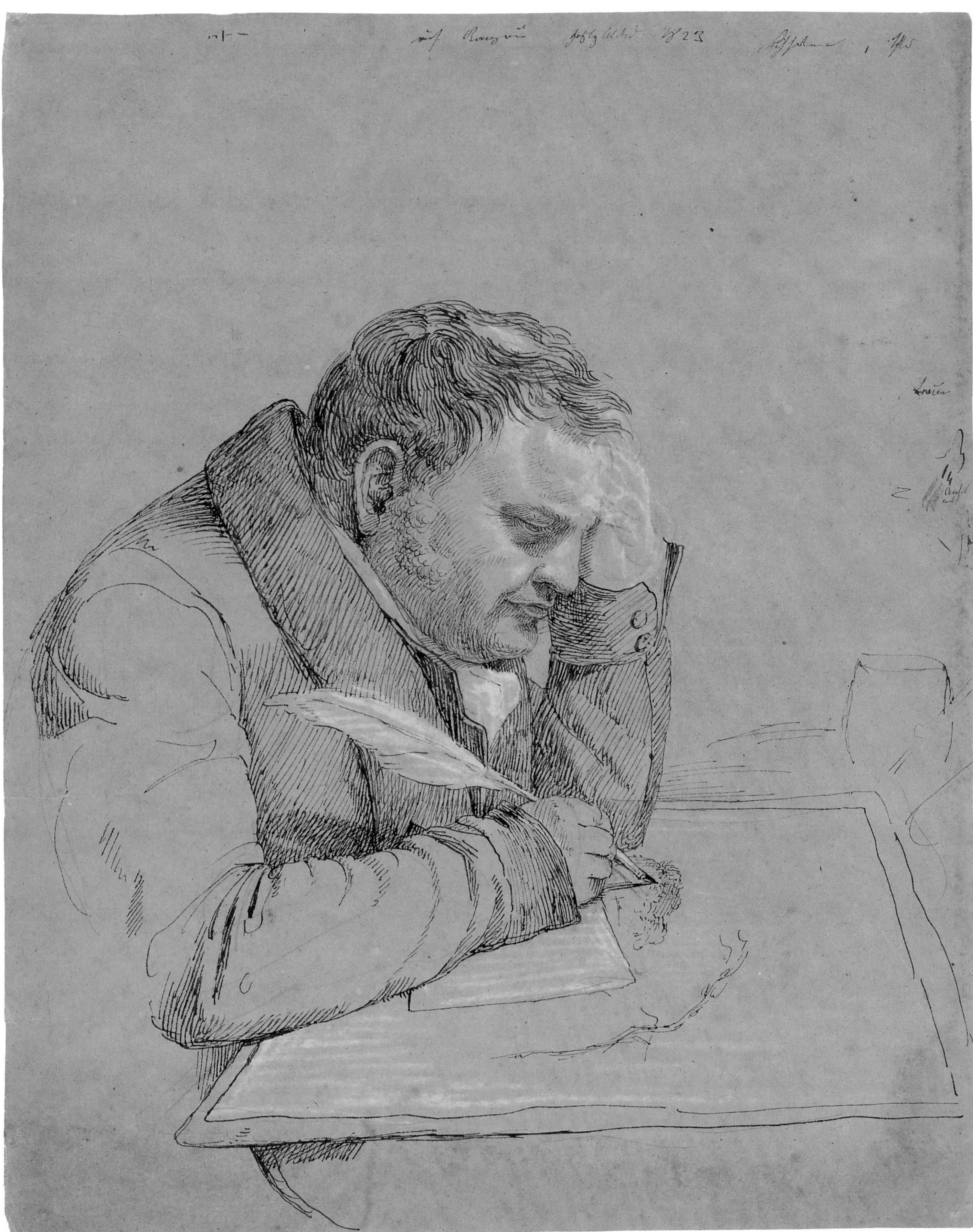

54
Carl Barth

Eisfeld 12 October 1787–11 September 1853 Cassel

Portrait of the Painter Theodor Rehbenitz,
c. 1817/18

Pencil on wove paper; 106 x 97 mm
Verso inscribed in pencil: "Rebenitz Maler / aus Kiel"
("Rebenitz painter from Kiel")

Provenance: Geheimrat Professor Ernst Ehlers, Göttingen;
Dr. Ponte, Leipzig; Haniel-Lüttichau, Wistinghausen

Bibliography: C. G. Boerner, 190th Auction, Leipzig,
27 November 1935, no. 25, repr. pl. 1; Walter Vontin, Carl
Barth, ein vergessener deutscher Bildniskünstler
(1787–1853) (Hildburghausen, 1938), pp. 58, 180, fig. 12;
Geller 1952, p. 91, no. 1065; Karl & Faber, 150th Auction,
Munich, 28 November 1979, no. 28 (Carl Philipp Fohr);
Wolf-Timm 1991, p. 25 (repr.)

Theodor Rehbenitz (1791–1861) initially studied
law in Heidelberg, but under the influence of the
Boisserée painting collection he decided on a

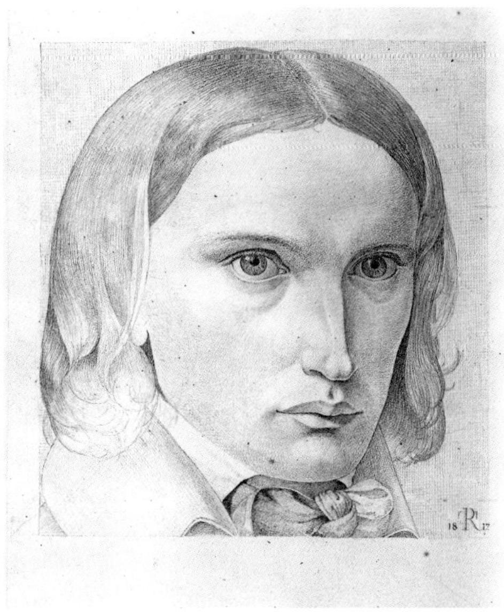

Theodor Rehbenitz, *Self-Portrait*, 1817. Pencil;
195 x 159 mm. Dresden, Kupferstichkabinett,
inv. no. C 3327

career as an artist. From 1813 to 1816 he pursued
his artistic training in Vienna in the circle
around Joseph Anton Koch, the Olivier brothers,
and Julius Schnorr von Carolsfeld. At the end of
1816 he went to Rome, where he developed a
close association with Friedrich Overbeck, to
whom he was related by marriage.[1]

Beginning in 1819, Rehbenitz and his friends
Friedrich Olivier and Julius Schnorr von Carolsfeld occupied the upper floor of the Palazzo Caffarelli on the Capitoline, the residence of the
Prussian envoy. Here the three Protestant
Nazarenes, known as the *Capitoliner*, participated actively in the ecclesiastical life of the
small Protestant community. Starting in 1819
they worked on a cycle of paintings on commission from the Naumburg canon Christian Lebe-
recht von Ampach. When Rehbenitz departed
from Rome in the summer of 1823, he left his
picture unfinished, and Schnorr completed it.
Rehbenitz had realized the limits of his artistic
abilities and accepted the consequences. He
made his way through Florence to Perugia,
where he stayed from 1824 to 1827. With the
help of Crown Prince Ludwig of Bavaria, he got
a job teaching German to the beautiful marchesa
Marianna Florenzi. Following another stint in
Rome from 1827 to 1832, Rehbenitz returned to
Germany and lived in Munich until 1842. In the
last years of his life he had a secure position as a
university drawing teacher in Kiel.

Rehbenitz's coolly stylized self-portrait of 1817
(fig.) aroused general admiration, and his early
Roman work gave rise to justified hopes of what
he might achieve. Schnorr wrote appreciatively
in 1819: "And Rehbenitz, too, is a thoughtful
artist and one of the most serious, who already in
Vienna produced some excellent work that was
received with deserved approbation."[2]

Rehbenitz was highly esteemed among the German artists. A likable person and a promising
artist, he was frequently portrayed during his
first years in Rome.[3] Thoughtfulness and seriousness radiate from Carl Barth's handsome
likeness. Here Barth shows his mastery of the
small-format portrait. Using a sharp pencil, he
composed it like a miniature. While the top of
the shoulders, the clothes, and part of the hair
that reaches down to the collar are summarily
sketched, the fine facial features are vividly and
precisely modeled in subtle gradations. The
drawing must have been executed during the
time when both artists were in Rome; 1817 or
1818 is the likely date. In stylistic terms, as well,
the drawing belongs to Barth's early Roman
period. It shows the ease, vigor, and elegance of
soft, silvery strokes that we find in his other
drawings from this time. The drawing not only
captures Rehbenitz's external appearance, but
also his serious demeanor, the emotional expression of his sincerity. Other factors support our
dating of the work: the youthful looks of the sitter; a comparison with a later likeness done by
Julius Milde in mid-1826, which shows him with
different hairstyle;[4] and the physiognomic similarity to Rehbenitz's early self-portrait (fig.). A
comparison with the latter shows the possible
stylistic alternatives: the natural, realistic
approach, on the one hand, and on the other, the
Nazarene approach, with the features stylized in
a timeless expression that gives them a carved,
solidified look (fig.). A similar intensity characterizes Barth's portraits of Ramboux, Fohr, and
Overbeck, which should also be dated to 1817 or
1818.[5]

Barth did not himself engrave his portrait drawing of Fohr, but had Amsler do it. According to
Vontin, Barth was so distraught over his friend's
tragic death, to which he had some connection,
that he declared himself incapable of executing
the engraving.[6] This portrait print attracted
attention at the 1819 exhibition of German artists
in the Palazzo Caffarelli; critics compared it to
Dürer's engraved likeness of Willibald Pirck-
heimer.[7] The plan was to use proceeds from the
sale of the print to erect a monument to Fohr. It
is conceivable that the drawing of Rehbenitz, as
well, was intended for an engraving. However,
small-format artist portraits were for the most
part private in nature; they remained souvenirs
(often exchanged), monuments to friendship,
similar to entries in an album amicorum. They
were engraved only under special circumstances,
as in the case of Fohr.

Carl Barth produced his best portraits of people
to whom he had an emotional connection. He
probably felt a close affinity for Rehbenitz, the
painter from Borstel in Holstein, which inspired
him to create this expressive portrait study, one
of the most beautiful in his oeuvre. Louise Seidler characterized the Thüringian engraver
Barth in her memoirs as "honest and upright...
a genuinely outstanding person, without guile, in
fact often honest and truthful to the point of
being indiscreet."[8] It is as though Barth saw his
own image reflected in the face of Rehbenitz.

1 Overbeck's older brother was married to Rehbenitz's sister.
2 Schnorr-Briefe, II, 3, p. 355. Letter from Rome to Rochlitz,
   dated 12 September 1818.
3 Fohr alone did three portraits of him in connection with
   the pencil studies he did between the end of 1817 and the
   spring of 1818 for the planned group-portrait etching of
   German artists in the Café Greco; cf. Heidelberg 1995,
   pp. 158 ff., 139 (repr.), p. 141 (repr.), cf. p. 18 (repr.). See also
   Geller 1952, nos. 55 (fig. 342), 1060 (fig. 396), 1061
   (fig. 395).
4 Formerly attributed to Ludwig Richter. Wolf-Timm 1991,
   p. 43 (repr.), n. 231.
5 For the Ramboux portrait see Bernhard 1974, p. 1202
   (repr.); for Fohr see Heidelberg 1995, pp. 214 f. (repr.); for
   Overbeck see ibid., pp. 216 f. (repr.) as well as Jens Christian Jensen, "Zwei Bildniszeichnungen, Overbeck darstel-
   lend, von Carl Barth," in *Niederdeutsche Beiträge zur
   Kunstgeschichte*, vol. 16 (Berlin, 1977), pp. 133–40, figs. 1
   and 6.
6 Vontin 1938, pp. 59, 61.
7 Kunstblatt, no. 80 (5 October 1820): 317; cf. also no. 66,
   17 August 1820, p. 262.
8 Seidler, p. 137.

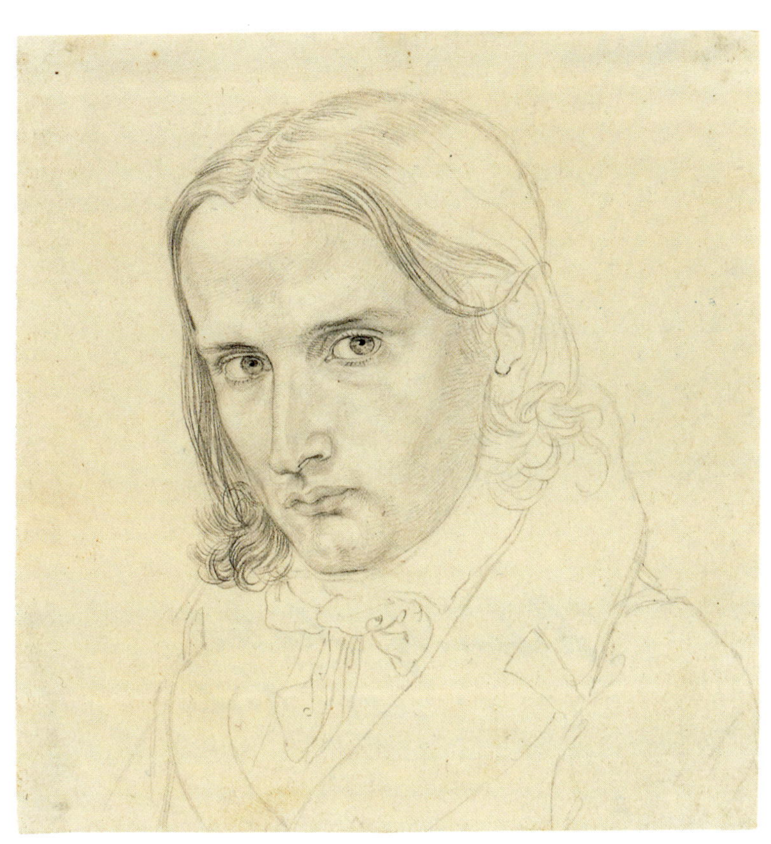

55
Moritz Michael Daffinger

Vienna 25 January 1790 – 22 August 1849 Vienna

Portrait of the Duke of Reichstadt, 1831

Pencil, watercolor, gouache, on stiff wove paper; water-mark: MONTGOLFIER; *224/6 x 162/4 mm. Legend inscribed by the duke's hand in pen and brown ink:*
"Arrivé près de moi—par un zèle sincère
Tu me contais alors l'histoire de mon père.
Tu sais combien mon âme, attentive à ta voix,
S'échauffait au récit de ses nobles exploits. (Racine.
Phèdre.)"

Provenance: Auguste Frédéric Louis Viesse de Marmont, duke of Ragusa, marshal of France

Bibliography: Leo Grünstein, "Moritz Michael Daffinger," in Thieme and Becker, vol. 8 (Leipzig, 1913), p. 263, left col.; Leo Grünstein, Moritz Michael Daffinger und sein Kreis (Vienna and Leipzig, 1923), pp. 25 f., p. 131.; Emil Pirchan, Moritz Michael Daffinger, Miniaturmaler des Vormärz (Vienna and Leipzig, 1943), p. 78

After the battle of Wagram, which ended in a victory for Napoleon, Austria and France concluded the Peace of Vienna on 14 October 1809. Napoleon had divorced Josephine Beauharnais on the grounds that she was childless, and on 2 April 1810, he married Marie Louise of Austria, daughter of the emperor Franz I. On 20 March 1811, at the height of Napoleon's power, she gave birth to his only legitimate son, Napoleon Franz Joseph Karl, with whom he sought to establish his dynasty. The son was given the title of king of Rome, and was baptized in the cathedral of Notre Dame on 9 June 1811. Napoleon saw Marie Louise and his son for the last time on 24 January 1814. Following the collapse of Napoleon's rule in 1814, they set out from Paris for Vienna and Schönbrunn, on orders from Metternich. Upon his return from Elba, when he remained in Paris for one hundred days, Napoleon tried in vain to prevail upon the Austrian emperor to send them back. Following the defeat at Waterloo, Napoleon abdicated the throne on 22 June 1815 in favor of his son Napoleon II.

In the meantime, Parma had been incorporated into the Austrian empire, and Marie Louise took over the reins of Parma's government in March of 1816. Her son remained behind in Vienna; he would see his mother only every few years, and their contact was chiefly through correspondence. In the Treaty of Paris of 1817, the Allies stripped the prince of his hereditary right to Parma. The following year, his grandfather, Emperor Franz I, granted him the small lordship of Reichstadt in Bohemia and the title of duke of Reichstadt. Surrounded by tutors, who introduced him early on to military science, he remained supervised and controlled. The life of young Napoleon unfolded between the Vienna Hofburg and Castle Schönbrunn as though he were in exile in a golden cage, shielded from the world, especially from his French relatives. He studied in detail the deeds and fate of his father, whom he passionately revered. His handlers withheld from him his father's last will, written on St. Helena in 1821, which left him with a generous inheritance.[1]

One of the most eminent field marshals in Napoleon's service had been Auguste Frédéric Marshal of Marmont (1774–1852). Beginning in 1796 he participated in Napoleon's military campaigns, including Egypt; owing to his battlefield successes, he had a splendid career. The marshal spent the last years of his life in Vienna and Venice. From 25 January to 6 April 1831, he gave the young duke of Reichstadt private lectures about his father's campaigns. As a token of gratitude, the duke presented to him "on the day of the last lecture a portrait of himself, painted very skillfully in watercolor by Daffinger, one of Vienna's best artists, who has surely best captured the profound and expressive features of the duke of Reichstadt. He is depicted seated across from a marble bust of his father, and he appears to be listening very attentively to something outside of the picture. Below the picture the duke wrote in his own hand[2] the allusive verses from Racine's *Phèdre*, which Hippolytus, the son of Theseus, addressed to his tutor Theramenes:
'You who were bound, sincerely bound to me
In Service, told me stories of my father.
You knew my soul, attentive to your voice,
Kindled at hearing of his noble deeds.'"[3]
In Racine's play, the verb at the beginning of the first line is more intimate than the one in the inscription: "*Attaché* près de moi par un zèle sincère…" Moritz I, count of Dietrichstein, the duke's chief tutor,[4] changed this verse to the version the duke wrote in his dedication,[5] a small example of how thorough the tutelage was under which the duke lived.

Among the most important works that the Austrian miniature painter Daffinger produced on commission from the imperial family are the more than one dozen portraits from the years 1830 to 1832 of the unfortunate duke of Reichstadt. These were usually ordered by the duke himself and used as presents. One of the most moving likenesses, the present watercolor for the marshal of Marmont was probably painted early in 1831 during one of the marshal's lectures on Napoleon. More strongly than the other portraits, it emphasizes the duke's resemblance to his father, particularly in his high and broad forehead. It shows the twenty-year-old duke deep in thought, seated in an armchair in front of a Neoclassical marble bust of his father, reminiscent of portrait busts of Roman emperors, especially Augustus.[6] The realistic rendering of the young duke includes conventional formulars of dignity, such as the Classical column in the background, lest there be any doubt about the social status of the person portrayed. Such courtly-aristocratic allusions to rank or pathos derive from English portrait-painting and the iconography of rulers developed by van Dyck, with which Daffinger had become acquainted in 1819 through Sir Thomas Lawrence. The present portrait of the duke of Reichstadt, an example of a natural, realistic portrait seems to evoke, nevertheless, a meditation on the era of the Empire and of Neoclassicism, which had come to an end with the reign of Napoleon.

The duke's realization of his hopeless situation and personal disappointments may have contributed to the tuberculosis he contracted early in 1832, which was misdiagnosed. He died at Schönbrunn on 22 July 1832 at the youthful age of 21, having just been promoted to colonel and "emancipated" from his tutors—a tragic figure who found his final resting place in the imperial crypt of the Capuchin church in Vienna.

1 *Das Testament Napoleons. Vollständige Faksimile des Testaments und der zugehörigen Dokumente in den Archives Nationales Paris* (Stuttgart, 1969).

2 Count Montbel, *Le duc de Reichstadt* (Paris, 1833); German ed. (Leipzig, 1833) p. 161.

3 Jean Racine, *Phèdre*, act I, scene I, trans. by Margaret Rawlings (New York, 1962), pp. 30 f. Cf. John Carteret-Grand, *L'Aiglon en images* (Paris, 1901), p. 129, and Frédéric Masson, *Napoléon et son fils* (Paris, 1904), pp. 278, 284.

4 Dietrichstein was the duke's chief tutor from 30 June 1815 to 14 June 1831.

5 Pirchan 1943, p. 78.

6 It is the type of biscuit bust of Napoleon that was manufactured and distributed by the Sèvres porcelain factory.

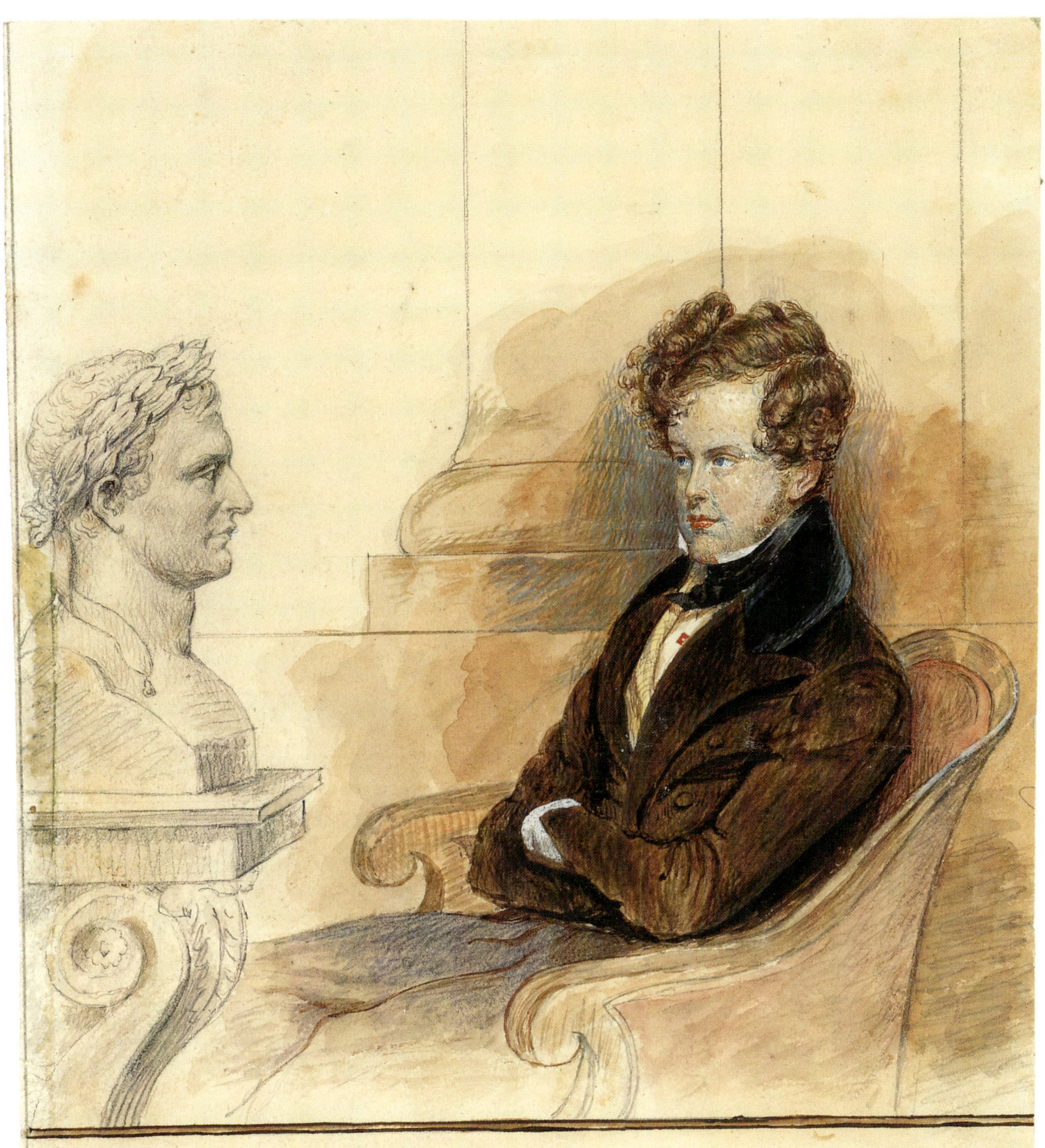

Arrivé près de moi — par un zèle sincère
Tu me contais alors l'histoire de mon père.
Tu sais combien mon âme, attentive à ta voix,
S'échauffait au récit de ses nobles exploits. [Racine. Phèdre.]

56

Ludwig Emil Grimm

Hanau 14 March 1790 – 4 April 1863 Cassel

Portrait of the Widow of the Painter Thomas Christian Wink, 1809.

Charcoal and black chalk, on laid paper; watermark:
coat of arms with a crowned lily; 376 x 239 mm
Inscribed in pen and brown ink, lower right: "1809.
München."

Provenance: Estate of the artist

Bibliography: Wilhelm Praesent, Ludwig Emil Grimm.
Ein deutsches Bilderbuch *(Cassel, no date [1939]), 2nd ed.*
1942, p. 26, pl. 23; Lübeck 1957, p. 20, no. 54; Munich 1958,
p. 30, no. 52; Lübeck 1969, pp. 40 f., no. 58 (repr.); Kassel 1985,
p. 64, no. 38 (repr.); Koszinowski and Leuschner 1990, vol. 1,
pp. 31 f., no. P 23, p. 33 (repr.)

The Protestant Ludwig Emil Grimm, who took a reserved attitude toward the artistic vision of the Nazarenes and rarely ventured into the field of historical and allegorical painting, was not concerned with lofty, idealized, or abstract subject matter, but rather with representing nature in a sober and objective manner.

The human being in his or her private environment (cf. cat. 57) and the human face lay at the center of his artistic interests. A talent for language, conspicuously developed in his family, may have given rise to his penchant for "excessively subtle" pictorial satire and caricature. In

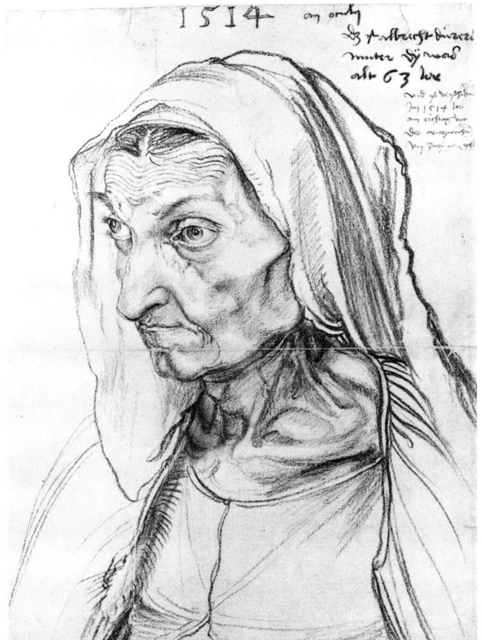

Albrecht Dürer, *Portrait of His Mother*, 1514.
Charcoal; 423 x 305 mm. Berlin, Staatliche Museen
Preussischer Kulturbesitz, Kupferstichkabinett

his numerous, natural, and unaffectedly realistic portraits of people of every age and from every social class, most drawn with the pencil, Grimm conveyed an image of humanity, informed by his family's intellectual and liberal background, that was quite unlike anything in the work of his Nazarene contemporaries. Like few artists of the age, he devoted himself to the theme of the child, though not in the metaphorically portentous sense of a Philipp Otto Runge, but out of sheer joy in observing creatures unspoiled by education. He was also fascinated by the beauty of young people, particularly young women and girls. His frequent depictions of aging people marked by life testify to his compassionate interest, which extended to outsiders and socially marginal figures. In this regard he was a precursor of Adolph Menzel, Käthe Kollwitz, and Max Liebermann.

In 1809, when he was a student at the newly established Munich Academy, Ludwig Emil Grimm drew this large portrait in charcoal and black chalk of his first landlady, the widow of the Munich Rococo court painter Thomas Christian Wink (1738–1797).[1] Rigorously faithful to reality, it shows the aged features of this woman who, as the wife of one of the busiest fresco painters of the second half of the eighteenth century, spent her youth in the court-dominated world of the Rococo. The realistic, monumental forcefulness of her face, depicted without cosmetic or artistic beautification, is reminiscent of Dürer's expressive portrait of his aged mother (fig.). Without flinching, Dürer depicted his mother's skeletal features—deeply stirring in their truthfulness—two months before her death. It was a portrait of a woman who, born into the world of the waning Middle Ages, had grown up in the traditions of the late Gothic period and had given birth to eighteen children; rendered by her son, she was seen through the realistic eyes of a man of the modern era. Here, as so often in Grimm's oeuvre, we find a parallel to Albrecht Dürer, whose works, especially the prints, Grimm had thoroughly studied.

Grimm had lost his own mother the year before he drew this portrait, an experience that may have made him particularly sensitive to the expression of human aging and decline. It is striking how often during this period he depicted older women: for example, the portrait of an old peasant woman from Haidhausen, also in 1809;[2] the 1810 and 1812 portraits of Frau Muxel, an odd and cantankerous old woman, who was his next-but-one landlady and the mother of his friends;[3] the 1814 portrait of the storyteller Catharina Dorothea Viehmann, who was so important for his brothers' fairy tale collection;[4] the portraits of the ninety-three-year-old gypsy Lore von Ungedanken from 1825[5] and 1826,[6] who belonged to that minority of socially excluded peo-

ple, and in whose dignified features he recognized the wisdom of an ancient prophetess;[7] and finally, the portraits of the 110-year-old Jewish woman Gidel David Salomo from 1827.[8] These portraits reveal a specific interest in the aging human physiognomy, an interest that for Grimm undoubtedly existed independent of a person's other character traits. That is also why the argument that our likeness could not be that of the widow Wink, because Grimm would not have felt any sympathy for her, is unconvincing.[9] In his memoirs, Grimm has left us a description of this woman, whose bigotry became intolerable for him.[10]

1 The plausible identification of our portrait drawing as
   the likeness of the widow Wink is based on information
   furnished by the Grimm scholar Wilhem Praesent 1939,
   even though he did not substantiate it in any detail.
   Elisabeth Schega, the daughter of the court medalist
   Andreas Schega, had married Thomas Wink in 1769.
2 Kassel 1985, p. 124, no. 105.
3 Koszinowski and Leuschner 1990, nos. P 42, P 60.
4 *Ibid.*, no. P 89.
5 *Ibid.*, nos. G 154–G 156.
6 *Ibid.*, nos. G 146, G 148–G 153.
7 Cf. Kassel 1985, p. 111 (Anton Merk).
8 Koszinowski and Leuschner 1990, no. G 157.
9 *Ibid.*, no. P 23.
10 "The woman was an arch-Catholic, in my room there
   were two small stoups on the wall, on my bed was a crucifix and another one hung on the wall. At table at noon-
   time (I had board from the old lady) it took a long time
   until we got around to eating; first came prayers, then
   the sign of the cross was made the appropriate number
   of times, then came noodle soup, followed by liver
   dumplings with sauerkraut, and finally the roast goose.
   Subsequently I was thoroughly questioned, whether I
   went to mass every day, when I had last been to confession, and so on. An old cousin ate with us. After a while
   I got very uncomfortable being around the old churchy
   women. On top of everything else, my landlady demanded that I go with her to mass every morning (it was
   winter) at five o'clock. I told her that I had other things to
   do than run to mass all the time. All this praying was not
   that important. I had come to Munich to study at the
   Academy, not to become a priest." (Grimm 1911,
   pp. 102 f.) Bettina Brentano wrote about Grimm's problems with his landlady to Achim von Arnim in December
   of 1808: "The only thing that is not for the best is his
   lodging with the two old women, who are very cantankerous. If he is not at home at six in the evening, he
   doesn't get anything to eat for supper." Quoted in
   Koszinowski and Leuschner, no. P 23.

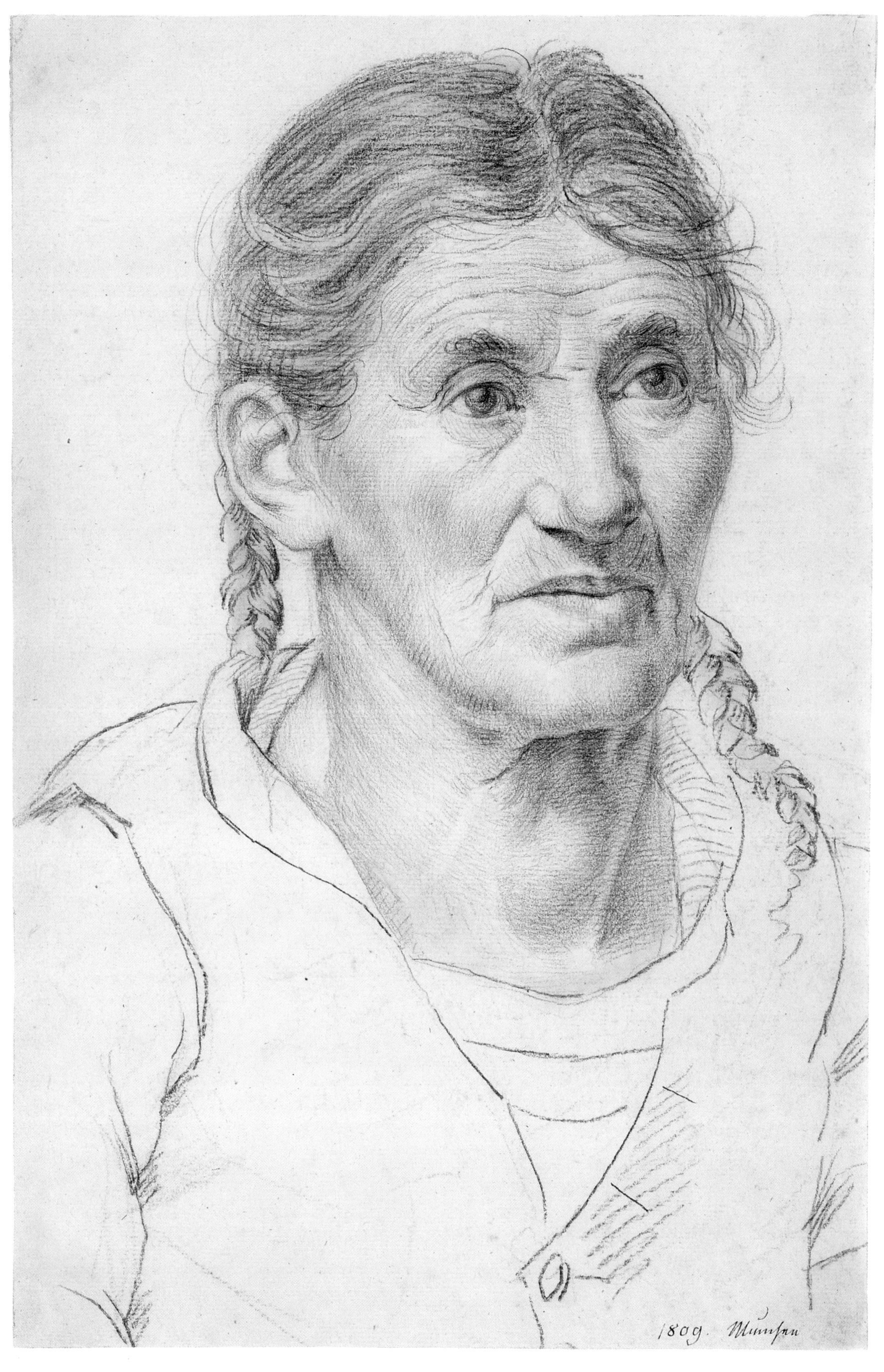

1809. München

57

Ludwig Emil Grimm

Lotte Grimm in Her Room, 1821

Watercolor over pencil, on wove paper; 325 x 245 mm; mounted on card
Inscribed and dated by the artist in pen and brown ink, lower right: "Der Lotte ihre Stube. gez. ad. v. Cassel d 21 Octob. 1821 v Ludwig Grimm" [Lotte's room. Drawn from life in Cassel October 21st 1821 by Ludwig Grimm]

Provenance: Estate of the artist; Robert Wölfle, Munich

Selected bibliography: Grimm 1950, pp. 208f., color pl. 7 and cover ill. in color; Lübeck 1957, p. 22, no. 60; Munich 1958, p. 30, no. 54 (frontispiece, repr. in color); Lübeck 1969, p. 41, no. 60, p. 43 (repr. in color); Cambridge 1972, no. 33 (repr.); Kassel 1985, pp. 109, 120, no. 96 (Anton Merk), p. 130 (color repr.); Koszinowski and Leuschner 1990, p. 96, no. P186 (color repr. on cover); Helmut Börsch-Supan, "Der dritte Bruder," Weltkunst (1992): 186

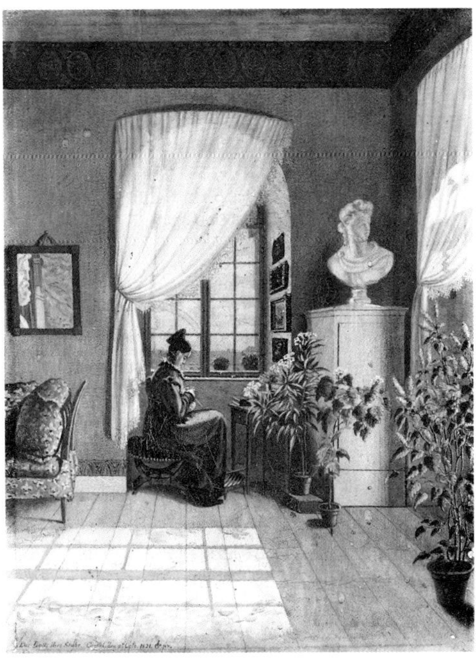

1 Ludwig Emil Grimm, *Lotte's Room*, 1821; oil on canvas, 377 x 288 mm (with frame); Bad Homburg v. d. H., Verwaltung der Staatlichen Schlösser und Gärten Hessen

Strong family bonds united the Grimm siblings throughout their lives. Early on, the brothers Jacob and Wilhelm Grimm (fig. 2) had become famous through their scholarly study of the German language and the publication of *Grimm's Fairy Tales* (1812 – 22). Time and again they used their social connections to help their brother Ludwig in his initially difficult life as an independent artist. That Ludwig was primarily a draftsman and etcher, and rarely made oil paint-

ings, certainly contributed to his problems. His natural artistic medium was the pencil, which he used with growing mastery for his realistic portraits and illustrations of everyday life. Family members and friends, in particular, were the subjects of his art. As Ludwig's nephew, the art historian Hermann Grimm, put it: "His artistic activity was from the very outset rooted in his own family, and in a certain way he never went beyond that."[1]

From 1814 to 1821, the Grimm family lived in the northern gatehouse, still extant, in the Wilhelmshöher Allee in Cassel. In the present watercolor, Grimm portrays in faithful detail the room of his beloved sister Lotte in this house. Charlotte Amalie Grimm (1793–1833) was the only sister and a favorite of the five Grimm brothers. Following their mother's early death in 1808, Lotte managed the household for her brothers until 1822, when she married the lawyer Ludwig Hassenpflug (1794–1862), who later became state minister of the electorate of Hesse. Ludwig had a particularly close relationship with his younger sister. From his youth on, he drew her portrait again and again, and after her early death, her six children became favorite subjects.

In an earlier watercolor from 1816, he showed her under a Gothic arcade, idealized as a patriotic, Christian, and virtuous woman.[2] In the watercolor here, by contrast, he observed her in her actual middle-class life: engaged in needlework, seated in a light-flooded room beneath a high, arched window. A rainbow outside is visible through the window above her head, like a halo. Potted plants on the windowsill, the sewing table, and the floor attest to the love of flowers and plants in the Grimm household. The light wood furniture, the light-blue wallpaper bordered at the top by a frieze of stylized leaves (which replaced the courtly lotus palmette frieze of the Empire style), and the floor of simple wooden planks constitute a characteristic image of a modest but tasteful middle-class interior of the Biedermeier period. The intellectual aspirations of this family, which became so important to Germany's cultural life, are expressed by plaster casts of antique sculptures, such as the bust of the *Apollo Belvedere* on top of the light-colored cabinet in the right corner, or the bust of the *Zeus of Otricoli*, visible in the mirror above the couch; these two busts were also on display in Goethe's house at the Frauenplan in Weimar.[3]

A comparison with other illustrations of interiors, all of which show the artists' interest in the subtle diffusion of light in a room, but which arouse very different emotions in the viewer, is instructive. Caspar David Friedrich's empty chamber, illuminated by indirect light, is both a devotional and a meditative image (cat. 22). Variations on Grimm's "woman's room" by Georg Friedrich Kersting (cat. 24) and Franz Pforr (cat. 32) show dark, closed interiors illuminated by the glow of table lamps. In these, unlike in Grimm's work, the women engaged in needlework appear restricted, with little prospect of change in their domestic roles.[4] By contrast, a few months before his sister's wedding, Grimm created a rather less constricted image of her and her social role as homemaker by emphasizing the open atmosphere of her surroundings: a Biedermeier scene of tranquil, middle-class life. This luminous watercolor is one of his most beautiful and renowned works.

Grimm executed a replica of this watercolor with a narrower pictorial space, and also repeated the scene in an oil painting of nearly identical format and dated the same year as the watercolor, 1821 (fig. 1).[5]

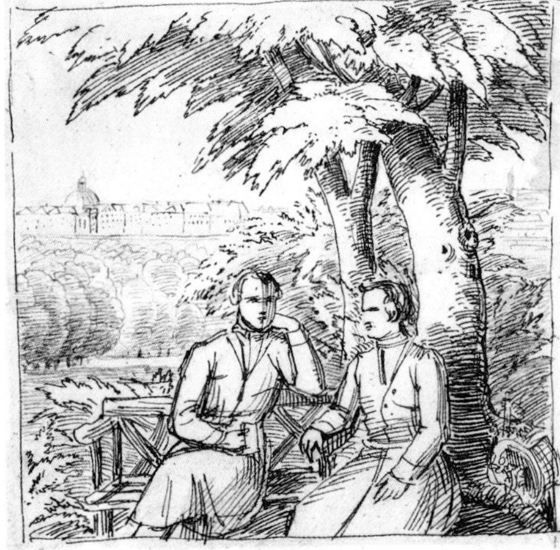

2 Ludwig Emil Grimm, *Wilhelm and Jacob Grimm in front of the Cityscape of Cassel*, 1829; pen and black-gray ink over pencil, on light-blue, tinted paper; 132 x 133 mm

1 Hermann Grimm, "Ludwig Emil Grimm," in *15 Essays*, 3rd series (Berlin, 1882), pp. 306 – 21, 306.
2 Cf. Kassel 1985, pp. 109, 120, no. 95 (Anton Merk), p. 131 (repr. in color).
3 Cf. Max Wegner, *Goethes Anschauung antiker Kunst* (Berlin, 1949), pp. 56 ff. (Apollo), fig. 26; pp. 58 f. (Zeus), fig. 24.
4 Cf. Westhoff-Krummacher 1995, pp. 114, 141 ff., 148, 165 ff. Cf. Cordula Grewe, "Shaping Reality through the Fictive: Images of Women Spinning in the Northern Renaissance," *RACAR* 19, nos. 1 – 2 (1992): 6 – 19.
5 Cf. Koszinowski and Leuschner 1990, p. 96, no. P 186, P 87 (watercolor, 250 x 195 mm), and pp. 387 f., Ö 10 (oil on canvas, 377 x 288 mm) (repr.).

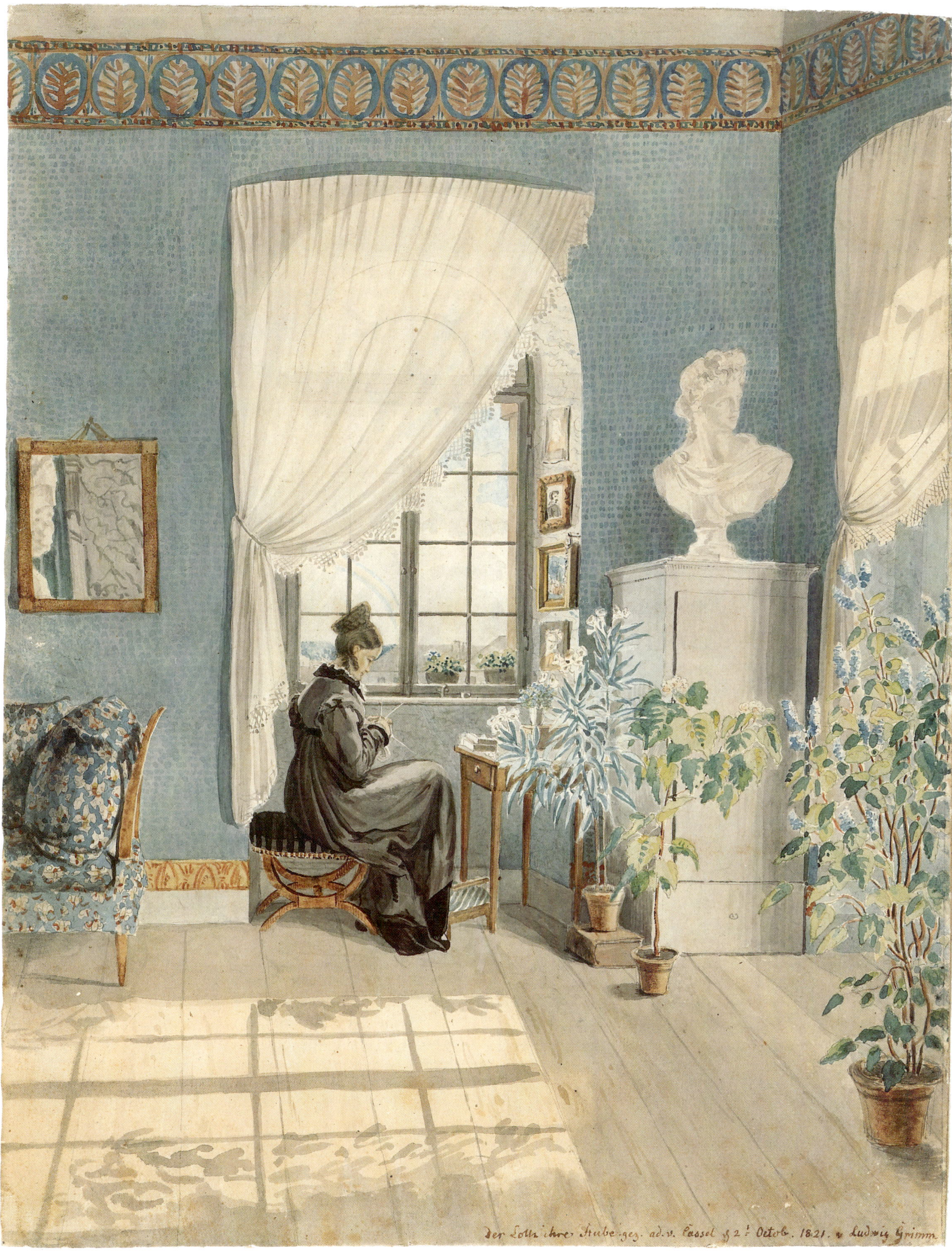

der Lotte ihre Stube gez. ad. v. Cassel d 2t Octob. 1821 v Ludwig Grimm

58
Moritz von Schwind

Vienna 21 January 1804 – 8 February 1871
Niederpöcking am Starnberger See

The Boat from Tasso, 1827

Pen and gray-black ink over pencil, on laid paper; water-
mark: C & I H O N I G; 224/8 x 290 mm

Provenance: Franz Graf von Pocci, Ammerland; Helmuth
Domizlaff, Munich

Bibliography: Stoessl 1924, pp. 54 ff.; Künstlerbriefe aus
dem 19. Jahrhundert (Berlin, 1914), pp. 184–86; Munich
1958, pp. 56 f., no. 162, fig. 24; Lübeck 1969, pp. 94 f., no. 180
(repr.); Bernhard 1974, vol. 2, p. 1778 (repr.); Bailey 1977,
vol. 1, pp. 44 ff., vol. 3, fig. 23; Doris Strack, "Moritz von
Schwinds Tasso Rezeption," in Torquato Tasso in
Deutschland: Seine Wirkung in Literatur, Kunst und
Musik seit der Mitte des 18. Jahrhunderts, ed. Achim
Aurnhammer (Berlin and New York, 1995), pp. 613,
622–26, fig. 5

As early as 1825, Schwind entertained the idea of traveling from Vienna to Munich, enticed by the royal painting gallery, potential commissions, and the prospect of meeting Peter Cornelius.[1] In August of 1827, he visited Munich and went to see Cornelius at the Glyptothek with a letter of introduction from his friend Franz Grillparzer. Cornelius would have liked to see some of his work, but Schwind had not brought anything with him from Vienna. In order to provide a sample of his skill, in one day Schwind drew the *Boat from Tasso* exhibited here, and he wrote about it at length to his friend Franz Schober in Vienna.[2]

He intentionally chose a theme from the epic *Gerusalemme liberata* by the Italian poet Torquato Tasso (1544–1595). This epic poem, set in the period of the Crusades and very popular among the Nazarenes, dealt with the liberation of Jerusalem and the holy Christian sites from the Islamic Saracens by the crusading knights.[3] Impressed by Cornelius's Glyptothek frescoes and as a tribute to him, Schwind chose a closely viewed, purely figural composition with an arched top similar to a lunette in one of the frescoes. This drawing was thus also intended to recommend the design for execution on a large scale in an architectural setting.

Schwind's theme, the crossing to Armida's island, had a long tradition as the title illustration to Canto 15 of Tasso's *Gerusalemme liberata*.[4] In the arched main scene, Schwind has depicted the two knights Ubaldo and Carlo in a symmetrical arrangement. With the help of the magic boat, which is steered by the good fairy in the center of the scene and which can sail more swiftly than an eagle flies, they cross to the island to liberate Rinaldo, the mightiest warrior of the Christian armies, from Armida's enchanted world. The youthful knight Carlo on the right, who turns toward the viewer, demonstratively holds the sword of the fallen Sveno, which he will hand over to Rinaldo as the instrument of revenge.[5] Following the late medieval typological narrative style, Schwind depicts in the spandrels the reason for and goal of the expedition shown in the main scene. Above left, the aged hermit Peter, the spiritual leader of the crusaders' army, and Godfrey of Bouillon, the military leader, look toward the fortress of Jerusalem, which can only be taken with Rinaldo's help. Meanwhile, above right, the youthful hero Rinaldo, without his armor and with the magic mirror in his right hand, engages obliviously in love play with Armida as Amor looks on.[6]

After moving to Munich in 1828, Schwind devoted himself once more to this theme from Tasso. He wrote to his friend Schober: "I want to use the morning, in the heated room I mentioned, to make studies and drawings for a picture, namely the boat I drew here last year…. Once I am done with the picture, I will draw a

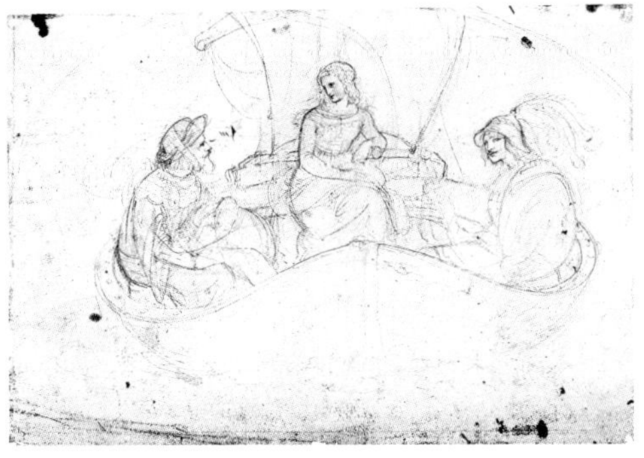

Moritz von Schwind, *The Boat from Tasso*, 1828.
Pencil, watercolor; 308 x 430 mm. Northern Germany,
private collection

suitable cartoon, for which a better occasion and instruction cannot be found anywhere else. I expect to learn the utmost from such a cartoon."[7] Doris Strack believes that the sheet here was a preliminary study for this painting, whose execution was planned for some future time.[8] She bases this view on the argument that the hatching alone would have taken Schwind a whole day. In fact, by 1827 Schwind was such a skillful draftsman that it is entirely conceivable that *The Boat from Tasso* was the work of a single day. The format (a quarter sheet), the finished composition with its borderlines, and the dexterous handling of the pen suggest that this is a presentation sheet, precisely the one that was shown to Cornelius. Schwind's description in the letter to Schober confirms this. Only recently, a second

drawing of *The Boat from Tasso* has appeared in a private collection, reproduced here for the first time (fig.).[9] This is a sketch of larger format. In some of the details it shows changes that seem to correct and clarify certain inconsistencies in the first version: for example, a less closely focused view of the figural composition; indications of Armida's island on the distant horizon at the left; a mast behind the fairy; the billowing of the sail in the direction the boat is moving; and the clearly seated posture of the fairy, whose face has been lightly touched with watercolor. Such changes suggest that this second work was a preliminary study for the planned oil painting, which was evidently never executed. Between 1834 and 1836, when Schwind, on commission from the crown prince Maximilian of Bavaria, executed watercolor designs for a cycle from *Gerusalemme liberata* in Hohenschwangau Castle, he did not use the composition of the crossing scene he had created in these two drawings.

1 Stoessl 1924, p. 44.
2 One day it was raining too much to go out, and I drew the boat from Tasso on a quarter sheet. Using the pen, I covered it with hatching, against my usual habit, with many strokes on top of each other, as many as possible up to the highest light…. I went to the Glyptothek and told him [Cornelius] I had done something; he should let me know when and where he wished to see it. Thereupon he invited me to dinner. (Letter dated 3 September 1827; Stoessl 1924, p. 54.) During the evening conversation, Cornelius asked about the drawing. He took it, stood in the light, and looked at it for a long time with his brow somewhat knitted…. He stood about three minutes, then he said: 'Decent.'… Then Cornelius came over to me, took the drawing into his hand and said almost quietly: "Your drawing shows talent—that's not what I am talking about—but for your age you have too much facility.' He pointed to some folds: 'This is not rigorous enough, too conventional, almost a mannerism. It would be bad if a history painter had to do everything from nature; one has to be able to draw naturally from memory. With a little more thought, it would have been good. One must be serious; one must not make a single stroke that falls short of one's best ability.'" (Stoessl 1924, p. 56.) During the course of the evening, Cornelius invited Schwind to come to Munich; *ibid.*, p. 58.
3 From May 1827 through 1828, Joseph von Führich finished the fresco cycle begun by Friedrich Overbeck in the Tasso room of the Casino Massimo in Rome.
4 Strack 1995, p. 623.
5 *Ibid.*, p. 624.
6 *Ibid.*, p. 623.
7 Stoessl 1924, p. 61.
8 Strack 1995, p. 625.
9 On the verso, *Emma Carries Eginhart through the Snow*; "Febr. 829"; cf. Karlsruhe 1996, pp. 119 f., no. 88, repr. (Friedrich Gross).

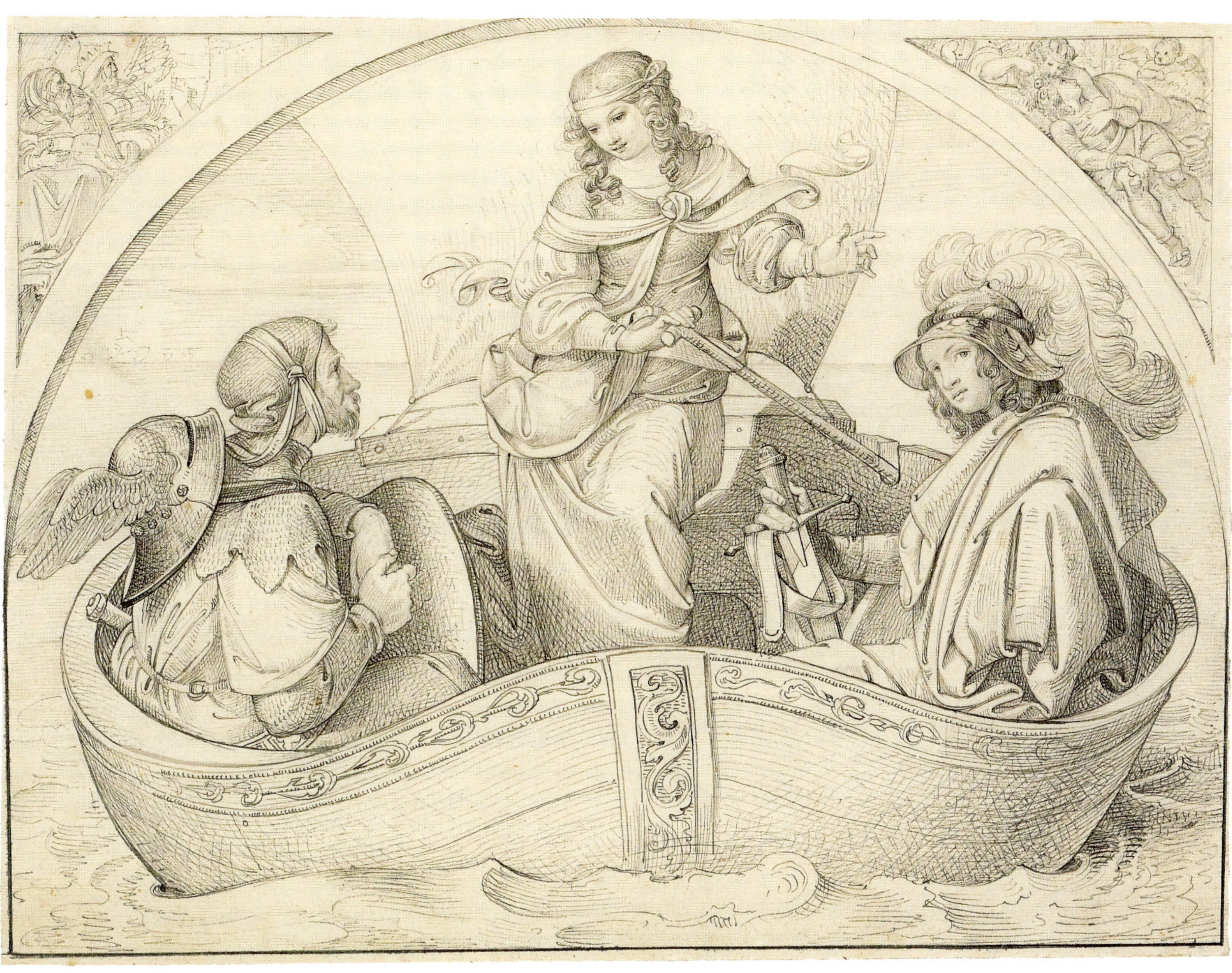

59

Moritz von Schwind

A Boatman in His Rowboat—Lorelei, 1840

*Pen and brown ink over traces of pencil, on laid paper;
watermark: D & C BLAUW; 296 x 192 mm
Signed in pen and brown ink, below right:
"MvSchwind 840"*

*Provenance: Oberlandesgerichtsrat Dr. Max Perger,
Baden near Vienna; Eduard Perger, Vienna*

*Bibliography: Berlin 1906, p. 123, no. 3128; Österreichische
Kunsttopographie, vol. 18: Die Denkmale des politischen
Bezirke Baden, ed. Dagobert Frey, with contributions by
Georg Kyrle and Fritz Eichler (Vienna, 1924), p. 78, no. 67,
p. 82, fig. 128; 310. Kunstauktion C. J. Wawra, Die
Aquarell- und Handzeichnungssammlung des verstorbenen Herrn Eduard Perger, Vienna 22–24 September 1930,
p. 35, no. 21 ("Man in a Boat"; repr.); Eugen Kalkschmidt,
Moritz von Schwind: Der Mann und das Werk (Munich,
1943), p. 57, fig. 14 ("River Trip"); Winterthur 1955, p. 62,
no. 271; Munich 1958, p. 57, no. 163, fig. 25; Heise 1959, p. 67,
fig. 47; Lübeck 1969, pp. 95 f.; Bernhard 1974, vol. 2, p. 1784
(repr.); Bailey 1977, vol. 2, pp. 489–91, vol. 3, fig. 121; Keller
1979, pp. 62 f. (repr.); Sieveking 1990, p. 58, 122 (fig. 17)*

The title of this drawing used to be given vari-
ously as *River Trip* or *Boatman in His Boat*.[1] Colin
J. Bailey offered the first thorough interpretation
of the subject of the drawing, and proposed the
appropriate title, in his unpublished dissertation
of 1977.[2] He considers the iconography to be
based on the ballad *The Boatman* by Schwind's
contemporary Johann Mayrhofer, which Franz
Schubert set to music in a song.[3] In support of his
thesis, Bailey offers a comparison with a watercolor of horizontal format by Leopold Kupelwieser. Although close to the ballad in mood and
atmosphere, it relates to Schwind's drawing only
in composition and motifs.[4] In the ballad, the
brave boatman, rain-soaked in his creaking boat,
defies the raging storm and lashing waves, the
threatening maelstrom and the reef. Nothing of
this dramatic mood is found in Schwind's drawing. Instead, we see a bright sunny day, the kind
of day the boatman in the ballad longs for in the
face of the storm. The river in Schwind's work
flows along so placidly that we cannot even tell
whether the boatman is rowing against the
stream. The closely held oar would seem to indicate that he is in fact steering his boat as it floats
with the current. In keeping with the ballad, Bailey reads in the boatman's face a look of grim
determination to defy the elements.[5] But the
knight in the boat is actually looking up along
the sheer rock. In order to do so more easily, he is
leaning back slightly and to the right, over the
edge of the boat.

The motif of the early German knight in a boat
leads back into the world of legend and fairy tale.
The collectors Max Perger and Alfred Winter-

stein already suspected that this masterful drawing was not created for its own sake from the
artist's imagination, but rather was inspired by
some literary source.[6] Both believed there was
some connection with the legend of the beautiful
Lorelei. Lurleberg or Lorelei is the name of a
sheer rock that rises 132 meters out of the Rhine,
between St. Goar and Oberwesel. Its resounding
echo was mentioned in travelers' descriptions as
early as the seventeenth century. The legend of
the sorceress on the Lorelei rock was invented by
Clemens Brentano around 1800 and published as
a song in his early novel *Godwi* in 1802 ("In
Bacharach on the Rhine there lives a sorceress
… "). Later he returned to the subject in his
Rhine tales. The legend of the siren Lorelei,
whose seductive song robs sailors of their sanity
and thus of control over their vessels, leading
them to their death as they founder against the
rock, was subsequently treated by many poets
and composers; the best-known work is Heinrich
Heine's poem of 1823/24, part of the cycle
Heimkehr: "Ich weiss nicht, was soll es bedeuten
…" [I know not what it must mean]. It was set to
music by various composers, among them Franz
Liszt.[7] With the musical setting by Friedrich
Silcher (1789–1860), it became a folk song that is
still popular today.

There can be no doubt that Schwind was inspired
by Heine's *Lorelei* in creating the present drawing. In a vertical format, which is filled by the
height of the steeply rising, craggy rock face that
underscores the impending danger to the boatman, he drew what he considered to be the song's
pivotal moment. Schwind often preferred the tall
format to heighten a work's expressive power;
later on, he used the vertical composition in his
"Reisebilder" [travel pictures]. At the bottom,
close to the rock, the boatman risks the fateful
look up toward the Lorelei, who can be heard but
not seen. Schwind's composition clearly corresponds to the fifth verse of Heine's song of the
Lorelei (see Appendix A). The hard, jagged rock
face, layered like crystal, appears as though chiseled; it has been drawn in a manner appropriate
to the material depicted, with steely, sharp, precise pen strokes reminiscent of the engraving
technique of the Dürer period. The engraving-
like sharpness with which Schwind has placed
the strokes in this drawing, and his lively handling of the line show that he had assimilated
Albrecht Dürer's style of drawing and engraving,
as well as the rhythmic touch of the draftsmen of
the Danube school. During his Vienna years, in
the circle of the Olivier brothers, Schwind had
studied original drawings and prints by early
German masters in the incomparable collections
of Duke Albert of Saxony-Teschen, the founder
of the modern-day Albertina, and in other private collections.[8] Ever since he had settled in
Munich, Schwind had maintained friendly con-

tact with Julius Schnorr von Carolsfeld, whose
precise draftsmanship, modeled after the engraving and drawing techniques of the early German
masters, likewise influenced him. With a
melodic fluidity in his sprightly stroke, Schwind
effortlessly drew this finished composition with
the pen over a summary pencil sketch; it is a virtuoso masterpiece. The work is also important
because it is dated and provides a reference point
for dating a group of stylistically similar drawings in Schwind's oeuvre.

1 In his youth, in a painting of 1823, Schwind treated the
   subject of a boatman in his boat. It shows a young man
   lying on his back in a drifting boat; propped up on his arm,
   he is looking up intently. This work is presumably based
   on Heine's poem *Die Loreley*; cf. Hans Tietze, "Aus dem
   Hause Olivier," in *Mitteilungen der Gesellschaft für ver-
   vielfältigende Kunst* (Vienna, 1910), fig. 7. In old age
   Schwind created the oil painting *The Boatwoman*; it shows
   a young woman standing in her boat in a long, strapless
   dress with a hat hanging from her hip. She steers the boat
   across a mountain lake in the moonlight; cf. Kalkschmidt
   1943, p. 203, fig. 121; in Weigmann 1906, p. 302 (repr.),
   the painting is entitled *Baroness Spaun Rowing Across
   Gmunden Lake*.
2 Bailey 1977, pp. 489–91.
3 Alfred Einstein, *Schubert*, trans. David Ascoli (London,
   1971), p. 167.
4 C. 1820. Sepia and watercolor over pencil. Vienna, private
   collection. Cf. Bailey 1977, pp. 490 f., fig. 120.
5 *Ibid.*, p. 491.
6 Winterstein expressed that view to Colin J. Bailey as well
   as to the present author; cf. Bailey 1977, p. 568, n. 260.
7 Fischer-Dieskau 1968, pp. 160 f.
8 Cf. Schwind's letter to Franz von Schober, written around
   the middle of August 1824, in which he wrote that in the
   house of Pinteric, which was full of early German art
   objects, he had seen Dürer's *Triumphal Procession* again;
   Stoessl 1924, pp. 36f.

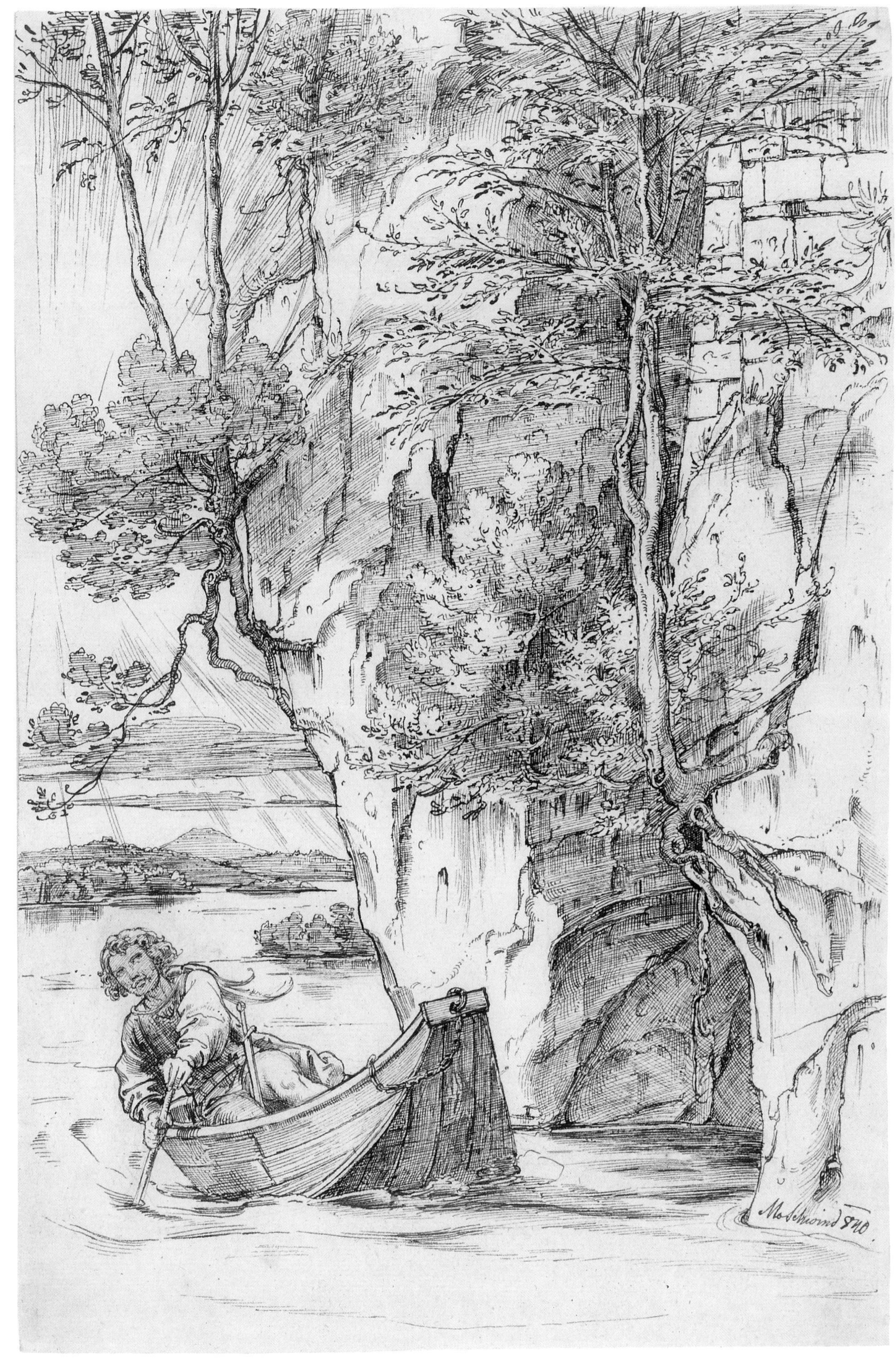
M. v. Schwind 840

60

Moritz von Schwind

In the Forest—Forest Solitude—
The Boy's Magic Horn, c. 1840–43

Pencil, brush and brown ink, on laid paper; watermark
(trimmed): NDERS; 291 x 228/230 mm
Signed in pencil, lower right: "Schwind"

Bibliography: Boetticher, vol. 2.2, p. 710, no. 76; Ludwig
Gurlitt, "Auf Schwind's Spuren, Neue Funde und Entdeck-
ungen," Westermanns Monatshefte 54 (October 1909):
119 f.; Moritz von Schwind, Zeichnungen und Aquarelle,
ed. Peter Halm, exh. cat., Staatliche Kunsthalle Karlsruhe
(Karlsruhe, 1937), p. 25, no. 89 ("Im Walde"); Arthur von
Schneider, "Moritz von Schwinds Zeichnungen und
Aquarelle, Zur Karlsruher Ausstellung von Handzeich-
nungen Schwinds," Die Kunst 77, no. 4 (January 1938):
99 (repr. facing p. 97); Schack-Galerie 1969, pp. 338 f.,
on inv. no. 11576, Vorzeichnungen (a); Bailey 1977, vol. 2,
pp. 389 94, 393, n. 141; Munich 1985, p. 276; Buberl 1989,
p. 81

This drawing, which only recently reappeared after having been believed lost for decades, is the first version of the subject. Schwind offered it for publication to the Düsseldorf publisher and art dealer Julius Buddeus in a letter from Karlsruhe dated 13 January 1843: "I have a drawing that needs little additional work, which you might be able to use as a title page. I did it as such, without any further purpose, as an illustration of *Des Knaben Wunderhorn* [The Boy's Magic Horn]."[1] We know from the collector Count Schack that Schwind later gave this same title to the oil version from around 1848.[2] In letters to Buddeus, Schwind also called the drawing *Horn Blower*. Between 1843 and 1845, Buddeus had it etched by Constantin Müller. On 7 July 1843, Schwind wrote to Buddeus from Karlsruhe that he was not satisfied with the etched copper plate, and he asked for information on "how the *Horn Blower* is faring and has fared."[3]

In his letter of 19 August, Schwind handed over three drawings to Buddeus, among them the *Horn Blower* for eighteen louis d'or.[4] From Frankfurt, to where he had moved at the end of May 1844, he complained in a letter of 19 November 1844 that "the engraving after the *Horn Blower* looked so hard and raw that he quite despaired of its ever getting done."[5] Constantin Müller's etching was eventually published by Buddeus in 1845/46 as an illustration to the poem *Im Walde* (see Appendix B) by the Düsseldorf writer Wolfgang Müller von Königswinter (1816–1873).[6]

Around 1848, Schwind returned to the motif—slightly enlarging the composition at the top, the bottom, and at the right—in two nearly identical painted versions.[7] According to Boetticher there was another drawing for the picture in the Schack-Galerie.[8] Schwind's own tracing after Constantin Müller's 1850 etching—now in the Kurpfälzisches Museum in Heidelberg[9]—has been published frequently in the absence of the drawing exhibited here, which only recently reappeared. Schwind wrote the text of Wolfgang Müller's poem underneath the tracing as a legend. This sheet was evidently a design for an engraving that was intended to combine picture and text on a single page.

The motif of the *Waldhorn* ["forest horn"] and Schwind's folk-song-like title recall the collection *Des Knaben Wunderhorn: Alte deutsche Lieder* [The Boy's Magic Horn: Early-German Songs], which had been published in three volumes between 1806 and 1808 by Ludwig Achim von Arnim and Clemens Brentano. "Like a horn of plenty, this collection brought together… German sagas, legends, and fairy tales in verse and song, and it would offer a splendid drinking horn (as Ludwig Emil Grimm depicted it in the title page etching of the second volume) from which the German people could drink a new youth, as it were."[10] But Schwind did not refer concretely to the content of this collection. The drawing here actually seems like a literal illustration to Müller's poem *Im Walde*, even though it was only later that Buddeus combined the poem with the drawing. In each of the four stanzas of his poem, Müller associated the notion of "forest solitude" with the happy feeling of youth, freedom, love, and songs, which the sonorous voice of the *Waldhorn* was to "proclaim and carry forth." In 1841, Ludwig Tieck wrote his novella *Waldeinsamkeit* [Forest Solitude] in which a short poem of the same title awakens the memory of the young Ferdinand von Linden: "Already as a boy I loved to stray and get lost in the forest of my home. In its innermost, nearly impenetrable parts, completely isolated from the world, I felt an indescribable happiness….And all this, and whatever yearnings I have ever felt for nature, just now came back fully alive in my bosom when the words 'forest solitude' were merely uttered."[11]

Schwind depicted his close-up nature scenes, especially of the forest, in an atmospheric and poetical way with human, legendary, or imaginary figures. The present subject is one of the most densely layered: it awakens a host of associations and allows a consequent range of interpretations reaching all the way to the profoundly psychological. The *Waldhorn* has echoes of the horn sound from Carl Maria von Weber's *Freischütz*. It exudes music that is orchestrated by the rustling and the voices of the forest. It is as though the horn were simultaneously a horn of plenty and a drinking horn collecting the fragrant forest air and the fresh dew, which the youth, a figure like Joseph Eichendorff's "Taugenichts" [Good-for-Nothing], seems to be drinking in eagerly. Wild roots and moss make a soft bed for the youth at the foot of an ancient oak, above a trickling spring and the damp forest ground. There are vague reminiscences of Philipp Otto Runge's paintings *Morning* and *The Spring*. The tree as a symbol of life carries allegorical meaning here in the image of the oak, not least as a symbol of the German unity aspired to at the time (1848–1871). With his crossed legs and raised arms, which resemble the outstretched limbs and branches of the tree, the youth has surrendered himself entirely to nature; he has become one with it. Wild and riotous growth is everywhere, the forest densely interwoven. Isolation in the forest is here a positive counterimage for the city dweller at a time of industrialization. An image of infinitude, the forest arouses yearnings and spurs the imagination, and has been a subject for German artists from Albrecht Altdorfer to Moritz von Schwind, from Max Ernst to Anselm Kiefer.

1 Gurlitt 1909, p. 119.

2 Munich, Bayerische Staatsgemäldesammlungen, Schack-Galerie, inv. no. 11576. "A blessed spring mood prevails in another painting, in which…a boy, only lightly clad, is lying on the ground and, a horn to his mouth, trumpets his heart's jubilation out into the world. Schwind used to call this painting *The Boy's Magic Horn*." Adolf Friedrich Graf von Schack, *Meine Gemäldesammlung*, 2nd ed. (Stuttgart, 1882), p. 55.

3 Gurlitt 1909, p. 119.

4 Ibid., p. 120.

5 Ibid.

6 In *Deutsche Dichtungen mit Randzeichungen deutscher Künstler*, ed. Julius Buddeus, vol. 2 (Düsseldorf, 1845/46), p. 16. Boetticher's view that the drawing was created in Frankfurt am Main after Wolfgang Müller's poem can therefore not be sustained; Boetticher, vol. 2.2, p. 710, no. 76. A reproduction of the etching can be found in Benz and Schneider 1939, p. 162, fig. 19, p. 213.

7 First version cf. *Verlorene Werke* 1931, p. 48 (repr.), 96. Second version: Schack-Galerie 1969, vol. 1, pp. 338–40, vol. 2, fig. 32; Buberl 1989, pp. 82 ff., no. 29, repr. in color.

8 Boetticher, vol. 2.2, p. 716, no. 265, pencil; 255 x 210 mm; Collection Dr. Eugen Lucius.

9 Pencil, pen and brush in gray ink, on yellowed tracing paper, mounted on Japan paper; sheet: 310 x 217 mm, image: 243 x 202 mm; below the picture is an inscription in four columns written in pencil by Schwind himself: three columns contain Wolfgang Müller's poem *Im Walde*, and the fourth column on the right contains the following: "Gedicht von Wolfgang Müller gez. von M. v. Schwind rad. von Const. Müller in der hl. Nacht 1850" [Poem by Wolfgang Müller drawn by M. v. Schwind etched by Const. Müller {with pen in gray ink} on Holy Night 1850]; Heidelberg, Kurpfälzisches Museum, Graphische Sammlung, inv. no. Z 1596a; Bailey 1977, vol. 2, pp. 391–93, vol. 3, fig. 96. Karlsruhe 1996, pp. 191 f., no. 298 (repr.) (Friedrich Gross).

10 Friedrich Gross, in Karlsruhe 1996, p. 192 (no. 298).

11 *Ludwig Tieck's gesammelte Novellen: Vollst. auf's Neue durchges. Ausg.*, 10 vols., in *Ludwig Tieck's Schriften*, 26 vols., *Novellen* (Berlin, 1854), pp. 477, 479ff.

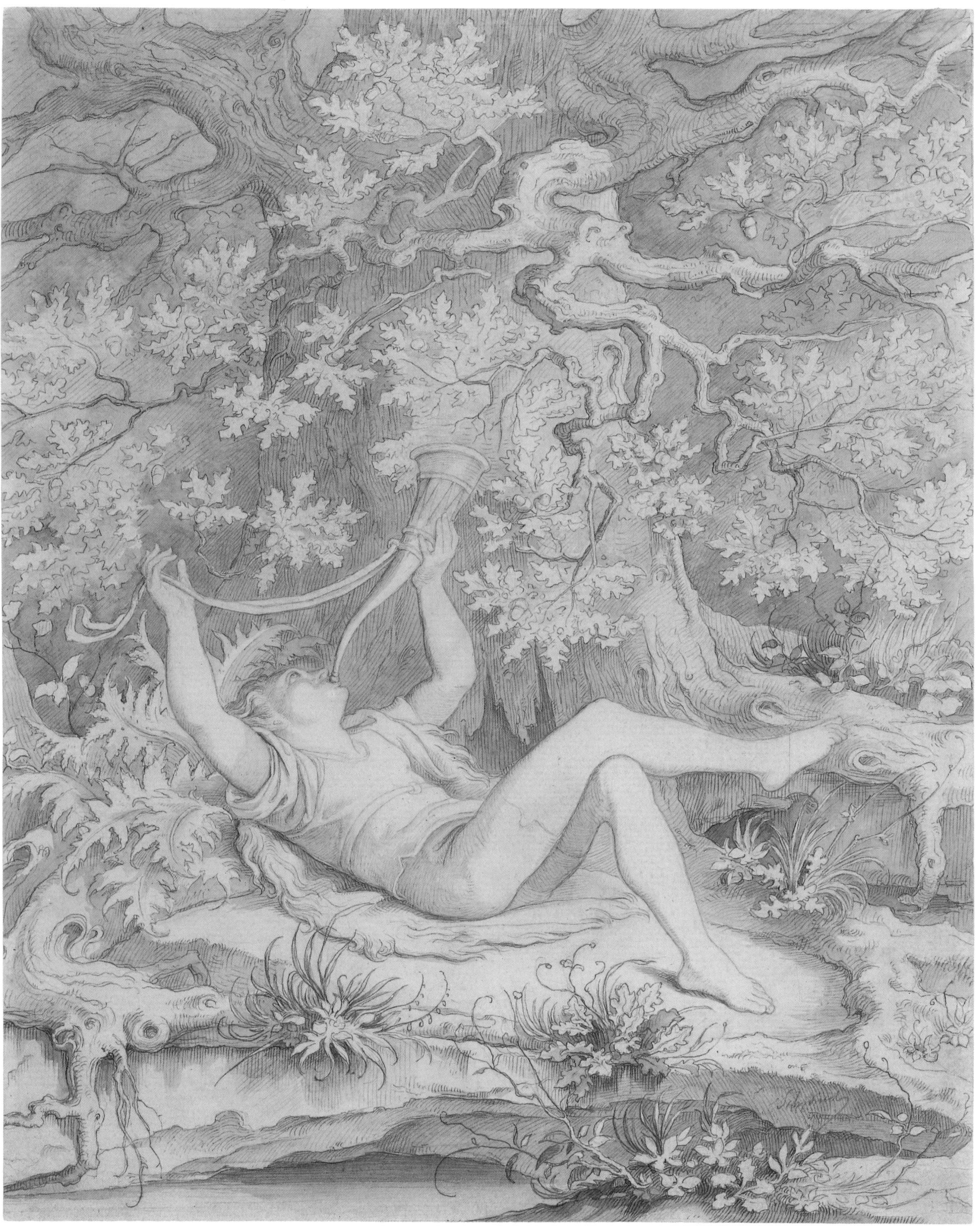

61

Simon Petrus Klotz

Baptized Mannheim 30 September 1776–1824
Munich

*An Excursion in the English Garden in
Munich*, 1795

*Pen and gray ink, watercolor, border in black ink, on laid
paper; 502/4 x 736/9 mm; laid down on its old mount of
heavy paper*
*By a later hand, in pen and black ink, a horizontal border
line parallel to the lower border; a signature in pen and
gray ink, still visible, below left: "Simon Klotz 1795 à
Munich" (covered over)*

Provenance: Katrin Bellinger, Munich

Bibliography: Sieveking 1988, pp. 154 ff. (repr. in color)

On 1 April 1792, the first public park in the
English style on the continent opened to the public (cat. 9). Its intellectual progenitor and true
founder was Sir Benjamin Thompson, the future
Count Rumford (cf. cat. 8). In the wake of the
French Revolution and the storming of the
Bastille in Paris on 14 July 1789, he advised the
elector Carl Theodor[1]—who was not popular in
Munich—to set up a public garden as a way of
preempting the spread of unrest and popular
insurrection. Carl Theodor, an absolutist ruler by
conviction, acceded to Rumford's liberal-demo-
cratic ideas, and signed a decree to establish the
English Garden as early as 13 August 1789.[2]
Rumford's idea was for the garden to benefit not
just one but all of the social classes. Significantly,
however, it was the educated class, which understood the garden's sociopolitical and iconological
meaning, that initially greeted it with enthusiasm. For the "untouched nature" of the English
Garden is in fact an artistic rendering of an idealized notion of what untouched nature should
look like—a notion modeled after, among other
things, French and Dutch landscape painting of
the seventeenth century, which was well known
among the higher social circles. All the elements
of the English Garden, those that existed and
those that were newly added (hills and hollows,
streams, trees, and bushes), were to be laid out so
that the visitor strolling along the marked paths
would be presented, both in close-up and at a distance, with a rich array of beautiful perspectives
and vistas. The visitor would encounter a random
sequence of scenery freely modeled after the
styles of Claude Lorrain or Anthonie Waterloo,
for example. To increase the garden's emotional
content, Rumford had decorative structures in
ancient Greek (cf. cat. 9), Gothic, and Chinese
styles incorporated into the landscape as staffage,
especially in the area of the old Hirschanger Forest (fig.).[3] Situated along a lovely winding path,
these structures were to be encountered sequen-
tially as a series of ever-new surprises, following
the principle of the gradual heightening of an
experience. The landscape garden thus presented
itself as untouched nature in three-dimensional,
walk-through images modeled after paintings.[4]
It is striking that nearly all artistic representations of the English Garden have as their primary focus the "sentimental" architectural
staffage (cat. 9). The visitor and the artist looking
for an encounter with nature were primarily
concerned with the visual experience of nature:
what was worth seeing and worth depicting.[5] In
the wake of early educational tourism, the characteristic landscape view with recognizable elements gained in importance as a souvenir.[6] It is
likely that the highly finished watercolor shown
here was also originally intended for this purpose. Klotz chose a vantage point that showed
two of the most prominent structures, embedded
in nature: the vista onto the park landscape with
the Chinese pagoda in the background at left,[7]
and the Officers' Mess, built in the Palladian-
Neoclassical style, on a rise in the right foreground.[8] The picturesque scenery is enlivened by
walkers and visitors to the Mess, dressed in fashionable clothes that identify them as members of
the upper classes. The viewer is invited to follow
the path that winds its way deep into the garden
and to surrender to the sentimental mood "in the
bosom of beautiful nature" (Sckell).
The nineteen-year-old Klotz mastered the difficult technique of watercolor and the large format
of the *veduta* with an effortless vigor and sound
painterly skill. In the use of a low horizon one
may detect the Dutch-trained eye of his teacher,
Johann Jakob Dorner the Elder. And even
though the uniform treatment of the trees recalls
the watercolor style of the Swiss *Kleinmeister*
["little masters"]—for example, that of Johann
Jakob Bidermann—Klotz has created an evocative, naturalistic scene of a late summer afternoon with finely nuanced coloration and subtle
observation of the light coming through the
gathering clouds. The sheet is an important document of the early artistic reception of the
English Garden, and is one of the earliest examples of the "painterly realism" of the Munich
landscape school. During the last decade of the
eighteenth century, Klotz created watercolors of
intense coloration, a significant number of which
are believed lost. The present watercolor, which
reappeared only a few years ago, is therefore an
important addition to our knowledge of Klotz's
early work.

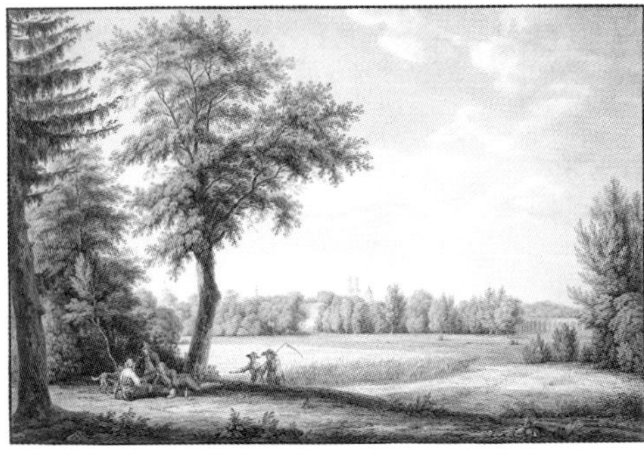

Simon Warnberger, *Summer in the English Garden in
Munich, View of the Chinese Pagoda, the Officers' Mess,
and the Amphitheater*, 1795. Watercolor, pen and gray
ink; 355 x 516 mm

1 The urbane elector Carl Theodor of the Palatinate (from
the Wittelsbach line of Zweibrücken-Salzburg) had transformed his Mannheim residence into one of the most
splendid German princely courts. He was a patron of
music, collected art, and created the gardens in Schwetzin-
gen, near Heidelberg. At the death of the elector Max III
Joseph in 1777, with whom the Bavarian line of the
Wittelsbach became extinct, Carl Theodor inherited
Bavaria and had to move his residence to Munich. There
the locals were offended by his preference for people from
the Palatinate, his strict censorship, his absolutist style
of rule, and his outlawing of the Order of the Illuminati.
What made him particularly unpopular was his offer to
Austria in 1785 to trade all of Bavaria for the Austrian
Netherlands and the title of king of Burgundy.
2 Pankraz Freiherr von Freyberg, "Die 'Geburtsurkunde'
des Englischen Gartens vom 13. August 1789—eine
Neuentdeckung," in von Freyberg 1988, pp. 77–83.
3 Verso inscribed: "S. Warnberger. nach Natur gezeichnet.
1795."
4 von Buttlar 1979, pp. 160 ff.
5 The recreational value of the garden in the modern sense
played a minor role.
6 This offered new areas of work and sources of income for
artists. Early views were reproduced in etchings and aquatints, later ones in lithographs and steel engravings in order
to meet the growing demand. Cf. Tübingen 1981, pp. 7–12.
7 The wooden Chinese pagoda was built between September
1789 and May 1790 by the Mannheim architect Joseph
Frey, who modeled it after the tall pagoda by William
Chambers in Kew Gardens, outside of London. The
Munich pagoda was originally intended as a lookout
tower. At a height of twenty-five meters, it towered over
the trees at the time it was built, allowing a sweeping view
of the city and the distant panorama of the Alps from its
upper stories.
8 The Officers' Mess was completed by the end of April 1791.
Built after a design by Johann Baptist Lechner, it incorporated a portico with Ionic columns in the Palladian-Neo-
classical Colonial style of New England, Rumford's birthplace. The building, later called Rumford Hall, with a
dining hall that could seat more than 150, was initially
used by the officers' corps, and later by court circles. It was
situated on a rise, which is no longer recognizable today,
since the surrounding area has been filled in.

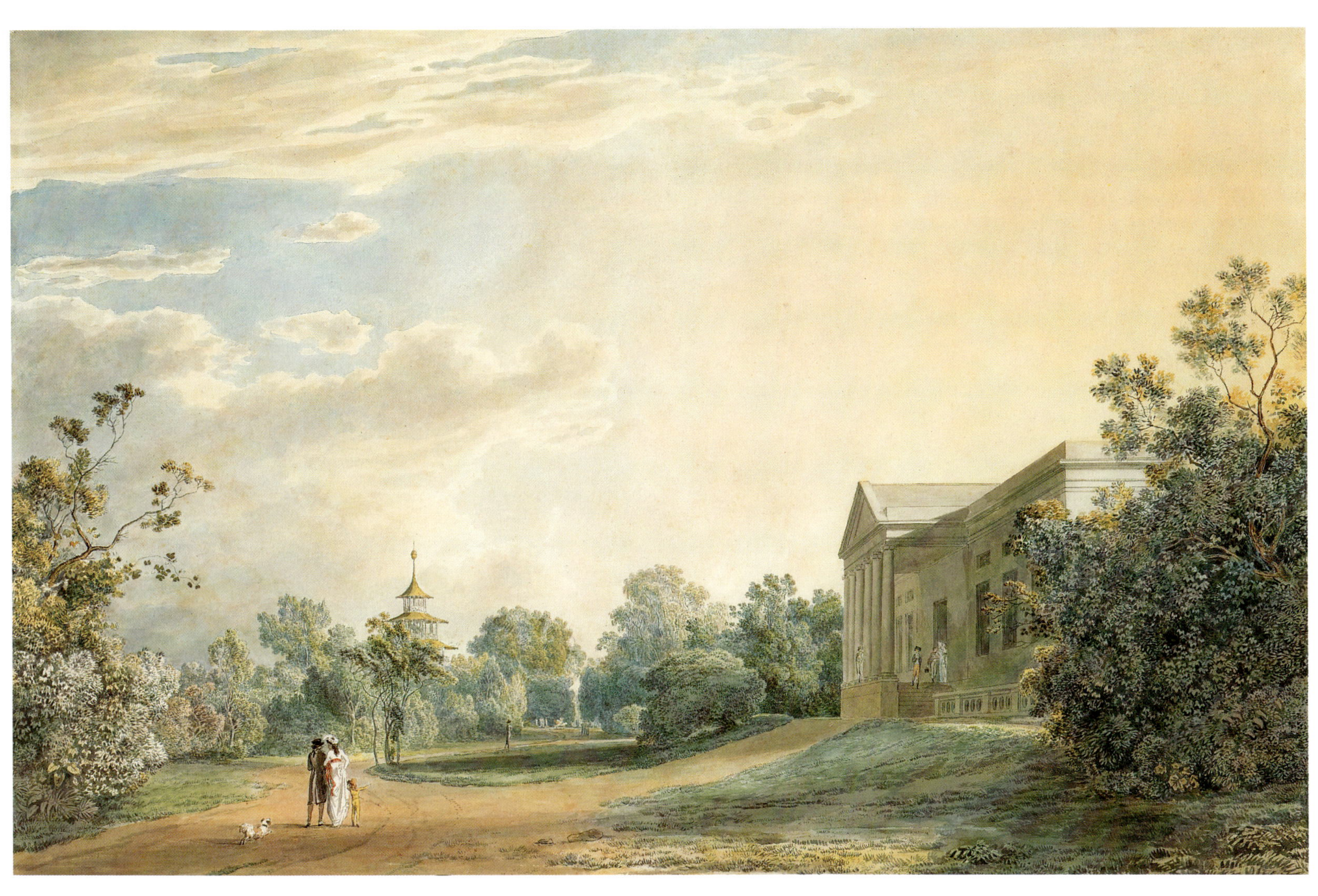

62

Max Joseph Wagenbauer

Baptized Grafing, Upper Bavaria
28 July 1775–12 May 1829 Munich

*The Weissenstein Ruin near Regen in the
Bavarian Forest*, 1805/06

*Pen and gray ink, watercolor, on heavy wove paper;
252 x 350 mm*

Provenance: J. A. G. Weigel, Leipzig

*Bibliography: Gutekunst, Stuttgart (15 May and following
days) 1883*, Versteigerungskatalog Nr. 1143; *Wiesbaden
1936, p. 53, no. 765; Barbara Heine*, Max Joseph Wagenbauer, *Oberbayerisches Archiv, vol. 95 (Munich, 1972),
p. 86, cat. raisonné no. 104; Munich 1979, pp. 242 f., no. 119
(repr.); Nuremberg 1989, p. 509, no. 414 (repr.)*

During the summer of 1805 and 1806, Wagenbauer went on extensive hikes through the
Bavarian Forest in Lower Bavaria. In numerous
drawings and watercolors, he discovered the

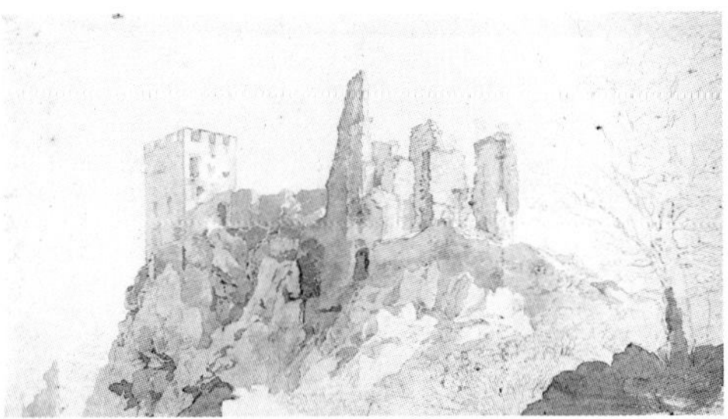

Max Joseph Wagenbauer, *Ruins of Castle Weissenstein
near Regen as Seen from the South*, 1805/06.
Pencil, watercolor; 245 x 420 mm. Munich, Staatliche
Graphische Sammlung, inv. no. 15201

beauty of this remote and little-explored landscape and its historical monuments. Northeast of
Deggendorf on the Danube, near the small city
of Regen, located on the Danube's tributary of
the same name, he was fascinated by the picturesque scene of the ruined Weissenstein Castle
perched on a narrow, rocky ridge. The ruin lies at
an elevation of 765 meters on the highest rise of
the "Pfahl," a mountain crest south of the Regen
valley. The castle, which dominates the region
for quite some distance, is one of the most
impressive in the Bavarian Forest.[1]
The medieval, early Wittelsbach fortification
was badly damaged during the Thirty Years
War. It was restored and made habitable again,
but a large section collapsed in 1740. The remain-
der was destroyed in 1742 by the Austrian Pan-
dour colonel Franz Freiherr von der Trenk
during the War of the Austrian Succession

(which had been provoked by the elector Karl
Albrecht of Bavaria).
Wagenbauer circled the ruin on top of the high
rocky ridge, executing three views on the spot,
from the south, east, and north, which he
sketched loosely with a pencil and worked up
lightly with watercolor.[2] All three attest to the
artist's effort to reproduce the topographical situation accurately; it is also noticeable that the
momentary effect of light is precisely observed in
each case.
The broadly composed sketch from the south
shows a panoramic view of the castle with the
keep on the western side, the same vantage point
as in the present watercolor, but closer (fig.).
Even the stand of trees on the right frame it as a
repoussoir. This sketch undoubtedly served as the
model for the watercolor,[3] and provides an
insight into the artist's working process. In the
studio, Wagenbauer used the pen and brush to
elaborate the motif recorded in the sketch into a
dense pictorial composition, whether on commission, in order to sell it, or for the purpose of reproduction. In the sketch, the castle is spread out
over the wide sheet, while in the finished watercolor it is seen from a greater distance and has
been moved to the right middle ground. The
entire foreground, in all likelihood an invented
addition, is placed in front of the castle like a
coulisse. In composing the picture, Wagenbauer
followed the classic conception of landscape, with
the framing stand of trees on the left as a *repoussoir* and the colors gradually lightening from the
lower edge of the sheet toward the top and into
the distance. With the utmost care he observed
the subtle incidence of the light from the morning sun, still low in the sky. The watercolors have
been applied in delicate nuances as local color, in
accordance with the gradations of light and
shade. In contrast to the sketch, the sky has also
been worked up, as far as the low horizon.
The picturesque ruin rises toward the sky in the
soft and clear sunlight like a Gothic vision from
the Middle Ages. Freestanding remains of the
wall jut up like steep rock projections formed by
nature. Nature and the transitory works of the
human hand have become one. The dominating,
illuminated ruin, witness to an idealized national
past, contrasts clearly with the poor wood huts in
the shadow at its foot, which are the shabby
dwellings of the present. Smoke rises from the
chimney of the first hut, and in the foreground
a peasant, setting out in the early morning hour,
carries his heavy load uphill. His solitary figure
recalls the motif of the wanderer. The *veduta* and
the invented foreground staffage have been
arranged with great artistry into a picturesque,
evocative image. Consciously or unconsciously,
in this work Wagenbauer went beyond the easy,
pure landscape description that usually dominates his work. Rainer Schoch has written that

"Wagenbauer sensed the aesthetic appeal resulting from the contrast of castle and hut, though
surely without any programmatic intent."[4] Still,
Wagenbauer's choice of this contrast was not
accidental, for it is striking how often he staged
the scene in his landscapes by contrasting castle
ruins with humble peasant huts.[5] There is certainly a symbolic undercurrent here that reveals
something about the mood of the time: the work
makes reference to the primeval and simple life
in nature, the opposition between social classes
and between rulers and ruled, and the yearning
for a glorious past in turbulent political times,
including the troubled present around 1806.

1 Cf. *Die Kunstdenkmäler von Niederbayern*, vol. 19: *Bezirks-
   amt Regen*, ed. Karl Gröber (Munich, 1928), pp. 114–19,
   figs. 85–89, pl. 9.
2 Heine 1972, p. 86, nos. 100, 101, 103.
3 *Ibid.*, p. 86, no. 103.
4 Rainer Schoch in Nuremberg 1989, p. 509, no. 414.
5 For example, *View of Diessenstein Castle* (Heine 1972),
   p. 85, no. 91, fig. 25; *View of Fürstenstein towards Englburg
   and Saldenburg, ibid.*, nos. 92, 93, figs. 29, 30; *View of Castle Leuchtenberg above the Village with Simple Peasant
   Huts in the Shadow in the Front, ibid.*, p. 91, nos. 146, 147.

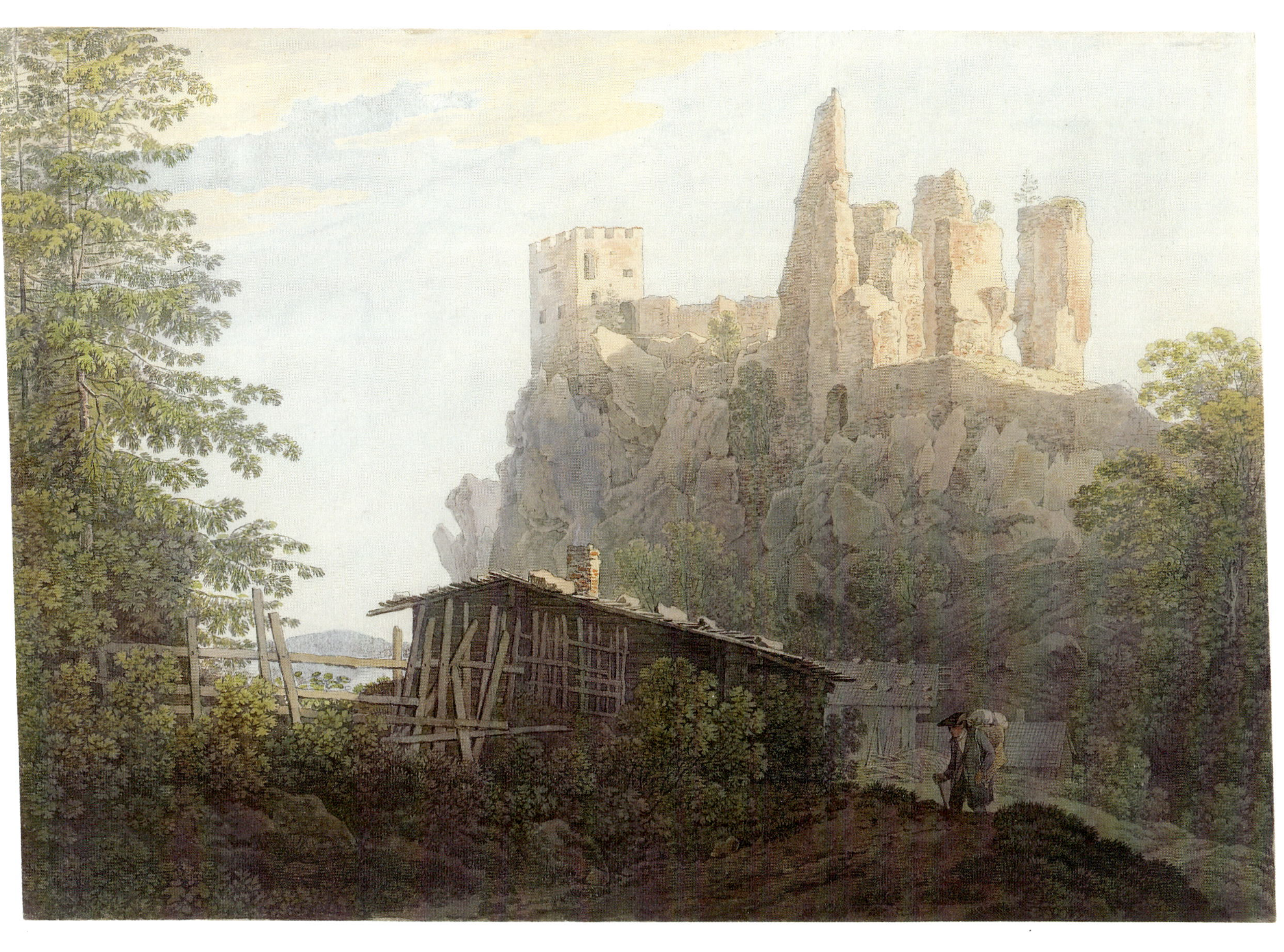

63

Johann Georg von Dillis

Grüngiebing above Schwindkirchen near
Haag / Upper Bavaria
26 December 1759 – 28 September 1841 Munich

Brook in Old Munich, c. 1790 –1800

Watercolor, pencil, pen and gray-black and brown ink,
black chalk, on laid paper; 259/261 x 366/8 mm

Bibliography: Munich 1958, p. 22, no.15; Lübeck 1969,
p. 24, no.19, p. 23 (repr.); Cambridge 1972, no.11 (repr.);
Munich 1991, pp. 86 f., no.11 (repr. in color)

German drawing of the late eighteenth century
was dominated by the fashionable monochrome
of the sepia manner and the gray-black wash
grisaille, on the one hand, and by painting in
opaque bodycolor or gouache, on the other. By
the end of the 1780s, however, Dillis preferred
the transparent watercolor (cat. 8, 9), a difficult
technique that flourished in eighteenth-cen-
tury England. Dillis soon acquired a mastery
unequaled in the German lands that placed him
in the ranks of the best English watercolor artists.
Dillis and Wilhelm von Kobell were among the
first artists in Germany who fostered the use of
watercolor as an independent medium, paving
the way for the flowering of watercolor painting
within the Munich school at the beginning of the
nineteenth century. Dillis contributed to this
development in his capacity as academy teacher,
as well as through the example of his work.
Dillis and Kobell also shared a love for the rural
idyll on the outskirts of the city,[1] which perhaps
grew from the influence on both men of seventeenth-century Dutch painters.[2] The suburban
idyll here also echoes the work of the Dutch masters. Although the precise location depicted here
is not identifiable, in all likelihood it is a view in
the southern Munich suburb of Au along one of
the city creeks diverted from the Isar River.[3] Dillis sketched the scene on the spot around noon on
a sunny summer day, presumably from a dry area
in the middle of the bed of the creek, whose flow
of water has declined to a trickle. In the middle
ground, above the creek, a precisely drawn
viaduct—a water pipe—catches the viewer's
eye. Simple wooden houses are visible behind the
banks of the stream, which are reinforced and
overgrown with trees and bushes. On the left is a
lively scene of everyday life: a man sitting on the
bank, a cow, fowl, and a woman with her back to
the viewer, evidently on her way to the usual
clothes-washing spot. Dillis has masterfully captured the momentary light in this characteristic
watercolor. We can also clearly observe his spontaneous and quick manner of working, as he goes
back and forth between the loose pen strokes in

various colors of ink and the brush charged with
a narrow range of colors, over the sketchy preliminary drawing in pencil. Sparing, carefully
balanced, and delicate watercolor accents have
been deployed with a sure hand, and together
with the reserves of the white paper they create a
pattern on the sheet. They may remind the modern viewer of Cézanne's manner in structuring
watercolor studies.

Dillis' watercolors have retained an astonishing
luminosity. He used choice painting materials,
presumably including the densely pigmented
English watercolors, and he also mixed his colors
according to his own recipes.[4]

In contrast to the highly finished picturesque and
topographically faithful *veduta* of Simon Klotz
(cat. 61), for example, this landscape exhibits a
sketchy quality, that suggests rather than
describes, and a bright transparency: an "impres-
sionistic" nature study of unusual freshness and
vividness. It is above all the reflections in the
shallow water that create the work's special
attraction and offer the loveliest testimony to the
artist's talent for the watercolor technique.
Sheets like this show why Dillis occupies a lofty
place as a watercolorist in German art of the late
eighteenth century.

1 For Dillis cf. Munich 1991, pp. 84 ff., nos. 9, 10 (repr. in
   color); the etchings of 1806: *The Large Isar Footbridge*
   (A.29), and *The Small Isar Footbridge* (A.28); and the
   painting *Excursion at the Schwabing Brook* (Messerer 1961,
   p. 84, no. 3, p. 118, repr.). For Wilhelm von Kobell, see for
   example the painting *River Landscape with Washerwomen
   in Front of Village and Bridge*, c. 1798 (Wichmann 1970,
   pp. 254 f., no. 474, repr.), and *Wolfratshausen on the
   Loisach River*, c. 1798 (*ibid.*, no. 478).

2 Dillis trained himself by, among other things, copying
   works of art, such as river landscapes by Jan van Goyen
   or by Jacob van Ruisdael and Salomon van Ruysdael;
   cf. Munich 1991, p. 86, no. 10, n. 3, pp. 306 ff., nos. 153 – 55
   (repr. in color). For Wilhelm von Kobell see cat. 65 – 67.

3 In the north of Munich, for example, there was the Eisbach or the Schwabinger Bach, in the south the Enten-
   bach, Glockenbach, or Mühlbach in der Au.

4 Dillis experimented with colors and techniques. Striking
   in his early work—as in this piece—is a fluorescent blue
   tone, probably Coelin blue, which was not mass-produced
   prior to 1805.

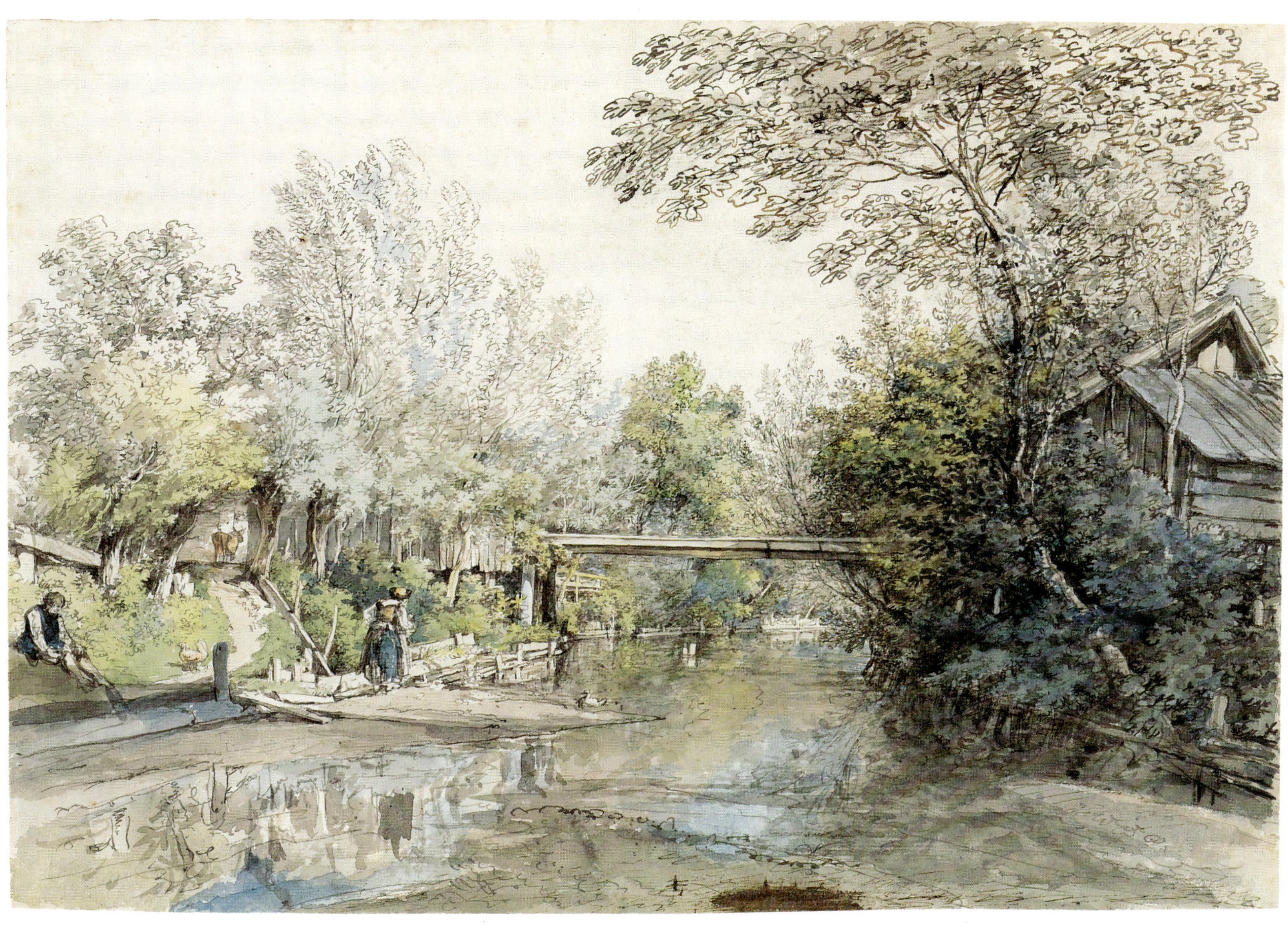

64

Johann Georg von Dillis

Common White Willows on Prater Island,
c. 1820–30

*Black chalk, brush and gray and brown wash, heightened
with white, on laid paper prepared with an ochre ground;
350 x 420 mm*

*Bibliography: Munich 1958, p. 23, no. 24, fig. 39; Heise 1959,
pp. 61 f., fig. 43; Munich 1991, pp. 96 f., no. 17 (repr. in color)*

The tree is a central motif in Dillis's experience of nature. Throughout his life he was fascinated by the strange shapes of old willows.[1] As early as 1794, he had done a painterly etching of an old, bent, and overgrown willow: situated at the bank of a river, it leans over the water with its interwoven limbs and branches and seems to become one with the water (fig. 1). The representation of nature in the Dutch style characterizes this and other early etchings by Dillis. Here he clearly paraphrases an etching by Jacob van Ruisdael (fig. 2). The comparison shows how close the two approaches are. Both men created images with strong emotional content: Ruisdael's is more soberly descriptive and Dillis's more densely atmospheric. Dillis's formulation reflects his pro-

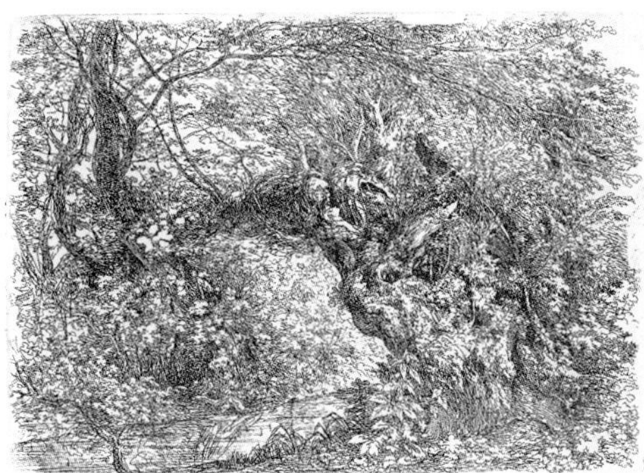

1 Johann Georg von Dillis, *The Old Willow by the Brook,*
1794, etching (A.30)

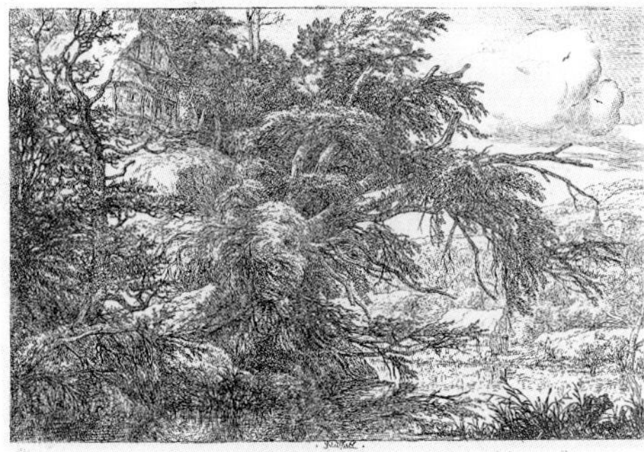

2 Jacob van Ruisdael, *The Big Tree on the Riverbank,*
etching (B.5). Munich, Staatliche Graphische Sammlung

found experience of processes like rampant growth, the expression of a sensitive, primal feeling for nature characteristic of the Sturm und Drang.

Dillis was the son of a forester, and his enduring bond with nature finds its loveliest expression in the present tree study, part of his late oeuvre. It was done directly from nature under the momentary impression of changing light. Dillis liked to search for motifs in nature, and he didn't have to go far from Munich to find them: the English Garden (cat. 9), Prater Island, and the meadows and banks of the Isar River, at that time still uncanalized. In the left background of the sheet here one can clearly make out, on the other side of the Isar, the military barracks built in 1810; today the site is occupied by the patent office.[2]

Dillis thus sketched a view from Prater Island toward the southwest. Fascinated by the wild growth of the trees and their appearance in the light, he observed the variety of their forms and gnarled deformities, modeling them in the evening light as picturesque motifs. The study is coherent and conveys an extraordinary chromatic effect, despite the very limited use of color, much like a grisaille. This is the result of the carefully pondered combination of the colored ground and heightening—here, for example, the layered application of brown washes. The charm of such a sheet lies not least in the fusion of its invented colors.

In his early work, Dillis expressed his exceptional colorism in his preference for the watercolor medium; in his later work his gift found expression in the imaginative use of colored papers. In addition to tinted paper, he used papers primed with color, which he prepared himself from a rich palette of ochre, brown, blue, and turquoise hues.[3] Dillis achieved highly painterly effects on the opaque and matte surfaces of these sheets. He preferred to use drawing materials that corresponded to the natural colors of his subject: for example, blue laid paper and white chalk for his many cloud studies around 1820,[4] and here, the warm ochre ground for the golden light of a summertime evening sun.

To what extent did Dillis adhere to academic traditions in the present study? To what extent did he transcend them? How far did he move artistically from his predecessors and contemporaries? The choice of the pictorial space still reveals a classically influenced composition in the tree and shrub *repoussoir* in the lower right corner and foreground. The common white willows echo the trees depicted by seventeenth-century Dutch painters, such as Adam Pijnacker or Aelbert Cuyp, which are modeled with luminous reflections of light. But in spite of clear reminiscences of the Dutch tradition, including also the works of Anthonie Waterloo or Jacob van Ruisdael, the impression of an immediate observation of

nature still predominates. Worlds separate Dillis's tree studies from the tree pictures of Jacob Philipp Hackert, which were still highly regarded in Dillis's day. Produced in series and executed monochromatically with brush and sepia, Hackert's trees seem dry and lifeless. Unlike Hackert's studies, Dillis's have nothing of the academic model-book conventionality about them,[5] and the painterly study here conveys not only the tree's appropriate botanical character, but also its unmistakable individuality. Dillis drew a large number of similar tree studies directly from nature, frequently as finished, autonomous works of art. He organized these studies as stock, perhaps in order to use them if needed in a larger landscape composition—for example, as a framing *repoussoir*.[6]

Dillis's tree studies, observed in the shifting light, provide a glimpse into essential aspects of his art. With great assuredness and an unfailing sense of proportion he set down these studies with the first sketch on the large sheets, leaving little margin for correction. In each case he followed the intrinsic rhythm of the trees in determining their placement in space and on the surface: in so doing, he created, in the 1820s, early examples of *plein air* painting and drawing. Unparalleled in their time in their freedom and boldness, Dillis's studies seem to anticipate the techniques of Adolph Menzel, Max Slevogt, and Max Liebermann.

1 Two types of willows, the weeping willow and the common white willow, have aroused eerie feelings in popular belief—see, for example, Goethe's ballad *Erlkönig*, which was set to music by Franz Schubert in 1815 and by Carl Loewe in 1818; cf. Fischer-Dieskau 1968, pp. 209 f.

2 Cf. Munich 1991, pp. 94 f., no. 16 (repr. in color).

3 Cf. Hinrich Sieveking, in Munich 1991, pp. 64 f., 96 ff., nos. 17–19 (repr. in color), pp. 110 ff., nos. 26–27 (repr. in color), pp. 193 ff., nos. 81–82 (repr. in color), pp. 290 f., no. 142 (repr. in color).

4 Munich 1991, pp. 106 f., no. 24 (repr. in color).

5 Max Joseph Wagenbauer (1774–1829) was still publishing tree models for landscapists between 1805 and 1824: *Studien verschiedener Baumgattungen,* 1805 (Heine L.17, Winkler no. 15–8), *Baumstudien für angehende Landschaftszeichner,* 1817 (Heine L.57, Winkler 54, 56), and *Baum- und Landschaftsstudien in Umrissen,* 1823/24 (Heine L. 61 / L. 62, Winkler 61–8/62); cf. Heine 1972, pp. 136–47; Winkler 1975, pp. 307–12; Nuremberg 1980, p. 95, no. 76 (1823).

6 In the Dillis estate is a portfolio entitled "Trees for Foregrounds"; cf. *Johann Georg von Dillis 1759–1841. Zeichnungen und Aquarelle aus den Sammlungen des Historischen Vereins von Oberbayern im Stadtarchiv München,* ed. Katrin Pollems, exh. cat., Bayerische Vereinsbank und Stadtarchiv München (Munich, 1989), p. 57. Cf. Munich 1991, pp. 96 f., no. 18, repr. in color, model for an oil painting: *Autumn Forest Excursion,* oil on copper; 445 x 595 mm., Messerer 1961, p. 92, no. 64, p. 148, repr.

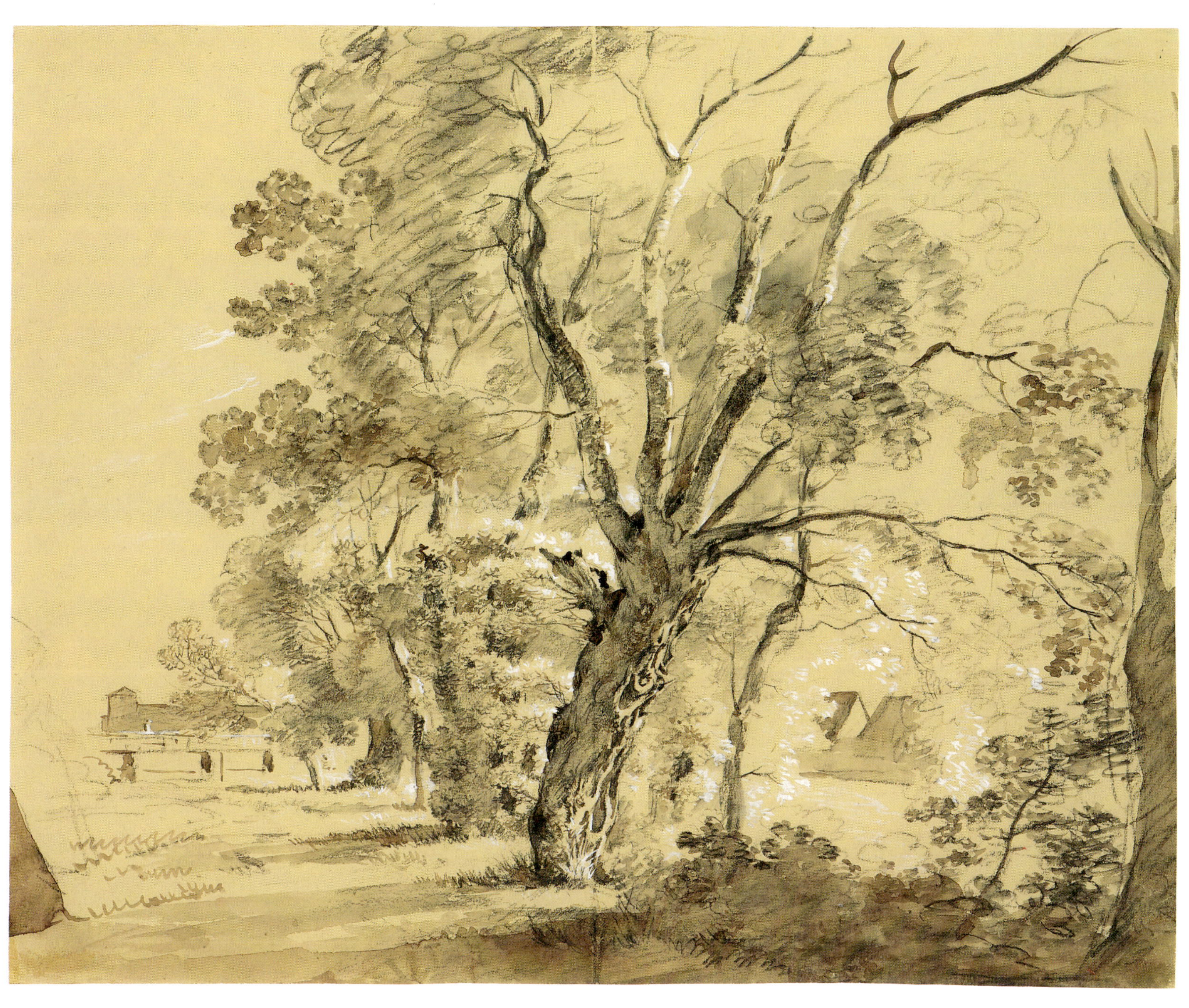

65

Wilhelm von Kobell

Mannheim 6 April 1766 – 15 July 1853 Munich

Staff Officers Listening to the Reading of the Day's Orders, c. 1795

Watercolor over pencil, pen and gray ink, border in pen and black ink on wove paper; watermark: 1794 / J. WHATMAN (trimmed); 393 x 506 mm
Signed in pen and gray ink, lower left: "Wilhelm Kobell"

Bibliography: Karl & Faber, Munich, catalogue of the 130th Auction, 2 December 1971, pp. 104 f., no. 454 (repr.); Siegfried Wichmann, Wilhelm von Kobell 1766 bis 1853. Erster Nachtrag zum Verzeichnis der Werke (Starnberg / Munich, 1973), no. 12, fig. 13; Karl & Faber, Munich, catalogue of the 189th Auction, 1 June 1995, p. 43, no. 234, pl. 12 (in color)

During the War of the First Coalition (1792–97), Austria and Prussia made common cause against the French revolutionary armies in an effort to preserve the monarchy in France and prevent the Revolution from spreading. Bavaria under the elector Carl Theodor joined Austria, while Prussia took a neutral stance after 1795. During this period of large-scale troop movements, Wilhelm von Kobell, a native of Mannheim who had been living in Munich since 1793 as court painter at the electoral court, created a large number of highly accurate military pieces in watercolor. These works won him great renown and subsequent commissions from the court for battle paintings. Kobell was particularly interested in the various and colorful uniforms of the soldiers, who were often brought together from far-away places.[1] In the present highly finished watercolor of around 1795, Kobell has depicted the uniforms with scrupulous accuracy down to the smallest details.

At the edge of a large encampment of allied troops, a general staff officer from the electorate of Bavaria, following a trumpet signal, reads the day's orders to the Austrian escort. Beyond the assembled officers on horseback the viewer's gaze sweeps across wide fields densely packed with tents. Tradition has it that the lowlands of the Danube Valley can be made out in the background, perhaps near Ulm. The trumpeter of the household bodyguards of the elector of Bavaria, placed slightly to the left of the vertical central axis of the picture, stands out among the crowd of soldiers by the color of his uniform: light blue with white cuffs and a dark, two-cornered hat with a plume. The blare of his trumpet directs the attention of the large number of assembled soldiers and onlookers to the electoral staff officer on horseback who reads the orders, surrounded by mounted officers. He is splendidly radiant in his blue uniform with purple cuffs and

a plumed two-cornered hat. The figure standing in the foreground between the begging children and the dog, his back to the viewer and looking toward the officer, is clad in the same radiant uniform of deep ultramarine blue. The officer who reads the orders is surrounded by mounted Austrian Chevaulegers, in white uniforms with blue cuffs, outfitted with rifles, sabers, and batons: the accompanying escort of the cavalry. They are wearing the casque, a simple, light leather helmet similar to what Count Rumford had introduced in the army of the electorate of Bavaria.[2] The gold embroidery shines on the royal-red of their saddle gear. On the caparison we can make out an S-shaped initial next to the Roman numeral "II" underneath a crown, evidently the figure "FII" for Emperor Franz II, who continued the coalition war against France after his father's death in 1792.[3] In the left foreground stands a figure who catches our eye because of the color of his uniform: clad in a green coat with red cuffs and a black hat, he is a Bavarian Chevauleger office; his wife is by his side, holding his arm.

Kobell devoted special attention to the genre scenes in the foreground, such as the begging children on the left and the activity in front of the tent of the sutler, or camp cook, on the right. They reveal his interest in the picturesque, but also his special empathy for figures at the margins of society, the kind of sympathetic feeling that is also evident in the work of Johann Georg von Dillis.[4] Sutlers played an important role in provisioning the troops, whom they accompanied on campaign.[5] In particular, they provided the encamped army with warm food. Here, the woman sutler kneeling on the ground prepares a stew on the open fire, while her husband sits on a bundle of wood, smoking a pipe and turning his attention to the reading of the daily orders. The mustachioed fusilier standing between the tent and the fire, clad in a cloak and a felt cap, is doing the same: he is an infantryman in the Volunteer Corps of the Austrian Army, a body of troops raised in the Hungarian border region. Other Hungarian infantrymen in similar dress are visible behind the cavalrymen. At the far right in the middleground is a neatly stacked pile of cannonballs under guard. For a brief moment the sun shines through a break in the clouds from the upper left, outside the picture, onto the nearest of the assembled figures. Here the colors of people and animals shine with radiant splendor, like precious jewels. Kobell has masterfully depicted the differences in the colors between the illuminated figures and those immediately behind the sunny spot. All the essential elements of his characteristic style are already evident in this early work: a foreground stage on which figures are additively assembled, as though from different contexts; a wide view into the landscape; and an

atmospheric staging of the light. The density and colorfulness of the figures are typical of Kobell's early works. Dutch elements remain inherent in Kobell's oeuvre in the choice of motifs, the composition with a low horizon, and the handling of the light. These elements were the result of his early, intensive preoccupation with Dutch seventeenth-century art, in particular through his reproductive prints in aquatint.

I owe a particular debt of gratitude to the military historian and retired *Oberzollrat* Hugo F. W. Schulz of Düsseldorf, a scholar and expert on the history of military uniforms, who identified the individual uniforms and explained the context of the events. His information provided the basis for my comments.

1 In this regard Kobell was a precursor of artists like Peter von Hess, Albrecht Adam, Johann Adam Klein, or Johann Christoph Erhard, who twenty years later, during the Wars of Liberation, created popular watercolors depicting the military and soldiers.

2 Rumford's military reforms in the years 1788–99 included cost-saving measures, especially in the area of uniforms; they also affected the diet and social security of the soldiers.

3 If one reads the figure as "LII," it would refer to his father, Emperor Leopold II, whose date of death would incline the dating of the watercolor to the year 1792. But such a dating can be ruled out on the basis of the watermark of the paper, which reads "1794," as well as on stylistic grounds.

4 Cf. Hardtwig 1984 and Günther Kapfhammer, "Hütkinder in Bayern als wirtschaftlich-soziales Problem," in *Wittelsbach und Bayern. Krone und Verfassung* (Munich, 1980), vol. 3.1, pp. 311–16.

5 They also sold spirits in their tent, for sterilizing the water; cf. Rotraud Wrede, "Uniformen und Schlachtendarstellungen im Werk Wilhelm von Kobells," in Wichmann 1970, p. 129.

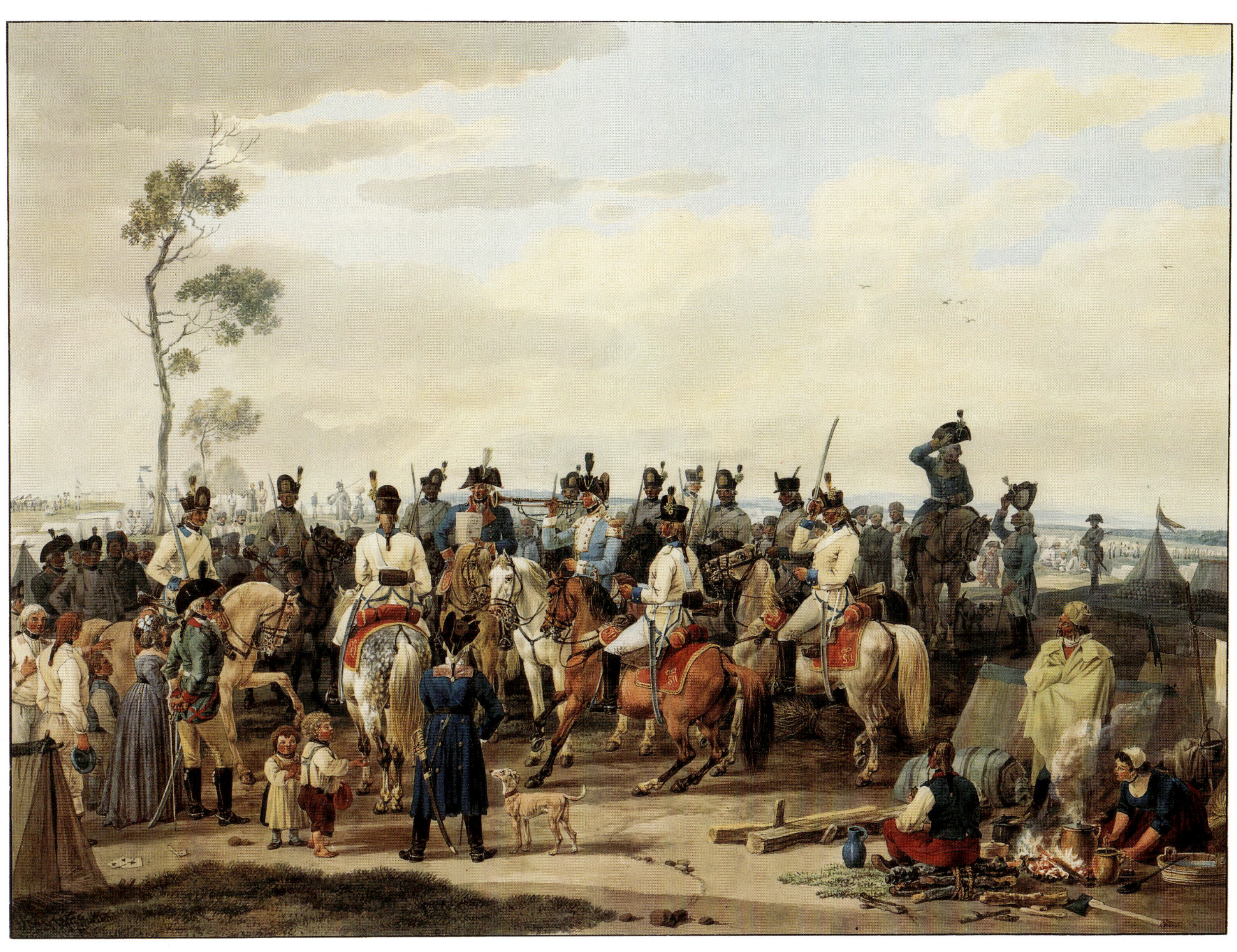

66

Wilhelm von Kobell

Postilion with Traveling Coach in the Fog,
c. 1798

Watercolor, border in black ink, on wove paper; watermark:
J. WHATMAN*; 371 x 500 mm*
Signed with pen or brush in gray ink, lower right:
"Wilhelm Kobell"

Provenance: Count Brühl; 1931, H.N., Munich

Bibliography: Ferdinand, Franz und Wilhelm Kobell:
Handzeichnungen, Aquarelle und Graphik, *ed. Gustav
Jacob, exh. cat., Städtisches Schlossmuseum (Mannheim,
1931), p.14, no.54; Wichmann 1970, p.252 f., no.461 (repr.);
Karl & Faber, 173rd Auction, 4 June 1987, Munich, p.53,
no.308, pl.15 (repr. in color)*

In this large, highly finished watercolor, Kobell depicts a passing three-horse travel coach in a rather bleak setting, against the backdrop of a hill that rises from the left edge of the picture toward the right. On the hill we can make out simple peasant dwellings. Usually this type of coach, or calash, had two horses, but since this was evidently fairly impassable and possibly mountainous terrain, a third horse, the so-called

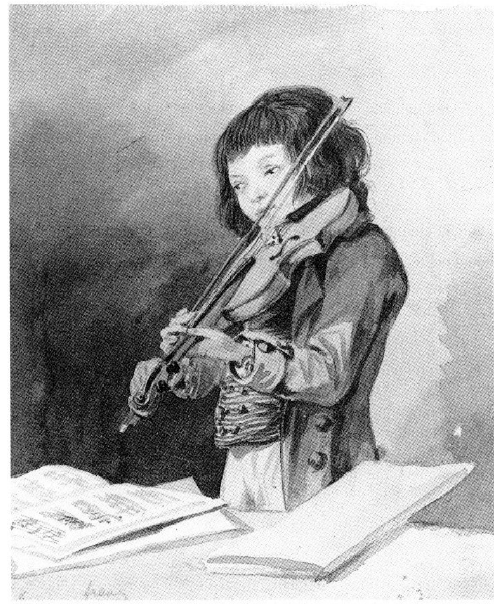

Wilhelm von Kobell, *The Artist's Brother Franz Playing
the Violin,* c. 1789. Watercolor, 221 x 179 mm

mountain horse, has been harnessed to the front. The horses, which are a leitmotif and favorite subject in Kobell's work, are not a particularly refined breed, but are simple draft animals. Under the open half-roof of the coach are two sleeping travelers, warmly dressed against the

harsh weather. Luggage has been loaded up front in place of the coach box: a large trunk, a duffel, and a hat; in the rear is feed for the horses. On the left behind the coach, two peasant children cross the open, sandy road. In this portion of the watercolor we can detect traces of white heightening, which was used to make a correction. In the background, above the horses, we can make out other figures at the farmsteads, as well as bare trees and bushes. The diminished scale of the figures helps us visualize the spatial depth. With the exception of the figural scene in the foreground, everything is shrouded in gray, creating the gloomy atmosphere of a cold, wet, foggy November day.

Compared to his crowded, colorful scene of a military encampment (cat.65), Kobell has limited the number of motifs in the composition and scaled back the color. Once again we can clearly recognize his compositional principles: a fore ground stage, through the middle of which a coach passes, the incorporation of the scene in a landscape context with a fairly low horizon, and finally, a very subtle handling of the light. As in cat.65, sunlight—albeit strongly filtered by the fog—falls from the upper left, illuminating the figural scene in the foreground (note the soft shadows on the ground) and making its contours stand out more clearly. Kobell's great mastery of the art of watercolor is evident in the colors of all the objects, which harmonize with the atmospheric gray background tones. In this way he truly created a masterpiece in the handling of diffuse light.

Next to Johann Georg von Dillis, Wilhelm von Kobell, who succeeded Dillis in 1814 as a teacher of landscape painting at the Munich Academy, is the most important exponent of watercolor as an autonomous artistic genre. Kobell executed his watercolors—which were intended for sale—in the studio, on the basis of careful preliminary drawings and sketches, and he did so with a precision bordering on pedantry. The finished works were given a border in black ink. Kobell's special talent for delicate, transparent watercolors had already revealed itself (much as it had with Dillis) in his quick, spontaneous watercolor studies of family members from life, which were rapidly sketched with the brush. For example, in one sensitive study he captured the childish grace of his younger brother Franz (born in 1779), deeply absorbed in his violin playing (fig.).

In the literature on this drawing, the coach has been erroneously described as a post coach. It is in fact a light, private, four-wheeled travel carriage, or calash, with a half-roof.[1] The rider on the saddled horse is the coachman, who drives and guides the carriage from this position. This way of driving a calash is called "riding à *postilion,*" though it does not necessarily mean that the rider was a postilion. The yellow color of his

coat, the "P" (perhaps for "post") inside a circle sewn onto his right sleeve, and the braided cord slung over his right shoulder (from which a post horn might be hanging down his back and therefore out of sight) make it likely that the coachman also worked for a postal service. Perhaps his employer was the house of Thurn and Taxis, which, following Bavaria's elevation to a kingdom, held the postal privilege until 1808, when it was replaced by a state-run postal service. No original example of this type of coach was believed to still exist, but recently one was discovered in private hands in Spain. A comparison reveals how accurately Kobell reproduced his model.[2]

Kobell, who liked to include all kinds of horse-drawn vehicles in his works, faithfully repeated the present motif of a coach with travelers, luggage, horses, and a rider in a different setting, a snowy winter landscape scene (cf. cat.67).[3]

1   I would like to thank Rudolf Wackernagel and Ulrike von Hase of Munich for identifying the type of coach and its function.

2   The calash is today in the Scheidel collection in Mannheim. Its appearance matches that of Kobell's carriage in the watercolor. I am grateful to Rudolf Wackernagel of Munich for providing me with this information.

3   Wichmann 1970, pp.252 f., no.462 (repr.).

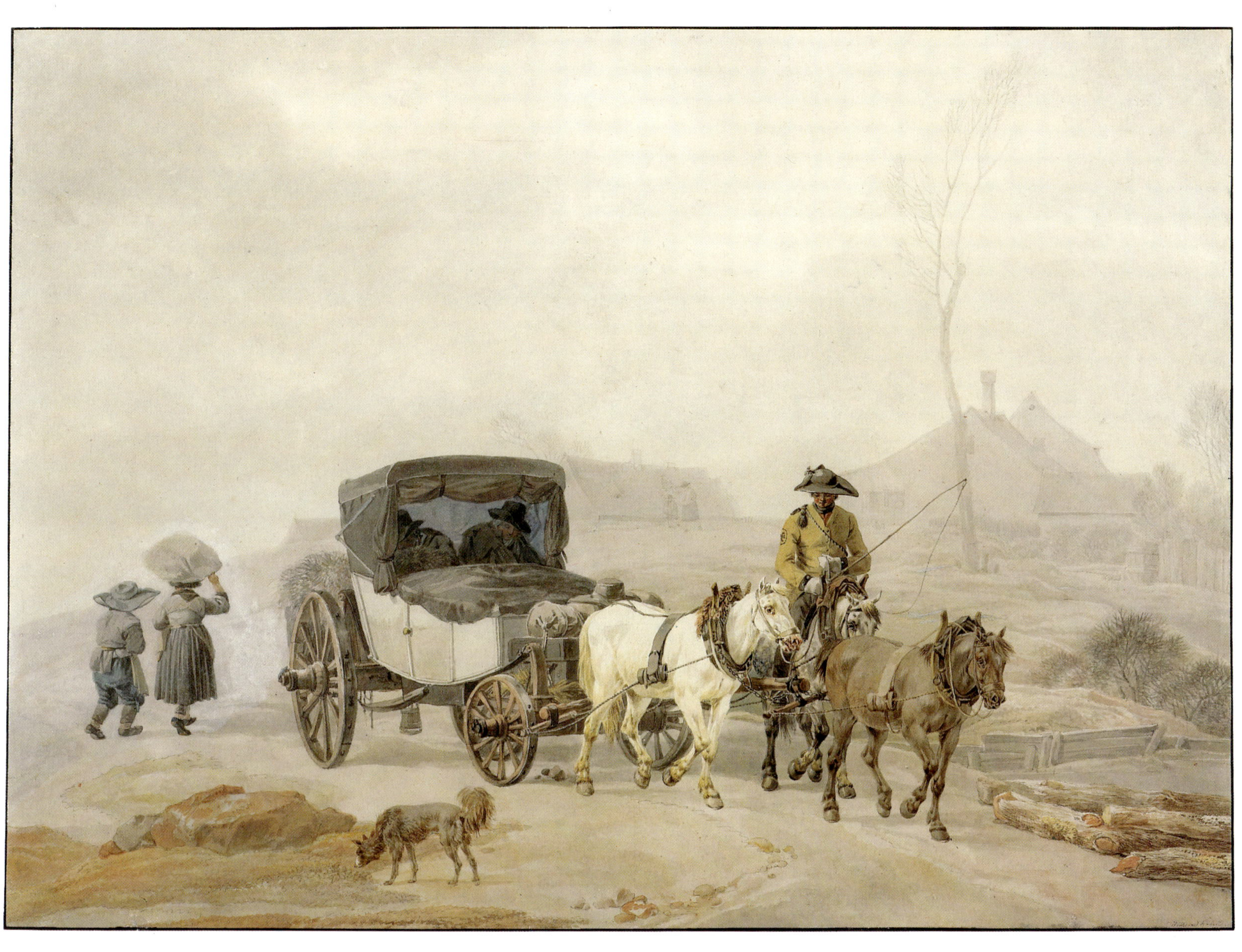

67

Wilhelm von Kobell

Horsemen at the Tegernsee, 1830

*Watercolor, lower border in black ink, on wove paper;
292 x 241 mm
Signed with brush or pen in gray-brown ink, lower right:
Wilhelm v. Kobell 1830*

*Provenance: Arthur von Mumm, Frankfurt am Main;
Dr. Fritz Nathan, St. Gallen; 1939 private collection,
Switzerland; Dr. Peter Nathan, Zurich*

*Bibliography: Hugo Helbing, 40th(?) Auction, Frankfurt
am Main, 31 May–2 June 1934, p. 20, no. 162, fig. pl. 24;*
Die Malerei des 19. Jahrhunderts, *ed. Paul Ortwin Rave
(Berlin, 1945), fig. pl. 63; Wichmann 1970, p. 474 f., no. 1479
(repr.)*

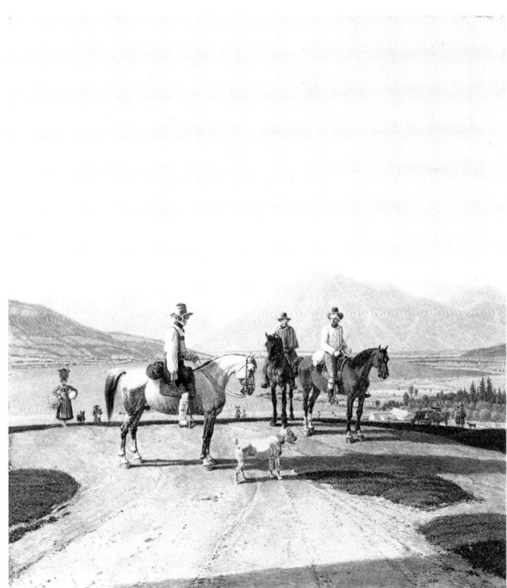

Wilhelm von Kobell, *Horsemen at the Tegernsee*, 1838.
Oil on wood; 290 x 259 mm. Private collection.

Among Wilhelm von Kobell's favorite landscape
backgrounds were the view of Munich from the
elevated bank across the Isar, and the vista across
the Tegernsee onto the foothills of the Bavarian
Alps. In the present Tegernsee landscape, one of
his most beautiful works, Kobell's watercolor
technique reaches its acme. While the compositional principles have remained the same as in
his previous works, the expressiveness has been
heightened here through the reduction and concentration of the motifs, and the refinement of
the delicately modulated watercolor tones has
been raised to the level of perfection. All this
becomes clear if we compare this work to his
watercolors executed more than thirty years earlier (cat. 65, 66). The figural composition on the
foreground stage remains the dominant feature.
With its clearly defined contours, the figure
group stands out silhouette-like against the

mountain scenery in the distance, which fades to
an airy and indistinct blue.

Compared to the earlier works, the composition
is freer. Due to the reduction in the number of
figures, which no longer overlap, and to their
inaction—literally a standstill—the image is
even more serene. Breathless calm and a glassy
clarity characterize the scene. Not a single breeze
stirs on this clear, fresh summer day. Long shadows indicate that the early morning sun is still
low in the sky. The country horsemen who have
encountered one another stand motionless under
the tall blue sky, each pausing in his momentary
position as though frozen or petrified, as in a photograph. The same is true for the figures in the
background. The last decade of Kobell's activity
would overlap chronologically with the earliest,
still-life-like products of photography, with
which his nephew, the mineralogist and poet
Franz von Kobell (1803–1882), experimented. In
the present watercolor, it almost seems as though
precious porcelain figurines have been composed
into a figural still life. Time itself seems to pause.
The desire to give permanence to what is unpretentiously picturesque, the harmonious and
happy moment when people meet in the beauty
of nature, may have inspired Kobell to create his
figural still lifes, which are unique in their technical precision. Their fascination results not so
much from the charm of naive simplicity as
from the magic of the static. In their isolation
and still-life-like character, the figures may
remind us of the pointillist works of the French
painter Georges Seurat. Both artists—Kobell
with an extreme realism of local color, Seurat
with a flat, abstracting screen of color—were
interested in the experience of light on the figures that was achieved by embedding them
within the natural fluctuation of light, though
the two did so with utterly different pictorial
techniques.

In Kobell's work there are many precursors for
every figure in its particular posture. Kobell
developed his figural types and landscape set-
tings into a visual vocabulary, and he knew how
to combine them again and again in new and
imaginative constellations, new pictorial poems
that also reflected the change of mood condi-
tioned by the weather (cf. cat. 66). Kobell also
exploited these possibilities commercially in his
etchings, which were circulated in editions: the
prints were worked up with watercolor and
finished to varying degrees, depending on the
price. The great mastery of this artist, who was so
important to the painting of the Biedermeier
period and for the early Munich landscape
school, expresses itself in his creativity in working with a limited repertoire. He presumably
owed his additive method to his uncle Franz
Kobell, with whom he lived in a joint household.
The latter had conceived of his landscapes as a

stage on which he constantly created new compositions with a limited stock of elements (cat. 3).
Eight years later, Kobell painted a second version
in oil after this watercolor, in which he paid
attention to the most minute detail (fig.).[1] The
painting is an exact copy; even the dimensions
are nearly identical. The width of the panel
exceeds that of the watercolor by about two cen-
timeters, with the motif extended correspond-
ingly, perhaps an indication that the watercolor
may have been trimmed slightly on the sides.
The existence of the oil attests that painted versions of a subject were occasionally commissioned after watercolor originals. As for the
motifs, there are only very minor, barely
detectable changes. Even the handling of the
light is the same, down to the narrow band of
shadow cast by the elevation at the upper edge of
the foreground plateau as a result of the sun's low
position in the sky. In the oil version, the white
horse in the watercolor has become a gray horse,
the patches of grass are green rather than a burnt
brown, and the wagon tracks are not as faint. On
the whole, the coloration is cooler and stronger in
the oil painting, more delicate and transparent in
the watercolor.

1 Wichmann 1970, no. 1587. The painting was sold in May
of 1993 by Christie's, London. I would like to thank Lord
Poltimore of Christie's for securing permission to reproduce the painting, and Christie's Images of London for
providing a slide of it.

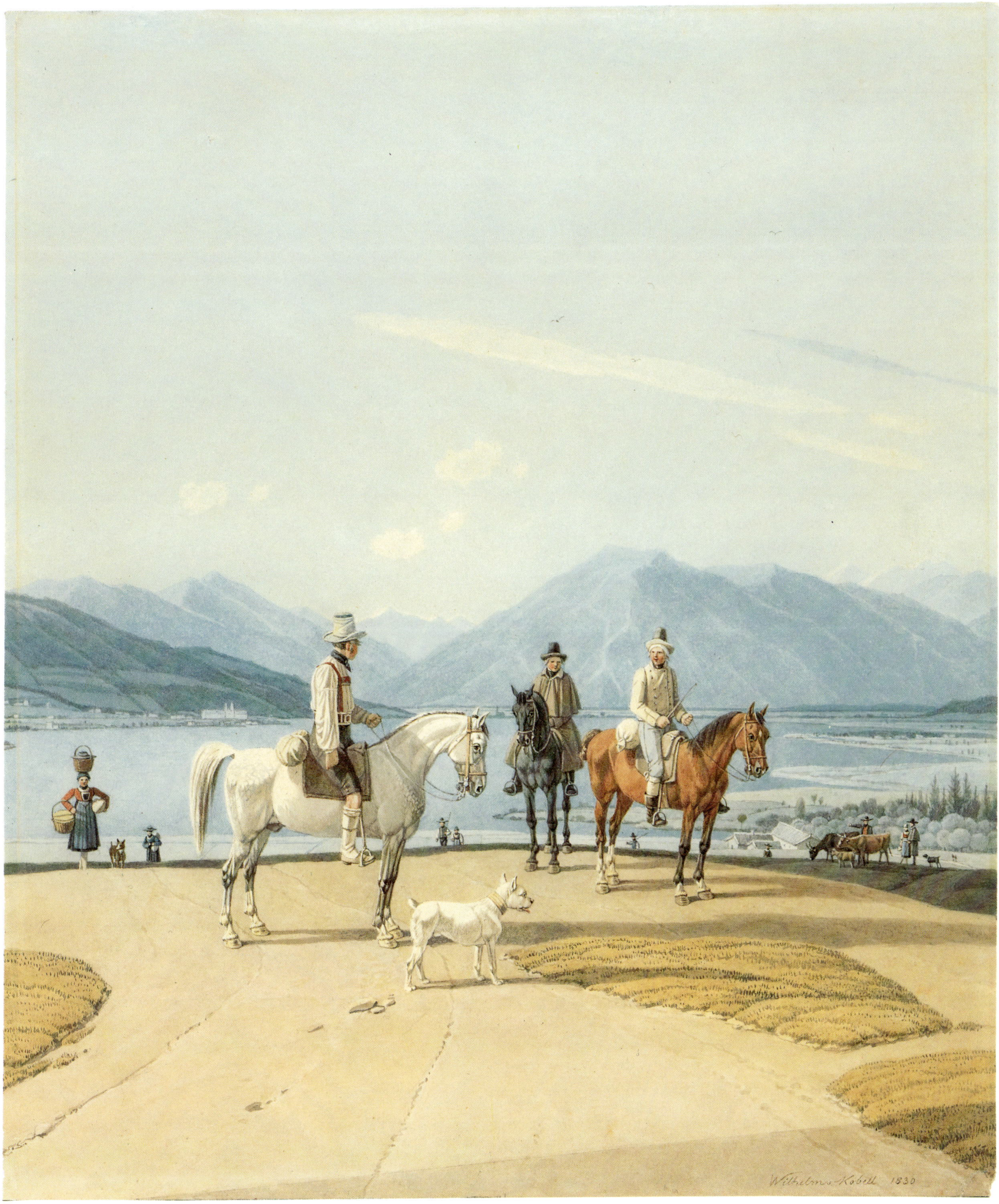
Wilhelm v. Kobell 1830

68

Joseph Karl Stieler

Mainz 1 November 1781–9 April 1858 Munich

Portrait of King Ludwig I of Bavaria, 1825/26

Watercolor over pencil on prepared paper; 493 x 402 mm; mounted on canvas

Provenance: Stieler estate, Munich

Bibliography: Munich 1958, p. 57, no. 165, p. 13 (repr.); Messerer 1966, fig. 1 (frontispiece); Lübeck 1969, p. 98, no. 187, p. 99 (repr.); Ulrike von Hase, Joseph Stieler 1781–1858: Sein Leben und Werk. Kritisches Verzeichnis der Werke (Munich, 1971), pp. 67–69, 68 f., 130 f., no. 122a (repr.)

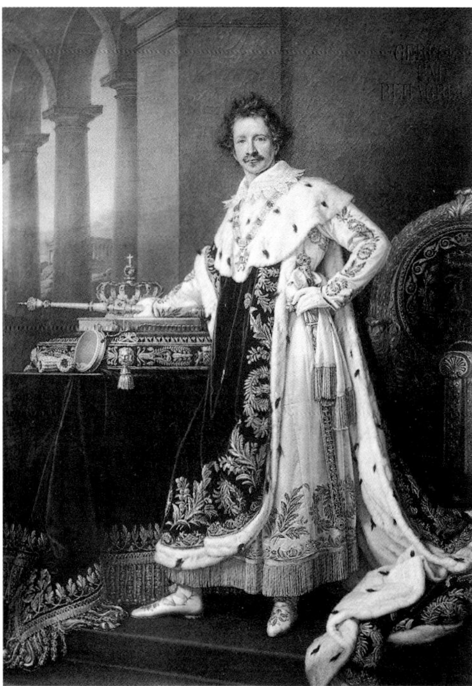

Joseph Stieler, *Ludwig I King of Bavaria in His Coronation Robes and Regalia*, 1826. Munich, Bayerische Staatsgemäldesammlungen, inv. no. 8235

Among the German princes of the nineteenth century, none played as important a role as a collector and a patron of architecture and art as the crown prince, later King Ludwig I of Bavaria—with the single exception of his own brother-in-law, Frederick William IV of Prussia. As sovereign, Ludwig combined political and artistic kingship in a unique way.[1]

Ludwig was born in 1786 in Strasbourg, the eldest son of Maximilian I Joseph, king of Bavaria, and his first wife, Wilhelmine Auguste, princess of Hesse Darmstadt. In 1810 Ludwig married Therese, princess of Saxony-Hildburghausen. He succeeded his father to the throne in 1825 and reigned until his resignation in 1848. Ludwig died in Nice in 1868 at the age of eighty-two.

Immediately following Ludwig's accession to the throne in October of 1825, Stieler was commissioned to paint the official portrait of the king in his coronation robes and regalia. With assistance from his student and nephew, Friedrich Dürck, he finished it in 1826 (fig.); various replicas of this painting exist.[2] There are very few works in Stieler's oeuvre whose process of creation is as well documented as that of the coronation picture, an important work for patron and artist alike. In preparation for his portraits, Stieler occasionally executed summary outline drawings in chalk or pencil that are studies of poses or proportions. One such study for the coronation picture has been preserved.[3] After that he usually began to paint directly on the final canvas without any detail studies. He used oil sketches primarily to clarify the colors. The reason he prepared a detailed study of the face in this case may be that Stieler needed it as the basis for his original painting and for replicas, since Ludwig was stingy with his time and was not available for additional sittings.

This frontal study—plain, spontaneous, and captured directly from life—recalls the portraits painted by Jacques Louis David, both stylistically and in the application of the colors like a wash on a light background. It shows the king in tangible proximity, and at the same time at a lonely distance, capturing both the individuality and royal dignity of the young ruler who has just ascended the throne. The study reflects intellectual alertness and open-mindedness. The view from below compels the viewer to look up at the face, but Ludwig does not appear to be fixing his gaze on the viewer with a sense of superiority, as he does in the finished painting; rather, he is self-conscious, with a pensive, shy air. In the slightly tilted head and on his lips lies the expression of a strong, almost stubborn "I," which bespeaks self-confidence and a sense of political responsibility. Ludwig's hairstyle contrasts with the shy seriousness and concentrated expression of his face. The locks that protrude ornamentally may have been a stylistic technique of Neoclassical portraiture intended to evoke heroic or geniuslike traits, or they may have been intended to express freedom, sovereignty, and a liberal attitude.[4] They surround his head like flickering flames. Ludwig had a burning passion for life, for beauty, and for art. His raised head with its lively hair suggests dynamic energy and creative restiveness, qualities that reflect the strong will and restlessness of Ludwig as a person and as a monarch.

This compelling study thus served as the model for the coronation picture. For the formal structure and decorative details of the latter, Stieler consciously drew on François Gérard's official portrait of Napoleon I in his coronation robes and regalia.[5] Ten years earlier, Ludwig, who had openly opposed Napoleon, had himself portrayed by Stieler dressed in an early German coat, a provocative sign of his patriotism. That he now had himself portrayed in the tradition of the Napoleonic ruler portrait reflects his affirmation of the young kingdom of Bavaria, established by Napoleon in 1806 through the Bavarian-French alliance. The official representative style created by French artists under Napoleon would exert a dominant influence in Bavaria. In contrast to the pose his father struck in his coronation picture of 1822,[6] Ludwig grasps the scepter, which rests on top of the constitutional charter, firmly in his right hand and rests his left hand on the sword by his side: programmatic clues that he is determined to rule on his own and to have his way, on the basis of the constitution and with faithfulness to the motto that is visible above the throne: "Just and steadfast."[7]

In the background of the finished coronation picture, Stieler includes a view of Valhalla, above which rays of sun symbolically break through. The final location of Valhalla in Donaustauf had been decided upon that same year, 1826. Its inclusion here is a programmatic allusion to Ludwig's patriotic desire for national unity, on the one hand, and to his love for art and architecture and his philhellenism, on the other. The arcade-like view takes up an architectural motif—modeled after Raphael's Vatican *Loggie*—in Klenze's plan for the Pinakothek, construction of which also began in 1826. This is a clear reference to Ludwig's prodigious building and collecting activities, the fruits of which remain essential for Munich's reputation as a city of the arts.

1 On Ludwig's personality, see Heinz Gollwitzer, *Ludwig I. von Bayern, Königtum im Vormärz: Eine politische Biographie* (Munich, 1986), pp. 248–61.
2 Von Hase 1971, p. 131, no. 123; p. 125, no. 72. Ludwig's portrait is exhibited in the Alte Pinakothek (Galerie der Stifter aus dem Hause Wittelsbach).
3 Von Hase no. 121.
4 Ludwig took a special interest in the depiction of the hair; von Hase 1971, p. 67 f., n. 306. Messerer 1966, p. 625, no. 574, letter dated 4 July 1827.
5 Von Hase 1971, pp. 67 ff., fig. A10.
6 *Ibid.*, p. 127, no. 88 (repr.).
7 Cf. *"Vorwärts, vorwärts sollst du schauen…." Geschichte, Politik und Kunst unter Ludwig I*, ed. Johannes Erichsen et al., exh. cat., Nuremberg, Germanisches Nationalmuseum (Munich, 1986), p. 26, no. 4, p. 82 (repr.).

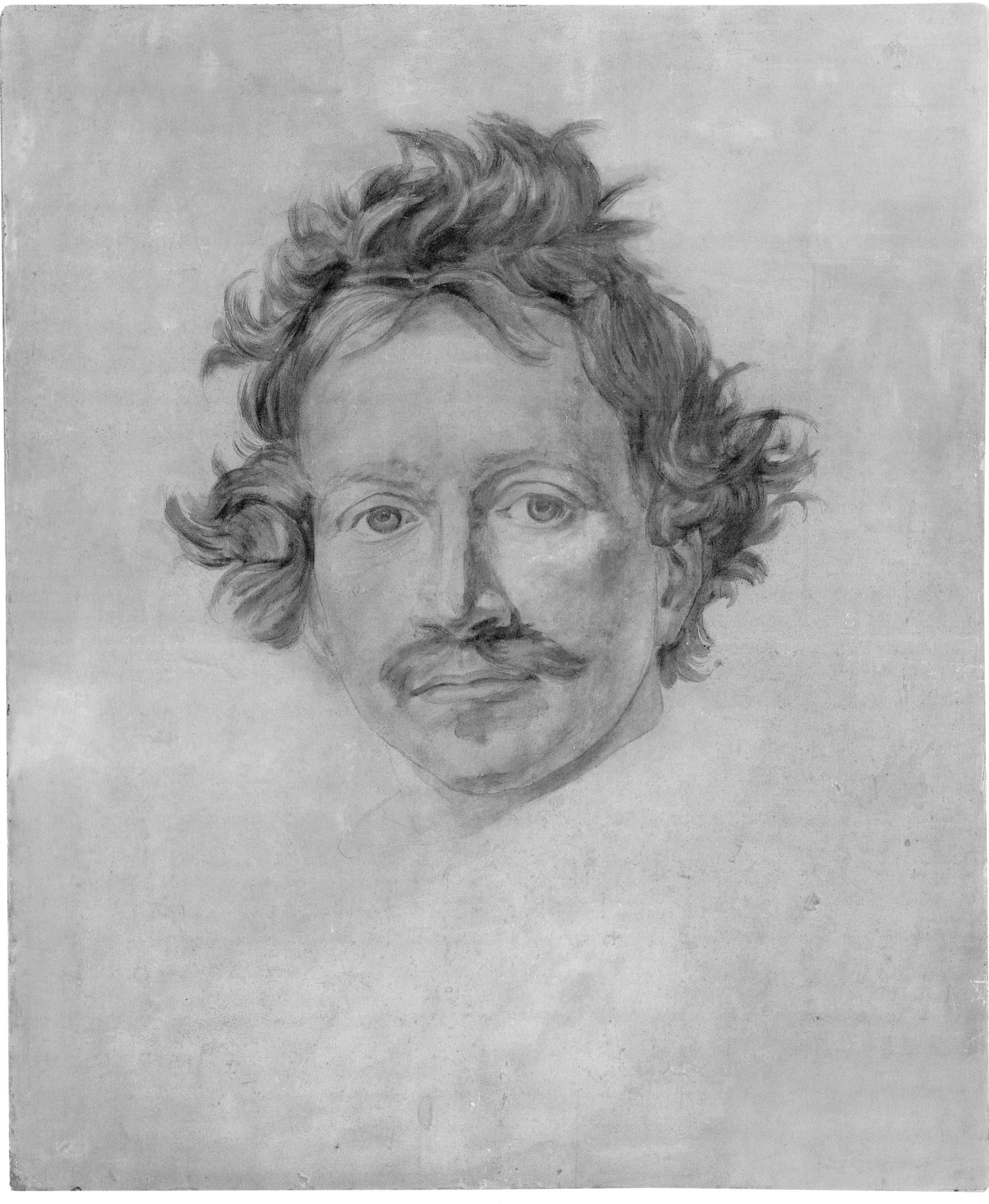

69

Leo von Klenze

Bockenem near Hildesheim
28 February 1784 – 27 January 1864 Munich

Terrace of the Inn "al Angelo" in Bellinzona,
1843

Watercolor over pencil, on heavy wove paper;
238 x 300 mm; partial border in pencil; trimmed on all sides
Provenance: Estate of Leo von Klenze

Bibliography: Munich 1958, p. 36, no. 80; Lübeck 1969,
p. 51, no. 83; Leo von Klenze als Maler und Zeichner
1784 –1864, ed. Norbert Lieb and Florian Hufnagl, with
contributions by Oswald Hederer and Norbert Lieb, exh.
cat., Bayerische Akademie der Schönen Künste (Munich,
1977), p. 129, no. Z.233a (repr.); Norbert Lieb and Florian
Hufnagl, Leo von Klenze: Gemälde und Zeichnungen
(Munich, 1979), p. 201, No. Z.271 (repr.)

In addition to his architectural designs, Klenze left behind an abundance of drawings, watercolors, and sketches, most of which he created during his travels. He traveled fairly frequently to northern Italy, in part for family reasons, since his wife was from Turin. All roads connecting the lands north of the Alps and Italy, which at the time led across the St. Gotthard and San Bernardino passes, crossed the narrow valley of Bellinzona, the capital of the Swiss canton of Ticino. Today the skyline of the town is still dominated by three massive medieval castles, which the Visconti and the Sforza, the rulers of Milan, erected against the Swiss Confederacy. Klenze occasionally stopped over in Bellinzona, and this is where he painted the present watercolor. We know that this site was in Bellinzona from a pencil drawing in Munich. Its view is largely identical with the one here, and Klenze inscribed it "Bellenz," the Swiss German name of the town, and dated it to 29 August 1843 (fig.).

We are probably looking at the roof terrace of one of the old fortifications, with a corner tower whose merlons are covered by a vine bower—a place with a lovely panoramic view of the surrounding mountains. Apparently the inn "al Angelo," where Klenze took lodging, had established itself in this picturesque location.

In the literature we find the unanimous opinion that the pencil drawing in Munich is a preliminary study for the watercolor. But a comparison of the two, which provides interesting insight into Klenze's manner of working, reveals that both were created independently on the spot. At first glance the two sheets already show significant differences in format and technique, and a closer look reveals that the artist chose a different vantage point for each. In the watercolor, the vantage point is elevated so much that the view of the landscape has been considerably expanded, and the corner tower of the citadel is perceived, not so much in close-up and from below as in the drawing, but almost at a distance and from above. Compared to the much smaller watercolor, the contour drawing in pencil offers a precise rendering of the scene, in the manner of a *veduta*. Klenze was given to drawing such views from nature in pencil with a fine contour line and careful attention to detail. On the left edge of the sheet he would often, as in the Munich drawing, divide off a narrow vertical margin for notes. There he would write, one below the other, a series of signs—such as a cross, a circle, and so on—and numerals, each with indications of color. He meticulously dispersed these signs, indicating local colors and the play of light, across the entire surface of the picture; to some, he added further handwritten notes. In this way the scene, including coloration, was securely recorded for subsequent reworking. And Klenze did in fact use these drawings for the execution of oil paintings at a later time; about twenty examples are known. The effect of such a composition transferred into an oil painting could be a static

one, reminiscent of colored *veduta* painting, but Klenze knew how to avoid such an impression by embedding the composition in an atmospheric light.

The present watercolor was composed differently, although its sketchlike, unfinished character indicates that it too was done on-site. First Klenze used a ruler to draw in the perspective lines of the terrace wall and the flagstones, in this way providing his composition with a grid for surface and depth. He applied the watercolor quickly over a summary pencil sketch, paying no attention to the color indications in the pencil drawing. The sunlight falling from the side and the strong shadow lines contribute to the impression of spatial depth and help shape the three-dimensional structures of the medieval architecture. The tension created by the perspective lines and the shadow lines leads the viewers gaze into depth, reinforced further by the tattered clouds that seem to hurry toward the vanishing point diagonally from the top left. Klenze's sense of color also reveals itself in the subtle observation of the bluish shadows. In the interplay between light and shadow, and in the clarity of the southern light, Klenze vividly and spontaneously captured his experience of this panoramic view.

A fondness for medieval architecture[1] links this watercolor to works by Gilly (cat. 75), Olivier (cat. 34), Blechen (cat. 77), and Wagenbauer (cat. 62). Klenze's linear perspectival construction, and the cubic, three-dimensional quality of the old building reveal the hand of the architect. The choice of subject also reveals the interest of the preservationist, architectural scholar, and archaeologist, further evidenced by the rendering of the stone slab leaning against the wall, which displays the serpentine coat of arms of the Visconti family. In his oil paintings, drawings, and watercolors, Klenze preferred the architectural object and architecture that had been integrated into the landscape. Depicting architecture was especially important to him, and he sought for it a "worthy scenographic picture," a kind of landscape passe-partout. The balanced relationship between architecture and surrounding landscape in this watercolor is characteristic of Klenze's work.

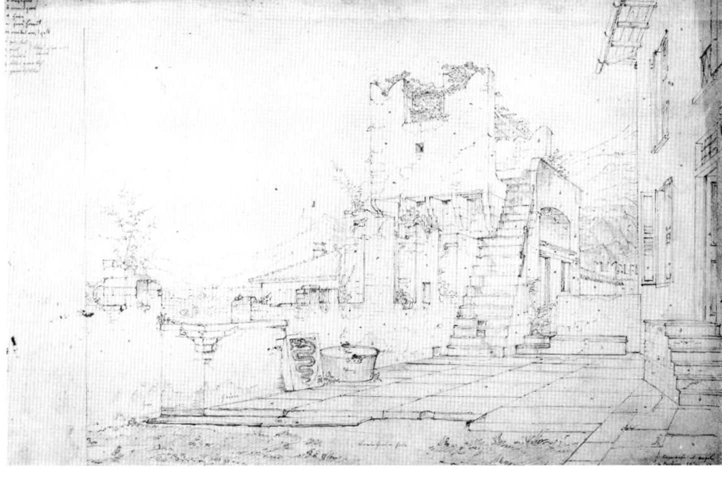

Leo von Klenze, *Terrace "al Angelo" in Bellenz, 29 Aug. 43.* Pencil, 333 x 502 mm. Munich, Staatliche Graphische Sammlung, inv. no. 27.778

---

1 Norbert Lieb, who saw a "Romantic" component in Klenze's fondness for medieval citadels, pointed to the influence of northern Italian and Venetian stage painting in Klenze's pictures of Bellinzona. On the pencil drawing of the inn "al Angelo" in Bellinzona, dated 1843, cf. Lieb and Hufnagl 1979, p. 51 f.

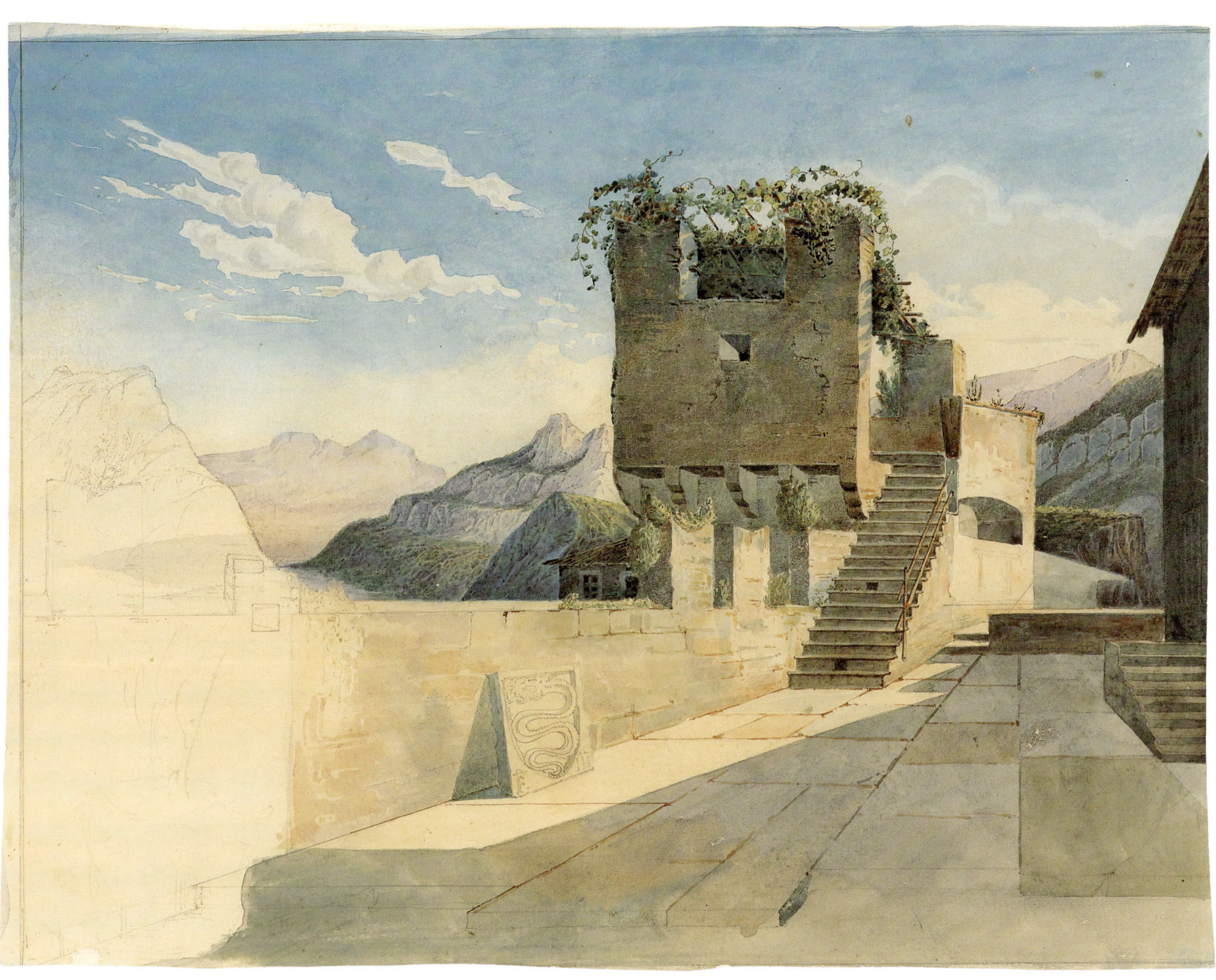

70

Carl Rottmann

Handschuhsheim near Heidelberg
11 January 1797–7 July 1850 Munich

Campagna Landscape near Aqua Acetosa,
1826/27

Watercolor over pencil, pen in gray-black ink, on heavy
wove paper; 337 x 581 mm
Inscribed in pencil, lower right: "Aqua Cetosa"
Verso, in pencil: study of the same view

Provenance: von Passavant-Gontard, Frankfurt am Main

Bibliography: "Carl Rottmann, Cartons und Naturstudien
aus dem künstlerischen Nachlasse desselben," in Verzeichnis der Werke hiesiger und auswärtiger Künstler, welche
auf der diesjährigen von der K. B. Akademie der bildenden Künste veranstalteten 13. Kunstausstellung sich be-
finden *(Munich, 1851), p. 35, no. 449; Decker 1957, p. 68,*
no. 249, fig. 50; Munich 1958, p. 50, no. 142; Robels 1974,
p. 92, pl. 51 (in color); Bierhaus-Rödiger 1978, p. 188,
cat. raisonné no. 92 (repr.); Munich 1979, p. 316, no. 280
(repr.); Carl Rottmann 1797–1850, Kartons, Aquarelle,
Zeichnungen, *ed. Barbara Strieder with a contribution by*
Peter Märker (Darmstadt, 1989), p. 50, under no. 14

A diary entry by Ludwig Richter helps us recapture some of the magic and uniqueness of the
landscape depicted here, today lost in the dull
uniformity of Rome's suburbs. Richter had just
left Rome to return to Germany when Rottmann
arrived in the city. On 6 December 1824, Richter
recorded his experience of the landscape, which
Rottmann depicted exactly two years later, also
in the winter from nearly the same vantage
point.

"In the afternoon I went out to Aqua Acetosa by
myself. I sat on the bank of the treacherous, rushing Tiber and drew. Here the river makes a bend
through the expansive valley of the Campagna,
where countless herds of sheep, cows, and horses
are pastured and give the area a truly oriental
appearance. Pallid clouds drifted in the still air,
the pale half-light of the slightly overcast sky
cast a charm all its own over the dying autumn
landscape, only here and there a little dark blue
shimmered through the streaky cloud cover. The
area made an impression on me quite like the
feelings I have in front of Nicolas Poussin's landscapes: a profound seriousness of emotion and a
gentle longing, which truly warms the heart.
The sweet silence that lay over the broad, tranquil fields aroused the feeling of solitude, only
the Tiber river, which spread out in front of me
broad and shining, rushed along in its meander-
ing path and sparkled in the distance; its turbid,
muddy surface concealed the dangerous depth.
Not far from there . . . was perhaps the spot where
the great and noble Fohr was pulled down by the
malicious water spirits.[1] There is splendor in a
broad river that winds its way shimmeringly
through the landscape, as in Raphael's *Draught*
of Fishes. . . . Evening fell. . . . It got cool; I sketched
quite a few other things besides."[2]

Rottmann drew and painted this watercolor
landscape study from nature during his winter
sojourn in Rome from 4 October 1826 to March
1827. The watercolor was done from a rise above
Aqua Acetosa, with a distant view northward
across the large loop of the Tiber and the Tiber
Valley in the Roman Campagna. In the far distance, more or less in the middle of the picture,
arises a landmark of the Campagna landscape:
the prominent silhouette of Mount Soracte, an
extraordinarily beautiful site that was depicted
many times by different artists.[3] Goethe, who
had tasted the waters of the mineral spring *(aqua*
acetosa) located there, already raved about the
place in 1787: "It is truly enough to drive you
crazy when you look at the clarity, the variety,
the airy transparency and heavenly coloration of
the landscape, especially the distance."[4]

The watercolor here, grandly composed in a
large, horizontal format, is marvelous for the way
it has captured the clarity of the light and the
immense distance. As the sky is reflected in the
water of the Tiber, the watercolor itself reflects
the artist's enthusiasm at finding himself face-to-
face with such natural beauty.

The artistic yield of Rottmann's first trip to Italy,
undertaken privately and at his own expense, as
well as the good offices of his friend Leo von
Klenze, court architect in Munich, won him an
important commission from King Ludwig I of
Bavaria: Rottmann was asked to decorate the
walls of the western arcades of the Hofgarten
with a fresco cycle of twenty-eight Italian landscapes. As part of the redesign of the Hofgarten,
a cycle with Greek landscapes was later planned
for the northern arcades (cf. cat. 71).

Rottmann undertook a second trip to Italy in
1829 at the king's request, and for the express
purpose of creating more landscapes. The king
decided on the pictorial program and exerted
considerable influence on the execution of the
individual paintings with respect to the vantage
point, composition, and choice of motifs. In the
manner of a "Journey to Italy in Pictures," the
landscapes followed a route from north to south,
with stops from Trent and the Gorge of Verona
down to Sicily, including Cefalu; the king added
descriptive couplets to each place. Aqua Acetosa
appeared between Perugia and Rome as the fifth
stop on this imaginary journey. This vantage
point at the old mineral spring, for which
Bernini had once erected a well house, had a very
personal meaning for Ludwig. To this day a marble plaque recalls that in 1821, Crown Prince
Ludwig of Bavaria had trees planted and benches
erected at this site. For the execution of the
fresco, Rottmann was able to consult the present
landscape, one of the few he could put to use
from his first trip to Italy. Compared to this
watercolor view, painted with unconstrained
freshness directly from nature, the finished
fresco shows a number of significant changes,
surely the result of Ludwig's influence. For
example, by manipulating the vantage point, he
increased Mount Soracte's height, pulled the
ruined well house into the center of the picture,
and moved the loop of the river to the right margin. The purpose of these changes was to increase
the impact of these scenically important motifs,
and to turn the landscape as a whole into something monumental.[5]

The cycle, executed by Rottmann in fresco
between 1830 and 1834, seems like a textbook of
a visionary history of Italy as seen through landscape, and at the same time a monument to its
royal patron, who had found his spiritual home
in that country. King Ludwig I composed this
distich for the finished fresco of Aqua Acetosa:

"Flieh aus den Mauern von Rom, um Rom das
alte zu fühlen,

Flieh in die Einsamkeit her, wo es sich lebet dem
Geist."

[Escape the walls of Rome to feel the Rome of
old,

Escape into this solitude, where it lives in the
spirit.]

1 Carl Philipp Fohr (1795–1818), cf. cat. 45–48.
2 Richter 1909, p. 523 f.
3 For example, in an "idealized" manner by J. A. Koch in
  1812, cf. Vienna 1990, p. 65, no. 8 (repr. in color).
4 Quoted in Femmel 1955, p. 35. Goethe himself sketched a
  view of "Acqua Acetosa," cf. ibid., p. 34 f., no. 15 (repr.).
  On 5 July 1787, he noted of the fountain: "In the morning
  I rise with the sun and go to Acqua Acetosa, a mineral
  spring, about half an hour from the gate where I am staying. I drink the water, which tastes like a weak Schwal-
  bacher [a German mineral water], but it is very effective
  in this climate." *Ibid.*
5 Cf. Bierhaus-Rödiger 1978, p. 188, no. 92 (repr.), pp. 214 f.,
  no. 169 (repr.), pp. 230 ff., nos. 205–7 (repr.).

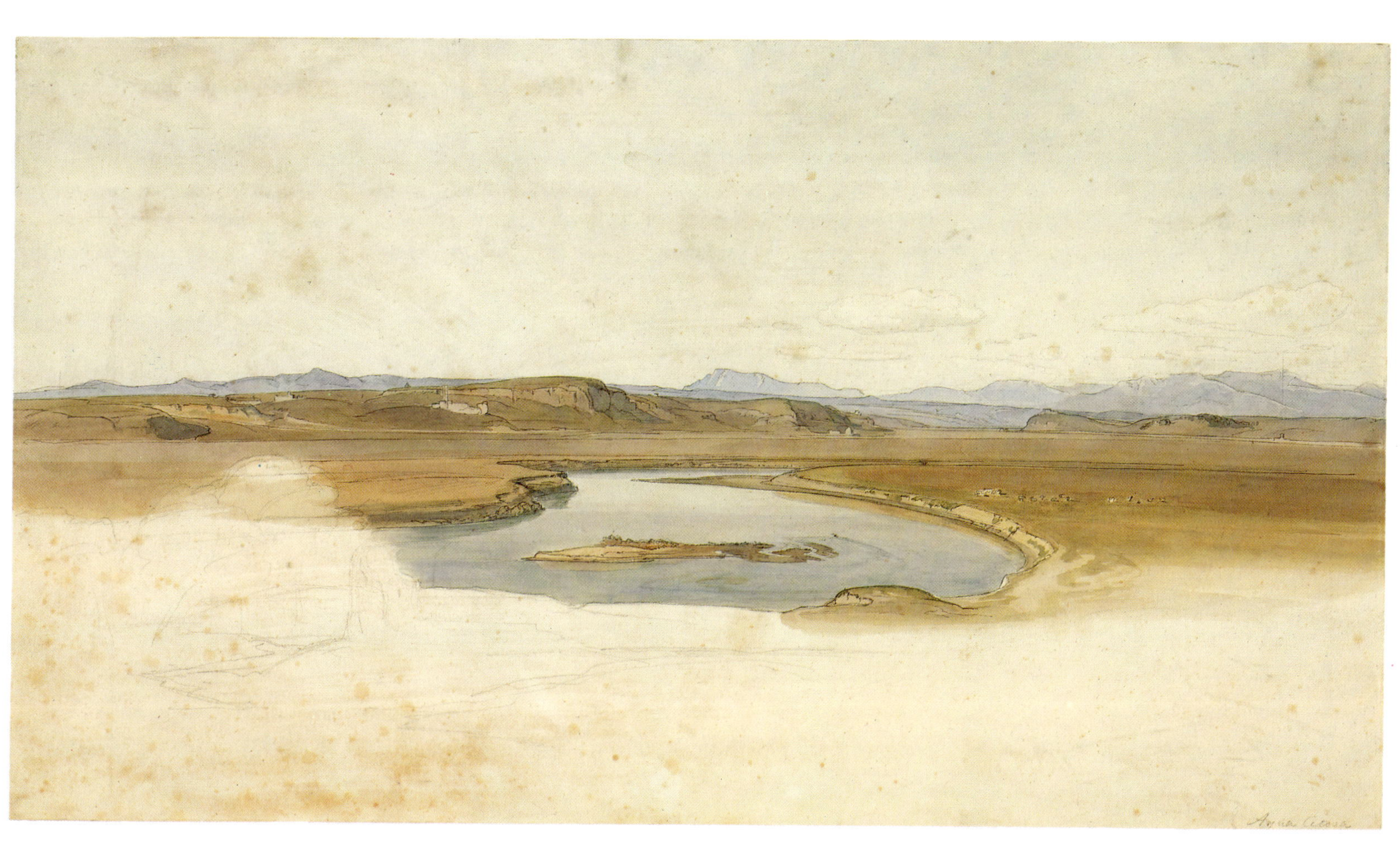
Aqua Cetosa

71

Carl Rottmann

Marathon, c. 1848

Watercolor, pencil, pen and gray and brown ink, height-
ened with white, on heavy brownish paper with rough
surface; 280/2 x 354/5 mm
Verso: sketch of the same landscape in pencil, squared

Provenance: Dr. von Bassermann-Jordan

Bibliography: Decker 1957, p. 90, no. 630; Munich 1958, p. 50
no. 143; Lübeck 1969, p. 80, no. 156

The enthusiasm for Greek art and civilization
cultivated by the humanistically educated King
Ludwig I of Bavaria was the driving force behind
many of his cultural achievements. He sought to
transform Munich into an Athens on the Isar. As
a philhellenic ruler he made a significant contribution in support of the Greeks' successful war of
independence against the Turks. As early as 1832
he planned an extensive cycle of thirty-eight
frescoes depicting Greek landscapes to decorate
the arcades of the Hofgarten in Munich, even

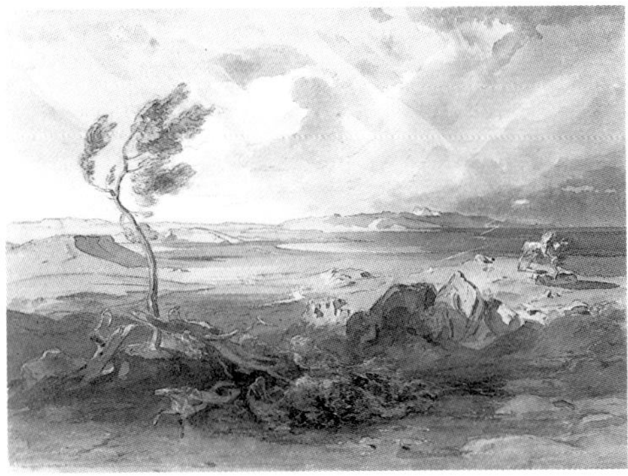

1 Carl Rottmann, *Marathon*, c. 1841.
Watercolor over pencil, 287 x 382 mm. Munich,
Staatliche Graphische Sammlung, inv. no. 21386

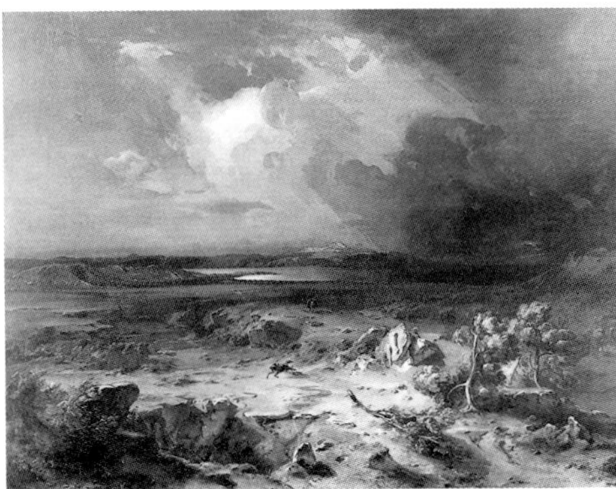

2 Carl Rottmann, *Marathon*, 1848. Encaustic on concrete;
157 x 200 cm. Munich, Bayerische Staatsgemäldesammlungen, inv. no. WAF 860; cat. raisonné 613

before the cycle with Italian landscapes was complete (cat. 70). Rottmann, who painted the Italian views in the Hofgarten arcades, was also
given the commission for Greek landscapes;
however, the latter were to be painted, not in
fresco, but in encaustic, that is, with wax as the
binding medium.

The occasion for this project was the proclamation of Otto I, Ludwig's son, as king of Greece. In
1833, Otto set foot on Greek soil. The following
year Rottmann traveled through Greece at Ludwig's behest to record the precise topographical
setting at sites of historical and mythological
importance. He returned in 1835 with a rich haul
of drawings and watercolors. His actual work on
the cycle, however, did not begin until 1838, and
it would drag on until 1850, the year of his death.
In 1839, the original plan of mounting the paintings under the arcades of the Hofgarten was
given up; in 1843, Ludwig I decided to give the
cycle a room in the Neue Pinakothek, then in the
planning stage. Finally, the number of pictures
was reduced from thirty-eight to twenty-three.
These constant changes had a considerable effect
on the preparatory process. The work was complicated and extensive, involving compositional
sketches in pencil done from nature and in the
studio, compositional designs in watercolor, oil
paintings, and the finished murals.

The encaustic painting *Marathon* was executed
between April and December of 1848. Early in
the summer of 1835, Rottmann had undertaken
an excursion from Athens to the nearby site of
Marathon. There he drew the topographical situation—the view across the Attic coast with the
bay of Marathon to the island of Euboea in the
background—that one can still recognize clearly
in the present watercolor. A pencil study, a pure
veduta created on the spot, has been preserved
in the Staatliche Graphische Sammlung in
Munich.[1] The catalogue raisonné by Erika Bierhaus-Rödiger lists various representations of
Marathon, from this initial pencil sketch to the
last oil painting (now in the Nationalgalerie,
Berlin),[2] a dramatically abstract work with a
Turnerlike battle of the elements. Among all
these versions, the present watercolor, which is
not listed in the catalogue, is closest to the final
encaustic painting in Munich in overall mood,
colors, and details of the motifs (fig. 2). It should
therefore be dated accordingly. Perhaps it was a
late alternative compositional design for the
painting, in which the artist did one more study
of the light; the squared drawing on the back
would support such a view. In all likelihood it
was created during the work on the large, commissioned piece. The careful, pictorial finish
indicates that it was probably intended for sale to
a collector.

In this watercolor, as in the encaustic painting of
1848, Rottmann interpreted the landscape of

Marathon, site of the Athenians' victory over the
Persians in the decisive battle in 490 B.C., as a
place of profound historical importance by making dramatic use of natural forces such as a thunderstorm. The unleashed powers of nature were
incorporated into the scene for the first time in
his watercolor design in the Staatliche Graphische Sammlung in Munich (fig. 1),[3] as was the
dramatic motif of the riderless horse galloping
away in fear, perhaps a reference to the Marathon run. In the present watercolor, Rottmann
was not concerned with rendering a topographically accurate landscape or illustrating the historical event; that would have been a theme for
the dominant genre of history painting. Instead,
his interest lay in the significance of this battle,
so decisive for the history of the West. The year
this watercolor was painted, 1848, was a year of
revolution and King Ludwig's abdication. In the
drama of the representation we can see reflections of the events of the day, as well as allusions
to the Greeks' war of independence against the
Turks. *Marathon* was thus both a historical as
well as a contemporary or "political" work,
which is confirmed by the high esteem it enjoyed
among contemporaries.[4] *Marathon* was considered to be the most beautiful painting in the
entire Greek landscape cycle.[5]

1 Cf. Bierhaus-Rödiger 1978, pp. 523 f., no. 442 (repr.).

2 *Ibid.*, pp. 523 f., no. 442 (pencil, Munich), pp. 383 ff.,
  nos. 609–13, p. 392, no. 625, p. 416, no. 698 (oil, Berlin),
  in each case with repr. Cf. also Decker 1957, p. 90.

3 Cf. Scheffler and Hardtwig 1979, p. 82, no. 90, color pl. 23.

4 Bierhaus-Rödiger 1978, pp. 384 f., no. 613 (repr.). Cf.
  Warnke 1992, p. 144, fig. 131; Busch 1985, pp. 298 ff., 300,
  fig. 101; Busch in Frankfurt 1994, p. 497, fig. 8. Cf. also
  Ludwig Lange, *Die griechischen Landschaftsgemälde von*
  Karl Rottmann in der königlichen Pinakothek zu München
  (Munich, 1854), pp. 22 f.

5 In 1854, the Munich Kunstverein published, as its annual
  gift, a galvanotype by Leo Schöninger after Rottmann's
  encaustic painting *The Battlefield of Marathon*; cf. Langenstein 1983, p. 293, 1854.

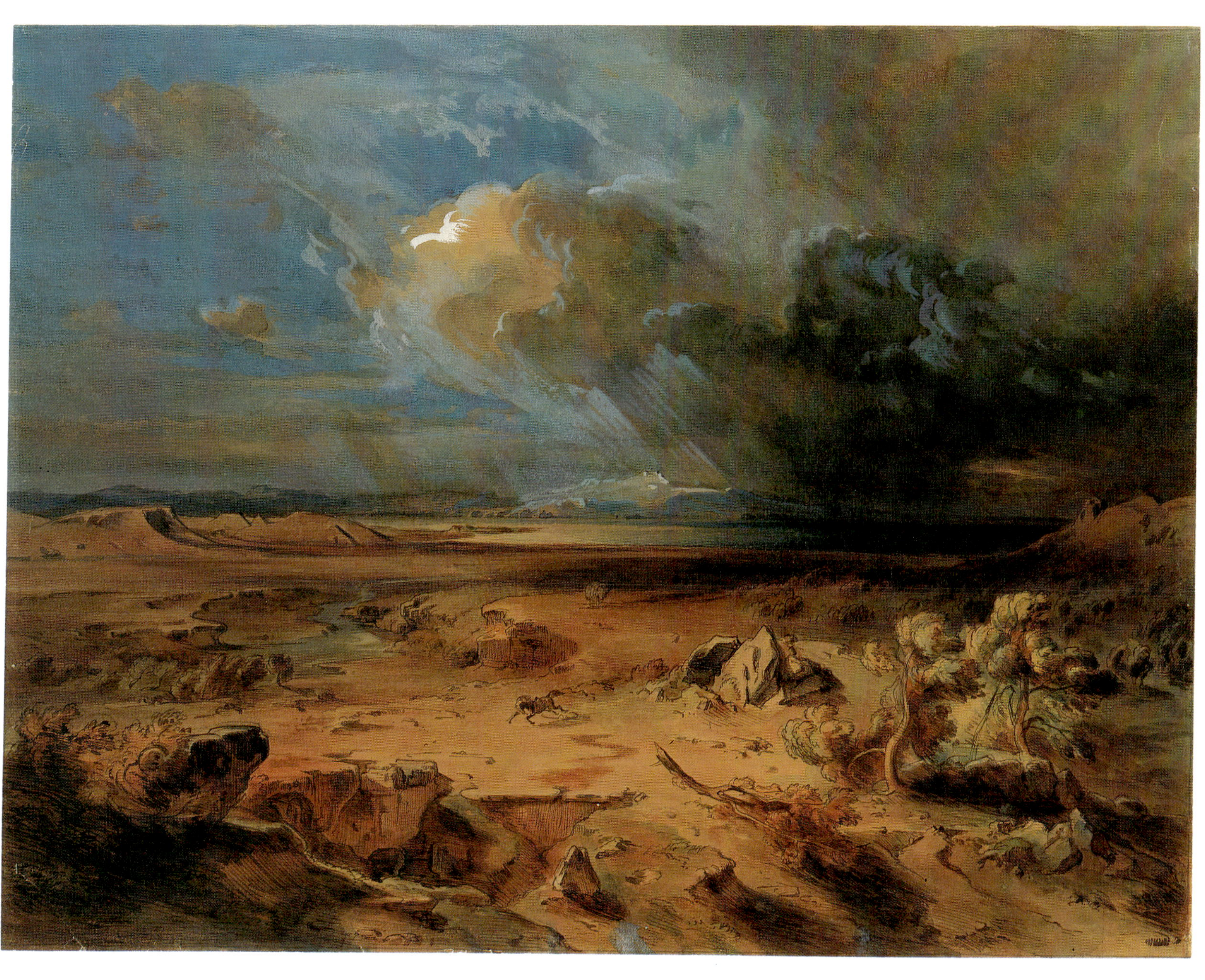

72

Carl Gustav Carus

Leipzig 3 January 1789 – 28 July 1869 Dresden

Castel dell' Ovo in Naples, 1828

Oil on pencil, on wove paper, mounted on card;
238 x 276 mm
Verso inscribed by another hand in indelible ink:
"C. G. Carus / Castel del Ovo"

Provenance: Johann Friedrich Lahmann, Dresden; Rudolf
Hintze, Stettin (Lugt 2215a)

Bibliography: Gerda Grashoff, "Carus als Maler"
(Ph.D. diss., Münster, 1926), pp. 37, 47; Munich 1958, p. 20,
no. 4; Heidelberg 1964, p. 36, no. 72; Lübeck 1969, p. 17, no. 6;
Munich 1995, p. 662, no. 94, p. 179 (repr. in color)

The physician and naturalist Carus, a man of universal talent and education, was also a very active artist and writer. In 1827 he became personal physician to the royal house of Saxony, and in that capacity he traveled to Italy in the spring of 1828 to accompany Prince Frederick August, who had an interest in art and the natural sciences. The trip involved stops in Rome and Naples. From May 4 to 19 the traveling party was in Naples, living in what is today the Via Chiatamone, "in the graceful and delicate Casino Reale—whose furnishings go back to Joachim Murat—at the edge of the bay and across from the old Castello dell'Ovo."

On the very first evening Carus separated from his companions to climb to the tomb of Virgil to draw, always keeping in sight "the view toward Castel S. Elmo and dell'Ovo, toward the sea and Vesuvius."[1] From his south-facing room he enjoyed a view of "Vesuvius, the sea, the castle, and the blue distance!" with the Sorrento peninsula and the island of Capri on the horizon. It was from here that he depicted the medieval Castel dell'Ovo in the present oil sketch; it is seen from the narrow side in a north-south orientation, a vantage point from which the castle, with its sparse architectural articulation, seems defiant and unfriendly.

Seen from the east or the west, the mighty fortress stretches out in a panorama. Situated on a long jetty, it juts out from the shore promenade into the bay like an island. It was here that Conradin of Hohenstaufen spent the final weeks before his tragic death in 1268. The citadel, with its eerie appearance, now more, now less massive depending on the weather, and with corresponding reflections in the water, was often depicted in art. Johann Georg von Dillis, in a hasty sketch made on the spot, was intent on capturing the atmospheric silhouette effect in the moonlight.[2] During his first trip to Italy in 1803, Karl Friedrich Schinkel did a faithful, *veduta* in pencil and watercolor from the east, with Capri in the left background.[3] In 1839/40, the Danish landscapist and portraitist Christen Købke (1810–1848) painted an oil sketch on the site: in it, the grimy, dark citadel seems gilded and weightless in the gleaming sunlight.[4]

Significantly, Carus chose for his view of the Castel dell' Ovo a rather melancholy mood, in keeping with his background in the Dresden school. What fascinated him was not the luminous color contrasts in the bright light of the sun, but rather the broken, diffuse light of a foggy, damp, and hazy midday atmosphere in which the sky and the surface of the water seem to merge. The infinitude of the sky reflected in the water arouses feelings of yearning. The silhouette of the mighty fortress rises gloomily on the horizon in the diffuse midday light. In the right foreground is a small fishing boat, and another is visible in the distance along with some sailboats; these are indicators of proportion and spatial depth. In keeping with his scientific background, Carus had a sober eye for objective data in nature that predestined him to be a realist as a painter. In this work he succeeded definitely in conveying the transitory nature of the passing mood by capturing the atmospheric conditions.

The Dresden Kupferstichkabinett possesses three other small oil sketches by Carus with views of the Bay of Naples and the Sorrento peninsula on the horizon. In technique and coloration they are identical to the present oil, and their creation is evidently closely connected to it.[5] They all have in common the technique of delicate, light blue glazes over a light reddish ground on white paper, which was subsequently mounted on card. These are the delicate impressions of color as perceived through the eyes of a northerner. In a similar way—albeit after his return from Italy and working from memory—Ernst Ferdinand Oehme, the Dresden painter and pupil of Caspar David Friedrich, used a northern, specifically Dresden-school style to "Romanticize" an Italian seascape in his 1827 *Moonlit Night on the Bay of Salerno*.[6] Carus was inspired to paint his spontaneous *plein air* oil studies by the Norwegian landscapist Johan Christian Claussen Dahl. As a teacher at the Dresden Academy, Dahl was influential, especially through his fresh and virtuosic oil sketches from nature and in particular through his cloud studies.

Carus owed a profound debt to the artistic inspiration of Friedrich, a close friend since 1817 and a lasting influence on his work. Following Friedrich's lead, Carus adhered closely to nature and imbued his landscapes with a strong mood. Carus offered a theoretical underpinning to this interest in his *Nine Letters on Landscape Painting*, written between 1815 and 1824 and published in 1831. Here he defined "the depiction of a certain state of mind (feeling) by means of the reproduction of a corresponding mood in the life of nature (truth)" as the central task of landscape art.[7] Conditions in nature should correspond to the artist's emotions. Without a doubt, Carus, who was occasionally prone to melancholy, achieved such a correspondence in his highly painterly rendering of the experience of the atmosphere at the Bay of Naples. Carus confessed that he felt a fondness for subdued moods. That was the reason he had composed "dark fog pictures…and the like"; he felt a need to "cleanse the innermost mystery of the soul from a heavy cloud," and to "finally, and always most importantly, bring relief—indeed, liberation—to myself."[8]

1 Naples, 4 May 1828; cf. *Carl Gustav Carus, Reisen und Briefe,* selected by Eckart von Sydow, Part 1: *Reise durch Deutschland, Italien und die Schweiz 1828* (Leipzig, 1926), pp. 92 f.
2 Cf. Bernhard 1974, p. 200 (repr.).
3 Cf. *Karl Friedrich Schinkel, Reisen nach Italien,* ed. Gottfried Riemann (Berlin, 1979), p. 71, fig. 70, p. 339. Bern 1985, p. 348, no. 228, p. 148 (repr.).
4 Cf. *Christen Købke 1810–1848,* ed. Hans Edvard Norregård-Nielsen and Kasper Monrad, exh. cat., Statens Museum for Kunst (Copenhagen, 1996), p. 298, fig. 209, p. 371, no. 139.
5 *View across the Bay of Naples toward Capri* (143 x 189 mm., inv. no. 1963–581); *The Bay of Naples with the Sorrento Peninsula* (78 x 81 mm., inv. no. 1963–583); *The Bay of Naples with the Sorrento Peninsula* (115 x 116 mm., inv. no. 1963–584). Dresden, Staatliche Kunstsammlungen, Kupferstichkabinett.
6 Cf. Dresden 1997, p. 70, no. 4 (repr. in color), p. 187, cat. raisonné no. 58 (Hans-Joachim Neidhardt).
7 Carl Gustav Carus, *Neun Briefe über Landschaftsmalerei. Geschrieben in den Jahren 1815 bis 1824, Zuvor ein Brief von Goethe als Einleitung,* 2nd ed. Ed. with an intro. by Kurt Gerstenberg (Dresden, no date [1955]), p. 49.
8 Carl Gustav Carus, *Lebenserinnerungen und Denkwüdigkeiten,* 4 parts in 2 vols. (Leipzig, 1865–66), 1, p. 128. Cf. Neidhardt 1976, p. 113.

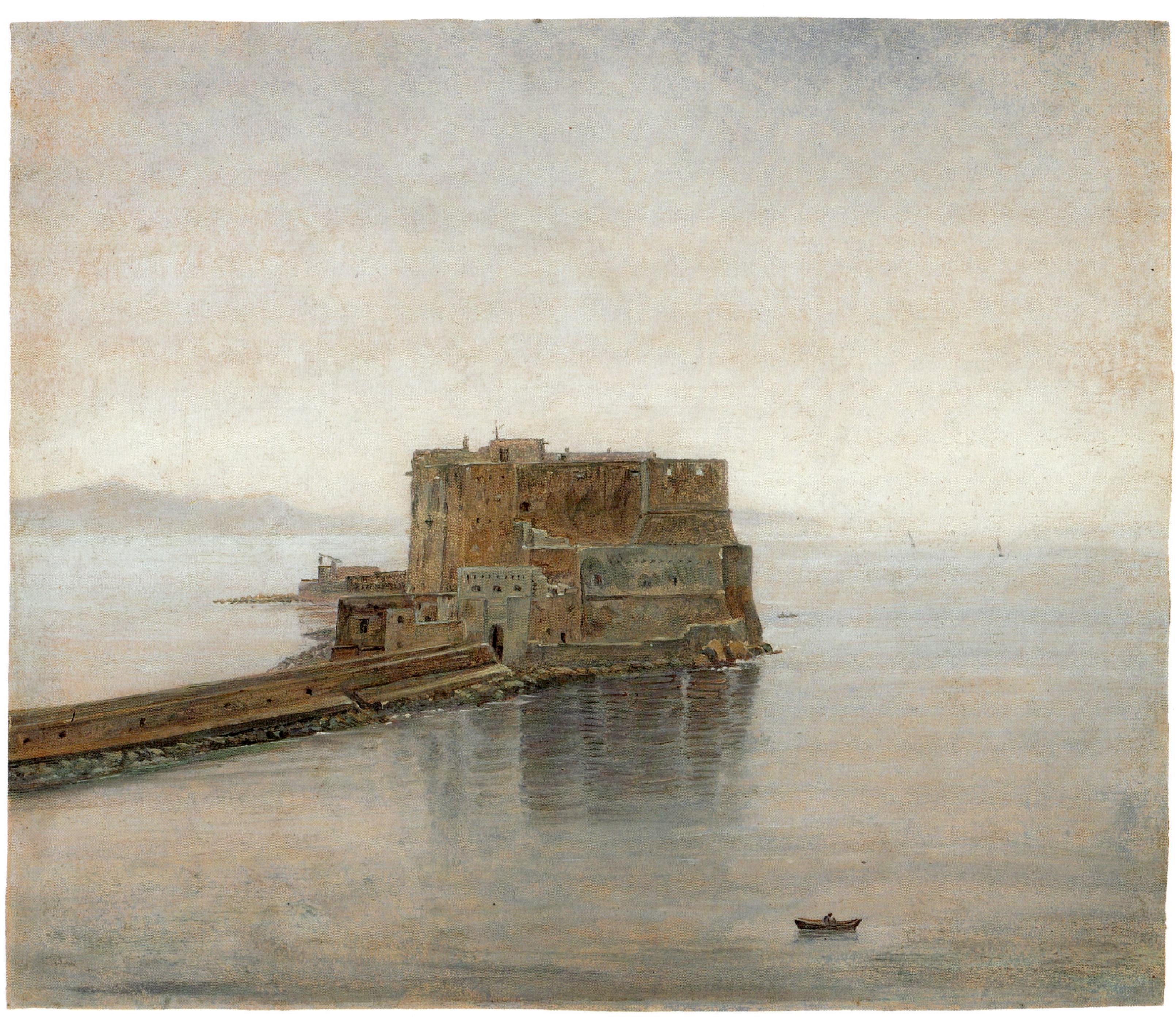

73

Ernst Ferdinand Oehme

Dresden 23 April 1797–10 September 1855 Dresden

Forest Chapel in the Snow, 1839

Pencil, watercolor, pen and gray ink, on wove paper;
155 x 235 mm
Signed in pencil, lower left: "E. Oehme. 1839"

Bibliography: Heidelberg 1964, p. 107, no. 433; Lübeck 1969,
p. 62, no. 108; Munich 1985, pp. 208 f., no. 104 (repr.); Berlin
1987, pp. 137 (repr.), 330; Dresden 1997, p. 199, cat. raisonné
no. 125 (repr.).

Oehme returned repeatedly to the theme of a forest chapel in the snow during different phases of his creative life. Variations on the theme course through his work like a leitmotif. For models we should look to Caspar David Friedrich, whose imagery had a lasting and decisive influence on Oehme: examples are Friedrich's *Abbey in the Oak Forest* of 1810,[1] and *Monastery Cemetery in the Snow*, a major work of 1819.[2] Common to all these models is the motif of a church—in ruins, to be sure—in a bare oak forest. During his student years at the Dresden Academy, Oehme had been a pupil of Friedrich's. In his first large painting, *Cathedral in Winter* (1821), he clearly engaged in a dialogue with his teacher's pictorial ideas and compositions. Despite the solemn, Friedrichean seriousness of this work, Oehme showed his own interpretation in that his painting was not a "memento mori, but rather a nostalgic transfiguration of the medieval Church and faith."[3] As late as 1850, Oehme created a variation on the theme in his *Mountain Chapel in Winter*. In the latter work, the symbolism has become entirely subordinated to nature. Oehme presented a second version of this late variation on the theme to King Ludwig I of Bavaria in the so-called King Ludwig Album.[4]

The location of the winter landscape exhibited here is imaginary. In the midst of a snowy clearing in an oak forest stands a chapel, a silent witness to medieval times, solitary and abandoned. No light burns inside. In contrast to the forest landscapes of Schwind (cf. cat. 60) and Ludwig Richter, not a soul is in sight. The motif of the composition remains rooted in Friedrich's pictorial world, though without Friedrich's symbolic power and sense of foreboding. A snowy landscape, a pagan, leafless oak forest, and a Christian church awaken a range of associations. Everything shimmers gently with the reflection of a subdued, wintry sun. Snow covers the landscape not like a shroud but like the mantle of a winter sleep. Neither a ruined church nor the gnarled oaks with broken and dead limbs mournfully evoke the transitory nature of existence: rather,

the trees seem to gesticulate vigorously, like living creatures.

At the same time, there is a quiet undercurrent of symbolic meaning in this natural, atmospheric winter landscape, a distant echo of the existential seriousness of Friedrich's art. The rather fairy-tale-like, enchanted forest reveals even more explicitly the influence of Ludwig Richter. It is easy to imagine this evocative scene enlivened by a few pilgrims in monastic garb or by the colorful procession of churchgoers returning home from mass in the style of Richter's figural inventions. Oehme clearly elaborated the structure of the gnarled oaks and their bark, as well as the shrubs and blades of grass in the snow, by working them over in detail with the pencil, and even the pencil strokes show Richter's style. Here we undoubtedly see the effect of Oehme's intimate friendship with Richter, which dates back to their time in Italy. Their relationship was so close that the two artists with their young families moved into the same house in Dresden in 1838, a situation Richter described in his memoirs: "These circumstances in which Oehme and I also lived in proximity merely increased the mutual involvement and artistic exchange in our work. If one of us reached an uncertain place in his painting, the neighbor was immediately called in, the matter was discussed and, if possible, clarified."[5]

Oehme showed his fondness for watercolor early on during his autodidactic beginnings as an artist, then during his years of study under Dahl, and later as an important result of his two-and-a-half years in Italy (1822–25). In the late 1830s and 1840s, there is a noticeable increase in Oehme's output of landscape studies lightly worked over in watercolor. These studies capture the appearance of landscapes in the light of transitional moments: in the twilight of dawn or dusk, before sunrise, or after sunset. They were done to record the fleeting impression of color, and they are accordingly inscribed in pencil. Oehme applied the lessons of these studies with great mastery in the delicate, atmospheric scene here. For example, the snow has not been painted by heightening with opaque white, but has been suggested by reserved areas of the white paper. The watercolor is carefully finished, with full signature and date—a complete cabinet piece for a collector, which explains why Oehme evidently sent it, via Ludwig Richter, to the Leipzig publisher Georg Wigand to be put up for sale.[6]

In contrast to the loose, abstracting rendering of a related theme in Carl Blechen's Castle Falkenstein (cat. 77), Oehme's watercolor remains conventionally representational. Using this approach, he has captured the light and color conditions of the wintry mood in the pale light of the winter sun with masterful subtlety. Although there is an undercurrent of ideas, the seriousness

of Friedrich's compositions has been transmuted into Biedermeier contemplativeness. Oehme's message is poetic, and in this regard, too, his work is more closely related to Ludwig Richter's. In his memoirs, Richter offered an assessment of Oehme's art that also applies to the present watercolor: "Later on, his most beautiful pictures were always mood pictures of a very unique and highly poetic kind. One could call him the [poet] Lenau among the painters: in the end, his deeply rooted artistic nature also won out over theoretical views, and he always employed his talent for the noblest purpose."[7]

1 Börsch-Supan and Jähnig 1973, pp. 304 f., no. 169 (repr.).
2 Destroyed in the war, cf. *ibid.*, pp. 351 f., no. 254 (repr.).
3 Hans-Joachim Neidhardt, in Dresden 1997, p. 71 (repr. in color).
4 *Ibid.*, p. 163, no. 95 (repr. in color), p. 216, cat. raisonné nos. 255, 256 (King Ludwig Album); cf. also p. 206, cat. raisonné no. 184, c. 1842.
5 Richter 1909, p. 375.
6 Richter sent the sheet together with another of Oehme's watercolors, a romantic landscape with a castle by the sea, along with a selection of works by other Dresden artists. We learn this from a letter by Ludwig Richter to Wigand, dated 28 April 1839, now in the Dresden Stadtarchiv, as reported by Hans-Joachim Neidhardt in Dresden 1997, p. 199, cat. raisonné 125.
7 Richter 1909, p. 218.

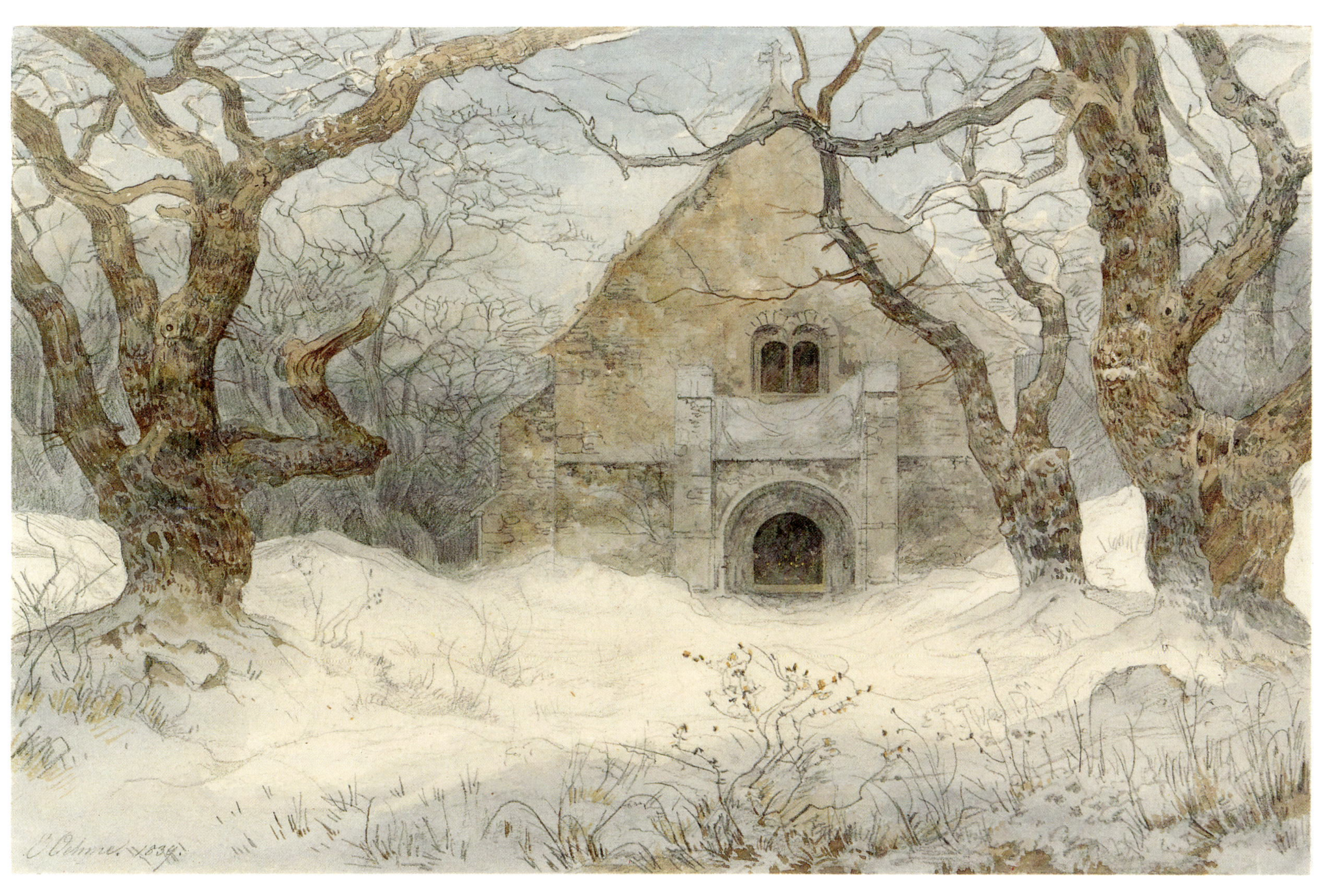

74

August Heinrich

Dresden 17 August 1794 – 27 September 1822
Innsbruck

A View near Loschwitz above the Elbe, 1822

Pencil, brush, and gray ink, on wove paper; 306 x 433/7 mm
Inscribed by another hand in pen and brown ink, lower left:
"G II.4" (Following a restoration, the numeral 4 was
errroneously retraced over 9.)
Verso inscribed in pen and brown-black ink: "Aussicht aus
dem Hohlweg, oberhalb Ryssels Weinberg" ("View from
the Hohlweg, above Ryssel's vineyard")

Provenance: Geheimrat Richard Schöne, Berlin;
Prof. Wolfgang Schöne, Hamburg

Bibliography: Andreas Aubert, "August Heinrich," in
Kunst und Künstler, *vol. 6 (1908), pp. 325 (repr.), 383;*
Ernst Sigismund, "August Heinrich," in Thieme and
Becker, vol. 16 (1923), p. 301; Gode Krämer, "Der Maler
und Zeichner August Heinrich (Dresden 1794–1822 Inns-
bruck)," (Ph.D. diss., Hamburg, Karlsruhe, no date [1979]),
pp. 77 f., 112 ff., 161, cat. no. 65, p. 263, fig. 58; Gode Krämer,
"August Heinrich — Tragik eines Malers," in Mitteilungen der Österreichischen Galerie, *vol. 26/27 (1982/83),*
no. 70/71: 175 ff., fig. 116

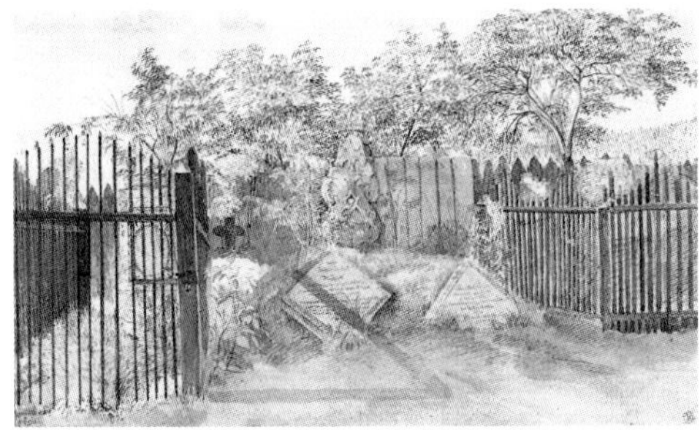

August Heinrich, *At the Loschwitz Cemetery*, 1822.
Pencil, brush, and gray wash; 96 x 156 mm

August Heinrich died of tuberculosis at the age of twenty-eight in Innsbruck, on his way to Italy, which he had so longed to see. Perhaps no one expressed the hopes and expectations that had been placed in Heinrich's artistry better than Caspar David Friedrich. In an expert opinion on Heinrich's 1820 painting *In the Uttewald Valley*, submitted in application for a stipend for travel to Italy, he wrote on 7 September 1820: "Upon closer inspection and analysis, the painting shows his skill at representation and a pure feeling and love for nature and truth. But perhaps we should give stronger consideration not to what Heinrich has accomplished to date but to what we can expect from him in the future. For Heinrich has a very vivid sense that, beneath the faithful reproduction of nature, art makes a higher demand on the artist, and conversely, human-

kind makes a higher demand on the work of art. I believe that it is precisely this pure, higher striving in Heinrich that should be appreciated and rewarded; all the more so because it is so rare."[1]

For the development of his personality and his art—specifically as a precise, naturalistic drafts-man—Heinrich was indebted to the crucial support of his teachers, Ferdinand Olivier in Vienna and Caspar David Friedrich in Dresden. That he accomplished his own goals and developed his own pictorial language, which differed from that of both of these eminent masters, attests to his artistic powers. At the same time, Heinrich did harbor a fondness for certain of their stock motifs. For example, several of his works represent cemeteries, which, as sites of devotion and meditation, were important to both his teachers. Heinrich did several drawings of the cemetery of the church in Loschwitz (fig.); perhaps he was thinking of his own imminent death, though the drawings do not convey a gloomy vision of transitoriness. The cemetery drawings, in particular, reveal his own strength and what set him apart from his teachers.

During the last two years of his life, Heinrich, seriously ill, gradually abandoned oil painting and devoted himself to drawing. This view from a sunken path above the Elbe was one of his last works, created about six weeks before his death. Heinrich himself described it as a pendant to his *Landscape with Walnut Tree in Loschwitz* (today in the Albertina in Vienna)—a view of the sunken path at Ryssel's vineyard in Loschwitz near Dresden.[2] A strong desire to turn the impressive study exhibited here into a painting compelled the artist, between 9 and 13 August 1822, to record in his diary careful notes on its motifs; he lists and painstakingly describes nearly every detail, including the coloration. For example: "The wall with the steps is the brightest part. The shadows cast on the steps by the leaves are very pure and ink-dark.... The entire wall and the wooden fence are brightly lit, the lilac casts lovely, pure leaf shadows on them.... Below the lilac there are many old, reddish-yellow leaves.... A lot of fresh green leaves grow at the top of the stairs.... the leaves of the walnut tree are the darkest part in the picture.... The leaves at the wall are lighter, a withered yellow-green, transparent yellow-green, white blue green...."[3]

In this drawing, Heinrich, with his love of detail, tried once more to cast a spell on the microcosm of nature. Above the wooden fence, cast in shadow by the backlight, the light of the sky is reflected on the Elbe River, where a boat glides by. The villages and fields beyond the Elbe are minutely described. There seems to be some significance in this configuration of motifs: a view from a sunken path over a fence closed by a gate,

across a river flowing by, and into the infinite distance. The viewer feels transported into the pictorial world of Caspar David Friedrich. What did Heinrich, his most gifted student, make of that world? He rejected Friedrich's deep symbolism, and transfiguration in the manner of Olivier. But given his fate, is there not an undertone of symbolism in this drawing, a deep yearning for eternity? In any case, cheerfulness does not characterize this view across the Elbe, which Heinrich rendered with an astonishing precision and faithfulness to nature in the brilliant light of the summer sun. What exists in it—and this may sound paradoxical—is the seriousness with which he observed nature from a deep sense of joy and rapture that almost seem religious. In this context, his diary is extremely revealing: its pages reflect his tremendous energy in the obsessively detailed description of his motifs and work, and in the acuity of his powers of observation. The present sheet, one of the small number of major drawings by Heinrich, is also a moving document of his will to survive through his art. Heinrich's extraordinary draftsmanship, so evident in this work, was certainly recognized by some of his artist contemporaries. Caspar David Friedrich owned about twelve drawings and watercolors by his favorite student.[4] Johan Christian Claussen Dahl—who had noted in his diary on 19 August 1819, "We can expect something from this man"—also acquired, after Heinrich's death, the artist's valuable diary and a total of thirty-seven drawings and watercolors, which he bequeathed to the National Gallery in Oslo. After Ludwig Richter became an instructor in landscape painting at the Dresden Academy in 1836, he often used Heinrich's drawings as models for the young landscapists.[5]

1 Krämer 1979, pp. 26, 132, no. 3, p. 237, fig. 25; cf. Neidhardt 1976, fig. 82 (in color). Hinz 1974, p. 130.

2 Krämer 1979, p. 166, no. 75, p. 261, fig. 56. The relevant diary entries from 31 July to 9 August 1822, *ibid.*, pp. 110 f.

3 Krämer 1979, pp. 112–14, 112.

4 The special esteem in which Friedrich held his student is revealed by the fact that in his painting *Two Men Contemplating the Moon*, of which he made various replicas, he depicted himself and August Heinrich as the two figures with their backs to the viewer; cf. Sumowski 1970, pp. 178 f. According to a list that Dahl drew up of works by other artists in Caspar David Friedrich's estate, there were about twelve watercolors and drawings by August Heinrich; cf. *ibid.*, p. 247.

5 Ernst Sigismund in Thieme and Becker, vol. 16, 1923, p. 300.

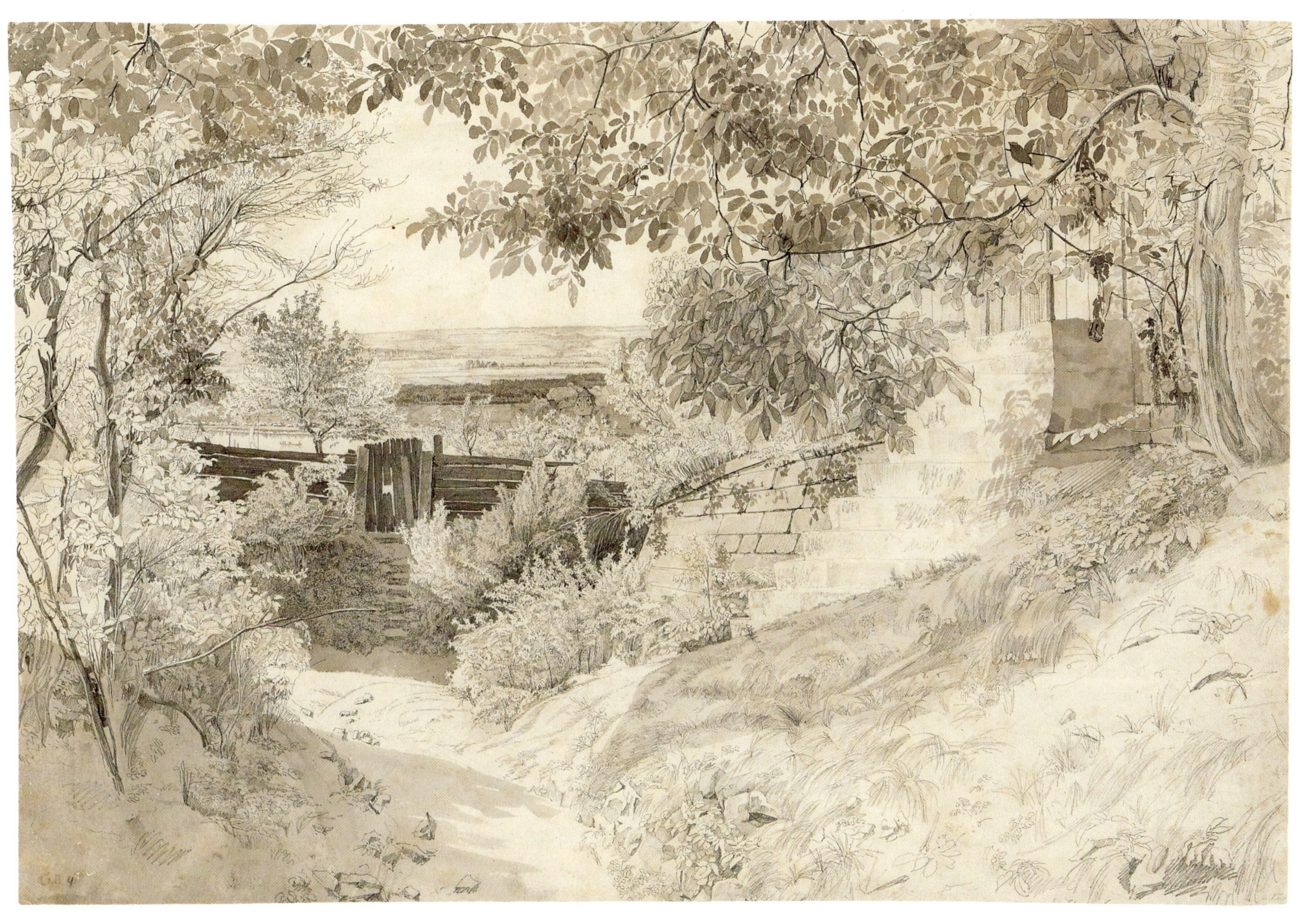

75

Friedrich Gilly

Altdamm near Stettin 16 February 1772 – 7 August 1800 Karlsbad

The Castle Church of the Marienburg, 1794

Watercolor, pen and gray-black ink; black decorative border, on laid paper; watermark: J. Honig & / Zoonen; 604 x 475 mm (sheet), 558 x 432 mm (image); upper left corner and lower right corner restored
Inscribed by another hand in pencil, lower right, below the image: "Marienburg"

Provenance: Leo von Klenze, Munich; 1946 Max Count Otting, Munich; Albin Ritter von Prybram-Gladona, Paris; Kurt Meissner, Zurich

Bibliography: Charlotte von Prybram-Gladona, Unbekannte Zeichnungen alter Meister aus europäischem Privatbesitz (Munich, 1969), p. 19, no. 16, plate 16

In 1794, twenty-two-year-old Friedrich Gilly accompanied his father on an official trip to the provinces of East and West Prussia. They also visited the Marienburg, which is located on the Nogar River south of Danzig. Founded in the thirteenth century by the Teutonic Knights as part of their missionary work among the pagan Prussians, the Marienburg was constructed in the fourteenth and fifteenth centuries and thereafter served as the residence of the grand master of the Order. From the fifteenth century to the eighteenth, it stood under Polish suzerainty. Following its recapture by Frederick the Great, it was used as a military barracks and ration depot, and became increasingly dilapidated.

After his inspection, David Gilly recommended that the ruins of the castle be torn down and used as a quarry for building projects in the surrounding area.[1] His son Friedrich, meanwhile, had done views of the Marienburg in watercolor and brown wash that would have momentous consequences. They attracted wide attention when they were shown at the Academy Exhibition in Berlin the following year, 1795.[2] Gilly had them published by Friedrich Frick in a sumptuous, monumental series of etchings with aquatint. They appeared between 1799 and 1803 in individual installments, partly reworked after his death and supplemented with additional views done on the site.[3] With the exception of the view of the entrance portal to the Marienburg, which reappeared in 1940 in private hands in Berlin, Gilly's originals were thought to be lost.[4] Recently this view of the castle church, surely the most beautiful of the series in the estate of Leo von Klenze reappeared—a precious addition to the small surviving oeuvre of the brilliant architect Gilly.[5]

This well-preserved sheet confirms the traditional account that Gilly used watercolor for his views of the Marienburg. This watercolor and the aquatint reproduction are completely identical in their dimensions[6] and nearly so in their details, except for minor changes; even the figures, solemn beholders of the church that are also meant to help us visualize perspective and scale, are identical. Frick merely added clouds to the sky, and he sensitively put merlons in place of the late Baroque, dilapidated roof on top of the slender tower, which Gilly had already left out.

Here Gilly has depicted the Marienburg from the land side, looking at the castle church from a southeasterly direction. Above the moat and the fortifications rises the two-story Gothic church structure, with the walled chapel of St. Anne below, the old crypt of the grand masters of the Order, and the bright castle church with its high windows on top. A colossal, polychrome statue of Mary with scepter and crown, about eight meters high, stands in the central space of the five-sided end of the choir. The stucco statue occupies a window niche with a gilt background framed by blue walls covered with golden stars—Mary as the Queen of Heaven. From this location, visible from far away, she greeted the rising sun every morning. The three-dimensional, sculpturally articulated structure of the high choir, with its reflective windows, glows like a jewel in a simple setting: the colorful accents of its reddish brick and yellow-blue mosaics sparkle in the noonday sun against the monochromatic, architecturally simple, and weakly articulated façades of the upper castle on the left and the middle castle with its former guest quarters on the right.

The painterly watercolor is composed with theatrically staged lighting. At this moment the position of the sun in the sky has placed the façades of the neighboring buildings in shadow, and they rise like silhouettes against the sky. In the text that accompanied the aquatint *Views of Marienburg*, which resonated with the romantic notions of the young, imaginative architect, Gilly emphasized the "special painterly effect" of the view of the castle church, and "a certain noble impression, which is heightened by the massive, half-ruined, and overgrown walls."[7] A magnificent conception and picturesque charm inform this watercolor, and they were already perceptible in Frick's print. Gilly admired the Marienburg as an example of "a truly great, simple style." The sober grandeur and affecting sublimity of the medieval architecture in this watercolor recall, despite the stylistic differences, the conceptual basis of French revolutionary architecture and Gilly's famous, revolutionary-Classicistic later design for a monument to Frederick the Great.

At the bottom of the two surviving views of Marienburg—in the present work, in the lower right—Gilly depicts fragments of antique or neoclassical architecture as a way of indicating that Gothic and antique ruins hold the same rank. Gilly's reversion to the architecture of the German Middle Ages had a precursor in Goethe's hymn to Erwin von Steinbach, *Von deutscher Baukunst* (1773), and shows a spiritual affinity and parallels to Wackenroder, whom Gilly had personally met in 1793.[8] Gilly's views of the Marienburg, which also stimulated the revival of the use of brick in northern German architecture, were an appeal to save a first-rate cultural monument, a national architectural mandate in the East comparable to the completion of the Cologne Cathedral in the West. This architectural mission, reformulated as a Prussian responsibility, eventually led to the restoration of the Marienburg under the influence of the historicist taste of the time.[9]

1 Cf. *Die Kunst hat nie ein Mensch allein besessen*, exh. cat., Akademie der Künste und Hochschule der Künste (Berlin, 1996), pp. 157 f., no. 2.2/108.

2 Cf. Börsch-Supan 1971, vol. 1, through 1795, no. 201.

3 Friedrich Frick, ed., *Schloss Marienburg in Preussen: Nach seinen vorzüglichsten aeussern und innern Ansichten dargestellt*, 18 plates and an engraved title page in aquatint after Gilly, Frick, Martin Friedrich Rabe, und Franz Ludwig Catel (Berlin, 1799–1803), view of the castle church, plate 7(6); *Schloss Marienburg in Preussen: Das Ansichtenwerk von Friedrich Gilly und Friedrich Frick. In Lieferungen erschienen von 1799–1803*, newly ed. by Wilhelm Salewski (Düsseldorf, 1965); *Friedrich Gilly 1772–1800 und die Privatgesellschaft junger Architekten*, ed. Rolf Bothe and Hella Reelfs, exh. cat., Berlin Museum (Berlin, 1987), pp. 100–104.

4 Pen and brush in brown ink; 378 x 242 mm. Now preserved in Berlin, Kupferstichkabinett; cf. Berlin 1994, pp. 88 f., no. 67 (repr. in color).

5 Cf. Alste Oncken, *Friedrich Gilly 1772–1800* (Berlin, 1935), pp. 101 f. The sheet with the view of the castle church must have made a powerful impression on contemporaries. It is said that the king himself acquired it; cf. Alfred Neumeyer, "Die Erweckung der Gotik in der deutschen Kunst des späten 18. Jahrhunderts: Ein Beitrag zur Vorgeschichte der Romantik," *Repertorium für Kunstwissenscahft* 19 (1928): 118 f. On the loss of Gilly's works during World War II see *Friedrich Gilly: Essays on Architecture 1796–1799*, intro. by Fritz Neumeyer, trans. David Britt (Santa Monica, 1994), p. 220.

6 The aquatint etching (image 522 x 412 mm) shows a detail of the watercolor in original size.

7 Excerpts reprinted in Alfred Rietdorf, *Gilly: Wiedergeburt der Architektur* (Berlin, 1940), pp. 24–28, on the castle church, see pp. 26 f.

8 Cf. Schmitz 1921, pp. 199–208, 203, 207, fig. 94 (castle church aquatint). Cf. Fritz Neumeyer (as n. 5), pp. 1 ff., nn. 2 and 6.

9 In 1804, Frederick William III decreed that the Marienburg should be preserved as a national monument. In 1844, Joseph von Eichendorff composed the official report "Die Wiederherstellung der Marienburg." The Marienburg was heavily damaged in 1945. It has since been undergoing restoration by the Polish monument authorities.

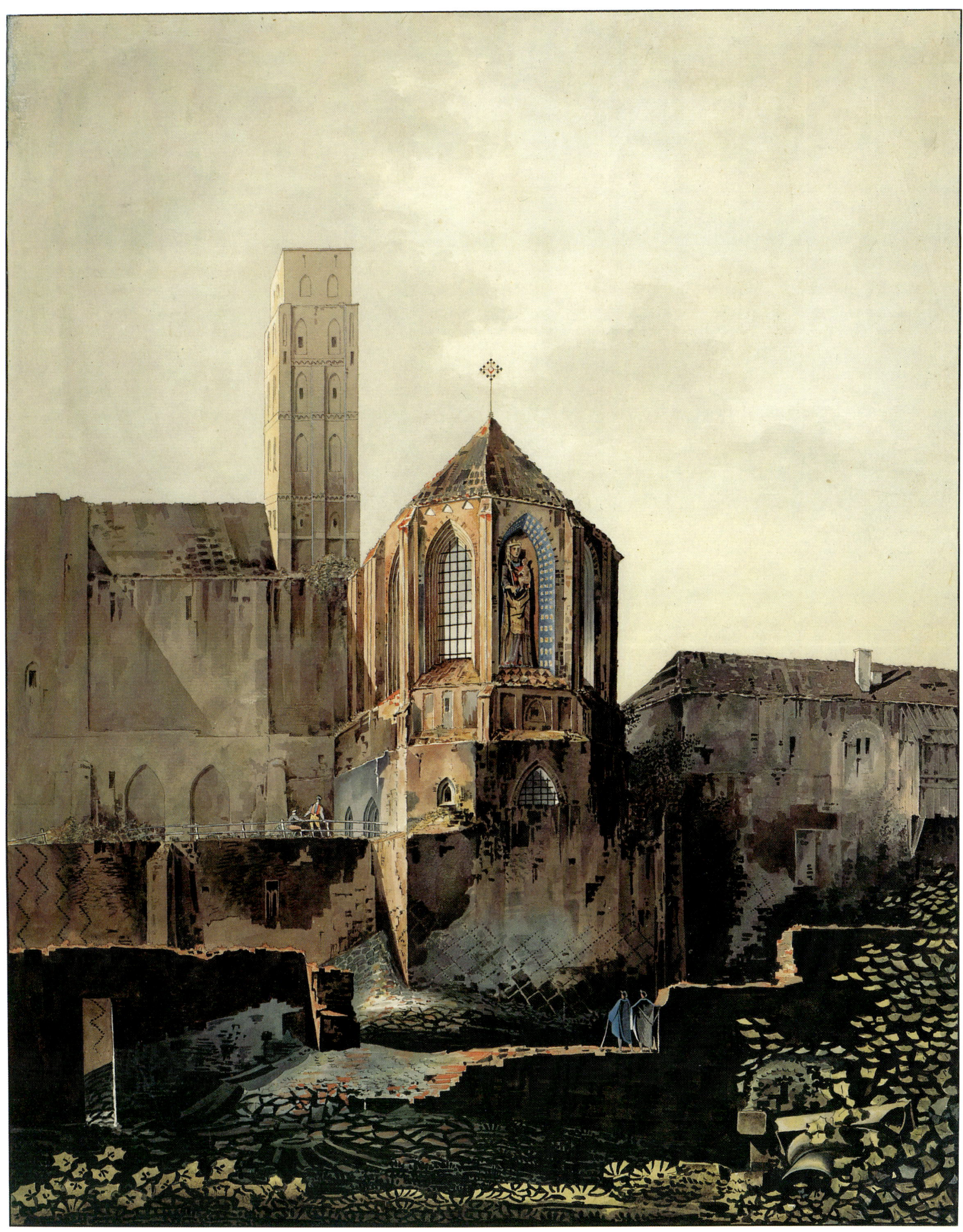

76

Karl Friedrich Schinkel

Neuruppin 13 March 1781 – 9 October 1841 Berlin

The People's Hall in the New Park outside Magdeburg, 1828

Pen and gray and black ink, border in black, on wove paper; 431 x 527 mm (sheet); 380 x 483 mm (framing line); horizontal crease under the center line
Signed lower right: "Schinkel Dez. 1828"
Verso inscribed in pencil: "Gesellschaftshaus in Friedrich Wilhelms Garten / bei Magdeburg / Carl Friedrich Schinkel fc" [Social hall in Frederick William's garden near Magdeburg. Carl Friedrich Schinkel fecit]
Provenance: Boguslav Jolles (Lugt 381 a); Dr. Berolzheimer; Ludwigsgalerie, Munich
Bibliography: Munich 1958, p. 53, no. 152; Lübeck 1969, p. 88, no. 170

Beginning in the eighteenth century, the social house, social hall, or casino became increasingly important as an architectural project. Having built between 1819 and 1825 a casino structure intended for social functions in Potsdam, in 1825 Schinkel submitted to the Lord Mayor of Magdeburg designs for a "People's Hall," to be erected in the city's Kloster Berge Garden. The garden, a landscaped park planned by Peter Joseph Lenné, was completed in 1831 on the site where the ruins of the medieval Benedictine monastery of St. Johannis auf dem Berge, south of Magdeburg's old city, had been removed in 1823–25. Schinkel's social house was to be a pavilion-like,

Neoclassical structure. He conceived it as a two-story building with a vigorously three-dimensional effect, a stucco structure with exterior flights of stairs, terraces, and loggias. The design was dominated by the center section, with a banquet hall that extended through both floors; similar to the casino in Potsdam, it was framed by colonnades.

An 1825 perspective view drawn with pencil and brush in gray wash shows the Neoclassical building in a picturesque park setting.[1] That drawing presumably formed the visual basis for a contract for the proposed commission. Three years later, Schinkel repeated the latter design in the upper portion of the present sheet, with minor changes in the staffage, and supplemented it in the lower portion with a façade elevation of the structure based on a corresponding preliminary drawing.[2] The present sheet then served as the direct model for the printmaker for reproduction in Schinkel's *Sammlung architektonischer Entwürfe* ("Collection of Architectural Designs"), published in 1829.[3]

In contrast to the preliminary drawing in pencil and wash, in the sheet exhibited here Schinkel anticipated the dry effect of the etching needle, using an extremely fine, sharp pen and short strokes without adding wash, and leaving out atmospheric elements such as clouds. Additional preliminary drawings for the building can be found among the works from Schinkel's estate in the Kupferstichkabinett in Berlin.[4]

In addition to the present drawing, Schinkel reproduced in his *Sammlung architektonischer Entwürfe* a second design for the "People's Hall," with "ground plans and section." He added an explanatory text to both sheets: "The building is nestled against a gentle slope and consists of a large main hall and four secondary halls. On the uphill side one steps out of the main hall directly into the garden. On the downhill side there is room for a basement to house the manager's apartment, the kitchens, and the cellars; on this side they have high windows and doors, on the uphill side regular basement windows. The people who arrive by coach get out here and enter the hall through the lower vestibule and up the stairs on either side that lead to the hall. Even larger staircases lead from the hall on both sides to the gallery that runs around it and to the terraces. In order to keep the entrance to the upper gallery on these stairs covered, a steplike elevation has been designed above the stairs; outside on the terrace on each side of the great hall, this elevation forms a flower stand...."[5] On a sheet that accompanies the preliminary drawings in the artist's estate, Schinkel further explains the functional aspects of his design: "At a place that is intended for entertainment, festivities, concerts, and so on, and is supposed to accommodate a considerable number of people, the essential

feature—aside from the most advantageous configuration of the rooms—is the most convenient and versatile connections between the rooms."[6] Schinkel's design for the "People's Hall" was never executed; the city of Magdeburg considered it too expensive. The building was, however, erected in 1829 based on new plans by an architect by the name of Siegfried, and it has survived, albeit altered, to this day.[7]

A portrait drawing in the Winterstein collection conveys an idea of Schinkel's appearance in those years (fig.).[8] It was done in 1824 in Rome during Schinkel's second trip to Italy by the miniaturist and portraitist August Grahl (1791–1868), an important collector of drawings. The miniature-like pencil portrait shows Schinkel from a slightly higher angle, and he appears more youthful than he does in the pencil portrait that Wilhelm Hensel evidently drew at the same sitting.[9]

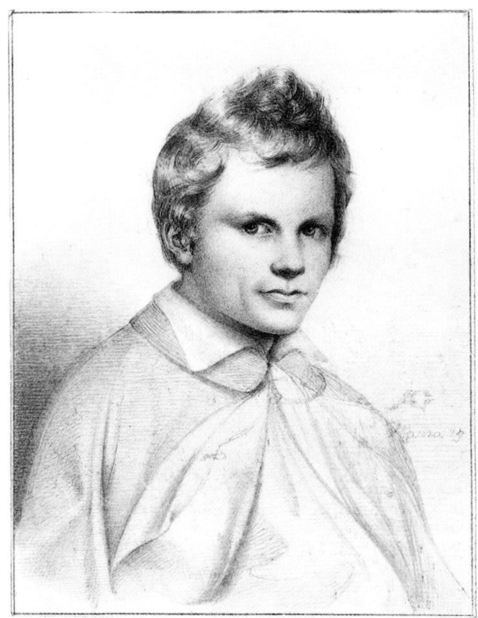

August Grahl, *Portrait of Karl Friedrich Schinkel*, Rome 1824. Pencil; 126 x 96 mm

1 *Perspective View of the People's Hall in the New Park near Magdeburg*, 1825. Pencil and gray wash; 316 x 483 mm. Inscribed below by the artist and signed lower right: "Perspectivische Ansicht des Volks-Saals in den neuen Anlagen bei Magdeburg ... Schinkel 1825." Berlin, Staatliche Museen Preussischer Kulturbesitz, Kupferstichkabinett, inv. no. SM 23.b.57; cf. *Karl Friedrich Schinkel: Eine Ausstellung aus der Deutschen Demokratischen Republik*, ed. Gottfried Riemann et al., exh. cat. (Berlin, 1982), pp. 22 f., no. 18.6, repr. (Gottfried Riemann).

2 I am grateful to Helmut Börsch-Supan of Berlin for calling my attention to this sheet and providing me with a photocopy. It can be found in the Schinkel estate under no. 23.b.-58. It shows the façade elevation in the upper half of the image (cf. n. 4).

3 *Sammlung architektonischer Entwürfe von Schinkel enthaltend theils Werke welche ausgeführt sind, theils Gegenstände deren Ausführung beabsichtigt wurde*, edited and published by Schinkel, 28 fascicles, 174 plates (Berlin, 1819–40); here, fascicle 16 (Berlin, 1829: L. W. Wittich), pl. 101.

4 Inv. nos. SM 23.b.57; 58; 59; 60.

5 *Sammlung architektonischer Entwürfe* (cf. n. 3), n. 1.

6 Quoted in Berlin 1980/81, pp. 293 f., no. 538, 539 (Gottfried Riemann).

7 I am grateful to Helmut Börsch-Supan of Berlin for information clarifying the matter; letter dated 14 March 1997.

8 Signed lower right: "AG [in ligature] / Roma 24"

9 As Schinkel noted in his travel diary on 19 October 1824: "In the evening Hensel and Grahl came to me. The former started to draw me...." Berlin 1981, pp. 64 f., no. 75.

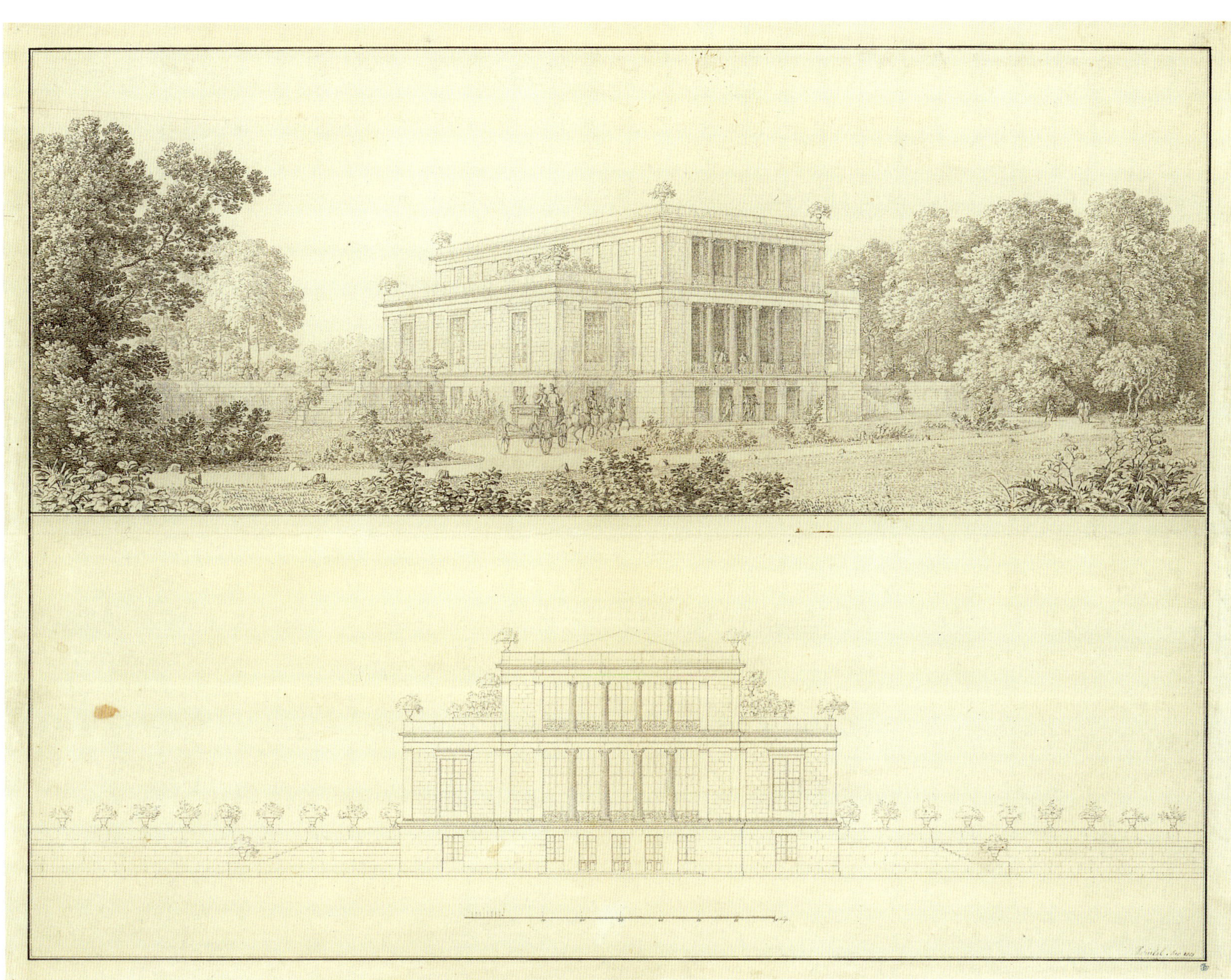

77

Carl Blechen

Cottbus 29 July 1798 – 23 July 1840 Berlin

Falkenstein Castle in the Selke Valley in the Harz Mountains, 1833

Watercolor over pencil, on wove paper; 229 x 327 mm
Inscribed in pencil, upper right: "Falkenstein"
Verso in pencil: tree studies; inscribed in pencil: "Blech-hütte b. Thale d. 21 t Sept" [Tin hut near Thale, 21 September]; stamps of the estate and collectors

Provenance: Estate of the artist (Lugt 263 b); H. Wilhelm F. Brose, Berlin (Lugt 307 c); Carl Brose, Berlin

Bibliography: Guido Joseph Kern, Karl Blechen: Sein Leben und seine Werke (Berlin, 1911), p. 170, col. 1, no. 14 (only the verso is mentioned); Hollstein und Puppel, Auktion XL, Sammlung Brose, Berlin, 8–10 November 1928. cat. no. 117, pl. 12; Paul Ortwin Rave, Karl Blechen. Leben, Würdigungen, Werk (Berlin, 1940), p. 455, no. 1857 (repr.); Munich 1958, p. 19, no. 2, fig. 43; Die Kunst 56, no. 9 (1958): 282 (repr.); Heidelberg 1965, p. 32, no. 27; Lübeck 1969, p. 15, no. 3; Munich 1972, p. 133, no. 162; Keller 1979, p. 68, pl. 86; Carl Blechen: Zwischen Romantik und Realismus, ed. Peter-Klaus Schuster, with contributions by Sigrid Achenbach et al., exh. cat., Nationalgalerie Berlin (Munich, 1990), p. 176, no. 234 (repr. in color).

Like other magnificent landscapes, the Harz Mountains were initially discovered, so to speak, by naturalists and then by artists who followed in their wake. Interest in the natural world had taken Goethe to the Harz Mountains early on, in 1777, 1783, and 1784. He worked his impressions of the landscape into his dramatic masterpiece, *Faust.* In 1811, Caspar David Friedrich traveled to the mountains, at the time still occupied by the French. The Harz region was then considered the native land of Hermann (Arminius; 18 B.C.– 21 A.D.), the heroic chief of the Germanic Cherusci tribe who fought the Roman oppressors and was regarded as a symbolic figure for the liberation from Napoleon's yoke. In a number of compositions inspired by this landscape,[1] Friedrich alluded metaphorically to the Harz as the homeland of German liberty. Carl Gustav Carus also traveled there in 1819, seeking inspiration for his atmospheric landscape paintings. In 1829, the young Hamburg painter Christian Morgenstern undertook a study trip through the mountains. Wilhelm Blumenhagen's *Wanderungen durch den Harz* [Excursions through the Harz Mountains], published in 1840 by Georg Wigand in Leipzig as part of the series "Picturesque and Romantic Germany," fostered the development of tourism. Blumenhagen's book contained steel-engraved illustrations after views drawn on the spot by Ludwig Richter in 1836, including Falkenstein Castle.[2] Between 12 and 22 September 1833, Carl Blechen, too, traveled through the

Harz Mountains. Of the many *plein air* studies he made there, thirty-six watercolors and drawings have been identified thus far.[3] They include this appealing watercolor with a view of Falkenstein Castle, a particular attraction of the region at the edge of the Selke Valley, which is closed in by forested mountains. The castle, built in the twelfth century above the Selke Valley, is located southeast of Quedlinburg and Gernrode, near Ballensted in the former province of Saxony. Just before the Selke River emerges from the mountains, Falkenstein rises like an inaccessible falcon's nest 135 meters above the river, on a mountain cone that is easily reached only from the high plateau. Renovated and expanded in the fifteenth and sixteenth centuries, it withstood all sieges over the centuries and is to this day the best-preserved medieval castle in the Harz Mountains.

It was here that the jurist Eike von Repgow, at the behest of Hoyer von Falkenstein, translated into Low German his *Sachsenspiegel*, the most important law book of the Middle Ages, originally written in Latin around 1250. In 1831/32, the architect Friedrich August Stüler redid the living quarters of the upper floor in a historicizing style. The similarly historicist furnishings of the manor house are presumably based on designs by Karl Friedrich Schinkel. An 1833 painting by Wilhelm von Kügelgen of the mistress of the castle, Bernhardine von der Asseburg, and her two sons adorns the hall.

It was at this very time, when the owners of the castle cultivated contacts with artists in Berlin and Dresden in connection with the restoration work, that Carl Blechen's excursion brought him to Falkenstein. Blechen's trip to the Harz Mountains occurred during the most mature phase of his development, only a few years before his tragic death. The artist was at the height of his artistic career. Beginning in 1831, he taught landscape painting at the Berlin Academy. Influenced by his many years as a set painter at the Königstädtische Theater in Berlin, he had developed a special feel for stagelike composition and a theatrical manipulation of light. During his trip to Italy in 1828/29, the experience of the southern light had liberated his art into a purely painterly conception of nature. In May of 1829 he filled a sketchbook with transparent, abstract, and light-suffused views of Amalfi and its environs, working outdoors with brush and sepia over pencil. This sketchbook is the most beautiful, and possibly the most important, document of his unique gift for *plein air* painting.

Still very much under the spell of what he had learned in Italy about the handling of light, Blechen, in this view of Falkenstein Castle, raised his already virtuosic command of the watercolor technique to a new dramatic level. With rapid, spontaneous strokes he freely sketched the

momentary impression of the scene on the spot, getting it down quickly on paper. Broad areas of the paper have been boldly left blank, the colors loosely applied in a sparing but lively manner with a heavily charged brush. It is astonishing how vividly Blechen has captured the basic chromatic atmosphere of this landscape in the delicate mixtures of his colors, reduced to blue, gray, and brown. The cropping of the pictorial space itself shows a stagelike composition; the castle seems to float weightlessly on the height, the symbolic vision of a transfigured Middle Ages. A comparison with Ferdinand Olivier's view of Hohensalzburg Citadel (cat. 34) shows that Blechen was here primarily concerned with the sensual, visual experience—the momentary impression—of this landscape and its historic building. By contrast, Olivier's meticulous rendering lifts the motif out of the flow of time and endows it with a quality of permanence. It is not surprising that the boldness and freedom of Blechen's art, focused on the experience of purely pictorial values, was understood by few contemporaries. With his fresh and painterly realism, Blechen's work strikes us today as highly modern, and a precursor to that of Menzel and similar late nineteenth-century artists.

1 Hans Spitzmann, "Der Harz in den Werken Dresdener Maler der Goethezeit," *Jahrbuch zur Pflege der Künste* 5 (1957): 164–85, 170 ff.

2 Ludwig Richter traveled once again to the Harz Mountains in September of 1842 with Ernst Ferdinand Oehme and Carl Peschel. Together with Wilhelm von Kügelgen they visited Falkenstein Castle, where they stayed at an inn. On this occasion, Oehme did various drawings and watercolors of the castle; cf. Dresden 1997, p. 206, no. 186 (repr.), p. 213, no. 232 (repr.).

3 Exh. cat., Berlin 1990, p. 174, no. 230.

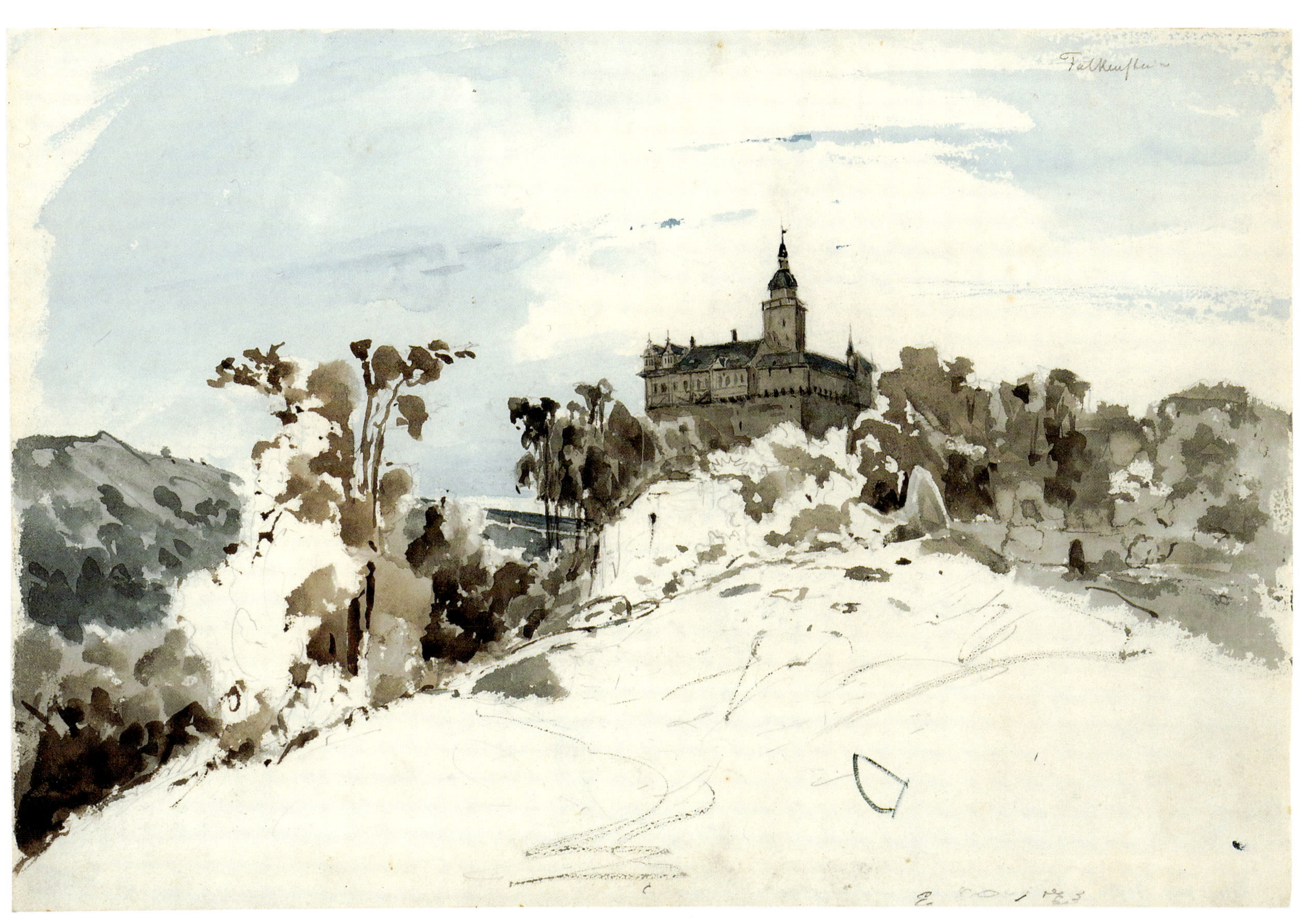

Falkenstein

78

Adolph Menzel

Breslau 8 December 1815 – 9 February 1905 Berlin

Choir of the Former Abbey Church in Berlin, 1838

Watercolor over pencil, on wove paper; 261 x 215 mm
Signed and dated with the brush, lower left: "Ad. Menzel 38"

Bibliography: Munich 1958, pp. 40 f., no. 101, fig. 45; Bremen 1963, p. 53, no. 1; Konrad Kaiser, Adolph Menzel— Der Maler (Stuttgart, no date [1965]), pp. 13, 38, pl. 2; Ebertshäuser 1976, p. 778 (repr.); Hamburg 1982, pp. 44 f., no. 3 (repr. in color).

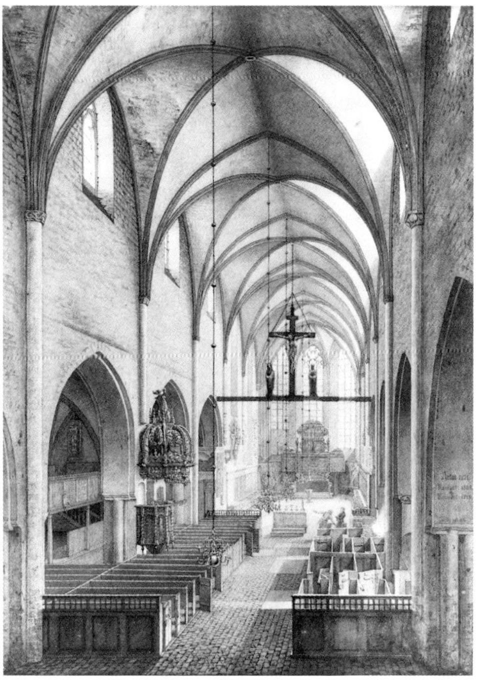

Carl Wilhelm Pohlke, *The Interior of the Abbey Church*, 1851. Watercolor; 578 x 414 mm. Berlin, Berlin Museum

The church of the former Franciscan abbey, dating from the thirteenth and fourteenth centuries, was destroyed in 1945; all that remains today are remnants of the outer walls. The no longer extant monastic buildings that adjoined the church housed the Gymnasium "Zum Grauen Kloster" (founded 1574), important as an educational institution for the Berlin middle class. Friedrich Ludwig Jahn, one of the founders of the German *Turnbewegung* [gymnastics movement], taught here during the Wars of Liberation, and Bismarck was a student at the school from 1830 to 1832.

At the beginning of the nineteenth century, the old abbey church, built in brick, was threatened by decay. A renovation was proposed in 1813, for which Karl Friedrich Schinkel drew a compre-

hensive plan. In 1836 there were renewed calls for the restoration of the church, which was to keep its function: providing religious services for the neighboring Gymnasium, public morning sermons, and a place of baptism for Jews. Although the plan to remove the old furnishings of the church was later dropped at the behest of the crown prince, it may have been the reason why Menzel, in 1838, drew his careful studies of the interior. At this time, general interest in preserving the church surged again, supported by the involvement of the crown prince, later King Frederick William IV of Prussia, who embarked upon the restoration immediately after assuming the reins of government in June of 1840.[1]

Menzel often drew inside the old Berlin abbey church in the late 1830s. In numerous pencil sketches he recorded the remnants of old furnishings, such as the choir stalls, baroque epitaphs set into the walls, and medieval booty.[2] It was also here that he did his first painterly "impressions" in watercolor, of which three others in addition to the present work still exist.[3] Menzel later wrote to his friend Paul Meyerheim about these works: "When I started doing my first watercolors here in the abbey church, a box of watercolors cost one thaler, which I didn't have. And so I fashioned a palette from the stiff cover of a diary, attached a rubber band underneath so that I could put my thumb through it, and bought five round Honig watercolor cakes, which I glued next to each other on the cover. With this contraption I worked for quite some time."[4] At that time Menzel was still in strained financial circumstances, having to earn a livelihood for his family.

In these works Menzel used watercolors in a kind of mixed technique with a pastel effect, a kind of prelude to his later fondness for gouache painting. The present, early sheet by the twenty-two-year-old artist already shows an original, willful, and totally effortless handling of a technique he tried and tested on his own. This approach would remain characteristic of Menzel, with his love of experimentation and his unconventional, technically innovative working process. In places the colors have been applied in such a brittle and dry manner that the structure of the paper is visible like a screen. Bright areas in the vault have been reworked with a wet brush to dilute the color; the strongest reflections of light, as seen, for example, in the window behind the organ or along the right wall, have been scratched out with a scalpel.

Menzel's affinity for the late baroque and its staging of light in architecture and sculpture manifested itself in his later work in numerous views of interiors of Baroque churches. That the young Menzel set his eye on a Gothic church interior surely also had something to do with the patriotic currents of the years leading up to the

revolution of 1848. Those currents awakened a new awareness of the cultural heritage of the Middle Ages and an interest in Gothic churches as monuments of a national past. Menzel's interior also documents the church's condition before the restoration that altered its appearance, though a watercolor by Carl Wilhelm Pohlke (born 1810) has captured it with much greater precision (fig.). A comparison with Pohlke's faithful *veduta* of 1851 makes it clear that Menzel was mainly interested in capturing not the architecture but the mysterious atmosphere of the medieval church space in its picturesque interplay with the light.

The restoration changed the appearance of the church inside and out so drastically that Franz Kugler was moved to recall the earlier conditions with nostalgia: "You remember the old, plain, early Gothic brick structure in the middle of our city, which stood there dilapidated and half-ruined amidst the noise of the day. A few times we took refuge inside, where we abandoned ourselves to dreams of times past.... These things [the restorations] don't really suit the venerable old building; it is as though the plain face of a matron wants to adorn itself with a flirtatious blond wig."[5]

Nearly ten years after the restoration, Menzel returned to the motif of his 1838 watercolor with the pulpit in the oil painting *Sermon in the Former Abbey Church* (1847). In the oil painting the scene inside the church, which was empty of people in the watercolor, has been enlivened by a pastor delivering a sermon to a solemnly assembled congregation. The church itself, however, is shown whitewashed, prior to the overpainting and decoration of the restoration: Menzel's affirmation of the authentic tradition and a statement against the distortion of the past by the new movement of historic preservation.[6]

1 Cf. Ernst Badstübner, "Die mittelalterlichen Kirchen Berlins im 19. Jahrhundert: Ein Kapitel Geschichte der Denkmalpflege," in *Studien zur Berliner Kunstgeschichte*, ed. Karl-Heinz Klingenburg (Leipzig, 1986), pp. 57–60, figs. 12, 13.

2 For example Berlin, Kupferstichkabinett, Menzel estate (formerly Nationalgalerie), inv. no. N-281, N-1126, N-1129, N-1185, N-1186. See also Berlin 1980, p. 341, no. 140 (pulpit).

3 Tschudi 1905, pp. 144–47, no. 160 (pulpit), 161 (gallery), 162 (organ front) with repr. All three watercolors have the identical format (260 x 220 mm) and are dated 1838.

4 Quoted in Munich 1958, p. 41, under no. 101 (Peter Halm).

5 Franz Kugler, *Kleine Schriften und Studien zur Kunstgeschichte*, vol. 3 (1854), p. 637.

6 Cf. Hamburg 1982, p. 44, no. 3 (Eckhard Schaar).

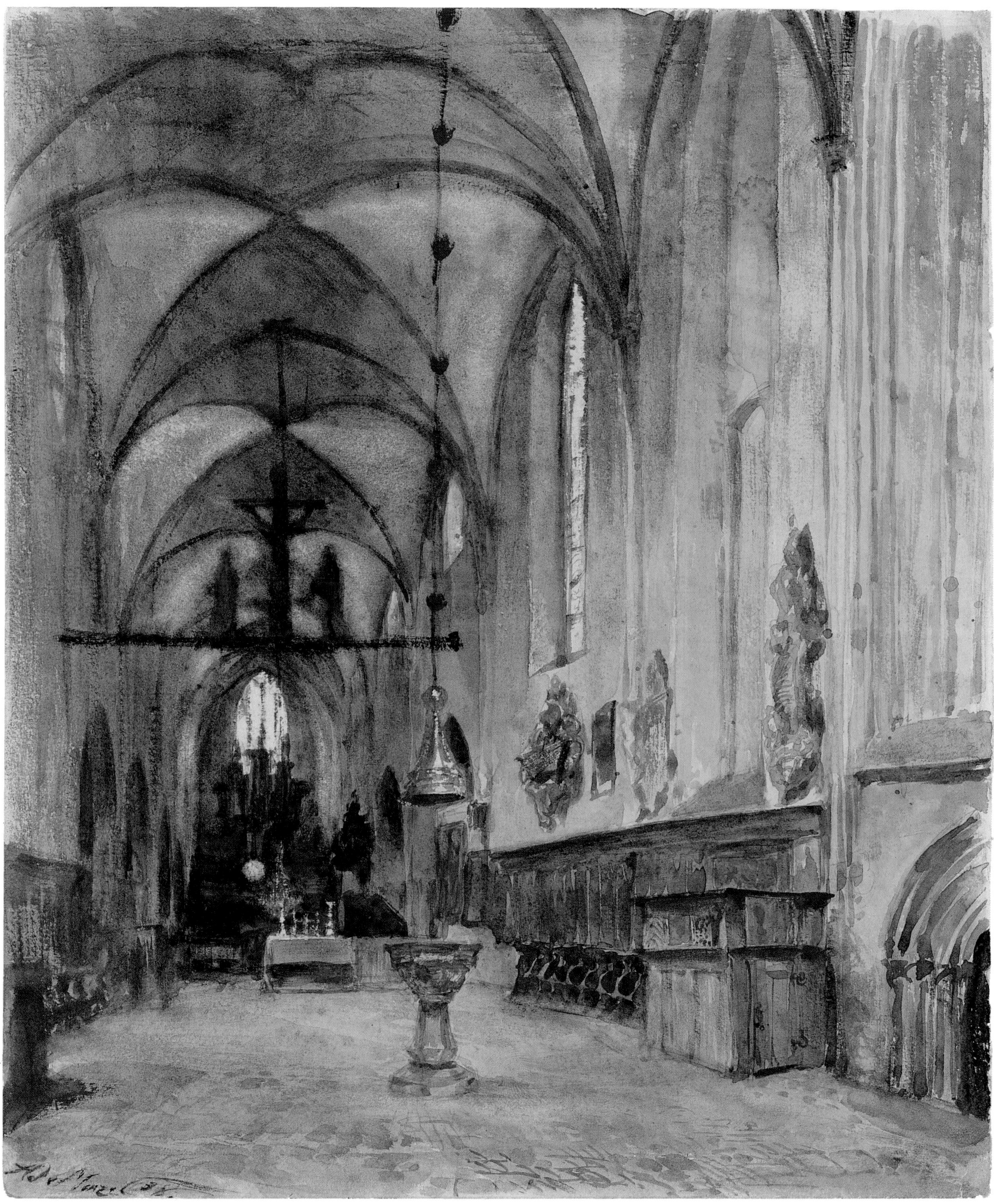

79
Adolph Menzel

Portrait of His Brother Richard, Study for the Lithograph "Molière," c. 1849

Pastel crayons, fixed, on rough, brown-tinted paper; 260 x 201 mm
Verso: old inscription (by the artist himself?) in pen and brown ink: "Adolph Menzel"; in pencil: "Original von/Adolph Menzel/bestätigt hiermit/Rudolph Lepke/f.202/1" [Original by Adolph Menzel, hereby verified, Rudolph Lepke f. 202/1]

Provenance: Auction House Hugo Helbing, Munich

Bibliography: Bremen 1953, p. 57, no. 43, p. 35 (repr.); Winterthur 1955, p. 60, no. 259, pl. 32; Munich 1958, p. 41, no. 103, fig. 47; Wolfgang Hütt, Adolph Menzel (Vienna and Munich, 1965), p. 41, pl. 15; Lübeck 1969, p. 59, no. 102; Hamburg 1982, pp. 100 f., no. 52 (repr. in color)

There have been various conjectures about the identity of the person depicted here. Because the subject holds the pen in the left hand, Peter Halm thought it possible that it was Menzel himself, drawn in front of a mirror. Others, most recently Eckhard Schaar, believe that the model was Menzel's brother Richard.[1]
Comparison with other self-portraits by Menzel and likenesses of his brother leaves no doubt that

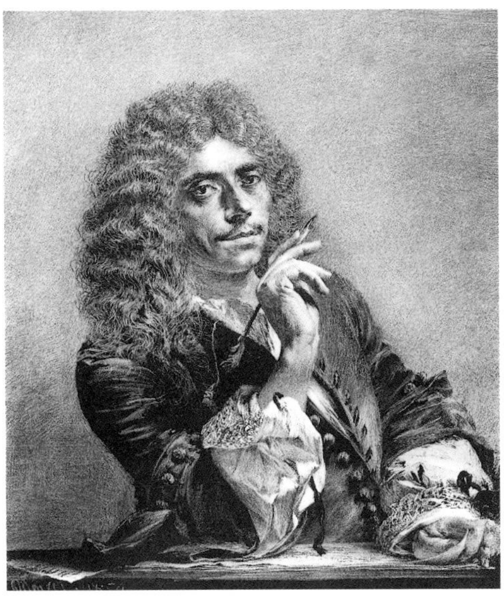

Adolph Menzel, *Molière*, 1850. Lithograph
(printed with ochre tone)

this is indeed a study of Richard Menzel (1826–1865), who had a gaunt figure and a highly arched forehead like that of his brother, though not as broad.[2] Before and after the death of their parents, Menzel looked after Richard (eleven years his junior), who was often sickly. With Menzel's financial help, Richard became a photographer and eventually acquired the photographic Art and Publishing Institute Gustav Schauer. Throughout his life, Menzel remained very close to his family. Along with his circle of close friends, it was an island of calm in his life; only here he did he feel truly safe and free; here he was loved and respected in every way. Because of his dwarflike stature, Menzel met "smiles of pity" when he ventured out, and as a result he was suspicious and withdrawn toward the outside world. Menzel often portrayed the family members with whom he shared a household throughout his life. His beloved sister Emilie, the only woman of importance in his life, was the subject of more than a hundred drawings, gouaches, and oil studies. These works—most of them utterly enchanting impressions—depict her in the most diverse, momentary situations. He also made many studies of his brother Richard, although, like this lively pastel drawn from life, they are not portraits in the sense of individual characterization. Rather, they are spontaneous sketches or studies of a specific activity or posture. Menzel used the present study of a pose and gesture as a model[3] for the 1850 lithograph showing a half-length portrait of the writer Molière. It was the first in a series of six lithographs that Menzel issued in 1851 with the Berlin publisher Carl Meder; the set has a title page that reads *Versuche auf Stein mit Pinsel und Schabeisen* [Essays on Stone with Brush and Scraper] (fig.).[4] He based Molière's likeness loosely on various older depictions, among them engravings after Mignard and Bourdon, and especially Lépicié's reproductive engraving after Charles Antoine Coypel's painted portrait. In the wake of the Restoration, interest in Molière's works revived in France. Between 1819 and 1846, five illustrated editions of his complete or collected works appeared, including the 1835 edition with eight hundred wood engravings after drawings by Tony Johannot, which Menzel used as a guide for his own illustrations for Kugler's *Geschichte Friedrichs des Grossen* [History of Frederick the Great].[5]
Franz Kugler described Menzel's 1850 lithograph in his review of the entire series in the *Kunstblatt*: "Half-length portrait of a male, whom we recognize as Molière. He is about to write and, resting the right arm with the pen on the table, is looking out at the viewer, absorbed in thought. This is a portrait that offers us not merely the particular physiognomy of an intellectually important man, but the person himself in a characteristic moment of his intellectual activity. This sheet, in particular, attests that this scraping technique is perfectly suited to full artistic expressiveness, far removed from any kind of facile sketch effect."[6]
Menzel, who took over his father's lithographic workshop at age sixteen, had already mastered the technique of lithography as a young man. The first art lithographs of his own design were executed with lithographic crayon or pen. In an effort to explore other possibilities of lithography, he experimented with tusche and the scraper. The stone was completely covered in lithographic ink; then the various gradations of light were scratched away with the scraper, and the result was overprinted with a tone with the light areas reserved. Thus Menzel revived in planographic printing effects of depth similar to the mezzotint manner of traditional intaglio printing. One of Menzel's models was the striking etching technique of Jean Jacques de Boissieu, whose art he admired.[7] As an artist who experimented with the technical possibilities and sought to expand them, Menzel would find a successor in the printmaker Max Klinger. In the series he modestly entitled "Essays," Menzel produced results of the utmost refinement in the effect of light and gave proof of his unequaled virtuosity in this technique. At the time, these lithographs were already highly prized as collector's pieces.

1 Cf. Munich 1958, p. 41, no. 103 (Peter Halm), and Hamburg 1982, p. 100, no. 52 (Eckhard Schaar).
2 Cf. Berlin 1997, pp. 125 f., no. 41 (repr.) (Marie Ursula Reimann-Reyher), with references to other portraits of his brother Richard.
3 A sketch in pastel crayon on brown paper of his brother Richard dates from this same period. Menzel evidently asked his brother to pose as a model for this sketch, which he used as a study for General von Stille in the painting *Company at the Table of Frederick II in Sanssouci* (1849/50); cf. Berlin 1980, p. 314, no. 20b, p. 174 (repr. in color).
4 Elfried Bock, *Adolph Menzel: Verzeichnis seines graphischen Werkes* (Berlin, 1923), pp. 260 ff., nos. 398–404, here no. 399-1. Half-length portrait of the writer Molière. Cf. Andresen, vol. 5, p. 45, nos. 167–73, here: no. 168, J. B. P. Molière.
5 Hamburg 1982, p. 100, no. 52 (Eckhard Schaar).
6 Franz Kugler, *Kleine Schriften und Studien zur Kunstgeschichte*, vol. 3 (Stuttgart, 1854), p. 637.
7 "…some years ago I once saw the entire work of Boissieu. He is indeed among the greatest in drawing and etching, and the sheets of his that I have here are among his best"; cf. *Adolph von Menzels Briefe*, ed. Hans Wolff (Berlin, 1914), p. 78.

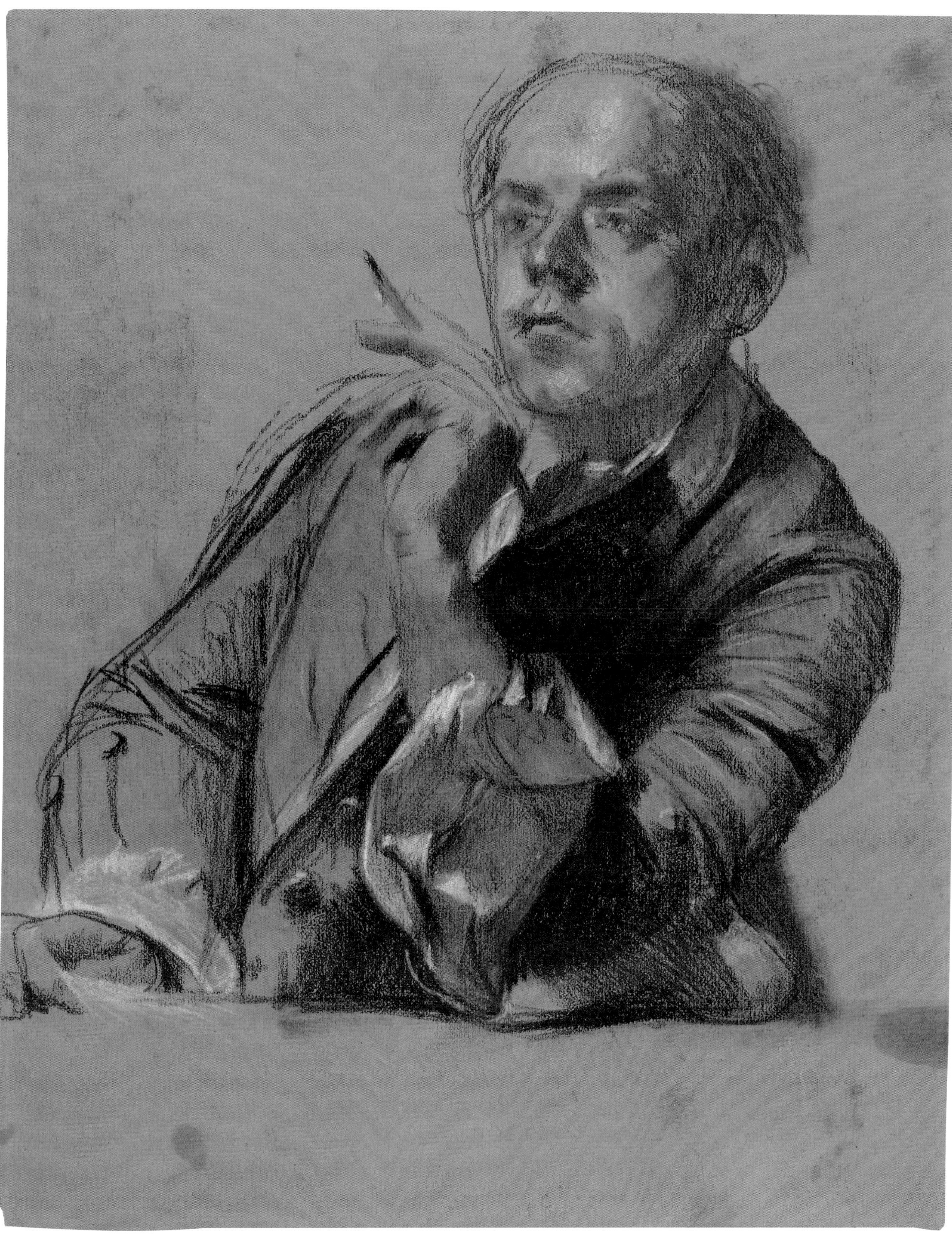

Adolph Menzel

The Opera Glass, c. 1850

Pastel on thin, cinnamon-colored tinted paper;
278 x 229 mm; left and upper edge trimmed
Inscribed by the artist in black chalk, upper left (trimmed):
"…n:/…pernhaus/(illegible)…August…(illegible)"
On the passe-partout verso, a stiff strip of paper with a
dedication in pencil by Menzel himself: "Director: 'Und
seht nur hin für wen Ihr schreibt' u.s.w. Davon sollst Du
Dir aber, Geliebtester die tragische Muse nicht degoutant
machen lassen. Nächstens ausführlich Dein A. M." [Direc-
tor: 'So just take a look for whom you are writing' and so on.
My dearest, don't let this make the tragic Muse distasteful
to you. More in greater detail soon. Your A.M.]

Provenance: A gift by Menzel with a dedication to the poet
and theater director Paul Heyse (1830–1914); from Heyse's
estate it was donated to a charity event in Munich;
Kunsthandlung Julius Böhler, Munich; after 1921, Julius
Böhler, Lucerne; W. Salzmann, Küsnacht; Georg Peyer-
Nilsson, Küsnacht/Zurich; Marianne Feilchenfeldt, Zurich

Menzel's subtle sense of color and his talent for atmospheric moods and "impressions" had manifested themselves early on in the richly nuanced tones of his interior of the former abbey church (cat. 78). These abilities continued to develop, and in the 1840s and 1850s the artist went through a productive phase in which he worked with pastels on tinted paper. These were the artistically fruitful years that saw the creation of the paintings *Balcony Room* (1845), *Sister Emilie in the Doorway* (1847), and *The Berlin-Potsdam Railroad* (1847). As the present sheet attests, his airy pastels, in which he effortlessly caught the effects of light and shadow, included masterpieces of the highest order, marking an artistic high point in his early work. The motif of a woman at the opera who is looking at the stage through her opera glass is one that Menzel depicted in several works; a delicate pastel in Berlin is closest to the one exhibited here.[1]

Menzel, who had a deep love for music, frequently attended concerts and operas. During these performances, as during visits to museums and exhibitions, he observed the audience with special curiosity.[2] In this work he is looking down at a woman who is watching the stage through her opera glass. What fascinated Menzel was not the action on stage but the reaction of the audience. Here he spontaneously captured the woman's situation: leaning forward on the balustrade of the gallery or box, she seems to be following the performance on stage with tense concentration, as though spellbound. She wears a fashionable capote hat, decorated on the side with a ribbon, which shields her face and points at the stage like a large eyeshade. Light falls from above onto her shoulders and onto the stole that gathers in folds over her right arm and slips off her back. The color contrast of the black hat heightens the experience of the light that has taken abstract shape on her dress and shawl. Menzel could not have drawn this scene with pastel crayons on the spot; that would have been too cumbersome and disruptive. But he scrutinized the woman very carefully and then committed her to his phenomenal memory; later, in the studio, he could draw the scene as if "from life" with bold and sweeping strokes. This sheet is also an example of Menzel's fondness for tackling complicated angles of view with a seemingly playful ease.

The inscription on the sheet, fragmentary because the left and upper edges have been trimmed, can be restored as follows: "(Erin)n:/ Opernhaus/(3.) August/(51)" [Remb.: opera house, 3 August (51)]. The date, however, is barely decipherable, and a different reading is possible. Menzel frequently inscribed his pastels with the word *Erinnerung* [remembrance], also abbreviated to *Erinn*. He did this to verify that these sheets, often loose and sketchlike, were not created directly on site but in the studio from memory. In many cases they were based on quick pencil sketches he drew in his sketchbook on the spot.

Menzel himself made a distinction between his official creative work that was completed at the best of his patrons and the court, and his independent creative work intended only for private use. He usually held back the free, subtly colored, painterly "impressions" of his airy pastels of the 1840s, in part because they served as a kind of archive for use as models in larger painted compositions. Only occasionally did he let go of them, finishing them for sale or as a gift to a close friend, as he did with both pastels of the lady with the opera glass: the Berlin sheet to the military physician Wilhelm Puhlmann, and this one to the poet Paul Heyse (1830–1914). Heyse was famous in his day, and his large body of work won him the Nobel Prize in 1911. Menzel had met him in 1850 at the home of the historian Franz Kugler, and a close friendship developed between the two men.[3] Menzel also dedicated a richly allusive black chalk drawing from 1855 to his friend Heyse. It shows an assembly of Weimar poets, a group portrait with Jean Paul, Schiller, Goethe, and Herder. The sheet is now in Cambridge, Massachusetts.[4]

The present pastel *The Opera Glass*, created around 1850, strikes us as highly modern. The farther back the viewer steps from it, the more its special charm becomes apparent. In the choice of subject matter as well as in its artistic execution —the boldness of the view from above, of the cropping of the image, and of the composition with unworked areas—Menzel shows himself to be a precursor to Degas and Toulouse-Lautrec, more than a decade before the influence of Japanese woodcut on avant-garde European art. Max Liebermann reported a conversation with Degas in which the latter had spoken to him about Menzel "with words of the utmost admiration, saying that he considered him the greatest living master, whose *Ball Supper* he had tried to copy from memory."[5]

1 *Lady with Opera Glass*, c. 1850. Pastel on yellow-brownish tinted paper; 282 x 194 mm. Inscribed by the artist: "Erinn"; Tschudi 1905, pp. 192 f., no. 254 (repr.). Berlin 1980, p. 312, no. 12, p. 170 (repr. in color); Berlin 1997, pp. 164 ff., no. 67 (repr. in color; Marie Ursula Riemann-Reyher); Berlin, Staatliche Museen Preussischer Kulturbesitz, Kupferstichkabinett.

2 See Tschudi 1905, pp. 22 f., no. 510 (repr.); pp. 170 f., no. 214 (repr.); pp. 188 f., no. 246 (repr.). See also Vienna 1990, pp. 248–53, nos. 142–45 (repr. in color).

3 A very vivid, urbane, and elegant portrait of Heyse, drawn in pastel, is evidence of this friendship. It was done in 1853, one year before Heyse, as a "Northern light," was called to Munich by King Maximilian II of Bavaria to promote the literary and cultural life there. Pastel on dark brown tinted paper; 445 x 295 mm. Nuremberg 1967, p. 194, no. 186, color pl. 186. Munich 1976, p. 1009 (repr.). *Adolph Menzel, Realist—Historist—Maler des Hofes. Gemälde, Gouachen, Aquarelle, Zeichnungen und Druckgraphik*, ed. Jens Christian Jensen, exh. cat., Kunsthalle, Kiel; Kunsthalle, Bremen; Museum für Kunst und Kulturgeschichte, Lübeck; Altes Rathaus der Stadt, Schweinfurt; Städtisches Kunstsammlungen, Augsburg (Schweinfurt, 1981), pp. 54 f., no. 9 (repr.).

4 Fogg Art Museum, Harvard University, inv. no. 1943–531; cf. Annette Schlagenhauff, *Adolph Menzel: Works in Harvard Collections* (Cambridge, 1991), pp. 10 f. (repr.).

5 Ebertshäuser 1976, p. 1364.

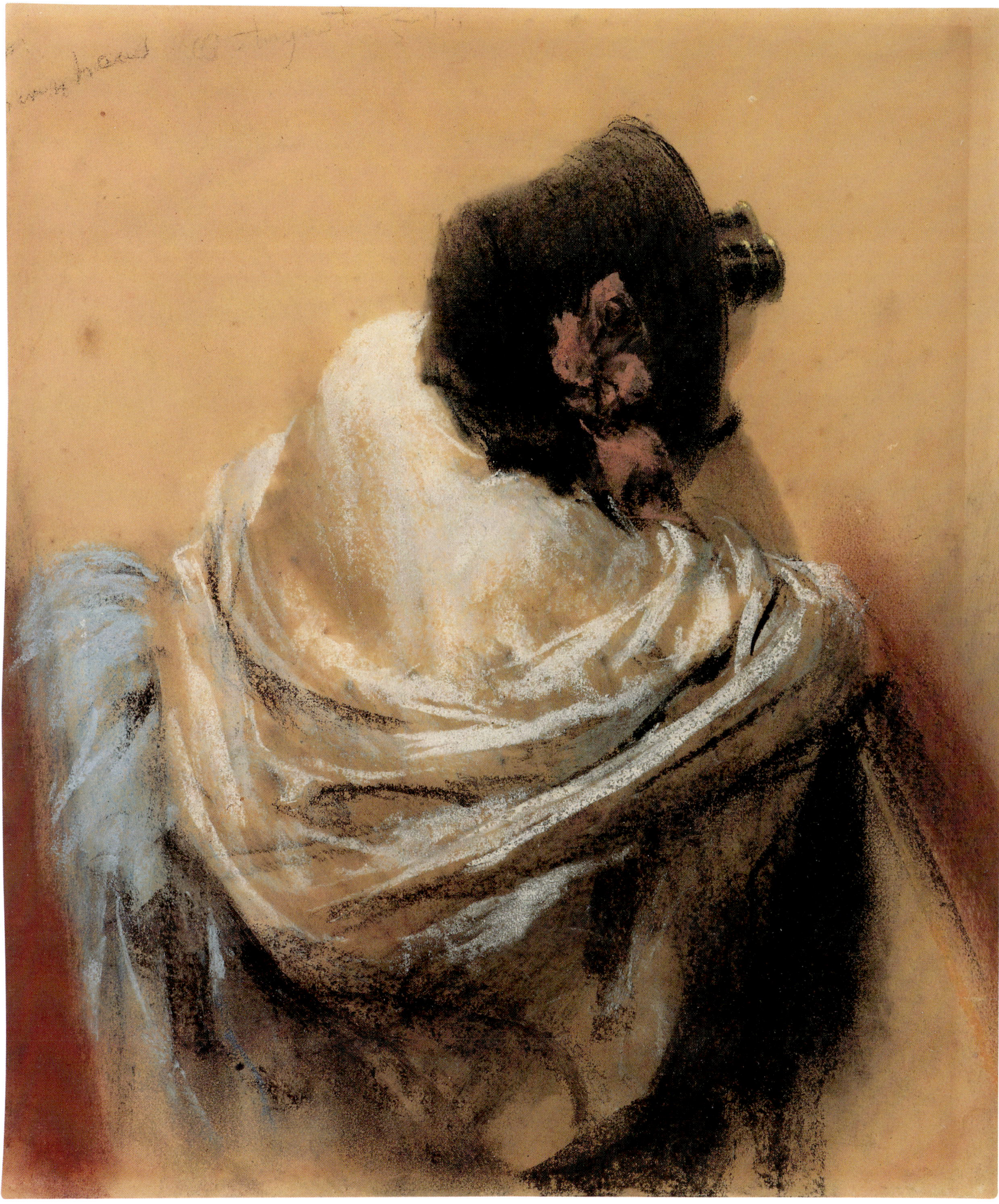

Epilogue

In addition to ongoing loans to special exhibitions, a selection of works from the Alfred Winterstein collection has only been exhibited twice before, in various German museums. For both these exhibitions, my father personally selected the works with great care; they were, above all, intended to offer examples of the artistic currents of a period which my father had made the focus of his collecting. But the exhibitions were also meant to express his pride in what he had achieved in decades of intensive study and diligent work. That might explain why my mother and I, following my father's death, had no plans for further exhibitions, although we were committed to expanding the collection in the same spirit.

It took the persuasive powers of James Cuno, the Elizabeth and John Moors Cabot Director of the Harvard University Art Museums in Cambridge, Massachusetts, with whom I have maintained a close friendship for years through the Friends of the Busch-Reisinger Museum, to convince me to show a selection of works to a wider public once more. He noted the importance of drawing in contemporary art, and the fact that many people, including those in the United States, have a stronger interest in this genre than one might expect. With the help of Peter Nisbet, the Daimler-Benz Curator of the Busch-Reisinger Museum, a selection was made of works from the Romantic era in Germany.

Hinrich Sieveking agreed to act as advisor to his American colleagues. In the present catalogue he describes the history of the collection with great sensitivity. His discussion of the individual works combines scholarship with an elucidation of the artistic developments of the time. His understanding of my father as a collector is more profound—or, certainly, more subtle—than anyone's, and today he is one of the preeminent experts on the German art of this period.

I am deeply grateful especially to these three individuals for the effort they invested in planning and preparing this exhibition. But I would also like to thank all the many others who have worked so hard to make the project a success. Of course, the greatest thanks and reward for all involved would be a warm reception of the exhibition by the public and a greater understanding of the artists and their ideas.

Wilhelm Winterstein

APPENDIX

<table>
<tr><td>

Die Loreley

Ich weiß nicht, was soll es bedeuten,
Daß ich so traurig bin;
Ein Märchen aus alten Zeiten,
das kommt mir nicht aus dem Sinn.

Die Luft ist kühl und es dunkelt,
Und ruhig fließt der Rhein;
Der Gipfel des Berges funkelt
Im Abendsonnenschein.

Die schönste Jungfrau sitzet
Dort oben wunderbar,
Ihr goldnes Geschmeide blitzet,
Sie kämmt ihr goldenes Haar.

Sie kämmt es mit goldenem Kamme,
Und singt ein Lied dabei;
Das hat eine wundersame,
Gewaltige Melodei.

Den Schiffer im kleinen Schiffe
Ergreift es mit wildem Weh;
Er schaut nicht die Felsenriffe,
Er schaut nur hinauf in die Höh'.

Ich glaube, die Wellen verschlingen
Am Ende Schiffer und Kahn;
Und das hat mit ihrem Singen
Die Loreley getan.

Heinrich Heine

</td><td>

The Loreley

I cannot explain the sadness
That's fallen on my breast.
An old, old fable haunts me,
And will not let me rest.

The air grows cool in the twilight,
And softly the Rhine flows on;
The peak of the mountain sparkles
Beneath the setting sun.

More lovely than a vision,
A girl sits high up there;
Her golden jewelry glistens,
She combs her golden hair.

With a comb of gold she combs it,
And sings an evensong;
The wonderful melody reaches
A boat, as its sails along.

The boatman hears, with an anguish
More wild than was ever known;
He's blind to the rocks around him;
His eyes are for her alone.

At last the waves devoured
The boat, and the boatman's cry;
And this she did with her singing,
The golden Loreley.

Translated by Aaron Kramer
In F. Ewen, ed., The Poetry and Prose of
Heinrich Heine *(New York, 1948)*

</td></tr>
</table>

Im Walde

Waldeinsamkeit! Ins schwellende Moos,
Da streck ich mich hin, hoch über mir groß
Wölbt grün sich das Dach von Zweigen;
Rings wilde Blumen blühn – und kühn,
So stürzt sich der rauschende Bach durchs Grün:
Sei gegrüßt, Du Jugendreigen!
Mein Horn soll es sagen und tragen,
Trariro, trariro
Wie bin ich der Jugend so froh, so froh
In den lustigen Sommertagen.

Waldeinsamkeit! O Du frische Schau
Durch der Blätter Spiel des Himmels Au
Das Blau durch die grünen Gipfel,
Und die Wolken fliegen daher – und hehr
Erhebt der Wald in der Lüfte Meer
Als Banner der Freiheit die Wipfel!
Mein Horn soll es sagen und tragen,
Trariro, trariro
Wie bin ich der Freiheit so froh, so froh
In den lustigen Sommertagen.

Waldeinsamkeit! Wie die Taube girrt,
Die Amsel als Herold zieht und schwirrt
In den Gipfeln singet sie sonnig.
Auf den Höhen der Falke schreit – und weit
Herauf tönt die alte und süße Zeit
O Liebe Du grüßest so wonnig!
Mein Horn soll es sagen und tragen
Trariro, trariro
Wie bin ich der Liebe so froh, so froh
In den lustigen Sommertagen.

Waldeinsamkeit! Wie der Wald rings spricht
Grüngoldene Strahlen und dämmriges Licht
Und Duften und Rauschen und Klingen,
Die Bäume die Vögel der Quell – und schnell
Durchtönen die Seele Gesänge mir hell,
Frischauf in den Wald sich zu schwingen!
Das Horn soll es sagen und tragen,
Trariro, trariro
Wie bin ich der Lieder so froh, so froh
In den lustigen Sommertagen.

Wolfgang Müller

In the Forest

Forest solitude! I lie down in the springy moss,
High above me there arches, large and green,
A roof of limbs and branches.
Wild flowers bloom all around, and boldly
The rushing stream flows through the green:
Greetings, you dance of youth!
My horn shall announce and proclaim it,
Trariro, trariro
How happy I am for youth, how happy,
In the pleasant days of summer.

Forest Solitude! O the fresh view of heaven's meadow
Through the play of the leaves,
The blue through the treetops of green.
The clouds drift along—and nobly
The forest raises its tops as a banner of freedom
In the sea of the sky!
My horn shall announce and proclaim it,
Trariro, trariro
How happy I am for freedom, how happy,
In the pleasant days of summer.

Forest solitude! As the dove coos,
The blackbird flies like a herald,
And in the treetops brightly sings.
On the heights the falcon screeches,
And the old, sweet time, resounds way up here,
O love your greeting is such a delight!
My horn shall announce and proclaim it,
Trariro, trariro
How happy I am for love, how happy,
In the pleasant days of summer.

Forest solitude! As the forest speaks all around
Golden-green rays and dusky light,
Sweet smells and rushing and ringing,
The trees the birds the spring—and quickly
The songs resound through my soul brightly,
To get up and into the forest!
My horn shall announce and proclaim it,
Trariro, trariro
How happy I am for songs, how happy,
In the pleasant days of summer.

Wolfgang Müller

Carl Barth

Eisfeld 12 October 1787 – 11 September 1853 Kassel

Carl Barth began his training with his father as a goldsmith's apprentice. His talent was recognized early, and in 1805 he began to receive support from Princess Therese von Thurn und Taxis. She enabled her protégé to study copper engraving from 1805 to 1812 with Johann Gotthard von Müller, a student of Wille's, at the Karlsschule in Stuttgart. There Barth learned the elegant "Parisian manner," rich in contrasts, and the faithful rendering of various materials and textures. In 1814 he went to Munich to continue his education, and there met Samuel Amsler and Carl Philipp Fohr.

Barth's most productive years, 1817 to 1821, were spent in Rome, where he shared lodgings with Amsler, an engraver, and with the painter Johann Anton Ramboux. A Protestant, he made contact with the inner circle of the Nazarenes and with Schnorr von Carolsfeld, who prompted him to study the engravings of Dürer and his contemporaries. The poet Friedrich Rückert became a lifelong friend. During his time in Rome Barth drew numerous and highly admired portraits of his fellow artists. In 1817 he and Amsler were commissioned to engrave the frontispiece to the *Nibelungenlied* illustrations of Peter Cornelius.

With Amsler and Ramboux, Barth was present when Carl Philipp Fohr drowned while swimming in the Tiber on 29 June 1818. Feelings of guilt for having encouraged his friend to go into the water and been unable to rescue him triggered a bout of depression, the first of a series that plagued Barth for the rest of his life. A serious fever contracted in 1821 forced him to return to Germany. After a stay in Nuremberg he went to Freiburg im Breisgau, where in 1824–25 he headed the copper-engraving shop of the Herder publishing house. After brief periods in Frankfurt and Darmstadt, Barth settled in Hildburghausen in 1830. For the next two decades he was employed, principally as a steel engraver, by the art-publishing department of the Bibliographical Institute headed by his friend, Joseph Meyer. In 1848 Barth was politically active for a time in the city parliament. Driven to despair by mental illness, he put an end to his life in 1853.

Barth's achievement lay in the dissemination of contemporary art, especially that of Thorvaldsen and of his own friends, the Nazarenes, through reproductions in an engraving style inspired by Dürer and Marcantonio Raimondi. His drawn and engraved portraits in particular, of which about four hundred have survived, show great talent. Barth also made a name for himself as an author of stories and poems, and as a translator and editor of Giuseppe Longhi's treatise on the art of copper engraving.

Carl Blechen

Cottbus 29 July 1798 – 23 July 1840 Berlin

Born to a poor Berlin family, Blechen began an apprenticeship in banking, but interrupted it in 1818 to do a year of voluntary military service with the Royal Corps of Guard-Engineers. A strong vocation led him to practice art in his spare time. Giving up his business career in 1822, Blechen enrolled in the Berlin Art Academy, where he concentrated on landscape.

On an 1823 journey through the mountains of Saxony and to Dresden he met Johann Christian Claussen Dahl and Caspar David Friedrich, whose art had a lasting influence on him. His works of the period attracted the interest of Karl Friedrich Schinkel, who in 1824 found him a post as a set painter at the recently opened Königstädtisches Theater. Blechen worked on theater productions for the next three years, an experience that accounts for the tendency toward a stagelike arrangement of planes and lighting effects in his later landscape compositions. He also concerned himself with lithography and etching.

The decisive event in Blechen's artistic development was his journey through Italy from October 1828 to November 1829, which brought his great painterly gifts to the fore. It was not the encounter with Italian art but the experience of light and color that opened his eyes to the beauty of landscape. Blechen's *plein air* oil sketches made him a forerunner of impressionism. Italy also inspired wonderfully airy brush drawings in sepia, and the famous views of his *Amalfi Sketchbook* (Kupferstichkabinett, Berlin), in which delimiting contours gave way to an open, painterly handling of color. In both his early and his radically different late work, atmospheric landscapes based on close observation were frequently given a romantic touch by the addition of such sentimental elements as Gothic church ruins or the figures of hermit monks.

In the years following his return to Germany, Blechen was at the height of his powers. He was appointed professor of landscape art at the Berlin Academy in 1831. Two years later he traveled through the Harz Mountains and to the island of Rügen. He became a full member of the Academy in 1835. But symptoms of a nervous disorder soon appeared, and in 1839 Blechen sank into a mental illness from which only death delivered him, at the age of forty-two. Most of his works can be found in Berlin.

Carl Gustav Carus

Leipzig 3 January 1789 – 28 July 1869 Dresden

In 1804, at the age of fifteen, Carus enrolled at Leipzig University to study physics and chemistry, among other sciences. Adding medicine in 1806, he graduated in 1811 with doctorates in both medicine and philosophy, as well as a master's in liberal arts. Throughout his life he practiced as a physician and gynecologist, becoming professor of obstetrics and head of the Dresden Maternity Clinic in 1814. Thirteen years later he was named physician to the king of Saxony.

As a university student the versatile Carus had begun taking lessons at the Leipzig Drawing Academy. Basically self-taught as a painter, he concentrated on landscapes, especially in moonlight. He was soon a member of the inner circle of romantic artists in Dresden, and became a close friend of Caspar David Friedrich, whose art influenced him significantly. His oil sketches from nature were inspired by the example of Johann Christian Claussen Dahl. Numerous journeys gave Carus the opportunity for artistic activity: he went to the island of Rügen in 1819; through the Riesengebirge in 1820; to Switzerland in 1821 and 1828; to Italy in 1821, 1828, and 1841; along the Rhein and to Paris in 1835; and to England and Scotland in 1844.

In writings on aesthetics the artist offered theoretical underpinnings for his approach to landscape, which was oriented less to subjective mood, in the style of Friedrich, than to the objective observation and realistic depiction of a scene, including the effects of atmosphere and illumination. From 1815 to 1824 he worked on his *Neun Briefe über Landschaftsmalerei* (Nine Letters on

Landscape Painting), which were published in 1831.

In 1818 he began a correspondence with Goethe on scientific issues. The two met in Marienbad in 1821, and shared intellectual interests led to a lifelong friendship. Carus also became Goethe's early biographer. Endowed with a universal talent of the kind Goethe envisaged, Carus was a key figure in Dresden romanticism. His accomplishments in medicine and other sciences were no less significant than his achievements in writing, art theory, and painting.

Daniel Chodowiecki

Danzig (now Gdansk) 16 October 1726 – 7 February 1801 Berlin)

In 1740, after his father's early death, Chodowiecki began a business apprenticeship in Danzig. He moved to Berlin in 1743 to work for his uncle, the proprietor of a gift shop, where for years he decorated small jars and boxes for sale. At the same time he was training in enamel painting with Johann Lorenz Haid of Augsburg, a student of Rugendas. Chodowiecki's work in this technique proved so successful that in 1754 he was able to establish his own studio.

Chodowiecki worked in the style of Watteau and Boucher. His family ties brought close contacts with the French Huguenot colony in Berlin. Though basically self-taught as an artist, he took classes in life drawing at Bernhard Rode's private academy and, eventually, classes in oil painting, a medium in which he first attracted attention in 1767, with *Jean Calas Bidding His Family Farewell*. In addition to conversation pieces in the French mode, he painted family scenes and Dutch-style interiors. Painting, however, played a relatively small role in his oeuvre; Chodowiecki's renown was based on his graphic art.

After becoming a member of the Berlin Academy in 1764, he promoted the reform of that institution and, in 1797, was named its director. Chodowiecki's original style in drawing and etching did not emerge until relatively late in his career. A master of the small format and the vignette, he illustrated countless calendars and almanacs, works of earlier and contemporary literature, and aesthetic and scientific treatises. His major achievements in this regard include illustrations for Lavater's *Physiognomic Fragments*, and for Basedow's standard work on education. Chodowiecki left an extremely rich graphic oeuvre comprising more than two thousand etchings and more than four thousand drawings. The creator of the style known as *Zopfstil*, or "pony-tail style," he was the major representative of the bourgeois art of rococo and Louis XVI during the period of Frederick the Great in Berlin. In contrast to the official, sensuous, and representational art of the court, Chodowiecki's was intimate, private, straightforward, and realistic. Today his large graphic œuvre offers a prime source for cultural history. Members of the rising middle class, whose values he disseminated in his works, felt themselves understood by him and rewarded him with a popularity unsurpassed in his day.

Peter Cornelius

Düsseldorf 23 September 1783 – 6 March 1867 Berlin

Cornelius's family, which probably came to Germany from the Netherlands, produced generation after generation of artists. He was first trained by his father, Aloys, inspector of the Düsseldorf Gallery. Then, beginning in 1795, he studied with the neoclassicist Peter Langer at the Düsseldorf Academy. After his father's early death, Cornelius supported the family by doing occasional illustrations and portraits.

Between 1803 and 1805 Cornelius entered the Weimar Art Competition three times without success, though his work did elicit praise from Goethe. In Cologne the artist made the acquaintance of the Boisserée brothers and Canon Ferdinand Franz Wallraf, and admired their collections of early German and Netherlandish art. Wallraf arranged for Cornelius's first important commission, the decoration of the cupola and choir of St. Quirin's in Neuss, executed in 1807–8. After moving to Frankfurt in 1809, Cornelius did illustrations for Goethe's *Faust (Part One)*, published the previous year, in which his original style emerged. Cornelius traveled through the Taunus Mountains with the painter Christian Xeller and then decided to continue with him, by way of Heidelberg and Switzerland, to Rome. There, in 1812, he joined the Nazarenes' Brotherhood of St. Luke, in which he later played leading role.

Initially Cornelius concerned himself with themes from the early German literature that the Nazarenes read together. He completed the remaining *Faust* illustrations; the first series, engraved by Thaeter and Ruscheweyh, was published in 1816 by Wenner in Frankfurt. He also drew illustrations for the *Nibelungenlied*, and Reimer, Berlin, published the engravings in 1817. From 1813 to 1816 Cornelius worked on an oil painting depicting the parable of the wise and foolish virgins.

Influenced by Luca Signorelli's frescoes in the Orvieto Cathedral, Cornelius was convinced that a renascence of German art could be achieved only through that medium. His first opportunity to try it came in 1816–17. The Prussian consul general, Jacob Salomon Bartholdy, commissioned Cornelius and other Prussian members of the Brotherhood of St. Luke to do frescoes in his apartments at Palazzo Zuccari depicting the biblical story of Joseph. Cornelius executed *Joseph Interprets the Pharaoh's Dreams* and *Joseph Recognized by His Brothers*, in which his own visual idiom came to full flower. Recognition for these works came immediately, when the Marchese Massimi commissioned him to decorate a room in the Casino Massimo with scenes from Dante's *Divine Comedy*. Preparatory drawings and cartoons followed for a ceiling fresco on the subject of Paradise.

Cornelius's meeting with Crown Prince Ludwig of Bavaria was a watershed in his life. The prince, wishing him to decorate the Glyptothek, took him to Munich in 1818. The Casino Massimo project was taken over by Philipp Veit. In 1819 Cornelius was named professor at the Munich Academy, where he soon attracted a large circle of students. From 1818 to 1830 he devoted himself to the Glypothek paintings. He devised a symbolic visual scheme based on classical mythology, but left the execution of the works largely to his students, which led to criticism of the paintings' supposed lack of unity and harmony.

From 1821 Cornelius served as director of the Düsseldorf Academy, teaching in the winter semesters, until he was named director of the Munich Academy in 1824. He was raised to the nobility the same year. From 1826 to 1836 he designed the decorations for the *loggie* of Leo von Klenze's Pinakothek, whose execution was entrusted to Clemens Zimmermann. A commission followed in 1829 for the decoration of Ludwigskirche, designed by Friedrich von Gärtner, and Cornelius spent years in Rome completing the designs. From 1836 to 1839, working alone, Cornelius painted the huge fresco representing the Last Judgment, but the result displeased King Ludwig and led to a break with him.

Ludwig's brother-in-law, King Friedrich Wilhelm IV of Prussia, thereupon called Cornelius to Berlin in 1840. He entrusted him with the decoration of the Campo Santo, a tomb for Prussian monarchs that was to be built adjacent to the cathedral. Though the artist devoted the rest of his life to making designs and cartoons for this project, it never came to fruition because political circumstances changed after the 1848 uprising.

Cornelius brought the ideas of the Nazarenes to Germany and put them into practice there. His rank as an artist rests above all on the abundance and originality of his ideas. He was more interested in conception than in execution, which he preferred to leave to others. Nor do his designs always reveal the hand of an outstanding draftsman. Cornelius shared the fate of Overbeck, in his earlier years earning the highest recognition and admiration and exerting a great influence on his students, but growing increasingly isolated and solitary with advancing age.

Moritz Michael Daffinger

Vienna 25 January 1790 – 22 August 1849 Vienna

After the untimely death of his father, a porcelain decorator, Moritz Michael Daffinger was apprenticed at age eleven to the Vienna Porcelain Manufacturing Company. In 1802 he also began attending the Academy of Visual Arts. Even before finishing his training and studies, Daffinger received several awards. He was employed by the porcelain company until 1812, decorating mugs, tobacco jars, plates, and cups with scenes from Greek and Roman mythology or copies of paintings in court collections. Portraits of members of the imperial house and personalities at court gave further proof of Daffinger's outstanding talent.

When French troops entered Vienna in 1809, he began his first series of portrait miniatures on ivory, depicting officers of Napoleon's army. In 1814 and 1815 the Congress of Vienna attracted numerous personalities of rank and fame to the city, and Daffinger was much in demand as a portraitist.

The artist's early work, relying on the tradition established by the French court artist Isabey, was characterized by a subdued palette. Influenced by English watercolor portraiture when Sir Thomas Lawrence came to Vienna in 1819, Daffinger developed an original, more decorative approach combined with stronger color. By the early 1820s his elegant and pleasing portraits had brought him wide acclaim, and he was all the fashion at court and among the aristocracy, which also put him in touch with Viennese literary circles. In the mid 1830s Daffinger reached the apex of his fame as a limner of feminine beauty in the Biedermeier mode.

After the death of his daughter in 1841, the artist gave up human portraiture and began depicting domestic flora, having special success with what were in effect portraits of flowers. He also collected prints, in particular by Rembrandt, whose style he emulated in a number of etchings during the last years of his life. Daffinger died of cholera, leaving behind a vast oeuvre that included more than one thousand portraits. Unlike the cool realism of a neoclassicist such as Füger, Daffinger's portraits have a lyrical, delicate touch. Their elegance, grace, and refinement mark the artist as a typical representative of Viennese art prior to the 1848 uprising.

Johann Georg von Dillis

Grüngiebing, Schwindkirchen near Haag, Upper Bavaria 26 December 1759 – 28 September 1841 Munich

Dillis was the son of a forester in the service of the electorate. The second of eleven children, he entered a Munich secondary school at an early age, his tuition being paid by his confirmation godfather, Prince-Elector Maximilian III Joseph. After studying philosophy and theology at the University of Ingolstadt from 1777, Dillis was ordained a priest. In 1786 he was released from clerical duties at his own request.

To supplement what he had taught himself, Dillis began formal art training in 1782 at the Munich Academy of Drawing (established in 1770) and worked as a drawing instructor in aristocratic Munich families. It was among the aristocracy, or in the "Illuminates" circle, which he joined in 1784 and in which he went by the name of "Timagoras," that Dillis met Sir Benjamin Thompson, an American with an influential position at the court of Prince-Elector Carl Theodor. Thompson, later Count Rumford, recognizing the young artist's outstanding gifts, helped further his artistic development and advance his career. In 1790, at Rumford's instigation, Dillis was appointed inspector of the new Electorate Gallery of Painting in Munich. Rumford also arranged for Dillis to accompany English aristocrats on their Continental tours; he went with Lord Palmerston and his family to Salzburg in 1794; with Sir Gilbert Elliot to Corsica in 1794–95; and with Lord Ossulton to the Bern Oberland, Switzerland, in 1797.

In 1796 and 1800, during the Wars of Coalition, Dillis organized the evacuation and safe storage of the painting collections in the face of advancing French troops. In 1803, as the libraries and art collections of Bavarian monasteries were being dissolved in the course of secularization, Dillis selected the most valuable paintings for the electorate collections. In 1806 he traveled to Paris in order to review, with Crown Prince Ludwig of Bavaria, the art treasures Napoleon had confiscated. From that point on he enjoyed a lifelong position of trust with Ludwig, later King Ludwig I of Bavaria.

In 1808 Dillis was raised to the nobility. The Munich Academy of Fine Arts was founded the same year, and Dillis became professor of landscape painting—a position he gave up in 1814 on the principle that "nature is the best teacher". In 1815, in Paris, he succeeded in having the most significant portion of the art booty taken by Napoleon returned to Munich. In 1822 Dillis succeeded Johann Christian von Mannlich as chief director of galleries. He rearranged the collections in Augsburg and Nuremberg and drew up an inventory.

Dillis contributed significantly to the expansion of the art collections Ludwig held—as crown prince and as king—by acquiring key individual works, by Raphael, for instance, or entire collections, such as the Boisserée and Wallerstein. He also supervised the construction of Leo von Klenze's Pinakothek, and the selection and hanging of the paintings there. Numerous journeys (eleven to Italy alone), frequently in the company of Ludwig, served Dillis's professional activities and further education. Dillis also managed to pursue his own art during his travels, especially drawings and watercolors.

Dillis's graphic legacy is estimated at over ten thousand works, of which about nine thousand are kept in the State Archive of the Upper Bavarian Historical Society and about 250 in the Staatliche Graphische Sammlung, Munich. Dillis also left some 250 oil sketches and paintings. His significance as a painter is now seen primarily in his fresh, innovative, wonderfully atmospheric oil sketches. With Wilhelm von Kobell and Carl Rottmann, Dillis was one of the most outstanding southern German landscapists of the day, and unique in terms of artistic aims that were far in advance of his times.

Carl Philipp Fohr

Heidelberg 26 November 1795 – 29 June 1818 Rome

The eldest son of a language teacher employed by the French reformed congregation, Carl Philipp Fohr grew up in humble circumstances. His drawing talent became evident at such an early age that his father apprenticed him, in about 1807, to the university drawing master Friedrich Rottmann, who also taught his own son, Carl, and Ernst Fries. In the summer of 1810, Fohr, then fourteen, was working outdoors in the Neckar Valley, drawing Stift Neuburg, when the landscapist Georg Wilhelm Issel came across him. Recognizing his unusual gifts, Issel encouraged the boy, instructing him in history and literature, and obtaining small illustration jobs for him. In 1811 Issel brought Fohr to Darmstadt, where he introduced him the following year to Philipp Dieffenbach, a historian and tutor to the princes at the Hessian court. The two soon became close friends.

It was Dieffenbach who introduced Fohr to a woman who would change his life: Princess Wilhelmine of Hesse, née Princess of Baden. In the winters of 1813–14 and 1814–15 the artist made two albums of superb watercolors for the princess, known as *The Sketchbook of the Neckar Region* and *The Baden Sketchbook*. In response Fohr's patroness granted him an annual salary of 400 guilders to ensure his livelihood.

In the early summer of 1814 Georg Moller, chief building councilor of Darmstadt, instructed Fohr in perspective and the rendering of shadows, and introduced him to medieval architecture. In Heidelberg Fohr attended lectures on German history at the university and frequently visited the Boisserée brothers' collection of early German and Netherlandish paintings. Fohr's enthusiasm for the Middle Ages, furthered by readings Dieffenbach suggested in the *Nibelungenlied*, sagas, and tales of chivalry, led to numerous depictions of related subjects.

From July 1815 to May 1816, Fohr studied at the Munich Academy under the neoclassical history painter Peter von Langer, copied works in the Gemäldegalerie, and discovered the landscapes of Joseph Anton Koch. In September and October of 1815, he walked by way of the Tyrol to Verona, Padua, and Venice, and on the return trip stayed in Salzburg. In Munich Fohr became friends with Ludwig Sigismund Ruhl, a painter from Kassel who shared his enthusiasm for the German late Middle Ages. The two collaborated on illustrations for poems by Friedrich de la Motte Fouqué and Ludwig Tieck. Ruhl and Domenico Quaglio introduced Fohr to painting in oils. During the summer of 1816 Fohr was back in Heidelberg, where he frequented the Teutonia students' association. In October and November he traveled to Rome, making the acquaintance of German artists, especially the Nazarenes. Fohr's reunion with Ruhl was apparently less happy, since they soon broke off their friendship.

In the meantime Fohr had made the acquaintance of Wilhelm von Harnier and Koch, an artist whose love of liberty matched his own. Working in Koch's studio, Fohr painted a series of works that included a commission for Johann David Passavant. From August to November 1817 he was incapacitated by a serious case of "Roman fever." Toward the end of the year he began preparatory work for a group portrait of German artists at the Café Greco—forty-eight portrait studies and four compositional designs for a planned etching—but apparently abandoned the project. For a farewell party German artists gave Crown Prince Ludwig of Bavaria in April 1818, Fohr painted landscapes on banners, which earned special recognition from the prince.

On 29 June 1818, Fohr drowned while swimming in the Tiber, as his friends Barth, Amsler, and Ramboux looked on helplessly. He was only twenty-two. His artistic legacy comprises seven oil paintings and an estimated seven hundred to eight hundred drawings and watercolors. In the fields of portraiture and landscape Fohr created works of the very highest quality. He remained independent of Nazarene influence, even during his stay in Rome. Though largely self-taught, particularly in drawing, Fohr was one of the major artistic talents of the Goethe period.

Caspar David Friedrich

Greifswald 5 September 1774–7 May 1840 Dresden

Caspar David Friedrich was the son of a soapmaker. The early loss of his mother, in 1781, and the death of his younger brother, who drowned before his eyes in 1787 after rescuing Caspar David during a skating accident, influenced his temperament profoundly.

Friedrich first received drawing instruction from Johann Gottfried Quistorp, an architect and university teacher who took him on walking tours that opened his eyes to the unique beauty of the northern German countryside. In 1794 he began a four-year study of the fundamentals of drawing at the Copenhagen Academy with Nicolai Abildgaard and Jens Juel. In 1798 Friedrich moved to Dresden, where, apart from occasional travels, he spent the rest of his life.

A key event was his 1802 reunion with Philipp Otto Runge, whom Friedrich had met the previous year. Dresden was developing into a center for romantic literature and art. Writers gathered around Friedrich Schlegel, Ludwig Tieck, Novalis, and, later, Heinrich von Kleist and Theodor Körner; artists included Gerhard von Kügelgen, Runge, Friedrich August von Klinckowström, the Riepenhausen brothers, Ferdinand Olivier, and, later, Carl Gustav Carus and Johann Christian Claussen Dahl. Friedrich soon stood at the focus of artistic endeavor in Dresden.

Submitting sepia drawings to Goethe's Weimar Competition of 1805, Friedrich was awarded half the prize. Personal contacts with Goethe ensued. Works in sepia were prominent in Friedrich's oeuvre, both early and late.

In 1806 the artist traveled through his home province of Pomerania and went on a walking tour of Rügen Island. The following year he began oil painting. The first oil to be shown publicly, in a studio exhibition of 1808, was *The Cross in the Mountains*, later known as the *Tetschen Altarpiece*, after its location in the chapel at Count Thun's Tetschen Castle. This landscape raised to the status of altar image drew harsh criticism, which led to a public dispute with the reviewer, Basilius von Ramdohr.

In the summer of 1810 Friedrich and his friend Georg Friedrich Kersting hiked through the Riesengebirge, a trip that yielded landscape sketches that eventually led to an entire series of late watercolors and oils. The following summer Friedrich went on a walking tour through the Harz Mountains, with similar artistic results. From 1808 to 1810 he painted his two major large-format works, *Monk by the Sea* and *Abbey in an Oak Wood*, which were included in the 1810 exhibition of the Berlin Academy and acquired by the king of Prussia at the behest of the crown prince. That year the artist was voted a member of the Academy by a slim majority. Membership in the Dresden Academy followed in 1816.

Friedrich married Christiane Caroline Bommer in 1818 and two years later moved with her into a building overlooking the River Elbe. Dahl became a neighbor in 1823. After visiting Friedrich's atelier in December 1820, the czar's son, Grand Duke Nicholas of Russia, began to collect his works. In 1824 the king of Saxony named Friedrich assistant professor, without permission to teach publicly, at the Dresden Academy. In 1835 the artist suffered a stroke that considerably hampered his ability to work and prompted him to spend a period at the spas in Teplitz.

One of the two major representatives of German romantic painting (Runge was the other), Friedrich died in isolation and poverty. His work was soon forgotten, despite its influence on Carus, Dahl, and others—despite, in fact, its having been the seed of an entire school. Friedrich's most gifted students were Ernst Ferdinand Oehme and August Heinrich. The existential content of his art would be rediscovered in the twentieth century, influencing post-World War II art in particular. Friedrich's estate comprised an estimated three hundred paintings, of which about half have survived, as well as a rich graphic oeuvre. This includes eighteen etchings, four woodcuts (executed by his brother, Christian), and approximately one thousand drawings, sepias, and watercolors, including seven transparencies.

Ernst Fries

Heidelberg 22 June 1801–12 October 1833 Karlsruhe

The son of a prosperous banker and art collector, Fries grew up in an artistic milieu. At the age of nine he joined his friends Carl Philipp Fohr and Carl Rottmann in drawing lessons with Rottmann's father, Friedrich. A crucial influence on his development was the Scottish landscapist George Augustus Wallis, who was active in Heidelberg from 1812 to 1815 and introduced Fries to oil painting and glaze technique. In 1815 Fries continued his training with court artist Karl Kuntz in Karlsruhe, then spent a year at the Munich Academy.

In 1818, Fries, Rottmann, and others took a journey along the Rhine and Mosel that yielded a great number of landscape studies. After taking courses in optics and perspective with the architect Georg Moller in Darmstadt in 1818–19, Fries returned to Munich for the year 1820–21, later taking study trips to the Salzburg region, Tyrol, and Switzerland. Then he decided to go to Italy.

Living in Rome from 1823–27, the artist frequented the circles of landscapists Joseph Anton Koch and Martin von Rohden. He became a close friend of the painter and draftsman Ludwig Richter, who described him in his memoirs as a "highly talented" artist who played a key role in the trends toward painterly technique and the use of colorism then emerging in Rome. Fries also befriended the French landscapist Camille

Corot, accompanying him on excursions in the Campagna, and drawing his portrait working outdoors. During a trip to the Gulf of Naples with another friend, the poet and painter August Kopisch, Fries rediscovered the Blue Grotto on Capri.

Returning to Germany, the artist went first to Heidelberg, where he married, and then back to Munich in 1829. He worked on paintings based on the numerous oil sketches, watercolors, and drawings he had done in Italy. In 1831 Fries was called to Karlsruhe to serve as artist to the Baden court, where, just two years later and at the height of his powers, he died of scarlet fever.

With Rottmann, Fries was one of the most outstanding landscapists of the younger generation, depicting the natural scene with a superb breadth of vision and richness of color. His sense of delicate, painterly tone gradations also came to the fore in his precise and atmospheric pencil drawings, and he produced lithographs as well.

Henry Fuseli
(Johann Heinrich Füssli)

Zurich 6 February 1741–16 April 1825 Putney Hill, near London

Füssli (later anglicized to Fuseli) came from an old Zurich family of artists. His father, Johann Caspar Füssli, was a portraitist, draftsman, and writer on art who published the writings of his friends Winckelmann and Mengs as well as his own *Geschichte der besten Künstler in der Schweiz* (History of the Best Artists in Switzerland). So Fuseli grew up in an artistically rich atmosphere and, at a young age, began to frequent the enlightened Zurich literary circle of Johann Jacob Bodmer. Here he was encouraged to read Homer, the Nibelung legends, Dante, Shakespeare, and Milton, whose works later provided subjects for drawings and paintings.

Since his father wished him to become a clergyman, Fuseli studied theology and in 1761 was ordained minister of the Reformed Evangelical Church. Then, only two years later, he was involved in a public scandal in Zurich. He and his boyhood friend, Johann Caspar Lavater, later author of *Physiognomic Fragments*, to which Fuseli contributed illustrations, produced evidence that led to the despotic Governor Grebel's conviction on corruption charges.

Forced to leave the city, the two found temporary refuge in Berlin. There Fuseli met the Swiss philosopher Johann Georg Sulzer, who advised him to go to England to facilitate contacts between English and German science and literature. In 1764 he settled in England, where he became acquainted with the intellectual elite of the Enlightenment and early romantic period. Fuseli earned his living by translating numerous French, Italian, and German books and essays into English, including Winckelmann's *Thoughts Concerning the Imitation of Greek Works in Painting and Sculpture*. But his artistic ambitions were not neglected in the process.

After Joshua Reynolds, favorably impressed with his drawings and early essays in painting, encouraged him in 1768 to make a career in art, Fuseli went to Italy to continue his education on his own. From 1770 to 1778 he lived in Rome, where classical art and Michelangelo's works profoundly influenced him. From that point on, the human figure stood at the center of Fuseli's concerns. He traveled to Venice in 1772 and to Naples in 1775. In 1778 he returned to Switzerland and the following year to England, resuming his activities as a translator, author, and editor. His breakthrough as an artist came with *Nightmare*, a painting exhibited in 1782 and thereafter often reproduced.

Subjects drawn from English literature contributed greatly to establishing Fuseli's reputation. The years 1786–90 were largely devoted to nine canvases from which engraved illustrations were to be made for the *Shakespeare Gallery*, a deluxe edition of the poet's complete works published by John Boydell. From 1790 to 1800 Fuseli created his major opus, the forty-seven paintings and more than one hundred drawings of the *Milton Gallery*, on which engraved illustrations to *Paradise Lost* were based. The painting cycle was exhibited three times and, though it was not especially well received by the public, it did further Fuseli's career.

Fuseli married in 1788. He became a member of the Royal Academy in 1790 and a professor there in 1799. His 1801 lectures on painting were received with great interest, and were published along with other writings on art. In 1804 he was named Inspector of the Royal Academy, and in 1816, at Canova's behest, a member of the Accademia di S. Luca in Rome. Fuseli continued to devote equal time to artistic and scholarly concerns into advanced age. He was buried in St. Paul's Cathedral in London.

Fuseli was one of the most fascinating and versatile figures of the Goethe period, a typical dual talent of the Sturm and Drang, a fine writer, but above all an artist of true originality, great inventiveness, imagination, and skill, whose unique gifts are especially evident in his many drawings.

Friedrich Gilly

Altdamm, near Stettin
16 February 1772 – 7 August 1800 Karlsbad

Gilly's father, descended from a Huguenot family that emigrated to Germany in 1689, was an architect who built several palaces for the Prussian royal house in the early German neoclassical style, and who wrote extensively on agriculture and hydraulic engineering. He recognized and furthered his son's talent early on, and took him along on official trips.

In 1788, after an apprenticeship in masonry and carpentry, Friedrich Gilly began studying with the architects Carl Gotthard Langhans and Friedrich Wilhelm von Erdmannsdorff, and at the Berlin Academy, where his teachers included Daniel Chodowiecki and Johann Gottfried Schadow. In 1790 he traveled to Westphalia and Holland to study hydraulic engineering, going on three years later to Paris, where he was intrigued by the consequences of the French Revolution, including revolutionary architecture.

In 1794 Gilly accompanied his father to East and West Prussia. Here he made drawings of the Marienburg, which, published in aquatints by Friedrich Frick, elicited great attention. The prints provided the impetus and the basis for the subsequent restoration of this castle and its declaration as a national monument. They also encouraged a renascence of northern German brick construction.

Two of Gilly's urban projects, though never put into practice, were highly admired and influential: his 1796 designs for a monument to Frederick the Great, and his 1797 designs for the Berlin Schauspielhaus, or theater. Named chief royal building inspector and given a government grant, he went on a study trip to England, France, southern Germany, Vienna, and Prague in 1797. The next year he became professor of optics, perspective, and architectural drawing at the newly inaugurated Building Academy and in 1799 he founded the "Private Society of Young Architects," in which he, Schinkel, and others concerned themselves with aesthetics and architectural theory. His design for the figurative frieze for the Berlin Mint, executed by Schadow, dates from that year.

A versatile talent, Gilly rapidly became a leading representative of the Berlin school of architecture, his drawings and designs moving it in the direction of a classical revival oriented to French revolutionary architecture and based on simplified geometric volumes. Called by his contemporaries "the greatest genius in the field of building," Gilly died at the age of twenty-eight. Only a few of his designs were ever built, and only one of these has survived, albeit in ruins, namely the Mausoleum in Dyhernfurth near Breslau. His ideas greatly influenced the next generation of architects, especially Leo von Klenze, and their effect on the work of his student Karl Friedrich Schinkel was epoch-making.

Johann Wolfgang von Goethe

Frankfurt am Main
28 August 1749–22 March 1832 Weimar

Thanks to his parents' interests, Goethe was immersed in art from earliest childhood. In September 1758 he began receiving drawing lessons from a private tutor. During his university years in Leipzig, Goethe was occasionally instructed by Adam Friedrich Oeser, director of the Academy, who also introduced him to art theory. Lessons in etching led to original attempts and to copies of landscapes by Alexander Thiele and others.

During various phases of his career, in Frankfurt, Strasbourg, and in the Merck circle in Darmstadt, Goethe drew landscapes, genre scenes, and portraits in the Dutch manner. Under the supervision of the painter and etcher Johann Andreas Nothnagel in Frankfurt, he tried his hand at oil painting, but with little success. Here, as later in Weimar, Goethe took drawing lessons with Georg Melchior Kraus, cofounder of the Ducal Free Drawing School in Weimar.

A decisive caesura in his life came with Goethe's Italian journey of 1786—88, which brought insight into both his vocation as a writer and his limitations as an artist. Yet in spite of his express intention to relinquish visual art entirely, he continued to draw throughout his career, especially during his journeys. In Italy, exchanges of ideas with J.H. Wilhelm Tischbein, with the draftsman of picturesque views Christoph Heinrich Kniep, and with painters Friedrich Bury and Jacob Philipp Hackert, helped Goethe develop a clearer and more defined style.

In 1806–7, a time of political turmoil, Goethe produced the delicately colored drawings of the delightful *Reise-, Zerstreuungs- und Trostbüchlein* (A Little Book of Travel, Diversion, and Consolation), made for Princess Caroline von Sachsen-Weimar. These drawings were followed in 1810 by a work to which Goethe attached great weight, a series of twenty-two depictions of Thuringian and, especially, Bohemian landscapes. In 1821 he had a small selection of his drawings published as etchings, accompanied by poems.

At his death Goethe's estate included approximately three thousand drawings, most of which are now in Weimar. They reflect his multifarious interests and his universal personality. The majority of the drawings are related to Goethe's professional concerns, such as theatrical practice, or to his scientific research in fields extending from color theory to anatomy, zoology, botany, geology, and meteorology. Drawing served Goethe as a means to sharpen his vision and memory, and, in the natural sciences, to increase his knowledge. This explains the importance he placed on the educational function of art, and his dedication to the Weimar School of Drawing and his competitions for young artists. As a draftsman Goethe remained a dilettante in the best sense of the word. Apart from the caesura through the Italian journey, it is difficult to detect any development in his work, because diverse means of expression coexisted throughout his career. Nevertheless, all of his visual creations are marked by a characteristic blend of objectivity and poetry.

Anton Graff

Winterthur, Switzerland
18 November 1736–22 June 1813 Dresden

The portraitist Anton Graff came of a family of pewter makers in Winterthur. After early training at the local drawing school run by Johann Ulrich Schellenberg, the young artist went to Augsburg, Germany, where he worked from 1753 to 1756 under Johann Jakob Haid, an engraver and master of mezzotint. In 1757 he moved to Ansbach, where he was employed by the portrait and miniature painter Leonhard Schneider in making copies of a portrait of Frederick the Great. From 1759 he was active as a portraitist, at first returning to Haid's studio in the prosperous trading center of Augsburg, where he stayed until 1764, then spending extended periods in Regensburg, seat of the German Reichstag, before returning to Winterthur and Zurich.

In 1766, Christian Ludwig Hagedorn offered Graff a position at the Dresden Academy as professor of portraiture and court painter to the prince-elector of Saxony. Commissions took him to Leipzig and Berlin, where in 1771, at the home of Johann Georg Sulzer, the Swiss philosopher, he met the poet Gotthold Ephraim Lessing and did his portrait. The same year Graff married Sulzer's daughter, Auguste. In 1783, at Teplitz, a spa in Bohemia, he made the acquaintance of an itinerant French artist by the name of Jean-Baptiste Carvelle, whose forte was miniature portraits in silverpoint. Graff quickly learned the technique and employed it from then on, mostly for miniature profile portraits.

A highly skilled craftsman and a tireless worker, Graff executed a total of almost two thousand portraits during his career. His order book (present whereabouts unknown) listed 1,655 oil paintings and 322 silverpoint drawings, with sitter's name and price paid. Graff's portraits are suffused by the Enlightenment spirit, reflecting an optimistic view of man. Thanks to their individual characterization and natural poses, they were highly regarded during his day, and many were reproduced and popularized in engravings by more than 130 craftsmen.

Ludwig Emil Grimm

Hanau 14 March 1790–4 April 1863 Kassel)

The youngest brother of the German philologists Jacob and Wilhelm Grimm, Ludwig Emil initially trained at the Kassel Academy from 1805 to 1807, developing his drawing and etching skills. Through his brothers he made contacts among the literary romantics associated with Achim von Arnim, Clemens and Bettina Brentano, and the jurist Friedrich Karl von Savigny. This led to collaboration on key literary projects, such as illustrations for the poetry anthology *Des Knaben Wunderhorn* (The Boy's Cornucopia) and for the *Zeitung für Einsiedler* (Hermits' Newspaper).

In 1808 Grimm was in the university town of Landshut with Brentano and Savigny, who arranged for his further education at the Munich Academy. He continued his studies there, with interruptions, until 1817, devoting himself to oil painting and to illustrating *Grimm's Fairy Tales*. In 1814 he fought in the War of Liberation from Napoleon, serving as a lieutenant in a Hessian regiment in the French campaign.

In September 1815 Grimm had a meeting in Frankfurt with Goethe, who praised his sketchbooks. The artist then went on to Heidelberg, to see the Boisserée Collection. In the spring of 1816 Grimm and Georg von Brentano set off on a three-month journey to Italy, where Grimm made contact with the Nazarenes. Some of the artist's abundant drawings which he acquired were subsequently published as etchings.

In the autumn of 1817 Grimm returned to Kassel. Five years later he drew portraits of twelve of the best-known professors at Göttingen University, which he published as two series of etchings, in 1823 and 1826. These, too, elicited Goethe's admiration. In 1828 Grimm participated in the Nuremberg ceremonies to commemorate the three-hundredth anniversary of Dürer's death. It was an experience he wrote about at length in his memoirs.

In 1842, after the death of his first wife, Grimm moved to Berlin temporarily to live with his brother Wilhelm. There he met Cornelius, Begas, and Menzel, and in 1843 executed the famous double-portrait etching of his brothers Jacob and Wilhelm. Ludwig Emil Grimm left only a small number of paintings—mainly portraits of family members, genre pictures, and works on religious themes. His gifts lay in drawing and etching, the media in which he produced a great range of portraits, landscapes, genre works, and depictions of animals. His most significant works are the portraits, particularly those of his early career.

August Heinrich

Dresden 17 August 1794 – 27 September 1822
Innsbruck

August Heinrich entered the Dresden Academy in 1810, and from 1812 studied in Vienna. Outside the academy, key impulses came from his friendships with Ferdinand Olivier and Julius Schnorr von Carolsfeld. In particular, the sophisticated, rigorous drawings Olivier made on his second trip to Salzburg, in 1817, exerted a lasting influence on Heinrich's naturalistic landscape studies. In 1818, having contracted a severe lung ailment, Heinrich returned to Dresden, where he became a pupil of Caspar David Friedrich and Johann Christian Claussen Dahl. Heinrich was the most gifted of Friedrich's students, and the two artists soon became friends.

With a scholarship from the king of Saxony, Heinrich was on his way to Italy in the summer of 1822 when he died of tuberculosis in Innsbruck. He was twenty-eight. He left behind a relatively small oeuvre, which was decimated during World War II. Five oil paintings and about one hundred drawings survive. Despite his limited output, Heinrich's painstaking investigations of nature and devoted immersion in its phenomena, his graphic discipline and subtle, detailed style in oils had a decisive influence on Dresden landscape painting, moving it in the direction of realism.

Franz Theobald Horny

Weimar 23 November 1798 – 23 June 1824
Olevano, Italy

Horny received his first instruction at the age of eight from his father, a painter and engraver who taught at the Weimar drawing school and who had decorated several rooms in Goethe's residence and the "Roman House" with surpassingly modest designs. Horny subsequently studied with Goethe's friend, Councillor Johann Heinrich Meyer, who set the boy to copying old masters and works by Jacob Philipp Hackert. Although this helped Horny learn formulas, it did not advance his technical skills significantly and it stifled his imagination.

In May 1815 Horny met Carl Friedrich von Rumohr, an encounter that proved decisive. Thirteen years his senior and a prosperous man, Rumohr became Horny's paternal friend, mentor, and patron, essentially supporting him for the rest of his life. He immediately invited him on his second journey to Italy, with an eye to shaping the young artist in accordance with his own educational ideals.

From Munich, where he had oriented himself at the academy and discovered the landscapes of Joseph Anton Koch, Horny proceeded to Italy with Rumohr in November 1816. Staying in Florence to the end of the year, he acquainted himself with early Italian painting under Rumohr's tutelage. In Rome he initially lived with Koch, studying in his studio for a year and assisting in the underpainting of landscapes. In June 1817 Rumohr took his protégé to Olevano, a mountain town southeast of Rome. Here, and in Frascati that August, Horny devoted himself to drawings and watercolors of plants, from nature. He met Peter Cornelius, who was likewise working in the area.

In September 1817 Cornelius was commissioned by the Marchese Massimi to decorate a room of his Casino Massimo with scenes from Dante's *Divine Comedy*. During the preparatory phase Cornelius employed Horny as an assistant in designing the ornamental festoons and garlands. The work did not proceed beyond the first three cartoons, however, because in the spring of 1818, Crown Prince Ludwig of Bavaria called Cornelius to Munich to decorate the Glyptothek, and his contract with Massimi was annulled. Thus Horny's involvement in the project ended. The period of his collaboration with Cornelius brought a strong Nazarene influence into his style.

In June 1818, Horny suffered his first bout of chronic tuberculosis, which at times severely curtailed his ability to work and necessitated a move to the more favorable climate of the Sabine Mountains. The artist lived at Casa Baldi, in Olevano, until his death.

In 1820–21 Horny created two highly finished watercolors for Rumohr, who rejected these inventions, however, as too cerebral. The artist's Nazarene friends, not surprisingly, were enthusiastic about the works. The contrasting responses gave rise to a fundamental theoretical debate between Rumohr and Johann David Passavant on the aims of contemporary art. In the process, Horny was involuntarily caught up in a quarrel with Rumohr that ended in a painful break.

It was ultimately the worsening state of his health that forced Horny to remove himself from the overweening influence of his Nazarene friends. In the beneficial air and solitude of the mountains around Olevano he finally arrived at his own style, creating his most beautiful landscape studies out of the immediate encounter with nature. But just as his work was beginning to come to full flower, Horny's life was cut short by tuberculosis at the age of twenty-five.

Though he referred to himself as a painter, he did not get beyond a few attempts in oils, most of which have since been lost. Horny's graphic talent, however, was as outstanding as Carl Philipp Fohr's. His estate, comprising three to four hundred drawings and watercolors and five sketchbooks, is largely to be found in his home town of Weimar.

Georg Friedrich Kersting

Güstrow 23 October 1785 – 1 July 1847 Meissen

After the early death of his father, a district glazier, Kersting grew up in straitened circumstances. In the fall of 1804 he began studies at the drawing school of the Copenhagen Academy, going on to the plaster and life class and finally to Nicolai Abildgaard's painting class, which he completed in the spring of 1808. To the Copenhagen Academy, which bestowed many honors on him, Kersting owed a masterful drawing technique and, in painting, a preference for the small format, a sense of subtle color values, and a delicate glaze technique.

In 1808 Kersting returned to his home town of Güstrow, where he joined the Freemasons the following year. In the footsteps of Philipp Otto Runge and Caspar David Friedrich, he then moved to Dresden, where he enrolled in the academy in 1810 and gave drawing lessons to the children of C.F. Frommann, a Jena publisher. Here Kersting established friendly ties with the families of Christian Gottfried Körner and Gerhard von Kügelgen, with Louise Seidler, Carl Gustav Carus, and above all, with Friedrich, whose art profoundly influenced him. In July of 1810 Kersting and Friedrich hiked through the Riesengebirge together. During these years the artist produced his finest so-called "room portraits," in which the sitters were depicted in their domestic ambiance. He had his first successful exhibitions in Dresden and Weimar. Out of his patriotic enthusiasm, Kersting followed Theodor Körner's proclamation, joined the Lützow Freikorps and in 1813–15 fought Napoleon's armies in the War of Liberation, distinguishing himself for bravery beyond the call of duty.

In 1816–18 he was active in Warsaw as a drawing instructor in the service of Princess Sapieha. On 1 July 1818 Kersting accepted what would be a lifetime post as supervisor of decoration at the Meissen Porcelain Factory, which left him little time for his own work. He introduced a new style of painted decoration and improvements in the gilding of porcelain which, with other technical innovations, led to greatly increased sales. Kersting supervised the manufacture of tableware for the Duke of Wellington in 1819. Business trips took him repeatedly to the Leipzig Fair or to industrial exhibitions in Berlin, and he traveled to Nuremberg for the Dürer jubilee of 1828.

Kersting's intimate interiors, done under the influence of seventeenth-century Dutch painting, represent a masterful and unique contribution to romantic art. Combining portrait and genre, they have an inimitable mood that derives from sophisticated lighting effects. As authentic records of bourgeois life in the Biedermeier period, the depictions are also of importance as cultural history.

Leo von Klenze

Schladen/Harz 28 February 1784–27 January 1864 Munich

The eldest of seven children of a well-to-do government attorney, Klenze received a humanistic education in Brunswick. In 1800 he enrolled at Berlin University to study law. But, encouraged by the works of the brilliant Friedrich Gilly, who had recently died, Klenze switched to architecture. He lived in the house of Friedrich's father, David Gilly, who was also his teacher. At the same time he attended Alois Hirt's classes in archaeology and classical architectural forms.

Going to Paris in 1803, Klenze continued his studies with Durand, Percier and Fontaine, who introduced him to the Empire style and its graceful ornamentation. He then took a trip to Italy that eventually had great consequences for his career.

From 1803 to 1813 Klenze served as court architect to King Jérôme of Westphalia, Napoleon's brother, who commissioned him to build the theater at Wilhelmshöhe Palace. During this period of his first successes, Klenze married the daughter of a composer from Turin.

In 1815 he traveled to the Congress of Vienna, hoping to find a new patron among the monarchs gathered there. He was disappointed in this regard, but on the way to Vienna Klenze had had a providential meeting with Crown Prince Ludwig of Bavaria, who asked him to submit to the design competition for the Munich Glyptothek. Their shared interest in classical architecture resulted in a lifelong bond between monarch and architect.

Klenze's commission to erect the Glyptothek (1816–30), a museum devoted solely to the history of sculpture, and one of the earliest public museums in the world, would have momentous consequences. In 1820 the architect was named court building supervisor and, after Ludwig I's accession to the throne, he was promoted in 1825 to royal building councillor and head of the General Building Administration. In this capacity Klenze served for decades as Munich's most influential architect and city planner. Like Schinkel in Berlin, he determined to a great extent the look of Munich in the nineteenth century, and indeed to the present day.

Klenze's major works included museum buildings that became prototypes for museum architecture far beyond Germany's borders: aside from the Glyptothek, he designed the Pinakothek, devoted to painting, which was built between 1826 and 1836, and the annex to the Hermitage in St. Petersburg, built between 1839 and 1851. Klenze also designed buildings for the expansion of the royal Munich Residence complex, including the King's Tract (begun in 1826) and the Festival Hall Building and Apothecary Wing (1832–42); the mansion for Eugène Beauharnais, Duke of Leuchtenberg (1816) and, opposite it, the Odeon (1826); and a series of national monuments: the Valhalla outside Regensburg (1830–32), the Hall of Fame in Munich (1843–54), and the Hall of Liberation in Kehlheim (1849–63).

As a city planner, Klenze left his most lasting mark on Munich by laying out axial boulevards and the open and enclosed squares that punctuate them: to the north, Ludwigstrasse with Odeonsplatz, and to the west, Brienner Strasse with Wittelsbacherplatz, Karolinenplatz (Obelisk), and Königsplatz, the site of Klenze's late work, the Propyläen (1846–60). After Ludwig's son, Otto I, became king of Greece in 1832, Klenze took an active part in the urban planning of Athens. In 1834 he spent nearly five months as an archaeologist and architectural historian in Greece, where he encouraged the restoration and maintenance of classical monuments.

A versatile and prolific man, like Schinkel, Klenze designed not only mansions, palaces, and monuments but also simple dwellings, churches, and railroad stations, as well as furniture and works of decorative art. His talents as a painter of architectural landscapes, draftsman, and watercolorist were considerable, and he was a significant collector of the art of his time. Klenze also wrote numerous publications based on his research in archaeology and architectural history, as well as travel books.

Klenze's significance in the German architecture of the first half of the nineteenth century was surpassed only by Schinkel. His literary estate is found in the manuscript collection of the Bayerische Staatsbibliothek (Klenzeana), and the greater part of his extensive graphic oeuvre is kept in the Staatliche Graphische Sammlung, Munich.

Simon Petrus Klotz

Mannheim (baptized)
30 September 1776–26 September 1824 Munich

When Prince-Elector Carl Theodor moved his court from Mannheim to Munich, Court Theater Painter Matthias Klotz followed with his family in 1778. He began teaching his second son, Simon, the basics of landscape, portrait, and miniature painting, lessons supplemented at the Academy of Drawing by Johann Jakob Dorner the Elder, a painter of landscapes, portraits, and historical pictures in the Netherlandish manner. In 1798 the young artist set off on the traditional journeyman's wanderings, continuing his training at the academies in Vienna, Dresden, Berlin, and Copenhagen and earning his livelihood by painting watercolor *vedute* and portraits. In 1804 he became a professor of the theory of the visual arts at the University of Landshut.

Klotz had already begun to employ the new technique of lithography for portraits and landscapes. His early, little-known work in drawing and watercolor was very dependent on the Munich landscape school. Neoclassical influences evidently stemmed from his study of classical art in Rome in 1804–5, and from a confrontation with the school of David in Paris.

Klotz owed his reputation above all to brooding history paintings on subjects of a religious or allegorical nature. However, only a few examples of his art have come down to us; one is *Night with Her Children Sleep and Death*, 1811 (Bayerische Staatsgemäldesammlungen, Munich, Inv. no. 8951). As P.F. Schmidt remarked, Klotz employed a "noble, sonorous" line and represented a "romantic classicism" akin to that of Carstens and Runge. The extent to which he may have been influenced by personal contacts with these artists, or by their works and reputation, remains unclear.

None of Klotz's large-scale works, such as ceiling paintings in the Royal Mint or the curtain for the Court Theater in Munich, have survived. The same holds for his major work, an 1809 cycle of landscape paintings evoking the four times of day. Not least on account of his evidently slim oeuvre, Klotz was eventually forgotten.

Franz Innocenz Kobell

Mannheim (baptized)
23 November 1749–14 January 1822 Munich

Franz Kobell was the grandson of Johann Heinrich Kobell, a Frankfurt grocer and spice dealer who sired the Kobell family of artists, with its Mannheim branch and its Dutch branch (Hendrik, Jan I, II, and III). After the premature deaths of his parents in 1762, Franz, then thirteen, was apprenticed by his guardians to a merchant in Mainz. He returned to Mannheim in 1766, determined to follow his artistic bent, even if it meant teaching himself. His brother Ferdinand, nine years older and himself a painter, draftsman, and etcher, took Franz under his wing, instructing him in the technique of landscape etching. Ferdinand had been employed as a set painter at the Mannheim Court Opera and had trained in Paris with Johann Georg Wille. His orientation to seventeenth-century Dutch art communicated itself to Franz, who at this period also attended the new Mannheim Drawing Academy (established in 1769).

In 1778 Franz applied to Prince-Elector Carl Theodor for a pension. It was granted, enabling him to live in Italy from 1779 to 1784. In Rome, where he spent most of that period, he made friends with the painter-poet Friedrich Müller, the sculptor Alexander Trippel, and the writer Wilhelm Heinse. The Italian years brought a profound reorientation in Franz Kobell's art. Deeply impressed by the Italian countryside, he discovered the classical landscape approach of seventeenth-century French and Italian artists. Relying strongly on Claude Lorrain, Gaspard Dughet, and Salvator Rosa, but also on the Dutch painters known as Italianates, such as Jan Both, Nicolas Berchem, and Carel Dujardin, Kobell arrived at a personal landscape style. On 3 August 1780 he was named court artist.

On returning to Germany, Franz became the first of the Kobells to settle in Munich, where Prince-Elector Carl Theodor had moved his residence in 1778. In 1793 he was joined there by his brother Ferdinand and his family, with whom he shared a garden house on Prannerstrasse. On 8 June 1808 Franz and his nephew, Wilhelm von Kobell, were nominated to the art committee at the inauguration of the Munich Academy of Arts, a position that entailed an annual pension supplement.

When he died at seventy-two, Franz Kobell left behind about a dozen oil paintings and innumerable drawings, most of them small. As a draftsman he remained beholden to the ideal and heroic landscape style exemplified by Lorrain. Kobell's work, which was highly regarded, influenced his friends Johann Georg von Dillis, Goethe, and Carl Friedrich von Rumohr, whose drawings are occasionally confused with his. Limited in subject matter and in manner— highly detailed drawings in brown ink—Franz Kobell's oeuvre resists chronological ordering, especially as he seldom dated his works. His late period, after 1800, is marked by very charming and effective landscapes and studies from nature, vivacious brush drawings done mostly in blackish-brown ink. Kobell's art was also made popularly available in aquatint reproductions.

Wilhelm Alexander Wolfgang von Kobell

Mannheim (baptized)
13 April 1766–15 July 1853 Munich

Son of landscapist and court artist Ferdinand Kobell and nephew of graphic artist Franz Kobell, Wilhelm von Kobell owed his artistic training primarily to his father. Ferdinand pointed out the importance of studying nature and recommended seventeenth-century Dutch painting, interests that Wilhelm pursued at the Mannheim Academy of Drawing. He put final touches on his Dutch manner by doing aquatint reproductions of Dutch paintings in Mannheim and Munich collections, prints that attracted wide attention. Seminal influences on his work were depictions of animals in the style of Potter, Cuyp, Berchem, and Wouwerman.

In 1792 Kobell was called to Munich to become court painter to Prince-Elector Carl Theodor, and he moved there with his parents the following year. During the next decade he produced numerous naturalistic, intimate portrait studies of family and friends, executed in colored chalks, brush and ink, or watercolors. In addition to genre pieces in watercolors and oils, Kobell was prompted during the Wars of Coalition to turn to military subjects, which earned him the reputation of a painter of battles. In 1806–7, for King Maximilian I Joseph of Bavaria, he executed a series of seven battle scenes depicting Napoleon's victories in the third War of Coalition. The series was intended as a gift to Maréchal Berthier, Napoleon's confidant.

A commission followed from Crown Prince Ludwig of Bavaria for a cycle of thirteen large-format battle paintings honoring soldiers of the Bavarian Army, which was allied with Napoleon. While executing the series, between 1808 and 1815, the artist undertook several journeys to the battlefields. His compositions were innovative in that they subordinated military events to the landscape and its atmosphere at a given time of day and year.

In 1814 Kobell succeeded Johann Georg von Dillis as professor of landscape at the Munich Academy, a post he filled until it was abolished by Peter Cornelius in 1826. In 1817 Kobell was granted personal nobility, followed by hereditary nobility in 1833. Until late in his life he remained true to an idiom he developed under the influence of baroque Netherlandish painting and, later, Biedermeier style. In his late work he favored the small format. Characteristic of his work were compositions with a low horizon, a foreground stage with various, usually static, figures and, beyond it, a spacious view into the depths of the Lower Alpine countryside, all unified by means of carefully considered lighting effects.

His highly sophisticated style made Wilhelm von Kobell one of the most outstanding representatives of the Munich school of landscape. He dedicated himself as much to watercolor as to oils and, along with Johann Georg von Dillis, contributed significantly to establishing watercolor as an independent and valid form of expression, one in which he achieved great mastery. Kobell also made a name for himself in graphic art, initially with popular aquatint reproductions and later with etchings designed for hand-tinting in watercolor. Multiple versions of these, reflecting various moods, were widely disseminated.

Joseph Anton Koch

Obergiblen/Lechtal, Tyrol
27 July 1768–12 January 1839 Rome

Koch came of a poor family of Tyrolean farm laborers. He was working as a shepherd boy when he first drew mountains, in 1781–82. The evident skill of these drawings attracted the attention of the suffragan bishop of Augsburg, supervisor of the Lech Valley churches, who decided to further the boy's training. After a brief apprenticeship with an Augsburg sculptor, Koch received a scholarship in 1785 to the notoriously strict Hohe Carlsschule in Stuttgart, an academy of science and art, where he learned the academic foundations of creative work.

In 1791, excited by the ideal of liberty promulgated by the French Revolution, Koch fled the regimentation of the school, as Friedrich Schiller had done a good decade earlier. When he was at a safe distance he cut off the pigtail that was compulsory at the school and sent it to his former teachers in Stuttgart. Via Strasbourg, where he met with Jacobins, Koch went to Switzerland, at first to Basel and Berne. Suspected of political agitation, however, he soon became persona non grata there. Finally Koch found a niche in Biel, and in nearby Neuchâtel came in contact with the English theologian and art collector Dr. George Nott, who was the first to buy his drawings and in time became Koch's principal patron and supporter.

During his time in Switzerland, Koch took numerous hiking tours that yielded Alpine views he used in later years as the basis for oils. He spent time in the Jungfrau region of the Berne Oberland in 1794. In late autumn of that year, Nott granted him a three-year Italian scholarship. Koch went by way of Milan, Bologna, and Florence to Rome and Naples, then settled in Rome. Here he immediately established contact with the group of artists associated with the equally freedom-loving and highly talented Asmus Jacob Carstens and his friend Carl Ludwig Fernow. The group was soon joined by Johann Christian Reinhart, Bertel Thorvaldsen, and Martin von Rohden. Carstens, the most outstanding German artist at that time in Rome, influenced Koch's work considerably toward a neoclassical figurative style, an emphasis on contours, and an integration of allegorical figures into the landscape.

In 1797 Koch began a correspondence with the Nuremberg publisher Johann Friedrich Frauenholz, offering to do business with him in the field of landscape etchings and illustrations. Inspired by his friend Carstens, who had died young, Koch in 1801 executed the first of what would become two hundred illustrations to Dante's *Divine Comedy*. On tours with Gottlieb Schick through the mountains east of Rome he discovered the beauties of the small wine-making town of Olevano —and of his local landlady's daughter, whom he married in 1806.

Rome remained Koch's second home until the end of his life. He left it only once, temporarily, to escape the unfavorable economic conditions that obtained under the French occupation. He moved with his family to Vienna, where from 1812 to 1815 he maintained close contacts with the anti-academic artists associated with Friedrich Schlegel, and made friends among the younger generation, the Olivier brothers and Julius Schnorr von Carolsfeld. Koch finished *Landscape with Rainbow*, a large-format canvas begun in 1804. It was acquired by the Munich Academy, where it had an enormous impact on young artists.

In spite of promising contacts made during the Congress of Vienna period, financial success eluded Koch, who soon returned to Rome when political circumstances were back to normal. In 1817 the young and highly gifted artists Franz Horny and Carl Philipp Fohr worked in his studio. Between 1820 and 1825 Koch painted a series of sublime Swiss Alpine motifs and completed the second version of the *Schmadribach Fall* (1822), one of his major works (Neue Pinakothek, Munich).

Though he was rather skeptical about the Nazarenes from the time they arrived in Rome, Koch was on friendly terms with them and enjoyed his role of mentor. In 1825–28, succeeding Cornelius and Veit, he completed the remaining decoration of the Dante Room at Casino Massimo, with scenes from the *Inferno*, a summing-up of his decades-long concern with Dante. In 1832, Koch made seven watercolor designs for decorations in music publisher Hermann Härtel's *Roman House* in Leipzig, but their execution, which was to be undertaken by Friedrich Preller, Sr., never came to pass.

Koch was a tough and vital man, original to the point of eccentricity, who defended his artistic stance with sharp-tongued acumen in a series of publications (including one entitled *Modern Art Chronicle…or, Rumford's Soup*, 1834). Though he earned the highest accolades as an artist, he lived in permanent financial distress. Nestor of the German artists' colony in Rome, Koch was admired and loved, and caricatured more often than any other artist. With his wondrously sublime, ideal, and heroic approach to landscape, linking elements of the classical art of Claude Lorrain and Nicholas Poussin with a careful observation of nature, he was an innovator and pathfinder for generations of artists to follow. Koch was the most significant painter of the ideal landscape in his Sturm und Drang generation. He left behind at least one hundred thirty oil paintings and far more than 1000 drawings and watercolors.

Carl Wilhelm Kolbe

Berlin 20 November 1757–13 January 1835 Dessau

Kolbe's father was a gold embroiderer and maker of wall coverings; his mother came from the French Huguenot colony. Immersed in French culture, Kolbe grew up bilingual in Berlin and attended the French Grammar School. In 1780 he became a French instructor at the famous Philanthropin School in Dessau, founded by Johann Bernhard Basedow, where he taught intermittently until the school closed in 1793. During that period Kolbe began devoting himself intensively to landscape drawing and experimenting in etching, with an eye to making a career in art. Encouraged by Daniel Chodowiecki, his aunt's husband, the artist returned to Berlin to continue his academic training with Johann Wilhelm Meil, Chodowiecki, and Asmus Jacob Carstens. So rapid was his progress that he was accepted as a member of the Academy in 1795.

Kolbe did not concern himself with painting; his talent lay in drawing and etching. Though his etching was self-taught, Duke Leopold Friedrich von Anhalt-Dessau named him court engraver in 1798. He also made him instructor of drawing and French at an upper school in Dessau, a post he retained until his retirement in 1829. Kolbe's pupils included the brothers Ferdinand and Friedrich Olivier. In 1805–7 Kolbe was given leave to go to Zurich to reproduce the landscape gouaches of Salomon Gessner (1730–1788) in large-format etchings.

Kolbe also made a name for himself as a linguist. His publications in the field earned him a doctorate from the faculty of philosophy at the University of Halle in 1810.

Kolbe's art, disseminated through his masterful etchings, remained influential into the twentieth century. His characteristic shifts in the proportions of motifs made him a predecessor of surrealism. Kolbe's principal themes were idyllic, Arcadian landscapes and plants and animals. His works reveal a close observation of nature as well as the influence of Anthonie Waterloo, Paulus Potter, and Salomon Gessner. His monumentally scaled renderings of herbs and often dramatic depictions of oak trees earned him the nicknames of "Herb Kolbe" and "Oak Kolbe."

Adolph Friedrich Erdmann von Menzel

Breslau 8 December 1815–9 February 1905 Berlin

To ensure a good artistic education for his talented son, Menzel's father moved in 1830 from Breslau to the capital, Berlin. Though a teacher by profession, he opened a lithographic printing shop, where young Adolph learned the craft. After his father's untimely death, the sixteen-year-old took over the business to support the family. From then on Menzel's training was in practical, commercial printing; as an artist he remained largely self-taught.

He first attracted attention in 1833–34 with six illustrations, printed from pen-and-ink drawings on the stone, to Goethe's *Künstlers Erdenwallen* (Artist's Pilgrimage). This work led to a commission for a series of twelve crayon lithographs on *Denkwürdigkeiten aus der Brandenburgisch Preussischen Geschichte* (Memorable Events of Brandenburg-Prussian History), published in 1834–36. Illustrations to Adalbert von Chamisso's *Peter Schlemihl* followed in 1838–39, and, in 1840–42, illustrations to Franz Kugler's *Geschichte Friedrichs des Grossen* (History of Frederick the Great), which led to a breakthrough for Menzel. His 398 drawings, cut into wood blocks under his personal supervision, set new standards for the art of wood engraving. The period of Frederick the Great was to concern Menzel throughout his career.

In about 1836 he began to work in oils as well as graphic media. By the mid-1840s Menzel was enjoying increasing patronage from the Prussian court. He worked first for King Frederick William IV, then for Emperors William I and William II. Yet despite his status as official history painter, Menzel retained his independence, producing a vast private oeuvre of drawings, pastels, and gouaches on subjects drawn from his immediate surroundings and from numerous journeys through Germany, Austria, France, and Italy. Menzel visited Paris three times, exhibiting there and meeting artists such as Courbet and Meissonier. His democratic stance came to the fore in 1848, in the unfinished oil *Aufbahrung der Märzgefallenen* (Laying Out of the March Dead). His *Eisenwalzwerk* (Iron-Rolling Mill), 1872–75, the first monumental German painting on the subject of industry and labor conditions, caused a great furor. Extremely dedicated and diligent, a born draftsman and master of graphic media, Menzel produced an enormous oeuvre of drawings and prints; the former National Gallery alone possessed 6190 drawings and 76 sketchbooks (now in the Kupferstichkabinett, Berlin).

Menzel was of dwarflike stature, only four feet six inches tall, a disadvantage that may partly explain his tireless and exclusive devotion to his work. Yet he was a giant among German artists of the nineteenth century. The recipient of many honors during his lifetime, Menzel was named Knight of the Black Eagle Order in 1898 and raised to the hereditary nobility.

Friedrich Nerly

Erfurt 24 November 1807 – 21 October 1878 Venice

Born Friedrich Nehrlich, Nerly adopted the name by which he is known in art history during his later, Italian period. After his father's premature death, Friedrich went to Hamburg to study with his uncle, the painter and lithographer Heinrich Joachim Herterich. He also worked in the lithography workshop of Johann Michael Speckter. Here he met Carl Friedrich von Rumohr, who recognized his talent, took the penurious seventeen-year-old into his home, and instructed him in art for nearly five years, 1823–28. Nerly was the ideal pupil for Rumohr, malleable and receptive to the older man's ideas of what an artist should be.

Nerly's great gifts as a painter emerged under Rumohr's tutelage, but came to full flower only when he had seen the landscapes of Johann Christian Reinhart and Joseph Anton Koch—and the reality of Italy, where Rumohr took him on his third Italian journey in 1828. From that year until 1835 Nerly lived in Rome, playing a leading role in German art circles (Ponte-Molle-Gesellschaft, Deutscher Kunstverein, Deutsches Künstler-Album). In 1835 the artist moved to Venice; he married there five years later and had a son who also became a painter (Friedrich Nerly, Jr.).

Nerly's principal achievement as a painter and draftsman lay in the free, painterly landscapes of the Roman period. Later, in Venice, he imposed certain restrictions on his talent—if not on his sales—by concentrating on the typical Venetian genre of *veduta*. Nerly's estate is kept largely in Erfurt (Anger Museum) and Bremen (Kunsthalle).

Ernst Ferdinand Oehme

Dresden 23 April 1797 – 10 September 1855

In 1819 Oehme became a student at the Dresden Academy and a private pupil of Johann Christian Claussen Dahl. The following year he studied with Caspar David Friedrich, whose style strongly influenced him. In the summer of 1820 Oehme traveled with his friend August Heinrich to Salzburg.

On a grant from the crown prince of Saxony, Oehme worked from 1822 to 1825 in Italy, where he was influenced by Joseph Anton Koch and became friends with Ludwig Richter. He and Richter hiked through the Sabine and Alban Mountains in 1824, assiduously drawing from nature. In Rome the two artists studied the drawings and watercolors of Carl Philipp Fohr and Franz Horny.

In 1825 Oehme returned to Dresden to assume the post of court artist. Stopping in the Swiss and Tyrolean Alps on the way, he painted superb watercolor views, some of which were later expanded into oils. Oehme's early enthusiasm for Caspar David Friedrich's style and philosophy remained undimmed throughout his career. In later years the fairy-tale mood of the popular art of Ludwig Richter, the friend who lived in the same Dresden house as Oehme from 1836 onward, gained increasing influence.

Oehme was made a member of the Academy in 1846. Because of the late romantic and increasingly painterly and realistic tendencies of his art, he became a major representative of the Dresden school of landscape. Among Oehme's most significant works are his numerous watercolor studies from nature.

Ferdinand Olivier

Dessau 1 April 1785 – 11 February 1841 Munich

The son of a court opera singer and an educator, Ferdinand Olivier received his first drawing instruction in Dessau in 1801–2 from Carl Wilhelm Kolbe, who was also a teacher of languages. His special interest in landscape was awakened by the extensive landscaped gardens laid out by Prince Franz von Anhalt-Dessau around Wörlitz. During brief stays in Berlin between 1802 and 1804, Olivier attended August Wilhelm Schlegel's lectures on literature and fine art.

In 1804 Ferdinand and his brother Heinrich went to Dresden to continue their education at the Academy, and Ferdinand copied paintings by Claude Lorrain and Jacob Ruisdael at the Gemäldegalerie. He met Caspar David Friedrich, whose profound allegorical landscapes made a lasting impression. Since he was fluent in French (his father having come from the Lausanne area), Olivier was sent in 1807 on a diplomatic mission to Paris, where he devoted his spare time to intensive study at the Musée Napoléon. Heinrich joined him in Paris, and various commissions from the brothers' patron, Prince Franz von Anhalt-Dessau, including a large portrait of Napoleon and two altar paintings, enabled them to extend their stay in the city until the spring of 1810.

That summer Ferdinand and his brother Friedrich traveled through the Harz Mountains, a trip whose artistic production clearly showed the influence of Caspar David Friedrich's approach to landscape. In 1811 Ferdinand moved with his brother Friedrich to Vienna, where he met Friedrich Schlegel, Joseph von Eichendorff, and Theodor Körner, and established friendly ties with Philipp Veit, Julius Schnorr von Carolsfeld, and Joseph Anton Koch. The Olivier residence formed a center for patriotically minded artists devoting themselves to a study of early German art, especially the prints and drawings of Dürer.

But it was Koch's landscapes that profoundly shaped Ferdinand Olivier's development. They helped him to find an original approach to historical landscape in which elements of early German art, especially the graphic art of the Dürer period, were delightfully blended with the close observation of nature that was then gaining prominence.

While his brother Friedrich fought with the Lützow Freikorps in the Wars of Liberation in 1813–14, Ferdinand, with a new family to consider—he had married a widowed Englishwoman with three children in 1812—did not participate. A devout Protestant, he was voted in absentia a member of the Brotherhood of St. Luke in Rome in 1816. Ferdinand Olivier was the sole Nazarene who never set foot on Italian soil.

His fame rests largely on his having discovered the beauties of the Salzburg region for art. After the Wars of Liberation he journeyed through the area twice, the first time in 1815 with Philipp Veit, and the second in 1817 with his brother Friedrich and Julius Schnorr von Carolsfeld. The resulting drawings, and those done in Vienna and environs up to about 1825, show Olivier at a peak of creativity and skill that remained unmatched in his later work. His stringent landscape drawings combine the Mediterranean ideal landscape in the style of Koch with the Nordic, meditative, painterly approach of Caspar David Friedrich. A number of these works, as Ludwig Grote said, are among "the loveliest and most moving documents of the art of drawing in Germany" during this period.

The year 1823 marked the publication of the artist's major graphic work, also a major work of romantic art. This was a series of nine lithographs, drawn with sharp crayon and printed over a homogeneous tone plate by Adolph Kunicke in Vienna, titled *Seven Areas around Salzburg and Berchtesgaden, Arranged According to the Seven Days of the Week, Linked by Two Allegorical Prints.*

In 1818–19 Olivier was also active as a writer and as the editor of the art journal *Janus.* During the restoration period of the late 1820s in Vienna he was increasingly isolated as an artist. Olivier began to relax his rigorous Nazarene style in favor of ideal landscape compositions with figures. From about 1825 he painted small-format landscapes with a Mediterranean flair, based on the Italian drawings of his brother Friedrich. For his own drawings he now preferred soft pencil, black chalk, and sanguine to sharp, hard pencil.

With the aid of his friend Julius Schnorr, who had prospered thanks to the patronage of King Ludwig I of Bavaria, Olivier moved with his family and brother Friedrich to Munich in 1830. They resided with Schnorr and assisted him on his frescoes in the royal Residence. In 1833 Ferdinand Olivier was named Deputy Secretary General of the Academy and given a professorship in art history, duties that left him scant time for his own work.

Johann Friedrich Overbeck

Lübeck 3 July 1789–12 November 1869 Rome

The son of Christian Adolph Overbeck, a senator who became mayor of Lübeck and also made a name for himself as a composer of *lieder*, Friedrich Overbeck grew up in a cultivated Protestant household. Interested in art from an early age, he first received drawing instruction at fifteen, in the atelier of Nicolaus Peroux. In 1805 August von Kestner introduced him to drawings made by the Riepenhausen brothers after fourteenth- and fifteenth-century Italian paintings. After Overbeck moved to Hamburg, J.H. Wilhelm Tischbein and Philipp Otto Runge encouraged him to make a career in art. In 1806 he enrolled in the Vienna Academy, but the monotony of the instruction and the eclecticism of its director, Füger, soon frustrated him.

Overbeck became close friends with Franz Pforr, a fellow student from Frankfurt. Encouraged by Eberhard Wächter, a friend of Carstens, Overbeck, Pforr, and other like-minded students began to experiment in oil painting, teaching themselves by studying the old masters in the public Liechtenstein and Belvedere Galleries. Regular meetings of the friends united in their opposition to the academy finally led to the founding, on 10 July 1809, of the Lukasbund, or Brotherhood of St. Luke. This was the seed of the Nazarene movement, devoted to a renewal of art through Christian faith.

In October 1809 Overbeck, Pforr, Konrad Hottinger, and Ludwig Vogel set out for Rome, traveling by way of Venice, Bologna, and Raphael's birthplace, Urbino, and arriving the following May. After a brief stay at Villa Malta, the Brotherhood of St. Luke moved into San Isidoro, an abandoned monastery, where they pursued their ideal of a monastic, ascetic life in the service of art and religion. Overbeck remained the spiritual and artistic mentor of the group. Living in the capital of the Christian world, they oriented themselves less to its classical past than to the flowering of Christian art in the Middle Ages and the Renaissance.

After the premature death of Franz Pforr in 1812, Overbeck experienced a religious crisis that led him to convert to Catholicism the following year. In 1816 the Prussian Consul General, Jacob Salomon Bartholdy, commissioned members of the brotherhood to decorate his apartment in the Palazzo Zuccari, with frescoes on the biblical story of Joseph. In 1817 Overbeck completed *The Sale of Joseph into Egypt* and *The Seven Lean Years*. Then the group was asked by the Marchese Massimi to do frescoes on themes from Dante, Ariosto, and Tasso at his Casino Massimo. Overbeck was entrusted with decorating a room with designs based on Tasso's *Gerusalemme liberata*. During the next ten years he finished frescoes on the vaulting, three walls, and part of the socle friezes. Then, wishing to devote himself to other concerns, Overbeck relinquished the rest of the task to Joseph von Führich.

In 1818 Overbeck had married Anna Schiffenhuber-Hartl of Vienna, who subsequently talked him into declining several offers of prestigious posts in Germany. Deciding in 1829 to devote himself solely to religious painting, he executed *The Miracle of the Rose* on the gable end of the Portiuncula Chapel in Assisi. In addition to architectural decorations, he completed many paintings, some large in format, including *Italy and Germany* (1828), *Triumph of Religion in the Arts* (1840) for Frankfurt, *Mourning of Christ* (1846) for Lübeck and *Christ Eludes His Tormentors* (1847–57) for Pope Pius IX. In 1847 Overbeck began working on the *Seven Sacraments* cycle (drawings in the Vatican). During the last years of his life he produced designs for the cathedral at Djakovo, Croatia.

Overbeck left an extensive graphic oeuvre. With the possible exception of Julius Schnorr von Carolsfeld, he was the most outstanding draftsman of the Nazarene circle. Thanks to his great talent, his high ethical standards in life and art, and his personal charisma, Overbeck played a key role in German artistic life in Rome. Overbeck had a profound influence as both man and artist, enjoyed an international reputation, and was showered with awards and honors. Because he clung to the artistic ideals and goals of his youth, however, he grew increasingly isolated with age as developments in contemporary art passed him by.

Franz Pforr

Frankfurt am Main
5 April 1788–16 June 1812 Albano, near Rome

Franz Pforr was orphaned at the age of thirteen. His father, Johann Georg Pforr, a much-admired painter of animals, died in 1798, followed two years later by his mother, Johanna Christiane Tischbein. She was a younger sister of artists J.H. Wilhelm Tischbein ("Goethe Tischbein") and Johann Heinrich Tischbein, Jr. A number of deep friendships would partially compensate Pforr for the loss of his family.

In the fall of 1801, his guardians in Frankfurt, Johann David Passavant, Sr., and Alderman Sarasin-Chiron, arranged for an apprenticeship with Pforr's uncle, Johann Heinrich Tischbein, an academy professor and inspector of galleries in Kassel. Wearied by the mechanical nature of the training, however, Pforr returned in 1805 to Frankfurt, where he became a close friend of his guardian's son, Johann David Passavant, Jr. That fall Pforr transferred to the Vienna Academy and continued his studies under a stricter regimen.

The turning point in his life came in 1806 when he became acquainted with Friedrich Overbeck. The two young artists began to study the works of early Italian and German masters in the Vienna public collections. Their opposition to academic instruction methods and their shared artistic interests soon attracted several like-minded friends. In the summer of 1808 they formed an alliance which led, on 10 July 1809, to the establishment of the Brotherhood of St. Luke and eventually to secession from the academy. The most significant part of Pforr's slim oeuvre was done in Vienna. Of a series of oils, several were lost, but extant are *The Duke of Habsburg and The Priests* and *St. George*. Pforr also did illustrations to Cervantes's *Don Quixote* and to Goethe's *Götz von Berlichingen*. Today his Goethe illustrations are considered the first images congenial to the poet's work.

In May 1810, the nucleus of the Brotherhood of St. Luke—Pforr, Overbeck, Konrad Hottinger, and Ludwig Vogel—settled in Rome, where they initially lived in Villa Malta, on the Pincio. Soon they were able to move to an abandoned monastery nearby, San Isidoro, where for the next few years they lived and worked as a monastic community. They held "evening academies," sitting for one another in a voluminous cloak Pforr had bought in Venice on the way to Rome. Pforr continued his series of illustrations to *Götz von Berlichingen* (which were never engraved), and in 1810, completed a painting begun in Vienna, *The Entry of Kaiser Rudolf von Habsburg into Basel*. By this time it had become obvious that Pforr was seriously ill with tuberculosis. In May 1812 he went to Albano for the healthier climate, but he died there only a few weeks later, at the age of twenty-four.

With Overbeck, Pforr was a guiding light of the Brotherhood of St. Luke, and together they gave Nazarene art its direction. While Overbeck devoted himself to religious themes in a Raphaelesque style, Pforr preferred the early German masters, whose simplicity and integrity impressed him. In addition to Christian legends, he concentrated on subjects from German history and literature, such as the story of the Habsburgs and Schiller's *Wilhelm Tell*. Pforr's drawing style is characterized by a rigorous, abstracting contour line of the type propagated by his uncle, Wilhelm Tischbein. Pforr's legacy comprises only four oil paintings, including a major work completed in Italy, *Sulamith and Mary*, and about two hundred drawings.

Johann Anton (Alban) Ramboux

Trier 5 October 1790 – 2 October 1866 Cologne

Ramboux's father came from Conflans, in Savoy, and his mother from an old Cologne family known for its goldsmiths. After taking private drawing lessons in Trier, Ramboux went on to study from 1803 to 1807 with the Benedictine monk Frère Abraham d'Orval in Florenville, Luxembourg. He spent the years 1808–12 in Paris, working in the atelier of Jacques-Louis David, who had a profound influence on Ramboux' portraiture. Ramboux earned his living in Trier between 1812 and 1815 by painting portraits.

In 1815 the artist studied at the Munich Academy, where he became friends with the Eberhard brothers and the Swiss artist Samuel Amsler. The following year he and Amsler undertook a walking tour, spending a few months in Switzerland and then going on to Rome, where the two found lodgings with Carl Barth at the Palazzo Zuccari. Ramboux established close contacts with the Nazarenes, but did not join the Brotherhood of St. Luke. In 1818 he completed his first major work in oil, *Adam and Eve after Banishment from Eden.* Carl Friedrich von Rumohr, recognizing the artist's ability to assume styles of the past, encouraged him to copy the works of Old Masters. For several years Ramboux wandered through Umbria and Toscana, studying and copying fourteenth- and fifteenth-century frescoes, but also producing superb landscape studies and portraits. While in Rome in 1822, Ramboux executed his finest double portrait, of the Eberhard brothers. On the return journey to Trier before the year was out, he made a lithograph version of this portrait during a stopover in Munich.

Back in Trier, Ramboux drew views of the Mosel Valley and tinted them with watercolor, selecting sixteen for publication as lithographs, issued between 1824 and 1827. After executing frescoes in the residence of vintner M.J. Hayn in 1826, he designed frescoes for the choir of Trier Cathedral, but these were never executed. In 1830–31 Ramboux concentrated on drawings, watercolors, and cartoons to illustrate works of Italian literature (Boccaccio, Dante, Petrarch). Between 1832 and 1842 he was back in Italy, combing the country and preparing more than two thousand tracings and more than three hundred twenty-five watercolors after frescoes and mosaics by early Italian masters.

From 1844 Ramboux, himself a collector of note, served as curator of the Wallraf Collection (seed of the later Wallraf-Richartz Museum) in Cologne, where he was also active as a restorer and watercolor copyist. In 1854 he went on a pilgrimage to Jerusalem. Apart from portraiture, Ramboux' significance derives from his drawings, including those made after early Italian works. They are important to art history since many of the originals have since been lost.

Johann Christian Reinhart

Hof, Upper Franconia
24 January 1761 – 9 June 1847 Rome

Reinhart's father, a Protestant clergyman, died young. The son began theology studies in Leipzig in 1779, but soon abandoned them for art. He attended the Leipzig Academy until 1782, working under Adam Friedrich Oeser, who also took him into his home. The highly cultivated Oeser, a friend of Winckelmann, gave the young man a classical education and inculcated what would become the lifelong concern of his art: an attempt to create ideal form that transcended reality.

In 1782 Reinhart began to teach himself etching. He spent the next two years in Dresden, where, influenced by his friends Johann Christian Klengel and Konrad Gessner, he devoted himself intensively to a study of nature, outside the academy. In 1785 he met the poet Friedrich Schiller, who shared his love of liberty and was to become a crucial lifelong friend. In 1786–89 Reinhart lived in Meiningen, in a close friendship with his exact contemporary, the Duke of Meiningen. Based on his sensitivity to natural phenomena, he developed an original approach to landscape from which all Netherlandish style had been expunged.

In late 1789 Reinhart left for Italy, which became his second home. In 1792, for the Nuremberg publisher Frauenholz, he began a series of etchings on landscape and animal subjects, including twenty-four sheets of *Malerisch radierten Prospecten aus Italien* (Painterly Etchings of Italian Views), which heralded a new approach to landscape. About three years later he arrived at the heroic style of landscape that characterized his subsequent work, in part resulting from his close exchange with Asmus Jakob Carstens, Joseph Anton Koch, and Johann Martin von Rohden.

From 1825 to 1829 Reinhart executed eight landscapes in tempera as wall decorations for the Palazzo Massimi in Rome. Since 1825 he had been receiving a stipend from King Ludwig I of Bavaria, who commissioned a series of four views of Rome from the Villa Malta, executed between 1829 and 1835.

The aging Reinhart penned sharp attacks against German art critics such as J. Heinrich Meyer and Ludwig Schorn, who had reported on the Roman art scene. In 1839 he became an honorary member of the Munich Academy, and was named Bavarian court artist. Reinhart was a vital, eloquent man, as his drawings suggest, and was talented at poetry and philosophy. He led a free and unconventional life, and was highly regarded by the other German artists in his circle. With Koch and von Rohden, he was at the center of the new German ideal landscape painting in Rome. Reinhart died at eighty-six, leaving behind an oeuvre of limited size. On record are about thirty-five of an estimated one hundred eighty oils, approximately five hundred drawings, and one hundred eighty prints.

Johannes Riepenhausen

Göttingen 1788 – 11 September 1860 Rome

Johannes Riepenhausen and his brother, Franz, received their initial artistic training from their father, the engraver Ernst Ludwig Riepenhausen. In 1800, the brothers met Johann Heinrich Wilhelm Tischbein, who had returned to Göttingen from Naples, and assisted Tischbein in engraving his illustrations to Homer, based on ancient Greek and Roman monuments. Modest talents but important influences and mediators, the Riepenhausen brothers collaborated so closely throughout their careers that it is hardly possible to distinguish their hands from one another.

In 1803 they sent Goethe a series of twelve sheets depicting an imaginative reconstruction, based on Pausanius's description, of Polygnot's frescoes in the assembly hall of the Cnidians at Delphi, which prompted Goethe to write an essay on the topic. In 1804 the brothers studied with Johann Heinrich Tischbein, Jr., at the Kassel Academy, transferring the next year to Dresden. There they executed drawings based on the legend of Genevieve, which were published in Frankfurt in 1806. The brothers also converted to Catholicism during this period.

In 1805 they went to Rome with Carl Friedrich von Rumohr and the brothers Ludwig and Friedrich Tieck and remained there to the end of their lives. They became friends with Joseph Anton Koch and Bertel Thorvaldsen and subsequently established close contacts with the Nazarenes. They collaborated on many images of the Virgin, including a *Coronation of the Virgin* (1806) for the German church S. Maria dell' Anima, and created portfolios such as *The History of Painting in Italy, as Regards its Development, Advancement, and Perfection.* Only the first two series of the portfolio, twenty-four contour engravings after Italian masters, were published, in 1810. In addition, they did engravings after Thorvaldsen's works and a cycle of twelve drawings on the life of Raphael, which were first published as engravings in Frankfurt in 1816. Further editions, including a smaller variant issued from 1833 onward, contributed markedly to disseminating the Raphael cult and to the reception of his work during the romantic period.

After the death of his brother Franz in 1831, Johannes Riepenhausen remained true to their common dedication to ecclesiastical and historical art in the Neoclassical and Nazarene style.

Carl Rottmann

Handschuhsheim, near Heidelberg
11 January 1797–7 July 1850 Munich

With Carl Philipp Fohr and Ernst Fries, Rottmann received his first drawing lessons from his father, Christian Friedrich Rottmann, a university drawing instructor. His next teacher was Johann Christian Xeller, who encouraged him to visit the Boisserée Collection. He was apparently introduced to oil painting by the Scottish painter George Augustus Wallis, who lived in Heidelberg from 1812 to 1815 and drew Rottmann's attention to the art of Claude Lorrain and Nicolas Poussin.

With Fries, Xeller, Daniel Fohr, and others, Rottmann undertook his first journey as a landscapist in 1818, traveling along the Rhine and the Mosel to draw panoramic views for the publisher Joseph Engelmann. Attending the Munich Academy from 1821, Rottmann encountered the art of Joseph Anton Koch and copied one of his heroic landscapes. Walking tours from Munich yielded studies of the Salzburg, Upper Bavarian, and Tyrolean countryside. In 1824 the artist married his cousin, Friederike von Sckell.

Funds from the sales of his paintings enabled Rottmann to make his first trip to Italy, in 1826–27. The following year, in Munich, he showed several works done in Rome, which made King Ludwig I of Bavaria pursue the idea of having the walls of the Hofgarten arcades decorated with frescoes of famous Italian landscapes. Aided by Leo von Klenze, Rottmann received the commission, and returned at the king's behest to Italy in 1829–30 to prepare studies for the frescoes on site. Between 1830 and 1833 the artist developed his twenty-eight landscapes based on King Ludwig's program, which was intended to convey the impression of a journey through Italy from north to south, with stops at the relevant sites.

When his son, Otto I, became King of Greece in 1832, Ludwig planned a second, Grecian landscape cycle for the Hofgarten arcades. Envisaging landscapes hallowed by mythology and history, he sent Rottmann to Greece in 1834–35 to prepare the requisite studies from nature. After the cornerstone was laid for the New Pinakothek, this Hofgarten project was altered. Of the thirty-eight Greek Hofgarten landscapes originally planned, twenty-three were executed in encaustic on stone slabs for the New Pinakothek, where they were subsequently displayed as a panorama in the Rottmann Room.

Having gained renown as a painter of historical landscapes, Rottmann was named court artist in 1841. His final years were overshadowed by an eye ailment that threatened him with blindness. Rottmann's strength was an ability to capture the natural scene in all its spaciousness and grandeur. He was the major representative of the Munich school of landscape in his own generation, and had a great influence on subsequent generations of landscape artists.

Philipp Otto Runge

Wolgast, near Greifswald
23 July 1777–2 December 1810 Hamburg

The ninth of a shipowner's eleven children, Runge grew up in a strict Protestant household. In 1795 he followed his older brother Daniel to Hamburg, entering his business as an apprentice. Recognizing Philipp Otto's talent, Daniel introduced him to his intellectual friends, who included the poet Matthias Claudius and the publisher Friedrich Perthes. Daniel remained his younger brother's principal patron throughout his life.

Runge began taking drawing lessons in 1797, devoting much of his spare time to them. After convincing his father of his artistic vocation, he entered the Copenhagen Academy in 1799, studying with Nicolai Abildgaard and Jens Juel until March 1801. Then he went on to the Dresden Academy until 1804. In Dresden the artist came in contact with romantic writers such as Henrik Steffens, Friedrich Schlegel, and Ludwig Tieck, the composer Ludwig Berger, and the painters Anton Graff and Caspar David Friedrich. After an unsuccessful submission to Goethe's Weimar Competition of 1801, Runge abandoned neoclassicism.

From that point on, Runge's goal was nothing less than a "new landscape painting." In 1802–3 he created a series of four contour drawings titled *Four Times of Day—Morning, Midday, Evening, and Night*, which were engraved in Dresden and published in 1805; a second edition came out in 1807. Reflecting a universal philosophy couched in allegorical terms, the images symbolized the times of day and seasons of the year, the ages of man, historical eras, and the natural cycles of growth and decay. In this cycle Runge formulated ideas whose intellectual and aesthetic development would determine all his future work. He envisaged his *Times* as monumental murals on the walls of a neo-Gothic structure erected expressly for them and reverberating with the sound of music. His premature death prevented the realization of this *Gesamtkunstwerk*.

In preparation for it, in about 1805, Runge began a theoretical investigation of the phenomenon of colors, their meaning and psychological effects; he corresponded with Goethe and others on the subject. The results of this work were published as *Die Farbenkugel* (The Color Sphere) in 1810. Runge began translating his *Times* series into paint in 1808, with a picture now known as the *Small Morning*. This was followed in 1809 by a second, fragmentary version known as the *Large Morning*.

In 1804 Runge married fifteen-year-old Pauline Bassenge of Dresden. During the next several years his reputation as a portraitist grew, especially as a result of such group portraits as *We Three* (1805) and *The Hülsenbeck Children* (1806). From early youth Runge was amazingly dexterous at cut-paper silhouettes, which he later created in the hope that their wide distribution for interior decorating would help improve popular taste. The same hope led him to produce numerous illustrations, decorative almanac covers, and even playing-card designs. Runge also recorded two Low German fairy tales, "The Fisherman and His Wife" and "The Juniper Tree" for the anthology of the Brothers Grimm. Runge died of tuberculosis at thirty-three, his pursuit of a new art cut short. Valuable sources for an understanding of his art and intentions are his letters and *Hinterlassene Schriften* (Posthumous Writings), edited by Daniel Runge in 1840. Apart from Caspar David Friedrich, Runge was the most outstanding artist of German romanticism. His work influenced his contemporaries Friedrich and Schinkel, and his ideas still held their fascination for the Blaue Reiter and Bauhaus artists in the twentieth century.

Johann Gottfried Schadow

Berlin 20 May 1764–27 January 1850

The sculptor Johann Gottfried Schadow learned his art in the sculpture workshop of the Berlin court with Antoine Tassaert, a Paris-trained Flemish sculptor. He fled to Italy in order to marry Marianne Devidels, daughter of a Jewish banker in Vienna, and lived in from 1785 to 1787 in Rome, where he became friends with Canova. From 1787 to the end of his life, Schadow played a key role in the cultural life of Berlin. Initially he worked for the Royal Porcelain Manufactory. In 1788 he became head of the Court Sculpture Workshop, and in 1815 director of the Academy of Arts. Schadow is considered the most significant German sculptor of the period around 1800. His style is characterized by fidelity to nature, grace, and sensuousness—qualities not typical of the strict neoclassicism of the day. His oeuvre comprises approximately three hundred sculptures, including numerous busts, and a great range of graphic works, mostly from the latter half of his career. These number about fifteen hundred drawings and one hundred fifty etchings and lithographs, many of them caricatures. Schadow's major works were done in the decade after his return from Rome: the wall sepulcher for Count von der Mark (1788–91), the Quadriga on Brandenburg Gate (1789–94), marble statues of Zieten and Frederick the Great in contemporary costume (1793), and the marble group of Princesses Luise and Friederike (1795–97). Two of Schadow's sons became successful artists: Ridolfo a sculptor (until his untimely death) and Wilhelm a painter. In old age Schadow made a name for himself as a writer on art. His memoirs (1849) have since become a standard source on the history of Berlin art and culture.

Johann Evangelist Scheffer von Leonhardshoff

Vienna 30 October 1795–12 January 1822

Scheffer came of a pious Christian family of the lesser nobility. His education at the Vienna Academy began at an early age. From Hubert Maurer he learned the fundamentals of drawing, based on the strict rules of the Füger school. In 1809, at fourteen, he joined the Academy Corps to fight Napoleon, finishing his service as a lieutenant.

A crucial point in his life was his meeting with Joseph Sutter, a member of the Brotherhood of St. Luke who had stayed behind in Vienna and who introduced him to Nazarene concerns. Also seminal to his artistic development was his first journey, in 1812, to northern Italy, including Venice, to visit his sister, who had married there. On the return trip Scheffer stopped over in Klagenfurt, where he met the resident prince-bishop, Cardinal Franz Xaver Altgraf Salm-Reifferscheidt, who later became his patron and eventually named him Chamber Artist. The cardinal financed Scheffer's second trip to Italy, which included a stay in Rome from 1814 to 1816, and arranged a commission to do a portrait of Pope Pius VII, who awarded Scheffer the Order of Christ for the results.

Digesting influences from Michelangelo, Raphael, and Perugino, Scheffer arrived at his personal style. Thanks to his close friendship with Friedrich Overbeck, he belonged for a time to the inner circle of the Nazarenes, who admired his unusual gifts and affectionately called him "Raffaelino." On 24 October 1815 Scheffer was ceremoniously inducted into the brotherhood "as youngest among the brethren, the first successor of dear departed Pforr."

When he developed tuberculosis, Scheffer returned to Austria, living mainly in Klagenfurt and in Vienna, where he was a friend and frequent guest of the Olivier circle. There, in 1816, he met Julius Schnorr von Carolsfeld, who drew

his portrait. Despite occasional support from Duke Albert von Sachsen-Teschen and other aristocrats, Scheffer was continually on the brink of poverty, and depended for income on the annual exhibition at St. Anna's, Vienna, where he showed various key works, such as *St. Cecilia Playing the Organ*. In 1820–21 he returned to Rome, where he created his major work, *The Dying St. Cecilia*. His worsening condition forced Scheffer to return to Vienna, where he died a year later, at twenty-six.

Scheffer's small oeuvre shows him to have been a gifted draftsman and painter capable of profound thought and deep emotion. He made a significant contribution to the revival of the devotional and altar image that was a goal of the Nazarenes.

Karl Friedrich Schinkel

Neuruppin 13 March 1781–9 October 1841 Berlin

After his father's early death, Schinkel and his family moved in 1794 to Berlin, where he attended the Zum Grauen Kloster secondary school until 1798. Deciding to study architecture, he entered the office of David and Friedrich Gilly, with whom he lodged and soon became close friends. In 1799–1800 Schinkel attended the recently inaugurated Bauakademie, or Building Academy.

When Friedrich Gilly died, Schinkel assumed responsibility for the execution of several of his mentor's uncompleted projects, then began producing his own architectural designs. From 1803 to 1805 Schinkel traveled through Italy, stopping over in Rome, Naples, and Sicily, where he made numerous landscape and architectural drawings that revealed a versatile talent.

Because of political tensions during the following decade—Prussia was under French occupation from 1806—there was little demand for architects. Schinkel began to concentrate on painting, especially on architectural landscapes. These often included neo-Gothic churches, monuments, and visionary architecture, motifs that reflected the artist's patriotism and symbolized a national renewal in the spirit of Christian German culture. After the War of Liberation, Schinkel designed a Gothic cathedral to be located on the key battlefield outside Leipzig and serve as a monument of national unity.

As a result of his 1815 promotion to Chief Building Councilor, Schinkel became responsible for monuments in the Rhineland, which had been annexed by Prussia. These included Cologne Cathedral, the future symbol of German national unity, whose completion Schinkel supervised from 1816 on. Also, a revival of building activity in Berlin brought him a series of important projects. By 1830 Schinkel had produced many of his

major works, in a Greek revival style that was modified to suit each building's function. They were brilliantly integrated into their urban environment, forming focal points: the Neue Wache (New Sentry Post) on Unter den Linden (1817–18), the Schauspielhaus (Theater) at Gendarmenmarkt (1819–21), and the Old Museum at the Lustgarten, opposite the City Palace (1824–28).

In addition to the classical repertoire, Schinkel mastered the neo-Gothic, using it alternatively in designs for individual projects. Werder Church, for instance, was finally built in an English-influenced neo-Gothic style with façades of unstuccoed brick (1821–30).

The architect derived a great deal of inspiration from his many study trips, such as his second Italian journey, in 1824. But it was his 1826 trip to France, England, and Scotland that proved especially significant. The plain, strictly functional architecture of early industrial England left a deep impression on Schinkel. It encouraged him to begin emphasizing structural factors over historical revival details, as seen in his Building Academy (1831–36) and in his designs (never executed) for a department store and a stock exchange.

Projects that were realized included buildings in and around Potsdam, the Charlottenhof Estate with Roman Baths (1826–27) and the domed St. Nicholas Church (1830–49). His unbuilt projects included designs for a royal palace on the Acropolis in Athens (1834) and for Orianda Palace in the Crimea (1838).

Schinkel's architecture decisively shaped the face of Berlin. With the possible exception of Leo von Klenze, Schinkel was the most significant German architect of the era. His oeuvre had a range without precedent, encompassing practically every architectural task of the period, from modest private houses to magnificent palaces, from urban planning to the preservation of monuments, as well as designs for sculptural building ornaments, murals, furniture, and decorative art of many varieties. Schinkel also produced dioramas and stage designs, including a set for Mozart's *Magic Flute*. Even as a landscape painter and portraitist his achievement was extraordinary.

Schinkel edited a variety of publications on his works, including the widely disseminated *Sammlung architektonischer Entwürfe* (Collection of Architectural Designs), which appeared in 28 issues between 1819 and 1840. In addition to significant literary writings, published posthumously by Alfred von Wolzogen (1862–64), Schinkel left an extensive graphic oeuvre, the greater part of which—over forty-four hundred drawings, gouaches, watercolors, and lithographs—is now in the Kupferstichkabinett, Berlin.

Julius Veit Hans Schnorr
von Carolsfeld

Leipzig 26 March 1794 – 24 May 1872 Dresden

Son of Veit Hans Schnorr von Carolsfeld, a painter and teacher at the Leipzig Academy, Julius received instruction in art from an early age. He mastered the technique of contour etching so rapidly that his father asked him to assist on illustrations in this manner after John Flaxman for Homer's *Iliad* (1804) and a *Manual of the Art of Drawing* (1810). An emphasis on contour line remained a characteristic of Schnorr von Carolsfeld's art throughout his career.

With an eye to becoming a history painter, Schnorr attended the Vienna Academy, studying with Friedrich Heinrich Füger. From 1811 to 1817 he lived in Vienna, during the politically heady period of the War of Liberation and the Peace Congress. He entered Füger's class shortly after Overbeck, Pforr, and others had left; soon he, too, formed an aversion to Füger's baroque-tinged neoclassical eclecticism and preferred to continue his training on his own.

Schnorr frequented romantic literary circles, meeting Joseph von Eichendorff, Theodor Körner, Friedrich Schlegel, and others. He found his greatest artistic challenge in Joseph Anton Koch, who lived in Vienna from 1812 to 1815, and in the patriotic brothers Ferdinand and Friedrich Olivier. He moved into the brothers' home, forming a friendship with them that lasted a lifetime. Like the Oliviers, Schnorr oriented himself toward early German and Netherlandish art, particularly Dürer's prints. Under the brothers' influence he concentrated on developing a precise linear style in the early German Renaissance manner. Schnorr's eminent graphic talent and virtuoso pen handling came to full flower in Vienna. In late 1817 he left for Italy, where he initially lived in Florence with Carl Friedrich von Rumohr. In the spring of 1818 he went to Rome, a city in which his gifts as a draftsman and a painter of oils and frescoes unfolded in nature studies, nudes, portraits and landscapes, as well as in history paintings, a field Schnorr considered his forte. He was accepted into the Brotherhood of St. Luke immediately after arriving in Rome. Together with Friedrich Olivier and Theodor Rehbenitz he lived in the Palazzo Caffarelli, the seat of the Prussian legation on the Capitol, and was active in the Protestant congregation as a singer and organist. Schnorr became the nucleus of the Protestant Nazarenes, who were known as "Capitolines." During these years he produced major landscapes and portraits, which he compiled in his *Book of Italian Landscapes* and *Book of Roman Portraits*. He also began laying the groundwork for a Bible in pictures, a project that lasted nearly four decades.

In the spring of 1818 Schnorr was commissioned to decorate a room in the Casino Massimo with scenes from Ariosto's *Orlando Furioso*. Unable to begin work until 1821, he completed the project in the summer of 1827. It made such an impression on Crown Prince Ludwig of Bavaria, who was frequently in Rome, that shortly after his accession in 1825 he called Schnorr to Munich to serve as professor of history painting at the academy. The artist's Munich years, 1827–46, were dominated by King Ludwig's commissions for monumental murals in the annexes to his residence, designed by Leo von Klenze. Schnorr began his decorations in 1831 with the Nibelungen Rooms in the Royal Wing, and went on the next year to the Salon de Service. A new project interrupted this work from 1835 to 1842: decoration of the three Imperial Rooms in the Festival Hall Wing with paintings on the history of Charlemagne, Friedrich Barbarossa, and Rudolf von Habsburg. Schnorr drew all of the designs and cartoons for this project (which are extant), and entrusted pupils with the execution.

In 1840 he began illustrations for an edition of the *Nibelungenlied*, published by Cotta in 1843. In 1846 he received the post of director of the Dresden Academy and Gallery of Paintings. As gallery director he supervised the move into Gottfried Semper's new building and the arrangement of the permanent exhibition. Schnorr went blind in his left eye in 1848.

After producing illustrations for the "Cotta Bible" (1846–50), Schnorr finally completed those for the *Bible in Pictures*, his major work. Published as wood engravings in large editions between 1852 and 1860, it became a household book in Germany. The *Nibelungen* frescoes in Munich were finally completed by his pupils in 1867. Still working at an advanced age, Schnorr produced designs for Meissen china and—a sign of his international reputation—for the choir windows of St. Paul's Cathedral in London. He was among the most significant artists of the romantic period and, along with Friedrich Overbeck, one of the finest graphic artists among the Nazarenes.

Moritz von Schwind

Vienna 21 January 1804 – 8 February 1871
Niederpöcking on Lake Starnberg

The fifth of six children of Court Secretary and Embassy Councilor Franz von Schwind, Moritz grew up in a highly cultured environment. After secondary schooling at the Vienna Schottenkloster, he studied philosophy at Vienna University from 1818 to 1821. When his father died in 1818, Moritz began earning his own living as an illustrator and draftsman. Goethe praised his vignettes for an edition of *Arabian Nights*.

In the summer of 1821 von Schwind decided to make art his career, and spent the next two years at the Vienna Academy as a student of Ludwig Schnorr von Carolsfeld and Peter Kraft. Leopold Kupelwieser instructed him in oil painting, but thereafter his growing skills were largely the result of independent work. From 1821 to 1828 von Schwind was a close friend of Franz Schubert and his circle, which included the playwright Franz Grillparzer and the artist brothers Olivier. In 1827 von Schwind went to Munich, where he met Peter Cornelius, who convinced him to move there the following year.

Thanks to Cornelius's influence he received commissions from the Bavarian Royal House for his first monumental murals: in 1832, decorations for the queen's library at the royal residence, based on Ludwig Tieck's *Phantasus*; in 1835–36, watercolor designs for Crown Prince Maximilian's Hohenschwangau Castle, based on subjects from Germanic sagas, the legendary youth of Charlemagne, and Tasso's works. In 1835 von Schwind traveled to Italy, where he spent a good five months, visiting Naples and Pompeii, and staying for some time in Rome, working on a painting based on Goethe's ballad "Ritter Kurts Brautfahrt" (not finished until 1839). Between 1838 and 1840 he executed a fresco cycle influenced by Raphael on the theme of Amor and Psyche, in the garden room of Rüdigsdorf Palace near Altenburg, Saxony. In Karlsruhe between 1840 and 1844 he executed various large-scale mural commissions, first in the Ständehaus, then in the Kunsthalle, where four large rooms and the stairwell were to be decorated.

In 1844 the artist moved to Frankfurt am Main, becoming history painter at the Städelsches Institut and painting *Bards' Contest at the Wartburg*. The post of professor of history painting at the Munich Academy was awarded him in 1847. A journey to Thuringia and connections with the Weimar court brought a commission from the Grand Duke of Weimar for frescoes at Wartburg Castle, which he executed in 1853–54, when he was at the height of his powers.

Between 1848 and 1864 von Schwind produced what he called "Travel Pictures," private works not initially intended for show or sale. The series comprised about forty lyrical small-format paintings, many of which expanded on drawings from von Schwind's youth (1822). In 1869 he sold twenty-five of these pictures to Count Schack, who, with a total of thirty-three paintings, owned the largest von Schwind collection of the day (now in the Schack-Galerie, Munich). Influenced by Pompeiian murals and the work of his friend Eugen Napoleon Neureuther, the artist created idiosyncratic compositions, narrative visual sequences within an encompassing frame. The major works of the series, prepared in numerous detailed drawings, were done in the spring of 1852 (*The Symphony*) and during the next three years (*The Story of Cinderella*).

In 1863 von Schwind began decorating the loggia of the Vienna Opera with scenes from Mozart's *Magic Flute*; he then executed ceiling paintings and lunettes in the foyer on themes from various operas, completing the work in late 1867. He also did a series of paintings to prepare murals for what were to be the Schubert and Beethoven rooms, but these were never executed.

Throughout his career von Schwind continued to work as an illustrator. In Munich he drew for humor and family magazines such as *Fliegende Blätter* and *Münchner Bilderbogen*. In addition to an extensive oeuvre in painting and murals, he left behind a vast number of graphic works, especially drawings and watercolors. He was doubtless one of the greatest draftsmen of the period, and the major representative of the literary, illustrative strain in late romanticism. Because of his affinities with music, with German history, and with the world of sagas and fairy tales, von Schwind held a special place in nineteenth-century art: his work remained popularly accessible and, not least on account of its pervading humor, valued and admired to the end of his life.

Edward Jakob von Steinle

Vienna 2 July 1810 – 18 September 1886
Frankfurt am Main

Edward Steinle was the son of an engraver. At thirteen he was already a student at the Vienna Academy, first with Vinzenz Georg Kininger, later with Leopold Kupelwieser, on whose advice he copied works by Fra Angelico and went to Rome in 1828. There he formed close friendships with Friedrich Overbeck, Philipp Veit, and Joseph von Führich, and continued to hone his painting skills on his own. Steinle's tie with Overbeck proved decisive for his development.

In 1829 Overbeck asked him to assist him on a fresco, *The Miracle of the Rose*, in the Portiuncula Chapel near Assisi. Steinle then drew cartoons for frescoes in S. Trinità dei Monti, which were executed by Joseph Tunner when he had to return to Vienna for a few months in 1830 after his father's death. Until 1833 he lived in Rome, intensively studying Italian Renaissance works. On returning to Vienna again he executed several altar paintings, concentrated on designs for applied art, and illustrated books, including Thomas von Kempen's *Von der Nachfolge Christi* (On the Imitation of Christ).

Steinle's development was further influenced by Friedrich Schlegel and his romantic circle, with whom he maintained close contact. In 1837 Steinle was commissioned to decorate the chapel of Rheineck Castle, near Remagen. To prepare himself for the task and to train in fresco tech-

nique, the artist went to Munich in 1838 to assist Cornelius on his frescoes in the Pinakothek and Ludwigskirche. After moving to Frankfurt in 1839, Steinle became the nucleus of a group of Catholic-oriented artists. With the aid of his friend Philipp Veit he secured the use of a studio at the Städelsches Institut. Work in Rheineck was finished in 1841, and two years later Steinle and Veit founded an independent art school known as Deutsches Haus, which attracted artists such as Alfred Rethel and Moritz von Schwind. The latter's influence effected a fruitful opening and expansion of Steinle's approach; apart from religious themes he now began addressing secular and literary subjects in a romantic vein.

In 1850 Steinle was named professor of history painting at the Städelsches Institut. During the following decades he designed ambitious mural cycles, most of which were executed by assistants, for Cologne, Münster, Aachen (1865 – 66), Kleinheubach (1870 – 71), Strasbourg (1877 – 79), and other locations. Steinle also drew cartoons for murals at the Städelsches Institut and the Opera House, as well as preparing designs for Frankfurt Cathedral. In 1879 he was raised to the nobility.

In conservative Catholic circles Steinle remained highly admired to the end. He was a Nazarene in the original sense of the word, though of the second generation. With amazing tenacity he maintained the ideals of the movement into old age; he was lonely, rigid, and alien in a completely changed world. His art, difficult of access today, is best appreciated through his significant work in drawing and printmaking. A highly gifted draftsman, Steinle produced masterly and often marvelous imagery on paper. His illustrations, for the Brothers Grimm or the works of his friend Clemens Brentano, among others, "reveal a draftsman of the highest sensibility, capable of conjuring up fairy-tale atmospheres of Schwindian power and poetry" (Hans Vollmer).

Joseph Karl Stieler

Mainz 1 November 1781 – 9 April 1858 Munich

Joseph Stieler was the fifth child of a respected master minter in the Electorate of Mainz. After his father's early death, Joseph taught himself to paint by copying portrait miniatures—so successfully that he was able to help support his family while still a boy. The years 1798 to 1800 brought crucial employment at the Electorate Court. Stieler worked for the influential Carl Theodor Freiherr von Dalberg, in Aschaffenburg and Mainz, then in Würzburg, where the artist earned enough to take a two-year apprenticeship with Christoph Fesel, a pupil of Mengs and a renowned history and portrait painter.

In 1800 Stieler went to Vienna, where he studied from 1802 to 1805 with Friedrich Heinrich Füger at the academy and copied old masters in the Gemäldegalerie. Füger advised him to give up miniature painting in favor of large-format oils, and influenced him toward portraiture in the English manner. Numerous portrait commissions took Stieler to Hungary, Galicia, and Poland. He was occupied in Cracow for ten months and in Warsaw for an entire year, producing about twenty-six portraits. To round off his training the artist spent the years 1807 – 8 in Paris, studying official portraiture in the service of Napoleon, and becoming a student of the neoclassical state painter François Gérard. At this point a change of approach occurred that would define his subsequent oeuvre: a stronger emphasis on contour, combined with a cooler palette and a restrained idealization of the sitter.

Stieler's Paris period was overshadowed by an eye ailment that prevented him from pursuing his profitable miniature painting. Lack of funds prompted him to go to the prosperous business center of Frankfurt, where he was inundated with commissions and earned enough to permit an extended Italian journey. Stieler was in Rome from 1810 to 1812, concurrently with the first Nazarenes, though he established no close contact with them. A stroke of luck came with a six-month stay in Milan, where Stieler did family portraits for Eugène de Beauharnais, Vice Regent of Italy and Duke of Leuchtenberg, and his wife Auguste Amalie, a daughter of King Maximilian I Joseph of Bavaria. Ties with the Bavarian royal house resulted, and Stieler went to Munich, where he was employed by the court from then on. At the court's behest he returned to Vienna in 1816 to paint Emperor Franz and his wife. Remaining for several years, Stieler also executed a portrait of Beethoven (1819). In 1820 he settled in Munich and was named court artist. He became a founding member of the city's Kunstverein, or art association, in 1824.

Into advanced age Stieler continued to enjoy commissions from emperors and monarchs, painting portraits of such illustrious intellectuals as Ludwig Tieck and Alexander von Humboldt. His best-known works, however, were done on commission from King Ludwig I of Bavaria. These included the 1828 portrait of the elderly Goethe, and the famous "Gallery of Beauties" for the Festival Hall Wing of the Munich Residence, to which he devoted decades. Characteristic of Stieler's manner was a verisimilitude tempered by an idealization derived from official French portraiture of the Napoleonic era.

Johann Heinrich Wilhelm Tischbein

Haina, Hesse 15 February 1751–26 June 1829
Eutin, Holstein

Wilhelm Tischbein came from an extensive family rich in artistic talent. His connection with Goethe brought him a nickname that distinguished him from the more than twenty artists with the same family name: he was "Goethe Tischbein." The son of a cabinetmaker, Wilhelm received his first training from his uncles, Johann Heinrich, Sr., a significant Kassel portraitist of the late rococo, and Jacob Tischbein, of Hamburg.

Wilhelm Tischbein lived the life of an itinerant painter, moving from Holland to Bremen and finally to Berlin, where he became a successful portraitist. A scholarship from the Kassel Academy enabled him to take his first trip to Italy, in 1779, and there he branched out into landscape painting. On the return journey Tischbein stopped in Zurich, spending the years 1781–82 in the company of Lavater, Bodmer, and Gessner. His second Italian sojourn, in 1783, was facilitated by the Duke of Gotha, for whom he executed his first history painting, *Konradin von Hohenstaufen*. In 1786 Tischbein met Goethe in Rome, to whom he gave drawing instruction, and whose famous portrait in the Campagna he completed the following year.

Tischbein began teaching at the Naples Academy in 1787 and was named its director in 1789. Two years later he started publishing sequences of etchings based on Greek vases in the Hamilton Collection, a series entitled *Homer, Drawn from Antiques*, and studies of animal physiognomies. After the French conquest of Naples in 1799, Tischbein returned to Germany, settling in Hamburg. Here he made contact with Romantic artists of the younger generation, such as Philipp Otto Runge and Friedrich Overbeck. From 1808 to the end of his life Tischbein was active in Eutin as court artist and inspector of galleries under Duke Peter von Oldenburg, to whom he had sold his art collection in 1804.

Tischbein's versatile talent extended to collecting and writing on art. His diverse historical, archaeological, scientific, and educational interests can in fact be said to have dissipated his artistic powers. As draftsman and etcher he left behind an extensive oeuvre of more than two thousand sheets, in which the variety of visual idioms in the Goethe period is reflected in an unusual way. Tischbein's characteristic graphic touch bespeaks an original personality and a sense of humor. In his own period Tischbein was admired as a skilled portraitist and history painter who oriented himself both to nature and to the art of classical antiquity.

Philipp Veit

Berlin 13 February 1793–18 December 1877 Mainz

The son of a Jewish banker, Veit grew up in Berlin. His mother was the eldest daughter of the philosopher Moses Mendelssohn. Her second husband, whom she married in 1799, was Friedrich Schlegel, author, cultural philosopher, and literary historian. Philipp lived with his mother and stepfather in Jena, Paris, and Cologne.

In 1809 he went with his brother, Johannes, to Dresden, enrolling in the Academy and studying for a time with Caspar David Friedrich. While visiting his parents in Vienna in 1810, Veit followed their example and converted to Catholicism. The following spring he returned to his stepfather's residence, a focus of Viennese cultural life. Veit met, among others, Joseph von Eichendorff, Theodor Körner, the Olivier brothers, and Joseph Anton Koch, who greatly influenced his development. In the spring of 1813 he and Eichendorff entered the Lützow Freikorps to fight the French. Veit, by then an officer, participated in the allied capture of Paris in 1814.

Veit returned to Vienna but embarked on an Italian journey in the summer of 1815. In Rome he made connections with Overbeck and Cornelius, and the following year collaborated with them on a fresco cycle in the residence of his uncle, Jakob Salomon Bartholdy. Then, at Antonio Canova's instigation, Veit was commissioned to paint a fresco in the new Museo Chiaramonti in the Vatican. After Cornelius relinquished the task of decorating the Dante Room at Casino Massimo Veit took it over in 1818, but completed just the ceiling fresco representing Paradise, in 1822–24. Then he, too, withdrew from the project.

In 1821 Veit married Karolina Pulini, a fifteen-year-old Roman girl. During the next few years he produced a series of important portraits. In 1829 the artist became director of the recently inaugurated Städelsches Kunstinstitut, with the associated Städel-Schule, in Frankfurt am Main, and moved there the following year.

The years 1834–36 were devoted to executing a three-part mural in the new building, comprising *The Introduction of the Arts into Germany by Christianity* and two wing panels, *Germania* and *Italia*, a Nazarene program picture which showed Veit at the height of his powers. Veit's fame attracted many students to the school, including Moritz von Schwind, Alfred Rethel, and Edward von Steinle. Yet a growing conflict between the advocates of the Nazarene style and the progressive forces of the Düsseldorf school eventually led Veit to resign his directorship in 1843 and establish his own school.

From 1853 the artist lived in Mainz, where he drew cartoons for the decoration of the cathedral, which were executed by his students from 1859 to 1864. In 1854 Veit became head of the Städtische Kunstgalerie, the municipal museum (now Landesmuseum Mainz) that eventually acquired his estate. Late in life Veit emerged as a writer on art. Central to his oeuvre are his outstanding portraits, both drawn and painted.

Max Joseph Wagenbauer

Grafing, Upper Bavaria (baptized)
28 July 1775–12 May 1829 Munich

After attending the Wilhelmsgymnasium in Munich, Wagenbauer began training in 1793 at the Munich Academy of Drawing under J. J. Dorner, Sr., and J. C. von Mannlich. In 1802 he was named court and chamber draftsman to the electorate court. The next year he taught drawing in the family of Count Lodron, at Haag Castle on the Ammer. From then on he resided permanently in Munich. He began to teach himself watercolor technique, and during the following summers took long journeys on foot through Upper and Lower Bavaria, the Upper Palatinate, the Bavarian Forest, and the northern region of Lake Constance. A series of landscapes resulted, for the most part watercolors. Though conventionally composed, these views exhibited a quality of light that gave them a heightened atmosphere. The lucidity and delicacy of Wagenbauer's colors and his mastery of the difficult technique made him an outstanding watercolorist.

From 1810 on he devoted himself principally to oils. His favorite theme remained cattle grazing in the Upper Bavarian countryside, and he soon established a reputation as an animal and landscape painter. Although he initially oriented his work toward Netherlandish models, such as Aelbert Cuyp and Paulus Potter, after 1820 he began to develop his own, straightforward approach to the topography of Upper Bavaria.

In 1815 Wagenbauer was named inspector of galleries. He enjoyed the support of King Maximilian I. Joseph of Bavaria, who acquired several of his paintings. An involvement with lithography beginning in 1810 made Wagenbauer one of the first artists to employ this technique for artistic ends. He created a number of model lithograph sequences on the art of animal and landscape depiction, which, since they were used for instruction in drawing schools, had widespread influence.

Friedrich Georg Weitsch

Braunschweig (Brunswick)
8 August 1758 – 30 May 1828 Berlin

After years of training with his father, the landscapist and animal painter Johann Friedrich "Pasha" Weitsch, Friedrich Georg entered the employ of the Stobwasser Lacquerware Company in Brunswick, where he decorated jars and trays with landscapes and idyllic scenes. In 1783 – 84 he honed his skills by copying Potter and Rosa da Tivoli in the Düsseldorf Gallery. Study trips to Holland and Italy followed in 1784 – 87. Weitsch was named court painter in Brunswick in 1787. He later moved to Berlin, where in 1794 he became a member of the Academy and four years later its rector, as well as Prussian court painter.

Weitsch's best and most admired work was done in portraiture. Schooled by Anton Graff's work, he was oriented toward French Neoclassical portrait painting of the Empire period. With a sharp eye for physiognomy, character, and personal aura, Weitsch created a series of significant portrayals, principally of scholars and artists prominent in the cultural life of Berlin. They included Alois Hirt painted (in Rome) in 1785; Johann Gottfried Schadow, in 1795; and Alexander von Humboldt, in 1806.

Weitsch also devoted himself to landscape and history painting, genre and still life. Here, however, his eclecticism revealed the limitations of his talent. In landscape he took his cues from disparate sources: from Claude Lorrain and Gaspard Dughet, as well as from both the Italianate Netherlandish and the realistic Dutch landscape art of the seventeenth century. In his history paintings the artist favored subjects from German history, from the legendary past to the present day. He also did a number of religious paintings.

His diverse drawings, like his paintings, show Weitsch to have been an eclectic artist whose work greatly fluctuated in originality and quality. Sanguine drawings from the Italian period, for instance, reflect the influence of Hubert Robert's drawing style and that of the French Academy in Rome. Weitsch's most successful drawings were his portraits, which have great vitality and natural charm.

Caspar Wolf

Muri, Aargau, Switzerland
3 May 1735 – 6 October 1783 Heidelberg

After beginning his artistic training with an apprenticeship in decoration and church painting in Constance, Caspar Wolf worked as a journeyman for a *veduta* painter in Augsburg. Then he set out on journeys that took him to Munich and Passau. All of these cities were centers of southern German rococo.

After returning to Switzerland, Wolf was employed from 1760 to 1768 by the Princely Abbey in Muri, where he painted decorative landscapes. These reflected his penchant for bizarre rock formations and waterfalls, as well as his vivid and imaginative formal idiom. In 1769 the artist went by way of Basel to Paris, where he spent some time in the atelier of Philippe-Jacques de Loutherbourg and was influenced by Joseph Vernet. During this period the Alpine landscape was a fashionable topic of conversation in Paris, thanks to publications such as Marmontel's *La Bergère des Alpes* (1759), Rousseau's *Nouvelle Héloïse* (1761), and translations of Salomon Gessner's works (1761).

Wolf returned to Muri in late 1771. Traveling through the Swiss interior in 1773, he executed topographical studies that attracted the attention of Abraham Wagner, Jr., a publisher in Berne. Wagner, intending to publish a reference work on the Alps, was on the lookout for an artist who could supply the requisite illustrations. Two prominent Berne personalities had already been recruited for the project: poet and scholar Albrecht von Haller, to write the introduction, and natural scientist Samuel Wyttenbach, to provide captions for the plates. Wolf was eventually commissioned to paint more than one hundred fifty Alpine motifs, a task that occupied him until 1779.

Immense effort went into ensuring the authenticity of these depictions. After making oil sketches on cardboard on site, Wolf transferred them to canvas in the studio, then carried his paintings—winter storms or no—back to the remotest of mountain crannies to make corrections. The job of reproducing Wolf's paintings—some as etchings, others as hand-colored engravings—was never completed. Only ten of them were transferred to plates, in 1776 – 77. The selection was edited by Balthasar Anton Dunker, and published by Wagner in 1777 as the first issue of the artist's major work, under the title *Alpes Helveticae*. When Wolf's paintings were shown in Paris in 1779, Jean-François Janinet, a master of color aquatint and four-color engraving, created superb color engravings of twenty-four of the works, under the supervision of Horace Vernet. These were published in 1780 – 82, as *Vues remarquables des montagnes de la Suisse avec leur description*, again by Wagner of Berne.

Wolf was the first artist to make the Alps the central theme of his oils, watercolors, gouaches, and drawings. The 1773 – 79 painting cycle reveals a new vision of the mountains, which, instead of appearing forbidding, frightening, and chaotic, are depicted as natural phenomena, unsullied and sublime. Here, as in the landscape and architectural views of his final period, begun in September 1780 in the Rhineland and Paris, Wolf proves to have been a forerunner of nineteenth-century landscape realism.

Selected Bibliography

ADB
Allgemeine Deutsche Biographie. Leipzig, 1875–1912.

A./Andresen
Andreas Andresen, *Die Deutschen Maler-Radirer (Peintres-Graveurs) des neunzehnten Jahrhunderts nach ihren Leben und Werken.* Leipzig, 1866–74; reprint Hildesheim-New York, 1971.

Andrews 1964
Keith Andrews, *The Nazarenes: A Brotherhood of German Painters in Rome.* Oxford.

Andrews 1967
Keith Andrews, *I Nazareni.* Milan.

Bächtold-Stäubli
Hanns Bächtold-Stäubli and E. Hoffmann-Krayer, *Handwörterbuch des deutschen Aberglaubens.* Vols. 1–10. Berlin and Leipzig, 1927–42.

Bailey 1977
Colin J. Bailey, "Moritz von Schwind and His Illustrations to Contemporary German Literature." Vols. 1–3. Ph.D. dissertation. Nottingham.

Bailey 1987
Colin J. Bailey, *German Nineteenth Century Drawings, Ashmolean Museum Oxford. Catalogue of the Collection of Drawings.* Vol. 5. Oxford.

Basel 1982
Zeichnungen deutscher Künstler des 19. Jahrhunderts aus dem Basler Kupferstichkabinett. Edited by Eva Maria Krafft. Exhibition catalogue, Kunstmuseum Basel, Kupferstichkabinett.

Bauer 1982
Jens-Heiner Bauer, *Daniel Nikolaus Chodowiecki, Danzig 1726–1801 Berlin. Das druckgraphische Werk. Die Sammlung Wilhelm Burggraf zu Dohna-Schlobitten. Ein Bildband mit 2340 Abbildungen in Ergänzung zum Werkverzeichnis von Wilhelm Engelmann.* Hannover.

Benz and Schneider 1939
Richard Benz and Arthur von Schneider, *Die Kunst der deutschen Romantik.* Munich.

Berckenhagen 1967
Ekhart Berckenhagen, *Anton Graff. Leben und Werk.* Berlin.

Berlin 1906
Deutsche Jahrhundert-Ausstellung. Katalog der Ausstellung Deutscher Kunst aus der Zeit von 1775–1875. Zeichnungen, Aquarelle, Pastelle, Ölstudien, Miniaturen und Möbel. Exhibition catalogue, Königliche Nationalgalerie, Berlin.

Berlin 1980
Adolph Menzel. Gemälde, Zeichnungen. Published by the Staatliche Museen zu Berlin (GDR). With contributions by Peter H. Feist, Françoise Forster-Hahn, Gerd Bartoschek, Edit Trost, Claude Keisch, Ursula Nündel. Exhibition catalogue, Nationalgalerie, Berlin.

Berlin 1980/81
Karl Friedrich Schinkel 1781–1841. Text by Ernst Badstübner, Sibylle Badstübner-Gröger, Gert Bartoschek, Götz Eckart, Hansjoachim Giersberg, Gottfried Riemann, Ursula Riemann-Reyher, Adelheid Schendel, et al. Exhibition catalogue, Staatliche Museen zu Berlin (GDR), Altes Museum.

Berlin 1981
Preussische Bildnisse des 19. Jahrhunderts. Zeichnungen von Wilhelm Hensel. Text by Cécile Lowenthal-Hensel, with contributions by Lucius Grisebach and Cécile Lowenthal-Hensel. Exhibition catalogue, Staatliche Museen Preussischer Kulturbesitz, Nationalgalerie, Berlin.

Berlin 1987
Waldungen. Die Deutschen und ihr Wald. Text by Bernd Weyergraf in collaboration with Annemarie Hürlimann. Exhibition catalogue, Akademie der Künste, Akademie-Katalog 149. Berlin.

Berlin 1994
Gottfried Riemann, with Claudia Czok and Marie Ursula Riemann-Reyher, *Ahnung und Gegenwart. Zeichnungen und Aquarelle der deutschen Romantik im Berliner Kupferstichkabinett.* Exhibition catalogue, Kupferstichkabinett, Berlin; Altenkamp Estate, Exhibition Center, Papenburg-Aschendorf.

Berlin 1997
Adolph Menzel 1815–1905. Das Labyrinth der Wirklichkeit. Edited by Claude Keisch and Marie Ursula Riemann-Reyher, with contributions by Helmut Börsch-Supan, Werner Busch, et al. Exhibition catalogue, Musée d'Orsay, Paris, 1996; National Gallery of Art, Washington, D.C.; Nationalgalerie im Alten Museum, Berlin, 1997. Cologne, 1996.

Bern 1985
Traum und Wahrheit. Deutsche Romantik aus Museen der Deutschen Demokratischen Republik. Edited by Jürgen Glaesemer, with contributions by Willi Geismeier, Jürgen Glaesemer, Joseph Helfenstein, Hans-Joachim Neidhardt, Hans Christoph von Tavel, Christa Wolf. Exhibition catalogue, Kunstmuseum Bern.

Bernhard 1974
Deutsche Romantik. Handzeichnungen. Edited by Marianne Bernhard, afterword by Petra Kipphoff. 2nd, revised edition. 2 vols. Munich.

Bernhard (Hinz) 1974
Caspar David Friedrich. Das gesamte graphische Werk. Edited by Marianne Bernhard (after Sigrid Hinz), afterword by Hans H. Hofstätter. Munich.

Bierhaus-Rödiger 1978
Erika Bierhaus-Rödiger, *Carl Rottmann 1797–1850. Monographie und kritischer Werkkatalog.* With contributions by Hugo Decker and Barbara Eschenburg. Munich.

C. G. Boerner/Arnold Otto Meyer
C. G. Boerner, 123.–125. Auktion. *Handzeichnungssammlung Arnold Otto Meyer*, Hamburg. Auction catalogue. Vols. 1–3. Leipzig, 1914.

Börsch-Supan and Jähnig 1973
Helmut Börsch-Supan and Karl Wilhelm Jähnig, *Caspar David Friedrich. Gemälde, Druckgraphik und bildmässige Zeichnungen.* Munich.

Börsch-Supan 1971
Die Kataloge der Berliner Akademie-Ausstellungen 1786–1850. Edited by Helmut Börsch-Supan. Berlin.

Börsch-Supan 1972
Helmut Börsch-Supan, *Deutsche Romantiker. Deutsche Maler zwischen 1800 und 1850.* Munich, Gütersloh, and Vienna.

Börsch-Supan 1987
Helmut Börsch-Supan, *Caspar David Friedrich.* 4th, revised, and expanded edition. Munich (1973).

Börsch-Supan 1988
Helmut Börsch-Supan, *Die deutsche Malerei von Anton Graff bis Hans von Marées 1760–1870.* Munich.

Boetticher
Friedrich von Boetticher, *Malerwerke des 19. Jahrhunderts.* Dresden, 1891–1901. Reprint: Hofheim im Taunus, 1979.

Bremen 1961
Julius Schnorr von Carolsfeld. Ausgewählte Handzeichnungen (leaflet). Bremen.

Bremen 1963
Adolph Menzel. Handzeichnungen. Text by Günter Busch and Christian von Heusinger. Exhibition catalogue, Kunsthalle Bremen.

Bruford 1979
Walter H. Bruford, *Die gesellschaftlichen Grundlagen der Goethezeit.* With bibliographical notes by Reinhardt Habel. Unabridged text of the German ed., Weimar, 1936. Frankfurt am Main, Berlin, and Vienna. English ed., *Culture and Society in Classical Weimar, 1775–1806.* London, 1962.

Buberl 1989
Brigitte Buberl, *Erlkönig und Alpenbraut. Dichtung, Märchen und Sage in Bildern der Schack-Galerie.* Exhibition catalogue, Bayerische Staatsgemäldesammlungen, Studio-Ausstellung 12, Schack-Galerie, Munich.

Büttner 1980
Frank Büttner, *Peter Cornelius. Fresken und Freskenprojekte.* Vol. 1. Wiesbaden.

Busch 1985
Werner Busch, *Die notwendige Arabeske. Wirklichkeitsaneignung und Stilisierung in der deutschen Kunst des 19. Jahrhunderts.* Berlin.

Busch 1994
Werner Busch, "Der Berg als Gegenstand von Naturwissenschaft und Kunst. Zu Goethes geologischem Begriff," in Frankfurt 1994, pp. 485–97.

von Buttlar 1979
Adrian von Buttlar, "Der Garten als Bild–das Bild des Gartens. Zum Englischen Garten in München," in Munich 1979, pp. 160–72.

Cambridge 1972
German Master Drawings of the Nineteenth Century. Edited by Hedy B. Landman, with John David Farmer, John R. Aldermann, Michael Conforti, Gregory Frucht, A. Rand Gordon, Anthony F. Janson, Nenette H. Sexton. Exhibition catalogue, Busch-Reisinger Museum, Harvard University; Metropolitan Museum of Art, New York; National Gallery of Canada, Ottawa; Minneapolis Institute of Art. Cambridge, Mass.

Cologne 1973
Sehnsucht nach Italien. Deutsche Zeichner im Süden 1770–1830. Exhibition catalogue, Wallraf-Richartz-Museum, Cologne.

Cologne 1984
Heroismus und Idylle. Formen der Landschaft um 1800 bei Jacob Philipp Hackert, Joseph Anton Koch und Johann Christian Reinhart. Published by the Wallraf-Richartz-Museum with contributions by Götz Czymmek, Joachim Gaus, Wolfgang Krönig, Ekkehard Mai, Albert Schug. Text by Ulrike Bühler et al. Exhibition catalogue, Wallraf-Richartz-Museum, Cologne.

Decker 1957
Hugo Decker, *Carl Rottmann*. Berlin.

Dieffenbach 1823
Philipp Dieffenbach, *Das Leben des Malers Karl Fohr,
zunächst für dessen Freunde und Bekannte geschrieben.* Darmstadt. Reprint with a foreword by Paul Ferdinand Schmidt,
newly edited by Rudolf Schrey. Frankfurt am Main, 1918.

Dörries 1943
Deutsche Zeichnungen des 18. Jahrhunderts. With an introduction by Bernhard Dörries. Munich.

Dresden 1997
*Ernst Ferdinand Oehme 1797–1855. Ein Landschaftsmaler der
Romantik.* Edited by Ulrich Bischoff, with contributions by
Ulrich Bischoff, Werner Kohlert, Petra Kuhlmann-Hodick,
Hans-Joachim Neidhardt, Gerd Spitzer, and Gregor J. M.
Weber. Catalogue raisonné of the paintings and pictorial
drawings by Hans-Joachim Neidhardt. Exhibition catalogue,
Staatliche Kunstsammlungen, Gemäldegalerie Neue Meister,
Dresden; Museum für Kunst und Kulturgeschichte, Lübeck.
Dresden.

Ebertshäuser 1976
Adolph von Menzel. Das graphische Werk. Selected by Heidi
Ebertshäuser, with a foreword by Jens Christian Jensen and
an essay by Max Liebermann. Vol. 2. Munich.

Erwerbungen 1982–1989
*Erwerbungen 1982–1989: Ankäufe und Geschenke – eine
Auswahl.* Text by Holm Bevers, Tilman Falk, Richard
Harprath, Wolfgang Holler, Dieter Kuhrmann, Gisela
Scheffler, and Thea Vignau-Wilberg. Exhibition catalogue,
Staatliche Graphische Sammlung. Munich, 1990.

Femmel 1955
Gerhard Femmel, *Die Goethezeichnungen aus Schloss
Hirschhügel bei Rudolstadt.* Leipzig.

Feuchtmayr 1975
Inge Feuchtmayr, *Johann Christian Reinhart, 1761–1847:
Monographie und Werkverzeichnis.* Munich.

Fischer-Dieskau 1968
Dietrich Fischer-Dieskau, *Texte deutscher Lieder: Ein Handbuch.* Munich.

Frankfurt 1968
Karl Philipp Fohr, 1795–1818. Text by Hans-Joachim
Ziemke, with an introduction by Kurt Schwarzweller.
Exhibition catalogue, Städelsches Kunstinstitut, Frankfurt
am Main.

Frankfurt 1977
Die Nazarener. Edited by Klaus Gallwitz, with contributions
by Henri Dorra, Paul Eich, Klaus Gallwitz, Christian Lenz,
Peter Märker, Anton Merk, Günter Metken, Sigrid Metken,
Ellen Spickernagel, Margret Stuffmann, Hans-Joachim
Ziemke. Exhibition catalogue, Städtische Galerie im
Städelschen Kunstinstitut, Frankfurt am Main.

Frankfurt 1991
*Peter Cornelius. Zeichnungen zu Goethes Faust aus der
Graphischen Sammlung im Städel.* Text by Martin
Sonnabend. Exhibition catalogue, Städtische Galerie im
Städelschen Kunstinstitut, Frankfurt am Main.

Frankfurt 1994
Goethe und die Kunst. Edited by Sabine Schulze, with con-
tributions by Friedmar Apel, Ilsebill Barta Fliedl, Andreas
Beyer, Helmut Börsch-Supan, Frank Büttner, Werner Busch,
Gudrun Körner, Detlev Kreikenboom, Petra Maisak,
Hermann Mildenberger, Norbert Miller, Jutta Müller-
Tamm, Margarete Oppel, Ernst Osterkamp, Anja Petz,
Sabine Schulze, Annette Seemann, and Bettina-Martine
Wolter. Exhibition catalogue, Schirn Kunsthalle, Frankfurt
am Main; Kunstsammlungen, Schlossmuseum, Weimar.
Ostfildern.

Frenzel 1846
J. G. A. Frenzel, *Die Kunstsammlung des Freiherrn C. F. L. F.
von Rumohr.* Dresden auction catalogue (from 19 October
1846). Lübeck.

von Freyberg 1988
*200 Jahre Englischer Garten München 1789–1989. Offizielle
Festschrift.* Compiled by Pankraz Freiherr von Freyberg.
Munich.

Geller 1952
Hans Geller, *Die Bildnisse der deutschen Künstler in Rom
1800–1830. Mit einer Einführung in die Kunst der
Deutschrömer von Herbert von Einem.* Berlin.

Geller 1955
Hans Geller, *Curiosa. Merkwürdige Zeichnungen aus dem
19. Jahrhundert.* Leipzig.

Gerstenberg and Rave 1934
Kurt Gerstenberg and Paul Ortwin Rave, *Die Wandgemälde
der deutschen Romantiker im Casino Massimo zu Rom.*
Berlin.

Goethe-Corpus 1958 ff.
Corpus der Goethezeichnungen. Text by Gerhard Femmel et
al. Vols. 1–7. Leipzig, 1958–1978.

Griffiths and Carey 1994
Anthony Griffiths and Frances Carey, *German Printmaking
in the Age of Goethe.* Exhibition catalogue, The British
Museum, Department of Prints and Drawings, London.

Grimm 1911
Ludwig Emil Grimm, *Erinnerungen aus meinem Leben.*
Edited and supplemented by Adolf Stoll. Leipzig.

Grimm 1950
Ludwig Emil Grimm, *Erinnerungen aus meinem Leben.*
Edited by Wilhelm Praesent. Kassel and Basel.

Grote 1938
Ludwig Grote, *Die Brüder Olivier und die deutsche Romantik.*
Forschungen zur deutschen Kunstgeschichte. Vol. 31. Berlin.

Grote 1944
Ludwig Grote, *Das Antlitz eines Jugendbundes. Zeichnungen
von Carl Philipp Fohr. Der Kunstbrief.* Edited by Carl Georg
Heise, no. 15. Berlin, no date (1944).

Grotkamp-Schepers 1980
Barbara Grotkamp-Schepers, *Die Mannheimer Zeich-
nungsakademie (1756/69–1803) und die Werke der ihr
angeschlossenen Maler und Stecher.* Frankfurt am Main.

Hamburg 1969
*Katalog der Meister des 19. Jahrhunderts in der Hamburger
Kunsthalle.* Text by Eva Maria Krafft and Carl-Wolfgang
Schümann. Hamburg.

Hamburg 1974
Caspar David Friedrich 1774–1840. Edited by Werner Hof-
mann, with contributions by Werner Hofmann and Siegmar
Holsten; text by Hans Werner Grohn, Eleonore Reichert,
and Eckhard Schaar. Exhibition catalogue, Hamburger
Kunsthalle. Munich.

Hamburg 1977
Runge in seiner Zeit. Edited by Werner Hofmann, with con-
tributions by Werner Hofmann, Peter-Klaus Schuster and
Georg Syamken; text by Werner Hofmann, Hanna Hohl,
Siegmar Holsten, Gisela Hopp, and Peter-Klaus Schuster.
Exhibition catalogue, Hamburger Kunsthalle. Munich.

Hamburg 1982
Menzel – der Beobachter. Edited by Werner Hofmann; text
by Gisela Hopp and Eckhard Schaar, with contributions by
Werner Hofmann, Carsten Meyer, Elke von Radziewsky.
Exhibition catalogue, Hamburger Kunsthalle. Munich.

Hardenberg and Schilling 1925
Kuno Graf Hardenberg and Edmund Schilling, *Karl Philipp
Fohr. Leben und Werk eines deutschen Malers der Romantik.*
Freiburg im Breisgau.

Hardtwig 1984
Barbara Hardtwig, "Johann Georg von Dillis und das Portrait um 1800 – 'Armeleutekunst' und Individualität."
Münchner Jahrbuch der bildenden Kunst, 3rd series, vol. 25:
157–88. Munich.

Hasse 1969
Max Hasse, "Ein unvollendetes Aquarell Franz Pforrs."
Städel-Jahrbuch n.s. 2 (1969): 301–9.

Heidelberg 1925
Carl Fohr 1795–1818 und die Maler um ihn. Text by Karl
Lohmeyer. Exhibition catalogue, Kurpfälzisches Museum,
Heidelberg.

Heidelberg 1964
Jens Christian Jensen, *Kunst in Dresden 18.–20. Jahrhundert.
Aquarelle, Zeichnungen, Druckgraphik. Ausstellung zur Erin-
nerung an die Gründung der Dresdner Kunstakademie 1764.*
Exhibition catalogue, Kurpfälzisches Museum, Heidelberg.

Heidelberg 1965
*Schlösser, Burgen, Ruinen in der Malerei der Romantik.
Gemälde, Aquarelle und Graphik deutscher, österreichischer
und schweizer Künstler 1770–1860.* Text by Anneliese
Stemper (topography) and Jens Christian Jensen (art his-
tory). Exhibition catalogue, Kurpfälzisches Museum,
Heidelberg.

Heidelberg 1968
Jens Christian Jensen, *Carl Philipp Fohr 1795–1818.* Vol. 1:
Skizzenbuch der Neckargegend und Badisches Skizzenbuch.
Vol. 2: *Die Werke Carl Philipp Fohrs im Besitz des
Kurpfälzischen Museums.* With an introduction by Klaus
Mugdan. Exhibition catalogue, Kurpfälzisches Museum,
Heidelberg.

Heidelberg 1995
Carl Philipp Fohr und seine Künstlerfreunde in Rom. Text by
Ulrike Andersson and Annette Frese. Exhibition catalogue,
Kurpfälzisches Museum, Heidelberg.

Heine 1972
Barbara Heine, *Max Joseph Wagenbauer.* Oberbayerisches
Archiv, vol. 95. Munich

Heise 1928
Carl Georg Heise, ed., *Overbeck und sein Kreis. Hundert
Bildtafeln mit dem Festvortrag "Kunst und Kunstgeist der
Nazarener" von Kurt Karl Eberlein zur Erinnerung an die
Ausstellung in Lübeck im Sommer 1926.* Munich.

Heise 1959
Carl Georg Heise, *Grosse Zeichner des 19. Jahrhunderts.*
Berlin.

Hinz 1966
Sigrid Hinz, "Caspar David Friedrich als Zeichner. Ein
Beitrag zur stilistischen Entwicklung der Zeichnungen und
ihrer Bedeutung für die Datierung der Gemälde." Ph. D. dissertation. Greifswald.

Hinz 1974
Caspar David Friedrich in Briefen und Bekenntnissen. Edited
by Sigrid Hinz. 2nd revised and expanded ed. Munich.

Hofmann 1995
Werner Hofmann, *Das entzweite Jahrhundert. Kunst zwischen 1750 und 1830.* Munich.

Howitt 1886
Margaret Howitt, *Friedrich Overbeck: Sein Leben und sein
Schaffen. Nach seinen Briefen und anderen Dokumenten des
handschriftlichen Nachlasses.* Edited by Franz Binder. 2 vols.
Freiburg im Breisgau.

Hutter and Lhotsky 1973
Heribert Hutter and Wanda Lhotsky, *Julius Schnorr von
Carolsfeld. Römisches Portraitbuch im Kupferstichkabinett der
Akademie der bildenden Künste in Wien.* Vienna.

Jensen 1958
Jens Christian Jensen, "Über die Gründung des Lukasbundes." *Der Wagen. Ein lübeckisches Jahrbuch* (1958): 105–22.

Jensen 1968
Jens Christian Jensen, *Carl Philipp Fohr in Heidelberg und
im Neckartal. Landschaften und Bildnisse.* Karlsruhe.

Jensen 1974
Jens Christian Jensen, *Caspar David Friedrich. Leben und
Werk.* Cologne.

Jensen 1977
Jens Christian Jensen, *Philipp Otto Runge. Leben und Werk.* Cologne.

Jensen 1978
Jens Christian Jensen, *Aquarelle und Zeichnungen der deutschen Romantik.* Cologne.

Karlsruhe 1996
Moritz von Schwind. Meister der Spätromantik. Text by Siegmar Holsten, with Susanne Richter, Barbara Rommé, Friedrich Gross, Doris Strack, Ulrike Olbrich, Sebastian Giesen, Helene Seifert, Rudolf Theilmann, Dietmar Lüdke, Anne Reuter-Rautenberg. Exhibition catalogue, Staatliche Kunsthalle, Karlsruhe; Museum der bildenden Künste, Leipzig. Karlsruhe.

Kassel 1985
Ludwig Emil Grimm 1790–1863. Maler, Zeichner, Radierer. Text by Cornelia Barth, Barbara Hardtwig, Erich Herzog, Alfred Höck, Egbert Koolman, Ingrid Koszinowski, Vera Leuschner, Karin Mayer-Pasinski, Anton Merk. Exhibition catalogue, Museum Fridericianum, Kassel; Schloss Steinheim, Hanau. Kassel.

Keller 1979
Horst Keller, *Deutsche Maler des 19. Jahrhunderts.* Munich.

Kemp 1979
Wolfgang Kemp, *…einen wahrhaft bildenden Zeichenunterricht überall einzuführen. Zeichnen und Zeichenunterricht der Laien 1500–1870. Ein Handbuch.* Frankfurt am Main.

Koerner 1990
Joseph Leo Koerner, *Caspar David Friedrich and the Subject of Landscape.* London.

Koschatzky 1981
Walter Koschatzky, *Die Kunst der Zeichnung. Technik, Geschichte, Meisterwerke* (Salzburg, 1977). Munich.

Koszinowski and Leuschner 1990
Ingrid Koszinowski and Vera Leuschner, *Ludwig Emil Grimm. Zeichnungen und Gemälde. Werkverzeichnis.* Vol. 1: *Portrait, Historie, Illustrationen, Alben, Varia, Ölbilder.* Marburg.

Krapf 1977
Michael Krapf, *Johann Evangelist Scheffer von Leonhardshoff, 1795–1822. Ein Mitglied des Lukasbundes aus Wien.* With a contribution by Hans Bisanz. Exhibition catalogue, Österreichische Galerie and Historisches Museum der Stadt Wien im Oberen Belvedere, Vienna.

Kurth 1941
Willy Kurth, *Berliner Zeichner.* Berlin.

Lammel 1992
Gisold Lammel, *Karikatur der Goethezeit.* Berlin.

Landsberger 1908
Franz Landsberger, *Wilhelm Tischbein. Ein Künstlerleben des 18. Jahrhunderts.* Leipzig.

Langenstein 1983
York Langenstein, *Der Münchner Kunstverein im 19. Jahrhundert. Ein Beitrag zur Entwicklung des Kunstmarkts und des Ausstellungswesens.* Munich.

Lankheit 1952
Klaus Lankheit, *Das Freundschaftsbild der Romantik.* Heidelberg.

Lankheit 1959
Klaus Lankheit, "Deutsche Zeichenkunst der Goethezeit, Handzeichnungen und Aquarelle aus der Sammlung Winterstein, München." Exhibition review. *Kunstchronik* 12 (1959): 64–67, 73–75 (figs. 1–3).

Larsen 1961
Egon Larsen, *Graf Rumford. Ein Amerikaner in München.* Munich.

Lavater 1775–78
Johann Caspar Lavater, *Physiognomische Fragmente zur Beförderung der Menschenkenntnis und Menschenliebe.* 4 vols. Leipzig.

Lehr 1924
Fritz Herbert Lehr, *Die Blütezeit romantischer Bildkunst. Franz Pforr, der Meister des Lukasbundes. Mit einem Anhang bisher unveröffentlichter Manuskripte romantischer Maler u. Zeichner. Pforr, Overbeck, Cornelius u. a.* Marburg.

Leipzig 1994
Julius Schnorr von Carolsfeld 1794–1872. Edited by Herwig Guratzsch. Text by Karl-Heinz Mehnert, Dietulf Sander et al. Exhibition catalogue, Museum der bildenden Künste, Leipzig; Kunsthalle, Bremen. Leipzig.

Lohmeyer 1935
Karl Lohmeyer, *Heidelberger Maler der Romantik.* Heidelberg.

London 1972
The Age of Neo-Classicism. The Fourteenth Exhibition of the Council of Europe. Exhibition catalogue, The Royal Academy and The Victoria & Albert Museum, London.

London-Tate 1972
William Vaughan, Helmut Börsch-Supan, and Hans Joachim Neidhardt, *Caspar David Friedrich 1774–1840. Romantic Landscape Painting in Dresden.* Exhibition catalogue, The Tate Gallery, London.

Ludwigsgalerie 1927
Carl Philipp Fohr (1795–1818) nebst einigen Arbeiten von anderen Künstlern seiner Zeit. Exhibition catalogue, Ludwigsgalerie, Otto H. Nathan. Munich.

Lübeck 1957.
Die Bildniszeichnung der deutschen Romantik. Text by Jens Christian Jensen. *Exhibition catalogue, St.-Annen-Museum and Overbeck-Gesellschaft, Lübeck.*

Lübeck 1969
Deutsche Zeichnungen 1800–1850 aus der Sammlung Winterstein. Ausstellung zum 100. Todestag Friedrich Overbecks. Text by Peter Vignau-Wilberg, with introduction by Jens Christian Jensen. Exhibition catalogue, Museen für Kunst und Kulturgeschichte, Lübeck.

Lübeck 1989
Johann Friedrich Overbeck 1789–1869. Zur zweihundertsten Wiederkehr seines Geburtstages. Edited by Andreas Blühm and Gerhard Gerkens, with contributions by Frank Büttner, Rachel Esner, Jens Christian Jensen, M. Piotr Michalowski, Ulrich Pietsch. Exhibition catalogue, Museum für Kunst und Kulturgeschichte der Hansestadt Lübeck—Behnhaus. Lübeck.

Lübeck 1990
Goethezeit und Romantik. Einhundert Meisterzeichnungen aus einer Privatsammlung. Introduction by Hans Werner Grohn. Text by Andreas Blühm, Gerhard Gerkens, and Hinrich Sieveking. Exhibition catalogue, Niedersächsische Landesgalerie and Forum des Landesmuseums, Hannover; Museum für Kunst und Kulturgeschichte and St.-Annen-Museum, Lübeck.

Lugt
Frits Lugt, *Les marques de collections de dessins et d'estampes.* Amsterdam, 1921/Supplément, The Hague, 1956.

Luther 1988
Edith Luther, *Johann Friedrich Frauenholz (1758–1822). Kunsthändler und Verleger in Nürnberg.* Nuremberg.

Lutterotti 1940
Otto R. von Lutterotti, *Joseph Anton Koch, 1768–1839. Mit Werkverzeichnis und Briefen des Künstlers.* Berlin.

Lutterotti 1944
Otto R. von Lutterotti, *Joseph Anton Koch, 1768–1839. Heroische und romantische Landschaft.* Innsbruck.

Lutterotti 1985
Otto R. von Lutterotti, *Joseph Anton Koch, 1768–1839. Leben und Werk. Mit einem vollständigen Werkverzeichnis.* Vienna and Munich.

Märker 1984
Peter Märker, *Bürgerliches Leben im 18. Jahrhundert. Daniel Chodowiecki 1726–1801. Zeichnungen und Druckgraphik.* Exhibition catalogue, Städelsches Kunstinstitut und Städtische Galerie, Frankfurt am Main.

Mainz 1986
"…auf classischem Boden begeistert," Goethe in Italien. Edited by Jörn Göres in collaboration with Horst Claussen, Roland Daube-Schackat, Ingrid Felber, Christina Florack-Kröll, Wilfried Franz, Petra Maisak, Doris Maurer, Wolfgang Schiering, Hartmut Schmidt, Hein-Theodor Schulze Altcappenberg, Gundula Sroka, Andrea Wagener. Exhibition catalogue, Wissenschaftszentrum, Bonn; Goethehaus, Frankfurt am Main; Goethe-Museum, Düsseldorf; Landesbibliothek, Kiel, and other locations in Italy. Mainz.

Mainz 1993
Unter Glas und Rahmen. Druckgraphik der Romantik aus den Beständen des Landesmuseums Mainz und aus Privatbesitz. Text by Stephan Seeliger and Norbert Suhr. Exhibition catalogue, Landesmuseum, Mainz.

Maisak 1996
Petra Maisak, *Johann Wolfgang Goethe. Zeichnungen.* Stuttgart.

Mannheim 1993
Nazarenische Zeichenkunst. Text by Pia Müller-Tamm. Exhibition catalogue, Kunsthalle, Mannheim. Die Zeichnungen und Aquarelle des 19. Jahrhunderts der Kunsthalle Mannheim. Vol. 4. Berlin.

Marbach 1966
Auch ich in Arcadien. Kunstreisen nach Italien 1600–1900. Text by Dorothea Kuhn in collaboration with Anneliese Hofmann and Anneliese Kunz. Exhibition catalogue, 2nd ed. Schiller-Nationalmuseum, Marbach am Neckar.

Martius 1956
Lilli Martius, *Schleswig-holsteinische Malerei im 19. Jahrhundert.* Neumünster.

Maximilian-Gebetbuch
Das Gebetbuch Kaiser Maximilians. Der Münchner Teil mit den Randzeichnungen von Albrecht Dürer und Lucas Cranach d. Ae. Reconstructed reproduction. Introduction by Hinrich Sieveking. Munich, 1987.

Meder 1923
Joseph Meder, *Die Handzeichnung. Ihre Technik und Entwicklung.* 2nd., rev. ed. Vienna.

Mende and Hebecker 1973
Matthias Mende and Inge Hebecker, *Das Dürer-Stammbuch von 1828.* Nuremberg.

Messerer 1961
Richard Messerer, *Georg von Dillis. Leben und Werk.* Oberbayerisches Archiv. Vol. 84. Munich.

Messerer 1966
Briefwechsel zwischen Ludwig I. von Bayern und Georg von Dillis. Edited and text by Richard Messerer. Munich.

Munich 1958
Peter Halm, *Deutsche Zeichenkunst der Goethezeit. Handzeichnungen und Aquarelle aus der Sammlung Winterstein.* Exhibition catalogue, Staatliche Graphische Sammlung, Munich; Germanisches Nationalmuseum, Nuremberg; Kunsthalle, Hamburg; Kurpfälzisches Museum, Heidelberg, and other locations. Munich.

Munich 1972
Das Aquarell, 1400–1950. Text by Walter Koschatzky and Herbert Pée. Exhibition catalogue, Haus der Kunst, Munich.

Munich 1979
Münchner Landschaftsmalerei 1800–1850. Edited by Armin Zweite. Exhibition catalogue, Städtische Galerie im Lenbachhaus, Munich.

Munich 1981
Deutsche Künstler um Ludwig I. in Rom. Text by Gisela Scheffler. Exhibition catalogue, Staatliche Graphische Sammlung, Munich.

Munich 1985
Deutsche Romantiker. Bildthemen der Zeit von 1800 bis 1850.
Edited by Christoph Heilmann. Text by Christoph Heilmann, Peter Vignau-Wilberg, and Thea Vignau-Wilberg, with a contribution by Walter Koschatzky. Exhibition catalogue, Kunsthalle der Hypo-Kulturstiftung, Munich.

Munich 1991
Johann Georg von Dillis 1759–1841. Landschaft und Menschenbild. Edited by Christoph Heilmann, with contributions by Barbara Hardtwig, Christoph Heilmann, Konrad Laudenbacher, and Hinrich Sieveking. Exhibition catalogue, Bayerische Staatsgemäldesammlungen, Neue Pinakothek, Munich; Staatliche Kunstsammlungen, Albertinum, Dresden. Munich.

Munich 1993
Ideal and Natur. Aquarelle und Zeichnungen im Lenbachhaus 1780–1850. Text by Dorothee Zanker von Meyer. With an essay by Joseph von Westphalen. Edited by Helmut Friedel. Exhibition catalogue, Städtische Galerie im Lenbachhaus, Munich; Saarland Museum, Saarbrücken. Munich.

Munich 1994
Julius Schnorr von Carolsfeld. Zeichnungen. With contributions by Stephan Seeliger, Hinrich Sieveking, and Norbert Suhr. Exhibition catalogue, Landesmuseum, Mainz; Bayerische Vereinsbank and Palais Preysing, Munich.

Munich 1995
Ernste Spiele. Der Geist der Romantik in der deutschen Kunst 1790–1990. Edited by Christoph Vitali. Exhibition catalogue, Haus der Kunst, Munich.

Neidhardt 1976
Hans Joachim Neidhardt, *Die Malerei der Romantik in Dresden.* Leipzig.

New York 1981
Germans Masters of the Nineteenth Century. Paintings and Drawings from the Federal Republic of Germany. With contributions by Gert Schiff and Stephan Waetzoldt. Exhibition catalogue, The Metropolitan Museum of Art, New York; The Art Gallery of Ontario. New York.

New York 1988
The Romantic Spirit. German Drawings, 1780–1850, from the Nationalgalerie (Staatliche Museen, Berlin), and the Kupferstichkabinett (Staatliche Kunstsammlungen, Dresden), German Democratic Republic. Text by Peter Betthausen, Claude Keisch, Matthias Kühn, Gertraute Lippold, Gottfried Riemann, Maria Ursula Riemann-Reyher, and Werner Schmidt. Edited by Gottfried Riemann (Berlin) and William W. Robinson (New York), in collaboration with Pamela T. Barr. Exhibition catalogue, The Pierpont Morgan Library. New York.

Noack 1927
Friedrich Noack, *Das Deutschtum in Rom seit dem Ausgang des Mittelalters.* 2 vols. Stuttgart, Berlin, and Leipzig.

Nuremberg 1966
Klassizismus und Romantik in Deutschland. Gemälde und Zeichnungen aus der Sammlung Georg Schäfer, Schweinfurt. Text by Konrad Kaiser, with contributions by Herbert von Einem, Jens Christian Jensen, Klaus Lankheit, Otto R. von Lutterotti, Hans Ost, Georg Poensgen, Werner Sumowski, and Siegfried Wichmann. Exhibition catalogue, Germanisches Nationalmuseum, Nuremberg. Schweinfurt.

Nuremberg 1967
Der frühe Realismus in Deutschland 1800–1850. Gemälde und Zeichnungen aus der Sammlung Georg Schäfer, Schweinfurt. Text by Konrad Kaiser, with contributions by Klaus Lankheit, Richard Messerer, Siegfried Wichmann et al. Exhibition catalogue, Germanisches Nationalmuseum, Nuremberg. Schweinfurt.

Nuremberg 1980
Nützliche Anweisung zur Zeichenkunst. Illustrierte Lehr- und Vorlagenbücher. Text by Gerlind Werner. Exhibition catalogue, Bibliothek des Germanischen Nationalmuseums. Nuremberg.

Nuremberg 1989
Freiheit, Gleichheit, Brüderlichkeit. 200 Jahre Französische Revolution in Deutschland. Text by Rainer Schoch in collaboration with Cornelia Foerster, Katrin Kusch, Edith Luther, Klaus-D. Pohl, Brigitte Schoch-Joswig, Jutta Zander-Seidel. Exhibition catalogue, Germanisches Nationalmuseum, Nuremberg.

Nuremberg 1991
Künstlerleben in Rom. Bertel Thorvaldsen (1770–1844). Der dänische Bildhauer und seine deutschen Freunde. Edited by Gerhard Bott and Heinz Spielmann. Text by Ursula Peters in collaboration with Andrea M. Kluxen, Peter Laub, Edith Luther, Harald C. Tesan. Exhibition catalogue, Germanisches Nationalmuseum, Nuremberg; Schleswig-Holsteinisches Landesmuseum Schloss Gottorf, Schleswig. Nuremberg.

Paris 1976
La peinture allemande à l'époque du Romantisme. Introduction by Michel Laclotte, with contributions by Werner Hofmann, Hans Joachim Neidhardt, and Youri Kouznetsov. Exhibition catalogue, Orangerie des Tuileries, Paris.

Paris 1984
Caspar David Friedrich, le tracé et la transparence. Edited by Jacqueline and Maurice Guillaud. Exhibition catalogue, Centre Culturel du Marais. Paris.

Pinnau 1965
Ruth Irmgard Pinnau, *Johann Martin von Rohden, 1778–1868. Leben und Werk.* Bielefeld.

Potsdam 1995
Friedrich Wilhelm IV., Künstler und König. Zum 200. Geburtstag. Exhibition catalogue, Neue Orangerie im Park von Sanssouci, Potsdam. Frankfurt am Main.

Rave 1949
Paul Ortwin Rave, *Das geistige Deutschland im Bildnis. Das Jahrhundert Goethes.* Berlin.

Rave 1965
Paul Ortwin Rave, *Kunst in Berlin.* Berlin.

RDK
Reallexikon zur deutschen Kunstgeschichte. Begun by Otto Schmitt, continued by Ernst Gall, Ludwig Heinrich Heydenreich, Hans Martin Freiherr von Erffa, and Karl August Wirth. Vols. 1–5. Stuttgart, 1937–67. From vol. 6 on, Munich, 1973ff.

Richter 1909
Ludwig Richter, *Lebenserinnerungen eines deutschen Malers. Selbstbiographie nebst Tagebuchniederschriften und Briefen.* Edited and supplemented by Heinrich Richter, introduction by Ferdinand Avenarius. 6th ed. Leipzig.

Robels 1974
Hella Robels, *Sehnsucht nach Italien. Bilder deutscher Romantiker.* Munich.

Rome 1981
Die Nazarener in Rom. Ein deutscher Künstlerbund der Romantik. Edited by Klaus Gallwitz, with contributions by Christoph Heilmann, Judith Huber, Jens Christian Jensen, Michael Krapf, Günter Metken, Sigrid Metken, and Gianna Piantoni. Exhibition catalogue, Galleria Nazionale d'Arte Moderna, Rome. Munich.

Rosenblum 1975
Robert Rosenblum, *Modern Painting and the Northern Romantic Tradition: Friedrich to Rothko.* London.

Rumohr 1832
Carl Friedrich von Rumohr, *Drey Reisen nach Italien. Erinnerungen.* Leipzig.

Schack-Galerie 1969
Gemäldekataloge. Published by the Bayerische Staatsgemäldesammlungen. Vol. 2: *Schack-Galerie.* Complete catalogue. Text by Eberhard Ruhmer and Rosel Gollek, Christoph Heilmann, Hermann Kühn, and Regina Löwe. Munich.

Scheffler and Hardtwig 1979
Von Dillis bis Piloty. Deutsche und österreichische Zeichnungen, Aquarelle, Ölskizzen, 1790–1850, aus eigenem Besitz. Text by Gisela Scheffler and Barbara Hardtwig. Exhibition catalogue, Staatliche Graphische Sammlung, Munich. Munich.

Scheidig 1954
Walther Scheidig, *Franz Horny, 1798 Weimar—Olevano 1824.* Berlin.

Scheidig 1958
Walther Scheidig, *Goethes Preisaufgaben für bildende Künstler 1799–1805.* Weimar.

Schellenberg 1926
Ernst Ludwig Schellenberg, ed., *Der Maler Franz Horny. Briefe und Zeugnisse.* Berlin.

Schiff 1973
Gert Schiff, *Johann Heinrich Füssli, 1741–1825.* Vol. 1: Text und Ouevrekatalog. Vol. 2: Abbildungen. Zurich and Munich.

Schmitz 1921
Hermann Schmitz, *Die Gotik im deutschen Kunst- und Geistesleben.* Berlin.

Schmoll 1970
Josef Adolf Schmoll, called Eisenwerth, "Fensterbilder. Motivketten in der europäischen Malerei." In *Beiträge zur Motivkunde des 19. Jahrhunderts* (Munich), pp. 13–165.

Schnell 1994
Werner Schnell, *Georg Friedrich Kersting (1785–1847). Das zeichnerische und malerische Werk mit Oeuvrekatalog.* Berlin.

Schnorr-Briefe
Julius Schnorr von Carolsfeld. Briefe aus Italien geschrieben in den Jahren 1817 bis 1827. Ein Beitrag zur Geschichte seines Lebens und der Kunstbestrebungen seiner Zeit. Edited by Franz Schnorr von Carolsfeld. Gotha, 1886.

Schuchardt 1848
Christian Schuchardt, *Goethe's Kunstsammlungen.* 2 vols. Jena.

Schwarz 1957
Heinrich Schwarz, *Salzburg und das Salzkammergut. Die künstlerische Entdeckung der Stadt und Landschaft im 19. Jahrhundert.* 3rd, substantially expanded ed. Vienna and Munich (no date).

Schweinfurt 1968
Romantik und Realismus in Österreich. Gemälde und Zeichnungen aus der Sammlung Georg Schäfer, Schweinfurt. Text by Konrad Kaiser, with contributions by Keith Andrews, Rupert Feuchtmüller, Eva Frodl-Kraft, Otto R. von Lutterotti et al. Exhibition catalogue, Schloss Laxenburg near Vienna. Schweinfurt.

Seidler 1922
Luise Seidler, *Erinnerungen.* Edited by Hermann Uhde. New ed. Berlin.

Sieveking 1975
Hinrich Sieveking, "Franz Horny." *Die Kunst und das schöne Heim* 87 (1975): 745–52.

Sieveking 1988
Hinrich Sieveking, "'Nach der Natur gezeichnet…' Beobachtungen zur frühen künstlerischen Rezeption des Englischen Gartens in München, zu Johann Georg von Dillis und zur Entstehung der Landschaftsmalerei." In von Freyberg 1988, pp. 144–61.

Sieveking 1990
Hinrich Sieveking, "Zeichen der Zeit—von Füssli bis Menzel – Aspekte deutscher Zeichenkunst der Goethezeit." In *Zeichnung und Moderne. Modelle zeichnerischer Verfahren,* edited by Bernd Growe. Alsfeld.

Skreiner-Festschrift 1992
Kontinuität und Identität, Festschrift für Wilfried Skreiner. Edited by Peter Weibel, Christa Steinle, Götz Pochat. Vienna, Cologne, Weimar.

Steinle 1977
Christa Steinle, "Thema, Ikonographie und Form im graphischen Frühwerk der Nazarener und ihre Beziehungen zur altdeutschen und altitalienischen Kunst, unter besonderer Berücksichtigung des Einflusses Dürers und Raffaels." Ph.D. dissertation, Graz.

Stoessl 1924
Moritz von Schwind. Briefe. Edited with commentary by Otto Stoessl. Leipzig.

Strixner 1808
Johann Nepomuk Strixner (lithographs), Johann Christoph von Aretin (preface), *Albrecht Dürers Christlich-mythologische Handzeichnungen.* Munich.

Stuttgart 1980
Christian von Holst, *Dante—Vergil—Geryon. Der 17. Höllengesang der Göttlichen Komödie in der bildenden Kunst.* Exhibition catalogue, Staatsgalerie Stuttgart.

Stuttgart 1989
Christian von Holst, *Joseph Anton Koch, 1768–1839. Ansichten der Natur.* Exhibition catalogue, Staatsgalerie Stuttgart.

Suhr 1991
Norbert Suhr, *Philipp Veit (1793–1877). Leben und Werk eines Nazareners. Monographie und Werkverzeichnis.* Weinheim.

Sulzer 1771/1774
Johann Georg Sulzer, *Allgemeine Theorie der Schönen Künste.* 2 vols. Leipzig.

Sumowski 1970
Werner Sumowski, *Caspar David Friedrich-Studien.* Wiesbaden.

Thieme and Becker
Ulrich Thieme and Felix Becker, *Allgemeines Lexikon der bildenden Künstler von der Antike bis zur Gegenwart.* 37 vols. Leipzig, 1907–50.

Traeger 1975
Jörg Traeger, *Philipp Otto Runge und sein Werk. Monographie und kritischer Katalog.* Munich.

Traeger 1977
Jörg Traeger, *Philipp Otto Runge oder Die Geburt einer neuen Kunst.* Munich.

Tschudi 1905
Hugo von Tschudi, ed., *Adolph von Menzel. Abbildungen seiner Gemälde und Studien aufgrund der von der Kgl. Nationalgalerie im Frühjahr 1905 veranstalteten Ausstellung unter Mitwirkung von E. Schwedeler-Meyer and J. Kern.* Munich.

Tübingen 1981
Peter Märker, Monika Wagner et al., *Mit dem Auge des Touristen. Zur Geschichte des Reisebildes.* Exhibition catalogue, Kunsthalle, Tübingen.

Vienna 1990
Von Caspar David Friedrich bis Adolph Menzel. Aquarelle und Zeichnungen der Romantik aus der Nationalgalerie Berlin/DDR. Edited by Gottfried Riemann and Klaus Albrecht Schröder. With contributions by Peter Betthausen, Ingried Brugger, Bernhard Maaz, Claude Keisch, Gottfried Riemann, Marie Ursula Riemann, Klaus Albrecht Schröder, and Angelika Wesenberg. Exhibition catalogue, Kunstforum Länderbank Wien. Munich.

Warnke 1992
Martin Warnke, *Politische Landschaft. Zur Kunstgeschichte der Natur.* Munich.

Washington, D.C. 1996
In the Light of Italy. Corot and Early Open-Air Painting. Text by Philip Conisbee, Sarah Faunce, and Jeremy Strick. Peter Galassi, guest curator. Exhibition catalogue, National Gallery of Art, Washington, D.C.; The Brooklyn Museum; The Saint Louis Art Museum. Washington D.C., New Haven, and London.

Wegmann 1993
Peter Wegmann, *Museum Stiftung Oskar Reinhart Winterthur. Deutsche, österreichische und schweizerische Malerei aus dem 18., 19. und frühen 20. Jahrhundert.* With contributions by Franz Zelger and Matthias Wohlgemuth. Frankfurt am Main and Leipzig.

Weigmann 1906
Otto Weigmann, ed., *Schwind. Des Meisters Werke in 1265 Abbildungen.* Stuttgart and Leipzig.

Westhoff-Krummacher 1995
Hildegard Westhoff-Krummacher, *Als die Frauen noch sanft und engelsgleich waren. Die Sicht der Frau in der Zeit der Aufklärung und des Biedermeier.* Exhibition catalogue, Westfälisches Landesmuseum für Kunst und Kulturgeschichte, Münster.

Wichmann 1970
Siegfried Wichmann, *Wilhelm von Kobell. Monographie und kritisches Verzeichnis der Werke.* With contributions by Heinz Bauer, Irmgard Gierl, and Rotraud Wrede. Munich.

Wiesbaden 1936
Zwei Jahrhunderte deutscher Landschaftsmalerei. Edited by Hermann Voss. Text by Juliane Harms. Exhibition catalogue, Nassauisches Landesmuseum, Wiesbaden.

Winkler 1975
R. Arnim Winkler, *Die Frühzeit der deutschen Lithographie. Katalog der Bilddrucke von 1796–1821.* Munich.

Winterthur 1955
Europäische Meister 1790–1910. Text by Lisbeth Stähelin. Exhibition catalogue, Kunstmuseum, Wintherthur.

Wirth 1990
Irmgard Wirth, *Berliner Malerei im 19. Jahrhundert. Von der Zeit Friedrichs des Grossen bis zum Ersten Weltkrieg.* Berlin.

Wolf-Timm 1991
Telse Wolf-Timm, *Theodor Rehbenitz 1791–1861. Persönlichkeit und Werk mit kritischem Werkkatalog.* Kiel.

Zurich 1990
Martin Bircher, Gisold Lammel, et al., *Helvetien in Deutschland. Schweizer Kunst aus Residenzen deutscher Klassik 1770–1830.* Reihe Strauhof Zurich, vol. 5. Zurich.

Index of Proper Names

Numbers in italics refer to illustrations

Photographic Credits

The works in the Winterstein Collection have been
photographed by Engelbert Seehuber, Munich.
Unless otherwise stated, all other pictorial material in this
publication has been kindly provided by the owners, as
indicated in the picture captions.

Jörg P. Anders, Berlin 60, 66, 82, 148

Berlin, Nationalgalerie 142 bottom

Cambridge, Mass., President and Fellows, Harvard College,
Harvard University Art Museums 122 bottom

Christie's Images, London 170

Darmstadt, Hessisches Landesmuseum 126, 128, 132

Dresden, Staatliche Kunstsammlungen 102, 144

Fischer-Daber, Hamburg 22 top and bottom

Heidelberg, Kurpfälzisches Museum 130

Kassel, Brüder Grimm-Museum 150 left

Ralph Kleinhempel, Hamburg 23

Munich, Bayerische Staatsgemäldesammlungen 15,
29 bottom, 62 right, 172, 178 bottom

– Bayerische Verwaltung der staatlichen Schlösser,
Gärten und Seen 112

– Staatliche Graphische Sammlung 21, 24, 27 top and
bottom, 94, 104 bottom, 124, 160 (Christina Pahnke),
164 top and bottom, 174, 178 top

Rheinisches Bildarchiv, Cologne 120

Hinrich Sieveking, Munich 10, 20 left

Stuttgart, Staatsgalerie 92

Vienna, Museen der Stadt Wien 116

Weimar, Stiftung Weimarer Klassik 48 left (Sigrid Geske),
48 bottom

Elke Walford, Hamburg 56

Zürich, Schweizerisches Institut für Kunstwissenschaft
62 left

Index of Artists